ADVANCED COMPUTER ARCHITECTURE

A Systems Design Approach

RICHARD Y. KAIN

Department of Electrical Engineering
University of Minnesota

PRENTICE HALL, Englewood Cliffs, New Jersey 07632

Library of Congress Cataloging-in-Publication Data

Kain, Richard Y.
    Advanced computer architecture : a systems design approach
  Richard Y. Kain
      p. cm.
    Includes bibliological references and index.
    ISBN: 0-13-007741-0 (hard cover)
    1. Computer architecture I . Title.
  QA76.9.A73K363 1996
  004.2'2--dc20   95-18657
                                               CIP

Acquisitions editor: **Alan Apt**
Production editor: **Bayani Mendoza deLeon**
Copy editor: **Peter Zurita**
Cover designer: **Bruce Kenselaar**
Buyer: **Donna Sullivan**
Editorial assistant: **Shirley McGuire**

© 1996 by Prentice-Hall, Inc.
A Simon & Schuster Company
Englewood Cliffs, New Jersey 07632

The author and publisher of this book have used their best efforts in preparing this book. These efforts include the
development, research, and testing of the theories and programs to determine their effectiveness. The author and
publisher make no warranty of any kind, expressed or implied, with regard to these programs or the documentation
contained in this book. The author and publisher shall not be liable in any event for incidental or consequential damages
in connection with, or arising out of, the furnishing, performance, or use of these programs.

Printed in the United States of America

10 9 8 7 6 5 4 3 2

cover photograph copyright 1992 by Richard Y. Kain

ISBN 0-13-007741-0

Prentice-Hall International (UK) Limited, London
Prentice-Hall of Australia Pty. Limited, Sydney
Prentice-Hall Canada Inc., Toronto
Prentice-Hall Hispanoamericana, S.A., Mexico
Prentice-Hall of India Private Limited, New Delhi
Prentice-Hall of Japan, Inc., Tokyo
Simon & Schuster Asia Pte. Ltd., Singapore
Editora Prentice-Hall do Brasil, Ltda., Rio de Janeiro

To Kathie

CONTENTS

Contents

PREFACE

*The man who sees two or three generations
is like one who sits in the conjurer's booth at a fair,
and sees the tricks two or three times.
They are meant to be seen only once.*

— Schopenhauer

Often tricks are repeated over generations, but are still meant to surprise the audience, according to Schopenhauer. It is instructive to view this from the other side—the magician must learn basic tricks before performing and astounding an audience. The history of computer design follows this pattern: Architectures have progressed through several "generations," usually defined in terms of the implementation technology, and many "tricks" have been rediscovered and re-used. Many techniques have been reinvented, because the old ones have been forgotten. I believe that although designers face different trade-offs in different technologies, they work with the same basic bag of tricks to conjure up new architectures.

In this book, I describe many architectural tricks and position them within a useful structure. The structure should clarify the similarities and differences between architectures by exhibiting not only the basic tricks and techniques, but also the relationships between software and hardware levels of system implementation and operation.

As designers ponder basic design trade-offs and seek good solutions to their design challenges, they should study the requirements and design options for the complete system. The system will include many modules arranged in

xix

levels, ranging from the processor outward to operating systems, programming languages, and application structures. For a number of years, it has been obvious that the design questions, design options, and approaches to the design questions have many similarities across the levels of the system. By being aware of the needs of the application, programming language structure, and operating system functions when designing the processor architecture, a design that supports a more efficient system might be developed.

Historical Designs. The book includes examples from a number of programming languages, operating systems, and processor designs, some new and some old. By exposing you to diverse examples, I hope to convince you that many design options are feasible, at least in the context of specific design environments. I also show you details needed to complete the designs, or I challenge you to find the details as you work through the problems.

Even though an arbitrary combination of design choices might not produce an effective system, we should consider and remember design techniques developed by our predecessors, because their techniques might be useful in many situations.

Many old design strategies are revived or reinvented as technology evolves and the design environment changes. We should not let the good designs of the past be forgotten, because once forgotten, it is a waste of time and energy to reinvent them later. And then they will have to be debugged all over again!

Why Did I Choose this Approach? Klapp [KLAP86] suggests that one contributor to the current "lag in meaning" is that people do not have enough time to ponder recent ideas. Time for "wondering" is time for finding new connections and relationships. The rapid introduction of new computer systems, programming languages, and myriad applications keeps designers and implementers busy meeting pressing deadlines. This may leave them with insufficient time to wonder about and ponder the overall scene.

My musings about how to approach architectural issues resulted in this book; this is the current version of my ongoing quest for a coherent personation of computer design issues. I am trying to join issues and techniques from software and hardware levels. I believe that better system designs can be achieved when designers start with a clear conception of the design problem and are familiar with the approaches used by their predecessors to solve similar problems at all levels of the overall system.

I have chosen to present a coherent approach to computer system design that encompasses many, if not most, of the design problems and solution options, starting from the structures of contemporary programming languages and operating systems, extending inward to the processor's architecture and its implementation. Many common design issues and certain approaches and solution options could be applied at several levels of system implementation. To emphasize the commonalty and to impose structure on the presentation, I tend to place general principles and design approaches at the beginning of each chapter and then progress in a top–down manner (from programming languages toward the processor and its implementation), using examples from actual programming languages, operating systems, and processors. In this manner, I detail and illustrate the problems and the designs that solve those problems.

There is considerable overlap between the material in some sections of this book and parts of certain computer science courses, particularly courses on the structure of high-level languages and operating systems, with a pinch of database topics thrown in. A reader who has studied these topics before might skim over these sections to see how I present the material (which does not always conform to the conventional terminology used in the specialized field). Although these topics might not be considered to be architectural topics by some purists, they are connected with processor architectures and with features that lead to high performance in real applications environments. Recall that the ultimate purpose of computer science is to understand how to develop algorithms and data structures that use computing machines to effectively solve large, difficult problems. Therefore, techniques that are useful in computer science have to be implemented somewhere within the total system. Thus, one should look with an eye toward how they can be supported within a system's architecture. The ultimate outcome of this thinking might be a software solution, but it might suggest direct processor support for features that otherwise might not be considered important. For example, if one were taking a view that functional necessity (in a mathematical sense) is the only criterion for including a feature within a processor, one would have difficulty implementing a secure system.

This book is a major rewrite that started from my earlier two-volume book [KAIN89]. I changed the emphasis in programming examples from Ada to C++ and from the MC68020 processor to RISC processors. I expanded and clarified examples and explanations and added more examples from contemporary systems. I added more details about sharing and coordination between cooperating processes. I reduced the explanations of many introductory topics and rely now on the reader's background with programming in C++ or a similar language and with the design of RISC processors, at the level of Patterson and Hennessy [PATT93]. Some background material and some specialized topics have been moved into appendices. The fact that some material has moved to an appendix does not reduce its importance; it merely suggests that it could be skipped by a reader desiring to obtain an overview of the majority view of what constitutes computer architecture. I believe that with sufficient basic background, the reader can progress through the chapters, referring to the appendices only for detailed information about certain processors. Along this vein, note that the last appendix contains a listing of significant portions of several processor instruction sets; thus the reader can perform exercises that involve writing realistic programs for these processors, which will give an appreciation for the significant differences among several design approaches.

About Performance Topics. In contemporary practice, to get a paper accepted for publication in a computer architecture journal or conference, the authors must simulate the proposed design and exercise that simulator against "typical" programs. Many performance tables are presented. I have chosen to downplay this aspect of architectural studies, because they do not affect the logical structure of the architect's design options. Furthermore, the ultimate measure of a system's performance requires an incredibly detailed simulation of the complete design, which clearly reaches to the scope of a large project, and therefore is beyond the scope of this text.

Another reason for omitting performance measures is that the results depend upon the particular programs used to exercise the simulator. In many studies, these are quite narrow, typically relying on certain Unix programs that use few, if any, floating-point operations or on numeric applications that heavily exercise floating-point arithmetic. One might question the degree to which these represent "typical" programs. And often one sees a significant variance among the results across the set of programs. These comments should not be taken as criticism of all papers that contain performance statistics; rather I wish to raise your level of skepticism about performance results that do appear in the literature. A careful look at what was simulated and what programs were used should give a hint about the degree to which the results might apply to a different environment.

General and Specific Designs. The book presents optional ways to satisfy many real-world goals that challenge designers of contemporary systems and processors. In most chapters and appendices, one basic problem domain and the fundamental approaches to those problems are developed at the beginning. Uses of these basic approaches to specific situations at various levels are amplified in the chapter. Some concepts, design details, and comparisons are presented and detailed in problems rather than in the text. Therefore, designers are advised to look at the problems in conjunction with the text.

Background. I assume that the reader is familiar with at least one processor design, one operating system, one programming language (preferably C++), and the design of basic pipelined RISC processors. I do not assume any experience with multithread systems or with secure systems, which are covered extensively in Chapters 6 through 9.

Structure of the Book. The book's structure and approach reflect my belief that the best way to understand a set of related problems and design issues is first, to see the general techniques that could be used, and, second, to see how those have been applied, both in straight and varied manners and in various combinations, within real systems. To illustrate the common features, it is necessary to structure the text around common problems or around common elements of the system design. The book can be divided into three parts. The first part has a structure based on the von Neumann breakdown of a uniprocessor system—there are memory, control, and functional elements to each design. The second part addresses issues that arise when multiple threads of control or thought are simultaneously active within the overall system. The third part deals with the additional constraints imposed on the system by protection and security concerns. A brief outline of the topics in each chapter and appendix follows:

Chapter 1. Illusions: An introduction to the basic assumptions or illusions that programmers use to cope with the complexity of computer systems. The illusions reappear in the other chapters, where we point out how design options can support the illusions.

Chapter 2. Instruction Set Design: A quick review of basic ideas in processor structure, which become the basis for many examples in the following chapters. This is supplemented by material in Appendices A through D, where specific processor architectures are detailed.

Chapter 3. Memory Organization: The process of getting from the name of a memory object to an access to a physical location holding a set of bits; issues of name mapping implementations (from symbol tables to hash tables and hierarchical tables); linking; segmentation; paging; cache memories; memory interconnection structures. The material in Appendices E and F provides an essential background for the discussion in this chapter. Appendix G discusses the functions of associative memories and their implementation.

Chapter 4. Single-Stream Control: Basic structures for specifying control flow through a sequentially processed program; Harvard and von Neumann architectures; instruction representations; and brief comments regarding microprogramming. This material is supplemented by Appendix H, which covers the nonsequential control structures in Prolog.

Chapter 5. Object-Oriented Processing: Object types and classes; type-based modularization; and processor and system support for type-based modularization. This material is supplemented by Appendix I, covering the LISP language and the design of a machine to support that language.

Chapter 6. Single I-Stream Parallelism: Importance of static discovery or development of parallelism; ways to express parallelism within programs; finding and adding parallelism to programs; SIMD array processors; MIMD array processors; pipeline and barrel processors; and VLIW processors. Dynamic detection of parallelism; superscalar architectures. Ways to restructure programs to enhance the possibility of parallel execution. Appendix J covers systolic arrays, which can perform special algorithms using static parallelism.

Chapter 7. Parallelism by Message Passing: Models of message passing; functional correctness; programming models; interprocess and intermodule communication; and input/output interactions. This material is supplemented by Appendix K, covering data flow systems and their implementation. Some correctness proof arguments in Appendix L relate directly to these models.

Chapter 8. Shared-Resource Systems: Shared-memory systems; functional correctness models; synchronization and coherence for programs and caches; basic uninterruptible instructions and their usage; implementations that support the single copy and program order illusions; barrier instructions. Appendix L discusses some reasoning strategies useful with shared-resource systems.

Chapter 9. Protection and Security: Protection schemes using page and segment structures. Security requirements and their logical consequences, including the Bell and LaPadula security model and the Biba integrity model; basic design approaches that might assure security properties; reference monitor design approaches; and capability and type enforcement approaches to secure system design.

Appendix A. SPARC Summary: The essential architectural features of the SPARC processors, which has evolved from the early Berkeley RISC designs.

Appendix B. Alpha AXP: Essential features of this DEC microprocessor design, which is based on several interesting design options, including the use of low-level software to implement essential functions.

Appendix C. MC680x0 Processors: Some features of this architecture, with emphasis on the MC68020, chosen because it includes some interesting features that disappeared in later "compatible" processors; these include a flexible coprocessor interface design and instructions for calling modules that execute somewhat independently. These processors were inside all initial models of the Macintosh family of personal computers.

Appendix D. Stack-Oriented Systems: The B 5700 and HP 3000 systems; stack structures to support stacked allocations for activation blocks; special addressing modes that access local objects allocated within the stacked activation blocks. The B 5700 uses the stack in place of registers in a load/store architecture.

Appendix E. Naming Memory Objects: Techniques for specifying objects in programming languages and within processor instructions. Special emphasis on nested naming environments and two-dimensional addressing, because these pose important design problems and implementation options.

Appendix F. Memory Allocation: Basic allocation policies and the supporting management data structures; and options for processor support for these functions.

Appendix G. Associative Memories: Operations provided in general-purpose associative memories (more flexible than the simple equality-search memories used in memory accessing). Several implementation strategies.

Appendix H. Prolog: The structure of this language based on "facts" and "rules" collected within a database that serves as both the memory and the program. Some emphasis on the difficulties of implementing this language with parallelism.

Appendix I. List Processing: Structure of a list processing language, emphasizing the data structures, the run-time definition capabilities, and the overlap between data and program in this language. An overview of the Symbolics processors designed for efficient execution of LISP programs. Some emphasis on their choice of list representations, which led to efficiency.

Appendix J. Systolic Arrays: Structure of systolic arrays, demonstrating the difference between passing a program across data (the conventional view) and passing data through an array (the systolic view). Mathematical descriptions of these systems. Unfortunately, this approach seems to apply to only a few classes of algorithms.

Appendix K. Data Flow Systems: Structure and implementation of these systems, which are based on asynchronous activations of processing modules that communicate by passing tokens across communication paths. These structures provide a basis for some proofs discussed in the next appendix.

Appendix L. Reasoning and Proofs: A few approaches to proving properties of systems and programs. History matrices and induction arguments.

Examples. The text's programming examples use various programming languages, frequently C++, which is only partially explained in the text. In a similar manner, the processor examples emphasize features of several microprocessors—the SPARC, the DEC Alpha AXP, and the Motorola MC680x0, especially the MC68020.[1] These three processor architectures are surveyed in Appendices A through C. Processors that directly support stack and list structures are presented in Appendices D and I.

Many examples are based on features from other programming languages, operating systems, multiprocessor structures, and processor designs. I have not tried to make you an expert on all details of any of these designs; there are always myriad details needed to fashion a practical realization of an effective system.

Trends and Concept List. Each chapter (or appendix) ends with three sections, the first, titled "Trends," contains a brief projection of some apparent trends related to the material covered in the chapter. The second section, entitled "Concept List," contains a listing of the important concepts that were discussed in the chapter. And the third is the problem section.

Problems. I believe that solving problems is an important part of learning from a text, for only in this way can you appreciate the subtle design details or the subtle consequences of choosing certain design options. Some problems are

---

[1] I have received several comments to the effect that this architecture has been supplanted by subsequent developments, which is indeed true. I continue to use it because two of its features are architecturally interesting, but have been dropped from subsequent processors in the same series.

straightforward. Other problems pose design goals that may not be completely specified. Therefore, part of your problem time will be spent interpreting the problem statement. Some interesting and challenging problems place you in the role of design consultant and critic—you will be given a design proposal to critique and asked to examine its implications for the complete system. The critique problems should be considered thoughtfully; I do not recommend trying to solve them in a single session. You should think about the proposal and then give your mind at least overnight to ruminate on the proposal's effects on a complete system before you complete your critique. Except for the introductory first chapter, every chapter and appendix contains some problems related to the material in the chapter or appendix.

The Book as a Text. The book is written for use as a text. Seniors majoring in computer science and graduate students in electrical engineering should be able to cover the material in two quarters or in an intense single semester course. A single semester schedule may require compressing things, making it a challenge to leave sufficient time for reflection and thought about the points being made. The single semester schedule will require eliminating many of the appendices from the classroom presentation.

The Book as a Design Tool. The book is useful as a design tool. It incorporates the essential features of and the concepts behind many diverse designs. For this reason, it should be useful to both architects and implementers, enabling architects to have more design options at their command and implementers to understand the roles of their module(s) within a complete system.

About the Language (in the Book). Contemporary writers face many problems concerning the "correct" usage of the English language. Regarding computer systems or other technological artifacts, there is the problem of when the systems or languages are, or were, in common usage. This difficulty leads the author to question which tenses should be used when discussing these artifacts. I want to explain my approach to these difficulties immediately, so the choices will not lead the reader into incorrect or deceptive interpretations or conclusions. I have chosen the following linguistic options:

1. All languages, systems, and designs are described in the present tense, even though some of them are obviously obsolete as I write and others may become obsolete soon after the book becomes available. A design or language can become obsolete for many nontechnical reasons. These factors do not imply that all ideas within the design are not useful, but rather, the design environment might have changed as technology or applications evolve.
2. I use C++ syntax for all programs that could be written in C++ and for programs incorporating concepts or structures that could become compatible extensions of C++. However, C++ is not a "rich" language, in the sense that

it does not present all possible general structures and implementation challenges. Thus, some programming examples illustrate structures or concepts that would never be considered compatible with C++. One example is the static nesting of procedure definitions. Examples that are unlikely to be considered compatible with C++ are expressed in a Pascal/Ada syntax, which is not explained in detail. The reader should be able to read these programs and understand their structures by working from the first chapter forward; except in a few easily detected places, the reader is not asked to produce any programs incompatible with C++ or common assembly language structures. I believe that most, if not all, example programs are syntactically correct, but this is not a programming text, so it should not be used as an accurate reference for program syntax.

3. Programming languages do not support boldface symbols, but I do use boldface to emphasize keywords within programs and to distinguish keywords from common English words within the body of the text. For example, I talk about the **for** loop structure using a boldface font for **for** when it denotes the keyword in the text or in programs. I also put all symbols that appear in programs into the same sans-serif font used for programs.

4. Within assembly-level programs, I have tried to use the manufacturer's syntax, explaining it only as it seems necessary.

5. All comments in C++ programs are marked using the C++ style—with double slashes to set off each comment, which runs to the end of the line. This comment structure may not be compatible with the conventions of the programming language used in the remainder of the line. Comments in other programs are sometimes expressed in the Ada style, using a double dash to set off the comment.

Best Wishes. I hope that you will learn interesting and useful things from the book. In particular, I hope that you will appreciate the connections between software and hardware design issues, leading you to a better appreciation of the interlocking nature of these issues and their solutions. I hope that you will learn optional ways to approach difficult, but not impossible, design goals and constraints. Also, I hope that you will learn about a few historically important designs that were innovative in their times; many deserve continuing study to assist the understanding of future designers. Perhaps in your time you will write a book that follows this tradition and that you will contribute to keeping alive my approach of integrating contemporary, historical, and untried (but logically interesting) design approaches!

Richard Y. Kain
Minneapolis, Minnesota

ACKNOWLEDGMENTS

My students and colleagues have provided many helpful suggestions for improving this text, and essential encouragement for this project. The students in my classes have tolerated sketchy drafts of this book.

I extend special thanks to Mark Smotherman and Matthew Frank for voluntary reviews of the manuscript; they gave very helpful suggestions. Three students from my class contributed significant editorial suggestions; I thank Derek Lee, Scott vander Linde, and Greg Younker for this assistance.

The Prentice Hall reviewers, who made many helpful suggestions, include Stephen J. Hartley, Dan C. Marinescu, Paul W. Ross, Robert Seban, and Douglas Reeves. Several of them suggested that the draft had too much material; this led me into a vast late-stage reorganization that moved one-third of the material into the appendices. Of course, they are not responsible for any of the contents of the book—after all, they probably do not agree with all of it anyhow!

I received some interesting suggestions from people watching the comp.arch bulletin board on the Internet, though I did not place priority on all of their suggestions. Special thanks go to George Papp, who saw my appeal and responded with helpful processor manuals.

The original impetus for this book came from Prentice Hall editors who suggested that I make a significant revision of the previous book, compressing it and updating material; Tom McElwee was the impetus in that direction. When he moved to marketing, Bill Zobrist ably took over and reined me in to complete the project. Chris Certain, the local representative, was quite helpful in getting materials in a timely manner. The production editing was started by Bayani DeLeon and finished by Rose Kernan, an able production editor who tolerated last minute changes, including adding her name to these acknowledgments.

People at the AmiPro help line also deserve some thanks for getting me out of several binds during the writing and production stages of this project.

Many people contributed to the previous book from which this was derived by a tortuous process; those not mentioned here influenced this text, indirectly through the old version.

Special thanks go to my wife, Katherine Simon Frank, without whose help and encouragement this would not have been possible. Now we can both enjoy life more as we celebrate the fact that the book is done!

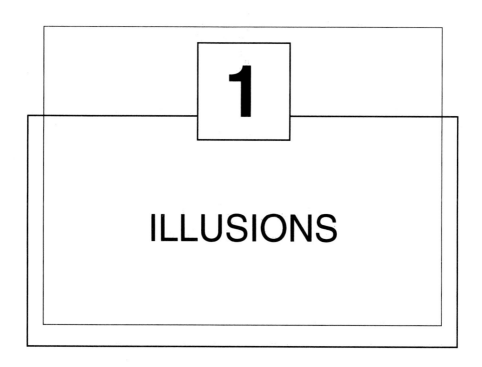

ILLUSIONS

*All architecture is what you do to it
when you look on it.*

— Walt Whitman

An architect designs structures covered up by surfaces (or *interfaces*) that create *illusions*. The surface might be a surface of reflective glass, making a building look lighter, or it may be a solid, heavy skin, making a building look important. In any case, the interface hides the building's internal structure. What do we want to see when we look at the structure, and how do we want to use it? These important questions define our methods for dealing with complexity.

We can deal with complexity by simplifying it—by creating new views, or *illusions*. A computer system is inherently complex. Several important illusions help us understand the behavior of a computer system. First, we accept the illusion that the computer behaves as though the processor executes a single sequence (or *stream*) of instructions or statements from a programming language. Second, we accept the illusion that there is a simple memory system, which performs reads and writes to memory locations that have names or addresses. Third, we accept the illusion that each perceived action, whether it be a memory read, a memory write, or the execution of a processor instruction, is a single *atomic* action and that nothing can interfere with its execution or completion.

Fourth, we might accept the illusion that the processor is manipulating complex objects, such as vectors, matrices, character strings, and lists.

However, reality may be quite discordant with the illusions: We know that a modern high-performance processor may execute instructions in parallel, and that a high-performance system might include many processors cooperating to execute the program, though these details could be hidden from the programmer. We know that the memory system may make parallel accesses to several objects. We know that some operations (at least the complex ones) might be interrupted. And we know that each processor actually handles only simple objects during each instruction. These real design features promote system speed and functionality, but they do add complexity to the implementation so that the user's illusions are supported and users can cope with the system's complexity.

We do need to hold on to our simplifying illusions so we can cope with the complexity of our applications without having to face any additional complexity introduced by the system itself.

When computers were first introduced in the 1940s, processor architectures were relatively simple, with few registers, small memories, and simple functionality. These limitations arose from the implementation technology; logic gates were expensive and it was difficult to keep the processor running without failure until the next scheduled checkout period. The illusion and the reality conformed with each other! Programming was difficult because the programmer had to deal with the internal details of the processor and its input/output devices. Operating systems (that hide resource management and communication details) had not been developed. High-level languages and other forms of abstraction were developed later; these provided a new view (or illusion) of the system's behavior by permitting the programmer to think in terms of more complex operations (e.g., expressions could be evaluated) and control structures (e.g., loop structures were codified). Modern programming languages support object-oriented illusions, whereby the system is viewed as performing complex atomic operations on complex data objects. We still hold to the illusion that there is a single control point governing the processing of named objects located within a memory system, and that the operations proceed without interruption.

While these software developments unfolded, the implementation technology evolved and new "generations" of systems were devised, many of them later becoming obsolete. Today we use superscalar processors that contain over a million active devices and provide fast execution; they reach this high performance level by violating the user's illusions within their implementations. Their designs do preserve the user's illusions when viewed from the outside: Even though a processor may execute several instructions simultaneously, it behaves in accordance with the illusion that there is a single control point governing the execution of one atomic instruction at a time. The gap between the programmer's illusions about the computer's structure and the reality of its design and implementation is very wide!

Crossing a wide gap is difficult unless the gap can be divided into a set of smaller gaps. Thus, the implementation of a high-level program on a modern processor is divided into several stages, including compilation, compiler optimization (which may introduce parallelism), operating system support, special sequences of program steps introduced by the compiler and hidden from the programmer, complex run-time decisions made within the processor's control logic, and finally information transfers among registers, memory, and functional units within the processor. The designers of the modules implementing these steps will be able to do a better job if they are aware of the interrelationships among the modules and the module design options that are available. Of particular importance is the question: "How is the responsibility for maintaining the illusions spread among the modules within the implementation?"

In this book I cover the basic illusions, many optional strategies that support those illusions, and basic design options that underlie system implementation strategies. You will see how the same set of basic options often can be useful at several levels within the implementation to support the programmer's illusions.

1.1 FORMALIZED ILLUSIONS

We start by formalizing and labeling the basic illusions.

Simple Memory Illusion. All objects within the computer system are stored within a memory system that contains a single copy of each item. An individual object within the memory is identified by its *name*. The atomic operations involving memory objects include *read* and *write*, which transfer a value of an object from or to (respectively) memory.

Control Point Illusion. The sequence of execution of a program is governed by the progress of a single conceptual *control point* whose position indicates the step being executed. The control point does not move from one step to the next one until the previous step has been completed. The semantics of the steps determine the order of execution of the program steps; this order is known as the *program order*. The single control point progresses in accordance with the program order.

Object Type Illusion. The computer system can manipulate objects of various types; the definition of an object's type includes the definition of all permissible operations on objects of the corresponding type.

Atomic Action Illusion. Each action initiated by the computer system is performed in its entirety without interruption. If it does get interrupted, its effects are canceled and it is reexecuted without interruption (if this is not possible, the system has detected an *error*, which will be handled in some other manner).

Operator Illusion. Each action performed by the computer system is an operator whose operands and effects are unambiguously specified.

Definition. A system component or module *supports an illusion* if it provides an interface through which the illusion appears to hold to an outsider.

The simple von Neumann processor model supports all of these illusions. In this model the processor executes instructions that are fetched from memory. Each instruction that makes a data access to memory contains the address of the data item. Each instruction is completed before the next one is fetched. Now compare this against the illusions: (1) Each data object located in memory is identified by a memory address in the instruction that desires access to the object; thus, the simple memory illusion is supported. (2) The single processor executes a single instruction that has been fetched from the memory location whose address was in the program counter (PC), and the PC is updated according to the instruction's semantics; thus, the single control point illusion is supported. (3) All objects are integers; thus the object type illusion is supported, albeit with a single object type, which is quite limiting. (4) There are no interrupts to interfere with this activity; thus, the atomic action illusion is supported. (5) The operators are the operations built into the processor's logic.

Our simple example shows that real machines might directly support the user's illusions, provided that the user is willing to be exposed to (and cope with) all details of the machine's design. To support the illusions with a different set of object types, a different control structure or a different definition of the operators, one can devise a logical structure that gives the appearance of being a machine. One can build this "machine" in various ways, such as by defining a program that presents the appearance of behaving like the specified machine. For example, one can support the appearance of a machine that directly executes C++ programs by writing a C++ compiler that translates C++ programs into processor-level programs that support the illusions that go with all C++ semantics. This C++ "machine" is not real, in the sense that it is not just hardware, but as far as the user is concerned, it is real, because it can be used to execute programs and perform useful work. A machine like this, which is not built from hardware, is conventionally called a "virtual machine."

> **Definition.** A *virtual machine* is an implementation giving the appearance of being a computing machine.

Because a virtual machine appears to be a machine, it would be helpful if it supported the illusions of a von Neumann system. There is a program whose steps control the machine's actions, there is a memory holding data objects, and there is a control unit that manages the activities. Although the implementation might not support the user's illusions, the machine's behavior would be more comprehensible when the illusions are supported. The difference between the simple von Neumann machine and a virtual machine might lie in the types of objects supported by the virtual machine or the organization of the memory system.

The definition of the machine (whether real or virtual) includes the semantics of its operations. These, in turn, define the correct, or functional, behavior of the machine.

> **Definition.** The *functional behavior*, or *correct behavior*, of a virtual machine is behavior that conforms to the illusions specified for that machine. In particular, the machine executes a sequence of nonoverlapped atomic actions whose operands are located in the simple memory and whose semantics are specified.

The designer's challenge is to support all of these illusions, particularly providing functional behavior, within a system designed for speed and efficiency, using the millions of devices that can exist within a single processor. A hierarchy of illusions created by a hierarchy of virtual machines implemented by hardware or software modules or other mechanisms might be required to bridge the wide illusion gap between the virtual machine and the physical processor.

1.2 HIERARCHICAL ILLUSIONS

In modern complex computer systems the user's illusions are far from the processor's reality. The wide gap is bridged by a sequence of mechanisms or modules that implement virtual machines. For example, the illusion that a system can process a floating-point value (called a *float* in C++) can be provided in several different ways:

1. The processor can include float registers and instructions that perform arithmetic on float objects.

2. The processor might not implement float operations directly, but it does detect the occurrence of float operations that it does not implement and then it does cause an interrupt that invokes software that does emulate the behavior of the float operations.
3. The compiler can insert calls to library routines that use integer operations to implement each float operation that is needed.
4. The compiler can insert into the program ("inline") a sequence of integer instructions that will perform each requested float operation.
5. The user can write routines that perform the float operations using integer operations; the user includes these routines within the definition of an object *class*. The compiler inserts calls to the defined routines as required.
6. The user can write subroutines like those in the previous option, but the user specifically codes calls to those routines when they are required.
7. The user can write programs without using any objects of type float.

Several important observations can be made from this set of options:

1. The user's illusion that the system supports float objects is maintained from option 1 through option 4, and a limited version of that illusion is still present in option 5. In option 6, the illusion partially disappears. It is completely absent in option 7.
2. The algorithms that implement float operations using integer operations do not have to change with the selection of any option (except option 7, which does not support them at all).
3. The system module mentioned in options i .. 7 can freely use float objects if one of options 1 .. $(i-1)$ is chosen, because the module can operate under the illusion that the system supports float objects.

The generalization of the second observation is the important notion that the same implementation options are available at all levels of the system. Of course, technological and efficiency considerations might identify some options as outrageous choices, but still they would satisfy the logical requirements by supporting correct functional behavior. In this book we discuss many implementation options and show how each one could be used within the computer system. We will see, for example, CISC implementations that push support for a linguistic feature into hardware; however, the compiler for a modern RISC system might insert a sequence of processor instructions to support the same feature.

1.3 LIMITS AND RESPONSIBILITIES

Every module has limits. For example, not all bit patterns represent a valid memory address (unless the memory is fully expanded). And not all bit patterns represent valid instructions.

How are the module limits handled within the system's design? And if there are limits, where is the responsibility for checking those limits? Three possibilities arise with respect to memory addressing:

1. The system's hardware checks each address for validity.
2. The compiler design guarantees that the program will never produce an invalid memory address.
3. The system is designed and configured so that every bit pattern does represent a valid memory address.

These possibilities represent three basic ways to handle the module's limitations. To complete a system, the designer must choose an implementation structure and a set of module functions that is compatible with each module's functionality and limitations. The choices behind a particular module design might imply that some responsibility must be assigned to higher-level modules (the compiler in our addressing example) in order to support the illusions.

We introduce descriptive terms for the three basic design approaches.

Definition. A module design follows the *everything checked* approach if it checks every request for conformance with the module's limitations.

Definition. A module design follows the *nothing illegal* approach if it makes no conformance checks, relying on the fact that the request source will never generate a request that exceeds the module's limitations.

Definition. A module design follows the *anything goes* approach if its design does not limit the requests that it can handle.

Most computer system modules check everything before performing the operation. Some are designed on the assumption that another (higher) module will never make unreasonable requests. For example, the implementation of a language relies on the compiler not to produce programs that inappropriately cross the boundaries of program modules. The anything goes approach appears rarely in computer systems.

Under all approaches, it is important that the designer recognize the consequences of design decisions, especially the responsibilities imposed on other modules as a consequence of choosing each option.

1.4 HISTORIC DESIGNS

Both contemporary and historic designs include viable design approaches that can support the illusions in an efficient manner. Therefore the book exposes many system design issues and common design options that can support the illusions. We examine each issue at different implementation levels to understand the set of design options and the interrelationships among the levels. We emphasize RISC processor implementations and high-level programming languages (especially C++) to illustrate some important contemporary approaches to these issues. We present examples and design issues arising from many other programming languages and processor architectures to illustrate the wide scope of techniques available to the computer architect.

A holistic view can be helpful: first, study the functional and performance requirements derived from applications and the illusions supported by programming languages; then move inward to the compiler and the operating system and finally to the processor's instruction set. This book follows this holistic approach, reaching from the high-level language down to the choice of the processor's instruction set and occasionally to the processor's implementation, where we examine the interconnections of functional units and sections of processor chips. At each level we examine many options from important contemporary and historic (even obsolete!) designs. Both contemporary and obsolete designs contain important lessons for future designers and illustrate ways to implement system functionality.

1.5 OVERVIEW

Computer systems are complex entities; their hardware and software are designed to support a few basic illusions that make them understandable to human beings. An important illusion is that a virtual machine provides functional behavior, conforming to all of the illusions it supports. But every virtual and real machine must have limits and boundaries. The methods by which these boundaries are enforced are very important. The choice of the design approach not only defines the module's requirements, but may also assign requirements (or responsibilities) to other virtual machines in the implementation hierarchy. In all of this, the requirement for functional behavior must be satisfied.

In the remainder of the book we study computer system design options spanning the range from software to hardware. We show relationships among the design issues and available options. We show how the illusions can be supported in all parts of the system. We approach this task in the following order. In Chapters 2 through 5 we explore the design of single instruction stream systems: first, the programmer's views of the structures of their processors (Chapter 2), followed by their memories (Chapter 3), their control sections (Chapter 4), and their object manipulation units (Chapter 5). In Chapters 6 through 8 we explore the use of parallelism to enhance system performance. We start with parallelism imposed atop a virtual machine that has a single instruction stream (Chapter 6).

Then we turn to two classes of models in which cooperating processes communicate by passing messages (Chapter 7) or by sharing resources (Chapter 8). We complete our study in Chapter 9 with an overview of computer system support for protection and security; the latter must satisfy another illusion—that accesses to shared resources and objects are limited in accordance with a specified security policy. The appendices cover both background material and specialized architectural topics and programming systems (the latter chosen because they are based on illusions that differ from those behind the conventional single processor system discussed before).

1.6 TRENDS

A trends section at the end of each chapter surveys some important trends related to the topics covered within the chapter. We try to extrapolate the present into the future, which is risky! It is difficult to base trends on the basic concepts presented here, so we will start this in a meaningful way in Chapter 2.

1.7 CONCEPT LIST

At the end of each chapter we list the key concepts mentioned in that chapter. Here they relate to the illusions and the design approach options.

1. Simple memory illusion
2. Control point illusion
3. Object type illusion
4. Atomic action illusion
5. Operator illusion
6. Support for illusions
7. Virtual machines
8. Functional behavior
9. Hierarchical realizations
10. Everything checked approach
11. Nothing illegal approach
12. Anything goes approach
13. Responsibilities for functional behavior

2

INSTRUCTION SET DESIGN

It is not enough to have a good mind.
The main thing is to use it well.

— *Descartes*

Methods are habits of the mind
and economies of the memory.

— *A. Rivarol*

The design of the processor's instruction set is an important architectural issue. A specification of the instruction set choice includes the description of the portion of the processor's structure that is visible to the assembly language programmer. This structure and the functionality of the instructions define the processor's behavior. It is important that the instruction set be compatible with the programmer's illusions and that it efficiently support those illusions. In particular, as we design the instruction set we must provide ways to use the computer well.

There are several options in the instruction set choice, including (1) choosing a minimal, yet functionally complete, design; (2) choosing instructions based on their speed of execution; and (3) choosing a more elaborate instruction set encapsulating frequent (or habitual) sequences into single processor operations. The first class of options gives a design that is simply implemented, though this design might not be relevant under current technology, which permits millions of devices within a single processor module. The second (Reduced Instruction Set Computer—RISC) option is commonly chosen because the instructions can be performed so quickly that even if more instructions are required to complete the job, their improved execution speed more than makes up the difference. Under this option, it is likely that the number of instructions in the program and the space that the program occupies will increase to perform the same job, but one can design processor logic so the instructions can be executed quickly in a pipeline. Under the third (Complex Instruction Set Computer—CISC) option, the processor's instructions are more complex than in a RISC machine, so they cannot be performed as quickly, but the same task can be performed using fewer instructions. In this chapter we survey some important issues and options in the design of a processor's instruction set.

The instruction set simultaneously reflects the programmer's view of the system's state, the primitive operand types (that are manipulated by the underlying system), and the basic operations that can be performed on those operands. Finally, the instructions specify how memory operands are accessed—specifically, how operand addresses are determined from fields within the instruction and the contents of processor registers and memory locations. Thus the instruction set defines the view of the illusions about the memory, the control point, the object types, the operators, and the notion that those operators are performed in an atomic manner. Support for any additional features, accessing modes, or object types has to be provided through software built upon the basic processor architecture.

In this book we show how the processor's limitations can be supplemented by high-level programming, by strategies implementing virtual machines that execute statements from high-level languages, and other support (from the operating system, for example) to give an applications programmer the overall illusion that the system supports both the programming language and the application correctly, efficiently, and in an understandable modular manner.

After reading this chapter you will know the representations and functions of some processor instructions. You will learn the fundamentals of processor architectures and be prepared for the processor-level discussions in succeeding chapters. Detailed information about several processor designs is given in Appendices A through D.[1]

---

[1]   We discuss additional features of these machines in many other chapters.

2.1 BASIC CONCEPTS

Each processor design conforms to the basic illusions described in Chapter 1: (1) there is a single execution point; (2) there is a single memory containing one copy of each object; (3) instructions are executed atomically in sequential order; (4) operations are defined; and (5) the first four assumptions define functional (correct) behavior.

To understand the processor's behavior as it executes instructions, we need to have a model of its internal structure, as seen by a machine-language programmer.

A processor's architecture has four major aspects:

1. Processor state
2. Memory system
3. Program control instructions
4. Object manipulation instructions

The *processor state* includes the information in programmer-visible registers (including every control register, such as the program counter), which conceptually[2] is stored within the processor. The *memory system* describes both the information stored in memory and the addressing techniques used to select information from memory during program execution. The *program control instructions* specify instruction sequencing for correct program execution. Finally, the *object manipulation instructions* specify how values can be manipulated by the processor. Most of these aspects relate directly to the illusions that we try to support. The memory system's design supports the simple memory illusion. The program control instructions support the control point illusion. The object manipulation instructions support the object type illusion. Finally, by the way that actions are sequenced, the control unit's design supports the atomic action illusion. Together we obtain functional behavior.

2.2 PROCESSOR STATE

The complete processor state includes portions not visible when the processor is in the user mode. The programmer-visible portion of the state is our focus here. The first important state information is the mode information in a status register; this defines that the processor is in the user mode or another mode. The other programmer-visible registers can be divided into several categories:

1. Status register
2. Integer registers

---

[2]   We use the word "conceptually" because the implementer may choose to store the information outside the processor itself, but the programmer does not have to know the details.

3. Float registers
4. Address registers
5. Program counter
6. Condition code registers
7. Pointer registers

Often the roles of these registers overlap—the stack pointer might be taken from an integer or an address register, and the program counter likewise. Some processors contain separate float registers, and other processors do not support floating-point operations in their instruction sets.

A specification of the processor registers states their sizes, their numbers, and their roles during instruction execution. Usually the size is a number of bits that is a power of 2. Usually the number of registers is another power of 2.

2.3 MEMORY STRUCTURE

In the conventional view, the contents of memory are organized as a series of addressable bytes. The program can access directly certain locations within memory. Even though each memory address designates an individual byte, the amount of information accessed during a single instruction may encompass several bytes. Some important memory design issues include the following:

1. How wide objects are constructed from consecutive memory objects.
2. Whether wide object addresses are constrained.
3. How addresses are determined within the processor.

Wide Object Construction. The first question determines how wide objects are constructed from individual bytes. There are two possibilities:

Definition. A *big-endian* machine forms wide objects from memory bytes by placing the byte with the lowest address at the most-significant end of the wide object.

Definition. A *small-endian* machine forms wide objects from memory bytes by placing the byte with the lowest address at the least-significant end of the wide object.

These definitions specify the location of the byte at one end of the wide object; the other bytes are ordered within the wide object in increasing or decreasing order according to the order of their memory addresses.

Wide Object Addresses. A second question concerns whether the processor/memory design restricts the addresses of wide objects. Under the natural alignment option, the addresses of all items in memory must be compatible with their lengths:

> **Definition.** An item stored in memory and comprising 2^n addressable units is *naturally aligned* (or simply *aligned*) if the n least significant bits of its address are all zero.

Imposing natural alignment permits the system to assure fast access to objects, because the memory structure can be adjusted so that a complete object can be accessed in one memory cycle.

Address Construction. The third question concerns the methods by which addresses are computed within the processor itself. In most RISC machines there are only two methods. Both add the contents of one register to a value obtained either from another register or from the instruction. In contrast, CISC machines often have many addressing modes, including the following:

1. Direct addressing (it comes from the instruction)
2. Register indirect addressing (it comes from a specified register)
3. Memory indirect addressing (the contents of a memory location contain the address)
4. Indexing
5. Preincrement/postincrement/decrement

Many early processor designs limit their support to direct, indexed, and memory indirect addressing.

The rules for interpreting addresses and the assignment of registers to hold special pointers can produce an important benefit in supporting structured high-level languages; some processor designs incorporate these rules and semantics within their instruction sets, as we will see later.

Additional rules governing the translation of addresses from a "virtual" memory space to a "physical" memory space relate closely to the use of paged or segmented address mappings; these, in turn, support the operating system's memory management functions.

2.4 INSTRUCTION FORMATS

Two dimensions of the instruction format question concern the variability of the overall instruction widths and the subdivision of individual instructions into fields, each with contents that encode a portion of the functional specification, such as a register number or the operation code.

The program counter (PC) register tracks the location of the instruction under execution or the next instruction to be executed (the correct choice depends upon the time within the execution cycle when you examine the register); at the conclusion of an instruction, PC contains the location of the next instruction to be executed.[3] How is the program counter updated during program execution? If each instruction has the same width, during sequential program execution the PC can be incremented by that width at any point during instruction execution. However, if instructions can have different widths, the instruction being executed must be decoded to determine its width (and, of course, other specifications critical to its correct execution). But to properly handle unusual situations, such as interrupts, the program counter may have to be supplemented with auxiliary registers, as shown in the following examples.

Example 2-1

> The MC680x0 processors (e.g., [MOTO84]) have variable width instructions, some using a second (16-bit) word to complete the instruction specification, whereas others use *extension words* to complete certain address specifications (this depends upon the addressing mode). There is a conventional PC register and a ScanPC register (not visible to the programmer) tracking which words have been interpreted so far. For instruction retry and for returns after interrupts that occur within delay slots, PC must be used, but for instruction fetching, ScanPC is needed. Updating ScanPC is simple because it deals with word-sized objects.

Example 2-2

> The SPARC processors ([SPAR92] and [WEAV94]) have a fixed instruction width (32 bits); the implementation utilizes overlapped execution, so the processor must track the location of more than one instruction to correctly recover from an interruption or exception. The programmer does not see the duplicity, but within the processor (and within the state it saves upon the occurrence of an interrupt), there are two PC registers—PC and nPC, the latter holding the location of the next instruction to be executed.

To execute an instruction, a processor must perform the following generic steps:

> G1. Fetch the instruction;
> G2. Advance PC;
> G3. Decode the instruction;
> G4. Perform the instruction.

Step G2 can be moved to a later position without affecting functionality if the implementation of step G4 is adjusted properly.

---

[3]   If the processor utilizes pipelined or overlapped execution, this description has to be modified.

2.5 CONTROL INSTRUCTIONS

A processor's control instructions and the implicit rules in other instructions governing changes in the contents of the PC register together determine the program's flow of execution. In conventional architectures, any instruction not in the control instruction class changes the PC by advancing it to the byte following the instruction being executed. Thus instructions are performed in the same order that they are stored in memory. This simple sequencing rule is not adequate to perform general algorithms, so to permit general algorithms to be performed, we need at least one conditional program control instruction to allow exceptions to the otherwise rigid sequential control flow.

To support structured programming, we also need instructions that support subroutine call and return, though they are not functionally necessary. Additional control instructions support loop structures.

Several design questions arise when selecting control instructions:

1. What conditions are checked by conditional branch instructions?
2. How are branch destinations specified?
3. What structured programming support is provided?
4. How much functionality is built into the semantics of control instructions?

Conditions to Be Checked. What conditions can be checked by conditional instructions? A typical processor design includes a *condition code register* (which might be implemented as part of a general status register), whose state can be modified during the execution of some processor instructions. Early designs simply tested the status of the (single) accumulator within the processor; some contemporary designs are returning to this style, testing register contents, because the condition code register can become a bottleneck that impedes certain kinds of parallelism used to speed execution, as we will see in Chapter 6.

A typical set of condition bits includes the following:

1. Zero (Z)
2. Carry (C)
3. Negative (N)
4. Overflow (V)

The conditions that can be tested in a SPARC conditional branch instruction, specified in Table 2-1, are typical of those available in a processor using a condition code register.

Branch Destination Specifications. The addressing options for branch destination specifications include absolute addressing, specifying a complete memory address, and relative addressing, specifying an (signed) offset from the contents of the program counter. PC-relative addressing is typically used to

TABLE 2-1   SPARC INTEGER BRANCH INSTRUCTION CONDITIONS

	Condition (C_1)			Complementary Condition (C_1')	
Mnemonic	Name	Logical Condition	Mnemonic	Name	
A	Always	1	N	Never	
E	Equal	Z	NE	Not equal	
LE	Less or equal	Z + (N XOR V)	G	Greater	
L	Less	N XOR V	GE	Greater or equal	
LEU	Less or equal unsigned	C + Z	GU	Greater, unsigned	
CS	Carry set	C	CC	Carry clear	
NEG	Negative	N	POS	Positive	
VS	Overflow set	V	VC	Overflow clear	

specify destinations of loop termination instructions, because the offset can occupy a few bits and therefore can fit into the branch instruction itself. Complete memory addressing is used for subroutine call instructions, because the locations of the call instruction and the entry to the subroutine are independently chosen.

Additional Functionality.   An important design option concerns the functions performed during a control instruction, particularly those that correspond to changes in the execution environment, such as subroutine call and return. At a minimum, the PC must be saved on CALL, to assure correct return to the calling program, but other state changes, particularly related to object addressing, can be included in the CALL semantics; these options are explored in Chapter 4.

2.6 DATA TYPES

Every computer supports objects of types integer and Boolean. Most realistic machines support diverse data types in their processor operations. Floating-point operands are often supported; we call them *float*, conforming to C++ conventions. Many processors support character string operands, with the strings held in memory and their descriptors held within the processor.

In conventional designs, the types of the objects participating in an operation are determined by decoding the function code from the instruction; other options in this regard are presented in Chapter 5. Some architectures provide a separate set of registers to hold float operands; this division can assist the efficient implementation of overlapped execution, as in RISC machines.

2.7 OBJECT MANIPULATION

In principle, all object manipulation can be performed by a two-operand subtract instruction (SUB) whose operands are the contents of a memory location and the contents of a processor register. Clearly, this structure is quite limiting and inefficient, so a rich set of operations is provided in most processor architectures. In addition to selecting the operation set, a design team must choose the following:

1. Operand width
2. Operand and result locations
3. The possibility of immediate (literal) operands

Operation Set Selection. Independently chosen operation sets are available for each data type. Integer operations include all arithmetic operations, with the possible exception of division (which is slow to execute, and which can be approximated by other techniques). Float operations also include all arithmetic operations, possibly without division. Some processors support square root operations.

The large market for machines that support COBOL programs for business applications drives many designers to provide a rich set of character string operations; we will not discuss these operations in this book.

Software structures based on object class definitions can expand the functions of the virtual machine visualized by a programmer; these extensions are handled within the compiler. They result in sequences of instructions using the basic data types supported in the processor's design.

Operand Widths. It is possible to design a processor in which this number is variable (the B 1700 processor takes this approach; see [BURR72]), but the benefits are few and the penalties in both speed and logical complexity are high enough. Thus, contemporary architectures support only a small number of operand widths. Table 2-2 illustrates the width selections available in some processors. Having only a small number of widths tends to make instruction execution more efficient; the Alpha AXP processors [SITE92] support integer arithmetic only on 32-bit and 64-bit operands.

Operand and Result Locations. Some processor designs are stack-based, with the operands popped from the top of the stack and the results pushed on the stack when the operation is completed. Most processors have a set of registers that are visible to the programmer. In these designs, at least one operand (for an operation that has two operands) comes from a register. Where are the other operands and the result located? The possibilities include other registers, the top of a stack, or a memory location. In a *load/store* architecture, the operands

TABLE 2-2   SOME OPERAND WIDTH SELECTIONS

Processor	Integer Size(s)	Float Size(s)
MC680x0	8, 16, 32	N/A
Intel x86	8, 16, 32	N/A
B 1700	1 .. 24	N/A
B 5700	39, 78	48, 96
Alpha AXP	32, 64	32, 64
PowerPC 601	32	32, 64
SPARC-V9	64	32, 64, 128

and results of object manipulation instructions never come from memory (they may come from the program stream as immediate values or from the top of the stack).

> **Definition.** In a *load/store architecture*, data references to memory addresses (not the top of the stack) can only copy object values, not manipulate them in any manner (transforming formats between register-size objects and memory items to maintain compatibility with the memory's big/small-endian layout is permitted).

Table 2-3 indicates some choices concerning load/store designs and the locations of operands and results of instructions that manipulate integers.

Immediate Operands.   Many programs frequently perform arithmetic using constant values, which themselves are often small. Therefore one might consider placing the constant values within the program itself as *literal* (or *immediate*)

TABLE 2-3   OPTIONS FOR ARITHMETIC OPERAND/RESULT LOCATIONS[a]

Processor	Operand_1	Operand_2	Result	Load/Store Design?
MC680x0	R	R/M/I	R/M	No
Intel x86	R	R/M/I	R/M	No
B 5700	S	S	S	Yes
Alpha AXP	R	R	R	Yes
SPARC	R	R	R	Yes

[a] The codes are I = immediate; M = memory; R = register; S = stack.

operands. A common design style is that immediate operands can replace memory addresses in those instructions that read a value from memory. This option imposes length restrictions on the immediate values, which therefore limit the range of values that can be retrieved from immediate operands. The advantage of immediate operands is greater than this simple argument suggests, however, because the constant values that appear most frequently in real programs are small integer values that easily fit within the size restrictions imposed on immediate operands.

Changing anything within the program during its execution requires writing to the program object, which introduces complexity in understanding and implementation. Using memory writes to modify the program being executed is discouraged by all advocates of good programming practice. It also complicates the design of instruction buffers. Therefore, immediate operands should be used only for constant values that are fixed prior to program execution.

2.8 SUMMARY

Several obvious reasons make minimal processor designs undesirable, including the following:

1. Programs that perform "simple" functions are long and awkward.
2. Program execution will be slow.
3. Having only a few registers forces an excess amount of object copying between the processor and memory.

On the other hand, there is one obvious reason why minimal designs might be desirable—it requires little logic to implement their functionality. This criterion is not important in this age of integrated circuits.

Various interesting processor designs are summarized in Appendices A through D.

Computer architects use the term "orthogonal" to indicate that two design features can be specified independently. It does not appear that there are interesting processors with completely orthogonal instruction sets, because complete orthogonality implies that every portion of the instruction must have a compatible meaning within the context of every possible function that has to be supported. It is desirable to have some degree of independence, meaning that the exceptions to the "common" interpretation of the instruction bits are infrequently encountered during program execution.

Orthogonality not only simplifies the programmer's task of remembering usage constraints, but it also simplifies the compiler's code generation logic, especially if the options concerning operand addressing and location are independent of the operation being performed.

At the hardware design level, instruction set orthogonality can decrease delays and can simplify implementation logic, because the logic that implements an orthogonal feature can be enabled before having to check another portion of the instruction to decide whether that particular logical function is actually required during the instruction's execution.[4]

Even if the processor has a complex instruction set supporting many object types, there is a wide gap between the semantics behind high-level programs and the processor's limited capabilities. This gap must be bridged by software structures supported by the compiler, assembler, linker, and run-time libraries, with assistance from the operating system. A processor designed with these needs in mind can execute the required functions more efficiently. The interactions between processor design issues and the semantic requirements coming from higher levels is a major theme affecting the presentation in this book. After completing the book, the reader should understand the reasons for many requirements and desires for processor features that otherwise might seem arbitrary.

2.9 TRENDS

The major trend that influences processor architectures is the trend toward RISC implementations, which favor the use of register-based processors, simple addressing modes, no indirection, and a large dependency on software to optimize program to improve the execution speed and to accommodate the overlapped nature of the processor's implementation.

Some important older processor designs incorporated mechanisms to support language semantics and operating system functions. Their lessons remain. First, the linguistic semantics do have to be supported, which can be difficult without adequate hardware support. Second, it is not wise to build policies into the processor design. Third, fundamental difficulties with stack management make it undesirable to structure a processor around a stack that holds operands and results from instructions.

These themes and trends are explored in this book, with particular attention to the need to support the semantics of programming languages.

2.10 CONCEPT LIST

   1. Processor register structures
   2. Program order sequencing

---

[4]   Alternately, a processor can initiate the action based on an assumption about the use of the bits and later discard the results if the assumption turns out to be incorrect—we discuss this design option in Chapter 6.

3. Big-endian and small-endian memory organizations
4. Natural alignment of memory objects
5. Extension words in instructions
6. Condition codes
7. Load/store architectures
8. Immediate operands

2.11 PROBLEMS

2-1. A designer proposes the following technique for enforcing a separation among virtual machines that run on a single processor system. Assume that the separation of memory spaces is the only concern. To attack this problem, the designer proposes restricting the formation of addresses by restricting the use of the processor's addressing modes. The proposed restriction would be enforced by designing the operating system so that it permits the execution of only programs produced by "certified" assemblers and compilers. The following questions probe important parts of this argument.

(a) Assume that the proposed enforcement mechanism guarantees that the prohibited addressing modes are never used. Can you then certify that two programs will always be separated in memory? In other words, is it possible to select a few addressing modes, restrict address generation to these modes, and then guarantee that certain addresses cannot be generated? Remember that the assembler does know the address information that is placed in the program when it is written.

(b) Now ignore the question of whether the mode restriction really guarantees the desired separation and consider whether the assemblers and compilers can check for the nonuse of the prohibited modes. Can this checking mechanism work properly? Explain.

2-2. Contrast the big-endian memory ordering against the small-endian ordering by comparing the order of memory accesses required to perform (i) sign testing and (ii) subtraction. You should support extended-precision operands (those longer than the longest operand width handled by processor instructions). Assume that two's complement representations are used in both cases.

3

MEMORY ORGANIZATION

The existence of forgetting has never been proved;
we only know that some things do not come to mind
when we want them.

— Nietzsche

Under the simple memory illusion we view the memory system as a set of places (which hold objects) coupled with a scheme for naming those places. There are four basic modes of access to an object within memory: Read (R), Execute (E), Write (W), and Read/Modify/Write (RMW). Execute access is used to obtain program bytes. Read/modify/write access is used to coordinate object sharing among processes simultaneously executing programs in one or more processors. During an RMW access, an atomic operation reads the old contents of the location, modifies it, and writes a new value back into the location.

First, we briefly review some major issues concerning the design of computer memory systems. The policies and mechanisms that support memory systems include schemes for naming objects, schemes for allocating space to hold the objects, and schemes for accessing the objects stored in the memory system. These activities take place at many levels of the system's implementation, including the high-level language program, the compiler, the processor-level program, the operating system, and the system hardware. The design issues and implementation options are similar at many of these levels.

How does a name in a C++ program, such as this_name, become converted into a bit pattern that can be sent as an address to memory when the named item is to be accessed? The necessary actions may be performed during different phases of system activity. We emphasize three phases of system activity that affect and influence memory system design. The first activity is *translation*, the term we use not only for the compilation of a high-level language program into a lower-level representation, but also for the translation of symbolic assembly language programs. Translation reduces a program containing symbolic names to a program in which the only symbolic names are those necessary for linking. The second activity is *linking*, the act of combining several separately translated programs to form a single larger program for execution. The third activity is *execution*, the running of the linked program.

Some memory system actions in this scenario are the following:

1. The programmer chooses a legal name.
2. The programmer places an object declaration within the program so that the compiler will allocate space with an appropriate lifetime.
3. The compiler allocates space for the object.
4. The compiler produces processor instructions to access the object.
5. The linker logically connects program modules to form the complete program.
6. The operating system allocates space for the process.
7. The operating system establishes memory mapping data so that the processor will access the proper location.
8. The processor allocates space for a group of objects.
9. The processor computes the effective address specified by an instruction accessing the object.
10. The hardware translates the effective address to an absolute memory address.
11. The cache looks for the object within itself.
12. The cache allocates space for the object.
13. The cache asks the memory to access the object.
14. The cache loads the block containing the object.
15. The cache accesses the object.

The major types of activity in this process are naming, allocation, and accessing, with the latter including name translation. We present memory systems issues following this breakdown, to illustrate the common issues and solution techniques used to approach similar problems at different levels of the system hierarchy. The naming issues in Appendix E and the allocation issues in Appendix F provide background for the accessing issues presented in this chapter.

An effective memory accessing design provides access to information in the computer when the processor needs access. It should satisfy the simple memory illusion; in particular, it should not let the computer forget anything and it should support object naming. For efficiency, it should not allow the information to get too far from the processor, unless the information is accessed infrequently. Thus to do its job effectively, the allocation mechanism may move information closer to or farther from the processor, depending on its frequency of use. To implement these moves and keep track of the closest location of each object, the accessing mechanism must be able to map names among name spaces as objects move among memory modules. Clearly these activities require assistance from the memory allocator.

In this chapter we discuss memory accessing for single process systems in support of the simple memory illusion. We start with a quick review of the naming and allocation issues presented in Appendices E and F. Then we start the accessing process with name written in a high-level program. To access the named object, the system must translate the object's name from one name space (such as the space of symbolic names) to another name space (such as the space of absolute memory addresses that can be interpreted by the memory system's hardware). The mapping may be performed in several stages. In this chapter we explore structured techniques for implementing these mappings. The presentation in this chapter is presented on the assumption that you know the material in Appendices E and F, along with some machine details from other appendices.

In general, the structure of object names or memory addresses for one virtual machine may not correspond directly to the structure of memory addresses for an underlying virtual machine. The correspondences between names in the higher machine and locations in the lower machine are defined by address transformations, that can be simple, complex, static, dynamic, system-controlled, or programmer-controlled. Certainly some name transformations can be performed during program translation, but other transformations cannot be performed until the program is in execution. For the run-time mappings, the mapping speed can be an important criterion for selecting the mapping technique. If one is very pressed for speed, one might consider including special hardware to support useful name mappings.

In this chapter you will learn basic mapping techniques and then explore their usage within the implementation of languages and systems. You will learn the reasons for the selections designers have made. After completing the chapter you should be a good critic and an understanding and sympathetic observer of name mapping functions.

The structure of this chapter is as follows. We first present the basic techniques used to implement name mappings. Then we explore their usage at different levels of the virtual machine hierarchy. We start with the translation of programs before program execution; this translation is started by the compiler or assembler and completed by the linker. Then we turn to name mappings performed during program execution. These include the computations of effective addresses and the interpretation of addresses that select component objects from a dynamic structure, such as a stack that contains activation blocks corresponding to procedure calls that are still active. Then we examine mappings that are usually performed in hardware, such as translations mapping virtual addresses to physical addresses. We look at the interface between the processor and the memory system, where we examine cache memory, memory interleaving, and other design options that have important effects on system speed. Throughout this discussion we utilize table lookup techniques, which can be implemented in specialized associative memory modules. Appendix G is an extension of the chapter; in it we digress from the narrow application of associative memories to name mappings and present some implementations of general associative memory functions.

In this chapter we learn various techniques for accessing memory; different designs are appropriate depending on the characteristics of the environment. For name mapping and accessing, two important characteristics of the environment are the size of the name space and the density of name usage in the space. If the name space is very large, its usage will be sparse on the average, but the usage could be locally dense if the names are clustered within a small region of the name space. If the name space is small, it will be well-used, and the mapping techniques appropriate for the sparse situation might be inappropriate. We will see the gradual transition from hashed table implementations (for sparse usage) to set-associative table implementations as the usage patterns shift along this continuum. We start with a quick review of basic name mapping techniques.

3.1 BASIC NAMING TECHNIQUES

Appendix E includes many ways that one can specify the name of an object or of a place within a program. Some important ideas from that discussion underlie the major discussion in this chapter, which concerns accessing techniques.

All naming starts from symbolic names created by a programmer; the translator converts these into address specifications that are interpreted directly by either operating system or innate processor algorithms. One special exception to this comment lies in Algol's call-by-name parameter-passing method, which is supported by the translator producing a short function whose result is a pointer to the object that is desired.

At the processor level, names are integers or pairs of integers. The latter case corresponds to a segmented address space. In most of this chapter we deal with addresses that comprise single integers.

3.2 BASIC ALLOCATION TECHNIQUES

Allocation, the second part of building a memory structure, is covered in detail in Appendix F. To obtain maximum benefit from the remainder of this chapter, you should be familiar with stack- and frame-based allocation techniques.

Stack allocation is important in the implementation of block-structured languages, because stacked blocks hold the parameters and local objects for the execution of (possibly recursive) procedures. By stacking these allocations, the design guarantees that a minimum amount of memory space will be accessed during the execution of the program. All processors support stack structures in some manner, though in many the support is hidden within the description of some processor instructions.

Frame-based allocation is important because it is used to obtain space within physical main memory to hold pages of programs or data. The accessing mechanism can help the allocator do a better job by collecting information about the program's accessing patterns; this is usually achieved through a "used" bit in page descriptors.

3.3 BASIC ACCESSING TECHNIQUES

After we review naming options, mapping formalisms, and terminology, we discuss several commonly used name mapping structures.

3.3.1 Object Designation Options

To access a memory object, the object must be selected, either on the basis of its location or its contents.

> **Definition**. An object is selected by *location addressing* if it is selected because of its location within a memory address space.

Location addressing is the common well-understood case, so we will not detail this illusion, preferring to spend time on the associative memory structure, which we discuss as though it is implemented in hardware, though clearly one could devise a software package to support the associative memory's functionality without special hardware mechanisms.

> **Definition**. An object is selected by *content addressing* (or *associatively*) if it is selected because a specified portion of its representation—the key—meets a match condition with respect to a selector value.

This definition defines the *key* as a component of the object in the memory and the *selector* as the external (input) value describing the entry to be accessed.

Now we look quickly into the hardware implementation of an associative memory. The location of the key within each entry in the associative memory may be fixed within the hardware design or the hardware might be designed so that it may be specified by a bit pattern contained in a *mask register*, M. To perform the logical search function, a match check is made against every word in the associative memory; for each word in the memory the result of that check is stored in a *match bit* associated with the word. If the system wants to access entries that met the selection test, the match bit can be used to select the associated word (see Figure 3-1). This description is independent of the match criterion; various match criteria could be used; equality searches are useful for mapping memory names. A formal statement of the equality match condition, along with other interesting match conditions and ways to implement associative memories, is presented in Appendix G.

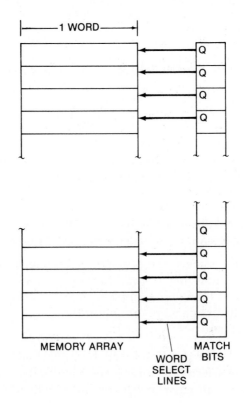

Figure 3-1　Associative memory array with word select lines driven by match bits

TABLE 3-1   EFFECTS OF AN ASSOCIATIVE SEARCH AGAINST A WORD CONTAINING 0xA3B672

Search Mask	Selector Value	Match Bit Result
0xF00000	0xA00000	1
0xF0F000	0xA0B012	1
0xF0F000	0xA3B149	1
0xFFF000	0xA3B149	1
0xFFF000	0xB3B149	0

Example 3-1

Consider a single object in an associative memory that contains A3B672 (hexadecimal). Suppose that the associative memory has a loadable mask register. A "1" mask bit value denotes a bit position in which the selector value and the memory location's contents participate in the match decision. To satisfy an equality match condition, the hardware tests all bits in positions where the search mask is "1"; in each tested position the bit in the memory word must equal the corresponding bit in the selector. Table 3-1 shows some search mask and selector values, and the corresponding match bit results.

In specialized processors associative addressing may be used to select operands;[1] here our interest in associative memories arises from their use to implement name mappings efficiently. In an associative memory used to map memory addresses, the search information is all or a portion of an address. In this situation, the type and form of the search information is known before the hardware is designed. Therefore, the designer can fix the bit positions within the key, which become a fixed field within each memory entry. Furthermore, a match condition demanding equality between the selector value and the contents of the key field will be adequate for all associative memory functions supporting name mapping.

One important difference between an associative memory and a location-addressed memory is that any valid address is the unique identifier of an object, which we will call a *word*. Thus any access request to a location-addressed memory selects a simple memory word. An associative memory, on the other hand, may contain more than one entry that matches a particular selector value, so an access request may set the match bits of several memory entries. It is also possible that the associative memory does not contain any matching entries. These points are important for the implementation and use of an associative memory.

---

[1]   For example, we might find all locations where there is a description of an airplane that is likely to cross an altitude boundary, so that we can call attention to a human traffic controller.

3.3.2 Object Name Mapping Strategies

Object names serve a role like addresses in a location-addressed memory system. There may exist different types of object names within a computer system; these are collected into *separate* name spaces. A *name mapping* transforms addresses between name spaces. A system may remap a name many times to obtain the hardware-recognizable address of the proper physical location. Because many maps may be used, and their time delays may be important in determining system performance, the efficiency of the name mapping process can be a matter of concern. In this section we explore several name mapping options; in later sections we will discuss their utility for various steps in the overall name mapping process. This section formally covers general mapping methods. We turn to practical mappings and present basic implementations of these mappings in Section 3.4.

The translation from a name n_1 in name space N_1 to the corresponding name n_2 in name space N_2 can be expressed by a formal mapping function f_{12}:

$$n_2 = f_{12}(n_1) \tag{3-1}$$

Such a formal description is conceptually complete, but not very useful in implementing the function.

To show how mapping functions might be implemented, we start with two extreme cases based on the following representation schemes:

    1. Algorithmic representations
    2. Tabular representations

An *algorithmic representation* of a name mapping can be encapsulated in a procedure. Any mapping can be implemented by a (sufficiently complex) procedure, which may execute slowly. "Simple" algorithmic mappings reduce the mapper's execution time, so they are interesting. For example, one simple algorithmic mapping encodes the input and output names, using an arithmetic function to convert between the encoded names.

A *tabular representation* of a name mapping specifies the output name corresponding to each possible input name. Because the set of names actually used is finite, a finite table completely describes such a mapping. However, the finite table can be large and therefore can be inefficient. By restructuring a table that is logically a single table into a hierarchy of tables, many disadvantages of the single table design can be ameliorated.

Another representation of a tabular mapping expresses the table's contents as a binary relation. If two items I_1 and I_2 satisfy the binary relation R, we say that the pair (I_1, I_2) belongs to the relation R. The complete relation can be described by listing all pairs that belong to the relation. Clearly the relation's pair list is equivalent to a tabular listing. A pair satisfying the mapping is similar to an entry in a hash table implementation of the mapping.

> **Definition.** The *domain* of a mapping is the set of input values for which the mapping is defined.

> **Definition.** The *range* of a mapping is the set of output values produced by the mapping.

Example 3-2

If a compiler assigns the variables with symbolic names X, Y, and Z to memory addresses 100, 105, and 130, respectively, its name mapping relation is

$$R = \{(X,100),(Y,105),(Z,130)\} \tag{3-2}$$

Tabular name mappings are used frequently in computer systems—the table is called a *symbol table* when the input names are symbolic; it is called a *segment table* when the input names are segment names; and so on.

3.3.3 Name Mapping Lifetimes

An important attribute of a name mapping is the time interval (its *lifetime*) during which the mapping remains valid. We must maintain a correct mapping during its lifetime, and we can discard the mapping information when we know that it will never be required again. Allocation designers must be concerned with the relationship between the lifetime of a program block and the lifetime of the mapping of its names.

The following questions and definitions delineate some important categories.

1. Is the mapping identical during all executions of the program?
2. Might the mapping change during program execution?

Here are some terms that describe the categories.

> **Definition.** A *fixed* name mapping is the same for all executions of a program.

> **Definition.** A *variable* name mapping is not the same for all executions of the program.

> **Definition.** If the same name mapping function is used during an entire execution of the program, it is a *static* name mapping.

Definition. If the name mapping function may change during program execution, it is a *dynamic* name mapping.

Notice that a fixed mapping must be static. If we were technically correct, we would define separate terminology to distinguish between a complete name mapping and the mapping of a single name within the domain of the map. Rather than collect many definitions, we rely on context to resolve any ambiguity between the complete map and the mapping of a single name. If the mapping of any name is either variable or dynamic, then the complete mapping has the same attribute. In the following we discuss name mappings of the objects that have direct names visible in the programming language; this excludes the names of objects that have been allocated space by using the **new** operator, and that are then located through pointer objects. The problem of mapping the names of these objects is different from the name mapping problems that we discuss here.

Example 3-3

A C++ compiler may allocate the objects local to procedure P in an activation block that will be allocated on a stack for the duration of P's execution. The resulting mapping of a local object's name to a stack location is variable and dynamic, because the procedure call history prior to the call to P affects the stack allocations during P's execution. However, the mapping of the name of a local object to an offset within the activation block is fixed and static.

A fixed name mapping can be performed during program compilation; first, the compiler makes its allocations and stores the allocation information in a symbol table. Later, when the compiler generates the program, the target names to be inserted within the program are determined by consulting the symbol table.

Name mappings that are not fixed cannot be performed during compilation; either the map is variable (and requires an adjustment for each program execution) or it is dynamic (and may change during program execution). In either case, the translation cannot be completed until run time, or just prior to program execution.

Because performing an allocation is tantamount to defining a name mapping for the allocated objects, some name mapping is implicitly modified whenever an allocation is changed. In Appendix F we mention three times when an allocation may be performed:

1. During translation (compilation or assembly)
2. During linking
3. During program execution

If name mappings change during program execution, hardware support may be desired for effecting the mappings speedily. In the next section we explore several algorithmic options and their hardware implementations.

3.4 NAME MAPPING IMPLEMENTATIONS

Now we discuss automatic name mappings, excluding the mappings implemented by pointer objects. The system design can provide support for efficient mappings of user-allocated objects by providing indirect addressing. The other name mapping problems require a different types of support, as we see presently.

Name mapping functions are implemented by one of these simple mechanisms:

1. Additive relocation
2. Locator structures
3. Table structures

For simplicity in the following discussion, assume that each name is an integer or a vector of integers.[2]

3.4.1 Additive Relocation

An additive relocation mapping uses this functional mapping:

$$n_2 = f_{12}(n_1) = n_1 + R_{12} \tag{3-3}$$

Note that R_{12} is the origin of the N_1 (target) space within the N_2 (host) space. Figure 3-2 depicts this mapping. Additive relocation simply positions a replica of the target name space within the host name space. Additive relocation may not be possible in multidimensional name spaces. An additive relocation mapping is simple and easily implemented. However, it has disadvantages:

1. N_2 must be larger than N_1.
2. N_1 must be a subset of N_2.
3. N_1 must be allocated contiguous space within N_2.
4. The map mechanism must include an adder that must propagate carries, slowing the mapping process.

3.4.2 Blocked-Pointer Relocation

A blocked-pointer relocation mapping divides the input address space into independently located blocks. Suppose that every name n_1 contains p bits, divided into a q-bit "block number" Q and a $(p - q)$-bit object address A (within the block). Then a 2^q-entry table MAP containing pointers defines the mapping, which is given by

---

[2]   This does not represent a loss of generality, because any symbolic name can be converted to an integer by performing arithmetic algorithms on the internal codes used to denote printable characters.

$$n_2 = \text{MAP}(n_1.Q) + n_1.A \qquad\qquad (3\text{-}4)$$

Figure 3-3 depicts this transformation. The addition implies that adjacent addresses within a block are mapped to contiguous locations, but the table lookup of block origins implies that the positions of the blocks can be completely arbitrary.

Blocked-pointer mappings are quite general. When $p = q$, the blocked-pointer technique implements a completely arbitrary mapping because the entire name is the block number and each block holds one map entry. With an appropriate block size, blocked-pointer mappings can overcome some disadvantages of additive relocation schemes:

1. Additive relocation requires that the output name space be not smaller than the input name space. Blocked-pointer mappings can circumvent this restriction because all possible input names need not have images in the output name space; a null entry or a flag in the mapping table can denote such an unmapped portion of the input name space.[3]
2. Additive relocation requires a contiguous allocation for all of N_1 within N_2. A blocked-pointer mapping requires contiguous allocation within each block, but the blocks may be arbitrarily located. Thus, though an allocation for N_1 must utilize a fixed number of blocks, they may be located anywhere within N_2, and, in particular, the blocks need not be contiguous.

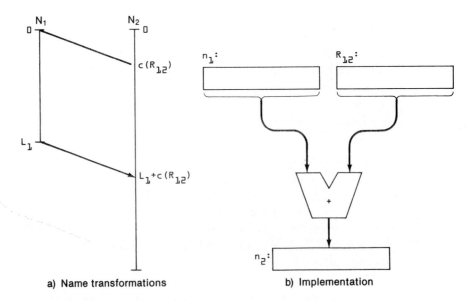

a) Name transformations   b) Implementation

Figure 3-2   Additive relocation

3. Finally, additive relocation requires an addition with carry propagation. This need can be removed in block mappings by allocating the blocks to *aligned* spaces (in N_2) beginning at addresses whose last $(p - q)$ bits are zero. The addition becomes concatenation, which is trivial. This leads to the simple mapping mechanism shown in Figure 3-4.

Block relocation does, however, have its own disadvantages:

1. If the block size is large, allocations for small objects require large space allocations that are not entirely used.

2. If the block size is small, the map table is large.

3. The map table must contain an entry for every block, whether used or not.

These conflicting observations give the designer an opportunity to choose space usage patterns by selecting the block size.

3.4.3 Tabular Mappings

A tabular mapping lists the mapped image of each discrete point within the domain of the map. A table entry contains each mapped name; it may be selected by indexing on the input name, if that is an integer, or by an associative fetch

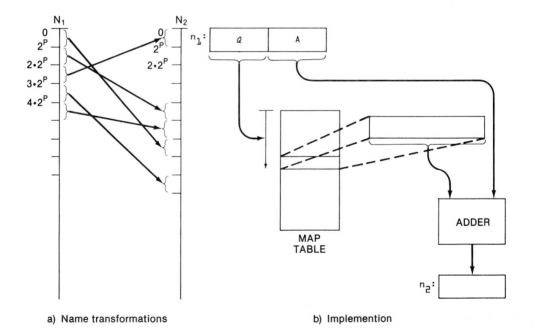

a) Name transformations   b) Implemention

Figure 3-3   Blocked-pointer relocation

from the table with the input name serving as the search key in an equality
match. The following paragraphs describe six alternative implementations of
tabular mappings:

1. Indexed table
2. Linked list
3. General associative table
4. Hash table
5. Hierarchical mapping tables
6. Ordered mapping tables

Notice that knowing the search algorithm defines both the search process
and the underlying data structure. Here we will not discuss algorithms for operations other than table search because the other algorithms are easily determined once the search algorithm is known. Some implementations rely on the
fact that the table entries are ordered by key values; for such an implementation,
it is essential that all table accesses use the same key field. Thus the table entries
can be ordered by their key values. We assume that this condition holds here,
and that there is a single key (which is the input name). Now we turn to the details of the mapping options.

Indexed Table. An indexed table map uses the integer input name as an
index value to select the table entry that contains the result of the mapping. This
mechanization of a tabular map realizes the mapping by this table lookup:

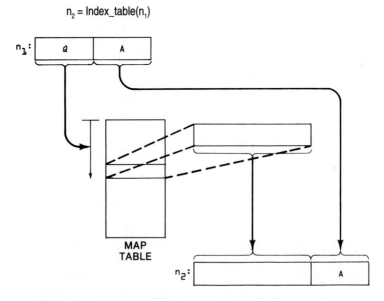

$$n_2 = \text{Index\_table}(n_1)$$

Figure 3-4   Blocked-pointer relocation using concatenation

An indexed table mapping can be useful if the name set is small and fills most of the target name space, because then the index table will be small and most of its entries will contain valid mapping information.

Linked List. In a linked list map implementation, each list bead contains one pair from the relation describing the map. The input name is the key for an associative list search for an equality match. The following program shows the search algorithm for this map representation, assuming that the list is linked in order of increasing key values:

```
class list_bead {
public:
     int key;
     int value;
     list_bead *next;
}
list_bead *map_list_head;        //The pointer to the head of the list
int map_selector( int selector, boolean *success) {   //assume boolean declared
     list_bead *here = map_list_head;      //Pointer to the current bead
     while ( selector < here.key )
          here = here.next;               //Move to the next bead
     if ( selector == here.key ) {
          *success = true;               //Indicate successful search
          return here.value;        //Return the mapped name
     }
     else {
          *success = false;          //This indicates no match found
          return 0;
     }
}
```

The linked list mapping is space-efficient; it contains a bead for each member of the relation, but each bead incorporates a pointer to the next item, which costs space. However, the mapper will be slow because accessing the list is slow, as the pointers must be followed to traverse the list. There is no practical way to compute the location of a matching list entry from the selector by evaluating an expression. If the list were ordered by the key value, it could be easier to detect missing entries, because the entire list would not have to be searched when there is no match for the selector, as shown in the preceding program.

General Associative Table. A general associative memory implementation of a tabular mapping contains all pairs that belong to the mapping relation.

---

[3]   The system must contain a mechanism to detect such flags or null entries and handle the exceptional situations.

An equality search using the complete input name as the selector will find the entry containing the corresponding mapping pair that contains the mapped name. This type of search was used for the linked list implementation of the map. The differences between the general associative table and the linked list are as follows:

1. With an associative memory, many comparisons can be made simultaneously.
2. In the associative memory, no space is consumed by pointers.
3. The associative search requires more logic or more time (see Appendix G).

Because general associative tables are expensive or slow, they are not often used for name mappings—the hash table or simpler associative schemes that we discuss now are used whenever the performance requirements permit.

Hash Table. A hash table can implement an efficient associative mapping if all search requests desire an equality match with the same predefined key field. For address mapping, each hash table entry contains one pair from the mapping relation:

Definition. A *hash table entry* is a pair (key, value). Also, a *validity bit* distinguishes positions that contain meaningful information from those that do not. The validity bit is set if the corresponding entry contains valid information. If the validity bit is clear, the entry is considered to be *empty* or *invalid*.

We could also describe the hash table entry's structure as

```
class hash_entry {
public:
    int key;
    int value;
    boolean valid;
}
```

A search request is "Find the answer that corresponds to the key value K." To search for an entry, one uses this general algorithm:

```
1. i = hash( K );      //K is the value sought
2. Access table[i];
3. If ((table[i].key == selector) && table[i].valid) then return the pair (i, table[i].value);
4. Invoke secondary search;
5. Return answer and success/failure status.
```

Step 4 is intentionally vague; there are many feasible options, as we shall see.

A common use of the hash table is to implement the symbol table in a compiler. Whether implemented in software or hardware, the hash table has

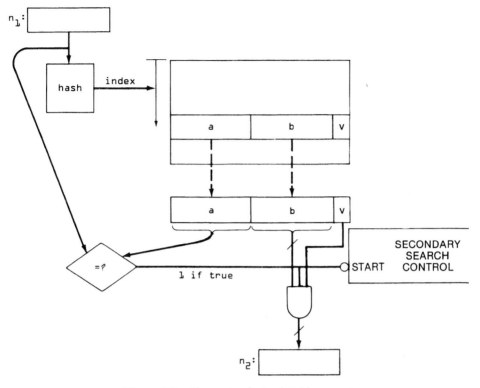

Figure 3-5   Elements of a hash table mapping

some common functional elements, including an indexed table, a hashing function, comparison testing, and a secondary search algorithm. An implementation is diagrammed in Figure 3-5.

The *hashing function* used in the first step performs a many-to-one mapping that compresses the space of key values to the space of table indices. Many different selector values will hash to the same table index, so the table index is not a unique specification of the desired answer. To resolve the uncertainty, each table entry must contain both a validity bit and the key value corresponding to the map pair that is stored in the entry. If the match test fails for every table entry in the slot and all of them are valid, we say that a *collision* has occurred. If any table entry is not valid and the match test fails, we can deduce that the answer is not in the table; why?[4]

We can generalize the hash table by permitting each table entry to hold more than one of the tabular map's relation pairs.

> **Definition.** A *table slot* is a position within the indexed table that may hold one or more entries from the tabular mapping.

---

[4]   Because map entries are never deleted.

In contrast to a slot, a table entry contains only one pair from the mapping function's binary relation. In step 3, the table slot chosen by the hashed selector value is examined to determine whether the key field in any of its valid table entries indeed matches the desired key value K.

If the equality check in step 3 fails and the table slot is full, the desired entry may be located in another place. This combination of conditions might occur because the hash function is many-to-one and other keys that map to the same hash value might be present in the table, or other overflow entries might have occupied this entry. The secondary search procedure determines whether the desired entry is in any other table entry. The simplest secondary search algorithm makes a circular scan of the table, starting with the slot after the one where the match try failed.

The simple sequential search algorithm works only if no table entry is ever deleted. Name mapping tables can be managed so that their entries never have to be deleted,[5] or special control bits can be used to permit sequential searching despite entry deletions (see Problem 3-5).

There exist many other data structures and corresponding algorithms for secondary searches; we briefly look at an interesting one that uses a hierarchy of tables.

Definition. A *hierarchy of hash tables* is a set of hash tables with the following properties:

1. The set implements a single overall associative table lookup function.
2. The tables in the set use different hashing functions.
3. Each table contains information about map entries not found in the other tables in the set.

Figure 3-6 illustrates a sequence of tables in a hierarchy (the sequence being ordered from left to right). The mth table is named table[m]; its ith entry will be denoted by table[m,i]. The tables need not have the same length. Our search strategy uses a different hash function at each table; these functions are denoted hash(m, key). The search strategy is as follows: first, examine the slot whose index is table[1, hash(1, K)]; if it suffers a collision, then examine the slot whose index is table[2, hash(2, K)], and so forth. If the hashed search in the last table suffers a collision, secondary searching within that table completes the search.

Although hashed mappings have the advantage of a short access time, they do have disadvantages. These include the following:

1. The hash table size must match the size of the range of the hashing function.

---

[5] We achieve this by structuring the table lifetimes so that the only deletions erase an entire table. This strategy is similar to allocating objects to pools based on the lifetimes of the pool and the object being allocated.

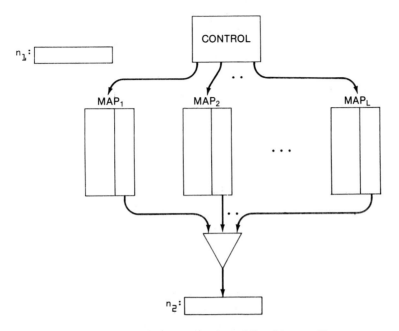

Figure 3-6   A multilevel map table

2. The hash table cannot be expanded easily.

3. The entire table space must be allocated even if the table contains only a few entries.

In addition, several speed concerns may mitigate against the use of hash tables to implement an associative mapping; these include the following:

1. Hashing time

2. Search time after finding a collision

3. Time to make the equality test

The multilevel map table structures we discuss in the next section should be considered when the first two speed issues seem important.

Hierarchical Mapping Tables. A multimemory hierarchical table mapping is not a multilevel hash table, but rather is structured as a sequence of successively inclusive tables. We name the constituent tables T_1 .. T_n, in the order they are used during a search for a table entry. In the multilevel hash table, table T_{i+1} contains entries different from those in tables T_1 .. T_i. In the table hierarchy, on the other hand, table T_{i+1} contains *all* of the entries from its predecessor T_i (and, by extension, of all of its predecessors).

A major advantage of a hierarchical mapping table is that the successive tables can reside in different levels of the memory hierarchy. A search failure in the first-level table initiates a search in the second-level table, which implies accessing a slower memory system. This strategy trades the use of expensive high-speed memory against slower access for entries found in lower tables—with programs exhibiting locality this implementation will not suffer too much time penalty compared to a strategy in which the entire mapping table is kept in high-speed memory. The situation is like virtual memory management: A table manager can move map entries among the constituent tables to speed the mapping process without expending excess space in expensive memory. The goal is to have frequently used entries in the first-level table, with less frequently used entries relegated to tables lower in the hierarchy. All component tables in a multilevel hash table might be allocated space in the same memory, but this allocation strategy would be unwise with the multimemory table, because there is little point in repeating all of the entries from a predecessor (in terms of the search process) table within another table occupying space in the same memory.

How should one manage the composition of the table at each level of the hierarchy? It is almost correct to reason that the strategy for deciding when to move a table entry among the levels could be similar to the strategy for managing virtual memory (see Section F.5), because the goals are similar. Some flaws in this analogy are explored in Problem 3-33.

An interesting special case, the *set-associative table*, is a two-level hierarchical table. In many systems, a set-associative map implements the name mapping for a cache memory and translates virtual memory addresses to physical addresses. Another interesting multimemory mapping uses a tree structure to implement a map with a large domain, which may be the case in a file system or a large database system.

The *set-associative* map is a two-level hierarchical table; the first level is used like a hashed table with a trivial hashing function (for speed). Often, the slot index is the verbatim contents of a selector subfield, such as the n least significant[6] bits. There are four important differences between a set-associative mapping and a hashed mapping:

1. Simplicity of the hash function
2. Slot size
3. Collision handling
4. Table state after a collision

We mentioned hash function simplicity earlier; in the set-associative mapping, hashing is performed by field selection, sometimes supplemented by a trivial computation.

---

[6]   The least significant end is chosen to obtain a better hashing distribution across the table indices.

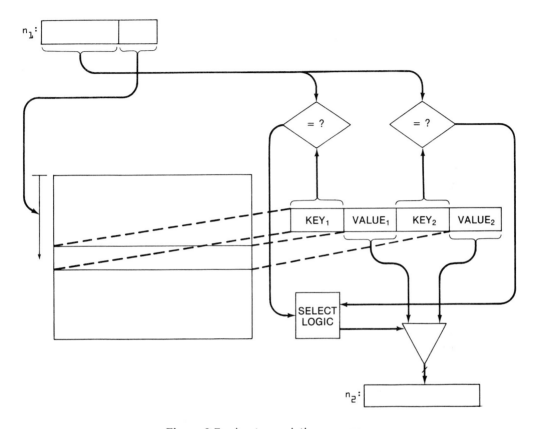

Figure 3-7   A set-associative memory

The slot size for a hashed mapping is usually 1. For the set-associative mapping, the slot size may be, and usually is, greater than 1, and the selector must be compared against all map entries in the selected slot. Comparing the selector against the keys in all entries requires multiple copies of the match checking logic; Figure 3-7 illustrates a set-associative table with slot_size = 2.

After a collision[7] in a set-associative table, a secondary search is made in the second-level table. Contrast this with the hashed table, whose secondary search algorithm looks at other entries within the primary table.

After the desired entry is found in the secondary table, a table manager may decide to promote it to the primary table to speed future accesses. Thus, the state of the primary set-associative table may change after a collision, unlike the hashed table, whose state changes only when table entries are inserted or deleted.

---

[7]   No entry in the slot matched the selector.

The set-associative structure does not dictate how the second-level table is implemented.

Here are some important decisions to be made during the design of a set-associative memory:

1. Select the bits to be used for the index subfield.
2. Choose the hashing function, if any.
3. Choose the number of slots in the table.
4. Choose the number of table entries per slot.
5. Select the policy for placing entries in the first-level table.
6. Select the implementation of the second-level table.

The index subfield bit selection, along with the hash computation, determines which key information constitutes the slot index in the set-associative memory. The choice may affect the statistical slot usage patterns, which affects performance. Sizing the first-level table determines the statistical spread achieved through the use of the index to find the table's slot to be accessed. The hardware cost is also affected by this selection. By varying the number of slots, the designer can move between a *fully-associative* table (with all entries in one slot) and a *direct-mapped* table (with one entry per slot). The selection of the number of entries per slot affects both the hardware complexity and the table size (once the previous selections have been fixed). The policy for placing entries in the first-level map determines when an entry is put into the set-associative table and where in the table the new entry shall be placed. The specific implementation of the second-level map is not very critical, because the system's performance advantage is achieved by attaining a high hit ratio in the first-level table. In an efficient system, the slower accesses to the second-level table are infrequet, so their delay does not impact significantly the average access time.

Comparing the set-associative mechanism against other table-searching mechanisms, we see that this mechanism requires wider table entries and more comparison logic per entry, but never requires more than one fetch from the first-level table. Furthermore, the table index is easily determined from the selector, so the mechanism can operate very quickly when the desired entry is indeed found in the first-level table.

To assist in making intelligent allocation decisions after a collision in a set-associative memory, the mechanism could collect some usage and status information. Because set-associative memories are usually used in environments requiring a fast response to each query, data collection hardware is necessary to obtain usage and status information. For example, when a new entry must be copied to the first-level table, information about recent usage of the entries in the first-level table can help select the entry to be displaced. One simple policy retains in the slot the entry that was accessed most recently; the manager replaces the other one (accessed less recently). This is a trivial special case of a least recently used (LRU) policy that can be supported by using recency bits to collect usage statistics (see Section F.6.3).

Set-associative maps are often used when rapid name translation is needed; often they are implemented in hardware modules. Collisions may be handled by hardware, firmware, or software modules, depending on the speed requirements.

Ordered Mapping Tables. Some address mapping functions are sparse in the sense that the map's domain includes only a small fraction of its input name space. A realization using a general associative mapping, requiring special hardware, may be too expensive. Hashing and set-associative maps provide effective implementations simulating general associative maps, but require the entire table stored at the lowest level of the hierarchy. In some situations, the map table has a very large domain; it is stored in several levels of the memory hierarchy. Ordering the table entries can assist accessing. A small ordered table can be searched using binary search, but this necessitates storing the table contiguously in some address space and having random access[8] to the table. If the table is too large to be stored in a contiguous address range, a multimemory mapping might be appropriate.

There are several ways to organize a multimemory mapping; here we present the tree structure and a mixed version—the indexed-sequential structure. In a tree-structured multimemory mapping, the access path depends on the selector value. Each tree node holds one entry; they are inserted into the tree in order by their key values, so a simple search algorithm suffices. At each stage of the search process an arithmetic comparison determines search success, search failure, and directs the continuation of the search, if required. If we generalize the tree by having each node contain a table of map entries, we can use other searching options within the node. For example, binary search requires a table contained in a contiguous section of a linearly addressable space in a random-access memory; that algorithm makes a less-than/equal/greater-than test to direct the search (see Problem 3-10). For binary search, the average search time is proportional to the logarithm of the table size.

A disadvantage of a tree structure is that pointers have to be traversed to effect the search algorithm, and chasing pointers is often slower than performing address arithmetic. This is a significant problem in highly overlapped processors, because the address for the next memory access is found after completing the previous memory access, making it difficult to keep a pipelined instruction processor busy. On the other hand, the use of pointers in a tree can be considered to be an advantage, because any pointer could direct the search to information in slower memory. For example, one might place all nodes just beneath the root node on the disk; then the pointers in the root table contain disk addresses.

---

[8]   This means that the access times are identical for all entries.

A second important ordered table structure is the *indexed sequential* table. The entries in this table are grouped into consecutive sets, much as the two-level tree. There are four levels of the mapping (see Figure 3-8). The key value in an entry at the first, second, or third level is the highest key contained in the set beneath. In the second level there is a table of the third-level structures; alternate entries in the third level distinguish whether the actual entry is found in a sequentially stored vector or in a linked data structure. The sequential list of entries is located in a fixed-length pool; the linked list chains together all "overflow" items—those that would not fit into the fixed-length pool. Assists for indexed sequential searching can be designed into disk controller modules.

3.4.4 Comments

Name mappings are essential to the process of accessing an object in a computer's memory system. The complete name mapping may be implemented in several stages. At each stage the name map may be implemented by a simple mechanism that allows little usage flexibility or by a complex mechanism that uses more space or takes more time to provide more flexibility. Three general name mappings suffice for all practical situations: additive relocation, blocked-pointer mapping, and tabular mapping. Different mapping functions and implementations may be appropriate at the compiler, linker, and run-time levels of the system, in addition to the processor and the memory interface hardware. After all, there is a different emphasis on speed, size, or flexibility in different situations. We explore these issues in the remainder of the chapter.

3.5 NAME TRANSLATION BEFORE PROGRAM EXECUTION

Static name mappings do not change during program execution, so they can be performed before program execution. We use the common compile-link paradigm to describe the preexecution activities. The compiler can define static allocations for block-local objects and for objects local to the compilation unit. These static allocations provide the basis for a static name translation performed before program execution. In a similar manner, the linker allocates space and thus defines names that link a set of program modules to each other; these names can be translated before program execution. The compiler maps names within one module; the linker maps names that couple modules to each other. Between them, all names can be mapped before program execution. There may be some benefit (in certain environments) to deferring the linking process until the program executes on the processor; we describe this option here even though it is a run-time activity, because it involves the same logical structures.

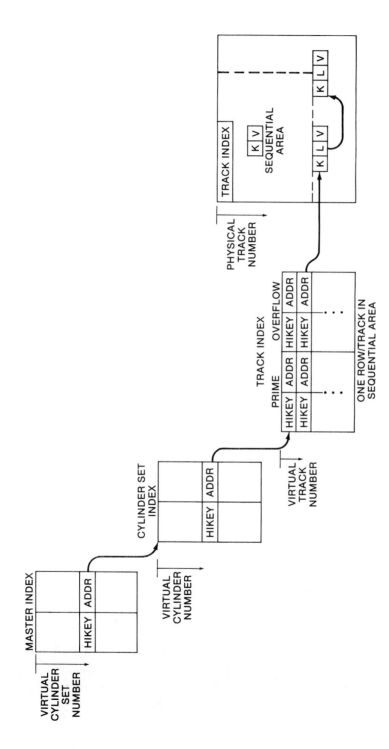

Figure 3-8   The structure of an indexed sequential file

3.5.1 Mapping Names in an Isolated Program Module

Any translation program, such as an assembler or a compiler, must perform name mappings. Similar design issues arise; they have similar solutions for both the assembler and the compiler. We discuss compilation, without loss of generality.

Four major issues relate to the name translation process:

1. Structure of the input name space
2. Structure of the output name space
3. Choice of the name mapping techniques
4. Implementation of changes in the name map

Structure of the Input Name Space. For compilation, the input name space is the space of symbolic names constructed according to the rules of the language. The space is structured by the rules defining how a programmer can name components of data structures. This space is sparsely used.

Structure of the Output Name Space. For compilation, the output name space is the space of address specification techniques that can be used in object programs. The space can be simple if the program makes only simple references to memory and only simple data structures appear in the program. This simplicity restriction also applies to addressing in RISC processors with limited addressing modes. Dynamically allocated objects, however, must be accessed through locator objects, indirection, or algorithms that compute addresses, the latter being necessary with RISC processors. Here are four important name representations:

2a. Integer value
2b. Parameters for a processor-supported addressing mode computation
2c. Search algorithm
2d. Index within a table filled by the linker

Name Mapping Techniques. The name mapping process involves both name definition and name replacement, which can be separated into two phases. During the name definition phase, the translator scans the program, accumulates a list of all input names, and allocates space, as appropriate. During the name replacement phase, the translator scans the program and replaces each input name with its output name.

Because the input name space is sparsely used, the translator might use an associative name mapping for its symbol table. Although associative mappings may be supported by hardware, speed is not critical in these translators, so the use of specialized name translation hardware is not indicated. Therefore, software-implemented hash tables are used to effect these name mappings.

Changing the Map. There are two situations in which the translator's name map must be changed dynamically during the translation process. One situation occurs when a new name is declared in the program; this name must be added to the program's name map.

A map update is required as the compiler's scanner moves across a naming context boundary. As the naming context changes, the translator's name mapping table must change. If the scanner leaves a completed context, the translator can discard the old symbol table and either resume use of the one for the old context that is being reentered or start a new one for the new context that was just entered. Many programming languages have nested naming contexts requiring that the compiler maintain every naming context until it is closed off by the token signaling block termination, such as the right brace in C++ procedure bodies. With static nesting, the compiler can stack the mapping tables, there being one for each naming context in the nest. Each map table can be a hash table.

Whenever the scanner enters a new name context, a new name table is created by pushing it on a stack and its contents are initialized to be empty. As the scanner leaves a completed name context, the name table at the top of the stack is deleted. The stack ordering reflects the block nesting, with the current block's map table at the top of the stack. When a declaration is scanned, the new name and its attributes are entered in the table at the top of the stack. Whenever a name has to be translated, the tables are searched backward from the top of the stack.[9] If all hash tables are the same size, stacking these hash tables is quite easily accomplished.

In summary, the translator converts symbolic names from the input program to names in the *translator name space* associated with the *translation unit*, the set of programs translated together. The translator uses a hash table to hold the required name mappings. The output names produced by the translator are input to the linking step. During linking, the translator name spaces of several independent translation units may be combined. The translation must provide symbol table information to assist the linker; the details of this information and its format depend upon the chosen linking method. We discuss some linking options now.

---

[9]   Due to the structure imposed by static nesting rules, the tables on such a stack contain all symbols that are permitted in the current naming context—no unnecessary block symbol tables are present.

3.5.2 Combining Translated Program Modules

The *linker* builds a program from separate translation units, combining appropriate ones to form a logically consistent single program. The links can be established prior to or during program execution. During this process, the linker combines the translator name spaces and modifies program addresses to be compatible with the space allocations for the composite program. In conventional designs, all of the program's parts must be gathered into a single address space before the program can be executed. The linker can be designed to make the logical connections and to place all of the required programs into the same address space. But these two actions do not have to be performed together. Linking and collection are separate acts:

> **Definition**. *Linking* is the act of establishing appropriate logical connections between separately translated programs.

> **Definition**. *Collection* is the act of gathering together appropriate separately translated programs to form a single program occupying a single address space.

An important design decision concerns the timing of the linking process. There are two major options, static linking and dynamic linking. *Static linking* occurs before program execution. *Dynamic linking* occurs during program execution. It is easy to guess that static linking is more efficient but less flexible than dynamic linking. Dynamic linking requires a supporting mechanism to test each access attempt to ascertain whether it is, in fact, a reference to an unresolved name. This requirement has a significant impact on processor design; it is discussed in detail in Section 3.4.4.

The data structures used during linking include the following:

1. A list of all externally defined (ED) symbols imported by each module, along with a list of all locations in each module where each ED symbol is used
2. A list of all externally visible (EV) symbols exported from each module, along with a list of the addresses of the (defining) locations within the module to which each EV symbol corresponds
3. A list of file names specifying a search path

The translator must provide the first two; the first one comprises a table expressing the imported symbols and their usage in the program module; this is called the *import table*. Similarly, the externally available symbols and their definitions are collected into an *export table*. The symbol definitions contained in the tables are relative to the origin of the space allocated by the compiler for the module when it is considered as a separate entity. Figure 3-9 contains a diagrammatic

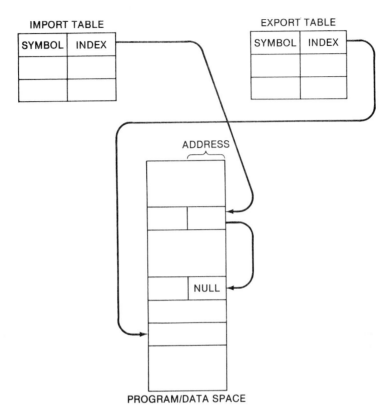

Figure 3-9   Import/export name lists. (The pointer
structure links together all uses of the imported name.)

representation[10] of these import and export tables and the data structures connecting them to the program.

The linker's job is to discover the meanings of all the externally defined
names that were used in each program; it starts by choosing an unlinked ED
name and then trying to find the corresponding external object. To do this, the
linker searches files that contain EV object definitions, following the search order
prescribed in the search list. Once the linker finds the corresponding definition,
the linker links the defining module into the composite program by adjusting the
access path to the referenced ED object so that it reaches the appropriate location
within the defining module. To achieve this, it may replace all references to the
object with the correct address or it may form an indirect address chain reaching
to the desired object.

---

[10]   This applies only to one linking scheme.

The final step in the linking process modifies addresses in programs so that correct accesses will be attempted during program execution. Several data structures and addressing modes play important roles in making address modifications. In addition, the choice of static versus dynamic linking has a profound effect on these aspects of the design. The underlying support for dynamic linking must be visible during program execution to detect unresolved links.

We detail two methods to link modules together and mention a variation on one of them. We base the following discussion on a processor design in which memory addresses appear as contiguous bits within programs.[11] In the first method, the linker establishes links by changing address information in the importing module. This technique cannot be used if a program is to be shared but still be linked into different naming environments. To make this linking method feasible, the translation program creates a list of all uses of an imported symbol. There is such a list for each imported name; the list could be an appendage of the symbol table. However, it may be efficient to structure this list as a linked structure that starts at a head pointer in the symbol table and continues with pointers in the address fields that will be used to reference the external object. The list pointers could be represented by the relative (or absolute) offset of the next location in the chain. With this chaining of all references to each imported symbol, as shown in Figure 3-10a, the linker can simply follow the chain of address pointers to find all locations where the imported name is used; at each of these locations, the pointer is changed to an address reference to the external object. The result of this operation is shown in Figure 3-10b. This technique is very efficient and straightforward; its only disadvantage is that the importing program is modified. Some details of this process are discussed in Problem 3-19.

In the second method, the translator replaces every reference to an imported object with an indirect address pointing to a table that the linker will fill with the addresses corresponding to the imported symbols. The compiler translates every reference to an ED object into an indirection to an entry in this table. When the imported symbol is resolved by the linker, the table entry is filled in. During execution, the imported object is accessed indirectly. Note that under this method, the using program is not changed during linking. Thus this method permits a program to be shared even though it may be linked to different environments. However, more memory accesses and more memory space are required during execution, compared to the first linking method. Figure 3-11a shows the data structures created by the translator to support this linking technique. The effect of linking is displayed in Figure 3-11b.

A variant of the second linking technique uses indirection through the export table of the defining module instead of a direct reference to access an

---

[11]   This situation does not apply to the SPARC and Alpha AXP machines in which immediate values appearing in programs are shorter than complete virtual addresses.

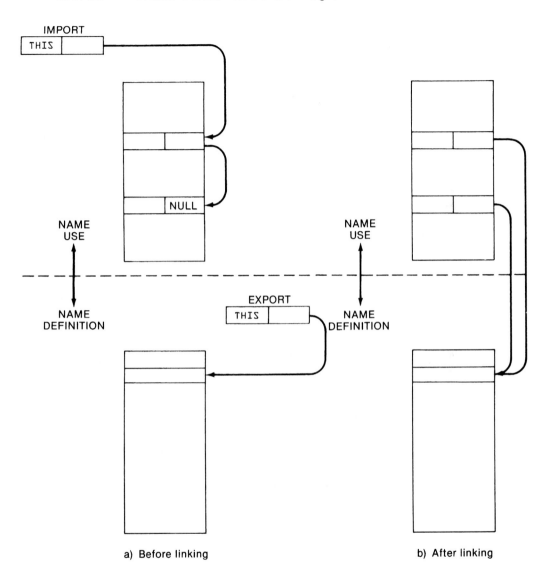

a) Before linking

b) After linking

Figure 3-10   Linking by changing addresses within the program

imported object. This option is not useful in most environments, as it requires
yet another memory access to reference an imported object, and it adds only the
flexibility to redefine the exporting module without having to relink the environment. Figure 3-12 shows the data structures under this variation.

The following examples illustrate some situations in which various linking
techniques are attractive.

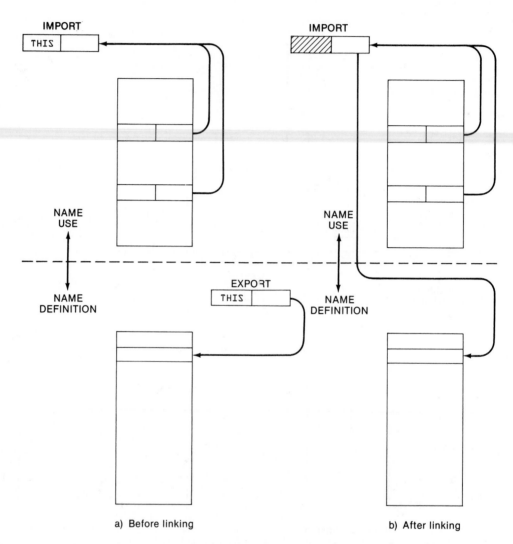

a) Before linking   b) After linking

Figure 3-11   Linking by indirect addressing using simple indirection

Example 3-4

We wish to defer the definition of imported symbols until program execution so that programs could be executed without being completely linked together. Each indirect address to an unlinked reference must be marked so that the processor can take an interrupt and the linker be invoked on any attempt to use an unlinked reference. After the link has been resolved, the address could be modified to access

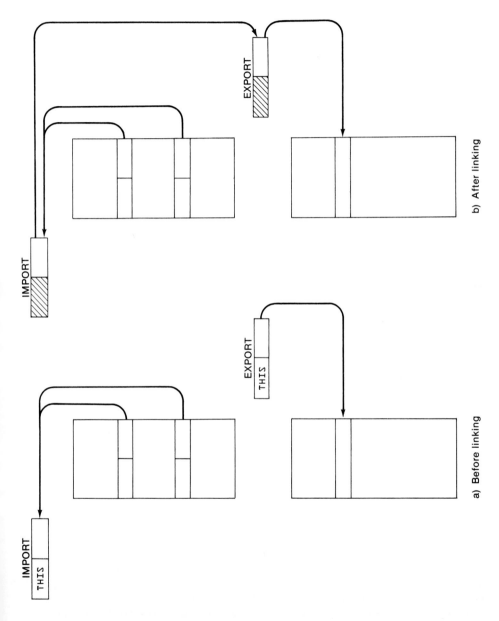

a) Before linking

b) After linking

Figure 3-12   Linking by indirect addressing using double indirection

the external object without using the linker again; then succeeding access attempts may proceed without linker intervention.

Unlinked entries can be flagged by placing the flag value in a special mark bit or by using a reserved (*signaling*) address value (such as all 1's). The mark bit or address[12] must be checked before each reference to any item anywhere in the system. This imposes two forms of overhead:

1. Space for the mark bit or logic to detect the signaling address value
2. Time for checking the mark bit and invoking the linker when an unlinked reference is detected

Example 3-5

We want to design a system so that it can use the same copy of a program, without modification, in different linking environments. Several needs must be met to satisfy this desire. First, we must keep variable data out of the shared program. This creates a program that is never modified; such a program is called a *pure procedure* or a *reentrant program*.[13] Second, we need to allocate a separate memory space for each user's local variables.[14] Third, we need to keep the linkage information separate for each process.[15] All of these needs can be met by giving each process its own copy of the linkage information, referenced indirectly through a locator private to the process.

Collection is the final process that might be performed while joining separately compiled program units. The collector allocates memory space for each program that is needed to resolve the links arising from the other programs. If addressing is one-dimensional, the collector allocates space to the programs in a first-come-first-allocated manner. The process of collecting may require that addresses internal to the program be modified to reflect the new location of the program, because the translator assumes that each object program starts at address zero; all addressing is relative to this assumed origin.

The details of the collection process depend on the addressing modes supported by the processor. Internal addresses that are expressed relative to the program counter do not need to be changed due to relocation, because the relative positions of the instruction and an object declared in the same address space cannot be changed by the relocation process. Addresses that serve as links between separate compilation units or that are not PC-relative do have to be changed by the collector. The locations of such addresses must be marked by the compiler or translator so that the collector can find those addresses that require

---

[12]   The address has to be checked to determine whether it is equal to the reserved value that signals an unlinked table entry. All bits of the address may have to be examined to make this decision.
[13]   Informally, a reentrant program can be reused without housecleaning, whether a previous invocation of the same program may have been suspended, exited, or terminated.
[14]   This requirement means that each program will have to access its private objects through an access object.
[15]   This requirement demands a separate copy of the link vector for each copy of the program.

modification. If external names may appear in address expressions (such as external[3]), there are two approaches:

1. The translator constructs an address computation to evaluate the address during program execution.
2. The linker completely resolves the address.

It is straightforward to compute an address during program execution; the translator assumes that the linker has provided a pointer to the origin of the relevant object, and the program treats this value as an address base.

However, if the linker is to completely resolve the address, the relocation information produced by the translator must provide guidance for the linker. One problem concerns the role of the linked address within a run-time address computation, such as indexing and indirection, because the representation of the address may depend on its role.[16] Another problem arises in processor designs (such as SPARC and Alpha AXP) where a complete address specification within a program cannot be formatted as a single field of contiguous bits; the linker has to insert code to access a table of linked addresses or the linker itself must divide each resolved address into appropriate parts and insert them correctly.

Linking becomes simpler if addresses within modules are one-dimensional and the processor has a second address dimension that the linker can use to hold module identification numbers. Then intramodule addresses do not require modification during the collection process, but segment numbers are changed. This scheme does not support hierarchical collection because every collection step adds an extra dimension to each address.

Example 3-6

In the Burroughs B 5700 family [BURR73], each module collected to form a complete user program is allocated a separate slot in a user-level vector of descriptors stored at level 1 of the address space. In a corresponding manner, system module descriptors occupy a system-level vector at level 0. As the collector constructs the user-level vector of descriptors, it does the following:

1. Adds a segment descriptor of the space to the user-level object list.
2. Builds either a *space descriptor* for each (static) ED data object or a *program control word* (PCW) for each ED entry point.

These steps are detailed in Section D.1.7.

3.5.3 Comments

Many steps in the name translation process can be made by translators and linkers before program execution begins. We have seen several strategies for implementing these mappings. The results of the mappings are address specifications

---

[16]   Sections 2.6 and 2.7 of [ORGA72] describe how multiple options are handled in the Multics system.

that can be used by the processor's effective address computation mechanisms, which are discussed next.

3.6 NAME TRANSLATION BY AN EXECUTING PROGRAM

Processor programs may have to complete the translation of object names and compute object addresses at run time. These actions may have been deferred until run time because some information required to determine an address did not become available until the program was executed. Here are some general reasons why the system might not be able to determine an object address before the program executes:

1. A virtual address is data-dependent.
2. Locator values are used in the address determination.
3. A physical address is context-dependent.
4. The address (that refers to an externally defined object) will be linked dynamically.

A *data-dependent virtual address* accesses an element from an array, a record, or another data structure. A conventional addressing mode's computation suffices for most of these situations, but the problems may be more complicated in a RISC environment.

A *locator* might be passed as a procedure parameter. Again, the address computation of a conventional addressing mode suffices, except possibly in a RISC environment.

A *context-dependent* address might be used to access a dynamically allocated space, such as a stacked activation block. In this case, conventional addressing modes cannot be used directly, unless the mapping between the level number and the physical origin of the corresponding activation block has been defined in a data structure compatible with a processor-supported addressing mode.

A *dynamically linked* address is used to access an externally defined object. The method used to represent resolved dynamic links may restrict the choice of processor addressing modes that can be used within the linked program.

An address resulting from a run-time address computation is called an effective virtual address (EVA). It is effective because it is an actual address used during object access. It is virtual because further translation[17] may be required to determine the corresponding physical address.

The virtual address of a dynamically allocated object cannot be determined until after the allocation has been made and the dynamically determined parameters of the object have been fixed. Table 3-2 summarizes the situations.

---

[17]   This (set of) translation(s) is controlled by the operating system. It is discussed in Section 3.5.

TABLE 3-2   SUMMARY OF RUN-TIME EVA COMPUTATIONS

Object	Address Components	Fixed	Variable
Automatic object	Block origin		•
	Object offset	•	
Procedure parameter	Block origin		•
	Object offset	•	
User-controlled object	Object origin		•
Component of user-controlled object	Object origin		•
	Component index	•	
Dynamically linked simple ED object	Origin of external space		•
	Object origin within external space	•	•

3.6.1 Automatic Objects

Automatic objects are statically allocated space (by the translator) within frames that are dynamically allocated upon procedure calls.[18] Thus, the address of each simple automatic object can be computed by adding a statically determined offset to a dynamically determined pointer that indicates the origin of the activation block (or stack frame) that holds the object.

In this section we describe this process and show how a processor can be designed to assist in this computation, either by assisting in the determination of the frame pointer or by assisting in the address computation and selection of the proper frame pointer.

Frame Pointers.   A new frame pointer value is determined whenever a new addressing context is entered. Processor instructions can assist by saving the frame pointer in a register from which it can be used in address computations. For proper interpretation of statically nested addresses, frame pointers for the statically enclosing blocks may have to be found; the processor can also assist in establishing pointer structures that lead to those frame pointers. Using a frame pointer to locate an activation block implements a blocked-pointer mapping of the names of local (and, possibly, parameter) objects.

In one implementation supporting frame pointers, there is a processor instruction that saves the stack pointer in a register and links the old pointer values into a chain within the stack itself.

---

[18]   In some languages, new frames are allocated after certain other context changes.

Example 3-7

The MC68020 instructions LINK/UNLK (unlink) form a complementary pair that allocates/deallocates and chains together activation blocks on the stack. The instruction LINK An,#<displacement> pushes the contents of An on the stack, loads An with the stack pointer, and then adds the displacement to the stack pointer. If the selected address register was used as the pointer to the topmost activation block, this instruction reloads that pointer with the address of a new block created at the top of the stack. Figure 3-13 illustrates these changes. UNLK simply reverses the allocation by reloading SP from the address register and reloading the address register with the value that had been previously pushed on the stack.

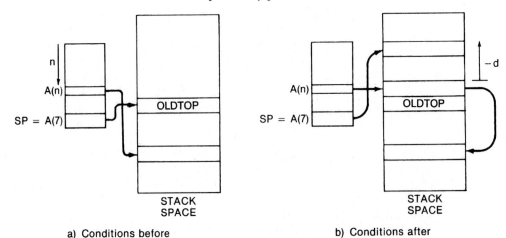

a) Conditions before   b) Conditions after

Figure 3-13   The MC680x0 LINK An,#d instruction (d < 0)

In register-transfer style, these operations perform the following algorithms:

LINK	UNLK An,#d
SP = SP - 4;	SP = A(n);
Memory[SP] = A(n);	Memory[SP] = A(n);
A(n) = SP;	SP = SP + 4;
SP = SP + d;	

These operations do not affect any address mappings, but they do create and maintain the data structure that chains the activation blocks together in dynamic order. The pointers in the address register and within the stack form the list of block pointers for mapping the addresses of local objects and parameters.

Example 3-8

In SPARC, the block chain is established by preserving the stack pointer during a SAVE instruction. Recall that the SAVE instruction moves to the next register window, with the effect that the stack pointer (that was in register %r14 before the SAVE) is located in %r30 after the save. During the SAVE instruction, an ADD operation is also performed, with the operands taken from the old register set and the result stored within the new register set. Therefore, the instruction SAVE %r14,%r0,%r14 has the effect of copying the stack pointer to register %r14 in the new register window. So there is always a correct stack pointer in %r14, and there is a frame pointer set to point at the location where the stack pointer was pointing when the SAVE was executed.

There are no built-in mechanisms that maintain or form the tree structure of frame pointers that can be used to make static nesting work properly. Therefore, the program must contain instructions to maintain this data structure for accessing global objects. There are several difficulties in producing this software. First, the information that has been pushed into register windows is not easily accessible. This problem is handled by a system call that forces the register windows to be stored in addressable memory; this method consumes a system call and many processor cycles. After the register values are saved in memory, the program can follow the pointers to get around within the structure. The second problem is that there is no processor support for recording level numbers when procedures are called. The software can accomplish this task by placing the level number into a register designated by convention (into %r13,[19] for example). Finally, there is no convention about the database used to establish the correct enclosing block for each new block. This information is needed to build the tree structure.

Two-Dimensional Addresses. In addition to its use to aid linking, a *two-dimensional address* containing two integers can be used to select an object in an activation block. In this case, the first integer is the level number, which has to be translated into the activation block origin. The second integer is the element's offset relative to the block origin. The addition of the block origin to the element offset produces the EVA for the element. To support this addressing method, we need a technique that efficiently translates the level number to the origin of the corresponding activation block. The design issue is to select the best mapping technique and to implement that mapping technique. Because there is no algorithmic relationship between the level number and the origin of the corresponding activation block, the address mapping must be enumerated in a table, a list, or a combination of those two. We examine the list map implementation and an implementation using a combination of a table for fast translations and a list for efficient management of the mapping function. Then we turn to the important problem of designing the system to properly maintain the map from block_number to block_origin.

Map Representation. The list representation of the tabular name map is constructed as a tree structure with the pointers pointing back toward the root of the tree. There is a list bead for each active context. Each bead contains information about the location of the corresponding activation block and a pointer to the statically enclosing activation block.

---

[19]   This consumes space that could be available for parameters passed in registers.

Example 3-9

Figure 3-14 depicts the tree structure for the following program skeleton[20] and history.

```
procedure a is ..
    procedure b is ..
    procedure c is ..
    procedure d is ..
        procedure e is ..
    procedure f is ..
        procedure g is ..
        procedure h is ..  ..


call a;
call b;
call c;
call d;
call c;
call d;
call e;
call f;
call g;
call h;
call f;
call h;
```

In the tree, a branch always connects a node at level m with a node at level $m - 1$. The tree has several branches that appear to be duplicates; these correspond to procedures c, d, f, and h, which have more than one activation in use. There is no ambiguity about the execution context for any procedure because the proper context is determined by following the pointers back toward the tree's root from the activation most recently created, which corresponds to the currently executing context.

Although a tree with reversed pointers, this data structure can be viewed as a set of lists, each one starting at a leaf of the tree, linked back toward the root (which corresponds to the outermost program block). So the tree can be used as the linked list implementation of a tabular name map. The list is linked according to the static program structure, with the current context at the head of the list. Each list for a current context starts at the leaf of the tree that corresponds to the current context and extends backward to the root of the tree. The processor traverses the list to translate a name. The number of list beads that must be traversed depends on the level numbers of the execution point and the address

---

[20]   The skeleton omits the **end**s and procedure specifications that would be required to make the program correct.

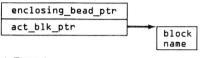

a) Format

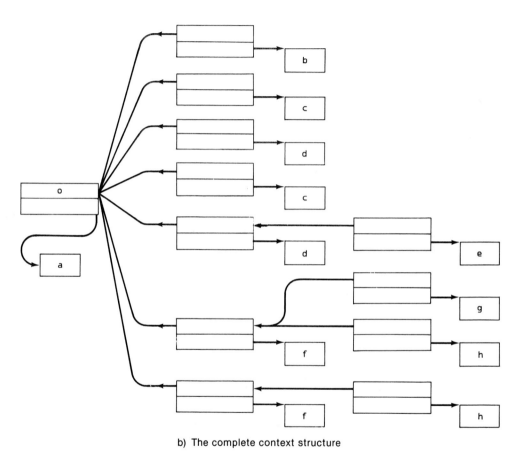

b) The complete context structure

Figure 3-14   A list representation of a context structure

desired. We can terminate the list searching algorithms in this structure either by finding a match for the target's level number or by knowing the distance down the list from the present context to the target context (by subtracting the level numbers).

Another implementation technique combines the table and linked list approaches. A linked data structure defines the map, and the processor transforms the data into a table format to speed accesses during program execution. The tabular representation is used to perform the actual name mappings. As the execution context changes, it will be necessary to modify the list and/or reload the tabular version of the map.

Map Updates. The address map must be updated whenever the addressing environment changes. Will the map be updated by hardware or software? We discuss implementations with processor support for map updating on context changes. This design is likely to be coupled with the design of the mapping mechanism itself, as it is in the Burroughs B 5700 designs ([BURR69], [BURR73]).

Example 3-10

> The B 5700 processor contains 32 "display" registers, named D[0] .. D[31]. During program execution, register D[L] contains the address of the MSCW at the bottom of the activation block for the visible nested block at level L. The translation of the virtual address (L, i) to an effective address EA is

> $$EA = D[L] + i;$$

> This address mapping process and its consequences for the rest of the system's design, such as the process for updating the map on context changes, are discussed in Section D.1.

Problem D-9 describes an alternate design[21] in which programmer accessible registers hold both display information and problem data.

The choice of the method for accessing automatic objects within activation blocks depends on the number of subroutine calls and the nesting depths of the nonlocal references made within the subroutines. In particular, the time cost of updating display registers can exceed the benefit of having loaded them automatically on procedure call. Designers of RISC processors optimize for the case in which almost all references are to local objects, but then an algorithm akin to the display update algorithm must be executed to find the origins of nonlocal blocks and thus to access visible nonlocal automatic objects.

Components of Automatic Objects. Accessing a component of an automatic object is simple unless one or more automatic objects have dynamic properties. In the simple case all automatic objects have only static properties; then they can be allocated in a static manner and the translator can determine the static offset from the frame pointer to any component part of any compound object. We illustrate this with a simple example.

---

[21] The reader is encouraged to evaluate this design proposal in the questions asked in Problem D-9. We neither disparage nor endorse the proposal here.

Example 3-11

```
class four_type {
private:
    int first, second;
}
void ex(..) {
    four_type black;
    .. ;
    black.second = 3;
    .. ;
}
```

Because the object black has a static internal structure, the compiler can allocate space its components relative to the origin of the structure. Because black is declared local to the procedure, space for it will be allocated within the activation block on entry to procedure ex. Then the element black.second will be located at the address A given by

$$A = AB\_location + black\_offset + second\_offset \qquad (3\text{-}5)$$

Figure 3-15 depicts these entities and shows the EVA reaching black.second. Here second_offset denotes the amount of the (static) offset by which second is displaced from the structure's origin, black_offset denotes the offset of the origin of the

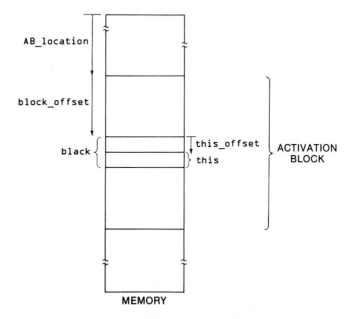

Figure 3-15   Accumulating offsets to access an item in a record in a block on a stack (Example 3-11)

structure named black with respect to the origin of the activation block, and AB_location denotes the origin of the activation block.[22]

3.6.2 Procedure Parameters

Special memory accessing modes may be required to access efficiently the actual value of a parameter from within a procedure. The details depend on the method that the processor supports for placing parameters on the stack. In Section F.4 we discuss two options for positioning the parameter block relative to the activation block allocated for the called procedure. One option places the parameters in the first part of the activation block; the other option places the parameters below the activation block. In the former option, parameters are included with local objects, and the addressing modes used to access local objects can access parameters as well. When the parameters are placed outside the activation block, as in the HP 3000 design (see Section D.2), a special memory addressing mode may be required to access procedure parameters.

Example 3-12

> Three registers in the HP 3000 processor [HEWL73] point to the stack space; they are S, which points to the top of the stack,[23] Q, which points to the top of the control region of the activation block, and DB, which points to a space at the bottom of the stack segment that is the base of the stack (but not necessarily the beginning of the segment containing the stack). The details in Section D.2 show that the HP 3000 stack grows toward higher addresses, and that procedure parameters are placed on the stack before the control words that start the activation block. This means that the parameters are found at addresses beneath that designated by Q, whereas the local objects are stored in locations above that in Q. Because there are likely to be more local objects than parameters, the addressing mode encoding is designed to permit longer displacements going positively from Q (toward local objects) than going negatively (toward parameters).
>
> The HP 3000 addressing mode details are covered in Section D.2.

3.6.3 User-Controlled Objects

The programmer specifies an access to a user-controlled object by specifying the pointer used to locate the object; accessing the object can be assisted by an indirect addressing mode built into the processor. Without this possibility, the program must load the pointer into a register and then use that as the source of the

---

[22]   The value named AB_location is not visible to or accessible from within the high-level program. The name is used only for expository purposes.

[23]   Actually, there is a register SM that points to the top of the stack in memory and a register SR that counts the number of stack words held in processor registers. Ignoring the effects of buffering the stack contents in processor registers, together SM and SR define the logical top of the stack, which is the basis for addressing. We proceed as though all stacked objects are located in a memory stack, whose top is in register S.

address for a memory access. If the user-controlled object is itself a compound object, further address manipulation is required to access a component within the object. Indirection followed by indexing is useful in this situation. When the compound object has a variant structure, the program itself must check the actual parameters defining which variant is about to be accessed before it can determine the correct indices to be used for the access (see Problem 3-15).

3.6.4 Dynamic Linking

Processor instructions and processor mechanisms are required to support dynamic linking among compilation units. Recall that the linking process connects imported symbols to symbols exported from other program modules. Under static linking, all such connections are established prior to program execution. Under dynamic linking, the links are evaluated (the jargon for this is "snapped") during program execution.

As a consequence of dynamic linking, the link vector may contain a mixture of snapped and unsnapped links. To support dynamic linking, the processor and the support software must be designed to detect when an access attempt reaches an unlinked entry in the import table. An interrupt (to activate the dynamic linker) should be signaled when an unlinked entry is detected. The following description of the situation is generic, as it does not depend on whether the instruction space is shared with other programs. First, we describe the situation for *every* access that uses an entry in the link vector as the pointer to reach the actual object.

Suppose that the processor register named B_{link} points to the link vector for the compilation unit. Any processor attempt to make an indirect reference through $B_{link} + k$ must evoke a test of the entry at $B_{link} + k$ to determine whether it refers to a snapped or an unsnapped link; the necessary information can be placed in a linked_flag bit within each link vector entry—the flag is true if the corresponding link has been snapped; the format is shown in Figures 3-16a and 3-16b.

The accessing process becomes

        1. Fetch the indirect word into ADDRESS;
        2. If the linked_flag is false, interrupt the processor;
        3. Access the address in ADDRESS;

Figures 3-16c and 3-16d illustrate the access paths and pointers used with dynamic linking. In Figure 3-16c we see the situation before the link has been snapped. Notice that the pointer in the link word is used to point to the symbolic ED name requiring linking; the first byte of the name space is the count of the number of bytes comprising the name. When the linker has been invoked, it searches for the corresponding object definition and then replaces the unsnapped link with an indirect word, completing the double indirection used in future

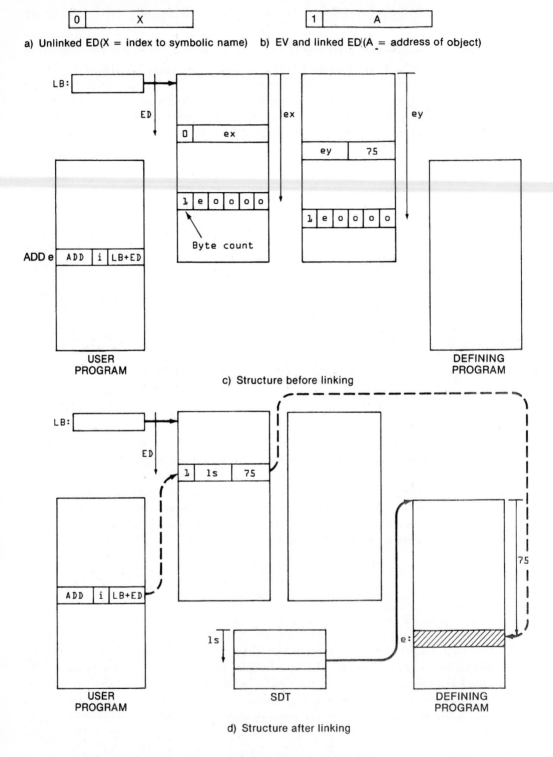

a) Unlinked ED(X = index to symbolic name)   b) EV and linked ED (A = address of object)

c) Structure before linking

d) Structure after linking

Figure 3-16   Multics dynamic linking (simple conceptual case—access direct to a simple object)

accesses to the ED object. By changing the link vector entry (see Figure 3-16d) on snapping the link (rather than the instruction referring to the link vector), the snapped link can be used to complete subsequent references to the same link vector entry without further linker calls. The cost of this saving is the extra memory access made to complete the second indirection. After the linker has made these changes, it returns control to the interrupt handler, which directs the processor to retry the instruction that caused the trap.[24]

Example 3-13

> The HP 3000 processor supports dynamic linking through link spaces at the end of each code segment. The last object in the segment is a count of the number of link entries included in the table, which is indexed backwards from the end of the segment. The table contains links corresponding to both ED and EV names. Two control bits in each link entry indicate whether the link is local (i.e., corresponding to an EV name) or global (i.e., corresponding to an ED name), and, for each local name, whether it can be called. A local link entry contains the offset of the object within the local code segment. A global link entry contains the number of the code segment containing the object and the offset of the object within that segment. Notice that by claiming that an entry is local and uncallable, it is possible to cause a trap that could invoke dynamic linking.

> Links can access procedure entry points directly from CALL instructions. Each CALL instruction contains an offset into the current code segment's link space. The offset is checked against the limit to check for validity. Then the selected entry is examined to determine whether the access is local or global. Global accesses look in the link section of the designated segment to find the address of the local object; again, there is a check against the maximum length (carried in the front of the segment). All code segments within the system are accessed through descriptors found in a table whose origin is the address found in memory location 0. Short pointers dictate that the code segment numbers are limited to 255 and the access indices used in making the second table access in a global access are limited to 127 (because 1 bit was used up to mark the entry as a global reference).

> The processor instruction LOADLABEL generates a local label (in global label format) and pushes it on the top of the stack. The (immediate) parameter of this instruction is the link offset to the object's pointer. The segment number portion of the global address is copied from the current code segment number register.

> Two aspects of this design are noteworthy. First, by placing the link information within the code segment itself, only a single segment number is needed to find both the code and the associated segment number. But this comes at the cost that code segments cannot be shared among processes that desire different link structures.

An important option is provided in the Multics dynamic linker design. The problem is that when a module is loaded the first time, its objects must be initialized in accordance with the declarations. One cannot support this functionality

---

[24]   This way the linker does not have to know about the internal register we called ADDRESS in the algorithm.

by just initializing the values when the module is entered because the initialization should occur only when the module is loaded for the first time. So the Multics design provides a flag interpreted by the linker; the linker causes a trap before the object has been loaded and the trap response is to initialize the object.

3.6.5 Comments

In this section we have explored several design issues concerning the computation of addresses during program execution. We introduced several addressing modes and techniques that could be added to the "conventional" addressing modes. We saw how these modes could support certain important high-level language constructs, such as parameter addressing, accessing objects in nested blocks, and accessing imported objects through link vectors.

3.7 OPERATING SYSTEM CONTROLLED ADDRESS TRANSLATIONS

The system must translate each EVA into a physical memory address (PMA). The operating system allocates memory resources, so the EVA → PMA mapping must be controlled by the operating system. The map parameters are stored in tables maintained by the operating system's memory allocator. The address translation mechanism retrieves table values to determine physical addresses for the program in execution. In this section we discuss the connection between memory allocation policies and the EVA → PMA mapping. In particular, we show how blocked-pointer mappings have been used in segmented and paged structures.

3.7.1 Segmentation

Because segment lengths vary, the address translation mechanism must check that the index value choosing a particular item within a segment specifies an object that lies within the segment's length. In addition, the EVA → PMA mapping must be performed. We study this mapping now.

Under segmentation, each EVA is separated into two parts: a segment number s and an item index i. The *segment descriptor table* (SDT) describes the memory space allocated for the segment and may contain access control information (see Chapter 9). Each SDT entry describes one segment; the entry for segment s is found by indexing by the segment number s. Each segment table entry contains at least the physical address[25] PMA of the origin of the segment and its length.

---

[25]   If the system implements paging beneath segmentation, the SDT entry contains the PMA of the first entry in the segment's page table.

The complete mapping of the address (s, i) is

$$PMA = SDT(s).physical\_origin + i \qquad (3\text{-}6)$$

The length check verifies that the following inequality is true:

$$i < SDT(s).length \qquad (3\text{-}7)$$

Using two adders can speed execution: While one adder performs the mapping addition, the other adder tests whether the address inequality holds. The comparison logic signals an interrupt if the index value exceeds the length. Figure 3-17 illustrates this addition and checking process.

The SDT represents the tabular mapping of the process' segment number space into another address space. The user program and/or the compiler/linker

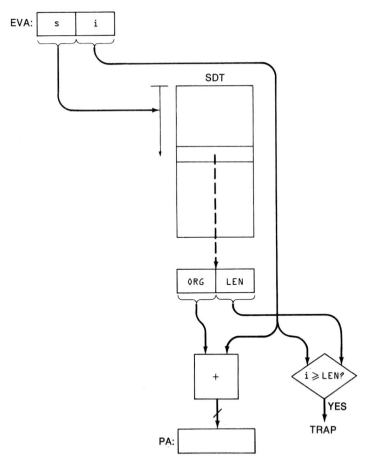

Figure 3-17 Mapping a two-dimensional address through a segment descriptor table (SDT)

determine which segments are loaded into the SDT. The operating system's memory allocator determines the physical addresses in the SDT entries. If protection mechanisms are in use, the protection policy module determines the contents of the access control fields in the descriptors (see Chapter 9).

Logically the SDT is a single table, and it could be implemented as one table.

The segment table might be separated into pieces in a manner visible to the executing process. The B 5700 system separates system objects (described at level 0) from user program objects (described at level 1). A global address is specified by a segment number and an index; the most significant bit of the segment number indicates which display register to use to translate the address. Figure D-5 shows this mapping.

In the Intel iAPX 432 ([TYNE81] and [ORGA83]) system, the segment number space is divided into four portions described by separate tables. The segment table used for a particular address translation is selected by the value of the two *low-order* segment number bits. This separation is visible to user programs. In particular, user programs may reload three of the four[26] table entries, thereby changing the set of accessible objects. Figure 3-18 illustrates this mapping strategy.

Alternatively, the SDT could be implemented as a tree of tables, with some bits of s selecting the subtable and the remaining bits selecting an entry. This design may be chosen for the convenience of the operating system; like paging, its existence would not be visible to any user program. Another design option is to manage the segment table like a set of pages, which might simplify the system's table and memory management functions.

3.7.2 Paging

A memory page is a block of memory allocated as a unit. The page size(s) is (are) fixed when the processor is designed. A typical page contains between 2048 and 8192 addressable units; the actual number having been chosen after simulation studies. There are many pages within the virtual address space. Pages are independently allocated memory space, so a blocked-pointer mapping is used; the complete mapping is described by the *page table*. Logically, there is a single page table, but because there are many pages and because programs exhibit locality, page address mappings may be performed by a two-level mapping table (see Section 3.4.3), with a set-associative table in front of the complete page table. In the IBM 370, the first-level table is called the Translation Lookaside Buffer (TLB).

---

[26]   The segment table numbered "0" contains pointers to the description of the process itself; therefore it cannot be changed during program execution.

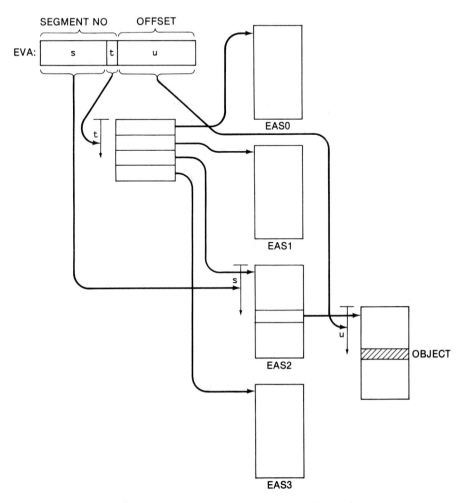

Figure 3-18   Segment address mapping in the Intel
iAPX 432 system

Figure 3-19 illustrates the page-address mapping through a TLB backed up by a complete page table contained in memory.[27]

The page table in memory can itself be paged; this structure has one major benefit and one major disadvantage. First, it allows one to represent a single mapping that has many gaps using a minimum amount of table space. However, to reach a general entry, the complete path from the root must be followed. In the Alpha AXP system, this structure is used to permit three sizes of the actual virtual address space.

---

[27]   Of course, the page table must not be accessible to user programs.

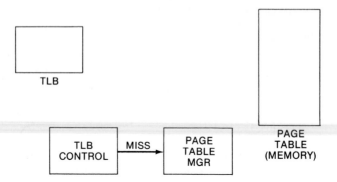

Figure 3-19   Modules in the Translation Lookaside
Buffer (TLB) and the page table

Example 3-14

In the Alpha AXP system's OpenVMS system, the page size is wired into the implementation; it may correspond to 13, 14, 15, or 16 bits of index value. Let P_B_Addr_Size denote the size of the byte address within a page. The width of the page index within a page table is three less than the width of the page index value (because each page table entry occupies 8 bytes). Three levels of page tables are used in address translation. Thus the number of virtual address bits that is supported is given by

$$4*(\text{P\_B\_Addr\_Size}) - 9$$

However, the physical address size is always given by (P_B_Addr_Size + 32).

To obtain maximum mapping speed, the TLB hardware must both compute the set-associative mapping and also manage the TLB's entries. Software intervention is not appropriate because it would be too slow for this frequently exercised function. When the EVA has a "hit" in the table, the PMA is constructed by concatenating the table entry with the "index" portion of the EVA. When the EVA's page is not present in the TLB, the hardware TLB control logic accesses the complete page table in main memory and loads the proper page description into the TLB, displacing some TLB entry. The entry to be deleted might be chosen by an LRU policy, described in Section F.5. The TLB can use a small set size and the LRU data can be recorded in a small set of recency-comparison bits.

3.7.3 Paged Segments

It is possible to divide segments and their descriptor tables into pages; the modifications to the points in the previous discussion to cover this option are straightforward. We should note in particular that under this option, the physical origin field of a segment descriptor would contain the location of the page table defining the space occupied by the segment.

3.8 THE PROCESSOR-MEMORY INTERFACE

The interface between the processor and the memory determines many system properties, including its performance. A hardware designer can increase system speed by incorporating mechanisms that speed memory accesses or that compute and translate effective memory addresses. The memory hardware design affects system expansion possibilities, system speed, and system reliability. Finally, special modules in the processor–memory interface can modify the addressing granularity, thereby decoupling the memory granularity seen at the processor from the granularity of the memory modules themselves. We discuss these issues in this section.

The time required for the processor to access an item stored in memory often is a fundamental limit to system speed. Under many designs, the memory access time is not identical for all memory access attempts, so the performance of the memory system is characterized by the *average* amount of time required for a memory access. This time is called the *effective memory access time*. The effective memory speed can be improved by changing logical structures in the processor–memory interface or by changing the memory technology. A technology change does not directly change the system's architecture and therefore is beyond the scope of this book; but technology changes do modify the cost/performance parameters and thereby affect the trade-offs that designers must consider.

The architectural techniques we discuss in this section include the following:

1. Memory management units
2. Cache memories
3. Multiple, independent memory modules
4. Memory bandwidth improvement
5. Memory granularity adjustments

A memory management unit reduces access time by speeding the memory address mapping process, which must be performed before most memory accesses. A cache memory statistically reduces the access time. Having multiple memory units statistically reduces the waiting time before an access attempt can be initiated at the memory, and therefore reduces the effective access time as seen from the processor. Memory bandwidth increases will increase system speed by decreasing the address sizes or increasing the amount of data accessed during one memory cycle. Data-width increases are helpful if the additional information accessed can actually be used by the processor. Granularity adjustment decouples the actual memory design from its logical interface viewed from the processor; this technique can be used to create one or more system(s) with different or flexible word sizes from the same set of memory modules. Other features of the processor–memory interface related to shared memory in multiprocessor systems and security in all systems are discussed in Chapters 8 and 9.

3.8.1 Memory Management Units

The memory management unit (MMU) is placed between the processor and the memory (Figure 3-20); it transforms virtual addresses to physical addresses and may check access rights to validate the acceptability of each access attempt.

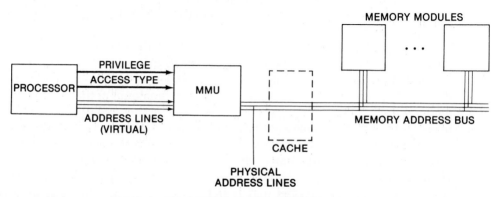

Figure 3-20   Placement of the MMU module

Assume, without loss of generality, that the MMU performs memory mapping on a page basis. Thus, the MMU logically maps each page number to the memory address of the corresponding page frame. The logical map table has one entry per virtual page frame. If the MMU receives a virtual address, which is usually the case, its mapping function has to be different for each executing process, and must be changed when the processor switches processes. The map table must span the virtual address space—a large address range. For good performance, speedy accesses are required, at least for those pages likely to be accessed. Thus although the translation time for pages likely to be accessed must be short, the translation for pages unlikely to be accessed can be slower. These observations suggest the use of a set-associative table within the MMU backed up by the complete address map held within main memory. MMU control logic must manage the composition of the set-associative table. Typically an LRU policy is used, with the LRU statistics represented by a set of recency-comparison bits within the table slots.

In a multiprogrammed system, the MMU's map table includes both physical location and access rights information for each page frame. The access rights bits define the types of access permitted to the executing process;[28] these access rights must be checked on each access attempt. To enforce this level of access control, the processor must notify the MMU of the type of each access being attempted. In some designs, all attributes of the executing process that determine its privilege are sent to the MMU with each request. These considerations suggest the processor–MMU interface signals shown in Figure 3-20.

Example 3-15

Each page table entry in the Alpha AXP Open VMS APX system contains 3 bits that indicate that a fault should be caused on any attempt to read, write, or execute any object within the page. Also, there are read and write enable bits for each of the four processor states (kernel, executive, supervisor, and user) controlling whether the processor is permitted to read and write when in the corresponding state.

For system integrity, all name mapping information in the table must be controlled by the operating system's memory management modules. This control ensures that the address mapping and access rights are consistent with the memory allocation and permission policy being enforced. Thus, the manager must control the contents of the memory copy of the memory map table, and it must define which map table is to be used by the MMU. There is no requirement concerning copying between the set-associative map and the mapping table because this copying is controlled at the MMU hardware level. If the MMU uses process number information to choose the map, switching among processes will be simple. However, if the MMU simply uses the user's virtual address, there must be a way for the operating system to invalidate all set-associative table entries when the scheduler dispatches a new process.

During a transition between from executing a user program to the operating system, it is necessary to instantly change the MMU's mapping function to that of the operating system. This requirement could be satisfied in two ways. One way is to include the operating system within the memory image of every user program and to have the processor granted all types of access to any section of the memory space while the processor is in its system mode. Another way is to include the operating system, as before, but provide a second set of access permission bits in the map. In this design, the set of access rights bits to be used on an access is selected based on the processor's mode. A third way to approach this dilemma is to provide two mapping tables and a means for instantly switching from one to the other. Figure 3-21 illustrates these options.

---

[28]   This fine granularity of access control is required to share memory correctly; see Chapters 8 and 9.

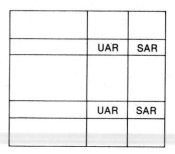

a) Operating
system has all access
rights everywhere

b) Operating system
has separate rights bits

USER
MAP TABLE

SYSTEM
MAP TABLE

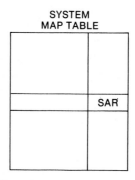

c) Operating system
has separate map table

Figure 3-21   User/operating system separation in the
MMU tables (UAR = user access rights; SAR = system
access rights)

Example 3-16

In i386 processors ([INTE89]), both the first- and second-level page tables contain
access control fields, with 2 bits in each field. In the processor's user mode, one of
these bits denies the user write permission (if it is zero) and the other specifies
whether any access is permitted from programs executing in the user mode. The
access permissions from the two levels are both consulted to determine denial of
access. Thus, user read access is denied if neither level permits user access, and
user write access requires permission at both levels. The supervisor is able to read
and write every page in the table.

Example 3-17

In SPARC and PowerPC 601 ([MOTO93]) processors, the processor state controls
the decoding of an access control field from the page table entry to determine access rights according to the entries in Table 3-3. Notice that SPARC provides

separate access control for execute accesses, and that neither processor supports a write-only combination. The elimination of the write-only and execute-only options can have deleterious effects in a system designed to support security policies (see Chapter 9).

TABLE 3-3   ACCESS CONTROLS IN POWERPC AND SPARC

Page Table Code	Power PC		SPARC	
	U[a]	S	U	S
000	—	R/W	R	R
001	R	R/W	R/W	R/W
010	R/W	R/W	R/E	R/E
011	R	R	R/W/E	R/W/E
100	Not used		E	E
101	Not used		R	R/W
110	Not used		—	R/E
111	Not used		—	R/W/E

[a] U = user mode; S = system mode.

Example 3-18

In the Alpha AXP Open VMS system, page table entries contain eight access control bits that independently permit read and write accesses from each of the four possible processor states (kernel, executive, supervisor, and user). However, the actions that occur if a write-only combination occurs is specified as "UNDEFINED."

The MMU must correctly restrict access to the map tables while the processor executes a user program, lest the user's program modify the table, thereby obtaining unauthorized access to information in the system. This issue may appear to be circular—the system must control accesses so that the access control mechanism works correctly! Actually, one way to approach this cycle is to deny access to the tables when user programs execute and permit table access only when the processor is executing in the supervisor mode. Another approach to this problem isolates the memory map information in a special device to which access is permitted only by executing special "privileged" instructions executable from the supervisor mode.

Now consider the location of the map table. It could be forced to be located at a fixed ("wired-down") location by the design of the MMU. If the MMU expects to find the memory map table at a fixed physical address, the system must copy the map table for the next process that will be dispatched to the fixed location where the MMU will find the table; this copying must occur before dispatching the process, and consumes many memory cycles. Because this delay would be significant, the MMU should be designed so that the address of the table origin (within main memory) is passed from the processor to the MMU. Because the mapping table does not have to be copied, this option permits changing the map quickly. Note that when it is necessary to reload the MMU's map, it must perform the same memory accesses under all design options, so the time to reload the map's cache does not affect the selection of an implementation technique. In this case, system assurance is based on the correct origin information being passed to the MMU upon process switch.

The mapping techniques just presented are appropriate for user processes, but to manage memory the system may have to access memory on the basis of physical addresses. Thus, when executing the memory management algorithms, the processor may have to bypass the MMU's memory mapping logic. How would this bypass be specified? One method for specifying the bypass decision uses the processor's mode. From the supervisor mode, for example, it could be ruled that all accesses bypass the MMU and are made directly to the memory. This choice is not wise, because many parts of the operating system would have to be written using absolute addressing, thereby placing a great burden on the programmers. It would be much better to provide a means by which the memory management function could be "buried" deep within the system, with the outer layers of the system written using virtual addressing. One design alternative makes the MMU bypass mode switchable while the processor is executing in the supervisor mode. With this option, the lowest levels of the operating system use absolute addressing, but the software for all levels above the memory manager can be written using virtual memory addresses.

Example 3-19

SPARC-V9 processors (see Appendix A) bypass the MMU's address translation mechanisms when the system is forced into the "RED" mode, which is invoked when traps overflow the system's capacity or when the system is reset or in the debug mode.

3.8.2 Cache Memory

A cache memory may be inserted between the MMU (if there is one) and the physical main memory (Figure 3-20) to give the processor the appearance of a faster main memory. The cache serves as the fastest, most expensive level of the memory hierarchy; it is inserted to decrease the average main memory access time as seen from the processor.

Logically, a cache memory is similar to a paged memory—information may be absent, the memory is the fastest in the system, and management algorithms are required. As with paging, the selection of the dumping policy is important. The problem of selecting the cache's dumping policy is not the same as selecting the page dumping policy because the speed ratio between the two memories involved is drastically different. With a high speed ratio, the cost of a poor decision is high, and the use of a complex decision algorithm can be justified. Thus, with a high speed ratio, a complex management policy can be implemented in software. On the other hand, if the speed ratio is low, the cost of a poor decision is low, and it is more important to make a quick decision than to make a really good decision, so a simple dumping policy can be adequate. The latter case applies to cache memory design, because the speed ratio between the cache memory and the main memory is less than 10:1, whereas the main memory to secondary memory speed ratio may be 10^3:1. Also, the cache memory is fast enough that very few logical operations can be performed during one cache memory cycle. Hence, all cache address translation and space management algorithms must be quite simple and must be implemented in hardware.

The cache provides fast access between the processor and any object stored in the cache. Frequent fast accesses reduce the average memory access time. The access time can be expressed in terms of the cache hit ratio:

> **Definition.** The *cache hit ratio h* is the fraction of access attempts that find the desired object within the cache.

If m is the average main memory access time and c the cache access time, then the average memory access time s is given by

$$s = hc + (1 - h)m \tag{3-8}$$

Because the cache memory is small and expensive, the size of the swapped unit must be much smaller than a page. Cache swapping units are called *blocks* or *lines*; their size lies in the range from 8 to 32 bytes. This size selection is based on hardware cost, the amount of physical space, the speed improvement, and the cost.

The high speed of the cache memory would be wasted unless it incorporates a high-speed mechanism that translates a memory address to a cache location. Due to program locality, a cache using a set-associative mapping will give good performance.

> **Definition.** The collection of entries in one slot of a set-associative cache mechanism is called a *set*.

Example 3-20

Figure 3-22 shows the complete TLB/cache mechanism used in the IBM 370/168 processor. The cache set selection is independent of the address translation for paging, which speeds up address translation because the cache index and the TLB can be accessed simultaneously.

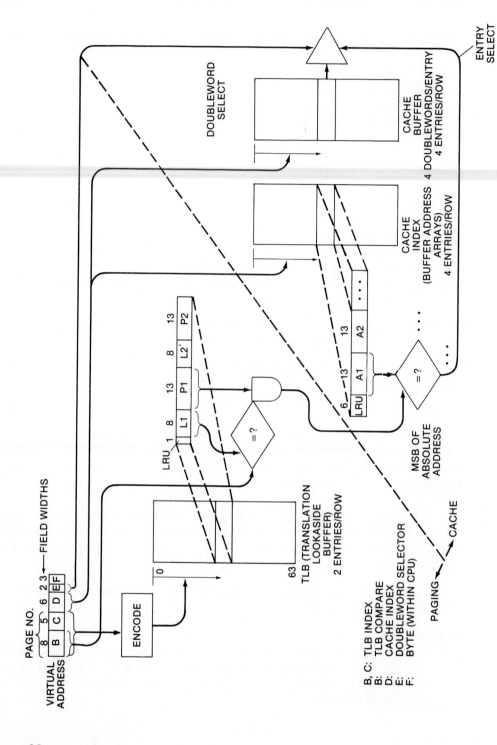

Figure 3-22 The paging/cache mechanism in the IBM 370/168 system

Several policy issues must be resolved to complete the design of a set-associative cache located between the processor and memory:

1. Cache block size
2. When to clean a cache block
3. When to load a cache block
4. When to dump a cache block
5. Cache position

Cache Block Size. Several issues affect one's choice of the size of a cache block, including the cache cost, the amount of information retrieved in a single memory access, and the amount of information accessed to replenish the instruction-processing pipeline (in a RISC processor). One would like to have all of these sizes match, but one might not be able to control the width of memory accesses. A secondary effect with respect to instruction issue is that it is desirable to have the instructions that are targets of branch instructions aligned with respect to the cache block size. Satisfying this alignment constraint will increase the chance that all program bytes that are accessed from the cache (and from other levels of the memory hierarchy) will be used during program execution.

Cache Block Cleaning. A cache memory, like a primary memory in a memory hierarchy, must occasionally receive new information to reflect a changed locality pattern. Old information must be replaced. Will the cache block to be replaced be clean? If it is not clean, its contents will have to be copied to main memory before a new block can be read in to take its place. The time penalty for this copying may reduce system performance. If the performance is unacceptable, we need to look for an alternate design. Could we design the cache so that its blocks are usually clean?

> **Definition.** A cache block is *clean* when its contents match the contents of the corresponding block of main memory. A block that is not clean is *dirty*.

What policies could be used for cleaning[29] cache blocks? Because a write cycle is the only activity that can dirty a block,[30] we consider the cache actions on a memory write. First, note that the only way that a dirty cache block can be cleaned is by writing it to main memory. So the block cleaning options amount to choosing the relationship between the write initiated from the processor and the write that cleans the cache block. We consider two policies:

---

[29]   Cleaning a cache block is like cleaning memory space.
[30]   Other situations requiring special attention, such as a write to a location that happens to be present in the cache from a direct-memory-access (DMA) device or from other processors in shared memory multiprocessor systems, will be considered later.

1. Write-through
2. Write-back

Under the *write-through* policy, during any write cycle, the cache generates a request to write the same information to main memory. A cache block never need be considered "dirty" if this policy is followed. This policy may slow the system because there will be many memory write requests. However, the designer can choose to include a queuing mechanism to buffer the write requests, because there is no logical reason that each write must be completed before the processor can proceed with successive instructions.[31]

Under the *write-back* policy, a block is not written to main memory until the cache decides to dump it, and then it is written to main memory only if it is dirty. This policy results in fewer main memory writes than the write-through policy. Under write-through, the write slowdown affects only memory write operations, whereas under write-back, the write slowdown may affect any memory access that causes a cache block to be loaded.

A mixture of the two policies can be implemented by adding a flag to each memory page or segment, the flag value signifying which policy is to be used for the associated information. A policy mixture may be useful in a multiprocessor system with hierarchical caches (see Section 8.8).

Example 3-21

> In the PowerPC 601, a write-through bit is included in each page descriptor; when it is set, the MMU will initiate a write to memory whenever a write to a location within the page occurs.

Cache Block Loading. Another cache design decision concerns the cache loading policy. It should be clear that if there is but a single program in the system, it always pays to load a block into the cache when the block is first read, for locality predicts that the program is likely to read other information from that same block in the near future. Within this policy, the designer has the option of including controlling hardware to permit the information in the memory block to be copied into the cache out of its natural (address-based) order, so that the information that is needed to proceed with instruction execution will be available as soon as possible (see Problem 3-39).

On write, however, the cache loading design issue is not quite so clear. It could be argued that once a block is written into, the same block is likely to be written into again soon. This argument suggests that the block should be loaded into the cache when the write operation is performed. This argument does not apply if the cache uses write-through, because under write-through, each write operation initiates a write cycle in the main memory, whether the block is located within the cache or not. It is easy to see that there is no advantage to

---

[31]   But this strategy does complicate cache coherency designs; see Section 8.8.

loading the written block into the cache if the cache uses the write-through policy and the block is never read. Furthermore, the written block will occupy cache space that otherwise could hold another block whose read accesses would be speeded up. Thus loading blocks into the cache on write misses may decrease the read hit ratio, which may increase the average memory access time.

Cache Block Dumping. A cache dumping policy is needed if each cache set includes more than one block. The dumping policy, like a page dumping policy, determines which block will be removed from the cache when a new block must be loaded within the set. Because there are few blocks per set, an LRU policy with usage data stored in a set of recency-comparison bits (Section F.5.2) can be used.

How does the selection of the dumping policy affect the cache performance? Recall that cache performance is characterized in terms of the "hit ratio," the fraction of access requests that are actually satisfied by the cache without reference to main memory. It is difficult to obtain any analytic characterizations of cache hit ratios except under unrealistic assumptions, so simulation must be used. Simulation studies are only as accurate as the characterization of the system's environment. With these caveats up front, let us look at one typical simulation study. The study by Smith and Goodman [SMIT83] is typical of these studies except that it studied only instruction referencing patterns. First, the authors obtain a "workload characterization;" memory reference strings are collected by an interpreting program. These reference strings are presented as input to the simulator. Different simulations emulate different cache policies for each reference string. The cache size and configuration were also varied. Their data show that the size of the cache is the most important factor determining the hit ratio. Furthermore, the performance is almost independent of the policy, especially in the region of interest (where the effective access time is small). These results are hardly surprising because caching is like paging and simulations of paging policies have shown that the choice of the page dumping policy does not have much effect on the performance of the paging system.

Cache Position. Should the cache memory be considered to be associated with the processor or with the memory? Figure 3-23 depicts the two alternatives. Our question raises an important design issue. If the cache is associated with the processor, only the (single) processor can submit access requests that will be handled by the cache. On the other hand, if the cache is associated with the memory, any memory requester can submit access requests to the cache.

Several issues complicate the selection among these alternatives:

1. Request competition
2. Multiple copies of data
3. Speed

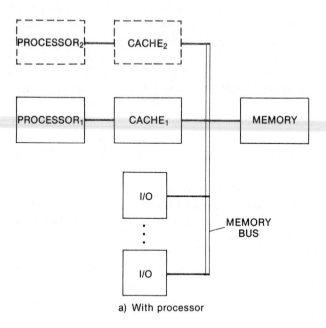

a) With processor

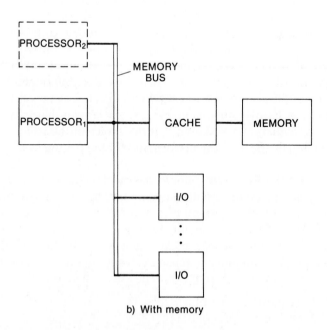

b) With memory

Figure 3-23   Cache position options

Request competition can be a problem if the cache is associated with the memory, because all processors and input/output devices may send access requests to the cache.[32] Competing requests may make the cache unavailable to a processor; this lengthens the average access time. This effect is not present if the cache is associated with the processor.

Multiple data copies may be present in a multiprocessor system; if there are several copies of the same memory item in different caches and any processor changes its copy, we have a problem. Immediately, the copies located within other caches contain obsolete information. The problem of keeping all views of the shared data consistent is known as the *cache coherence problem*. The logical synchronization aspects of this situation are covered in Chapter 8. In one solution to the coherence problem, each cache monitors memory write requests on the system bus and takes an appropriate action when it sees a write re₁uest. The cache may have to invalidate a block or update the copy held in the cache using the new value (that can be copied from the memory data bus). The overhead of these activities may decrease the cache speed. The effect is present only if the caches are associated with the processors. If all caches are associated with the memory, a cache entry effectively replaces the memory copy for all access attempts so there is only a single (visible) copy of each memory item. Therefore, all processors see the result of any memory write, and the coherence problem vanishes.

The *effective cache speed* is affected by both the speed of the cache itself and the propagation delay between the processor and the cache. If the cache is associated with the processor, the propagation delay from the processor to the cache will be short, and the effective cache access time will be the smallest possible for the given cache implementation. For this reason, the cache memory is usually associated with the processor, and is often incorporated within the processor chip—but this implies that the cache consistency problem will have to be solved somewhere else within the system, but will require processor support.

Another important design option is to include two independent caches, one for all instruction accesses and the other for all data accesses.[33] Because every instruction access is a read, blocks in the instruction cache never become dirty. Also, having the data and instruction separation permits simultaneous accesses to proceed to both caches, which opens another design option similar to the Harvard design separating instructions from data in the memory space, as discussed in Section 4.1.

---

[32]   At first reading, this statement might make the reader conclude immediately that there is no reason to want the cache at the memory. Actually, placing separate caches in front of separate memory modules does spread the demand, and the effect of the competition may not be more serious than the contrary effect of the cache coherence problem discussed in the next paragraph.

[33]   These are usually called the *I-cache* and the *D-cache*.

Finally, a designer can consider extending the memory hierarchy by placing a *second-level cache* between the primary cache and the memory system. This option has several attractive features:

1. The size of the secondary cache is not limited by the amount of space on the processor chip.
2. The secondary cache can make the implementation of certain coherence mechanisms more efficient by reducing the number of requests that have to be handled by the first-level cache (see Section 8.8).

Summary. The cache cleaning policy selection affects both the system's logical properties and the speed of memory write operations through the cache. If the cache is associated with the processor, the selection affects the logical properties, because delayed writing may affect the consistency of the memory views as seen by different processors. On the other hand, a system with memory-associated caches always presents the external world with a single view of the memory, regardless of the policy for writing information to memory. The effective memory speed is affected by the choice of the cache block cleaning policy because a memory write operation takes longer when the block must actually be written to main memory. The slowdown only affects write accesses, which typically constitute about 15% of all memory accesses.

3.8.3 Memory Interleaving

It is possible to construct a complete memory system using a simple memory module, but there are many reasons why this strategy is undesirable. First, the design poses reliability problems. Second, the design limits system expansion. Third, the design cannot allow overlapping access requests from several different requesters, because the module cannot handle a second access request while another one is being completed. Request overlapping can improve system performance; we discuss this effect in Chapter 6.

Here we present some alternative methods for constructing a memory system from several separate memory modules. The design issues center on the method used to select which memory module contains the object being addressed. It is safe to say that memory module selection is based on the values of some memory address bits; although this is certainly true, the observation does not illuminate the selection issues or the designer's options. In this section we discuss several options, including interleaving.

If the number of modules is a multiple of 2, the module selection should use bit values taken from the ends of the physical address, but not from its middle. The design decision concerns how many bits are to be used from each end of the address; the selection affects the randomness of the request distribution among modules, the memory expansion possibilities, and the effects of failures on the system's capacity.[34]

If the number of modules is not a multiple of 2, nontrivial address mapping logic will be required. In the following subsections we discuss some interleaving options, as follows:

1. No interleaving
2. Power-of-2 interleaving
3. Prime-way interleaving

No Interleaving.   For no interleaving, the memory module number is taken from the most significant address bits. Each memory module will hold a set of contiguous addresses. The accessing pattern is not likely to be randomly distributed across the set of memory modules, because a long block of consecutive addresses[35] is located in the same module. This design does, however, have a memory system expansion advantage; the expansion increment is a single module, providing system configuration flexibility.

Interleaving by a Power of 2.   Memory interleaving maps any pair of consecutive addresses to different physical modules. The degree of interleaving is the length of the cycle by which addresses are mapped into module numbers. Suppose that address zero maps into module zero (a common condition!) and that the next address that maps into module zero is L. Then L is the degree of interleaving. With L-way interleaving, a memory address M is mapped into a module number N and a local address A using the relations

$$N = M \textbf{ mod } L;$$
$$A = \lfloor (M/L) \rfloor; \qquad // integer\_part\_of(M/L)$$

With this module selection scheme, memory must be expanded by adding a complete interleaved set of modules, thereby adding a contiguous set of addresses to the memory.

When L is a power of 2, the residue and quotient operations amount to selecting physical address bits. In particular, N is the set of $\log_2 L$ bits from the right end of M, and A constitutes the remaining bits of M.

At the module level, the referencing pattern to an interleaved memory will be randomly distributed among the modules unless the program exhibits a repetitive pattern with an addressing increment A satisfying $\gcd(A, L) > 1$. Otherwise the probability that an arbitrary memory access request will select a particular memory module will be $1/L$.

---

[34] This concern may not be important unless the system should be able to operate in a degraded mode after a module failure; we will not discuss it in detail.

[35] Recall that consecutive addressing is common inside loops and when processing many data structures.

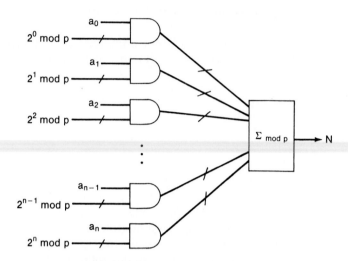

Figure 3-24   Determining the module number when prime-way interleaving is used

It is possible to specify dynamically which address bits should be used for the module number; witness this scheme used in the CRAY T3D [KOEN94]:

Example 3-22

> The CRAY T3D multiprocessor system supports block transfers from the global memory space to memory local to a processing node. Each global address contains two fields, a node number and an address within the memory local to that node. The block within the global address space is defined by an incremented address value, which is divided into a module number and the local address under control of a mask register that specifies how address bits are to be routed to the node number portion of the physical address. For example, the leftmost bit of the node number is taken from the address bit position that corresponds to the position of the leftmost set bit in the mask value. More details of this scheme, including its implication of a large fan-in within the routing logic, are given in Problem 3-43.

Prime-Way Interleaving.   It might seem that prime-way interleaving would be terribly inefficient and its implementation awkward due to the need for division by the prime number. It is possible to exploit some properties of prime numbers to simplify the design, provided that some waste space can be tolerated. We first present a simple way to find the module number N from the address M. Then we tackle the determination of the local address, which does require either a division or an allocation with unused space.[36]

To find the module number, we must divide the address M by the prime number P (we use P rather than L, as before, to emphasize the fact that the value is a prime number). Now express M in terms of its binary representation:

---

[36]   This scheme was first described in [LAWR82].

TABLE 3-4   RESIDUES OF 2^i mod P

			P		
i	11	13	17	19	37
0	1	1	1	1	1
1	2	2	2	2	2
2	4	4	4	4	4
3	8	8	8	8	8
4	5	3	16	16	16
5	10	6	15	13	32
6	9	12	13	7	27
7	7	11	9	14	17
8	3	9	1	9	34
9	6	5	2	18	31
10	1	10	4	17	25
11	2	7	8	15	13
12	4	1	16	11	26
13	8	2	15	3	15
Period (of residues)	10	12	8	18	36

$$M = \sum_{i=0}^{a-1} m_i 2^i \qquad (3\text{-}9)$$

The module number N is given by

$$N = M \bmod P = \left[\sum_{i=0}^{a-1} m_i 2^i\right] \bmod P = \left[\sum_{i=0}^{a-1} m_i(2^i \bmod P)\right] \bmod P \qquad (3\text{-}10)$$

The quantity in parentheses is a constant for each i, independent of the value of m_i. In other words, Equation (3-10) states that the m_i's select some constant values to be summed (see Figure 3-24), with the summation being performed modulo P. The constants exhibit cyclical values as a function of i, as shown in Table 3-4 for a few interesting values of P. We can easily argue that the period of this cycle has to be a divisor of $(P - 1)$. The shortest period among the entries in the table occurs for $P = 17$.

The remaining part of the prime-interleave design concerns the selection of the local address A. Theoretically, we should use the quotient resulting from the division of M by P; we have already noted that this requires a difficult

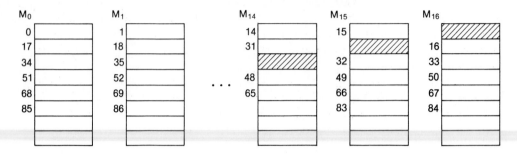

Figure 3-25   Address mapping with a 17-way interleave. (Unused space shaded; addresses expressed in decimal notation.)

computation (which could itself take much longer than a memory cycle!). If we are willing to sacrifice some memory space to obtain simplicity in the addressing mechanism, we use instead the quotient on division by a power of 2 less than P. This choice guarantees that (1) the address can be found by bit selection, (2) every address is at least as high as the correct one, and (3) that the mapping from M to A is one-to-one. Let R denote the selected power of 2. With $P = 17$, we choose $R = 16$. Figure 3-25 illustrates the mapping of physical addresses into the memory modules for $P = 17$ and $R = 16$. It is easy to see that the fraction of useful space is R/P, which indicates that the greatest power of 2 less than P should be used for R and that choosing P close to a power of 2 is desirable.

3.8.4 Memory Bandwidth

The bandwidth of the memory system can be a system bottleneck. Here we present some simple system structuring techniques that modify the processor–memory interface. These techniques reduce the address bandwidth requirement or increase the data bandwidth by increasing parallelism. Drastic system restructuring to allow several operations to be performed on an object between the time it is read from memory and the time a result is written back to memory can reduce the impact of any memory system bandwidth limitation. Some such designs are discussed in Chapter 8.

    Address Bandwidth. This is less likely to be a bottleneck than the data bandwidth. The address bandwidth requirement can be reduced by moving address translation from the processor if the physical addresses are wider than the virtual addresses. Under such a design the processor would send a short virtual address across the bus and the memory system would translate it to its long form. Whatever mapping scheme is used, from the processor side the operating system must modify the mapping mechanism on every mapping change; with the translation moved to the memory system, the transaction redefining the mapping consumes bus bandwidth. For example, using this strategy to translate the B 5700's context-dependent addresses in the memory system would require that the display information be available within the memory system.

Another way to reduce the address bandwidth uses a simple form of context-dependent addressing for instruction fetching. Suppose that every instruction is the same size. Now move the program counter logic to the memory system. For sequential instruction fetching, a single-bit request "fetch next instruction" is adequate; no address need be sent from the processor to the memory. A new address must be sent from the processor only when a branch is to be taken. The Fairchild F8 microprocessor system uses this bandwidth reduction technique.

Data Bandwidth. These constraints are more likely to affect system performance than address bandwidth constraints. A simple approach that can relieve this bottleneck is to access many objects in parallel during one memory access. If the additional objects are likely be used, the parallel access may be worthwhile. With a specialized application such as vector processing, it is very likely that the additional objects will be used. Thus, vector-oriented large-scale machines are designed with a wide data path to memory.

Example 3-23

The CDC STAR-100 [CONT70], a vector machine, is designed to access 512 information bits and 16 parity bits on every memory cycle. This is achieved by a parallel interconnection of a set of smaller memory modules, each one holding 64-bit words. All modules in a parallel set receive the same address. The wide data path to the processor is constructed by concatenating the data paths to the modules in the parallel set, as illustrated in Figure 3-26.

A memory with a wide data path can be used to speed transfers between a processor cache and main memory. Many bits from the same cache block can be accessed simultaneously during one memory cycle. The bits can be sent from memory to the cache as a sequence of objects smaller than the entire cache block, with each transfer taking much less time than a complete memory access. The cache response time would be reduced even further if the memory's control logic were redesigned to send the addressed object in the first bus transaction that passes data to the cache. Sequencing through the remaining words starting from the addressed one is adequate to load the complete block.

Example 3-24

Suppose that the memory width is eight words, and that a block of eight words is to be loaded into the cache using word-size transfers on the bus. After the cache misses when it attempts to access location 35, the memory accesses locations 30 .. 37 in one cycle. The controller than sends the words to the processor in the order 35, 36, 37, 30, 31, 32, 33, 34, which allows the cache to respond to the processor immediately after the first word is received from the memory.

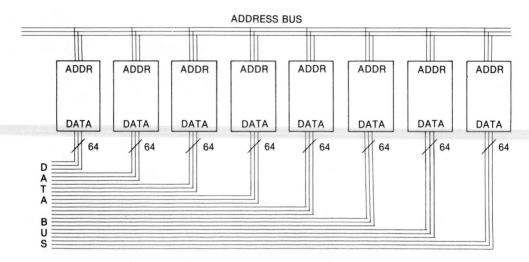

Figure 3-26   The memory organization in the CDC STAR-100 system

There is some difference of opinion about whether this strategy provides sufficient benefit; another approach is to align information in memory based on the
positions of cache block boundaries. The Alpha AXP literature, for example, es-
pouses such alignments, telling one how to choose the granularity of these alignments so that most (if not all) implementations will see the object aligned on a
cache block boundary. Having instructions that are jump targets aligned at the
granularity of a cache line is beneficial, because this alignment makes it likely
that all instructions fetched with the target will be accessed (because there are
not any predecessors that are not likely to be executed). The alignment can be
managed by the compiler's code generator.

3.8.5 Granularity

The simple memory illusion suggests that each memory access reaches an object
whose size is defined by the object's type. This defines the granularity for object
naming and data transfers when memory accesses are made. If the actual widths
of the object and the memory system are incompatible, adjustments must be
made to support the simple memory illusion. If the object width is greater than
the memory width, multiple accesses will have to be used to support the illusion.
A simple case of this design style is a memory system attached to a processor
that has a fixed object size (such as 64 bits in the Alpha AXP design) where the
memory's width is a multiple of the fixed object size. A similar simplicity occurs

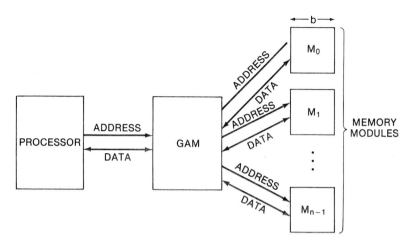

Figure 3-27   Placement of the GAM module

when the processor is designed to handle varying object sizes, but all these sizes are multiples of a single size (such as 1 byte).

On the other hand, if the object is not an exact multiple of the memory width or is smaller than the memory width, masking and shifting will be required to give the illusion that only a single object has been accessed. In particular, suppose that the processor's object sizes do not have any simple relationship among themselves. For example, the processor might support object sizes at bit granularity.

To support this illusion, one might use a granularity adjustment module (GAM) interposed between the memory system and processor (Figure 3-27) to handle width mismatches. Now let b denote the number of bits each memory module accesses in a single cycle. Bit addresses are interleaved among n modules in b-bit chunks. Thus, the sequence of the (bit) addresses of the bits within module 0 begins as follows:

$$0, 1, 2, \ldots, b-1, nb, nb+1, nb+2, \ldots, (n+1)b-1, 2nb, \ldots$$

In any reasonable design, both n and b should be powers of 2, so we assume this condition as we continue the discussion. We also assume that each access request from the processor includes both a starting bit address and a bit count (object length).

To achieve the illusion, the GAM divides the incoming (starting) address into N, D, and B fields, as shown in Figure 3-28. To illustrate the GAM's computation, consider accessing a single bit located at address A. The contents of the N field within A determines which memory module contains the addressed bit. The

Figure 3-28 Fields within
an address in a system
using a GAM module

D	N	B

B field tells which single bit within the "word" accessed in that module is being designated as the starting bit of the object. The D field selects the word within the selected module where the addressed (first) bit is stored. If the request asked for more than 1 bit, the bits immediately following the first one may be located within the same word as the first bit, or, if the addressed bit was the last bit of the word, in the next module (next being interpreted modulo the number of modules). It is easy to see that, in general, the GAM should send addresses to the memory modules according to the following:

> **GAM Addressing Rule**. The module-local word address w of the information is $D + 1$ in module i for $0 \leq i \leq N - 1$ and D in module i for $N \leq i \leq n$.

By using this addressing rule, the GAM can access at least $(n - 1)b + 1$ consecutive bits starting at any bit address.

After the GAM has accessed the desired bits, it must reformat them for presentation to the processor, to support the illusion that the processor receives the accessed data in an aligned position within the processor–memory data path. For reading, the alignment process will require both shifting and masking. To write into the memory, the GAM must supervise a sequence of actions: read, shift, mask, and write.

Example 3-25

> In the Burroughs B 1700 series, memory addressing is to the bit, and the processor can make variable-length memory requests for up to 24 consecutive bits. A GAM is used with the configuration parameters $n = 4$, $b = 8$.

3.9 SUMMARY

In this chapter we reviewed naming and allocation issues that underly memory systems. We also covered the address mappings required to translate a high-level name into a sequence of signals that would access the correct location in a physical memory. We showed different implementations of general address mappings, including the use of associative memories, hash tables, computed addresses, and set-associative memories. We showed the use of these techniques in different stages of the accessing sequence. For example, hash tables are used in compilers, tabular mappings are used in segmentation and paging, and set-associative mappings are used to speed up page table and cache mappings. All of these mechanisms perform the same basic address mapping, translating

TABLE 3-5   SUMMARY OF MEMORY NAME MAPPINGS

| Address Mapper | Input Name Space | | |
	Form	Size	Usage Density
Translator	Symbolic	Vast	Very Low
Linker	One or two integers symbolic	Large	Low
Processor	One or two integers[a]	Large	Low
Operating system	(Virtual) integers	Large	High (in blocks)
Memory interface hardware	(Absolute) integers	Large	High (in blocks)
Cache controller	(Absolute) integers	Large	High (in blocks)
Memory module	Integers	Moderate	High

[a]Or parameters of an algorithm that produces an integer.

names from one name space to another name space. Table 3-5 summarizes the name mapping problems encountered at the different stages of accessing.

In Chapters 6, 8, and 9, we consider other memory-related issues, showing how parallelism and sharing can yield speed or logical improvements, but at the same time can create consistency and privacy problems.

3.10 TRENDS

Name mapping techniques have stabilized and are well-understood. Most systems use paging with wide virtual addresses. In this system structure, segments are not really needed, because separate objects can be placed into separate sets of contiguous pages, the only disadvantage being that any length checks are constrained to the granularity of a single page size. Set-associative techniques are used in caches that are located within processor chips, because the time delays associated with sending requests off the chip are too long. Designers of MMU tables and access control information need to be sensitive to the need for protection and security, as discussed in Chapter 9.

3.11 CONCEPT LIST

1. Location addressing versus associative addressing
2. Name mapping properties—domain and range
3. Name mapping lifetimes
4. Hash tables
5. Set-associative tables

6. Table slots
7. Translator name space
8. Linking
9. Collection
10. Link vector—export and import tables
11. Dynamic linking
12. Frame pointers
13. Two-dimensional context-dependent addressing
14. Environment stuffing
15. Display registers
16. Segmented memory addressing
17. Segment descriptor table
18. Paged memory addressing
19. Page tables
20. Translation Lookaside Buffer (TLB)
21. Memory management unit (MMU)
22. MMU access rights checks
23. Cache memory
24. Write-through and write-back policies
25. Cache coherence problem
26. Memory interleaving
27. Granularity adjustment module (GAM)
28. Associative memory functions

3.12 PROBLEMS

3-1. This problem asks you to specify a mapping of multidimensional subscripts into one-dimensional subscripts which requires a minimum number of multiplications for execution. The mapping is to be performed during program execution.
(a) Specify such a mapping.
(b) Give formulas for the numbers of additions and multiplications required to map an n-dimensional subscript vector into a single index value.
(c) Specify the minimum set of parameters needed to define the function.

3-2. Write an algorithm that performs an equality search in a hash table with p (> 1) entries per slot. Use sequential search for collision resolution.

3-3. A hash table controller resolves collisions by using a sequential search starting just after the location at which it discovered the collision. Table entries are never deleted. The search keys are alphabetic strings. The simple hashing function uses the alphabetic position of the first letter in the string as the (1-origin) table index (this simple hashing function is not recommended for general use!). Thus, a string starting with "a" hashes into the first table entry, and one starting with "d" hashes into the fourth table entry.

TABLE 3-6 SNAPSHOT OF A
HASH TABLE

Location	Key
1	alan
2	brad
3	alex
4	dick
5	ellen
6	cindy

A snapshot is taken and the contents of the table are observed; Table 3-6 shows the hash table contents at the snapshot.

(a) Based on the snapshot, write inequalities that state the strongest timing relationships that you can find concerning the ordering of the times that these entries were added to the table. For example, if you conclude that "ellen" was entered after "alan," write

ellen > alan

Do include a relation concerning any pair of keys about which you can determine a timing relationship from the information in the snapshot. Do not include redundant relations. For example, if you decide that the following three relationships are true, omit the third one from your answer, because it can be discerned from the other two. The three relations are

ellen > alan
alan > brad
ellen > brad

(b) Construct a table showing the number of table entries that are examined in the searches. Make a row for each entry in the table and show the number of table entries accessed during the search to reach that entry.

3-4. You are given a hashing function

index hash(**int** key, size)

Its parameters are a key and a table size. Its result is an index value within the range 1 .. size. You will use this hashing function to construct a hash table using sequential searching after a collision.

(a) Specify a hash table search procedure that will work correctly even if the hash table is completely filled (i.e., there are no null entries in the entire table). If a search fails, have the procedure leave **true** in the global object missing_entry. (Otherwise, missing_entry will contain **false** when the procedure returns.)

(b) Write a hash table class supporting the following operations: insert, search, and initialize. The hash table length is given in a global compile-time constant hash_table_size.

3-5. Hash table search procedures used after a collision can have problems entries if table entries may be deleted. To alleviate this problem, a designer proposes that one include in all hash table entries, in addition to the valid bit, a mark bit called reserved. The idea is to set the reserved bit when an entry is deleted from the table.
(a) Why not just clear the valid bit in the slot that held the deleted entry?
(b) Write out as a sequence of steps the algorithms supporting this type of hash table, with the operations: insert, search, initialize (the complete table), and delete (a single table entry). Be sure to specify all important values.

3-6. Write a description of the hash table search algorithm if the table uses a set of J hash functions to perform the secondary search. There is only one table.

3-7. An address mapping is implemented using a hierarchy of hash tables. Let htab(i, j) denote the jth $(1 \leq j \leq N)^{37}$ entry in the ith $(1 \leq i \leq L)$ table of the hierarchy. The same hashing function is used to access the tables at all levels of the hierarchy. In case of a collision in the ith table, the next search is made in table $(i + 1)$—using the same hash function. If there is a collision at level L, one of the following strategies is used:
   1. Use sequential searching in the table at level L; if this fails, quit.
   2. Search sequentially, as in strategy 1, but if that fails, try sequential searching in table $(L - 1)$, and so on; failure occurs if the sequential search at level 1 fails.
(a) Write out the steps of the search algorithm for each design.
(b) Contrast these designs with the following more conventional designs:
   (i)   A single hash table with one entry per slot and LN slots.
   (ii) A single hash table with L entries per slot and N slots.

3-8. Specify a procedure that will expand a hash table, placing its former entries properly into a larger table space. Assume that there is a hash function:

index hash(**int** key, size);

Each table entry contains three fields: valid, key, and value. When should this reconstruction/expansion procedure be invoked?

3-9. Consider a set of entries to be entered into a hash table. For each entry E_i, its probability of use p_i is given. Let arrangement A be the arrangement of hash table entries achieved by inserting the entries in a time sequence by the decreasing order of their usage probabilities. Show that arrangement A is optimal in the sense that the expected (i.e., average) number of table fetches to retrieve an entry will be minimized.

3-10. Use the conditional move instruction from the Alpha AXP processor (see Section B.6) to implement a binary search algorithm for an ordered list. Your program should need only one branch instruction to complete the loop that makes subdivisions of the list and a second one to exit the loop when the matching entry has been found. The program should leave the index of the entry that matched in register R4, or zero if there was no matching entry in the list.

---

[37]   Yes, all tables are the same length! Why?

3-11. Suppose we implement the mapping of Table 3-8 with a four-slot direct-mapped table that uses the least significant two bits of the key value as the table index. The primary table entries change with time. Assume that the direct-mapped table is initialized with invalid entries, and that an LRU replacement policy is used.

  (a) Suppose that each table slot holds one map entry. Construct a history showing the entry events and the times when an entry must be moved out of the first-level table.

  (b) Repeat part (a) using a table with two entries per slot.

TABLE 3-8   NAME MAPPING FOR PROBLEM
3-11 (IN ORDER OF ENTRY INTO THE TABLE)

Target Name (hex)	Host Name (hex)
3	0B2
E	1A1
10	6
8	110
1A	32
1C	05B
13	138
6	1A6
0	1AB
16	10A
1E	69
F	1B7

3-12. A designer might consider using an n-ary tree to hold an associatively searched table. The data structure of such a tree is depicted in Figure 3-29 (n is the number of objects in each bead within the tree). In the figure, notice the tags associated with the pointers in the data structure; each tag signifies whether the described space contains data or further pointers. Also notice that the highest key value within the subtree is placed in the entry that points to the next lower level of the table. This structure is designed for efficient execution of a search algorithm that stops when the value from the table is not less than the selector. When the search stops, the tag of the object can be examined to determine whether the desired entry has been found; if the tag signifies a pointer, the described space is then scanned following the same algorithm. Notice that you can flag an empty entry by placing the highest possible key in that location (provided that either (1) there are no deletions from the table or (2) the deletion algorithm rearranges entries as required).

  (a) Write a search algorithm that returns a flag indicating success or failure and a pointer to the entry that matched the search value.

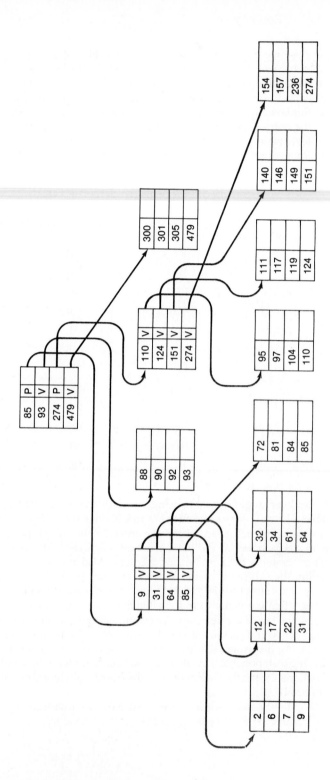

Figure 3-29 The structure of an *n*-ary tree

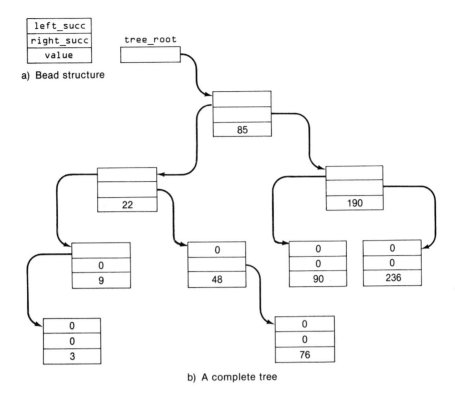

a) Bead structure

b) A complete tree

Figure 3-30   The structure of a balanced binary tree

(b) We explore the coding for an empty entry now. Explain the reason for the implication that using the highest possible key as a flag for an empty entry will not work if deletions do not rearrange the table. In your answer, describe a table organization rule such that the effects of deletions are always confined to the subtree

(c) Write an algorithm that inserts a new entry into the table.

(d) Write an algorithm that deletes a table entry.

(e) Discuss the advantages and disadvantages of "balancing" the tree. A tree is balanced when the lengths of the longest and shortest access paths from the root to any object differ by at most one.

3-13. You need to access an entry in an ordered table containing n entries. Two designs are being compared; they are a binary balanced tree (with one value at each intermediate node, as in Figure 3-30) and an ordered list that is searched by a binary search algorithm. It is argued that because both searches examine the same table entries, the choice between the two designs is arbitrary (in other words, the two are equally desirable).

(a) Is the premise of the statement correct (that both designs will search the same table entries)?

(b) Is the conclusion correct? Explain your answers.

3-14. This problem concerns the implementation of a mapping function through an *n*-ary tree structure. Each node contains either *n* pointers to other nodes or *n* values. Let *T* denote the number of entries in the table (which comprises the entire tree).

   (a) Find a mathematical expression that gives the processing time expended at one node as a function of *n*. A binary search algorithm is used for searches within the node.

   (b) Find an expression for the total time expended in a complete search (for a fixed total table size) as a function of *n*. (Do not account for the access time to reach a new node—which might have to come from a slower memory.) Assume that all table entries are at the leaves of the tree.

   (c) How is the answer to part (b) changed if each internal node contains *n* table entries in addition to the tree links? To answer this, you must take into account the probability of finding a match at an internal node of the tree.

3-15. Consider the variant object structures of Example E-9. This problem concerns the computation of the address of the city component of the structure.

   (a) Assume that the components within an object are allocated space in the order of their declaration. Thus the component named country is last in the block allocated for the object. Write out an algorithm that determines the location of this component within a specific instance of the object. The specific instance is identified by the contents of a pointer contained in the object named address_pointer. (Specify any assumptions you make regarding the encoding of the discriminant information.)

   (b) How could the difficulties of part (a) be alleviated by reordering the components? Explain any modifications you make to allocation and accessing.

   (c) Explain why the techniques used in part (b) cannot be used to remove entirely the difficulties exhibited in part (a).

3-16. An indexed-sequential structure may be used to hold a single large disk file containing records that will be retrieved individually. In this structure the root-level table selects the set of "cylinders" on which the data resides (this corresponds to selecting the disk pack holding the information). The second level table selects one cylinder in the set (this corresponds to positioning the heads on that disk pack). The third level table is stored at the beginning of the selected cylinder; it holds an index of all information on that cylinder, which is separated into two parts: (1) a portion that is ordered by key value and stored sequentially on the disk, and (2) a portion that is structured as a linked list. Both structures are ordered by increasing key values. The space allocated for the sequential information is statically allocated, so insertions might require allocating beads in the linked list portion.

   The index entries alternate; the odd-numbered entries specify the highest key value in a block of sequentially stored information, along with the number of the head that should be selected to access this information; the even-numbered entries specify the highest key value in the linked list portion holding overflows from the previous sequential block, along with a pointer to the first bead in that list. A linked list is not used for all entries because following a linked list on a disk is expensive (a complete revolution may separate one list entry from its successor).

(a) Compare this structure with the *n*-ary tree structure described in Problem 3-12. Indicate the advantages and disadvantages of each structure if the structure is stored in (1) random-access memory and (2) disk memory.

(b) Explain why restructuring the database to remove overflow records should be considered after inserting an item into the structure.

3-17. In this problem you will write a C++ class implementation for the structure of an indexed sequential data structure (see Problem 3-16 for more details about this structure, including a scheme for marking empty entries). Your class should include operations to insert and find table entries based on an exact match with the search key. Do not consider restructuring the overflow information when you insert an entry in the table. Assume that there are no deletions and that the last entry in the cylinder index contains the disk address of the first free space available for an overflow bead.

(a) Explain why it is adequate that the free overflow space be described by a single pointer.

(b) Write the search algorithm.

(c) Write the insertion algorithm.

(d) Complete the class definition.

3-18. This problem explores the situations described in Table 3-2.

(a) Give examples from a high-level language that illustrate each of the situations in the table.

(b) Draw a figure describing the allocation and effective address computation for each situation in the table.

3-19. Here is a sketch of the reference replacement algorithm that is used by a linker to replace a chain of uses of an address with the definition. The following assumes that a complete address will fit into a single instruction's address field.

> 1. Let S be the next unlinked imported symbol; (If there are no more, exit.)
> 2. Let A be the address in the entry where S was found;
> 3. Find the declaration linked to S, and let D be its value;[38]
> 4. Let B be the contents of the address part of M(A);[39] (This is the pointer to the next entry.)
> 5. Store D in the address part of M(A);
> 6. Copy B into A; if this is not 0, go to step 4;
> 7. Go to step 1;

Modify this algorithm so that it will function correctly if a complete address does not fit into an instruction's address field. You can assume that the following two functions are available:

> hi(A);   //result is the high-order part of the address A
> lo(A);   //result is the low-order part of the address A

Be sure to specify in your answer how all address objects are represented, including the pointers that form the chain linking the places where the address is needed. Also discuss why this technique is not very good for performing linking.

---

[38]   This value is actually an address.

[39]   This denotes the contents of the location with address A.

3-20. A program uses a user-allocated array of structures created by the following C++ fragment

```
class problem {
public:
        int this;
        int that;
}
problem *examplea;

..
examplea = new problem[10];          //examplea is a local object within a procedure.
```

(a) Devise a data structure that provides appropriate information for an Alpha AXP processor to be able to access the entry examplea[i].that.

(b) Show how the Alpha AXP processor could be programmed to read that entry, given that R15 contains the frame pointer for the local context, and that there is a known (static) offset a_offset describing the location of the pointer named examplea within the activation block.

3-21. Design a method to implement call-by-name in ALGOL for a processor that does not support tagging in memory objects.

3-22. One option for passing subroutine parameters is to place them in the calling sequence (i.e., in the calling program itself). A designer proposes to use this convention to call recursive procedures. Is this feasible? Describe what additional manipulations the recursive procedure would have to perform (in addition to those necessary if the procedure were nonrecursive).

3-23. Five "needs" that may enter into the selection of one linking scheme over another are:
   1. The ability to establish linkages during program execution.
   2. The ability to change existing links during program execution.
   3. Speed of program execution.
   4. Speed of establishing links.
   5. The ability to share instruction segments.
      Order these five "needs" in relative importance for each situation:
   (a) Execution of C++ programs.
   (b) Execution of Pascal or Ada programs.

3-24. This problem concerns the number of beads of the context tree that the processor must examine to fill the display. Let n denote the current level; the level numbers increase inwards, starting from the user's outermost program block, which is at level 2. In a system using the Burroughs B 5700 design, how many block pointers will be examined to construct the new display in each of the following situations? Write a skeleton of a program in some block-structured language (specify the language you are using) to illustrate the situations in parts (a) through (d).

(a) The main program calls a procedure declared within the declarations of the main program.

(b) A program at level n calls a procedure declared within its declarations.

(c) The program returns to its caller, the call having been made in a situation like that described in part (a).

(d) The program recursively calls itself.

(e) The operating system schedules another process for execution; the new process will resume execution in a block at level *n* (*n* should be a parameter of your answer). Do not attempt to write a program skeleton for this situation.

3-25. Specify a SPARC stack allocation scheme that allocates space for display information to be used in the implementation of a statically nested language, such as Pascal.

3-26. Suppose that a SPARC processor is executing a program from a statically nested language.

(a) Explain why one cannot leave the parameter values in the registers and perform a program with the following (Pascal) skeleton (which shows all declarations):

```
procedure a( i : integer ) is
        procedure b( j : integer ) is
                procedure c( k : integer ) is
                begin
                        k = i;
                        ..
                end c;
                x : integer;
        begin
                ..
                x := c(x);
                ..
        end b;
        y : integer;
begin
        ..
        y := b(y);
        ..
end a;
```

(b) Outline how stacking can be used to provide access to satisfy these global accesses to formal parameters within the procedure nest. Warning: Be careful about the frame pointers disappearing behind register windows!

(c) How can the compiler detect these situations to know when to stack parameters that have been passed in registers? Why can't the calling program know to stack the parameters rather than pass them in registers? Explain.

3-27. Draw a diagram illustrating access paths for completing each variety of linked addressing possible in the HP 3000 architecture (see Example 3-13).

3-28. The iAPX 432 segment numbers are translated by a four-way interleaved table structure, with one of the four component tables reserved for static objects that define the execution context for the program associated with the context. The component table used to translate an address is selected by the two lowest-order bits of the segment number. This problem asks you to compare the Intel scheme against a scheme in which there are also four tables, but the component table is selected by the two highest-order segment number bits.

(a) If all segment number fields have the same width, which scheme do you prefer? Why?

(b) Repeat part (a) if the segment number fields have two widths, call them narrow (N) and wide (W).

3-29. A set-associative memory is designed specifically for use to map page numbers into origin addresses (this might be used inside an MMU). Here is the design: The associative memory is a buffer in front of a memory-resident table whose origin is 800_{16}. Each associative memory entry contains a validity bit V (which is set if the entry is valid). The V bit value can be controlled from the processor by executing one of two special instructions CLRV and SETV, which clear and set the V bit of the page selected by the address in the instruction, respectively. These operations have no effect if the page fails the associative search (i.e., is not found in the associative memory). When a new entry is written into the memory, its V bit is automatically set. The associative memory inserts a replacement entry from the memory-resident page table whenever an associative match (used to try to find the mapping of a page number) fails. An LRU discipline is used to determine which entry should be replaced.

(a) Is there any need for a WRITEAM instruction that writes a new entry from a processor register into the associative memory? It would specify an associative memory entry by using the memory address as a selector. Explain.

(b) Discuss the need for the SETV instruction.

3-30. A paged system might utilize three tables (described in what follows) to assist in memory accessing and memory management. Two of these tables, which we will call the "short table" and the "long table," are searched using the virtual page number. The third table, which we will call the "reverse table," is searched using the physical page origin.

When a virtual address is to be translated, the short table is consulted. If the desired entry is not found in the short table, the long table is used for a second search attempt. The reverse table might be used during page fault handling.

In this problem you are asked to determine what information should be stored in the entries in each table. You should try to shorten the table entries as much as possible (in other words, an answer stating that all information is in each table is not satisfactory). Your selection criterion should be that you wish to maximize the speed of common operations, while providing sufficient information to implement the management policies and to provide logically correct behavior. Fill out a table formatted like Table 3-7, placing marks that indicate information that should be present in a table entry.

Complete the table twice—once for LRU management and once for FIFO management. If you think that other information should be present that is not listed, add rows to your table.

3-31. Here is a proposed method for keeping usage data for pages. Place a counter in each page descriptor in the main memory map. The counter manipulation rules are: (1) A counter is incremented on each attempt to access the page; (2) all counters are decreased by the same value, which is proportional to the number of memory accesses made to the entire memory since the last time a page fault

TABLE 3-7   INFORMATION IN PAGE TABLE ENTRIES

Field Contents	Short Table	Long Table	Reverse Table
Virtual page origin			
Physical page origin			
Dirty bit			
Time of last use			
Used bit			
Length			
Access rights			

occurred, whenever a page fault occurs. The pages having the lowest count values are the first candidates for replacement.

(a) Discuss the relationship of the proposed scheme to LRU management with respect to both effect and implementation.

(b) When a new page is loaded, the counter is initialized to a constant value. How should the (fixed) initial value for the counter be determined? Explain.

(c) Discuss the advantages and disadvantages of the proposed scheme.

(d) Consider a modification of the count decrease rule in which the amount of decrement in a count value is proportional to the present value held in the counter. Does this variation approximate LRU better than the original scheme?

3-32. It could be argued that processor registers are just like another level of the memory hierarchy. After all, they are faster than a cache memory and they do store values.

(a) If this argument were accepted, what form of operand specification would you expect to find in a processor's ADD instruction that adds together the contents of two registers? Explain.

(b) Do you think that this memory hierarchy argument provides a basis for a reasonable system design? In other words, would you recommend designing a system around this argument? Explain.

3-33. Consider using page management policies to manage the placement in memory of the pieces of a hierarchical mapping table. In particular, we examine their use when the table holds the mapping for names in a static name map. In this situation table entries are rarely (if ever) changed, and the complete table can be allocated space at the bottom of the memory hierarchy. Thus there is never a "dirty" entry in any table.

(a) If table entries are never changed, which management question(s) have trivial answers? Explain.

(b) How can the memory management algorithms be simplified under the assumptions of part (a)?

3-34. Determine logical expressions that specify access permissions for user programs executing in the Intel i386 processor. See Example 3-16 for a description of the access control method. Use the following symbols: U_i is the user access permission bit at level i, and W_i is the write permission bit at level i; for i = 1, 2.

(a) Write an expression that is true if the user is able to read the page.

(b) Write an expression that is true if the user is able to write the page.

3-35. A designer proposes associating a cache memory with each memory module. We could assign certain memory modules for instructions and others for data. Because program references are more local than data references, smaller caches could be used with the instruction memory modules, maintaining the same hit ratios, yet the overall system cost would be decreased in comparison to a design in which a separate (but equal) cache is associated with every memory module. Discuss:

(a) The hypotheses of the claim.

(b) The factors that influence the system cost of the proposed design.

(c) Any software support required to achieve the claimed advantages.

3-36. A designer proposes that a cache memory be constructed from a fully associative memory. Another designer favors the set-associative approach. The fully associative proponent argues that that design can do everything that the set-associative memory can, and also is more able to adapt to changing loads and referencing patterns. Discuss this argument and describe why the set-associative implementation is always preferred.

3-37. State one (simple) reason why using a general hashing algorithm applied to a memory address is not recommended for finding a cache entry holding the contents of the memory location.

3-38. Show that the hc term in Equation (3-8) should be replaced by just c if the main memory access cycle is not initiated until after the cache miss is detected. Explain why this detail makes little difference in the overall results if h is close to 1. Thus, argue that the average memory access time is a linear function of h.

3-39. In this problem we compute the speed advantage that could be obtained by reordering the sequence of transmissions between memory and the cache. The parameters of the problem are as follows:

1. The latency of memory accesses, L.
2. The size of a memory block, measured in units of bus blocks (groups that can be transferred between memory and the cache in one bus cycle), B.
3. The transfer time T required to transfer a bus block to the cache.
   The time required to access and transfer one bus block to the cache is L + T.

(a) Given that there is a cache miss for a data read access, find the average speedup of data accesses that can be achieved by not necessarily ordering the bus blocks in order of memory addresses.

(b) Repeat part (a) for instruction accesses after a cache miss.

3-40. Find the longest signal path through the TLB/cache structure in the IBM 370/168 design described in Example 3-20.

3-41. An interleaved memory system has m modules arranged in an n-way interleave. What is the probability that two simultaneous memory access requests to unrelated addresses will desire access to the same module?

3-42. Prove that in an L-way interleaved memory, an addressing pattern in which the nth access request presents the address $B + nK$ (here B and K are arbitrary constants) will result in some modules never being selected if $\gcd(K, L) \neq 1$.

3-43. Consider the use of a bit mask to determine the module number in an interleaved memory system. The mask works as follows: The leftmost bit of the module number result is the bit from the address in the position of the leftmost set bit of the mask. The next leftmost bit of the result comes from the address bit that corresponds to the next leftmost bit of the mask, and so forth, ending with the rightmost result bit coming from the address bit in the position corresponding to the rightmost set bit in the mask. For this analysis, let a denote the width of an address, let m denote the width of a module number, and assume that the mask value is legitimate (exactly m bits in the mask are set). Find the fan-in of the logic determining the module number. Also find the fan-in of the logic determining the address within a module (which comprises the address bits that did not appear in the module number).

3-44. The randomness advantage of interleaving can be traded against the small expansion increment advantage of a noninterleaved system by taking some module selection bits from each end of the address. To be specific, suppose that L bits from the left end of the address and R bits from the right end of the address are concatenated to construct the module number.
  (a) What is the increment for expanding the memory size?
  (b) What is the degree of interleave for accessing consecutive memory addresses?

3-45. Draw a diagram showing an interconnection of adders that perform modulo arithmetic to compute the module number from a memory address when the 17-way interleaving scheme discussed in Section 3.8.3 is used.

3-46. A designer proposes increasing the memory bandwidth by providing two memory buses; one handling READ requests and the other devoted to WRITE requests.
  (a) Draw a diagram of this memory system configuration.
  (b) Describe the bus event sequences to implement a READ/MODIFY/WRITE memory cycle.
  (c) Compare the performance of this design against the performance of a conventional one-bus design with twice the bandwidth.

3-47. A system uses a GAM to cause the processor to feel that the memory contains 23-bit objects, even though the memory has 8-bit entities in its basic modules. The system is to be designed to permit arbitrary bit addressing for the origins of the 23-bit objects being accessed.
  (a) What is the minimum number of memory modules that could be used if the system is to permit access to any contiguous 23-bit word in a simple memory cycle?
  (b) A designer proposes inserting a cache holding 23-bit items between the processor and the GAM. The cache would accept a bit address A and hold the values of the 23 bits for locations A, A + 1, . . . , A + 22 in one cache entry. Comment on this design, particularly whether it will provide the correct functionality (recall that any cache should be logically transparent, still supporting the single memory illusion). Be sure to consider both write-through and write-back caching.

4

SINGLE STREAM CONTROL

It is harder to command than to obey.

— F. Nietzsche

It is not enough to have a good mind.
The main thing is to use it wisely.

— Descartes

The computer's control section supervises the system's operation to support the control point illusion. To perform this function, the control unit must "know" where to find individual program elements (statements or instructions), it must "know" the interpretation (meaning) of the program elements, and it must "know" how to command the other parts of the system to effect the desired functions. The control unit is responsible for all bookkeeping concerning the location of the execution point, and it may be responsible for performing certain auxiliary operations, such as those required to maintain information about the memory address mapping as the execution point moves among naming contexts. The conventional view of these operations is based on the illusion of a single "control point" progressing through a "program."

Some languages, like Prolog, take a radically different view. The Prolog view is that the system consists of only a database in which searches are activated when the user asks a question. Under this view, the system tries to answer the question by database searches; it seeks some way to meet the "goal" specified by the question. During the search, other actions might be performed, depending on the contents of the database. This paradigm is discussed in more detail in Appendix H.

In Chapter 2, we described simple microprocessor control structures. In this chapter, we study general control functions in a single virtual machine performing atomic actions (i.e., there is no overlapping). We present sequence control constructs and describe how they might be implemented at lower levels. We also consider the location and representations of the instructions themselves and the use of lower-level sequencing in the implementation of higher-level functions.

We present a small set of simple control structures, a set of constructs for high-level languages, and discuss some criteria for selecting modifications to the control function set. Then we present enhancements at various levels of system description, starting from high levels and working down to low levels. We show some techniques used to implement low-level control constructs.

After you have studied this chapter, you should be familiar with control functions and structures for single virtual machines supporting the control point illusion. These structures will provide the basis for generalizations to systems with multiple activities, giving the impression of parallelism under a single control point (covered in Chapter 6), and systems with multiple processes, to be covered in Chapters 7 and 8.

4.1 BASIC CONTROL CONCEPTS

We divide the control design issues into four groups; design options for each will be discussed at various levels of the system within this chapter. We phrase these issues in terms of the simple paradigm depicted in Figure 4-1. The program is stored in an *addressable memory*; a *program counter* (PC) contains the location of either the current instruction or of the next instruction;[1] an *instruction register* (IR) holds the current instruction; and a *sequencer* issues control signals to system components to properly implement the specified actions.

The four design issue groups concern the choices of the following:

1. Program sequencing constructs
2. Program location
3. Control implementation techniques
4. Instruction representations

---

[1]   At some point during the execution cycle, the PC is updated to point to the next instruction.

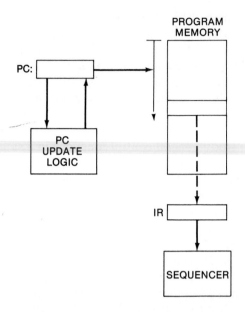

Figure 4-1   Basic control sequencing modules

Program sequencing constructs determine the order of program execution. The choice of sequencing constructs may affect the readability of the program and the ease of correctly specifying the program. *Program location issues* determine the relationship between the memory that holds programs and the memory that holds data. Program location issues may affect the integrity of the program and the flexibility of memory management. *Control implementation decisions* determine the rigidity of the implementation. The selection of a control implementation technique may affect the ease of correcting implementation errors and the speed of program execution. *Instruction representation issues* determine how an instruction is encoded. Instruction representation decisions may affect program size, the complexity of the control unit, and the execution speed.

Design decisions taken within each of these issue groups have different effects. Now we examine these general options in more detail.

4.1.1 Sequencing Constructs

Sequential execution is a basic sequencing construct, with instructions executed in the order in which they are stored. The PC update logic (Figure 4-1) controls the execution sequence. Usually the PC is incremented during instruction execution so that it moves to the next sequential instruction. If an instruction specifies a branch or jump, the PC is loaded with the destination of the branch and the next instruction is taken from the new location.

In principle, all possible control sequencing constructs can be built up from sequential execution and one conditional branch instruction (such as JNG). Although it is true that all conceivable control structures can be constructed from this simple model, any interesting program would be terribly inefficient because it would need many steps to implement other desirable control constructs. Thus we desire a more comprehensive set of control structures.

As we expand the set of control structures, we keep in mind reasonable selection criteria, which include the following:

1. Understandability (simplicity)
2. Provability and testability
3. Closeness to structures at neighboring abstraction levels
4. Performance

Understandability reflects the ability of humans to comprehend (and, therefore, to use) the sequencing structures. Understandability is closely related to (1) the ease of reasoning about the program's behavior and (2) the closeness of the control structures to those used by the virtual machines adjacent in the hierarchy. For example, sequencing abstractions that closely reflect the requirements of an application would provide a convenient framework for programming that application. Simplicity is closely related to understandability; structures that are complex are more difficult to understand and fewer people can use them effectively and correctly.

Provability and *testability* are also closely related to understandability; to reason about an implementation of an algorithm, one must either understand both the algorithm and the implementation or construct an automated procedure that does. Any argument must consider both the sequence of operations and their semantics. Sequencing must be considered so that the reasoning process can equate the machine's state after the execution of one instruction to the machine's state before the execution of the next instruction. The semantics of each program step determine the relationship between the machine's state before the instruction and the machine's state after the instruction. These notions are expanded in Appendix L.

Test design is closely related to reasoning about program structures. Clearly, there is a similar intent; both proofs and tests are devised to convince one that the system does in fact perform in a functional manner. Just as reasoning structures are closely related to the execution sequence, so, too, test designs must be based on the execution sequence. Therefore, system designs and implementations that improve understandability by improving structure will enhance both the test design process and the reasoning processes.

Closeness impacts the understandability of the relationship between neighboring levels of the implementation; if the structures being implemented and the structures available to implement them are similar, then the implementation will require few steps. Closeness may speed implementation, improve understanding, simplify reasoning, and simplify testing. It may, on the other hand, degrade performance, because more intermediate levels will be required to bridge the gap between the application and the hardware implementation of the system. Having more levels in the design does not necessarily slow execution, however, because the level structure might have only minor effects on the actual implementation.[2]

Performance is an important criterion in all computer designs. Some sets of system requirements may emphasize performance, whereas others may emphasize other system properties, such as cost or reliability. Performance is especially important at lower levels, as these levels form the basis for implementing all higher-level functions. Performance can be improved if the high-level functionality can be achieved in fewer atomic actions in the implementation.

Thus, we observe a trade of understandability against performance— schemes that are more understandable seem to require more support for adequate performance, and the maximum performance seems to be achieved by implementing the system with one of the least understandable schemes. One could, of course, construct counterexamples to this statement, and it is not meant as a challenge for the reader to waste time.

4.1.2 Program Location Options

Two design issues concern the program's location. The first determines whether there are separate data and program memories. The second determines whether separate program and data memories can reverse their roles.[3]

It may seem that a scheme providing complete separation of instructions from data is reasonable, but at the very least there must be some means for writing the program memory to load a new program. Another exception to the simple separation arises if the instruction set permits immediate data operands to be read from the program memory.[4] The control unit can be designed to detect immediate addressing and to make an appropriate memory request when necessary. This rule does not assist with loading program memory, because it is not possible by a simple examination of the program sequencer status to distinguish writes used for program copying from other data writes.

A machine with a separate program memory is often called a *Harvard Machine*, because the first computers built at Harvard in the 1940s used a separate paper tape for their programs; this tape was logically similar to a separate read-only program memory. Machines that intermix programs and data in the same

---

[2]   It is a straightforward matter to develop an algorithmic method for reducing any multilevel implementation to a single program level, while preserving functionality.

[3]   The issue concerns whether it is possible to read and write programs as though their instructions were data objects, and whether it is possible to execute data objects as though they were programs.

[4]   There is no logical requirement for immediate addressing.

memory are called *von Neumann Machines*, or *Princeton Machines*, because the first machine built by von Neumann at Princeton placed the program and the data in the same memory unit. Sharing the same memory has an allocation advantage, because there is a better chance that an arbitrary combination of program and data space requirements can be fit into a single larger address space than into their own separated smaller spaces. However, the different locality patterns for instruction and data references suggest that a designer consider using separate caches and memory management policies for programs and data. The Harvard architecture, while less common at the processor level than the von Neumann architecture, has some advantages: It permits more overlap of instruction fetching with instruction execution.[5] In addition, the program memory can be a read-only structure during program execution; this feature implies that the program can be reentrant—that is, it can be shared by two processes without changing its representation.

The second location issue concerns reversing the program and data roles. This design decision does determine whether programs can be loaded and whether immediate operand values can be read from the instruction memory. One way to overcome the limitations is to design several processor instructions that access the program memory for data references. Simple store and load instructions would suffice (in a logical sense). To attain the advantages of the Harvard separation, the programmer would have to limit the use of these instructions. Another way to attain the separation is to permit the program to branch to the data memory.[6] This scheme for transferring control does not solve the immediate addressing issue.

A third location issue concerns the space allocation for the program and data components of a process. If both share the same memory space, the total space will be adequate if it adds up to more than the total instruction and data spaces for the process. If the memory spaces are separate, each portion of the memory must be large enough to hold its portion of the space required for the process. The allocation advantage of allocating space from a pool is lost when the spaces are separated.

What criteria might affect the selection between the two options? First, the sizes of memory addresses may differ. Second, program comprehensibility is affected.[7]

---

[5]   If instructions were to contain immediate operand values, an exception must be made to this statement; the fetch of an immediate value cannot be overlapped with the next instruction fetch, because both are located in the same memory.

[6]   This change might also imply a reversal of the memory roles. A simultaneous role reversal still permits execution speedup by overlapping data and instruction fetches.

[7]   The ability to use data as a program or a program as data may mask the program's structure.

4.1.3 Control Implementation Options

Implementation choices can affect the rigidity of the implementation of control functions, including instruction interpretation, sequencing to implement instruction semantics, and instructions that modify the control sequencing. The control implementation can be static, in which case one would "wire" the implementation into the mechanism, or dynamic, in which case the implementation would be effected by a piece of software that interprets the instructions being executed.

The designer of a dynamic implementation chooses both the nature and timing of implementation changes; each change might completely redefine the instruction set. A special instruction set could match the processor to the needs of an executing program. For example, if a program used only floating-point data objects, integer arithmetic operations could be removed without penalty.

What system measures are affected by these choices? Flexibility is obviously increased if the implementation is dynamic. However, consulting dynamic state information to interpret each instruction slows instruction execution. So, because system speed is a major concern, dynamic implementations are usually limited to infrequent operations. If the system supports a dynamic instruction set, all instruction set changes made by a process become part of the state of that process, and the system must manage this information along with the conventional parts of the process state, such as the contents of the processor registers.

4.1.4 Instruction Representation Options

An instruction, like all information in the computer, is represented by a set of bits. These options choose the interpretation of the bits in each instruction. Some typical questions in this group are: How is the function code extracted from the instruction? Where are operand addresses, if any, to be found? Are there, in fact, any operand addresses?

Choosing among these options determines the *instruction format*. An important design dichotomy separates *fixed* from *variable* instruction formats. If the format is variable, we ask whether individual fields can have lengths that may vary in different instructions? Can the length of a single instruction depend on information within the instruction itself? The MC68020 has variable instruction formats and variable instruction lengths (all instruction lengths are multiples of 16 bits); this flexibility is used to accommodate certain operand addressing modes. In the MC68020, instruction execution and the function to be performed are determined by the contents of the first word of each instruction. RISC designs have fixed instruction lengths to support pipelined execution, which requires that the each instruction be fetched before its predecessor has been completely interpreted.

What advantages might be obtained by changing the instruction format? First, making instruction lengths variable and their formats variable can reduce overall program size, which reduces the number of memory references required to access the program; this effect might speed program execution. On the other hand, decoding and extracting instruction fields whose sizes may vary is more difficult than extracting fields from fixed-format instructions, so control units that can handle variable formats may be inherently slower than control units that do not have to handle more than one instruction format. In addition, the data path structure in a hardware interpretation mechanism will be complex if formats are flexible, increasing system design and implementation times and costs, and possibly slowing program execution. Furthermore, engineers may have to reduce the clock speed if longer physical interconnections are required to implement a flexible format design.

4.1.5 Comments

Four important issues in the design of the single-process control section are the selections of (1) the sequencing constructs to be supported; (2) the location of the program, in contrast with the location of its data objects; (3) the implementation of the control section; and (4) the representation of the control information, in particular, its instructions. These four themes will structure the majority of the discussion in this chapter.

Many opposing forces act to favor or disfavor design options. At different design levels, different considerations may dominate, so different selections may be appropriate. Now we start with the high-level language level, where understandability is very important, and progress eventually to the microprogramming level, where speed is important and the understandability can be very low.

4.2 HIGH-LEVEL LANGUAGES

In this section, we consider control design issues and show how the language structure can affect the option choices outlined before. Our focus is on languages that adopt the traditional view of a program as a sequentially executed set of statements. A different view forms the basis for nonsequential languages such as Prolog, discussed in Appendix H.

4.2.1 Sequencing Constructs

At the high-level language level, the control construct selection is often based on the ease of understanding program structures. We start with these basic control structures:

1. Sequential execution
2. Conditional execution
3. Loops
4. Subroutines
5. Goto statements
6. Exceptions

At the end of the section, we introduce a few control structures that are not present in many programming languages but that can be useful for specification, implementation, modularization, or understanding.

Sequential Execution. Sequential execution is the default mode of operation; this sequencing pattern applies unless otherwise specified. In most high-level languages, statements are executed in the order they are written in the program text unless a specific sequence control statement or the end of the program block (such as a loop body) is reached.

Conditional Execution. A conditional execution structure specifies the execution of a set of statements only if a stated Boolean condition is met, or, more generally, if a stated expression has a specified value. In C++, these two situations are specified by the **if** and **switch** control constructs, respectively.

Loops. *Loop structures* specify the repetitive execution of a list of statements, which together comprise the body of the loop. The loop's control flow is governed by its termination structure. The basic structures include[8] the indefinite loop, the **while** loop, the **until** loop, and the counting loop. A normal exit from a loop structure occurs when the termination condition at the head of the loop is satisfied. However, loop exits can also be made by executing the **break** (**exit**, in some languages) statement, which forces loop termination before the loop's normal termination condition is met. The **break** statement obviates the need for a **goto** statement to exit the loop.[9]

Loop exits may be forced by exceptions, as discussed later.

Subroutines. Decomposing a program into functions or procedures is an important modularization technique. From the point of view of the calling procedure, the call statement along with the execution of the called procedure can be considered to be a single operation of an "enhanced machine," with the enhanced machine's program counter remaining at the call statement during the execution of the called procedure. In other words, we could take the view that the PC for the caller remains at the call statement while the procedure or function is

---

[8]   Not all of these structures are provided in all languages.

[9]   An exit using a **goto** statement is not favored because the **goto** statement provides a means for constructing flow structures that are difficult to comprehend.

performed. This view, ignoring the details of the called procedure, is consistent with procedural modular decomposition, with class-oriented encapsulation, and with the implementation inside processors (which "save" the program counter during subroutine execution).

Subroutine structures must be supported by control constructs for procedure call and return. We present simple cases in this section.

A call statement transfers control to a procedure or function. The procedure executing the call statement is known as the *calling procedure*, and the procedure to which control is transferred is the *called procedure*. A **return** statement transfers control from a called procedure back to the calling procedure. Under the hierarchical view, the execution of **return** signifies completion of the single high-level operation by the underlying implementation level, so the caller can proceed to its next action.

Every call-return mechanism should permit *recursion*; with recursion, a procedure can be called from a program even though that process currently has an uncompleted invocation of that same procedure. In the implementation, a LIFO stack that saves the state of each invocation above the saved states of all earlier invocations of the same procedure is required to support recursion. Most contemporary languages, including C, C++, ALGOL, PL/1, Pascal, Ada, and Modula, permit recursion. Thus the system must support some means of stacking the saved program counter contents.

Goto Statements. A goto statement specifies an immediate change in the execution point, without saving the location from which the **goto** was taken. It may seem obvious that **goto**s are required for programming generality, because program completeness is guaranteed by the existence of the conditional **goto**. This "obvious" conclusion is not correct. In fact, the **goto** is not necessary if conditional and loop control constructs are available. In other words, the conditional and loop control constructs together are logically sufficient to express any arbitrary control sequence, and the **goto** construct is not required!

The following example shows that though a syntactic analysis may conclude that a program has good structure, a complex structure may be hidden beneath the beautiful syntactic structure. Thus, good structuring cannot be imposed by linguistic rules alone; the programmer must be committed to good structure in the first place. In a similar manner, we conclude that one cannot design a program analyzer or a language translator that enforces good programming practices or warns against poor practices. But one can devise language structures that make it difficult to circumvent good structuring practices.

Example 4-1

One can emulate the actions of any general-purpose computer using a single **loop** statement containing a single **switch** statement. If the range of instruction addresses is 1 .. n, the emulation program is

```
void emulate() {
    int program_counter, n = highest_address;
    while ( program_counter <= n )      //n is the upper bound
        switch ( program_counter ) {
            case 1:
                <first_instruction's_effect>;
                break;
            case 2:
                <second_instruction's_effect>;
                break;

              ..

            case n:
                <last_instruction's_effect>;
                break;
            default:
                return;
        }
}
```

Because any of the instruction effect clauses can assign a new value to the variable program_counter, arbitrary control structures can be emulated by this program structure. We hasten to point out that the reader should not take this design as an example of good programming practice! Rather, it is perhaps best to treat it simply as a demonstration of the possibility of reducing the number of control structures.

The **goto** statement is a controversial addition to the basic repertoire. Because any **goto** can shift control to any visible label in the program, a programmer can create complex flow structures using **goto**s. In fact, one can construct sequencing structures so complex that people may have difficulty comprehending them—even the original programmer may have trouble upon returning to the program after an extended absence. Nevertheless, the possibility of arbitrary sequencing supported by the **goto** can be useful for handling errors and exceptional conditions.

The control flow complexities possible with the **goto** statement prompted Dijkstra [DIJK68a] to title a famous note "Goto Statement Considered Harmful."[10] Many advocates of structured programming overreacted by defining structured programming as the absence of **goto**s. Though complex sequencing structures can be created without using **goto**s, albeit with difficulty, this strict definition of structured programming is not realistic.

Whereas the **goto** construct is not desirable in structured programs, it is necessary for the efficient implementation of many low-level system functions. After all, there is a basic requirement to be able to violate the restrictive sequential sequencing straitjacket. Consider, for example, designing an efficient implementation of the **if** construct. There is no way that the program can be arranged

---

[10]   This note started the structured programming movement in earnest. It also prompted a spate of papers with titles of the form "_____ considered harmful!"

so that no **goto**s are required, because certainly there must be a way to skip past the instructions that correspond to the statement_list that was not selected by the Boolean test.

Frequently, **goto**s have destinations (or "targets") that are statically determined; this case might be a consequence of the design of the language, or of the usage in a particular program. In this case, the translator can be designed to take care of many details. On the other hand, dynamic **goto**s, whose destinations cannot be determined from a static examination of the program, are more difficult to handle. Dynamic destinations complicate matters because the program may be difficult to understand and because the system must determine the actual destination each time the dynamic **goto** is executed. Furthermore, if the language permits the execution of a **goto** to change the naming context, the system must detect and make all context changes implied by location of the actual destination within the modular structure. Notice that reasoning about program behavior is difficult with static **goto**s and almost impossible with dynamic ones. Nevertheless, some languages support dynamic **goto**s. Ada and C++ do not.

Two basic techniques for specifying dynamic **goto** destinations are

1. Selected **goto**s
2. Label variables

The *selected* **goto**[11] statement contains a list of all possible destinations. One of the listed destinations is selected based on the value of an expression in the statement. In FORTRAN, a computed **goto** looks like

GOTO (23,30,25,79,45)S

The value of S, which is an integer, is used as a (one-origin) index into the list of statement numbers to find the statement number of the next statement to be executed. Any selected **goto** can be reduced easily to a **switch** statement with static destinations. Because the set of possible destinations of a selected **goto** is static, even if the language permits naming context changes as a consequence of a **goto**, the translator can determine the legality of each possible destination of the selected **goto** and thus can insert calls to appropriate management functions as needed.[12] These compile-time implementation details can be "hidden" from the programmer's view, but the appearance that the structure is static can be illusory.

In its original version, COBOL permits one to change the destination of a GO TO statement under restricted conditions.[13]

---

[11]   This is called a "computed goto" in FORTRAN, and is also available in APL.
[12]   These requirements will be discussed later.
[13]   Most people consider the use of this "feature" to constitute a bad programming practice.

Example 4-2

> The ALTER operation in the original version of COBOL allows a programmer to change a **goto**'s destination in a restricted manner. To understand the restrictions, one must know some basic COBOL program structuring notions. Program blocks in a COBOL program are called "paragraphs." If a COBOL paragraph consists only of a GO TO, its destination can be modified by executing an ALTER statement anywhere in the program. Consider this paragraph
>
> ```
>         A.
>              GO TO FIRST.
> ```
>
> Here A is the "name" of the paragraph. Execution of the statement
>
> ```
>       ALTER A TO PROCEED TO SECOND.
> ```
>
> changes the destination of A's GO TO to SECOND.

This ALTER possibility introduces difficulty in program understanding—an apparently static **goto** is really not static because another statement anywhere in the program might change its destination.

   Label variables constitute the second way to specify the destination of a dynamic **goto**. A label variable is an object whose value identifies a location within the program. Performing an assignment to a label variable may redefine the destination denoted by the variable. The execution of the statement

```
       goto label_variable;           //not C++
```

causes a transfer of control to the statement whose label is held within the label variable. Although this description makes the implementation seem simple, several complexities are not far beneath the surface! Recall, for example, that object name interpretation may depend on the execution context; this implies that after the transfer to the destination statement, the proper name interpretation rules must apply. So we must design things so that the label variable's "value" can be used to find (or specify) the execution context (which defines the naming context) to use after the **goto** is performed. Two significant implementation questions arise from this context identification question:

1. How to specify the execution context within the label variable's "value"
2. How to pass a label value from one context to another one

   This design problem is similar to the problem of passing object names among contexts (see Section E.3.2), so a similar approach can be used to "solve" the problem—we include within the "value" of each label variable a pointer to the activation block that defines the chosen naming context.

   A label variable may cause both data-dependent legality problems and data-dependent module exits. The following example illustrates one legality issue that might arise from the use of label variables.

Example 4-3

Consider this program fragment using label variables:

```
label label1;
    ..                      //for simplicity, not all objects used are explicitly declared here
label1 = "success";        //The label "success" is defined elsewhere
for ( i = 1, i <= n, i++ ) {
    if ( a[ i ] <= 6 )
            label1 = "fail";        //Not C++
fail:  y = y + 3;
}
goto label1;                //Not C++
```

The **goto** statement will cause a transfer of control to the middle of the loop if, for some i in the range 1 .. n, a[i] is less than or equal to 6. Such a transfer should be illegal, as it compromises the integrity of the loop module structure. If, for some execution of the program, every a[i] were greater than 6, however, the **goto** would not compromise the loop structure, and that execution of the program would not violate the program's structure. Because the legality of the **goto** is dependent on the data being processed, the compiler cannot tell whether the **goto** is legal. To be "safe," the compiler could be designed so that it would consider this program fragment to be erroneous.

If the execution of a **goto** implies a change of the naming environment and a change of the execution context, its implementation will have to check whether the environment really changes. If a change is needed, the system must progressively unwind (pop) stack frames until the one corresponding to the new execution environment has reached the top of the stack.

To avoid these problems, the designers of C++ did not permit label variables. Another way to remove this problem is to define, as in Ada, that a label name shall not be visible outside the program unit where it is defined. These rules prohibit transferring control among parallel constructs, such as among exception handlers or subprograms declared within the same encompassing program. They also remove the possibility of an execution context change as a side effect of the execution of any **goto**.

Example 4-4

Consider this Ada program (using C++ syntax for label declarations):

```
procedure f( .. ) is
    ..
    procedure g( .. ) is
    begin
        ..   //goto a would be illegal here
    end g;
    procedure h( .. ) is
```

```
          begin
             ..
             goto aa;   //illegal
          end h;
             ..
      begin
          ..
aa:   ..
          ..
b:    loop
             ..
             goto aa;        //legal
             ..
      end b;
          ..
   end f;
```

By Ada rules, the label aa declared within procedure f is visible inside f, but not in procedures g or h. Thus, a **goto** statement with destination aa is legal within f. Notice that the **goto** can be used to exit from loop b.[14] However, the same **goto** statement within g or h would be illegal unless another statement labeled aa appeared within the same procedure. These rules ensure that a **goto** cannot force a procedure exit (from procedure h to procedure f in this case).

A generalization of a label variable is a variable that points to a function or a procedure. These are legal in C++; they can be very useful for writing procedures that may call different versions of a utility program (such as a sorting program). Most of the difficulties associated with label variables do not arise from the use of pointers to functions, because calling a function cannot disrupt the caller's context. If all the procedures that a procedure pointer might designate are sufficiently similar in intent, the use of the pointers will not complicate program understanding. However, one can create program semantics that are quite confusing by using pointers to functions.

Exceptions. We distinguish exceptions, which are caused by the processor detecting conditions arising from the instructions being executed, from interrupts, which are caused by events external to the program in execution. Many programming languages do not give the programmer the option to program the response to an exception. In general, exception constructs may be used to handle errors, asynchronous events, or unexpected operand values. However, the exception semantics (discussed in what follows) may remove some of these possibilities.

Three basic design issues concerning exceptions are (1) whether the execution point is permitted to return, after the exception has been handled, to the

---

[14]   The destination would be the statement labeled "aa".

point where the exception was taken; (2) how the execution context to be used during the handler's execution is found; and (3) how the association of an exception handler with an exception event is established.

What's Next after an Exception Occurs? Suppose that an exception E has been declared and that a handler for E has been associated with E. Then if E occurs, control immediately passes to the associated handler, which is then executed. If the language permits handlers to return to the point of execution when the exception handler was activated, the handler would be written like a subroutine. In particular, the handler would execute a **return**, which would pass control back to the point where the exception condition was detected. Figure 4-2 illustrates this control flow; the circled numbers in the figure indicate the order of execution.

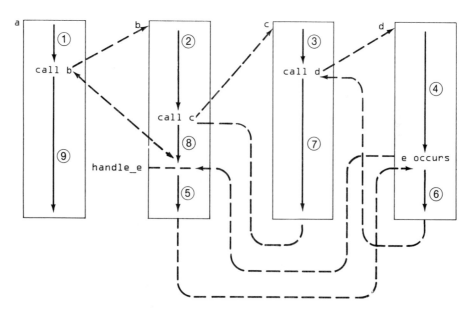

Figure 4-2   Control flow for exception handling with return allowed after the handler completes

Notice that if all exception handlers must force a return from the enclosing context, they cannot be used to handle unusual conditions that are not fatal. On the other hand, if they act like procedure calls, they can be used to handle such conditions.

If the language does not permit handlers to return, then when the handler is completed, some default control action is taken. In Ada and C++, exception handlers cannot return, and the procedure, function, or **try** block in which the

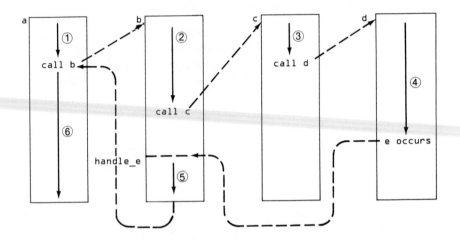

Figure 4-3   Control flow for Ada exception handling

handler was declared is terminated automatically when the handler has completed execution. This control structure is illustrated in Figure 4-3.

What Is the Exception Handler's Execution Context? Every exception handler is declared within a context, be it a nested block or a program. Let C_E denote the declaration context for handler E. The execution context for E (C_{EX}) should be some invocation to which C_E applies. The appropriate handler for an exception is found using dynamic nesting resolution rules (in C++, the nest is built from **try** blocks). The dynamic search starts with the execution context in force when the exception handler was invoked. We call this context C_{PC}—the context of the PC. There are two interesting combinations regarding these execution contexts.

In the simplest case, $C_{EX} = C_{PC}$. Control can pass to E without a context change, because the prior context was correct for E's execution. In the second case, $C_{EX} \neq C_{PC}$. To determine the appropriate action, we need to know the action upon completion of the handler. If the handler must be able to return to C_{PC} after the handler completes, the system must execute the handler using context C_{EX}, which may not be at the top of the stack.[15] On the other hand, if the handler must force a return from its context (C_{EX}), the stack cleaning associated with the eventual context shift should be coupled with the search to find the handler. During the search process, the system pops contexts off the activation block stack. The following example illustrates the actions supporting a C++ exception (in C++, the exception's occurrence forces a return from its defining context).

---

[15]   See Problem 4-3.

Example 4-5

```
void a () {
    try {
        ..
        b ();              //call to b, which will throw the exception
        ..
    }
    catch (ex& E) {
        ..                 //body of the handler for exception E
    }
}
void b() {                 //b does not catch any exceptions
    ..
    c();                   // b calls c, which initiates the throw
    ..
}
void c() throw( char* ) {  //the throw list declares the types associated with
                           //all exceptions that it might throw
    ..
    throw ("E");           //throw an exception whose name is E
    ..
}
```

Suppose that the history of this program is

```
call a;
call b;
call c;
E occurs;
```

Because the handler for E declared within procedure a is the appropriate one to take the exception, returns from blocks b and c must be forced before the exception can be handled. Figure 4-4 shows the activation block stack before E occurs and just as E's handler begins execution. After the handler terminates, block a is also deleted from the stack, as procedure a is automatically exited on completion of E's handler.

Associating a Handler with an Exception. The final exception design problem concerned how an association between an exception and a handler can be established. Languages differ greatly regarding the syntax used to specify this association, but these differences are not conceptually significant. We must be concerned, however, with whether the association is static or dynamic; a static association is established during compilation, whereas a dynamic association can be established and modified during program execution.

In Ada and C++, the association between exceptions and their handlers is static; the handlers are defined at the end of a program or **try** block; these associations apply during the execution of that block. Thus, block entry implies the

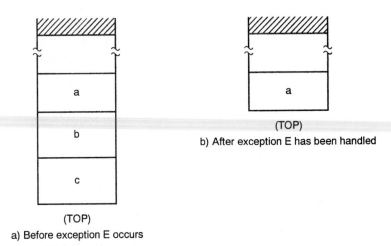

a) Before exception E occurs

b) After exception E has been handled

Figure 4-4   Stack cleansing after exception occurrence

automatic establishment of a handler-exception association for every exception handler declared along with the block. In some languages, such as PL/1, the handler-exception associations are dynamic. When a PL/1 block is entered, no automatic new handler-exception associations are created; rather, the associations that existed before the block entry remain in effect. A new (or revised) association can be established by executing the ON statement, which has the form

ON <exception> DO <statement>;

The semantics should be obvious from the keywords. A programmer can, in effect, make the associations static by placing all ON statements at the top of each block, because the associations will be established dynamically before the program executes the other statements in the block. Dynamic changes in the associations between handlers and exceptions may make a program difficult to understand.

Other Control Constructs. In this section we review several unusual control constructs that are not present in most languages, but that do present interesting semantic possibilities. The last two are useful in programming cooperating processes (see Chapter 7). The constructs we present are as follows:

1. Routine replacement subroutine calling
2. **one_of** conditional execution
3. Guarded **do** conditional looping
4. **wait** conditional pausing
5. **select** conditional pausing

Routine Replacement. In routine replacement subroutine calling the execution of the called routine replaces the execution of its caller. In particular, the caller is not resumed when the callee completes its algorithm. Rather, the callee returns control to the caller's return point. We use the keyword **rcall** to indicate a replacement call. The **rcall** semantics require destroying the caller's execution context (but saving its return conditions), creating an execution context for the called procedure, and transferring control to the called procedure.

The **rcall** activity bears some resemblance to exception handling in Ada; but it is not identical to exception handling (why?).

One_of. The **one_of** and guarded **do** are generalized conditional execution constructs that flexibly[16] select statements (to be executed conditionally) based on the evaluation of a set of Boolean expressions. These constructs can be useful for specifying program behavior because their semantics relate simply to the Boolean conditions; therefore, the conditions can be used when reasoning about program properties.

The **one_of** alternation construct is somewhat like a **switch** structure. To see the similarity, think of the **switch** structure as a specification of a set of (trivial) Boolean conditions. Under this view, when the **switch** is executed, the Boolean conditions are evaluated, and the statement list associated with the true condition[17] is executed. Because the conditions all test for equality with the same expression, they are both trivial and nonoverlapping—only one of them can be true (because the right sides of the equalities are all different). In the **one_of** structure, the Boolean conditions can be independently written by the programmer, and more than one of them may be true. During the execution of the **one_of** statement, all of the Boolean conditions are evaluated and one statement list selected (nondeterministically) from among those associated with true Boolean conditions is executed. We express the **one_of** statement in a manner similar to a **switch** statement:

```
one_of {                          //Not C++
    case (<boolean_1> ):
        <statement_list_1>;
        break;
    case (<boolean_2>):
        <statement_list_2>;
        break;

        ..

    case (<boolean_n>):
        <statement_list_n>;
        break;
}
```

---

[16]   These include nondeterministic possibilities.

[17]   It may be that all conditions are **false**, in which case no parts of the **switch** statement are executed.

A **one_of** statement does not include a **default** condition; if none of the Boolean conditions are true, execution proceeds to the next statement immediately; in that situation, the **one_of** is effectively a nooperation. The **one_of** construct is useful for specifying and modeling high-level policies that seem arbitrary at the level of abstraction of the model. No programming language has a **one_of** statement, but some do contain a **select** construct that has many similarities with the **one_of** construct. The **select** construct is used in conjunction with interprocess message communications, as discussed in Section 7.3.1.

Guarded do. The guarded **do** statement is a looping version of the **one_of** statement; like the **one_of** statement, a guarded **do** statement contains a set of Boolean conditions, each associated with a list of statements. It is also true that this structure is not present in programming languages intended for execution; nevertheless, we describe its semantics as though it were executable. Thus, we say that each time the statement is executed, all the Boolean conditions are evaluated. If all are false, the loop is terminated. If, however, one or more are true, one of the true ones is (nondeterministically) selected and the corresponding statement list executed. The control point then returns to the beginning of the one_of statement. All the Boolean conditions are then reevaluated, and the loop continues until all conditions are false. Here is our syntax for the guarded **do**:

```
do {                                    //Not C++
    when (<boolean_1>):
        <statement_list_1>;
        break;
    when (<boolean_2>):
        <statement_list_2>;
        break;

    ..
    when (boolean_n):
        <statement_list_n>;
        break;
};
```

After the guarded **do** loop has completed execution, the union (OR) of all of the Boolean conditions specified within the **do** must be false. This fact makes the guarded **do** an attractive structure for specifying and reasoning about program properties at a high level of abstraction.

Wait. The **wait** statement specifies conditional execution based on the value of a Boolean expression. The program will wait until the associated Boolean expression becomes true before proceeding with program execution. This rule is meaningless if there is no other activity within the system, because the value of the predicate cannot change in such an environment. It will be useful for programming cooperating processes, as we discuss in Chapters 7 and 8.

Select. The **select** statement also specifies conditional execution, with several predicates specified; the program waits if no predicate is true. If one of them becomes true, the corresponding statement list will be executed. If several conditions become true, one of those is chosen. This structure can be useful when several processes cooperate, and also in conjunction with a **delay** predicate (see Section 7.3.1). Here is our syntax for this statement:

```
select {                              //Not C++
    when (<boolean_1>):
        <statement_list_1>;
        break;
    when (<boolean_2>):
        <statement_list_2>;
        break;

        ..

    when (boolean_n):
        <statement_list_n>;
        break;
}
```

Summary. In this section we reviewed many sequencing constructs; most of them are present in some programming language, but most are not functionally required in any language. The richness of the constructs eases the tasks of program construction and of specifying and understanding program semantics.

4.2.2 Program Location

The design decision concerning whether program memory is separate from data memory is simple at the high-level language level.

Most languages clearly separate the roles of program and data objects, the only exceptions being label and entry point variables, both containing values that point to program locations in memory. Thus, conceptually, the system has a Harvard architecture. Furthermore, strong typing imposes a clean separation of name spaces between program objects and data objects. In particular, in C++, there is no way that data can become part of a program and no way that the program can be interpreted as data.

In LISP, on the other hand, data structures can be interpreted; for example, the LISP EVAL function executes the function that is the first element in the list argument of the EVAL command; the remainder of EVAL's list argument is the list of the actual arguments for the function. Furthermore, EVAL's argument can be a computed data structure. Thus EVAL(f <list>) has the effect of f(<list>), with the dynamic binding of the name f to a procedure body evaluated during program execution when EVAL is used.[18] A similar feature is available in SNOBOL. In

---

[18]   LISP is described in Appendix I.

Prolog,[19] there is no clear separation of program and data; in the programming model, the computer contains a set of data (but nothing identified as a program!) and that data are always processed by the same built-in algorithm. Thus, Prolog programmers view a von Neumann structure with program and data objects sharing the same memory.

4.2.3 Implementation

The implementation of high-level control semantics must provide the proper control sequences in an efficient manner. Whether these are implemented by compilation or interpretation makes no semantic difference. System performance is affected, however. Thus the frequency of use of various high-level programming constructs should influence the designer. Table 4-1 illustrates statistics collected from typical Pascal programs; statements that contain nonsequential control possibilities comprise about 50% of all statements. The high frequency of **call** and **return** shows the need for an efficient implementation of these constructs.

TABLE 4-1   STATEMENT
FREQUENCIES IN PASCAL PROGRAMS

Statement Type	Frequency (%)
Assignment	45
If .. then	29
Call/Return	15
Loop	5
With	5
Case	1
All others	<1

Source: [PATT82] © 1982 IEEE.

4.2.4 Representation

The design decision is trivial here—each program must be human-readable and therefore must be represented by a character string. The statement syntax is fixed in syntax but the statement length varies.

---

[19]   Prolog is described in Appendix H.

4.2.5 Comments

A large variety of control flow constructs have been included in high-level languages. Many of these constructs directly map to control constructs provided at the processor level. Some control constructs are useful for reasoning about program properties, and may not have "clean" implementations. Nevertheless, their logical properties make them attractive.

4.3 PROCESSOR-LEVEL CONTROL ISSUES

The control structures selected for a high-level language may be supported directly by the control structures and representations interpreted by the processor itself. The processor's implementation might reflect these structures. Thus many important control structures have direct analogs within the processor's instruction set. In this section we discuss the control structures that have analogs within the processor's instruction set, in addition to various ways the processor can be designed to support efficient execution of high-level languages.

4.3.1 Sequencing Constructs

Sequential execution, combined with a single type of conditional branch, is adequate for implementing (or simulating) all possible sequencing structures. But this restriction produces very lengthy programs and gives little benefit. The set of sequencing constructs within the instruction set must be expanded to improve system performance. First, we review the basic sequential and conditional sequencing constructs.

Sequential Execution. During sequential execution the processor's control logic increments the program counter (PC) by the length of each (non-branch) instruction as it is issued for execution. If all instructions have the same length (as in RISC designs), the processor can easily find all the boundaries between instructions. If there are variations in instruction length, those instruction fields that determine the length of an instruction must influence the PC update function, and the PC cannot be completely updated until the instruction has been decoded. Many processors with variable instruction length use a scanPC register to track the reads of extension words. In this design, scanPC contains the address of the first program element that has not yet been considered, and PC contains the starting address of the current instruction. Additional information about positions within the program is needed in two cases: (1) the instructions have variable lengths or (2) precise exceptions must be supported, despite any attempts at anticipatory execution within the processor.

Conditional Execution. Conditional execution is supported by branch instructions that test conditions within the processor. Three questions about this design concern

1. Branch target specifications
2. What object should be tested
3. Control flow structures

How Can the Branch Target Be Specified? Three important options are

1. Jump instructions
2. Branch instructions
3. Skip instructions

In most designs, the difference between jump and branch instructions is based on how the branch target location is specified. In a branch instruction, the address is specified relative to the location of the control transfer instruction. In a jump instruction, the target location is specified as a general memory address. The most flexible option uses general processor addressing modes to determine the destination address, but the target offsets in branch instructions are restricted to a small field size.

Skip instructions are like branch instructions except that when the condition is met, the target must be the one immediately following the instruction after the skip instruction.[20] Because a skip instruction is a special case of a branch instruction, one might ask, why introduce the skip construct? It may be attractive because it removes the need for a branch destination specification within the branch instruction. By choosing a skip instruction format that includes a memory address, an object in memory can be tested. Even if the skip instruction does not include a memory address, the skip instruction might be attractive because it can be represented using fewer bits, because it does not need any memory address specification.

Example 4-6

The IBM 704 [IBM55] has a skip-class instruction, CAS (Compare Accumulator with Storage) with one memory operand, whose contents Y are compared against the contents of the (single) accumulator A. The next instruction is one of the three immediately following the CAS instruction. If $A < Y$, the instruction after CAS will be next. If $A = Y$, the second instruction after CAS will be next. Finally, if $A > Y$, the third instruction after CAS will be next. Notice the relationship between this sequencing structure and the FORTRAN three-way IF. This coincidence is interesting, because FORTRAN was originally implemented on the IBM 704.

---

[20]   In other words, the instruction following **skip** is skipped!

It is easy to implement a skip instruction if every processor instruction has a fixed length, and difficult otherwise. There is no net space benefit if the skip instruction is immediately followed by a jump instruction, but the skip instruction might still be attractive because it does not impose a need for an expanded instruction format that includes two memory addresses. There is no advantage to having skip instructions if instruction execution is pipelined.

One special situation is worth noting: When the only action inside a conditional structure is a simple register load, the whole structure can be replaced by a conditional move instruction (see, e.g., Section A.6).

What Should Be Tested?   The conditional branch instructions in some processor designs, such as Alpha AXP and MIPS, can test only the contents of processor registers. In other designs, like the IBM 370, the MC68020, and the SPARC machines, the branch test is based on condition code values. Another possibility is to include instructions that implement multiway branches based on a value in a register or an instruction's outcome.

What Flow Structures Are Supported?   The mapping between branching constructs in high-level languages and instructions in the processor program is not a simple one-to-one mapping. One simple branch instruction is not sufficient to directly support the **if** .. **then** .. **else** language construct, because the **if** .. **then** .. **else** structure contains two alternatives. Nevertheless, only forward jumps are required to implement the **if** .. **then** .. **else** semantics.[21]

However, there are interesting alternatives at the processor level:

Example 4-7

All computational instructions in IBM System/38 machines [IBM81a] have an optional form using an extension of the operation code to define result conditions under which the next instruction will be taken from one of (up to) three branch "targets." Another optional form sets an "indicator" in a memory location if the specified condition testing the result of the computation is true. For each computational operation, one variant of the instruction forgoes condition testing.

Selected **goto**s can be supported at the processor level by using indexed addressing to determine the branch destination. An addressing mode using indirection after indexing to determine the branch instruction's destination gives a control structure analogous to FORTRAN's computed **goto**.

Example 4-8

A vector listing the destinations for a selected **goto** statement can implement the semantics of the FORTRAN indexed **goto** statement such as

GOTO (3, 6, 14, 10)S

---

[21]   This observation will become important when branch prediction is used to speed execution (see Section 6.6.3).

The following program fragment implements this statement if the granularity of the index value in S matches the size of the statement label addresses.

```
            load R_x with S;
            branchi dest_vec - 1, R_x;   //indirection with indexing first
dest_vec: label_3;
            label_6;
            label_14;
            label_10;
```

Example 4-9

The VAX CASE instruction [DIGI77] combines the indexed jump and jump table activities into a single processor instruction. The list of possible targets appears within the program. The VAX CASE instruction has the following arguments:

1. S, an integer selector value
2. B, an integer base value
3. L, an integer limit value
4. D[i], a list of destinations

If (S − B) is positive and not greater than L, the value (S − B) is used as an index into the list of destinations, and a branch is taken to the address selected from the destination list. However, if (S − B) is negative or exceeds L, no branch is taken.

Loop Support.   At the processor level, loop support can take several forms. First, processor implementations can be "tuned" for fast loop execution, as is discussed in Section 4.3.3. Second, branch predictions can be tuned for loops (also see Section 6.6.3). Third, instructions to test for loop continuation or completion can be provided. The MC68020 DBcc instructions are in this class. We illustrate the spectrum of options in several examples.

Example 4-10

The PDP-11 instruction SOB (Subtract One and Branch) contains a register number r and an offset value w [DIGI75]. Its semantics are:

```
1. PC = PC + 2;        //PC counts bytes but this instruction occupies 2 bytes
2. R_r = R_r - 1;
3. if ( R_r != 0 ) PC = PC - 2*w;        //to loop start
```

The branch is always taken backward to reach the beginning of the loop. By contrast, the VAX11-780 loop counting instructions interpret the offset as a signed quantity, even though the usefulness of the positive offset option is questionable.

Alternately, one can count in a register and specify the branch target in the loop instruction, as in the DBcc instructions in the MC68020.

Procedure Call and Return.   During procedure calling, the processor at least must save the PC and reload the PC with the location of the first instruction of the called procedure. The return instruction reverts control to the caller, so it reverses the actions taken on call, and thus there are few design decisions for the return once the call has been specified. For this reason, we discuss only the call design here. In the following, we assume that the PC value to be saved is to point to the location in the program following the CALL instruction.

Two important decisions within the CALL design are the following:

1. In what type of location will the PC be saved—in a register, in memory, on a stack, or elsewhere?
2. What additional actions should be included in CALL? The possibilities include saving processor registers, acquiring local space for the called procedure, changing the name map, and changing the protection state.

Where Is the PC Saved? Registers, memory, or stacks can be used.

With *register saving*, the CALL instruction has two operands—one specifies the register in which PC is to be saved, and the other specifies the entry point of the called procedure. Letting R and E denote these two values, the CALL involves the following steps:

    1. Update PC to point to the next instruction;
    2. Save PC in register R;
    3. Load PC with E

Register saving is quick, but the called procedure may have to copy the saved PC to a memory location to support nested or recursive procedure calls.[22] The Alpha AXP processor works this way.

Memory saving of the PC requires an extra memory cycle during CALL. Furthermore, the CALL instruction must specify two memory locations—one for PC saving and the other for the first instruction of the procedure being called. Let these two operands be S and E. Then the execution of CALL requires

    1. Update PC;
    2. Save PC in memory location S;
    3. Load PC with E.

To reduce the number of instruction bits, the designer might force a relation between the addresses E and S. For example, the relation E = S + 1 is used in the central processor of the CDC 6600 [CONT66] and in the DEC PDP-8 processor. The constraint between E and S does save address specification bits. This design does force the saved state to be mixed with instructions (with the CDC 6600 relation, the saved PC value is saved in the memory location immediately preceding the first instruction at the entry point), so the procedures

---

[22] This extra copying does destroy the speed advantage obtained by avoiding the memory reference during the CALL instruction. For this reason, register saving is desirable if the called procedure requires few registers, but undesirable if the called procedure (1) requires many registers and (2) recopies the saved PC to make another register available.

cannot be reentrant. Furthermore, placing the saved PC value within the program space introduces two new problems: (1) location S must not be reached by sequential instruction execution (thus the procedure entry point cannot occur in the midst of a sequential block of instructions[23]); and (2) proper coordination with instruction buffering is required (see Section 8.8.2).

A *memory stack* is the third option for a place to save the return address. This option eliminates the need for the CALL instruction's parameter that specifies where to save the PC, because there is (conventionally) only one stack (described by the pointer SP) onto which the saved PC will be pushed. If SP points to the top byte on the stack, with the stack growing toward lower memory addresses, the semantics of the CALL instruction are

        1. Update PC;
        2. SP = SP - address_size;
        3. Memory[SP] = PC;
        4. PC = E;

Recursion is directly supported in such a design, because any later saved states are automatically stacked atop earlier saved states.

A *combination of register saving and stack saving* is a fourth possibility for saving the return address. Under this option, the PC is saved in a register after the former contents of that register are pushed on the stack. If the selected register is denoted by R, the semantics are

        1. Update PC;
        2. Save R on the stack;   //see previous
        3. R = PC;
        4. PC = E;

Example 4-11

The PDP-11 subroutine call instruction JSR[24] has a register number operand; the previous contents of the designated register are pushed on the stack and the return address is then placed in the register.

One advantage of this option is that parameters transmitted in the caller's program can be easily retrieved by using indexed addressing; register R can be used as an index register that points directly to the instruction object following the call. This location would contain the value of the first parameter if parameters were passed in the instruction stream. Indirect addressing is used in the return instruction to reach the next instruction within the calling program.

---

[23]   It can be argued that it is useless to CALL in the middle of an instruction sequence anyhow, because it would be difficult to establish the execution environment for the called procedure.
[24]   This instruction disappeared in the PDP-11/780.

Additional Actions within CALL Instructions. To complete the CALL instruction design, one must select those actions beyond minimum PC saving that will be performed within the call instruction. These extensions could be designed to support high-level procedure structures. One interesting extension has the processor automatically save the old naming context. Another extension establishes some of the new execution context as the CALL is performed. In some designs, the execution context specifies the protection state of the processor; in such a processor, the protection state *must* be managed during the call instruction. A list of the possible extensions can be based on the actions necessary to establish a new environment for the execution of the called procedure. Here are some activities that might have to be completed before the called procedure can really begin executing its body; these become candidates for activities in a CALL instruction:

1. Save the program counter.
2. Establish the new protection state.
3. Save the caller's processor state.
4. Establish a new stack frame and frame pointer value.
5. Establish the new naming environment.
6. Allocate space for the called program's local objects.

Saving the program counter is clearly necessary to be able to resume the caller after the procedure has completed execution.

A new protection state may be required for execution of the called procedure—this must be handled within the CALL instruction to assure compliance. This topic is discussed in Chapter 9.

The *caller's processor state* must be saved if the called procedure is going to disturb this information in ways incompatible with the called procedure's defined interface.

A new stack frame and pointer will be needed if parameters have been passed or the new procedure requires stack space allocations to hold local objects during its execution.

A new naming environment will be required if the call causes the process to enter a new naming environment. This is necessary if the program relies on a statically nested naming environment and the implementation uses context-dependent encodings of object names.

Space for local objects may be required and also might have to be initialized. This space could be allocated on the stack.

In many situations,[25] all of these actions must be completed before the called procedure can be initiated. Therefore, the basic design trade-off is between including these activities within CALL and implementing them in other ways.

---

[25]   If the called procedure is very simple and does not use many processor resources, some of these could be bypassed.

TABLE 4-2 EVALUATION OF DESIGN OPTIONS CONCERNING ACTIONS NEEDED TO ESTABLISH THE ENVIRONMENT FOR A NEW PROCEDURE INVOCATION

Action	Where Done		Time Cost		Frequency
	CALL	Otherwise	CALL	Otherwise	
Save the PC	✓				
Set the new protection state	✓				
Save the caller's processor state					
Set a new frame pointer					
Set the new naming environment					
Allocate space for local objects					
Initialize local objects					

Table 4-2 outlines these items. In the table, we checked that the program counter must be saved within CALL. All other requirements present options, except the protection state, which must be established during CALL, for reasons discussed in Section 9.1. With the usage frequencies serving as weights on the execution time costs/benefits, one can develop an overall cost picture for each option. If the processor is pipelined and instruction fetches are effectively hidden behind data accesses to memory, most of the actions to establish the environment can be accomplished with little time penalty compared to a design in which they are included within the CALL operation (see Problem 4-15).

The following examples illustrate the implementation of some of these options within CALL instructions in actual machine designs.

Example 4-12

The B 5700 ENTER instruction establishes a new stack frame and addressing context and also links the new stack frame into the static addressing hierarchy. This operation is detailed in Section D.1.6.

Execution environment specifications can define the local addressing environment of the called procedure and/or the access rights accorded to the process while executing that procedure. To meet these requirements, an entirely separate execution environment, including a new stack space, might be needed. Notice that changing both local addressing and access rights supports the visibility limitations of C++ classes, and changing to new static spaces also supports the use of those classes to hold the global state internal to a package. These restrictions can be met by processor actions upon call, but similar restrictions can be enforced by assuring correct software.

By changing access rights during CALL, one can restrict information flow to conform to a specified security or protection policy, as discussed in Chapter 9.

Example 4-13

The VAX processors support two elaborate CALL instructions, CALLG and CALLS, designed so that the act of calling a procedure does indeed have minimum effect on the caller's processor state. An argument list location is one operand for CALLG. The operand specified in the instruction is the address of the "entry point," whose contents are an "entry mask" EM that specifies initial settings of the overflow trap enable bits and 12-bit mask denoting which of the registers $R_0, .. , R_{11}$ should be stacked for restoration upon return to the caller.[26] The stacking of registers R_{12} through R_{15} is not optional because they have special fixed roles, as follows:

1. R_{12}: argument pointer;   //also called AP
2. R_{13}: frame pointer;   //also called FP
3. R_{14}: stack pointer;   //also called SP
4. R_{15}: program counter.   //also called PC

The address of the first word of the argument list is in AP; the first word of that list contains the length of the argument list, and the argument values themselves are stored in subsequent words. The frame pointer contains the location of the base of the new activation record established by the CALL being executed; it is used for activation block addressing and for restoring the stack pointer during RETURN.

When the CALLG instruction is executed, the following actions are taken:

1. TEMP = SP_1, SP_0;   //TEMP saves the stack pointer alignment
2. SP is adjusted to be doubleword aligned;
3. EM = Memory[entry];
4. The registers selected by EM are pushed on the stack;
5. PC, FP, and AP are pushed on the stack;   //MUST save these for linking
6. Push EM save mask, the condition codes, TEMP bits, and clear SM.S;
7. A zero word is pushed on the stack;
    //this can hold the address of a trap handler
8. Set values in condition bits (0 or set as per the entry mask);
9. FP = SP;
10. AP = operand value;
11. PC = entry + 2;   //the address of the first program byte.

These actions place the processor in a known state, aligning the stack pointer, saving all processor registers that will be used by the called procedure, and transferring control to the called program. Figure 4-5 depicts the state after this operation has been completed. The return operator unwinds these actions to restore the processor's state when it does return to the calling program (see Problem 4-13).

The CALLS instruction supports parameter passing on the stack. The operation differs from the CALLG instruction, because (1) a word containing the number of arguments is pushed on the stack before step 2 of the CALL algorithm described before; (2) in step 10, AP is set to point to the location of the stack word containing the argument count; and (3) the SM.S flag is set. During return, if SM.S is set, the argument count is found in the stack and the arguments are removed from the stack.

---

[26] Because the entry mask information is a static attribute of the called procedure, placing it within the program space is consistent with having the program space be read-only.

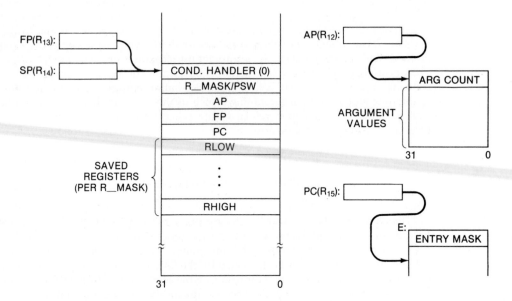

Figure 4-5   VAX stack configuration after CALLG E

Example 4-14

The CALLM instruction of the MC68020 processor is used to call a module, which is a separately translated program running in its own execution environment. The instruction's operands include (1) a "descriptor" and (2) the number of bytes occupied by arguments to be passed to the module. The instruction's effective address gives the location of the module's descriptor, which includes the module's entry point, whether the module requires a separate stack for execution (and the value of that stack pointer), and a pointer to the data area to be used by the called module. The use of this area is determined by how the module has been programmed; it could be used to hold the (private) link vector of that module (see Section 3.5.2). In actuality, the entry point location is not simply the location of the first instruction to be executed after the CALLM instruction is completed; rather, the first word at the entry point specifies the number of the processor register that is to be loaded with the pointer to the data area for the module; then the called program knows how to access the correct link vector.

To complete the module call, the processor needs the (static) entry point location and other information that may depend on the program using the module. The latter information is found in the module descriptor, which is private to the executing process.

When a module is called, the processor state is saved. In particular, the module descriptor pointer is placed in the saved state; this action permits the called module to access any user-defined[27] information that may have been placed in the

---

[27]   "User-defined" really means "not interpreted by the processor's built-in mechanisms."

module descriptor. The first word of the module descriptor and the first word of the saved stack frame contain access-level information related to data sharing and access control; its use is described in Section 9.7.2. The contents of the access-control information may force the processor to change stacks for the execution of the new module; if no change is required, the new activation block is pushed on the caller's stack.

The CALLM instruction requires many processor cycles; the actual number depends on n, the number of parameter words passed, and whether a new stack is required. The cycle count, in the worst case, reaches $71 + 6n$. By contrast, the BSR instruction, which calls an "ordinary" subroutine, takes at most 13 cycles. Clearly, the CALLM instruction should not be used where not necessary. It is no surprise that the RETM instruction takes up to 35 cycles, compared to only 12 cycles (worst case) for the ("normal") RTS return instruction.

The CALLM instruction was removed from the MC68030 and succeeding processor designs, despite its potential for supporting object-oriented concepts such as C++ classes. Apparently, the overhead was too high and software developers did not use it.

Example 4-15

The Intel iAPX 432 has two complex call instructions: CALL and CALL_THRU_DOMAIN. Both instructions have two operands containing three pieces of information:

1. Descriptor of the callee's static link
2. Pointer to the domain definition for the new procedure
3. Pointer to the entry point's instruction segment (relative to the new context)

The operands of these instructions can be taken from the stack, from memory locations, or from an immediate operand (this processor has no programmer-visible registers). The two pointer values are taken from the same object, which contains only static information. The operand location flexibility is adequate to permit the compiler to allocate the static information (the domain definition's location and the instruction segment pointer) within the program itself and dynamic information (the static link's location) within a process-local space.[28]

The domain structure defined by these structures could be used to support Ada packages or C++ classes; note that the domain can have different entry points (selected by the instruction segment index in the third operand) just as a C++ class can have several externally visible functions or procedures. However, the iAPX 432 processor design restricts the location of each entry point to the beginning of a segment, so there must be a separate segment for each visible entry point in the class definition.

The first data in the instruction segment specify static information about the execution environment for the called procedure. The first instruction follows this static information. The three parameters of the CALL instruction specify the domain index of the called domain, the address of the new static link, and the number of the instruction object that is being called. A large amount of other information is

---

[28]   Notice that the static link information is actually static with respect to the process, but may be different for each process that might be sharing the domain, so the linking information cannot be placed in a shared program segment; notice the distinction between the system's view and the process' view.

TABLE 4-3   CONTEXT CHANGES DURING DOMAIN CALL IN THE INTEL iAPX 432

Role of information	Assignment
Current context	context[..] = oldc.free_ctxt_ptr
Caller's context	context[..] = proc[cntxt]
Defining domain (address segment 0)	EAS[0] = context[..] = new_domain[operand1]
Address segment 1	EAS[1] = new_domain[operand1]
Static link	context[..] = old_context[operand3]
Program's segment number (new context)	proc.PC.seg_no = operand2
Program counter bit index	PC.bit = 0x40
Pointer to code's data object	context[..] = new_inst_obj[0]
Pointer to code's segment descriptor object	context[..] = new_inst_obj[..]
Pointer to domain's local constants	context[..] = new_domain[..]
Top of stack	proc.TOS = new_inst_obj[..]
Pointer to next free context	context[..] = <from storage mgr>
Top of storage management stack	context[..] = <from storage mgr>
Pointer to global constants	cntxt.g_cnst_ptr = oldcntxt.g_cnst_ptr

copied during the CALL_THROUGH_DOMAIN instruction; it is listed in Table 4-3. Particular offsets within objects have been omitted from the table; it is safe to assume that they are all different. The context objects themselves are maintained as a linked list; upon entry, a new one is allocated; the actions specified in the first two rows of the table maintain the (doubly linked) chain through the active contexts.

Example 4-16

In the i386, the CALL instruction might involve checking access rights and changing the processor's protection state, as detailed in Section 9.7. It can be supplemented by the 386 ENTER instruction, which is not a CALL instruction, but is used as the first instruction in a called procedure. The ENTER parameters include level, the lexical level of the new procedure, and local_space, the number of bytes to be allocated for local objects. When the ENTER instruction is executed, the processor performs the following actions:

1. Push the frame pointer.
2. Save the TOS in a temporary location (saveBP).
3. Copy level − 1 pointers from the old frame to the top of the stack.
4. Load the frame pointer (register BP) with the value in saveBP.
5. TOS = TOS - local_space   //allocate space for local objects.

This operation helps establish an addressing environment if the called procedure is nested within the calling procedure. Another use is supported by a special case in the semantics; if level is 0 or 1 the processor bypasses the pointer copying steps and simply allocates local space.

The complementary LEAVE instruction resets the stack pointer and the frame pointer from the values on the stack; it is executed as the last instruction in the procedure.

These examples show that complex context changes can establish the proper program execution context, but they are time-consuming. In [GEHR86], it was shown that a reassignment of the locations used for state information and an enhancement of the memory controller (to support an operation that clears a block of memory) could save over 50% of the iAPX 432 CALL's memory references, reducing its cost to a level comparable to procedure invocation in the MC68020.[29]

Performance. How could one quantify the performance of a processor during procedure calling? One might count the number of processor cycles required to execute CALL, until execution arrives at the first instruction corresponding to the first statement of the called procedure, with all machine conditions established for the execution of the called procedure. For a fair comparison, this count should include both the cycles consumed by the CALL instruction and the cycles expended during all prologue steps that establish the environment for the new procedure's execution. Designers have observed that by moving standard prologue functions into the CALL instruction, one could reduce the overall CALL cycle count, because additional instruction fetches would be eliminated. This argument has been used to justify placing enhanced features in CALL instructions. The high frequency of call/return instructions (see Table 4-1) emphasizes the importance of an efficient implementation of procedure call on the system's performance. However, the overlap of instruction executions within a pipelined processor may make the establishment of the new execution environment just as fast when the job is accomplished with instructions in the prologue of the called procedure (see Problem 4-15).

If the called procedure is complex, it is likely that the compiler will wish to establish an independent environment for its operation; then an enhanced CALL instruction will be helpful. On the other hand, a short procedure may not require many processor resources, and any effort expended to establish an independent execution environment, such as saving the complete processor state, will be wasted. Therefore, the designer may choose to provide not only a "complete" call instruction, but also a short version that does not establish an independent environment for the called procedure.

Example 4-17

The HP 3000 processor [HEWL73] supports two call instructions, named SCAL (subroutine call) and PCAL (procedure call). The SCAL instruction provides

---

[29]   This demonstrates that there may be a significant opportunity to enhance the speed of an implementation of complex instructions, and that the raw performance of one implementation cannot be used to judge the speed of the general implementation strategy.

minimum support, simply saving PC on the top of the stack and loading PC with the entry instruction address. When PCAL is used, a new activation block is created and the complete processor state is saved on the stack. The PCAL instruction is used whenever the called procedure is located in a separate instruction space.[30]

Interrupts. Interrupts are caused by events external to the program in execution. Because there is no relationship between the program in execution and the occurrence of the interrupt, the system must be designed so that when it reacts to the interrupt, it preserves the status of the program interrupted for the handler. The conventional approach to this requirement is to design the processor to treat the occurrence of the interrupt like a procedure call with no explicit parameters.

Several design issues remain after it has been decided that the interrupt's occurrence will be treated like a call:

1. When may interrupts be recognized?
2. Where is the process state saved?
3. What process state is saved?
4. How is the handler's entry point found?
5. Where does the program resume after the interrupt handler is completed?

When May Interrupts Be Recognized? If we interpret an interrupt as a signal to handle an external event and then return to the interrupted program, then the basic requirement is that when an interrupt occurs, the processor must be able to save state in such a manner that the execution point can return to the interrupted program. There are both microscopic and macroscopic aspects to this timing issue. The microscopic aspect concerns when an interrupt can occur within the execution of an instruction. The macroscopic aspect concerns when an interrupt can occur within the execution of a program.

A partial answer to the microscopic version of the question is "before starting a new instruction." Additional checks for interruptions may be added within the execution of long instructions to meet requirements concerning its response time—the delay between the occurrence of the interrupt and the execution of the first instruction of the interrupt handler.

The macroscopic version of the question involves delving into interactions among interrupt modules and process synchronization activities (see Section 8.8). One interesting question concerns what should happen if an interrupt handler is in execution when a new interrupt occurs? The following requirement is necessary: For it to be permissible that a new interrupt B be recognized after interrupt A has been recognized but before the A's handler has completed execution, the processor will have to be able to save the state of A's handler. There are three possible rules: (1) it is not possible to interrupt an interrupt handler, (2)

---

[30] A separate instruction space will exist if the caller and called procedures were compiled separately.

interrupts cannot be "recursive,"[31] or (3) the states of interrupted processes must be stored on a stack. Each rule has obvious implications concerning the times when an interrupt can be tolerated.

One important rule concerns the state of the interrupt system when an interrupt handler is initiated. The usual rule is that all interrupts (except fatal ones such as power failure) are turned off when any interrupt handler is initiated. After the handler has saved sufficient state that it would not be harmed by the occurrence of other interrupts, the software turns them back on.

Another important rule concerns the *masking* of interrupts. Most systems have a hierarchical rule—each interrupt has a *level*, and while an interrupt is being processed at level L, only interrupts of priority higher than L will be recognized. This rule prevents recursion within handlers, prioritizes them, and simplifies the process of saving state for a handler.

Example 4-18

The MC68020 processor state includes an interrupt priority level value; interrupts with higher priority than that value can be handled, but those with equal or lower priority must wait until the present handler has completed its job and the processor is restored to its former state (where the interrupt level will correspond to a lower priority).

Example 4-19

SPARC processors choose the highest priority trap when one is recognized. Other traps are turned off so that no others can be recognized until after that one has been processed.

Example 4-20

The Alpha AXP processor turns off all interrupts while processing a PALcode sequence. In this manner, these functions may appear to be *atomic*, that is, to have been completely performed without interruption, though this method for ensuring atomicity does not work correctly if there is more than one processor or more than one source of memory write requests (such as DMA devices) in the system. The need for atomic actions and their usefulness is detailed in Chapter 8. Turning off interrupts does increase interrupt response delays, which can be intolerable in some environments.

Most processor designs include a hierarchical scheme for trap processing. Each time that a trap occurs, the trap level within the processor's state is incremented. There is a limit to the number of levels, so special actions occur when the topmost level is about to be reached.

Example 4-21

SPARC processors must support at least four levels of trap processing. If the trap level indicates that a new trap is interrupting a trap handler, a different handler

---

[31]   Meaning that the same interrupt occurs a second time before the first occurrence has been handled.

entry point may be chosen.[32] If the new value of the trap level would be the maximum such value, a special interrupt is generated, and the processor enters a "RED" state that is used for "Reset, Error, and Debug." No further traps will be recognized and other unusual conditions apply, such as disabling the MMU mapping, while the processor is in this state.

The number of levels by which trap handling can be nested must be limited to guarantee that space will be available for use by the trap handlers.

Where Is the Process State Saved? If the processor architecture uses a stack to save the PC during a CALL, a stack is usually used for state saving on an interrupt.[33] If the processor state is saved on an interrupt exactly like it would be for a procedure call, it may seem that the same RETURN instruction as for a procedure's return can be used to terminate the interrupt handler. The apparent parallel between interrupts and a procedure call cannot be carried this far, unfortunately, because the processor's mode may be changed from user mode to supervisor mode to handle the interrupt. As a consequence, the execution mode before the interrupt occurred must be saved on an interrupt and restored on completion of the interrupt handler.

Example 4-22

On occurrence of an interrupt, the B 5700 processor saves the state on the stack the same way that the state is saved on a procedure call (see Section D.1.6). The same CALL and RETURN mechanisms can be used for both procedures and interrupts because the system design is based on the "nothing illegal" approach. Therefore, one knows that stacked mode information will not be compromised by any program.

If the system design is not based on the "nothing illegal" approach, the saved mode cannot both (1) be stored in a place writeable by a user process and (2) be restored on procedure return (see Problem 4-14), lest the system's integrity suffer. One way out of this dilemma is to add a (privileged) interrupt return instruction that restores the processor mode, whereas the user mode procedure return instruction cannot change the mode when it restores the execution state.

Example 4-23

The MC68020 has three stack pointers, a user stack pointer (USP), an interrupt stack pointer (ISP), and a master stack pointer (MSP). Bits 12 and 13 of the status register determine which of these three will be used for register A7. On the occurrence of an interrupt, the status register is saved on the stack and then set so that ISP will be used as the stack pointer. In this manner, the master stack can be reserved for the execution of system procedures directly requested from an application process. There are several return instructions differing in the amount of

---

[32] The flag indicating an interrupt of a trap handler is used to choose one half of the trap vector (see Figure 4-6).
[33] But there may be one or more separate supervisor stack(s) for saving the interrupted state and for use during the execution of the interrupt handler.

processor state information restored from the stack; the RTE (return from exception) instruction loads the processor's mode from standard information, so it cannot be executed while the processor is in the user mode.

What Process State Is Saved? One basic consideration in answering this question is that the processor must save sufficient state upon the occurrence of an interrupt that program execution can be resumed after the interrupt has been handled (if resumption is appropriate). One question concerns whether the interrupt was caused by the execution of an instruction that should be retried from the beginning, that absolutely cannot be retried, or that can be resumed from the point of interruption. It is straightforward to determine the information that should be saved to make this work properly. In a RISC machine such as SPARC, both PC and nPC have to be saved, because the interruption may occur when the instruction in a delay slot is ready to be executed next. An important general problem in a processor with delay slots is that the successor of each instruction cannot be determined by examining the instruction itself or its location in memory. Therefore, we need to save both the addresses of the next instruction and its successor.

Another important situation arises if an interrupt occurs during the execution of an instruction that might be restarted after the interrupt is processed. In this case, the saved PC should contain the address of the instruction in progress, because it is very difficult, if not impossible, to work backwards from the address of the next instruction to find the address of the previous instruction, due to control transfers and varying instruction lengths.

How Is the Handler's Entry Point Found? Many processor designs dedicate memory locations to hold interrupt entry points. Some information about how to save the process state may also be stored in specific memory locations. The big decision in this area concerns whether the processor automatically decodes the interrupt. If so, it chooses the handler's entry point using a computation based on the interrupt number.

Example 4-24

> On an external interruption, the IBM System/370 [IBM81b] saves the processor state (its PSW) in locations 24_{10}–31_{10} and takes the new PSW from memory locations 88_{10}–95_{10}. This PSW contains a saved PC, which defines the entry point for the interrupt handler. A word containing the interruption code is stored at a memory location chosen based on bits in the PSW. (Similar activities occur for internal interrupts.)

A simple condition decoding design multiplies the interrupt number by a constant (usually a power of 2, since the multiplication amounts to a shift operaiton) and uses the result as an address or a table index. The addressed location contains either the first instruction of the interrupt handler or the address of the first instruction of the interrupt handler.

Example 4-25

In SPARC-V9 [WEAV94], a trap number is associated with each possible trap cause. The trap number and the trap level are combined with the trap base address (TBA). The result is loaded into the program counters (PC and nPC) to initiate the trap handler. The field that receives the trap number is offset from the right end of the register by 5 bit positions (see Figure 4-6), so that the entry points are separated by 32 bytes (or eight instructions). Thus, the activity between the decision to handle an interrupt and the execution of the first instruction of the trap handler can be summarized as follows:

```
save_processor_state;
TL = TL + 1;
entry = (TBA && 0xFFFFFFFFFFFF8000) + 32*trap_number;   //a multiple of 16
if ( TL > 1 ) entry = entry + 0x4000;   //special entries if already in a handler
PC = entry;
nPC = entry + 4;
```

Example 4-26

The MC68020 distinguishes among 256 different exception conditions (of which 192 can be defined by the programmer). A table containing 1024 bytes defines the interrupt entry points. The origin of this table is held in the VBR (vector base register) processor register, which is accessible by the executing program only when the processor is in the supervisor state. Each table entry contains 4 bytes holding the address of the entry point of the associated exception handler. This table structure is depicted in Figure 4-7.

On occurrence of an interrupt or exception, at least 8 status bytes, and as many as 88 status bytes, are pushed on the stack; for details, see Chapter 6 in [MOTO84].

The status register saved at the top of the stack contains the mode and the interrupt priority level (used for prioritizing interrupts). Next on the stack is the saved

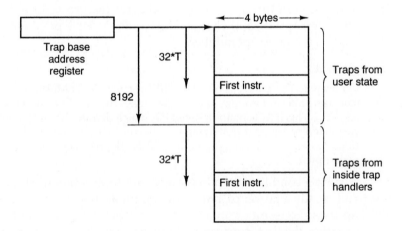

Figure 4-6   SPARC trap base register (TBR)

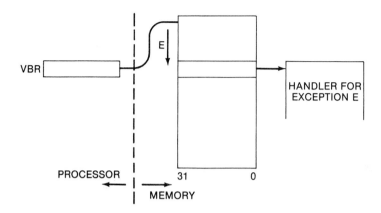

Figure 4-7   MC 68020 exception entry table. The table offset is 4*E (in bytes), there being 4 bytes per table entry

program counter, below which is a word containing the format and vector offset, the latter being an index into the exception entry table; its value serves as an indication of the type of exception that occurred. The format field specifies the format of the status information saved on the stack. Beneath these "standard items" is a space for "additional processor state information," which may contain from 0 to 40 (16-bit) words.

On completion of the interrupt handler, the processor executes the RTE instruction, which restores the entire state, examining the saved format information to determine which information was saved and how to resume the interrupted activity.

Where Does the Program Resume after the Interrupt Handler Is Completed? The answer to this important question depends on the type of interrupt and the decisions made in the interrupt handler. If the interrupted program should be resumed, the handler just executes the interrupt return instruction to restore the processor state and therefore to resume the interrupted program. If the interrupt was caused by a condition detected during instruction execution (such as a page fault), possibly the instruction should be retried after the interrupt handler has established conditions that permit successful execution of the instruction; in order to get back to the interrupting instruction, the system must have saved the address of the instruction that caused the interruption, or the system must have saved sufficient state about the execution progress to be able to resume execution in the midst of the instruction.

Routine Replacement.   Of the "other" control constructs mentioned in Section 4.1, only routine replacement has appeared at the processor level.

Example 4-27

> The IBM System/38 processor instruction "transfer control" (XCTL) performs a routine replacement call, passing an argument list to the replacement routine.

4.3.2 Program Location

Program location is the second basic issue concerning the control design space. Most processor designs are based on the von Neumann model and do not restrict program location. A few designs use the Harvard model. Many processor designs incorporate separate instruction and data caches, so the increased memory access bandwidth benefits of the Harvard design are obtained at the cache level. Also, it is easy to permit simultaneous instruction and data memory accesses; this simultaneity permits higher performance.

Example 4-28

> The MC68020 processor has an instruction cache within the processor chip; an external data cache may be added to the system. The internal instruction cache permits instruction fetching to proceed without going outside the chip.

Example 4-29

> Many RISC processors, such as SPARC, have separate instruction and data caches within the processor module.

Access control restrictions may be imposed to support protection and security of shared objects.[34] The access controls may imply restrictions on program location, because a program can be executed only if it is located in a memory space to which the processor has execute access. Execute access usually does not imply write access, and the program cannot modify itself during execution. Processor designs that write subroutine return addresses into the program are incompatible with program protection against inadvertent modification. If write access is permitted to the program's space, it may be subject to inadvertent modification. Furthermore, any write to the program space could cause problems if instructions might be buffered in the processor, as discussed in the next section.

4.3.3 Implementation

Processor control implementation choices affect the complexity of the processor's logic, its testability, and its speed. Microcoding (see Section 4.4) greatly enhances the regularity of the processor's implementation and makes its control section more easily testable, but slows execution.

Most processors have a supervisor mode in which all instructions can be executed and in which system control can be exerted. In contrast, in the user

---

[34] Chapter 9 discusses protection and security in more detail.

mode. some processor instructions will be proscribed and memory access may be restricted.

Other techniques that speed implementation include the use of parallel execution (see Chapter 6), instruction buffers, instruction caches, branch prediction, and designing instruction representations to facilitate their interpretation (see the next section).

Instruction Buffers.   Instruction lookbehind buffers and instruction caches help because programs exhibit locality, so recently executed instructions are likely to be executed in the near future, and instructions in successive locations are also likely prospects for execution.

The instruction buffer (or cache), like a memory cache, is located between the control unit and the memory. The design of either one presents the memory cache design issues. Loading, location, and dumping policies must be selected.

One buffer design holds the n most-recently executed instruction words, wherever they happen to be located in memory address space. A general associative search mechanism is required, giving the flexibility to hold any loop at the expense of lookup logic complexity. Because the sequentially executed instructions in a loop body can be placed in consecutive memory locations by the compiler, designing an instruction buffer that can handle the general case may not be a good strategy. One simplification is described in Problem 4-24. Another possibility is to use an instruction cache, which is identical to a general cache, but holding instructions only. Most programs do not rewrite their instructions during program execution. Therefore, the instruction cache is not designed to handle writes to the program space. If a program does write over its own instructions and the processor does have an instruction cache or buffer, specific synchronization instructions must be executed to notify the buffer that its contents might be invalid. These design issues are similar to design issues with object sharing; more details are provided in Chapter 8 where the general topic is presented.

Prefetching.   Instruction *prefetching* can speed accessing because instructions are sequentially executed. Under this design, on each (buffer or) cache reference, the cache is searched for the next block *after* the one referenced; if that block is absent, it is fetched. The Fairchild CLIPPER uses this strategy, which is used in the ILLIAC IV instruction buffer. The ILLIAC buffer design incorporates prefetching—instructions are fetched from memory in wide groups; when the first instruction in a group is issued, the buffer is checked for the presence of the next instruction group and it is fetched if it is not present already (see [BARN68] and [BOUK72]). In some prefetching schemes, page boundaries are significant; instructions will not be prefetched across page boundaries to prevent filling the TLB with information about pages that will not be used.

Branch Prediction. To increase performance, an overlapped processor will initiate instruction fetch and execution before previous instructions have completed execution. Therefore the outcomes of conditional branches might not be known when the processor would like to initiate the instruction after the branch. To provide more speedup for all programs, the control unit can be designed to guess (technically this is called *prediction*) the outcome of each conditional branch instruction, To produce functional behavior, the processor must be designed so that it can undo the effects of any instructions that were initiated speculatively if it turns out that a branch prediction was incorrect. If the predictions are correct most of the time, this technique will speed program execution. The details of these options are covered in Section 6.6.3.

Parallel Execution. Many opportunities for parallel execution can be designed into a processor implementation. The compiler's optimizer and code generator can look for statically observable parallel execution opportunities, and may be able to rearrange the object program to use these opportunities. Additionally, parallelism might be detected dynamically during program execution by the execution mechanism. These opportunities are discussed in Chapter 6.

4.3.4 Instruction Representation

Several design issues concern the representations used for processor instructions. The competing goals are control unit simplicity and program length.

Control unit *simplicity* can be enhanced by encoding instructions so that each bit within each instruction is used in only a small number of different ways. The RISC designs epitomize this approach, using almost all instruction bits in almost the same manner in all instructions. The MC68020 instruction set, on the other hand, requires complex decoding, there being over 40 instruction formats, and many bits that are used in different fields in different instructions.

Length savings can be achieved by allowing variable-length instructions, but at the cost of decoding complexity, because the actual length of an instruction may be determined by the function code or other parameters.

Definition. The *instruction granularity* of a processor is the greatest common divisor of the set of all instruction lengths used in that processor.

Definition. The *instruction size count of a processor instruction* is the number of different instruction lengths that can accompany the same function code.

Definition. The *instruction size count of a processor* is the maximum of the instruction size counts of the instructions in that processor.

In the MC68020, the instruction granularity is a word, and the instruction size count of the processor is 11.[35] In the B 5700, the instruction granularity is a byte and the instruction size count is 4. In the Intel iAPX 432, the instruction granularity is a bit and the number of operand specification possibilities pushes the instruction size count for the INCR (increment) instruction alone to 16.

The complexity of instruction fetching and decoding increases as the instruction size count increases, so mechanism complexity is the cost of shortening programs by encoding some instructions in few bits. Furthermore, it is really difficult to have both (1) instruction encodings such that the instruction has to be decoded to determine its boundaries and (2) instruction execution pipelines, because the pipelined processor attempts to fetch and decode an instruction before its predecessor has been completely decoded.

To determine an encoding that truly optimizes the instruction length, all usage frequencies must be known. Then one uses the Huffman coding algorithm [HUFF52], which produces a coding whose average code length is the shortest average code length possible. The drawbacks of fine instruction granularity and decoding complexity prevent Huffman coding from being used in computer instructions.

The decoding difficulty that arises from small length granularity variations can be alleviated by choosing a suboptimum encoding that uses a small set of lengths.

TABLE 4-4   ENCODING SPACE–TIME
TRADES; B 1700 STUDY

Encoding Scheme	Space	Decoding Time
All use 8 bits	1	1
Huffman	0.57	1.17
4, 6, or 10 bits	0.61	1.026

It is difficult to quantify the trade between length and decoding complexity. There is a small number of publicly available examples. In one, Wilner [WILN72] measured the trade of decoding time against space consumed by the instructions themselves. He studied instructions in the systems programming machine of the Burroughs B 1700 processor. The time measure is specific to the microcoded interpretation scheme used, so the trade-off information cannot be directly applied to other situations. Nevertheless, the results are instructive. Table 4-4 shows decoding time versus code space at three points in the design space. The shortest time and largest space correspond to function codes that have a single fixed length. The time and space measures are normalized to this

---

[35]   One word for the instruction and five extension words within each of two address specifications.

"best time" case. The smallest space and longest time correspond to Huffman coding. The third point corresponds to choosing three fixed code lengths and assigning codes for the most frequent instructions to the shortest length, and the least frequent instructions to the longest length. Although this midpoint does not achieve either the space or the time minimum, the differences between this point and the optimum points are quite small. The study highlights the importance of choosing length granularities wisely.

Another system using a small number of lengths is the Intel iAPX 432, in which operand specifications are encoded in varying lengths, with a bit in the instruction's format field indicating the width of the field.

4.3.5 Comments

Over the years, processor designers have made diverse design selections in their attempts to move some high-level language semantics into processor functions. We have seen many attempts in this direction, many associated with loop control and function calling. Some of these design decisions result in very complex instructions. Compared to a RISC design, these processors might be considered "very complex." But many, and frequently all, of the functions must be completed before the body of the called procedure can be executed.

Control unit designers can speed instruction execution by incorporating an instruction buffer or instruction cache and by employing branch prediction logic. The Alpha AXP uses a complex branch prediction scheme with a branch prediction stack to speed procedure return.

Many instruction representation techniques have been used. At two ends of the instruction size count spectrum are the iAPX 432, with bit granularity and over 16 instruction lengths, and RISC machines (e.g., the Alpha AXP) with one instruction length.

4.4 MICROCODE CONTROL STRUCTURES

Microcode implementations of processor functionality were commonplace before the advent of large-scale integrated technologies. The basic idea behind microprogramming is to implement the processor's control section as a programmed module, the lower-level program being called the microprogram.

A microcoded control unit includes a microprogram counter MPC that contains the address of the microinstruction to be fetched from the control memory. To perform the the fetched microinstruction it is copied into the microinstruction register MIR, whence it may be decoded to produce control signals that

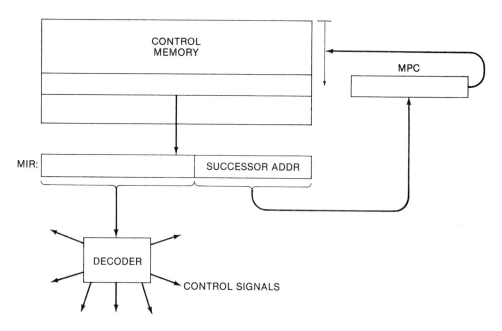

Figure 4-8   Basic elements in a microprogrammed control unit

enable register transfers, insert constant values, perform operations, and make microprogram sequencing decisions. Figure 4-8 depicts this general structure.

A sequence of microinstructions may by needed to perform the functions of a single processor instruction.

The use of microprogramming to implement a processor's functionality builds from a very primitive base (the host machine's architecture) to construct a more complex structure (the target machine's architecture). The implementation has several advantages, including regularity in the system's logic. Programming RISC machines at the assembly language level is analogous to microprogramming a host machine with primitive functions—there are many details that must be considered, and that the programmer would rather not have to consider. It is helpful to have program development tools when dealing with either RISC processor assembly language or a microprogramming language.

We briefly review the design decisions faced in constructing a microcoded implementation of a processor's functionality, to illustrate the similarities with the decisions that still remain for processor designers.

One basic design decision for a microcoded implementation of a target architecture concerns the microinstruction width; the terms vertical and horizontal microcode are used to describe the two extreme approaches in this design continuum.

Definition. A *horizontally microprogrammed processor* has wide microinstructions that require very little decoding, and many activities can be independently specified within a single microinstruction.

Definition. A *vertically microprogrammed processor* has microinstructions that are like instructions for a simple processor; choosing the "function code" of the instruction determines the entire sequence of actions for that instruction.

Notice that these "definitions" are not very precise; that is intentional, as there is no way to precisely specify this separation, and no implementations are devoid of encoded fields within microinstructions.

Within a vertically microprogrammed processor, the microprogram sequencer's functions are similar to those of a processor's control unit, but all instructions are simple, so the sequencer's complexity is much lower than the complexity of a sequencer for the target machine implemented without microprogramming. The "missing complexity" has been replaced by the larger control memory, which has a regular structure. A control unit implementation following this paradigm is said to be "vertically microprogrammed." Its microinstruction width may be as small as 16 bits. The typical vertical microinstruction is divided into fields that have interpretations similar to those of a processor instruction, such as the function code, the register number(s), and a field choosing the instruction variant to be performed.

At the horizontal end of the spectrum, the designer divides the host's microinstruction into "fields," with the contents of each field being decoded (if required) to choose the combination of control signals that should be sent to the corresponding partition of the host's logic. This design approach leads to the decoder structure shown in Figure 4-9. A horizontally microprogrammed microinstruction may have a width greater than 100 bits. There may be more than 15

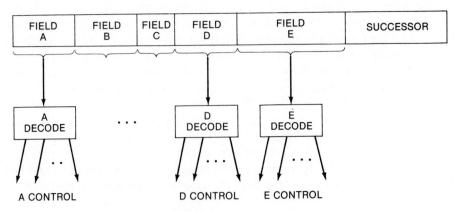

Figure 4-9   Decoding a field-based microinstruction

such fields; some may be decoded and others not. Wide microinstructions are typically found in high-performance systems, with the slower systems bearing the price of executing more microinstructions to effect the function that could be performed in fewer horizontal microinstructions.

The problem of designing microcode control structures is quite different for vertical microcode than it is for horizontal microcode. Because vertical microcode looks like a conventional processor program, the control design decisions for vertical microcode and for processor instructions are quite similar. Therefore, the control design selections for a vertical microcode implementation parallel those for processor control instructions, and the discussion of Section 4.3 can be adapted to the design of vertical microcode control structures. Therefore, we will not discuss vertical microcode designs further.

Several interesting design issues arise in horizontally microcoded systems. We adapt common control paradigm, with a program memory (microcode designs usually follow a Harvard architecture), a microcode program counter (MPC), and a microcode instruction register (MIR). Figure 4-8 illustrated these basic elements of the control section. In addition to these elements, a sequencer attached to the MIR outputs controls the issuance of control signals that implement the desired functions.

One important design problem concerns the determination of the parallelism possible within individual microinstructions; this problem is a version of the static parallelism detection problem that is discussed in Section 6.2.2.

4.4.1 Sequencing Structures

During microcode execution, many conditional sequencing decisions must be made; for example, they decode the instruction being interpreted and they select execution sequences based on the contents of the data and instruction objects being processed.

Sequential Execution. Sequential execution is not generally useful for horizontal microcode, because incrementing MPC takes time and requires special hardware, and conditional branches are quite frequent. Rather, to determine the next microinstruction address (NMA), one precomputes NMA and stores it in the microinstruction, from which it is copied to the MPC. This design saves execution time at the cost of space in the microcode memory. This NMA scheme, depicted in the format and data flow structure of Figure 4-8, was used in Wilkes' first proposal for microcoded control [WILK53].

Having the next microinstruction address taken from the NMA field of the microinstruction removes any need to correlate the program's flow structure with its location in memory address space. Thus, the microprogram execution sequences may merge and flow arbitrarily through the address space without incurring any execution time penalty. Some conditional execution designs are closely coupled to the NMA encodings.

Conditional Execution. Two-way conditional branching, of the form used in most conditional execution instructions at the host processor level, is not attractive within horizontal microcode. One detriment is the time delay to examine the condition value(s) and subsequently to gate the next instruction address into the MPC. Another detriment is that many consecutive two-way branches are required to implement a multiway branch.

A two-way conditional decision could be implemented by copying the condition bit being tested into part of NMA; the successor instruction would come from either of two locations, depending on the condition value. Figure 4-10 illustrates testing the carry bit by stuffing it into the least significant bit of NMA. In this design, the two branch destinations have consecutive addresses. This contiguity is not a difficulty, because each microinstruction can specify its successors' location with different contents in their NMA fields.

Another way to use a machine condition to affect the MPC is to OR the condition being tested with NMA from the microinstruction. Figure 4-11 illustrates the structure of the next address determination logic for this design option. If condition C affects bit position k, and if NMA_k is one, the value of condition C will not affect the effective next instruction address. Thus, the NMA encoding can be chosen to serve both as a base address and as a condition mask. Problem 4-29 illustrates some related issues.

Any computation of a conditional instruction address could slow execution. One could eliminate this bottleneck by using deferred branching to speed

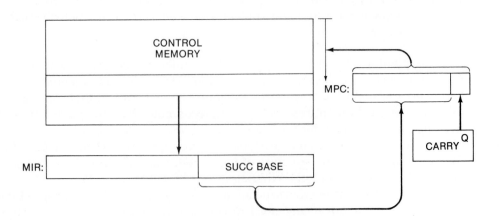

Figure 4-10   Condition bit stuffing for microcode
conditional sequencing

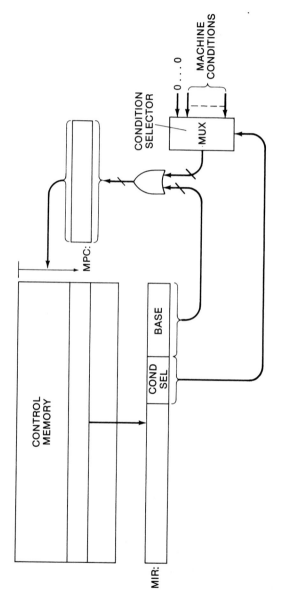

Figure 4-11 Conditional microcode sequencing implemented by ORed machine conditions

execution, even though the deferral makes programming more difficult, just as it does with any processor architecture that leaves delay slots in the instruction stream.

Example 4-30

The PDP-11/60 [TANN84] microinstruction sequence control uses a 12-bit microinstruction address, constructed from a 3-bit page number and a 9-bit index within the page. The page number is held in a "field" register (which actually could be the high-order bits of the MPC), so page changing requires special register transfers.[36] Control flow is determined by the 9-bit base address BA in the microinstruction and one of 32 selectable combinations of 6 bits determined from the machine status. Selectable patterns include useful subsets or functions of the function code, selected according to the target processor's instruction format.[37] The branch control field is ORed with the least significant bits of BA, as illustrated in Figure 4-12. Deferred branching is used.

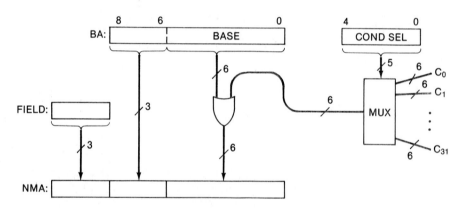

Figure 4-12 Information flows that determine the next microinstruction in a PDP-11/60

Two design decisions required to complete a multiway NMA branching design are as follows:

1. Choose the portions of the machine state to be available for NMA determination.
2. Choose the NMA bits that can be affected by the selected condition.

The second decision is unimportant. By contrast, a good selection of the machine state that can be tested can improve system speed by tailoring the host machine to the target architecture.

---

[36]   This is similar to one scheme for obtaining wide memory addresses, as discussed in Section E.4.2.
[37]   These patterns are selected to allow microcode to quickly dispatch to sequences performing important target processor functions.

Loop Support. Microcode loops could be used to emulate iterative processor instructions such as bit shifting and division. To support microinstruction counting loops, the designer could dedicate a host register for counting and connect special loop-termination test logic to the outputs of that register. The output from the termination test would be one condition input for NMA determination.

Another application for microprogram looping lies in the implementation of multiple precision operations. To determine precision, compare the host's word width against the word width in the target architecture. To perform the target's operation, use an iterative loop passing across all host-size components.

Example 4-31

The B 1700 is a vertically microprogrammed processor whose ALU width can range from 1 to 24 bits; the width for an operation is determined by the contents of the 16-bit field length register FL. If $C(FL) > 24$, the ALU width will be 24. The FL register and the 24-bit field address register FA contain the parameters for implementing multiprecision instructions whose operands might span many memory words. To do a multiprecision operation, the FL and FA registers are used in a microcode counting loop, with the COUNT microinstruction controlling the loop iterations. One COUNT operand is the amount of the counting increment. Variants of the COUNT microinstruction count these two registers singly or together, possibly in opposite directions. The choice of count direction on FA determines the order of memory accesses for operands, so it controls whether the operands are represented using the big-endian or small-endian convention and whether the operands are processed in right-to-left or left-to-right order.

With an increment quantity of 24 (the maximum ALU width), a loop could be easily constructed to perform serial operations on string or numeric operands. If the FL value should become negative or zero as a result of the COUNT operation, it is set to zero and a flag is set. This flag can be tested by a later instruction to complete the loop. Because the FL value defines the width of the ALU operands, this simple loop structure will correctly handle operands whose lengths are not multiples of 24, any residual fragment being handled last.

The B 1700 loop counting scheme is related in a clever manner to the ALU width control to simplify (micro-)programming to manipulate general operands.

Subroutines. Microcode subroutines are not usually supported, because speed is of concern, and the call/return overhead would be too great. A microprogrammer would not want to call a subroutine within the implementation of a commonly executed instruction.

Interrupts. In most designs, microcode is not directly interrupted. However, the microprogram must emulate the host machine architecture, which does respond to interrupts. To handle interrupts, a designer could include a specific "interrupt_occurred" bit in the host to signal the occurrence of an interrupt. This bit is added to the testable machine conditions. The host could be microprogrammed to capture the interrupt status in a host interrupt status register that copies the system's bus interrupt signals. The interrupt_occurred bit would be tested in microinstructions when it is convenient to respond to an interrupt.

4.4.2 Program Location

Harvard style microcode is often used; the microcode memory is not visible from processor instructions. This design has several advantages, including (1) the two levels of the system are separated and (2) short addresses can be used for microcode sequencing. In this section we discuss three variations on the basic Harvard design:

1. Multiple microcode memories
2. Writeable microcode memory
3. Microcode in main memory

The first variation has several control memories; each control memory can be programmed to support a separate processor architecture; this flexibility can "bridge" customers from a previous architecture to a new design. Under this strategy, one can implement a new architecture efficiently and the old architecture as efficiently as possible. The poorer performance of program running under the old architecture is an incentive for customers to change to the new architecture.

The second design variation allows processor instructions to write into microcode memory. With this design one could add interpretations for function codes unassigned in the basic target architecture. Such an expansion can permit an efficient implementation of operations on new data types or speed the execution of programs written in a particular language. There are two difficulties with writeable control memory: (1) The added microcode is part of process state. Thus, once a process writes to control memory, the operating system must assure that those changes remain intact during all time intervals when the process is in execution.[38] (2) A minor technical difficulty with writeable microcode concerns mismatches between the processor word size and the microprogram instruction size. If the microcode word is wider than the processor word, a sequence of write instructions has to be performed by the processor program to write one microinstruction word.

The third design variation interprets microinstructions taken from the processor's main memory. The variation can be used to cut system cost (if control memory is significantly more expensive than control memory). The microcode for the System 360 model 25 is taken from main memory. With today's lowered memory prices, this reason for choosing to place the control program in main memory has vanished.

---

[38] This requirement can be difficult to satisfy, because some processor designs that support writeable control memory do not provide any way to read the control memory—as would be useful to save the process state.

Example 4-32

The Burroughs B 1700 system supports several languages through "soft" interpreters. The person implementing a language on the B 1700 designs both a compiler and a "good" soft host machine for the language. The soft host machine is then implemented by microcode for the host machine hardware. Each program file is labeled to identify the soft host under which it should be executed. The operating system ensures that the proper microcode has been loaded before the program from the file begins execution. This design style requires some overlap between the control store for each soft machine language and the control store supporting the operating system. (See Problem 4-30.)

By placing microinstructions in main memory, the designer can eliminate the cost of a control memory. If microinstructions are executed directly from main memory, the microcode word width should equal the main memory word width, but it could be a multiple of the main memory word width. To improve performance, microcode caching can be added.

Example 4-33

The B 1700 systems place the (vertical) microcode in main memory, but larger models include a fast microcode memory. This memory acts like a microcode cache, except that it is loaded by specific microinstructions. Figure 4-13 depicts (a simplified version of) the logic for accessing microcode in this structure. The FFIELD register holds the value of the most significant bits of the microinstruction memory addresses corresponding to the block of microcode in the fast memory. A comparator examines MPC and FFIELD to determine whether to read the microinstruction from main memory or the fast microcode memory.

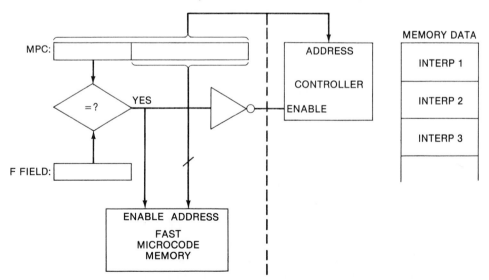

Figure 4-13   Microprogram access structures in the B 1700 processor

4.4.3 Implementation

Though adopting a Harvard architecture can be attractive for the microcode memory, variations might be considered to improve performance in special situations. Several additional implementation tricks at the microcode level may improve system performance. We consider microcode caching, field extraction units, and indirect specifications of common control program elements.

Microcode Caching. Caching microcode by using the design of a memory cache between processor-level memory and the processor itself is not useful. Why? The processor-level cache succeeds because there is a great speed difference between the cache and the next slower memory, and because there is locality in the referencing patterns of processor programs. At the microcode level, neither of these properties is true.

Field Extraction Units. A field extraction unit selects and aligns a contiguous subset of a register so that the subset can be processed as a single entity. This facility can be used in many ways within a microcoded host processor; it can dissect an instruction's fields, it can separate the exponent field within a float object from the mantissa field, or it can separate addressing-mode specifications from addresses. One major usage within a microprogrammed host is to separate target machine instructions into their constituent fields. The field contents can be used to select registers or microcode sequences that perform the host's instruction.

The control inputs to a field extraction unit specify the position p and width w of the field to be extracted. The internal logic can be simpler if the field position is a binary number counting from the end at which the output is aligned. For example, if the output field is right-justified, then p should be measured from the right end of the word. The data input is the object that contains the field to be extracted. Figure 4-14 depicts a field extraction module. Long logic chains or a large fan-in will be required in the field extraction logic.

Why use a field extraction module? After all, if the field format is fixed when the host is designed, the field can be extracted by routing wires from the source to the proper destinations. If the host machine is designed to emulate a single target architecture, all instruction and data object formats are known when the host is designed, and all fields to be extracted are also known. The host hardware register designations and selection logic can be customized to these field definitions. On the other hand, if the host machine must emulate several target processors, different instruction formats may have to be decoded, and specialized field extraction units may be useful.

It may be useful to think of this issue in terms of binding times. If hardware paths are used for field extraction, the field formats are bound at hardware

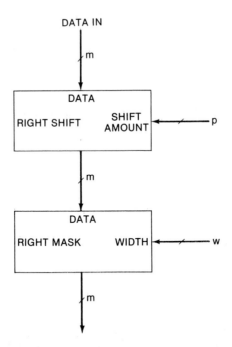

Figure 4-14   Field extraction logic (right-justified output)

design time. If general field extraction units are used, the field formats are bound when the microcode is written.

Example 4-34

The B 1700 processors are designed to support various target architectures, not all of them known when the hardware was designed. The designers chose many divisions (some of them overlapping) of the information in the registers and gave them individual names, as though they were separate registers. For example, the F register is divided into several named parts. Fields FA and FL, holding the values manipulated by the COUNT microinstruction (see Example 4-31), are both subsets of F.

Due to the delays they introduce, general field extraction units are not an attractive option for a high-performance host. Typical high-performance hosts are tailored to one target architecture and use wired-in field extraction.

Short Codes for Common Control Elements. Microcode can be shortened if common elements of the microprogram are represented by short codes. Some common elements that could be given short designations are constant values, register numbers, and sequences of microinstructions. We discuss the program simplifications that short coding can produce, and warn of the decreased system speed that might result.

Many host machine designs include short selector codes that feed constant values to ALU inputs. Others organize an array of constant values like a small memory, permitting "normal" addressing to select a constant from the memory. Because only a few constant values need be used to emulate a host architecture, a small fast memory holding these constants can be advantageous. Designs that do not provide short constant names must have some way of placing a complete constant value within a microinstruction.

The second opportunity for shorthand names lies in register naming. The host registers that emulate the target's address, data, and instruction registers are candidates for this special consideration.

Example 4-35

> The PDP-11/60's target architecture includes eight processor registers, but the host architecture includes a 16-register memory whose contents can be selected by a 4-bit code. The last four members of the memory can also be selected by a 2-bit code in certain contexts; these four elements contain three constant values (0, 1, and 2) and the memory buffer register.

A third opportunity for shortening microcode is to define short names for common sequences of microinstructions. Under this option, sometimes called nanoprogramming, a microinstruction may be implemented by a sequence of nanoinstructions, the latter specifying the host's behavior at a very low level of detail. The major problems here lie in the complexity of coding the lowest level and in the slow system speed resulting from the hierarchical implementation.

A fourth opportunity assigns short codes to common patterns. A short code serves as the address of a wide entry in a translation memory TM. In Figure 4-15, we show how values from TM could be used to form a wide microinstruction requiring little decoding before it is performed. This two-level structure is similar to the two-level microinstruction-nanocode design, but it is not identical to nanoprogramming because each low-level entity corresponds to a single high-level entity. The access delays in TM might slow execution.

A fifth opportunity for shortening microcode uses two-level decoding of the microinstruction fields. In this scheme, the interpretation of one field, say A, depends upon the value within another field B. The decoding logic either has a large fan-in (because the bits from both A and B must participate in the choices) or is a cascade of decisions—a decoder for B generating enables that select one of several decoders that are attached to A. Both of these options can slow program execution compared to using single-level decoding.

4.4.4 Representation

The representation of vertical microcode instructions is similar to the representation of processor instructions. With horizontal microcode, decoding can be reduced, especially if each field is assigned to a specialized unchanging role. Then

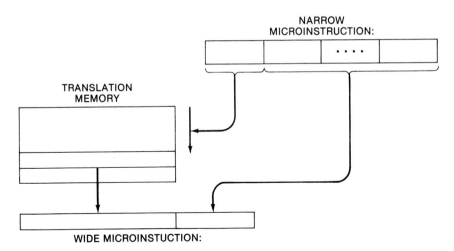

Figure 4-15   Using a translation memory (TM) to translate a short code into many microinstruction bits

only a small amount of decoding is needed. Although this desirable state of affairs requires wide microinstructions, it does speed execution.

4.4.5 Comments

Microprogramming is an important implementation technique because it gives a simple regular implementation and it allows modifications after the hardware has been completely designed. The choice of control structures for microprogramming are slightly different from those at higher levels, because the microprogram will be used for a long time and it is invisible from almost all people. Therefore, it can be worthwhile to precompute the addresses of the successor instructions and to place those values directly into the microinstructions themselves. In addition, stuffing machine conditions into the successor address gives a powerful and speedy mechanism for multiway branching. Wide, horizontal microinstructions can speed the implementation, because they require little, if any, decoding logic.

4.5 SUMMARY

We discussed options concerning the control of a single process within a computer system. We addressed several important design decisions such as the selection of sequencing structures, the separation of programs from data within memory, and the representation of the instructions themselves.

At high levels, where programs are frequently rewritten, the choice of control structures should be dominated by the desire for clarity in the program's structure. At lowest levels, by contrast, the designer is not very concerned with these niceties and system speed requirements dominate, such as in the design of RISC machines. Program location selections vary. We use a Harvard structure at the highest levels and at the microcode level, but we use a von Neumann structure at the processor level. The representations of the instructions themselves become more complex at lower levels.

4.6 TRENDS

Starting from the bottom up, microcoding will disappear, because the extra accesses to find the instructions are too time-consuming. The reasons that made it attractive have worn off—now people agree that extensive simulation prior to commitment to silicon should remove design errors, and any need to modify the design later can be handled by releasing a new version of the system.

Programmers will continue to use structured programming, and many will minimize the use of **goto**s in their programs, though many other programmers will continue to write unstructured programs using the **goto** construct. The view that programs and data are separate should continue to expand, except for special programming languages, such as LISP and Prolog, whose use will likely continue. But developing specialized processor hardware to support these languages will probably fade from the scene, because processor design has become so complex and expensive. Efficient programs running on high-performance general-purpose processors should adequately fill this niche.

Efficient instruction representation continues to be an important issue, because RISC machines must be able to decode and start instruction execution without too much delay waiting to decide what should be done. Unfortunately, compatibility goals restrict a designer's options. Valiant attempts by the designers of the Alpha AXP [SITE93] to provide automatic conversion of old program images have met with some success; this strategy will continue to provide good bridges between old and new architectures. Designs in which the control unit automatically replaces an instruction from the old instruction set with a sequence of instructions from the new instruction set might become a popular method for bridging the gap between old and new processor instruction sets.

The trend toward wider registers and wider buses connecting the processor to the memory seem not likely to extend to instruction widths; 32-bit instructions provide adequate selection of registers and space for address offsets that should be sufficient for most programs to execute quite efficiently. Furthermore, increasing the instruction width increases the instruction cache bandwidth requirement.

4.7 CONCEPT LIST

1. The simple program illusion
2. Simple sequencing structures
3. Control operations
4. Harvard machines
5. Von Neumann machines
6. Basic modular control structures—subroutines, loops, and switches
7. Undesirability, yet necessity of **goto** statements
8. Label variables and entry point variables that point to program steps
9. Exception handlers are found by following dynamic nesting rules
10. Limits on exception usage derive from the exception-handling model
11. Selective execution statements include those with certainty (**if**) and those without certainty (**one_of**)
12. Some languages mix the program with a database (e.g., LISP, Prolog)
13. Skip class instructions permit simple tests of memory objects
14. Condition codes or register contents can be tested for conditional sequencing
15. Procedure call/return instructions can be enhanced to support addressing, allocation, and changing contexts for new modules
16. Consistent interrupt handling requires care in managing nested structures and processor state
17. Hardware decoding of interrupt causes
18. Instruction buffers and caches
19. Instruction prefetching
20. Branch prediction
21. Instructions can have variable sizes
22. Microprogrammed control units
23. Successor addresses in microinstructions
24. Multiway branches can be implemented quickly by stuffing a selector value into the destination address
25. Modifiable microcode
26. Field extraction modules
27. Prolog has an unconventional system model; see Appendix H
28. LISP has an unconventional system model; see Appendix I

4.8 PROBLEMS

4-1. Describe a strategy for converting a COBOL program that contains dynamic **goto**s changed by ALTER to another COBOL program that uses only the selected **goto** for dynamic branching.

4-2.   We are trying to solve the following problem: A label variable, like an entry point variable, must be associated with an execution environment. In a recursive situation, each block may have been invoked several times. A label associated with any of the invocations might have been passed as a parameter to a context such that the label's execution environment is not part of the current execution context. The system should branch to the proper context if asked to **goto** the label variable.

Discuss and compare the following two proposed solutions to this problem:

1. The "value" of each label variable contains a pointer to an activation block defining the appropriate execution environment.

2. The "value" of each label variable does not contain any execution environment information. Rather, the dynamically most recent activation of the program block containing the label value's declaration will become the execution environment after the **goto** is taken.

For an example that illustrates the different semantics of the two proposals, consider this (Ada) program structure:

```
procedure k is
    procedure f( lab : in out label; .. ) is --Not Ada
        b1, b2, b3, b4 : boolean;
        procedure g is
            h1 : label;                 --Not Ada
        begin
            ..
        <<h>> if b2 then
                    h1 = h;             --Not Ada
            else
                    h1 = lab;           --Not Ada
            end if;
            ..
            lab = h1                    --Not Ada
            f( h1, .. );
        end g;
    begin
        ..
        if b1 then
                g;          --function call
        end if;
        ..
        if b4 then
                goto lab;
        end if;
    end f;
begin
    ..
    f( place, .. );
    ..
<<place>> ..
end k;
```

Take this execution history:

```
k calls f
f calls g
g calls f
f calls g
g calls f
```

After the last call, the stack contains six activation blocks.

Now assume that in this (third) activation of f condition b4 is true and the **goto** lab statement is executed. What is on the activation block stack after the **goto**? Under proposal 1, it would contain 1, 3, or 5 blocks. Under proposal 2, it would contain either 1 or 5 blocks. The exact numbers depend on the values of the Boolean quantities during previous invocations of the procedures. All activation blocks corresponding to modules that will be aborted as a consequence of the **goto** are to be discarded on execution of the **goto**.

4-3.   In Section 4.2.1, we discussed the possibility that an exception handler might execute with a local context that is associated with an activation record that is not the topmost one on the stack. This question concerns the consequences of this desire.

(a) Specify an algorithm for finding the frame pointer for the handler's execution context.

(b) Suppose that the exception handler needs to allocate or deallocate objects while it is in execution. Where would space for these objects be allocated? How would they be named from within the handler?

(c) Specify any ways in which the SPARC stack frame layout (see Example F-9) limits the selection of ways to handle the issues in the previous parts of this question. Explain your answer.

4-4.   This problem explores the relationship between exception control flow rules and the use of the stack by the exception-handling program. There is only one stack per process.

(a) Show an example that illustrates how the exception handler could use addressing relative to the top of the stack to access objects stored during the execution of the "normal" program for the block where the exception handler is defined. Assume that the Ada exception control flow model is being followed.

(b) Now construct an example to show why the scheme of part (a) cannot be used if the exception control flow rules allow a return to the procedure where the exception occurred.

4-5.   The following program includes a guarded **do** statement. Without any information available about the properties of the functions f and g, what can you say about conditions in the visible objects (x and y) after the **do** has been executed? Assume that the **do** does, in fact, terminate. (Can you actually tell whether this is the case?)

```
int x, y;
..
do {
    when ( x > 7 ):
        f( x, y );
```

```
                              break;
                         when ( x < 5 ):
                            g( x, y, 3 );
                            break;

             };
```

4-6. Construct a program whose control flow structure is equivalent to a guarded **do**. Do not use **goto**s. Provide two different solutions, one for each of the following options regarding the selection of the enabled statement that will be executed. Each solution should be equivalent to a strategy for converting an arbitrary guarded **do** statement into an "equivalent" program.

(a) Perform the first (in order of appearance in the program) enabled statement each time the **do** loop is performed.

(b) Perform a randomly selected one of the enabled statements each time the loop is performed.

4-7. A system designer argues that there is no logical requirement that a system support branch instructions with run-time modifiable destinations. It is trivial to see that a solution that simply emulates all statements will do the job. We seek other approaches to the problem.

(a) Show how the effect of label variables in a high-level language could be emulated in a system that allows only selected **goto**s. If your approach requires help from the compiler or the linker, specify the assistance needed from each.

(b) Explain why a designer might want to think of implementing dynamic destinations at the processor level.

(c) Discuss the relationship between this problem and the issues presented in Problem 4-2.

4-8. A designer is proposing a new processor instruction set. He suggests that the design would be simpler if the only conditional execution support were through conditional skip instructions. Each of these instructions tests processor status in a manner specified within the function code. The processor then skips the next instruction in the program if the condition is true.

Discuss the viability of this design philosophy at the processor level and also at the microcode level. In thinking about the microcode level, assume that the machine is to implement the instruction set of a general-purpose processor of conventional design, such as the MC 680x0.

4-9. Consider a **switch** structure in which the selection expression may have values in the range 0 .. 63, with all values within that range equally probable. Let c_i denote the count of the number of instruction words corresponding to a direct translation of the statement list for expression value i. (This count does not include any branch instructions that might be inserted at the end of the statement list to skip over the others and reach the instructions corresponding to the statement after the **switch** statement.) Table 4-5 specifies a frequency distribution of c_i.

TABLE 4-5   FREQUENCY DISTRIBUTION OF STATEMENT LENGTHS

Number of instruction words	0	1	2	3	4	5	6	7	8	9	10	13	15	18
Number of cases		2	4	10	18	9	7	4	3	2	1	1	1	1	1

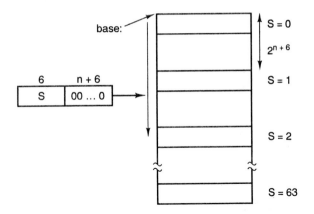

Figure 4-16   Determining the **switch** instruction address

In this problem, you will evaluate some design options concerning the imple-mentation of the **switch** branching using computed destination addresses. The branch address computation will use the value of the selector shifted by an amount that you will select; the result will be the destination address of the branch instruc-tion. Figure 4-16 illustrates this destination address computation. Note that the ini-tial instructions of the **switch** statement blocks are separated by 2^n words, where n is the amount of the shift. Define the "branch target area" to include the locations be-tween B and $B + 2^{n+6}$, where B is the "base" branch location used if the **switch** selec-tor is zero. In this problem consider $n = 2, 3$, and 4 only. If an instruction sequence does not fit into the space between branch destinations, then the maximum possi-ble subsequence of the instruction sequence will be placed there and the last word will be filled with a branch instruction that occupies the whole word. Figure 4-17 illustrates this program flow.

(a) Outline a strategy for placing the instruction words within memory.
(b) Determine I_n, the total number of instruction words required for the complete implementation of the **switch** statement, for $n = 2, 3$, and 4. Why is $I_n > \Sigma c_i$?
(c) What is the smallest n such that $I_n = I_{n+1}$?   [*Turn the page for part* (d)]

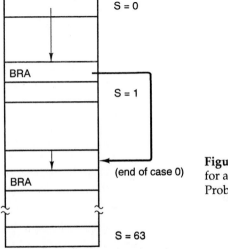

Figure 4-17   Program flow for a long sequence in Problem 4-9

(d) Let J_n denote the number of instruction words within the branch target area that contain instructions executed for statements in the **switch** statement lists. Find J_n, for all n. Include those branch instructions that pass control to the next statement as part of the set of instructions executed for the statements in the **switch** lists. Do not count any additional branch instructions that may have to be inserted to overcome the limitations imposed by the branch address computation.

4-10. A designer proposes a new general CASE instruction to be included in a processor design. The operands of the proposed instruction are a value V and the addresses of two tables. Value V is treated as an unsigned integer. To execute the instruction, the processor sequentially scans through table1 until an entry is found that exceeds or equals the operand value. Let i denote the position in table1 where the test is satisfied. Thus, we know that

value < table1[j]   for all j such that $1 \le j < i$
value $\ge$ table1[i]

The program counter will be loaded from table2[i].
(a) Discuss the relationship between this instruction and the C++ **switch** statement.
(b) Compare this instruction to the VAX CASE statement presented in Example 4-9.
(c) Do you recommend the inclusion of the proposed CASE instruction? Explain. Consider the execution of FORTRAN and C++ programs.

4-11. This problem concerns two ways to realize **while** loops, one using software and the other using a new processor instruction.
(a) Show that the effect of the construct

while (<boolean>)
   <statement>;

can be implemented using the construct

until (<boolean>)
   <statement>;

without any **goto** statements.
(b) Propose a processor instruction to assist the implementation of the **while** structure. Specify the operand(s) and semantics of the proposed implementation. Show how and where your proposed instruction would be inserted into the program by a compiler translating the **while** construct.

4-12. The examples in Section 4.3.1 cited several different processors and their instructions that support counting loops. We will see how these instructions could be used to perform the three FORTRAN DO loops whose headers are specified in what follows. The DO statement syntax is

DO n I = N1, N2, N3

Here n is a statement number, I is an integer variable name, and N1, N2, and N3 are integer-valued expressions, with N3 > 0. If N3 is omitted, it assumes the default value of one. The semantics are (1) the expressions N1, N2, and N3 are evaluated once before the loop body is executed; (2) the statements following the DO, up to and including the statement labeled n, constitute the loop body; (3) the mth time through the loop the counter I has the value

$$I = N1 + (m - 1)*N3$$

and (4) this progression of I values continues until I > N2, at which time the loop body is not executed, and the loop is completed. The loop body is always executed at least once, regardless of the values of the expressions Ni. Here are the three loop headers to consider:

> DO 3 I = 1, 10
> DO 3 I = 1, 10, 2
> DO 3 I = 6, 20, 3

(a) For each cited processor, state how you would initialize the counter and its decrement (or increment) quantity (state which you are defining).
(b) For each cited processor, draw the structure of the loop control flow.
(c) Would you recommend changing the processor's instruction set if N3 were an expression to be reevaluated during each iteration of the loop? Explain.

4-13. Here are three alternate proposals to provide the capability of saving processor state during the procedure calling process:

1. Save all registers as part of the CALL instruction.
2. Add a single instruction that saves all registers in a block of consecutive memory locations beginning at the effective address specified in the SAVE instruction.
3. Each register can be saved by a separate STORE instruction, which is executed within the called routine as needed.

In each case, a complementary capability to restore the processor's state will be provided.
(a) What are the advantages and disadvantages of the three proposals?
(b) To compare the speeds of these three designs, make the following speed assumptions:

1. Unless specified otherwise in the following list, each instruction requires two time units (this time includes both the instruction fetch and its execution).
2. In design 1, each instruction fetch and each register store takes one time unit.
3. In design 2, each register save requires two time units.
4. In design 3, the register-saving program loop takes seven time units per register saved, plus three time units for initialization.

You are asked to determine combinations of the frequency of procedure calls and the number of memory cycles used in executing an "average" procedure such that each design is better than the other designs. The comparison criterion is the execution time averaged over all procedures. Assume that the frequency distribution of the number of registers i required by a procedure is given by $f(i)$. The value of the function $f(i)$ gives the fraction of function calls (measured dynamically) for which the called procedure uses exactly i processor registers.

(c) Compare these schemes against the MC68020 scheme in which the entry mask specified with the entry point is consulted to determine the registers to be saved on the stack. Discuss the differences between the designs.

4-14. Example 4-13 described the VAX CALLG instruction. Recall that the argument list for the called procedure is not located on the stack. The VAX also has a CALLS instruction that would be executed after the argument values (4 bytes apiece) have been pushed on the stack; CALLS establishes conditions for the execution of the procedure. The CALLS operands are an argument count (the number of 4-byte objects to be passed as parameters to the subroutine) and the address of the entry mask for the procedure. A calling sequence is structured:

```
PUSH argument_n;
PUSH argument_( n - 1 );
..
PUSH argument_1;
CALLS n, proc_entry;
```

An address in the VAX is a byte address.
(a) Write a sequence of register transfers that performs CALLS.
(b) Draw a diagram showing the contents of significant registers and the top region of the stack upon completion of the CALLS.
(c) Write out the steps for performing the return instruction. Note that there is only one return instruction; a flag (saved with R_MASK on the stack upon CALL) indicates whether the call that entered the routine was CALLG or CALLS. If the call was CALLS, the return instruction removes the arguments from the stack.

4-15. In this problem we explore methods to establish the execution environment for a new procedure with a pipelined processor. Throughout the problem, assume that the processor can make simultaneous accesses to the I-cache and D-cache, and that all I-cache accesses succeed. (Thus, the only possible memory timing bottleneck arises from data accesses.)

In this problem we restrict our attention to the need to (1) save the stack pointer; (2) save the frame pointer; and (3) establish a new frame pointer.
(a) Assuming that CALL only saves the PC in a register, write a SPARC program fragment that does this job. Describe the sequence of data accesses used during the program fragment.
(b) Assume another design in which CALL includes the required activities. Describe the sequence of data accesses that will be made during CALL.
(c) Draw timing diagrams corresponding to the options of parts (a) and (b) and comment on any differences or similarities that you find.

4-16. Write a program fragment for the Alpha AXP architecture that emulates the i386 ENTER instruction that copies a block of pointers from locations within the stack to the top of the stack. Comment on the performance limitations that arise from the pipelined implementation of the processor (assume that the pipeline has four stages: fetch, decode, execute, and store, with forwarding to speed execution across dependencies).

4-17. A processor uses a hardware pushdown stack to save the PC during subroutines. The stack capacity is limited by the hardware configuration, so the stack control logic must be designed to prevent stack overflow. Notice that stack overflow could occur on any call. Interrupts and traps are handled like calls, necessitating saving the PC on the hardware stack. This problem concerns the design of a hardware stack controller that interrupts the processor if any action is attempted that would imply future stack overflow. Describe all control information needed to implement this feature and discuss (1) how it could be managed and (2) the tests that check for stack overflow.

4-18. A Harvard architecture contains a program memory separate from the data memory. A designer proposes that the same effect could be achieved by providing two memory maps in the MMU—the instruction address map would be used when fetching instructions and the data address map would be used when accessing data objects. Would this scheme provide all/some/none of the benefits claimed for the Harvard architecture? Explain.

4-19. One could design a "two-address" processor in which each instruction specifies the location of the next instruction to be executed, even if no branch is required. Two next instruction addresses must be specified in a conditional branch instruction or a CALL instruction. This capability might be useful for a number of reasons, including the following:

  1. Instructions might be stored in a memory device which does not support random access.

  2. Instruction execution times might be variable.

  Discuss the degree to which these reasons apply to the following cases. For each case, recommend whether two-address instructions should be used. All data objects are stored in the same memory device as the instructions.

  (a) All instructions and data are stored on a physically rotating memory device, and executed directly from this device (i.e., they are not buffered in a high-speed memory). A word stored in the rotating memory can be accessed only when the word is passing a fixed "read station."

  (b) Instructions are stored in a serial shift-register memory that requires frequent refreshing (by reading all objects in the memory). The memory's shift control logic permits an external controller to suspend shifting for a limited period of time. The shift control logic limits the suspension time by forcing shifting whenever the time since the last shift exceeds T.

4-20. In this problem we consider the relationships between the two styles of condition testing in conditional branch instructions. In particular, we look at the emulation of the conditional branch tests of the SPARC processor (see Table A-4) on a processor that can only test the sign of a register's contents or whether they are zero. We consider emulating the actions of the following SPARC program fragment

                ADD D1, D2, D3
                Bcc TARGET

For each possible condition test (represented by the cc field) available in a SPARC processor, write an equivalent sequence for the processor that tests register contents.

4-21. A processor designer proposes to include an instruction lookbehind buffer to decrease instruction fetch delays. The buffer holds the n most recently executed instructions, using a fully associative search to determine whether a desired instruction is present in the buffer.

(a) For what control flow patterns would the inclusion of the buffer actually decrease program execution times?

(b) Our designer further proposes that the processor-level program be allowed to explicitly control the loading of the lookbehind buffer. Two new processor instructions—"Start instruction saving" and "Stop instruction saving"—are proposed. The lookbehind buffer keeps the n most recently executed instructions fetched while the processor was saving instructions. The instructions controlling instruction saving are not themselves saved in the buffer. You are to recommend whether the designer's new instructions should be included in the repertoire. Answer the following questions related to this decision.

(i) Are there any situations in which program speed would be improved by including the new instructions? Explain.

(ii) Are there any situations in which program speed would be degraded by including the new instructions? Explain.

(iii) Do you recommend that the new instructions be included?

(c) Compare the proposed design against one with processor instructions BEGINLOOP and ENDLOOP. BEGINLOOP would initiate lookbehind saving and ENDLOOP would stop saving even if the buffer was not already filled. If the buffer filled up during the loop, it would automatically stop saving when it filled up, preserving the instructions that it had saved before it filled up.

4-22. Consider a processor with a lookbehind instruction buffer and relative addressing in branch instructions. A designer proposes that the buffer be controlled according to the following rules:

1. The buffer will be declared invalid if the processor executes a jump to an instruction not located within the buffer.
2. After a jump to a location within the buffer's address range, the processor will obtain the instruction from the buffer if the buffer location is valid.
3. Every instruction fetched from memory is loaded into the buffer when it is about to be executed.

(a) Define the logic for determining whether the destination of a jump instruction lies within the buffer. Be sure to consider cases in which jumps are taken from the middle of the buffer.

(b) Draw a register-level diagram showing the registers holding the information needed to determine where an instruction is found (include the PC). Show the logic modules needed to make the decision, indicating the data paths between the registers and the decision modules. Also describe the functions of all the modules.

4-23. This problem is concerned with the policies for changing register contents and validity bits that control an instruction lookbehind buffer. Suppose that the program counter is divided into two fields:

```
class pc {
public:
     int p, i;
}
pc program_counter;
```

The two registers pp and j specify the buffer's range in such a way that the validity of a buffer entry can be determined from the logical expression

$$\{ [(i < j) \wedge (p == pp+1)] \vee [(i \geq j) \wedge (p == pp)] \} \wedge \{buffer[\,i\,].v == true\}$$

Here buffer[i].v denotes the validity bit associated with the *i*th word of the buffer. Note that this test not only tells how to test a buffer entry for validity, but also implies how the buffer entries must be managed as the program is executed. The test is designed to allow the buffer to hold all instructions for a loop whose instructions are located in contiguous addresses and that is short enough to fit into the buffer.

Specify completely a consistent set of policies concerning changes in the values of the pp and j registers and the v bits in the buffer entries. Your solution should be compatible with implementations of the processor's functionality without the instruction buffer; in particular, you should not have to add processor instructions to control the buffer. A solution with the smallest number of special cases is considered to be best.

4-24. Contrast the use of an instruction cache with the use of an instruction lookbehind buffer (as described in Problem 4-21) with respect to the following:

(a) Performance versus complexity.

(b) The types of program structures that are speeded up by including the cache or buffer.

4-25. Consider a processor in which some instructions are shorter than one word; these short instructions are packed into single words. Suppose that when the program counter is saved, only the word address information is saved.

(a) Describe any constraints on program structure imposed by the restriction on PC saving.

(b) Define the interrupt response time to be the elapsed time between the (asynchronous) occurrence of the interrupt signal and the fetch of the first instruction of the interrupt handler. Are there restrictions on interrupt response times? What are their consequences? Relate the worst-case interrupt response time under these assumptions to the worst-case interrupt response time achieved if the remainder of the program counter could be loaded and stored.

(c) Comment on the possibility of handling an exception after the execution of any instruction within the program.

4-26. The Alpha AXP documentation provides guidelines for speeding program execution; one of these is that it is desirable to place the destinations of branch instructions at addresses that are naturally aligned with respect to the size of the blocks fetched into the instruction cache. Discuss any similarities and differences between this advice and the design described in Problem 4-25.

4-27. Here is a designer's reasoning and claim: The destination address for an unconditional microcode branch instruction could be computed by the same technique used for conditional branch instructions. For any conditional branch, the host forces a machine condition into the low-order bits of the MPC. The machine condition to be used in this manner is selected based on the contents of the "condition select" microinstruction field. One way to implement an unconditional branch is to take the selected condition bits directly from a microinstruction field (this has the effect of forcing a constant into the selection bit positions). A second way to implement unconditional branching places the complete destination address in the next instruction address field of the microinstruction; no selection is used.

The claim is that the former scheme allows shorter microinstructions than the latter scheme. Discuss this claim.

4-28. Consider a microcoded host design in which NMA bits may be modified by selected machine conditions when a next instruction address is being computed. The text claimed that the detailed selection of which bits were modified was not important. Consider two designs, A and B, that differ only in the selection of affected bits. In design A, a condition set C can affect bit i of NMA, whereas in design B, set C affects bit j ($j \neq i$) of NMA. Assume that bits i and j are not affected by any conditions not in set C in either design. Justify the claim by showing that a rearrangement of A's microprogram suffices to construct an equivalent microprogram for B.

4-29. Consider the microinstruction branching scheme in which the condition bits are combined with the next instruction address from a horizontal microinstruction by using an OR operation (see Figure 4-11).

(a) Does this mean that no condition mask or selector is required? Explain your answer.

(b) Someone claims that using NMA bits in this manner creates a bias toward using addresses containing bits set to 1, and that, as a consequence, certain portions of control memory might be sparsely utilized. Comment on this claim.

4-30. A designer proposes a microcode control instruction that behaves like the VAX CASE instruction (see Example 4-9). The claim is that this structure would be useful for multiway branching such as used for dispatching based on the function code of an instruction being emulated. Comment on this proposal.

4-31. Consider the following suggestion. A microcoded host machine designer wishes to remove the need for MPC saving during subroutine calls. She proposes to design the microcode so that conditional branches can be used to return from microcode subroutines. By selecting the branch conditions in the branch that performs the return to be identical to the branch conditions that caused the control flow to reach the point from which the call was made, the designer proposes to achieve a return flow that corresponds to the calls. As an example, pick a microcode routine that might be called during the execution of a MPY instruction or during the execution of a DIV instruction. Within the subroutine's return instruction function code, bits (from the target's IR) can be selected to distinguish the two instruction codes and thereby to reach the proper return points. In particular, a different return point would be reached depending on whether MPY or DIV was being performed.

(a) Discuss the reasonableness of the assumptions behind this design.

(b) In a second design (call it E), the microprogram establishes some coded conditions in a register R and then calls the routine; R's contents are used to select the branch destination that achieves the return. For the original design and design E, discuss whether the design restricts the use of subroutines in microcode. Explain your conclusions.

(c) For both designs, discuss whether the design saves anything when compared to a design with microprogram subroutine calling supported by saving MPC on a hardware stack.

4-32. Show that one could design an operating system for a processor with writeable microcode that would allow process swapping, despite the fact that the microprogram could not be read. Furthermore, there need not be any restrictions on the writing of microcode by any process in the system. The proposed strategy for achieving this goal is to force all microcode writing to be performed by a service within the operating system.

(a) What data would the operating system have to buffer to perform this task correctly?

(b) When the operating system wishes to swap processes, what steps related to the writeable microcode should be performed?

4-33. In Example 4-32, the text claimed that there must exist some overlap in the B 1700 design between (1) the S-interpreter used for executing user programs written in a particular programming language and (2) the S-interpreter for the programming language used to write operating system programs. Justify this claim.

4-34. A designer proposes building a microprogrammed host with two control memories having different speeds. The proposed strategy places the microcode for all frequently executed target instructions in the faster memory and the microcode for less frequent target instructions in the slower memory. Further, the designer proposes allocating a buffer within the fast memory into which a block of the slow memory's contents could be copied. This copying would be achieved by dividing the microcode in the slow memory into blocks based on the, pattern of data types of the target instruction's operands. When one instruction from a block of slow memory is executed, the entire block within which it is contained will be copied into the fast control memory, from which it will be executed.

Comment on this design proposal. Would it be functionally reasonable? What addressing logic would be required? Would it provide a reasonable cost/performance balance? Would you recommend implementing it? Explain.

4-35. We wish to modify the logic suggested in Figure 4-13 so that (1) the fast microcode memory address space is divided into four blocks, (2) a microinstruction within a block but not present in the fast memory will be loaded into fast memory only when some microinstruction in the same "slot" (of four microinstructions) is fetched, and (3) the selection of the four blocks that might be swapped into the fast memory is controlled by the microprogram. A BLOCK_CHANGE microinstruction is added to control which blocks are present in the fast memory. There are two operands for this instruction: (1) the block number (which is the most significant bits of the memory addresses within the block), and (2) the number of the block frame within the fast memory where the new block is to be positioned.

(a) Specify the controller's rules used to determine which memory will be used to read a microinstruction.

(b) Draw a picture of the modified control logic.

(c) Specify the actions required to implement the BLOCK_CHANGE instruction.

4-36. The text claimed that the logic within a field extraction unit would be simplified if the field's position were specified relative to the end of the register at which the result will be aligned. Justify this claim.

4-37. Draw a functional diagram showing the major components of a field extraction unit. There are n bits in the input word, and the output is to be a copy of the w bits starting in bit position b. The bit positions are numbered from right to left. So if $n = 32$, $w = 10$, and $b = 15$, the output is to be a copy of input bits $15 .. 6$. The output is to be right-justified within the n-bit output data path.

4-38. Discuss the relationship between the design of a field extraction unit and the design of a granularity adjustment module (see Section 3.8.5).

4-39. A designer claims that the use of a translation memory TM (Figure 4-15) has the following advantages and disadvantages:

1. System speed could be enhanced by overlapping execution; thus, the TM design has little speed penalty.
2. The cumulative number of memory bits required to specify an emulator will be reduced by using the TM design.
3. The TM memory's contents effectively replace decoding logic.
4. Determining a good TM implementation of an emulator to replace one that was horizontally microcoded is a straightforward task.

Comment on these claims, taking a position about whether each claim is justified (completely, partially, or not at all) and explaining your positions. If your answer claims that something is possible, your answer should demonstrate an approach to making that possible. If your answer claims that something is difficult, support your answer with a sketch of a difficult instance.

5

OBJECT-ORIENTED PROCESSING

The formula "Two and two make five"
is not without its attractions.

— F. Dostoevsky

Spurious moral grandeur
is generally attached
to any formulation computed
to a large number of decimal places.

— D. Berlinski

The computer's ability to manipulate information makes the computer more than just a filing system. The important illusions regarding object manipulation are the object type illusion (that all objects have types), the operator illusion (that all manipulations follow the unambiguous operation specification), and the atomic action illusion (that these operations are performed without interruption from other activities). Then we couple these with the single control point illusion, which governs the sequencing among the operations.

What set of types and operations do we need for generality? The answer is simple—an inefficient, but logically complete computer system can be constructed using only one manipulation operation—integer subtraction. What operations and types should we support in a realistic design? At the lowest level, surely integers and booleans. It is certainly convenient that programmers do not have to deal with the value encoding used to represent integer values. Similar statements can be made about float objects, though they might not be supported in the hardware of all processors. Working upwards, we define new data classes and corresponding operations. In this manner we encapsulate the object representation and operation implementation details, raising the level of abstraction. These actions create a virtual machine on which it should be easier to implement our algorithms efficiently. The ideal programming language for the top level of the hierarchy is "close" to the application.

At the bottom of the hierarchy, when the processor performs an operation, it does access some bits from somewhere and performs some operation on those bits. How does the processor know how many bits to handle? How does it know what to do with them? These answers come from the operation code and from the information about the types of the objects involved in the operation.

Overall, we wish to support the typing illusion:

> **Object Type Illusion.** The computer system can manipulate objects of various types; the definition of an object's type includes the definition of all permissible operations on objects of the corresponding type.

A related statement concerns *strong typing*, which, although it has been attributed almost mystical properties, is actually a simple extension of the object type illusion:

> **Definition.** If language L imposes object type rules such that the computer always interprets each object as a member of one (fixed) class, independent of the path used to access the object, we say that L is *strongly typed*.

In this chapter, we survey the creation of new object classes, object representations, operation specifications, and operation implementations. We will see how designers can provide efficient, yet extensible, language and system implementations. As an extension of this discussion, we present the design of a LISP-oriented processor in Appendix I. We also see how the low-level processor support can be extended to assist with operations on objects whose types are outside the base processor set of types.

How do these design decisions affect the structure of the underlying system? At the top level, adding a new object class specification to a C++ program has no effect on processor design. A C++ programmer may use classes to build abstractions that support new data types; these extensions create software procedures within the program. The compiler inserts appropriate procedure calls to invoke operations for the new classes. However, we do have the option, at the processor level, to add hardware modules that handle objects belonging to the new class. This change would significantly enhance system performance if the programs frequently took advantage of the hardware assist.

After reading this chapter, you will be familiar with the use of class-based abstractions and some modern approaches to supporting diverse data classes and their operations. You will see the advantages of a system design in which frequently used operations and classes are supported at the hardware level, with infrequently used operations and classes supported by slower mechanisms, such as optional coprocessors, microcode, or software.

5.1 BASIC CONCEPTS

In this section we survey some important concepts and design options related to object typing and object manipulation. The notion of type is quite important because it permits one to categorize objects and define appropriate interpretations of old and new procedures and functions that operate on objects of the new type.

First, we clarify some terminology: An object type defined by the programmer is called a *class* in C++ and a *type* in Ada; similar terminology is used in other languages. We use the word "class" for a defined type. We use the word "type" when describing this attribute of a particular object. Thus, after defining the class example, we might define object E and declare its "type" to be example. And then we would say that the type of E is example.

The terms "function" and "procedure" appear frequently in class definitions. Both terms refer to procedural objects; they differ only in whether they return a result. In many places, we should use the phrase "procedure or function" to be technically correct, but we simplify things by using only one or the other term; this should not add confusion.

5.1.1 Objects

An object is an entity that holds a value and has a type, which defines the interpretation of the value held within the object. Your intuitive notions regarding objects and types are probably correct; here we emphasize the relationships between an object and its type, and the consequent limitations on how the object can be manipulated.

Object-type binding may be static or dynamic. Static typing is established by a declaration in a program, such as

> `int x;`

Strong typing suggests that the type of an object be an immutable property of the object. A combination of good programming practices and strong typing leads one to the idea that each object's type should be a static property of the object. Thus, by extension, the type of an object declared in the program is known at compile time, so the compiler can be responsible for producing a correct program that manipulates the object in accordance with the class definition. In this case, no type checking is required during program execution. If, however, the type of an object cannot be determined at compile time,[1] the run-time system must include a mechanism that finds the object's actual type. Otherwise, the absence of representation-dependent behavior cannot be guaranteed, and the system is operating under the "nothing illegal" approach with respect to the programs.

There are many ways to specify an operand's type:

1. Static type declaration, with type information along the operator path
2. Type information along the access path
3. Type information within the object itself
4. A combination of the above

Figure 5-1 illustrates how a system designed based on these options determines an object type at runtime. The picture shows accesses that start from the number of a register that contains the memory address of a descriptor of the object itself.

The first option was illustrated before; the object type declaration removes any need for run-time data specifying object classes. Figure 5-1a depicts this option; dashed arrows indicate that the function code implies the object's type.

The second option places type information along the access path reaching the object. Such type information may be contained in a descriptor of the object or of the space within which the object is located. Figure 5-1b shows an object descriptor holding both the object's class and a pointer to the object itself. The other alternative places groups of objects of the same class into a single space whose descriptor contains the type information.

The third option places type information within the object itself. A typical design under this option places type information in a tag associated with the object (see Fig. 5-1c). We discuss this option in connection with object naming in Section E.3.3.

The final option separately declares two aspects of the object's type; a pair of the preceding options are used to specify each aspect of the type. For example, with Ada variant records the record type is static and a (dynamic) discriminant value within each object indicates which variant applies to that object (see Fig. 5-1d).

Comments. As we work our way from high-level languages to microcode or hardware realizations, implementation correctness is assured by making correct transformations among these schemes. These transformations depend on

---

[1]   In C++, this can happen if the object is pointed to by a nonspecific pointer (of type ***void**) or if the object's type is a **union** (e.g., the set of possible types is enumerated in the **union**'s declaration).

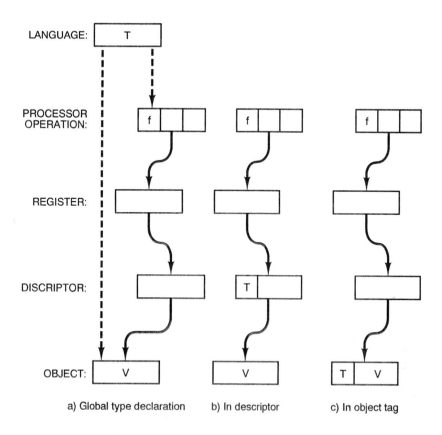

Figure 5-1   Location options for type information (key: T
= type field/tag; V = value; DV = discriminant value)

whether the object-type associations are static (fixed before program execution)
or dynamic (determined during program execution).

The great concern for a structured approach to typing (which is character-
istic of programming languages) is rapidly lost as one moves to lower system
levels. In the extreme, at the microprogram level, correct programming can be
assumed. At this level, the types of all operands are implied by the function
codes sent to the ALU. The individual operands correspond to components of
the representation of an object whose type is defined at a higher level of abstraction. In the middle, at the processor level, objects can be tagged or described by
type information along the access path from the operation or address specification; these techniques imply that type enforcement is built upon run-time checks
or processor implementation decisions. The designer makes a conscious choice
regarding the system design philosophy when she decides how classes are

bound to values at the processor level (is the execution correct because "everything was checked" or because "nothing illegal was requested?").

Example 5-1

It has been claimed that strong typing makes if difficult to write bad programs. This example shows how a weakly typed system can be emulated by a program written in a strongly typed language. Thus, one can misuse strong typing to produce arbitrarily bad programs!

One can construct a strongly typed emulator E_w that emulates the behavior of an arbitrary weakly typed language L. Suppose that the compiler for L converts the representations of all objects to groups of integers. The emulator handles integer objects, and will be strongly typed, in the sense that every object will be declared to be an integer, and will indeed be treated as an integer. The focus on integers is not restrictive, because integer operations can be used to separate bit collections into fields and to perform arbitrary operations. Clearly, we can build an algorithm that emulates any machine using only integers. There is nothing in the emulator that regulates the behavior of objects as a higher level of abstraction (what is a particular collection of integers being used to represent?). This argument sketches the construction of a strongly typed emulator of an arbitrary machine, including one that is not strongly typed.

We hasten to point out that this example presents an academic emulation designed to dispel the apparent magic surrounding strong typing. Strong static typing can give implementation ease, execution speed, and program understandability, but it does not guarantee these benefits.

Despite the advantages of strong typing, some languages allow the program to assign a value of any type to any named location. If one wished to ensure class consistency and thereby avoid the possibility of representation-dependent results within a system presenting this flexibility, one must either tag all objects with their classes or rely on correct programming. If all objects are tagged, the system design follows the "anything goes" approach. Reliance on correct programming follows the "nothing illegal" approach. Adopting the nothing illegal approach does not introduce any architectural problems, in the sense that there are no options that could be used in the lower levels to assist the system's correctness.

5.1.2 Specification of Programmer-Defined Types

It can be helpful to define a new type to handle complex objects that are represented as a collection of constituent objects. Each instance of the type will be treated as a single entity and its representation can be hidden from outsiders. The definition of a new type is more than a set of representation rules; it has to include rules about how the objects are to be manipulated and which portions of an object's representation should be visible and which portions of the procedures and functions should be available to programs that manipulate objects of other types. To form a boundary around the representation and implementation details, we encapsulate them within a class definition. Inside the definition, the details can be specified to be "hidden," which masks the details from programs outside the class definition.[2]

By hiding representation and implementation details, people can create virtual machines at a high level of abstraction, and only a few people have to know how the internal objects are represented and manipulated. In the following, we use the word "class" to denote an encapsulated definition that does hide representation details from the outsiders. It may be helpful to visualize the implementation of a class as a *module* within the system. It will not deceive you[3] to think of the hidden attributes of objects within the class as being stored within the class module. A *class specification* defines the module's interface, specifying all externally visible attributes and operations that can be used by programmers. It also specifies the externally hidden (but internally visible) object components and functions used to construct the class realization.

The Structure of a Class Definition.   Each class definition contains a specification section (which defines the interface of the class module) and an implementation section (which details the implementation of the class module and the objects assigned the new type). The major parts of a class definition are as follows:

1. The templates that describe how to call the externally visible functions that manipulate the objects
2. The representation of an object, including the externally visible components and other (internal) components encapsulated within the class
3. The hidden class-level objects used within the implementation
4. The bodies of the functions available for manipulating the objects

Representation Specifications.   All value representation schemes are built from simple, basic elements. Structured representations mirror the way we think about objects; one can use class, structure, or record constructs to collect objects of diverse types to represent the state of a single object within a new class. The representation choice affects the speed of access and the speed of object processing.

Object-Level Components.   Every object of a type is also considered to be an instance CI of the class. The representation of the state of instance CI uses a set of private component objects. For example, the representation of a float object

---

[2]   One has to be careful about the interpretation of this comment, because C++ permits some modules to be included logically within a class definition even though they are not syntactically enclosed within that definition.

[3]   This applies to the logical functionality, but certainly not to speed or efficiency questions.

uses two integers that represent the exponent and mantissa portions of the value; these two parts are not available individually.

Class-Level Components. Consider a class implementing memory pages. Within the class implementation, a space manager keeps information about free pages. Where is this free-space information? Clearly, it belongs within the class, but not within an individual instance of the class; these data are not specific to an individual page, but rather are used to manage the set of pages. This example illustrates the fact that the representations of some classes need objects related to the class as a whole, and not to specific instances of the class. These objects are declared within the class module, but outside an individual instance of the class, so they become visible inside procedures that manipulate individual entities within the class.

Procedure Specifications. Any class definition may include procedures having arbitrary names and arbitrary semantics; the procedure bodies are specified in a conventional manner. If the class completely encapsulates the objects, only the procedures defined inside the class definition may know the object representation conventions and may manipulate the instances of the class. In addition to the programmer-defined procedures within a class, a few "standard" operations, such as value copying and object creation, may have simple "standard" implementations. However, for some classes, the operations may require more complex algorithms specified as procedures overloaded on the names of the standard operations. A common set of standard operations includes **copy, equality_test, create,** and **destroy**.

The *copy* and *equality_test* operations seem obvious—two objects (of the same type) are equal if they contain the same bit patterns. Unfortunately, this is sufficient, but not always necessary. For example, we might wish to define two lists to be equal if they contain the same leaf values in the same order, with no requirement that the two be represented by the same bit patterns. (If two lists were implemented with pointers, and the two were located at different addresses, their bit patterns would differ even if their leaf values matched at the bit level.)

A *constructor* procedure initializes the value within a new object immediately after it has been created. When the constructor procedure has terminated, the entire class is left in a consistent state. A constructor may have parameters whose values determine the initial state of the new object. A *destructor* procedure destroys the value within an object immediately before the object itself is destroyed, again, leaving the entire class in a consistent state. An object should not be created without immediately calling the associated constructor, and an object should not be destroyed without first calling the associated destructor, because either omission could result in inconsistent class states.

Another warning needs to be raised about implied operations—in general, the integrity constraints must be satisfied after the assignment (provided that the integrity constraints were satisfied before the copying activity), and this means that with interdependent objects, simple instance copying is not likely to suffice.

To customize the meaning of equality (for example) for different object types, one needs a way to name procedures with operator symbols. Once this definition is made, the meaning of the equals sign has been redefined for different object types. In other words, the meaning of the operator depends upon the types of its operands. An operator whose interpretation depends upon the types of its operands is called an *overloaded operator*. Overloading exists at the processor level when it checks the operand types before choosing the operation to be performed.

What Is the Procedure Supposed to Do? Why not answer this question with "Just what I programmed it to do!"? This answer suggests that the individual defined the actions of the procedure in terms of the procedure itself, which is quite circular. In addition, because procedure bodies can be complicated objects themselves, using one as a specification might not aid understanding. What options do we have?

We could formalize a procedure's functionality, stating unambiguously the effects of performing the procedure. Specification by effect is useful in the abstract, because it decouples the specification from any implementation. The decoupling is achieved by expressing the effects as a relationship between the class state after the operation and the class state before the operation was initiated.

Example 5-2

We want to specify the effects of push on a stack object, whose representation has two parts: s, containing the stack itself, and t, containing the index of the top of the stack. A formal description of the action of pushing an object on the stack starts with this description of the states before and after the operation:

$$(st1.s, st1.t) = [push(st1, v)](st1.s', st1.t')$$

This states that the objects named st1.s and st1.t are changed by performing the operation push(st1, v). The apostrophes designate object values before the operation; bare symbols denote object values after the operation completes.

To specify the resulting state, we write

$$(st1.s, st1.t) = [push(st1, v)](st1.s', st1.t') = (concatenate(st1.s', v), st1.t'+1)$$

This statement could be read as though it were a function call: "The function push(st1, v) applied to stack st1 (whose state is denoted by (st1.s', st1.t')) leaves a state with st1.s' concatenated with v and st1.t = st1.t' + 1." Notice the close relationship between this statement and an implied internal representation.

Effect specifications can be powerful tools in certain proof realms.

Another abstract way to describe operations by their effects uses functional relationships to describe the externally visible results of applying a sequence of one or more functions to one or more objects. Many statements would be needed to specify the behavior of a stack object; these are typical ones:

```
pop(newstack) = error;
pop(push(stack, x)) = x;
```

To complete the behavioral description, we probably have to describe the internal state of the object along with the outputs. This returns us to the dilemma: One seeks to encapsulate representation details, but one needs some internal representation scheme in order to express correctness conditions.

The preceding development is based on the notion of tracking object state as it changes when operations are performed on the object. This approach is an extension of Hoare's predicate logic, used to reason from rules describing the effects of each program step to obtain conclusions about overall program behavior [HOAR69]. Appendix L explores proof techniques in more detail.

Comments. Each approach has its advantages. A specification by implementation gives an implementation. On the other hand, a specification by effect states the operation's results without biasing the implementation; this form may be more useful for reasoning about program properties. But both schemes have drawbacks. A specification by implementation does not suggest alternate implementations that are functionally equivalent. A specification by effect does not suggest any realization, so it might not be obvious how the functions might be implemented efficiently or even correctly.

Integrity Constraints. Can an arbitrary state exist within an object? Perhaps so, but not always! Certainly, any bit pattern is acceptable inside an integer object. But consider a record concerning airplane seat sales. Suppose that it includes a variable size holding the number of seats on the plane, a variable sold holding the number of seats that have been sold, and a variable empty holding the number of empty (unsold) seats. Clearly, the relation sold + empty = size must be satisfied. This simple *integrity constraint* will be true if the implementation has properly manipulated the object. The constraint restricts the object states.

An integrity constraint may restrict the state within a single object or the state of the class considered as a whole. Either situation can be described from two viewpoints:

1. Optimistic: Certain combinations are valid.
2. Pessimistic: Certain combinations signify that an error has occurred.

This discussion may seem to be theoretical, but it extends to important considerations in database systems. Also it can be used to detect errors within the system, because illegal combinations of object states can only occur if an error has occurred. We spend a few moments on this issue. We look at two levels: single objects and the entire set of objects within a class.

Object-Level Consistency. An integrity constraint at the object level defines the limits on the state of an object considered in isolation. If the representation of the object contains several component parts, the predicate may express a relationship between the values within these components.

Example 5-3

Floats represented using the IEEE convention [IEEE85] must admit the possibility of NaN (not a number) objects, which arise from operations that would produce infinite results, or from performing "normal" operations on operands that themselves are NaNs. Normal float values are represented in a normalized format. Values that are not normalized and have exponent values that lie in the middle of the range are illegal representations ("unnormalized"). Other illegal bit patterns include those with a zero mantissa and an exponent that is nonzero but is not the maximum exponent value.

Class-Level Consistency. An integrity constraint at the class level relates the states of several (or, more typically, all) of the instances of the class.

Example 5-4

A list object is constructed from "beads" that were obtained from a heap of free space. Suppose that each list is singly-linked. The module that manages the list class is responsible for acquiring and freeing the beads when they move on and off the list. Suppose also that the heads of all lists are held within the manager. Then the manager could traverse all lists and find their beads. All heap space should be reachable from user lists or the free list, and no user space should appear on the free list. These constraints define a consistent state for the list manager. This consistency cannot be ascertained by examining a single list object.

Reuse. The ability to reuse an old design to complete a new project is very important. The system structure and the interface structures determine the ease of this important activity. We briefly mention four levels at which definitions or designs might be reused, and we illustrate a few of these cases.

1. Create a new class definition by adding to an existing class definition.
2. Define parameterized classes.
3. Define parameterized structures.
4. Dynamically type objects.

Class Inheritance. Class inheritance allows one to reuse old class definitions when forming new classes. The basic idea is to include attributes from a previous class, including the representation and implementation, within the definition of the new class.

Programmers using languages like C++ and Ada can define new data types or classes based on old ones and thereby construct a hierarchical class structure. Several issues governing these constructions and guidelines for effective use of these constructions are very important, but because they are software and application design issues that have almost no effect on the underlying design, they are not discussed here. One might wish to exercise caution when constructing new representations, because one can easily construct representation structures that are difficult to support efficiently using the basic accessing structures available in the underlying system. For example, one could build a vector from a set of isolated objects, which is an interesting conceptual exercise, but this structure does not correspond to a simple implementation in a computer using a location-addressed memory system.

Parameterized Classes. Often, one can develop a class definition that has parameters; this structure permits one to complete one definition and then to create versions of the basic class by setting the parameters to particular values. The ability to use a type name as a parameter can be very important. For example, one could define a type that is a stack of objects of type T, where T is a parameter of the definition. The class would include the usual push, pop, and empty test operations. The definition of a class for stacks holding any particular object type this_type can be created by simply asking for a copy of the *generic* class with the type parameter set to this_type. The new class will come complete with correct operations if the basic stack definition was correctly implemented.

Among the potential difficulties with this scheme is the problem of determining whether two objects belong to the same class. The question may seem academic, but it is important in trying to achieve strong typing, because the act of assigning one variable to another is simple if they are of the same type, and is quite a different matter if their types differ.

Parameterized Structures. The benefits and issues concerning definitions of parameterized structures are similar to those concerning parameterized class definitions, except, of course, that the structure's definition does not include any information about procedures or operations that can be applied to the objects. In many programming languages these structures are called *variant records*. A variant record groups several related classes beneath a single declaration. The objects whose values choose the specific format of a particular instance are called *discriminants* in Ada. Each discriminant object must be of a type that has a finite set of discrete values. The description of the representation must specify the representation for every possible value of the discriminant. The discriminant value may affect both the space allocation for and the format of the information contained within an instance of the record type. Therefore, Ada requires that the actual type of each instance of a variant record be fixed when the instance is declared or allocated.

Dynamic Typing. Two ways that object types can be varied during program execution have significantly different consequences. The two possibilities are as follows:

1. An object's type is fixed when the object is (dynamically) created.
2. An object's type may vary during the lifetime of the object.

There is no problem with giving the compiler the responsibility for correct implementation of operations on objects whose type is fixed when they are created and never varying during their lifetimes. The second possibility, however, raises grave difficulties, including the fact that program errors due to type misuse cannot be blamed on the compiler. Rather, the responsibility lies completely on the programmer. Despite the advantages of static typing, limited usage of dynamic typing may be attractive; the simplest case is an array with dynamic dimensions, which is convenient for declaring a temporary local array for use within a procedure. The array's dimensions are fixed when the object is allocated. The implementation stores the actual dimensions and consults them as required.

Example 5-5

In ALGOL60, a dynamic array can be declared as a local object; its dimensions are evaluated during the procedure's prolog and appropriate space allocated at that time. Using Ada-like syntax, a procedure header might look like

```
procedure f( a, n : integer ) is
    b : array( n, n );              --not Ada or C++
```

The current value of n will be needed to compute the one-dimensional index of an array element. If that value had been static, it could have been placed in the program as an immediate value. But when it is not known to the compiler, the value will have to be read from a data object when the index computation is required.

An implementation of arrays with dynamic dimensions can be built without any other features of parameterized structures or parameterized classes.

Overloaded Operators. To determine the semantics of an operator, it is essential to know the types of the operands, so one needs to know the binding between an object and its type. The function's name or symbol designates the function to be performed. But if the function name is overloaded, the vector of operand types must be considered part of the operation's name.[4]

Visibility and Scope Rules for Objects and Classes. The object visibility rules discussed in Section E.2.3 apply equally to class definitions. If static nesting is used, class definitions can disappear and reappear during the execution of a single program. These changes imply not only object allocation but also initialization of static objects defined within the class. They also limit the regions

---

[4]   Suggestions for encodings applicable to C++ implementations are given in [ELLI90].

within which pointers to objects can exist, a property used in Ada to prevent dangling pointers (see Section F.3).

Comments. The reuse of object class definitions is an important tool for structuring complex programming tasks. The reuse of object type definitions appears at the hardware level, where logical module descriptions can be parameterized in a similar manner, saving design effort. Operator overloading and other concepts introduced above may affect the implementation of processor instructions.

5.1.3 Object Activity

One might view an object as a passive entity (a place holding a value that is merely the target for memory accesses or an actual parameter passed to a function or procedure) or as an active entity (which contains functions that can operate on the object itself). Our view affects how we position the implementation of the procedures that manipulate the object—is the procedure inside the object or is it separate? Of course, a realistic implementation places all procedures defined for a class within a class-level object that is shared among all instances of the class, however we choose to view the structure.

5.1.4 Associations between Operations and Operands

Static association rules bind operands with operators. We base our discussion on the options available in mathematical notation. Similar options exist at the processor instruction level, as we shall see. Programmers write expressions to specify a sequence of operations; algebraic precedence rules determine the corresponding operation–operand associations. Operation–operand associations also can be inferred from the use of functional notation to invoke an operation; in this case, parentheses determine the operation–operand associations.

To illustrate several mathematically equivalent techniques for writing and interpreting expressions, let f denote an operator with two operands x and y. If f is not commutative, the operands have different effects on the result and must be distinguished by their positions. There are three locations where f could be written (see Table 5-1).

In infix expressions with several operators, operator precedence rules and parentheses indicate the evaluation order (which amounts to defining the operation–operand associations). Both the prefix and postfix forms are unambiguous if each operator symbol implies a fixed number of operands; the expressions do not require parentheses or precedence rules. If, however, they are ambiguous, one could use parentheses or remove the ambiguity by introducing new operator symbols that do imply specific operand counts. Prefix notation is similar to

TABLE 5-1   ORDERING OPTIONS WITH TWO OPERANDS

Symbol Order	Option Name	Use in instruction
f x y	Prefix	2 registers
x f y	Infix	TOS and 1 register
x y f	Postfix	2 from TOS

functional notation, except that the parentheses used in functional notation are not present in the prefix form.

Two groupings in the symbol sequences of Table 5-1 suggest interesting interpretations of the operator and its operands. Conventional functional notation is obtained by adding parentheses to the prefix form, as in f(x, y). A second interesting variation groups the function name and its first parameter in parentheses, as in (f, x)(y); this description suggests that the function (f, x) be applied to the operand y.

Example 5-6

In the Smalltalk language [GOLD83], a request to perform a procedure is considered to be a message sent to the object that is the procedure's first parameter; the message contains the function name and the second (and subsequent) operand(s). Figure 5-2 depicts this view, showing how an object "contains" the procedures and functions of which the object can be the first parameter. The function bodies appear to exist within x, but in an implementation, all function bodies defined in one class could be collected together, as shown in the picture. The function bodies are not externally visible because they are accessed only through class pointers, as shown. In effect, the procedure's name is the pair (function_name, first_parameter).

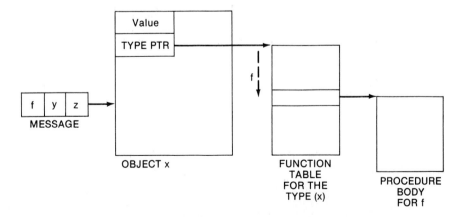

Figure 5-2   The object-oriented (Smalltalk) view of type-based procedures [calling f(x, y, z)]

Some formats place the operand names and the operator name on an equal footing within a data object that can later be performed as a program segment. For example, the LISP object (+ 5 6) expresses an addition if it is executed as a program fragment. But because this is also a data item, another program statement could make an assignment (during program execution) to the first position (where an operator name is expected) within a data structure that will be interpreted later as a program fragment. This option, which is similar to changing the function code in a processor instruction, also exists in Smalltalk.

Operand Specifications. Operands are specified by the name of the location where the operand is stored. This might be a memory location or a register. At the processor level, an implied location, such as the top of an evaluation stack, could be used, even though it does not have a specific name.

In high-level programs, object names specify memory locations, because registers and stacks are invisible implementation artifacts. In microprogrammed hosts, operands all come from registers, so they are specified by register numbers. In between (in processors, for example), all choices might be available.

5.1.5 Comments

The basic needs discussed here affect many levels of system design; the extent of the effect depends on the assignment of responsibility for correctly bounding access to object representations and for correctly implementing operations. We explore the effect of these options at the programming language and processor design levels.

5.2 HIGH-LEVEL LANGUAGES

Each programming language has a way of declaring objects and their types, often permitting the programmer to define new object classes. The details do not affect the system's architecture, though they do affect software, which assumes responsibility for correct support for the specified types and operations.

5.2.1 Classes and Types

All programs start with a few base classes from which all other objects are constructed. The implementations of the base classes are assumed correct. An expandable language permits programmer-defined classes and class-based modularization. What are our desires regarding the use of class declarations for language expansion? We wish to expand a flexible base by adding class definitions that support various applications. It should be easy to make these expansions with hierarchical modular program structures. We also wish to be able to reuse definitions without too much waste.

Class Interface Specifications.   Each class definition must specify the features that shall be visible to the outsider. These include externally visible (hereinafter called *public*) functions and procedures and may include information about the representation of objects belonging to the new class. We will not delve into the details of this software issue, simply pointing out the importance of having a clean interface and noting the types of information that need to be specified so that the interface can be used.

Representations.   Every language that allows a programmer to define new classes permits the programmer to specify the representation of an object of the new class. In some languages, such as Pascal, type definitions are limited to representation specifications and the structure of the representation is visible wherever the object is visible. This is not true in C++ and Ada, because a programmer can hide the representation by declaring it **private** or **protected**, which makes it invisible outside the definition of the class.

Dynamic Objects. Objects that are instances of classes are dynamic objects, coming and going as contexts change and objects are created and destroyed. The components of these objects are declared in C++ class definitions as **private** objects; in Ada, they appear as component of the representation, which must appear within the interface specification of the new class.

Static Objects. In C++, objects at the class level are declared **static** and must be initialized outside the class definition. In Ada, on the other hand, objects at the class level are simply declared to exist within the body of the class definition (hidden from the outside) and are automatically initialized when the class becomes visible as a consequence of entering a context within which the class definition occurs. In either Ada or C++, the representation of each individual instance of a new class can be encapsulated by declaring it to be **private**.

Summary.   One can establish class relationships to simplify class declarations and encapsulate certain semantic details. These possibilities are quite useful in high-level programming. Unfortunately, elaborate class declaration features are not available in many programming languages. Pascal, for example, permits class declarations that define object representations, but there is no facility for encapsulating these types, because their representations are visible wherever the class is visible. These structures assist programmers; a correct implementation of these features relies on the compiler.

Who is responsible for monitoring the boundaries of the encapsulation? In most schemes, the compiler is supposed to generate "correct" code to handle all operations on instances of declared classes, and is not supposed to allow one to see hidden objects or functions outside the defined boundaries.

5.2.2 Objects and Their Types

What are the consequences of strong typing? How are object types checked and their conformance enforced?

Simple strong typing occurs when the type of every object is declared within the object's declaration. The compiler uses this type information to optimize the implementation of operations; there is no run-time cost because run-time object type checks are not needed. Dynamic typing makes things difficult, as run-time checks are required to determine the actual types of objects.

Static Object–Type Associations. Each object declaration associates an object type with the object's declaration, thereby assigning a static type to the object. Like C++, most typed languages force static typing on objects, but may allow dynamic types to handle variants.

Every object–type binding scheme (except operator-based) has been used in some language. The importance of knowing object classes and of choosing correct operator variants (based on the actual operand types) cannot be overemphasized; an error may cause results that depend on the internal representation schemes—a possibility that we hope to eliminate by encapsulation so that it is not possible to write high-level language programs that exhibit representation-dependent behavior. In a weakly typed language, there exists some way to create two or more access paths to the same object (by two different names that are aliases, for example) permitting several distinct interpretations of the same bits (based on the assumed type of the object). By writing a value using one path and then reading that value using a different path, we induce representation-dependent behavior. This programming style defeats our goal of encapsulating representation choices.

Dynamic Object–Type Associations. If the association between an object and its type can vary during program execution, it will be difficult to support the strong typing illusion. Under one method, each object's representation includes type information that is checked before any operation is performed on the object. So to enforce strong typing in a system with dynamic object–type associations, one might have to pay a performance penalty.

Example 5-7

A C++ declaration of the *union* structure poses dynamic typing difficulties; a simple declaration of this dynamic type and an instance declaration looks like

```
union dynamic {
        int first_way;
        char second_way;
};
dynamic thing;
```

This fragment declares an object named thing whose type is named dynamic. There is only one component within the object, but treated as an integer if named as thing.first_way and treated as a character object if named as thing.second_way.

5.2.3 Class Specifications

We illustrate class specification techniques with a hierarchical C++ class definition as a running example. We will develop the structure of a hierarchical definition of a double-ended queue (deque) using inheritance from a definition of a single-ended queue (queue). Both queues will hold integer objects and will be implemented using a circular buffer to hold the queue's contents. Pointers to the head and tail of the queue will be required in the implementation.

Basic Structure

```
class int_queue {
public:    //The next two declare the two procedures that access the queue
    put( int new_one) {        //The queue itself is implied
        ..                          //and need not be listed as a parameter
    }
    int get( ) {            //This returns an integer; no queue parameter, as above
    }
    int_queue( ) {          //The constructor procedure
                            //A possible size parameter is omitted for simplicity
        head = tail = 0;
    }
protected:      //The following objects hold the implementation of a queue object
    int buffer[100];        //Fixed buffer size
    int head, tail;   //These indices point to empty entries delimiting the queue
    boolean full; //This removes ambiguities of the empty/full pointer patterns
};

class int_deque : public int_queue {  //Declares the inheritance;
                            //makes the functions in int_queue available here
public:     //The following adds two new functions for the reverse operations
    reverse_put( int new ) {
    }
    int reverse_get( ) {
    }
}
```

We will add to this template in the following; this skeleton omits the implementations of the procedures and functions. It shows that the representation of an int_queue object is hidden from outsiders; they cannot access the either head or tail pointers or the contents of the buffer holding the queue's contents. The components of int_queue are marked **protected** to permit them to be seen within any class that inherits from the int_queue class, yet to remain invisible outside these class definitions.

Basic Operations.   Our example shows a skeleton to which specialized operations, which are written as conventional procedures, can be added. The standard operations (create, destroy, copy, and equality_test) must be studied, and might require special declarations, as described in what follows.

Creation and Destruction Operations.   The creation operation is invoked whenever an object is created if its class definition specifies a creation operation. In C++, the creation operation is called a *constructor*, and its name is the same as the type name; the static declaration

```
int_queue new_queue;
```

causes invocation of the function int_queue() when the object is allocated. Similarly, a call to **new** int_queue will invoke the constructor. If the type definition is parameterized, the object declaration or **new** call must specify the actual parameter values defining the new instance.

Destructor procedures never require parameters, because the object being destroyed is self-describing. In C++, the destructor function is named by the type name preceded by a tilde, as in ~int_queue(). In our simple queue example, a special destruction operation is not required. All constructor and destructor procedures must satisfy the class's integrity constraints.

Copy Operations.   Object copying might involve a simple replication of the contents of the representation objects, but if it requires more than that, a function overloading the assignment operator must be defined. Within the equality testing discussion, we illustrate how the name can be specified. In general, object copying will require more than simple replication if the integrity constraint for the class involves a set of objects.

Equality_Test Operations.   Like copying, in some simple object classes, equality testing can be implemented by comparing the bits within the representations of two instances of the class. In our queue example, however, equality should mean that the two queues contain the same objects in the same order. Thus, a bit match between the contents is sufficient for equality, but not necessary. We need to overload the equality test operator with a new function. Here is a specification of the function, without its implementation:

```
int int_queue::operator== (const int_queue &right) {
    ..
}
```

We pass in the right operand as the single parameter; the left operand is an implied parameter (in the style of Smalltalk). The components of the implied parameter can be named without any explicit object name part. For example, to test whether the two queues in the equality_test body have identical head pointers, we write

```
head == right.head
```

5.2.4 Translation

The compiler and linker are responsible for correct implementation of the operations and the object-type bindings specified in the program. In addition, the compiler may try to optimize the implementation of the program. This process will introduce problems if the programmer worked from assumptions not shared with the compiler.

The compiler's code generator makes choices that can affect the execution speed. One technique reorders instructions that evaluate an expression. One problem with this technique arises from the semantics of the operations: a reordering that appears to be functionally neutral[5] may change the result values if the actual operators (1) have side effects or (2) do not satisfy the mathematical properties assumed to make the reordering functionally neutral (these properties include associativity, commutativity, and distributivity). Another set of problems arises from the limited precision of the finite representations of object values. We illustrate these problems with examples.

Example 5-8

Consider evaluating the Boolean expression "f(x) or g(y)" in which functions f and g return boolean results. From Boolean algebra, we know that the expression will be true if f(x) is true, independent of the value of g(y). Thus, we could avoid evaluating g(y) if we knew that f(x) were true. To save execution time, an optimizing compiler might produce a program that evaluates the general form

```
a or b
```

as follows:

```
if a then true else b
```

This is an example of the "short-circuit" evaluation strategy: the evaluation proceeds only as long as necessary to determine the expression's value. Under the short-circuit version, b might not be evaluated. This omission is acceptable if b has no side effects. But suppose that g(y) does have a side effect: it writes a new value

---

[5]   We say that a change is functionally neutral if it does not change the value of the eventual result.

into the location "side." Under the short-circuit evaluation, this write from g(y) would not occur if f(x) happened to be true. Thus, although the evaluation of the logical expression was correct, the overall result of the executing the expression was changed when g(y) was bypassed.

We cannot, unfortunately, rule out side effects; file manipulation programs exist to cause side effects in the file system. In Prolog (see Appendix H), all changes to the contents of variables occur as side effects of functions. Further, the occurrences of exceptions are side effects. It is certainly true that structured programming advocates abhor side effects, but exceptions and the file system example illustrate that side effects cannot be abolished at all implementation levels.

Representation Limits. Other problems arise because all object representations use a finite number of bits and cannot convey arbitrary accuracy.

Example 5-9

How do we compute the value of tan(120000)? The major problem is that we have to remove all multiples of 2π from the argument, which requires carrying many significant digits so that the result will be meaningful. If you tried to estimate the value of this quantity using interval arithmetic, you would have a big problem. Possibly all that you can say is that the result is a real number.

Mathematical Property Violations. Another problem with compiler optimization concerns violation of the assumed associative, commutative, and distributive properties by overloaded operator definitions. It is easy to construct an example illustrating this point—one simply overloads an associative arithmetic operator with one that is not associative.

Finally, a rearrangement by the compiler for optimization may introduce problems if the actual arithmetic operations do not obey their ideal mathematical properties. For example, an operator might not commute or associate if the actual operand values push beyond the limitations imposed by the representation conventions.

Example 5-10

In the following program fragment, suppose that all objects hold floats, whose representation conventions impose value limits to the value range 10^{-40} .. 10^{40}.

```
a = 10¹²;
b = 10⁻²⁵;
c = 10⁻²⁵;
d = a * b * c;
```

Mathematically, the product could be evaluated in any order, because multiplication is both commutative and associative. Evaluation in the order (a * b) * c gives the correct result. However, in an evaluation corresponding to a * (b * c), the first multiplication causes underflow and the final result will be incorrect. This illustrates that arithmetic operators do not associate when an intermediate value lies outside the range of values permitted by the representation conventions.

Notice that reversing the values of a and c reverses the consequences: The first ordering produces underflow and the second gives the correct result. Without foreknowledge of the approximate values assumed by the operands, the optimizer cannot choose an evaluation order that will give correct results every time.

In conclusion, the compiler may inadvertently change the program's results as it tries to reduce the program's execution time by rearranging the evaluation order. This effect may occur if program procedures have side effects or if the assumed mathematical properties are not satisfied; it can be eliminated only by eliminating optimization.

5.2.5 Comments

In this short survey of type specification and definition options within high-level languages, we saw how one can specify both the interfaces and implementations of new object types. By using special keywords, one can define encapsulations around the type definitions and the instances of the new object types. This leads one to question how these boundaries are enforced, and how the object-type associations are enforced within the implementation. Many systems rely on correct compilation, but others perform dynamic tests to find object types and then to choose the appropriate implementation. We now explore these questions at the processor level.

5.3 PROCESSOR LEVEL

There is little object type selection at the processor level, unless the designer is free to define support for new types or to add functional units, modules, or coprocessors to support new object types. In this section, we emphasize the options for expanding beyond the limitations of a "standard" instruction set and its implementation in standard ways. This support can take several forms, including the following:

1. Support for type module boundaries
2. Variations in object size
3. Variations in value-encoding schemes
4. Variations in operand location specification
5. Operations that depend on the types of their operands
6. Adding special operations to support certain object types

All operations within a computer are built up from the basic operations provided within the instruction set. We know that integer subtraction is logically

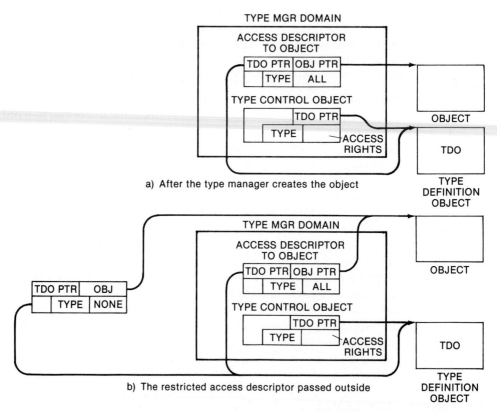

Figure 5-3   (a, b) An Intel iAPX432 type manager creates and uses an object

sufficient, but choosing it as the only operation certainly does not give an efficient system! Conventional designs support the four basic arithmetic operations on integers, and possibly on float objects. Some designs have eliminated division for two reasons: (1) it is not executed frequently and (2) it is almost impossible to speed its execution except by implementing it as a series of multiplications that obtain a successive approximation to the quotient. In general, one can implement frequently executed operations in a manner tuned for speedy execution, allowing less frequent operations to move more slowly.

5.3.1 General Type Support

Support for general programmer-defined classes is difficult to provide at the processor level. However, a processor can be designed to enforce boundaries around the class implementation.

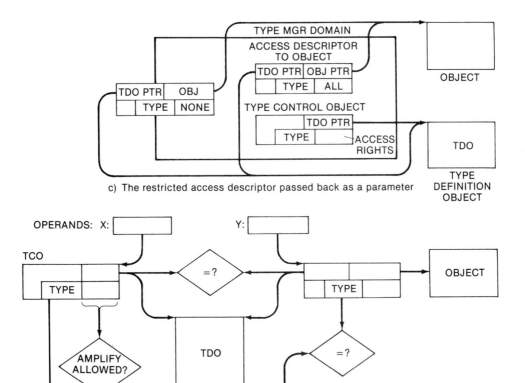

c) The restricted access descriptor passed back as a parameter

d) The manager expanding the rights. (Diamonds indicate validity checks that must succeed to amplify the rights.)

Figure 5-3   (c, d) An Intel iAPX432 type manager creates and uses an object

Example 5-11

The Intel iAPX 432 accesses objects through storage descriptors. Every object has a type, encoded within the object descriptor, which also contains a pointer to a type description object (if the type is user-defined) and a pointer to the space containing the object's representation. One type of object is a type manager, a module including the implementations of the functions defined for the new type.

A type manager can create a new instance (of the type it manages) by executing the processor instruction CREATE_TYPED_OBJECT, which returns a descriptor of the (uninitialized) new object.[6] One operand of this operation is a descriptor of the type object. The conditions after the typed object has been created are depicted in Figure 5-3a. Before releasing a descriptor of the object, the type manager copies the

---

[6]   A similar operation creates a "refinement," which is a subpart of a complete object, and assigns it a type. This important feature permits the type manager to collect a set of representation objects into a single storage segment, thereby saving memory allocation overhead.

descriptor and then executes the RESTRICT_ACCESS_RIGHTS instruction to restrict the holder of the copy from direct access to the object; Figure 5-3b shows the restricted descriptor that can be passed outside the type manager's domain. This restricted descriptor encapsulates the representation of the object itself, so it can be held, copied, and passed around as a procedure parameter outside the type manager without revealing the composition of the object.

A program outside the type manager can copy the restricted descriptor and eventually can ask that an operation be performed on the object. At this point, the program passes the restricted descriptor back to the type manager as an argument. Figure 5-3c illustrates the arrival of the restricted descriptor within the type manager. The manager takes the restricted descriptor and amplifies its rights. This should be possible only if it is the proper type manager, which is determined by testing whether the manager wishing to expand the access rights also holds the type description object for the type of the object described by the restricted descriptor. The amplification is obtained by executing the AMPLIFY_RIGHTS instruction, which has two operands: the descriptor to be amplified and the type control object pointing to the type definition object (see Figure 5-3d). The amplified descriptor gives the type manager access to the representation (which was not available outside the package); with this access, it can manipulate the representation to perform the requested function.

Other processor designs do not enforce boundaries around user-defined type definitions at this basic level, relying on correct compilation to ensure boundary enforcement.

5.3.2 Object Representations

Choosing the representation of data objects affects the difficulty of manipulating the objects; choosing the instruction representation affects decoding complexity and speed. Therefore, both choices affect the system's speed.

Object Sizes. Most contemporary processors have word lengths that are powers of 2. In the past, before ASCII character codes became the standard, several manufacturers used 6-bit character codes. Then the desire for compatibility among several types led to an interesting conjecture regarding the processor word length: In any "interesting" machine, the word length can be expressed as $2^n 3^m$, for n an integer, and m an integer in the range 0..2. The multiplier is a power of 2 so that every character can be given an easily interpreted address at a character granularity. Table 5-2 lists the word and character sizes of several machines.

An occasional design permits a limited set of integer widths. Usually, a designer's representation choices are limited by compatibility requirements, related to previous system designs and the desire for internal consistency among representations of various classes.

TABLE 5-2 WORD AND CHARACTER SIZES
FOR SOME INTERESTING MACHINES

	Size (bits)	
Machine	Word	Character
PDP-8	12	6
PDP-11, VAX	16	8
MC68000	16	8
PDP-1	18	6
B 1700	24	4, 6, 8
MC680x0 (x > 0)	32	8
IBM 370	32	8
IBM 704, 7094	36	6
B 5700	48	6, 8
CDC 6600	60	6
All CRAY	64	—
Alpha AXP	64	8

Example 5-12

The B 1700 processor supports arithmetic and logical operations on operands of any width between 1 and 24 bits. The width for each operation is taken from the processor's FL (field length) register. The objective was to make this design a good emulator for any processor architecture that the designer of a soft machine might devise.

A related width design question concerns the widths of objects that can be passed between the processor and the memory in both LOAD and STORE operations and as immediate values for other operations. Table 5-3 lists these widths for a variety of processors. The widths that are not a power of 2 are widths of

TABLE 5-3 OBJECT WIDTHS IN THE
PROCESOR–MEMORY INTERFACE

Machine	Widths (bits)
Intel x86	8, 16
MC680x0	3, 8, 16, 32
B 5700	8, 16, 48
Power PC601	8, 16, 32, 64
Alpha AXP	64
SPARC-V9	8, 13, 16, 32, 64

TABLE 5-4   REPRESENTATIONS OF
NONSTANDARD "VALUES" IN THE IEEE
STANDARD FLOAT FORMAT

	Representation	
Type	Exponent	Fraction
Infinity	Maximum	0
NaN	Maximum	$\neq 0$
Zero	0	0

immediate values taken from instruction words; typically, they are zero- or sign-extended.

Value Encoding. The conventional representation decision for integer objects chooses a two's complement encoding for signed values, with few exceptions.

Example 5-13

The MC680x0 design allows a 3-bit instruction field to hold coded integer values for the "Quick" instructions (that include this short value field). Because there is little use for a zero operand, the field is interpreted as eight when it contains zero. All integers in these quick instructions are positive.

However, some major exceptions occur with integers appearing in fields within float objects. Here we use a biased encoding for the exponent part and sign/magnitude encoding for the mantissa part (in the IEEE standard scheme [IEEE85]). The IEEE standard specifies representations for the three special values listed in Table 5-4. The "not a number" (NaN) case can be used in various ways; it could denote an uninitialized operand or the result of meaningless arithmetic operations, such as subtracting infinity from itself. Every zero is taken to be a positive number. Infinity can have either sign, indicated by the sign bit. The rules governing arithmetic define special cases for infinite and NaN operands; additional logic in the implementation detects these special cases and forces the results specified in the standard (which would not be computed by conventional arithmetic algorithms).

5.3.3 Associations between Operations and Operands

Each instruction is an operator, complete with object selectors, specifying the source(s) of the operand(s) and the destination(s) of the result(s). At this level, many implementation mechanisms are visible, so that the operand or result locations might be chosen from registers, the evaluation stack, and addressable memory, within limitations imposed by the processor design, which may be oriented toward one of these viewpoints. In a traditional design, the role of each named operand is determined by its location within the instruction.

Operand Specification Options.   A processor design may emphasize a stack or uses registers to hold operands of basic manipulation instructions, such as ADD and AND. RISC processor designs, using load/store architectures for speed, restrict operand sources and destinations to registers. Processors like the MC680x0 and the Intel ix86 series use registers, but permit other addressing modes so that operands or results can come from memory locations. In contrast, the B 5700 series uses stack operand and result locations exclusively. The Intel iAPX 432 system permits many options; a field within the instruction specifies the types of source and destination locations. These few examples do not show all options; in fact, practically all combinations of types of operand locations coupled with the location of the operand's specification can be found in some machine. Many possible combinations have only academic interest, such as starting with an address from the top of the stack that points to a descriptor of the operand which, in turn, is in memory.

Usually there is a direct correspondence between the location of an operand's specification and the operand's role in the operation; this correspondence is fixed by the function code. A more elaborate scheme allowing great flexibility in this regard is provided in the Intel iAPX 432.

Example 5-14

In each iAPX 432 instruction, the format field specifies which operands are accessed on the stack or through an operand addressing specification, and which operand specifications assume which roles (as both an operand and a result location).[7] With one operand/result, there are two possibilities (stack or addressed memory). With two operand/results, there are five combinations (see Table 5-5). Note the special case with both references made to the same memory address; this is useful for replacing an operand with the result (as in x = −x;).

Uncertain Register–Memory Associations.   The compiler can eliminate unnecessary stores and loads (to speed program execution) if it can recognize that the contents of a named object that is assigned to a memory location can be assigned to a register. Under this simple optimization method, the compiler changes all accesses that would make reference to the memory object into accesss to the register that is holding the object. One can say that the object has been *allocated* to the register for some portion of the program's execution interval. Clearly, making an allocation of this type will reduce the program's execution time.

---

[7]   There are no register options because this processor does not have any programmer-visible registers.

TABLE 5-5 OPERAND SPECIFICATION
POSSIBILITIES IN THE iAPX 432—AN INSTRUCTION
WITH TWO OPERANDS OR RESULTS

First Operand or Result	Second Operand or Result
Stack	Stack
Stack	Memory
Memory	Stack
Memory	Same memory location
Memory	Memory

It is a simple matter to devise algorithms that allocate objects to registers, *provided* that the memory locations that correspond to objects can be ascertained by the compiler. Difficulties arise if the object–memory associations cannot be determined before program execution. For example, references to vector components whose indices are variables introduce uncertainty about the corresponding memory locations. The compiler, not knowing which memory location might be denoted by a[i] and a[j], will have to assign these two to different registers, just in case i != j. But if i = j, the two should hold the same value, since they are both surrogates for the same memory object.

Example 5-15

A simple translation of this program fragment uses registers as surrogates for memory locations:

```
a[i] = 3;        LOAD    #3,D3    //D3 is surrogate for a[i]
a[j] = a[i];     MOVE    D3,D4    //D4 is surrogate for a[j]
a[i] = 6;        LOAD    #6,D3
x = a[j];        MOVE    D4,X
```

This translation does not work correctly if i = j, because the result stored in X should be 6 in that case, whereas it would be 3 after this fragment completes execution. To correct this possibility, the compiler will have to handle every ambiguous memory reference by inserting instructions that store every new value into the corresponding memory location, and fetch it back from that location. The extra instructions are not necessary if the compiler can determine that the correct value is still in the surrogate register (which will be the case when the references are not ambiguous).

In the sample fragment, the instructions corresponding to the first statement must store the new value into the memory location holding a[i], but the program does not have to fetch that object from memory to make the second assignment, since it is obvious that the correct value is present in D3. Similarly, the values stored during the execution of each of the first three statements have to be stored to memory, and the memory value has to be used in the fourth statement. These observations give the following memory referencing pattern:

```
LOAD    #3,D3
MOVE    D3,a[i]
MOVE    D3,D4
MOVE    D4,a[j]
LOAD    #6,D3
MOVE    D3,a[i]
MOVE    a[j],D4    //must reference memory, since the address is uncertain
MOVE    D4,X
```

One might improve program speed if one could reduce the need for these extra memory references when they are not actually required. This improvement requires runtime checks to determine whether two registers are acting as surrogates for the same memory location. Hardware checks can be accomplished after modifying the processor register to hold both the value and the address of the memory location for which the register is currently acting as a surrogate. The modification creates a *c-reg* (cache register). Special processor instructions can be added to load and store the contents of c-regs when necessary, and to replace the memory access with simple register copying when the surrogate addresses of two or more registers actually match. In the example, a processor with c-regs would store the updated value into D4 during the third statement, since D4 and D3 are surrogates for the same memory location. Details of this design approach are presented in [DAHL95].

5.3.4 Overloading; Type Dependence

How does the processor know the type associated with each object so it can be manipulated correctly? In a conventional design, operand-type information is implied by the function code in each instruction that manipulates the object. However, other design options have been used, ranging from tagging objects with type information to placing type information along the access path reaching to the object.

Operation Code Implies Operand Type.   In conventional designs, the function code specifies the operand types. Each operand is simply a set of bits, and the way that the bits are interpreted is determined by the function code.

Example 5-16

The Power PC601 instruction set contains three ADD instructions:

```
add     (add integers)
fadd    (add double-precision floats)
fadds   (add single-precision floats)
```

Thus, in this design, the operand types are conveyed within the function code.

The object type information implied by the function code will be assumed correct if the compiler has been assigned the responsibility got supporting the strong typing illusion.

Object Type Associated with the Object. If the system design does not obtain object types from the function code, the object type information must be associated with the objects themselves. Various type specification methods have been used in processor designs:

1. Types in object tags
2. Types in descriptors
3. Types limited by object location

An additional option, not discussed here, is that each object contains some type information that supplements the information specified by one of the methods just listed. The major example of this style is the use of discriminants to specify variant structure types and/or the size(s) of dynamically dimensioned arrays. These aspects are not apparent, however, at the level of processor instructions, because in most systems, correct software is required to support these variants.

Self-Identifying Objects. Tagged objects are self-identifying to the level specified by the tag encoding. If tagged objects are copied into processor registers, the tag information must be copied along with the data. This rule applies to programmer-visible registers and to invisible registers within the implementation, such as registers holding information from memory locations near the top of the stack. Value tagging in the B 5700 machines distinguishes numeric values from control objects, among numeric types, and among some classes of control objects.

Example 5-17

> In the Burroughs B 5700, the tag associated with a numeric object indicates whether the associated value is single- or double-precision.[8] The processor has one ADD instruction; its implementation determines the operand widths from their tags.[9]

This scheme has the obvious cost of providing space to hold type tag information for every item within the system; the tagging has to be at a fixed

---

[8] The processor does not support integer values; rather, the floating-point representation was chosen so that the mantissa field in the float format is interpreted as an integer with radix point at the right end. Furthermore, the exponent is encoded so that a zero in the exponent field does mean a zero exponent. Thus, if an integer value is small enough, its representation as a float is the same as its representation as a sign/magnitude integer, which is the convention chosen for the machine.

[9] A similar statement is true for subtraction, multiplication, and division.

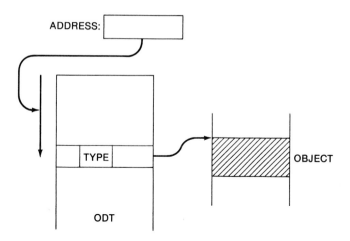

Figure 5-4   IBM AS/400 object-type information in the object definition table (ODT)

granularity, which corresponds to the granularity of the object representations. The cost of this space overhead pushes one to devise alternate schemes, such as collecting together groups of objects having the same class and then tagging the group.

Type Tags in Pointers to Memory Objects.   In processors without programmable registers, all operations are memory–memory or stack–stack. One example of this style is the iAPX 432, in which the pointer to an object contains the type code for the object. Rather than a predefined code, a pointer to the type descriptor object is used when the object's type is programmer-defined. A similar technique is used in the IBM System/38, with object-type information located in a centralized object table containing object descriptors (but there is no facility for user-defined object types).

Example 5-18

The IBM AS/400 contains object-type information in the ODT (object definition table); all computational operations are memory-to-memory. Figure 5-4 illustrates the access path to an operand leading through the ODT, where the type information is stored. Three numeric representations are supported: binary integers, packed decimal strings, and zoned decimal strings. There are two add instructions: ADDLC (unsigned) and ADDN (signed). As the processor executes these instructions, it obtains the types of both sources and the destination from the ODT to select appropriate algorithms and representation conversions.

Type Implied by Object Location.   In some designs, objects in certain locations will always be interpreted in the same manner. Specific registers, for example, hold integers, whereas others are dedicated to holding **float** objects or memory addresses.

We can extend this approach to memory and assign types to segments. The segment descriptor contains the type code describing all objects within the segment. This scheme is adequate to find the types of objects within memory.

Similar groupings of memory objects based on their type can be used to protect capabilities from unauthorized modification; these schemes are discussed in Section 9.5.1. A simple version of this scheme separates segments based on whether they contain capabilities or other data (or program) objects. A single bit is adequate to distinguish capabilities from other objects.

Comments. In a system that relies on instruction codes to specify types, the processor design is based on the "everything correct" approach, and object-type association problems do not affect the processor design. However, if type information is associated with each object, consistency dictates that all type information associated with an object must remain associated with the object throughout its existence. Thus, whenever an object is copied, its type information must maintain its association with the new copy, which may imply that the type information must also be copied. This implies that processor registers must contain type tags or be restricted to holding only objects of a single specified type, such a floats.

5.3.5 Extensions to the Operation Set

The instruction set selection does not affect functional completeness, but it can ease understanding and speed program execution. By extension, one might consider defining new processor-level operations by changing the logic or the

TABLE 5-6 SOME OPERATIONS FOR SPECIAL DATA TYPES AND SOME SPECIAL OPERATIONS FOR ORDINARY DATA TYPES

Data Type	Processor	Operations
Integers/ character strings	System/370	Binary–decimal conversion
Character strings	Mainframes	Edit
Floats	VAX 11/780	Polynomial evaluation
Decimal integers	MC680x0	Byte add/subtract
List	Symbolics 3600	(Many—see Appendix I)
Sorted list	B 5700 HP 3000	Lookup Lookup
Doubly linked lists	VAX 11/780 MC68020	Atomic insert and delete

microprogram. Likewise, changing the modular structure within the processor can enhance performance. We explore these possibilities now.

Design Special Operations in the Processor. Some processor instructions support particular object classes, without trying to encapsulate the class; thus, the instructions added to support class NC may not form a complete operation set for class NC. Rather, we aim for speed, and we might obtain a large performance improvement from encapsulating a frequently executed function in a processor instruction. Table 5-6 summarizes some representative instruction set expansions grouped by data type.

Example 5-19

The VAX 11/780 includes single- and double-precision polynomial-evaluation operations. The operands are an argument value, the degree of the polynomial, and a pointer to a memory-resident table of the polynomial's coefficients.[10] This operation utilizes processor registers R0 .. R3 (or R0 .. R5 if the instruction specifies double-precision values), and returns the result in register R0 (or the pair R0, R1). The implementation performs this algorithm (for single-precision evaluation):

```
1. R0 = 0; R2 = degree; R3 = coef_origin;
2. R1 = R0 * arg;
3. R0 = R1 + memory[R3];
4. R3 = R3 + 4;                    //4 bytes per coefficient
5. R2 = R2 - 1;
6. if ( R2 != 0 ), goto step 2;
7. R1 = 0;
```

Because it is difficult for a compiler to detect that an instruction of this type might be used to evaluate and expression, the instruction rarely appears in programs.

Example 5-20

The MC68020 provides partial support for insertion and deletion in doubly linked lists through its CAS2 instruction. For example, to insert a bead into a list, the program first reads and computes the proper values for the list update. Then the program executes CAS2. In Figure 5-5a, we see these values in the new bead about to be inserted into the list. Figure 5-5b shows the actions of CAS2 that update the doubly linked list. The final state of the queue is shown in Figure 5-5c. The instruction is valuable because it encapsulates all substitutions required to update a doubly linked list into a single uninterruptible operation sequence. Because this instruction is uninterruptible, it can be used (without other locks) to manipulate queues describing shared resources; this use of CAS2 is described in Section 8.5.4.

Contrast the MC68020's minimal list and queue support with the VAX, the AS/400, and the iAPX 432: The VAX has queue-manipulation operations that

---

[10]   The coefficients are stored in order with the coefficient of the highest power first and the constant term last.

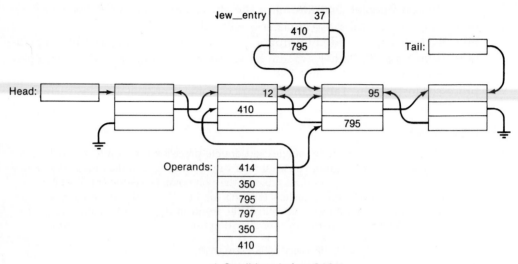

a) Conditions before CAS 2

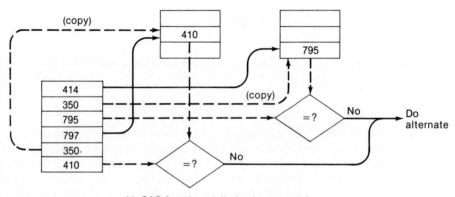

b) CAS 2 actions (all checks succeed)

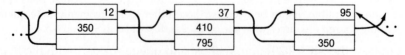

c) Conditions after CAS 2 (checks succeeded)

Figure 5-5   The MC68020 CAS2 instruction updates a doubly linked list (word width version)

both construct proper linkages and insert them. The iAPX 432 and the AS/400 queue-insertion instructions include searching the queue and finding the proper place to make the insertion, according to the discipline specified for the queue and the queue's current contents.

Example 5-21

> The VAX 11/780 has "queue"-insertion and -deletion instructions, INSQUE and REMQUE.[11] A queue is represented by a doubly linked list; the first bead entry contains the forward pointer and the second entry, the backward pointer. Both queue operations are performed with the interrupts turned off so that if there is only one processor in the system, proper synchronization can be achieved between processes that share the same queue.[12]

Example 5-22

> In the IBM AS/400, five processor operations support queue objects:
>
> > CREATE
> > DESTROY
> > ENQUEUE
> > DEQUEUE
> > COPY QUEUE DESCRIPTION
>
> This operation list encompasses the basic queue operations that one would encapsulate within the queue data class. In this system, each queue specification gives the format of the entries in the queue, including their sizes and classes. Each queue's descriptor specifies the queueing discipline, which can be LIFO, FIFO, or either of those queue classes ordered by priority. While making a queue insertion, the processor finds the proper location within the queue based on the queueing discipline (FIFO, priority, etc.) specified in the queue's description.

Customize the Instruction Set. Conventional wisdom holds that a processor's instruction set is fixed when the processor is designed and that this fixes the instruction sets of both the processor and all of its compatible successors. This is not true; it can be beneficial to modify or expand the instruction set. We explore several techniques that adjust the instruction set.

Couple Procedures to Instructions. Some processor designs allow the programmer to write a software routine and then couple it with a processor instruction. This technique can speed execution; it also gives the appearance that the processor's instruction set has been expanded by the functions available in the

---

[11]   We place the word queue in quotes because although DEC says that these operations support queues, in fact, they support doubly linked lists. We make the distinction because some expect that a queue instruction would use the queue discipline to find the spot for inserting a new entry, but here the program is charged with that task; the insert operation will do the right thing with the pointers, given the proper pointer as an operand.

[12]   We discuss synchronization of this variety in Chapter 8.

software. Logically, this scheme is identical to adding extensions to the mi-ⴸ
croprogram.

Example 5-23

> The Data General Eclipse architecture [DATA74] supports user-defined operations
> called XOPs (eXtended OPerators), implemented by software routines residing in
> user memory. During the invocation of one of the XOP operations, the following
> steps are performed:

> 1. The processor state is saved as if for procedure call;
> 2. The two effective operand addresses replace the stack locations where AC_2 and
> AC_3 were saved;
> 3. Bits 10..6 from the XOP instruction (which specify the software routine to be
>   invoked) are added to 24_{16}; call this sum S;
> 4. Transfer control to the location specified in memory location S;

> After the routine has completed execution, it executes a POP BLOCK instruction
> that removes the saved processor state from the stack, restores the stack pointer,
> and returns control to the calling context. Up to 32 new user-defined operations
> can be added in this manner.

An XOP implementation will be faster than a procedure call to perform the
operation because parameter fetching for the XOP instruction uses the built-in address evaluation mechanisms.[13]

Emulate Instructions inside the Operating System. One can expand the instruction set by adding interpretations to unused operation codes, hiding the implementations within the operating system. The execution scenario is that the
control unit interrupts program execution when it encounters the special function code value(s), and the operating system then activates the appropriate program. This technique is used in the Alpha AXP processor to implement PALcode
functions. One advantage of this approach is that the function's implementation
can be processor-specific (i.e., the code can exploit processor features that might
not be carried through all implementations of the processor family) without
changing the user's view of the processor's functions.

A possible problem with this strategy arises if the implementation assumes
that the processor turns off interrupts while the emulation program is executing.
This design can hide exceptions caused by "normal" instructions if the processor
utilizes overlapped execution to improve its performance. To eliminate this difficulty in the Alpha AXP design (which uses "PALcode" routines inside the operating system to perform some functions), a PALcode procedure will not be
initiated until it is certain that no preceding instruction will cause an exception to
be raised. This constraint satisfies the logical requirement, but the possible delay

---

[13]   A similar method can be used to add to the microprogram, but this technique is difficult to use and
the details depend upon the implementation of the particular machine model.

reduces the performance improvement expected from the overlapped execution used within the design.

Add Microcode. A microprogrammed host may be expanded by rewriting part of its microcode to support additional operations or object types. This strategy is an interesting option when the processor is not too highly overlapped. There are several problems even without overlapping, such as the fact that any changes made on behalf of a certain process must be treated as part of the state of that process. This means that this state will have to be saved and restored if the process is interrupted and rescheduled for later execution. When many activities occur simultaneously within the processor, it is difficult to write correct microcode that controls all actions.

Add Functional Units. One might want to add functional units to an existing processor design to improve the performance of existing instructions and to expand the instruction set. The first strategy is discussed (with other parallelism techniques) in Section 6.4. To expand the instruction set, one might add a functional unit within the processor to handle a new data type. This design change is similar to the addition of a coprocessor. Some processor families grow by adding functions that had been performed in a coprocessor to the processor module.

Add Coprocessors. A coprocessor encapsulates operations within a hardware module. Notice the strong resemblance between adding a coprocessor and encapsulating new object types in a class structure, but notice that encapsulation by programming requires correct programs.

Adding a coprocessor to support a new object type can make the operations involving instances of the new class more efficient. This strategy may face a limitation within the processor's instruction set—the processor might not be able to invoke operations in arbitrary coprocessors. The design of a general coprocessor interface is discussed in Section 7.8.3. Another option involves the processor with the coprocessor's details.

Example 5-24

The Intel 80x87 coprocessors support advanced arithmetic operations, including the computation of some transcendental functions and constant values of some transcendental constants such as the value of π. The coprocessor is invoked when the processor executes certain special operations that will cause traps to the operating system if the coprocessor is not present. The processor issues a single instruction to the coprocessor, which may be "busy." The coprocessor tells the processor when it thinks that the processor can continue operation along the instruction sequence. Before the main instruction sequence can invoke the coprocessor again or if there is a data dependency (see Chapter 6) between a memory operation in the coprocessor and a memory operation invoked from the main program, the main program must include a "wait" instruction. The WAIT instruction guarantees that all previous memory accesses will have been completed before the WAIT is deemed to have been finished.

Adding coprocessors offloads operations on new types from the processor, which might permit the processor to continue operating in parallel with the coprocessor's execution of a function within the type module.

One criticism of all previous schemes is that memory bandwidth demands from a coprocessor can become high if individual objects of the new type are complex and occupy many memory locations. This problem could be alleviated by storing the instances of the class within the physical module from which those objects can be accessed—in this case, the coprocessor. Allocating space within the coprocessor for the class instances increases the boundary protection within the implementation.

Combining These Options. Attractive combinations of the support options can be constructed. Basing implementation choices on the frequencies of use and the complexities of the operations can yield a good design compromise.

Example 5-25

Based on studied usage statistics, the DEC MicroVAX 32 [SUPN84] designers divide the data types into three categories for implementation in the processor chip, in the optional floating-point chip, and in conventional routines invoked from interrupt handler software (called "macrocode" in their paper). The assignment of the loci of support for each data type is tabulated in Table 5-7.

The usage statistics and the microprogram sizes for this design are summarized in Table 5-8. Notice that the space required for the microcode itself is reduced to 20%, yet less than 2% of the instructions executed (counted on a dynamic basis) by the processor cannot be executed from the processor's microcode. To approximate the performance loss, one must know the execution times of the instructions in question and the performance penalty for execution of an instruction outside the microprogram. The MicroVAX designers provided some performance assists within the chip's instruction set, thereby reducing the time penalty for execution outside the microcode to a factor of 4. The overall performance degradation amounted to 4%.

Detect Instruction Sequences. One might design logic to detect and speed the execution of common instruction sequences. This possibility may be attractive because the compiler's code generator generates a fixed pattern of instruction codes every time a particular language construct appears in the program.[14] Procedure calling, for example, translates into a fixed pattern, including standard algorithms for parameter evaluation, state saving, and stack

---

[14]   This describes the pattern prior to code optimization. But the code optimizer may preserve the type of code patterns that we are describing.

TABLE 5-7   MICROVAX 32 TYPE SUPPORT

Data Type	Means of Support			
	Host	Microcode	Optional Chip[a]	Macrocode
Byte integer	x			
Word integer	x			
Longword integer	x			
Quadword integer		x		
Variable bit field		x		
Variable character		x		
String		x		
Float (d-format)			x	
Float (f-format)			x	
Float (g-format)			x	
Float (h-format)				x
Octaword integer				x
Leading separate				x
Trailing numeric				x
Packed decimal				x

[a] If the chip is not present, these types are supported by macrocode.
Source: Based on data from [SUPN84]; © 1984, IEEE.

management. An effective address computation follows another template. These patterns may occur so frequently that it may be worthwhile to detect the occurrence of the pattern and perform the whole pattern more quickly by executing a special sequence of operations.

TABLE 5-8   MICROVAX INSTRUCTION STATISTICS

Percentage of Instances Based On	Locus of Implementation		
	Processor	Optional Chip	Macrocode
Static instruction count	57.6	23.0	19.4
Static microinstruction count	20.0	20.0	60.0
Dynamic microinstruction count	98.1	1.7	0.2

Source: [SUPN84], Table 2; © 1984, IEEE

Example 5-26

In the B 7700 processor, subscripted component selection (supporting access to objects with names like A[X]) is handled by a sequence of program operations. For loading the component's value, the sequence is

```
VALUECALL X
NAMECALL A
INDEX_AND_LOAD_VALUE
```

The index quantity is pushed onto the top of the stack by the first instruction. Then the common instruction sequence begins. The step pushing X is not included in the common instruction sequence because that subscript might have been computed by preceding instructions. The B 7700 processor's control unit detects this common sequence of two function codes, executing it as a single indexed load sequence. Time is saved in several ways, partly because the single indexed load avoids some mutually canceling top-of-stack manipulations inherent in a sequential execution of the two instructions.

Could the program fragment in the previous example be speeded up by introducing a new processor instruction? Certainly a new instruction would do the job. But introducing an instruction makes the new processor incompatible with previous models, and any program compiled for the previous model would not benefit from the speedup. Another difficulty blocking this option for the B 7700 design is that there is no space in the instruction encodings where one could encode a new operation containing an operand address unless one doubled the instruction length while using an extended instruction code. This change would make the program just as long as the version for the B 5700, so the only savings would occur through shortening the execution sequences.

5.3.6 Comments

Conventional implementations of processor operations were not covered because they are covered elsewhere. Interesting modifications to the processor's capabilities include extensions of the instruction set and varying operand widths. The processor can be designed to support class encapsulation and to enforce object–type associations.

Although it is appealing to promote complicated operations to processor instructions, there is an inherent incompatibility with RISC processor designs, in that most RISC pipelines and execution controllers are designed with the assumption that every processor operation can be performed with at most one memory reference. For this reason, any operation that requires several memory references will have to be moved to a coprocessor or a separate module within the processor, but outside the pipeline structure. A separate sequencer may be needed to control the operation.

Efficient implementations of basic operations rely on parallelism. Many techniques, including pipelining and overlapped execution, enhance performance; they are discussed in Chapter 6.

5.4 SUMMARY

Strong object typing and encapsulated class definitions can enhance program clarity and ease the implementation of operand manipulations. Class definitions can be reused to build hierarchical class definitions.

The value representation choice affects the ease of object manipulation. At high levels, a convenient representation may shorten programs; at the host machine level, the representation choice may produce the following types of savings:

1. Fewer logic gates (reducing complexity)
2. Reduced delay through the computational logic (speeding operations)
3. Improved memory accessing patterns (affecting caching efficiency)
4. Parallel or pipelined implementations become possible

Before an operation can be performed, several bindings must be made: a type to an object, an operation to a combination of operand classes, and the operation to its operands. These bindings may all be made during compilation and linking (as in Ada) or deferred until runtime. The timing of this binding determines the responsibility for supporting the strong typing illusion; if the type is not known, it cannot be enforced. And once it is enforced, say, by the compiler, the type information disappears from the object representation, and cannot be checked later.

Processor designs can be slanted toward certain languages and related object representations. A careful operand representation choice can save both memory space and processing time; this effect influenced the design of the Symbolics 3600 machines (see Appendix I), with, among other features, a special representation for a common list configuration.

A basic difficulty with building complex operations to support new object classes is that a RISC-style pipelined design is not compatible with instructions that require more than a single memory reference to access a data object.

There are several ways to speed program execution by changing the order of operations, the object representation technique, or by introducing parallelism. Special attention should be paid to frequently executed operations, because a great performance benefit can be obtained from speeding these operations.

Numerous parallelism techniques can further speed processors; they are presented in Chapters 6 through 8.

5.5 TRENDS

Software reuse and structuring techniques will lead to increasing use of object-oriented programming, which means that more programs will use class definitions built up in inheritance-based structures. But one should be careful to keep this trend in perspective, because there is little value in overlooking the reality of the basic operations and capabilities of the processor itself.

Under the current trend, RISC processor designs incorporate modules supporting common data types such as floats, without any low-level support for new class definitions. Activities that used to be implemented in coprocessors will migrate toward the processor for two fundamental reasons: (1) considerable delay is incurred in sending a signal off the processor chip, and (2) the growing number of active devices that can be placed in a single chip (a consequence of technological improvements) makes it easy to fit added functionality into the processor chip.

The responsibility for implementation correctness and class boundary enforcement will stay within compilers and code optimizers.

5.6 CONCEPT LIST

1. Static and dynamic object–type binding
2. Strong typing
3. Class specifications
4. Class encapsulation
5. Class-level components
6. Overloaded procedures
7. Standard procedures and the need to overload them
8. Functional specifications of procedures by implementation
9. Specification by effect
10. Integrity constraints
11. Class inheritance
12. Parameterized classes and structures
13. Operand–operator associations
14. Prefix, infix, and postfix notation
15. Object constructors and destructors
16. Discord between programmer assumptions and compiler reality
17. Contraction and expansion of access rights
18. Type-based implantation of processor instructions
19. Special operations for special object types
20. Instructions implemented by the operating system
21. Coprocessor instructions for new object types

5.7 PROBLEMS

5-1. Draw a picture illustrating two logically different paths reaching to an object x. Designate a place for type information in a location along each path to the object.

   (a) How can type consistency be assured if x is a local automatic object?

   (b) How can type consistency be checked if x is a component of a local automatic record? What if x is in a statically allocated record?

   (c) What part of the system bears the responsibility for correct type checking in each case? Explain.

5-2. In Section 5.1.4, we presented the option that object type information be found along the path to a storage object. Two designers argue about the semantics of the STORE operation in a register-based processor which uses this design option. Designer A argues that object type information should be specified by the class declaration in the high-level language; therefore, the type information along the access path to the object governs the representations that can be stored in the location. As a consequence, during the execution of a STORE operation, the value representation may have to be changed to conform to the destination's type designation. Designer B argues that the type of the value held in the processor register should govern the type actually stored. After all, she argues, the transformation proposed by designer A could destroy information that might fit into the destination location. Therefore, she continues, it is better to change the type information along the access path than to change the representation of the information. Any subsequent operation that needs the specified value can change its representation, if that seems to be necessary, she concludes.

   (a) Specify the behavior of the STORE operation under each option.

   (b) Discuss these two arguments with respect to compatibility with a C++ program.

   (c) Designer C argues that although it might be fine to store the value exactly as it was computed, without type constraints that result may be larger than the operands, and thus performing a sequence of operations on the values without any representation changes just makes the representations longer and longer. Discuss this argument in relation to the points claimed by designers A and B.

   (d) Which approach to the STORE operation do you recommend? Why?

5-3. It might be argued that there is little point to making the type tags on values so large that all classes could be designated by the tag value alone. Rather, the set of classes could be divided into class groups, such that a particular operation performed on an object of any class within class group A always produces a result having a type that belongs in class group A. For example, it might make sense to separate arithmetic values from bit strings because the result of performing arithmetic is never typed as a bit string and one never performs logical operations on numeric quantities.[15] The proposal continues with the suggestion that the function code of a processor instruction imply the class groups of the operands and the result; the tag information associated with the individual values would be used to identify a particular class within the class group.

---

[15]   Do not consider logical masking to extract field contents because such operations expose the encoding and representation that we are trying to encapsulate within the operation implementations.

(a) We wish to design an extension of the MC68020 processor that handles tagged values following the encoding scheme proposed before. To this end, divide the object classes supported by the MC68020 processor into groups so that the number of object tag bits is reduced. (*Hint*: Follow the separation rules suggested before.)

(b) List the arithmetic and logical operations that manipulate object values (not simply copying them). Construct a set of lists with tuples of class groups as list labels. A typical list label might be (arithmetic, arithmetic, arithmetic), where the first two entries represent the two class groups of operand classes and the last represents the class group of the result class. Place each arithmetic and logical MC68020 operation into the list corresponding to the combination of its class groups.

(c) Discuss how lists constructed by following the previous procedure could be used to find a smaller instruction set that encompasses all operations of a general machine. (Your answer should not be specific to the MC68020.)

5-4. Discuss the following argument: A processor-level object-manipulation architecture in which all operands and results are located in memory closely resembles the high-level language view. We also know that processors using operand registers can operate more quickly than those without registers, because memory accesses are not required to access operands and store results. But caching memory information is just like placing it in registers. Thus, caching memory objects is adequate for implementing high-level language functions efficiently while supporting an illusion of memory-to-memory object processing.

5-5. Complete the implementation of the int_deque class by giving correct procedure bodies. Use the operations available for the int_queue class whenever possible without ruining efficiency.

5-6. One way to define a new class in terms of an old class uses the notion of *value restriction*. Under this scheme, the objects in the new class have the same representation scheme and the same operations apply, *but* the range of possible values is restricted. In Ada, for example, one can define a new "subtype" as follows:

subtype ten_only **is** integer **range** 0 .. 9;

(a) Discuss the claim that there is advantage to this restriction with respect to space occupancy.

(b) Discuss the contrary claim that any attempt to enforce the restriction will slow the program excessively.

(c) Can you think of any way to modify the implementation to reduce the cost of range checking? Explain.

5-7. Define a class for a procedure_table data type for use in a C++ compiler that supports overloaded procedure definitions. A procedure_table object will be searched to find the appropriate entry point for a call to an overloaded procedure name. Your answer should be structured so that overloaded procedure names with different numbers of arguments and different combinations of argument classes will be handled correctly.

(a) Define the interface to a procedure_table class designed to encapsulate the procedure_table data class.

(b) When are entries added to the table?

(c) How is the table used to find the proper program to execute for each call?

(d) Comment on the viability of using this approach in a C++ compiler.

5-8. A processor designer proposes reducing the number of program bits required to specify a given algorithm by redesigning the instructions so that there is only a single processor instruction. The proposed instruction has four parameters:

> r: an integer selecting a processor register;
> i, j, k: addresses of words in memory.

Each instruction occupies a single word, which is the granularity of memory addressing. The execution of the instruction (r, i, j, k) has the following effects:

1. Subtract the contents of memory location i from the contents of register r.
2. Place the result of step 1 in both register r and memory location j.
3. If the result computed in step 1 was negative, jump to memory location k.

(a) The designer makes two claims:

1. The design is logically complete.
2. The design actually does save program bits.

Discuss these claims. Do you expect them to be true? Explain.

(b) Would your answers be changed if the direction of the subtraction in step 1 were reversed?

5-9. A designer wishes to support in the processor instruction set objects that are singly linked lists linked in increasing order of a (single) key value. In addition to the linked list lookup instruction (discussed in Example F-15), she proposes to add bead insertion and deletion operations.

(a) Specify these insertion and deletion operations, based on the B 5700 list format used for its linked list lookup instruction.

(b) Discuss the advantages and disadvantages of the proposal.

(c) Another designer proposes to speed linked list insertion and deletion by designing processor control logic to detect sequences of processor instructions that correspond to performing these list operations. The idea is to avoid generating intermediate results. Discuss, but do not implement, this suggestion; just compare this proposal with the proposed instruction set expansion.

5-10. Consider the queue insertion operations in Example 5-21. The queue's header is always present, through all manipulations of the queue, though its contents can change. The other beads in the queue are dynamic, and may be deleted at any time. Furthermore, a process can be interrupted at any time, with control passing to another process under control of the operating system's scheduler module. Considering these possibilities, comment on the difference between the VAX queue insertion operation and the MC68020 CAS2 instruction (see Example 5-20).

5-11. Write an algorithm for the AS/400's queue insertion operation when the list is ordered by priority (see Example 5-22). Define a bead format that contains an integer object in addition to the priority value used to order the list. If there are several beads with the same priority value, they should appear in FIFO order.

5-12. Under the Smalltalk view, a call to an overloaded function generates a message sent to the first operand containing the function name and its parameter list. A designer proposes an alternate design in which function calling is implemented by sending a similar message to the last operand (chosen because it would be on the top of the operand stack). Discuss the proposal, citing any advantages or disadvantages you can find.

5-13. For each of the three approaches listed in Section 5.3.4, write a description of a single add operator that will handle all combinations of integer and float operands. You should have three descriptions in your answer.

5-14. To speed the determination of the proper implementation of an overloaded operation, a designer proposes adding a cache within the processor. The cache entries would contain entries from the mapping

$$(\text{function\_name, operand\_type\_vector}) \rightarrow \text{entry\_address}$$

(a) Describe the role of the cache in the execution of a high-level function call.
(b) Where in the execution sequence would you use the cache to speed execution of the call?
(c) Are there any benefits from the design that includes the cache? Explain.

5-15. Here are two proposed methods for implementing operations on objects that are represented by Ada variant records. For simplicity, assume that all operands have the same record type (in other words, their type differences are restricted to differences in the values of their discriminant parts—you do not need to worry about verifying this assumption):
  1. Use the discriminant value(s) to select the function bodies.
  2. Use common operation implementation routines, with conditional execution based on actual discriminant values, to vary the basic operations when required.
     Compare these options. Consider the specification of the operations, the operand representations, the implementation complexity, and the execution times.

5-16. Describe the behavior of the program shown in Example 5-15 if it is executed by a machine with c-regs.
  (a) The address information associated with the cache-registers must be consulted to make program execution efficient and functionally correct. Describe these checks.
  (b) Illustrate the speed improvement by showing the actual memory accesses made during the execution of the program fragment from the example. You will need to compare the accesses made by a conventional processor against those made by the c-regs processor, for the cases when $i = j$ and when $i\ !=j$.

5-17. To save time while evaluating a complex arithmetic expression, an optimizing compiler looks for common subexpressions within the expression being evaluated. If the processor has registers, the compiler may assign a register to hold the value of the common subexpression between the time that it is evaluated and the time that it is last required during the process of evaluating the complete expression. If the processor design has an evaluation stack rather than a set of registers, retaining the subexpression's value between uses and then managing to have it at the top of the stack when it is required for later use may require tricky management of the entries near the top of the stack. To assist in this endeavor, a stack-based processor may have DUPLICATE and EXCHANGE instructions. DUPLICATE pushes a second copy of the top of the stack, whereas EXCHANGE interchanges the top two stack entries.

(a) What expression is evaluated by the following program fragment?

```
LOAD A
LOAD B
MULTIPLY
DUPLICATE
LOAD C
ADD
EXCHANGE
LOAD D
SUBTRACT
MULTIPLY
```

(b) It would be convenient to be able to address the intermediate values near the top of the stack as though they were located in registers. This could be accomplished by adding an addressing mode that names objects relative to the top of the stack. Write a program fragment that evaluates the same expression using this kind of operand addressing.

(c) Did your first attempt to write this program fragment leave the stack cleaned up after it completed execution? Explain. Discuss whether the opportunity to access operands within the stack saves instructions. Consider both this example and the general case.

5-18. This problem explores the possibility of shortening a program by redefining the interpretation of the instruction function code field in a context-sensitive manner. The basic idea is that if only a few instructions are going to be used in a given context, then only a few function code bits are really required to specify which instruction should be executed. The resulting reduction in program length would save both memory space and instruction fetch time (but for maximum benefit, it would require that the program counter address memory at bit granularity). The problem develops some alternate means for specifying these changes. For the purposes of this problem, you can assume that the execution context changes only during procedure CALL and procedure RETURN.

(a) In this option, the program may redefine any processor operation by changing its microprogram. The claim is made that by overwriting useless operations with useful ones, the total microcode space will not have to be increased, yet execution time will be speeded because the microinstruction instruction fetch time is short compared to the instruction fetch time. Is this claim valid? Specify a method for the program to change the interpretations of the function code field. Does your method achieve any of the claimed savings? Explain.

(b) This variation allows the compiler to add instructions for user-defined classes to the processor's instruction set. The declaration section of each program would state which built-in classes are not going to appear in the program very frequently. In addition, new class declarations include usage frequency estimate with each operation specification. The idea is that the compiler can use the frequency estimates to choose which operations to map to microcode.

5-19. Consider a stack-based processor (you can use the B 5700, if you want a specific design). This problem concerns the benefits of an implementation that groups successive instructions into single execution sequences, as suggested in the text for indexed loading. In this problem, we consider the instruction sequence

> LOADVALUE <address>
> ADD

Remember that one of the addition operands will be at the top of the stack before this sequence of instructions begins. Assume that the value at the indicated address can be read out in one memory cycle.

(a) How many push and pop operations will be performed on the stack while this sequence is executed?

(b) How many memory operations, excluding those for instruction fetching? Assume that the stack is held in memory.

(c) Repeat parts (a) and (b) if the processor contains registers that buffer the top of the stack.

(d) Repeat parts (a) and (b) if the control unit is designed to detect the sequence and execute it as a single instruction (which cannot be interrupted in the middle).

5-20. If a processor has to check operand types before it can initiate an operation, the result will be delayed. One design strategy that might alleviate this problem is illustrated by the following. Consider numeric values in a processor that mixes floats with integers in the same registers; each register has a tag to indicate whether its contents is an integer. In this design, when an ADD instruction is initiated, the processor sends the operands to an integer adder and a float adder so they can start their computations. While these are taking place, additional logic checks the operand types to choose which result should be copied to the destination register.

(a) Draw the data paths for this design, showing the enable logic for result gating.

(b) Discuss the types of environments in which this approach could gain speed. Do not criticize the tagged approach; merely accept that as a given for this problem. Your discussion should consider the following possibilities (the list is meant to be suggestive, but not complete):

1. Processor speed could be limited by the performance of other instructions.

2. The operand types might not be identical.

3. Only a few operations will be affected by the redesign.

6

SINGLE I-STREAM PARALLELISM

Coming together is a beginning;
keeping together is progress;
working together is success.

— T. Roosevelt

If you do not believe in cooperation,
look at what happens to a truck
when one wheel comes off.

— E. Filene

To realize system speed beyond that achievable by efficient coding and implementation of single instruction streams, the system must utilize parallelism. With several activities (which we hope are useful!) progressing at the same time, the system can produce more results within a given time interval. There are several difficulties in implementing parallelism: First, one must decide whether the parallel system should support the illusion that the processor or system is actually executing a program using a single control point. Second, one must find where parallelism can be used in an implementation, while preserving the system's functionality. Third, control mechanisms must be devised to coordinate the parallel activities. Fourth, when programming the system, one may have to exercise special care to implement an application efficiently, especially if the system's parallelism is not completely hidden by the illusion of a single point of execution.

Finally, one must try to preserve the opportunity to use modularity in system design and programming, as these support structured design.

In this chapter we discuss parallel system design based on specifying or finding parallelism opportunities within modules supporting a single instruction stream illusion. System designs supporting several instruction streams and the corresponding parallelism opportunities are covered in the next two chapters.

Parallelism within a single instruction stream can be *virtual* or *real*. Virtual parallelism is achieved when a program is written to give an illusion that it is executed by independent entities that are working in parallel, even though they might not be really working that way. Real parallelism is achieved when several functional units are simultaneously working on parts of the program specified within a single instruction stream. Virtual parallelism is a fiction introduced to retain modularity within a program specified as a series of somewhat independent modules. These modules interact in controlled ways, such that the behavior is compatible with the illusion that there is a single control stream running through the set of modules. Thus the system, despite its underlying parallelism, supports the single control point illusion.

Behind the illusion of a single instruction stream there can be real parallelism that is either *static* or *dynamic*.

> **Definition.** *Static parallelism* is parallelism detected during the design of the hardware and/or the software.

Introducing static parallelism can speed the execution of many programs in a manner that preserves the illusion of a single control point proceeding through the program in program order, so that the parallelism is invisible to the programmer. For example, a compiler can reorder instructions to promote parallelism. Specialized hardware designs that rely on parallelism detected before execution may be very effective for particular problem classes, and can provide large speedup for these classes of algorithms or problems. However, these same algorithms and design techniques may not speed the execution of algorithms outside the domain for which the system was designed. For example, a parallel system designed for solving partial differential equations may be totally inappropriate for handling database queries. A more general method for introducing hardware parallelism at the processor level allows each instruction specification to control several independent activities, such as multiple instructions issued during the same clock interval. A limitation is that, in many algorithms, not all available instruction execution slots can be filled with useful operations.

The second form of real parallelism relies on detection or management of parallelism during program execution.

> **Definition.** *Dynamic parallelism* is parallelism detected during program execution.

Implementing dynamic parallelism may require extensive hardware support, but can enhance system performance greatly. The improvement occurs because the control mechanism knows about the actual events that have occurred or might occur during program execution (such as the outcomes of conditional branch decisions). The logic that controls the parallelism checks conditions and restricts instruction issue so the basic illusions are supported and functional behavior is observed. Furthermore, the dynamic parallelism scheme can be tailored to the hardware configuration of a particular processor implementation (i.e., parallelism can be found that might not be visible in all realizations of the same instruction set).

At the processor level, systems utilizing static parallelism could be classed under the "everything correct" approach, because their correct behavior requires that the parallelism detection process that generated the actual processor program from the user's program support the system's illusions. No checking during program execution validates the choices made during the detection of static parallelism; omitting checks simplifies the implementation hardware and may shorten program execution times. But static parallelism might not provide maximum speedup if the program's execution presents uncertainties that cannot be clarified until program execution, for in those cases, the parallelism detection process must assume the worst case to preserve the illusion of correct program execution. For example, if array indices are computed during program execution, one cannot determine before execution whether two independent accesses to the same array (such as to $x[\,i\,]$ and $x[\,j\,]$) actually access the same component. Being conservative reduces the amount of parallelism and thus the program's speedup.

Another important—but uncertain—situation arises when several independent processors collaborate to perform a single task, for the execution times of the separate instruction streams cannot be known with sufficient precision to perform a static analysis of all interactions. Thus, static parallelism design strategies are not appropriate for systems with multiple independent processors.

In this chapter, you will learn techniques for specifying and performing parallel algorithms specified by a single instruction stream, with independent program modules and, at the hardware level, with both parallel and pipelined computing elements. You will learn how these parallelism techniques can speed execution. You will learn techniques for introducing parallelism prior to program execution by choosing good schedules and good instruction parallelism for very long instruction word (VLIW) processors. In addition, you will learn some logical constraints sufficient to assure that correct computations will be performed on the parallel system. These techniques are limited because static analyses are possible only if information is available regarding the actual operands, result destinations, and execution times of every system component. In particular, we cannot attempt static parallelism when the tasks are executed on independent processors because the timing is too uncertain. In general, static parallelism can enhance the speed of many programs, but dynamic parallelism detection produces the best performance in most cases. Thus, at the end of the chapter, we turn to superscalar processor design, in which dynamic detectors find parallelism within a single instruction stream, yet preserve the illusion of a single control point executing instructions atomically in program order. All high-performance processors rely on superscalar parallelism to achieve their high program execution speeds.

In the next two chapters you will learn techniques supporting dynamic parallel execution of independent instruction streams; more extensive run-time mechanisms are required to support this flexibility.

6.1 FUNCTIONAL CORRECTNESS

Introducing parallelism introduces the possibility of changing the behavior of a program. So the concept of *correctness* becomes extremely important. To define correctness, we need a precise model for the behavior of all program elements and their interactions. In this chapter, the programming model includes a common memory; the registers and functional units within the processor(s) are independent of each other. Parallel activities in the processors and the functional units contribute to system speed.

Functional behavior is behavior in accord with the user's expectations. Nonfunctional behavior, in contrast, is behavior not in accord with the users' expectations. What do users expect? In the single-thread model, one views the computer program as a sequence of atomic steps to be performed exactly in the sequence that they were written, without overlap. This sequence determines the program's functional behavior.

> **Definition.** The *functional behavior* of a program is the behavior exhibited by an atomic execution of the program's steps in program order.

This definition is compatible with single instruction stream programming models, in which it is easy to determine the execution sequence:

> **Definition.** The *program order* of instructions within a program is the sequence specified by the order in the program text, combined with the decisions made during the execution of conditional branch instructions.

Determining the program order can be difficult under some parallelism models if the synchronization primitives do not exactly constrain the relative timings among all program steps. We return to these issues in Chapters 7 and 8, where we study particular models concerning such interactions.

Under the single thread model, nonfunctional behavior might be introduced by interactions between tasks that are executed in nonsequential order. Nonsequential execution may result from (1) parallel execution among functional units or (2) out-of-order execution within a single functional unit.

Granularity. We may view a program at various levels of granularity; interesting granules are tasks, threads, individual instructions, and indivisible ("atomic") actions.

> **Definition.** A *task* is an independently scheduled thread of execution comprising a sequence of atomic actions, which are referred to as *steps*.

> **Definition.** An *atomic action* is an action that is performed in its entirety without interruption by other activities in the computer system.

We use this terminology to refer to all types of granules.

Interactions. In systems supporting parallelism with a single instruction stream, the only sharing in the programming model occurs through shared registers and memory locations. Under such a model, two tasks can interact if both access the contents of the same memory location or the same processor register, and in no other way. Each interaction with a shared object is a read (R) or a write (W) action. Reads do not affect the visible state of the shared object, whereas writes do change that state, affecting the values observed during subsequent reads.

A schedule that preserves program order gives functional behavior; however, schedules that do not obey program order might produce the same (functional) results more efficiently. Our goal is to find and use schedules that assure functional behavior even though they might not obey the program order constraint. We need to understand the constraints on these schedules that assure functional behavior.

Read and Write Sets. We use the following notation to specify the interactions among atomic actions. We denote tasks with integer labels. If task t reads (writes) object X, we write $R_{X,t}$ ($W_{X,t}$). To determine task scheduling constraints, we identify for each task T_i its *read set* $\mathcal{R}_i$, comprising the set of shared objects[1] that it will read, and its *write set* $\mathcal{W}_i$, comprising the set of shared objects that it

---

[1]   As mentioned before, these objects include both memory locations and processor registers but exclude all objects used privately by the task.

will write. There is no scheduling constraint among tasks T_i and T_j, if the following empty intersection conditions apply to these pairs of sets:

1. $\mathcal{R}_i \cap \mathcal{W}_j = \phi$
2. $\mathcal{W}_i \cap \mathcal{R}_j = \phi$
3. $\mathcal{W}_i \cap \mathcal{W}_j = \phi$

The fourth possible pairing—of two read sets—does not impose a constraint, because reads do not change the state of an object. In particular, in all schedules that differ only in the interleavings among only reads by any of the tasks, these reads will return identical values, regardless of their actual execution order. On the other hand, if any of the three empty intersection conditions is not satisfied, the two tasks are dependent, and to achieve functional behavior, the ordering among the accesses to the objects in the sets that do intersect must be compatible with the original program ordering.[2] Alternately, these sequencing requirements can be phrased as precedence constraints.

> **Definition.** A *precedence constraint* exists between tasks T_i and T_j, if the execution of T_j must follow the completion of T_i. The fact that this precedence constraint exists can be expressed by writing $T_i \rightarrow T_j$, or by stating that (i, j) belongs to the precedence relation P.

Three types of dependencies lead to precedence constraints. Their conventional names reflect the types and specified order of accesses to a shared object:

1. Dependency; also called an RAW dependency
2. Antidependency; also called a WAR dependency
3. Write ordering; also called a WAW dependency

Dependency Constraints

> **Definition.** Tasks T_1 and T_2 have a *dependency* precedence constraint from object X[3] if their accesses to object X are specified in the order $W_{X,1} R_{X,2}$. This is also called a *RAW (read after write)* dependency.

Under an execution schedule that violates a dependency constraint among T_1 and T_2 from object X, the second task will read the old value in X, when it should have read the new value that is the result of the write performed by T_1. In particular, a violation of the constraint occurs when accesses to object X were specified in the order $W_{X,1} R_{X,2}$, but occurred in the order $R_{X,2} W_{X,1}$.

---

[2]   If we wish to look within the tasks, we could consider the actual reads and writes by the tasks to determine whether the behavior of a particular execution schedule would be functional. But this is simply viewing the system at a lower level of detail, where logically identical problems arise. So we stay at the task level in the text.

[3]   In these definitions, object X denotes either a shared processor register or a shared memory location.

Antidependency Constraints

Definition. Tasks T_1 and T_2 have an *antidependency* precedence constraint from object X if their accesses to object X are specified in the order $R_{X,1} W_{X,2}$. This is also called a *WAR* (*write after read*) dependency.

Under an execution schedule that violates an antidependency constraint, the first task will read the new value in X instead of the old one held there. In particular, a violation of the constraint occurs when accesses to X were specified in the order $R_{X,1} W_{X,2}$, but occurred in the order $W_{X,2} R_{X,1}$.

Write Ordering Constraints

Definition. Tasks T_1 and T_2 have a *write ordering* precedence constraint from object X if their accesses to object X are specified in the order $W_{X,1} W_{X,2}$. This is also called a *WAW* (*write after write*) dependency.

Under an execution schedule that violates a write ordering constraint, the value left in X will be the value written by the first task T_1—an incorrect value. Future reads of the contents of X may produce incorrect results. In particular, a constraint violation occurs if accesses to object X were specified in the order $W_{X,1} W_{X,2}$, but occurred in the order $W_{X,2} W_{X,1}$.

A program's precedence constraints may result from (1) data read and write interactions and (2) uncertainties about the outcomes of conditional branch instructions within the program. A proper view of a conditional branch instruction gives it a read set containing the condition being tested and a write set containing the program counter. It is true that all instructions modify the program counter, but unlike conditional branch instructions, unconditional instructions change the PC in a predictable manner that does not depend upon the instruction's operands. Thus, the PC value after an unconditional instruction can be predicted with certainty and there is no need to await instruction completion to know which instruction follows in program order. But with conditional branches, the identity of the next instruction is uncertain. A conservative way to handle this uncertainly about the execution sequence is to install an *execution barrier*—all instructions preceding the barrier must be completed before those that follow can be initiated. Other techniques involving speculative execution are discussed later; the functional requirement is that the realization must give the appearance of a single execution point following the correct execution sequence.

Precedence Graphs. A directed graph depicts precedence constraints.

Definition. A *precedence graph* is a directed graph in which node t corresponds to task t and there is a directed branch from node i to node j if there is a precedence constraint demanding that T_i must precede T_j.

The task numbers that label a precedence graph's nodes are usually written inside the circles that represent the nodes; additional information may be added to the graph, as described later.

Schedules. A *schedule* depicts the timing of a set of events occurring during the performance of a task. The schedule of a single-thread program is constructed by placing the statements in program order. Three representations of a schedule are as follows:

1. A string of step names
2. A timing diagram
3. A list of start and finish times for the constituent steps

Example 6-1

A program for execution on a uniprocessor has five steps with precedence constraints $T_1 < T_3 < T_4 < T_5$ and ready times as follows:

$$T_1\colon 0; \quad T_2\colon 2; \quad \text{others according to precedence.}$$

The best schedule is shown in Figure 6-1. This schedule could have been represented by a string of the task names indicating their order of execution, as in:

$$T_1 T_2 T_3 T_4 T_5$$

Another option representing the schedule is a list of the start and finish times, as in

$$s_1 = 0; f_1 = 5; s_2 = 5; f_2 = 8; s_3 = 8; f_3 = 9; s_4 = 9; f_4 = 14; s_5 = 14; f_5 = 16.$$

A speed goal is to find a schedule that shortens the task's *makespan*. The makespan of the schedule in Example 6-1 is 16.

Definition. The *makespan* of a schedule or a program execution is the elapsed time between the initiation of the first task and the completion of the last task.

A logical requirement is that the actual schedule must preserve the program's functionality, which implies that the schedule must honor the logical interactions among the atomic actions within the tasks.

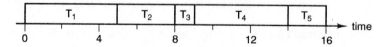

Figure 6-1   A timing diagram depicts a schedule (see Example 6-1)

Feasible Schedules

Definition.   A *feasible schedule* is a schedule that satisfies all precedence constraints among the program's steps.

Given a feasible uniprocessor schedule (i.e., without parallelism), some other feasible uniprocessor schedules can be generated by interchanging adjacent steps, provided that their order is not constrained through a precedence relationship.

Given a feasible schedule, a feasible parallel schedule can be constructed by scheduling parallel execution (i.e., as separate threads) of a set of adjacent steps that do not participate mutually in precedence constraints. At places in the schedule where precedence constraints must be satisfied, the relative progress of the threads can be controlled by scheduling synchronization actions or by predetermining a schedule that is controlled by a centralized coordination mechanism, which could be as simple as a common clocking scheme. General ways to specify synchronization constraints in shared resource systems are covered in Chapter 8.

Designers that attempt to schedule parallel activities in a load/store uniprocessor system must solve a restricted version of this problem. In this design context, the processor registers are the shared resource, the individual instructions are the tasks, and the schedule must meet the precedence constraints to behave in a functional manner. We present several approaches to this problem in Section 6.6. But first we explore the benefits of parallelism, the general scheduling problem, and techniques for exploiting parallelism opportunities at higher levels of abstraction.

6.2 PARALLELISM DETECTION AND PERFORMANCE

Before looking at the design of systems using parallelism to improve performance, we show that this technique can provide benefits. Next we find the types of information required to make an informed selection of activities that could be performed in parallel. Then we look at algorithms for detecting static parallelism.

6.2.1 Performance Advantages

Suppose that we need to complete n independent executions of the same task T. Let m denote the number of copies of a module able to perform that task in unit time. If $m = n$, the task set could be performed in unit time. In contrast, with only a single copy of the module, the execution of the task set would require n time units. The *speedup* S achieved by parallel execution is the ratio of these times, which is m. If m is a divisor of n, a speedup of exactly m can be achieved. The

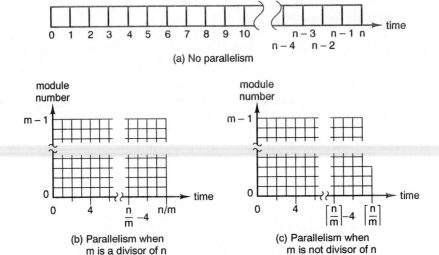

Figure 6-2   Schedules with overlap save time

execution schedules that correspond to these two situations are depicted in Figure 6-2. When m is not a divisor of n, some modules will be free during the last time unit (see Figure 6-2c). In general, the makespan is $\lceil n/m \rceil$ and the speedup is

$$S = n / \lceil n/m \rceil \qquad\qquad (6\text{-}1)$$

Except for the discontinuous behavior of the ceiling function, we have *linear speedup* proportional to the number of modules available to perform the task. Clearly, this is the best speedup that one can achieve, because the schedule keeps all modules busy during the execution interval. Linear speedup is the goal of all parallelism techniques. Usually, linear speedup is elusive because one or more of the assumptions that underlie the previous simple analysis are not valid. However, for some problems, one may be able to obtain superlinear speedup by restructuring the algorithm.

What assumptions led to linear speedup?

1. All tasks can be performed at any time.
2. All tasks are independent.
3. All tasks are identical.
4. All modules can perform all tasks.
5. All modules perform their tasks at the same speed.
6. Synchronization steps added to assure functionality do not add execution time.

The first two assumptions about the tasks themselves are closely related, because the major reason that some tasks cannot be performed at any time is that they participate in precedence constraints that specify an ordering relationship between the two tasks. The third assumption makes all tasks interchangeable with respect to where they can be executed and with respect to the amount of time they require for execution. The fourth and fifth assumptions state that the execution modules are *homogeneous*, which is not the case in many interesting situations. For example, an integer unit and a floating-point unit are not designed to perform the same operations, and certainly do not operate at the same speed. The final assumption is not realistic, because synchronization will be required and will add overhead.

The following example will be used as we study various instruction dispatching and reordering possibilities.

Example 6-2

Figure 6-3 shows a precedence graph for some tasks; each task number is shown within the corresponding node, and we have written next to each node the identity of a functional unit that will be able to perform the task, along with its execution time. This information is represented as $F_i(t)$, where i is the number of the functional unit, and t is the execution time.

A program and its precedence constraints, explicit or implicit, will be the input to a scheduling module that determines the actual order of instructions in a program or of events in a system. The goal is efficient program execution.

6.2.2 Scheduling Task Execution

A scheduler module can be incorporated into a program preprocessor to produce a static execution schedule for the program. The scheduler's decisions will be represented as a sequence of instruction *issues*. Each issue denotes the initiation of a task or instruction. The scheduler avoids nonfunctional behavior by

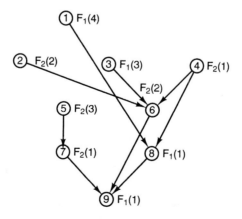

Figure 6-3   A precedence graph

delaying instruction issue until the danger of a precedence constraint violation has passed. Alternately, to promote parallelism, the scheduler could reorder instructions. In this section, we explore the general scheduling problem and several heuristic approaches to the algorithmically difficult problem of optimizing program makespans.

Scheduling Problem. The general scheduling problem involves the following elements:

1. A set of tasks $\{T_1 .. T_n\}$
2. A set of functional modules $\{M_1 .. M_m\}$
3. A set of precedence constraints $\{P_1 .. P_p\}$
4. A set of integer[4] execution times $\{E_{i,j}, 1 \le i \le n, \ 1 \le j \le m\}$; $E_{i,j}$ specifies the time that it would take to execute task T_i using module M_j (consider the execution time to be very large if the module cannot perform the task)
5. A set of shared objects $\{A .. Z\}$[5]
6. A program that specifies a sequential execution ordering of the tasks

The solution to the problem is a schedule for the execution of the tasks, expressed as (1) a graphical timing diagram, (2) a set of task start and finish times $\{s_i, 1 \le i \le n\}$ and $\{f_i, 1 \le i \le n\}$, or (3) a set of start lists $\{S_i, 1 \le i \le t\}$, where S_i contains the tasks initiated at time i. When scheduling instructions, we use the term *instruction issue* to denote the act of initiating instruction execution, usually by sending the command to a functional unit within the processor. We distinguish two sources of precedence constraints:

Definition. Task Y must precede task Z according to a *program precedence* constraint if Y precedes Z in the program's task ordering. In this case, we say that Y is a *program predecessor* of Z.

Definition. The *immediate logical predecessors* of task Y are those tasks whose results are the inputs for task Y.

In other words, the immediate logical predecessors of task Y are those tasks X_i for which there is a precedence relationship forcing X_i to precede Y. In a shared resource environment, these constraints arise from the RAW, WAR, and WAW ordering constraints.

Definition. The *logical predecessors* of task Y are those tasks in the transitive closure of the immediate logical predecessor relation to task Y.

---

[4]   The assumption that the execution times are integers does not lose generality.

[5]   This notation is meant to indicate that we will use capital letters to denote these shared objects, with no particular restrictions on the choice of letters, except to avoid name duplication.

In other words, the set of logical predecessors of task Y includes all tasks that must logically precede the initiation of task Y.

An important concept in many scheduling algorithms is that of an enabled task:

> **Definition.** Task W is *logically enabled* at time t if W has not been scheduled prior to time t and all of W's immediate logical predecessors have completed execution before time t.

> **Definition.** A task is *ready for execution* if it is logically enabled.

A correct scheduling algorithm must generate a feasible schedule. Usually, we desire a schedule that minimizes (optimizes) the schedule's *makespan*.

One can construct programs that make it difficult to find the optimum schedule, but their existence does not prove anything. They do, however, illustrate that the scheduling problem is difficult, and that the entire schedule must be considered to find the optimum point. The general scheduling problem is NP-hard [GARE79], which means that it is likely that in the worst case, a combinational number (based on the number of tasks involved) of schedules must be considered before one can be certain that the optimum schedule has been found. This inherent difficulty leads one to consider heuristic scheduling algorithms, such as list scheduling, which is used to dynamically schedule instruction issue in superscalar processors.

List Scheduling. This simple (greedy) scheduler works from a list that includes all program steps (in program order) that have not been scheduled. The output from our scheduler will be a list of start sets. In the simplest variety of list scheduling, a task can be scheduled when (1) it is ready for execution and (2) a functional unit that can perform the task is available to receive a new task. This rule permits parallel task initiation—each start set can have several members.

Let T denote the task at the head of the list, and let M_T be the set of modules that could perform T. Also let NRT(i) denote the next ready time t for module (i)—a module is *ready* at time t if it is able to accept a request to perform a new task at time t. Let $S(i)$ denote the start list for time i; it contains the names of the tasks that initiate execution at that time. The list schedule is generated as follows:[6]

1. Set the current time t = start_time.
2. For all i, set NFT(i) = start_time.
3. For all t, set $S(t) = \Phi$ (initialize the start lists to empty).
4. If the task at the head of the list is not enabled at time t, go to step 8; otherwise, let T denote that task.

---

[6]   This algorithm specification does not include precedence constraint evaluation; we assume that they are evaluated at the proper point in the algorithm (see Problem 6-2).

5. Choose an i such that module i can perform T and NFT(i) ≤ t.

   If there is no way to choose such an i, go to step 8.

6. Schedule T for issue at time t to module i

   (set: $s_T = t$, $f_T = E_{T,i} + t$, $NFT(i) = E_{T,i} + t$, $S(t) = S(t) \cup T$)

7. Go to step 4 if unscheduled tasks remain (otherwise, terminate).

8. t = t + 1; go to step 4.

This algorithm initiates the tasks in program order. Because t does not advance until no tasks remain that could be started at time t, several tasks can be assigned to the same start set. Thus, parallel activity is possible.

Example 6-3

Figure 6-4a shows a list schedule for the task precedence graph of Figure 6-3. The makespan for this schedule is 12. In subsequent examples, we show that this time can be reduced by modifying the scheduler's algorithm.

In terms of minimizing the makespan, the strict list scheduling strategy is conservative, because even though the next task in program order might not be able to be initiated at time t, still it might be possible to initiate another task out of program order.

Example 6-4

Consider three tasks and a system with two functional units A and B. The first two tasks can be performed only in unit A, and the third task can only be performed in unit B. We have the following dependencies and constraints:

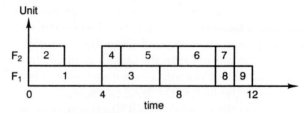

a) Simple list schedule with in-order issue

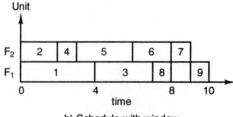

b) Schedule with window
width = 2

Figure 6-4   Some list schedules for the tasks of Figure 6-3

$$s_1 \geq 0 \qquad\qquad\qquad E_1 = 3$$
$$s_2 \geq 1 \qquad\qquad\qquad E_2 = 5$$
$$s_3 \geq f_2 \qquad\qquad\qquad E_3 = 3$$

The first two constraints come from precedences with previous activities, and the third from a precedence constraint between two of these tasks.

If we use the list scheduling algorithm on this problem, we obtain the schedule depicted in Figure 6-5a, whose makespan is 11.

In the preceding, we imposed the rule that the tasks are scheduled such that the relative start times of every pair of tasks does not violate the specified program order. By relaxing this restriction, we can improve the schedule, but taking full advantage of this possibility may require looking into the future and possibly leaving a functional unit idle even though there is an enabled task within the issue window.

Example 6-5

For the program in Example 6-4, a schedule better than a list schedule can be obtained by looking ahead at the beginning—Figure 6-5b displays a schedule with an idle moment at the beginning, permitting T_3 to be performed earlier, leading to completion at time 9. This example shows that a scheduling algorithm that does not look ahead might not be able to find the schedule with minimum makespan.

One can construct an example of difficult optimum scheduling by modifying the example to chain together a sequence of predecessors such that the example's situation would become apparent only after looking ahead by a large interval. Recall that such examples do not constitute a proof of anything, but

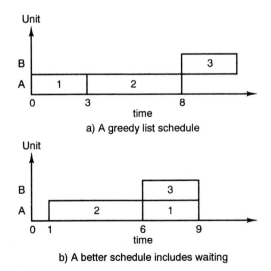

Figure 6-5   Schedules for the tasks in Example 6-4

they illustrate that the scheduling problem is difficult, and that the entire schedule must be considered to find the optimum point.

Execution Out of Order. New scheduling opportunities are opened up if task initiation can violate program order. A simple modification of the list scheduling algorithm adds an *issue window* of width w. Any enabled task within the issue window is a candidate for scheduling. As before, the scheduler's list includes the unscheduled tasks (in program order). Steps 4 and 5 of the scheduling algorithm are modified so that the algorithm examines all tasks within the issue window whose logical predecessors have completed and for which an execution module is available. Because a task must be enabled before it is scheduled, the schedule will be feasible and will produce functional behavior.

Example 6-6

Figure 6-4b shows the schedule for the graph of Figure 6-3 obtained by a scheduler that permits execution out of order using an issue window with width 4. The makespan is decreased to 10.

Superscalar processors use a similar issue algorithm; during program execution, they choose instructions to issue from a window of unissued instructions; we discuss this design approach in Section 6.6.

Assured Completion Ordering. One safe way to guarantee that the behavior of an overlapped machine matches the behavior of program order execution is to require (1) that each instruction not be issued until its operands are available, and (2) that each instruction not be permitted to write its results until all of its program predecessors have written their results. This statement does not constrain instruction issue to follow program order, but it does require that the precedence constraints be satisfied. We can design a system to assure completion in program order by deferring result writing until the results from all program predecessors have been written. The functional units would remain busy, and if they had pipelines, they could become congested with stalled intermediate results from issued instructions that cannot complete. A logical deadlock might occur if the processor were permitted to issue instructions out of order to a single pipeline and the write buffer filled up before the bottleneck could be broken.

Forcing instruction completion to occur in program order places a barrier after every instruction. In general, a *barrier* defines a point where we wish to assure that all instructions preceding in program order have completed execution before execution continues beyond the barrier. The barrier's presence places two constraints on instruction scheduling:

1. All preceding instructions must complete before the barrier can be passed.
2. All successor instructions must wait to start execution until the barrier has been passed.

Barriers in the program define points at which we know unambiguously whether any preceding instruction has caused an exception. Though we might not be able to tell *which* preceding instruction caused the exception, we do have the cause isolated to the region between two consecutive barrier instructions.

Many buffer management details have been avoided in this simple description of the approach toward in-order completion; see Problem 6-40.

6.3 SINGLE-THREAD PARALLEL-PROGRAMMING PARADIGMS

In this section we survey methods by which programmers can construct single-thread programs that specify the possibility of parallel activities. In one approach, a single-thread program with parallelism specifications appears to be constructed of several independent modules that act independently (unless, of course, they communicate via messages—see Chapter 7—or share data objects—see Chapter 8). The program structure incorporates modular separation, which suggests that we view each module as a separate process, even though the modules do not act independently. The programmer specifies control transfers among the processes; this controls the relative progress of the individual processes. An execution sequence specification in this style is tantamount to specifying the complete program order among the steps, and thus all interprocess synchronization. Because the execution sequence is completely specified, these specification schemes produce virtual parallelism.

Two specification techniques describe interleaved executions:

1. Remote procedure call
2. Remote resumes

The word "remote" is used because the program being executed by one process specifies control sequencing in another ("remote") process.

We desire interprocess flow specifications that preserve the integrity of the component processes. We want to be able to adapt processes written for independent execution for use in the parallel structure. (We hope this adaptation requires few changes, such as the addition of a small number of control statements.) Finally, fast execution should be possible. For fastest execution, one may tailor the process specifications to the machine executing the program.

6.3.1 Remote Procedure Call

A remote procedure call specifies a control transfer between two processes in which one process invokes a procedure within another process. The usual procedure calling conventions apply to the remote procedure call: The calling procedure (and process) are suspended until the called procedure completes execution. When the called procedure completes execution, the suspended caller is reactivated and continues its computation.

One stack of activation blocks is adequate to realize a program that utilizes remote procedure call. The caller's activation block stack can be used by the called process (even though it is within a different process), because the caller will not be reactivated until the called process has completed execution and cleaned up the stack. The context changes for **call** and **return** can be handled in exactly the same manner as for uniprocessor procedure calling.

Example 6-7

Process 1:	Process 2:	Process 3:
void F(..) {	**void** G(..) {	**void** H(..) {
..	..	..
G(2, x);	H(y);	..
..	..	..
}	}	}

The following execution history is compatible with these processes:

1. An outside procedure calls F;
2. F is executed down to the call to G;
3. G is called;
4. G is executed down to the call to H;
5. H is called;
6. H executes its complete procedure;
7. H returns to G;
8. G completes execution;
9. G returns to F;
10. F completes execution;
11. F returns to its caller;

Figure 6-6 depicts this sequencing; the circled numbers indicate the steps.

Even if the system has several independent physical processors, and even if the three processes had been allocated to three different physical processors, the execution sequence would have been identical to this history because the execution model states that there is a single execution point.

Remote procedure call semantics can be used to specify a distributed system algorithm even if a called procedure might be executed on a processor physically remote from the processor executing the calling process (see Problem 6-10).

A remote procedure call structure preserves the logical separation between the distributed processes, so each process can be designed independently. The virtual parallelism with modular separation supports structured design.

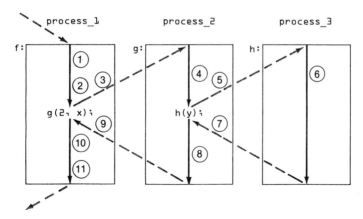

Figure 6-6   Control flow for remote procedure call

6.3.2 Remote Resumes

Under the remote resume paradigm, the (single) control point moves through the processes, but the behavior within each process is truly independent of actions in the other processes. Moving the control point to another process synchronizes the processes and may pass data, but otherwise does not disturb the state internal to the independent processes. In particular, when one process surrenders control to another process, its status is saved on its own stack. When the process is awakened later, its saved internal state will be retrieved from its own stack. Because the act of surrendering control is not coupled with procedure call or return, the activation block allocations do not obey a last-in-first-out discipline, and a single stack cannot be used to support the set of processes.

> **Definition.** A *coroutine* is a process whose control flow is governed by remote **resume** instructions.

There are three basic conditions for "good" usage of coroutines:

1. Interactions between the processes should be restricted to the control and data flows specified by the remote **resume** statements.
2. The execution of a process should be **resume**d from the point where it was suspended.
3. Each process should run to completion.

It is easy to design an implementation satisfying the first two conditions. It is difficult, however, to assure that the third condition will be met; once a coroutine surrenders control, it cannot finish if it is never resumed by some other coroutine. Thus, one cannot guarantee that a coroutine constructed in isolation will be resumed to run to completion.

Several statements support our programming paradigm:

process_name = **create** f(x, ..); —Create a new process, initialized to execute procedure f with the specified parameters. The new process is effectively placed in a suspended state, but is not activated by this statement. An identifying name that denotes the new process is returned and stored during the assignment specified in the statement.

resume process_name {**out**(x, ..)} {**in**(y, ..)}; —Resume a named suspended process from its point of suspension, suspending the caller (the process executing the **resume**). If an **out** list is given, the actual parameters listed are sent to the corresponding formal parameters listed in the **in** list specified in the **resume** statement at which control was relinquished.[7] The next time that a **resume** or **coreturn** that names the caller is executed, the caller will be resumed at the statement following this **resume**.

coreturn process_name {**out**(x, ..)}; —Terminate the executing process, resumeing the named process. Values may be passed to the resumed process, as described in the **resume** statement in that process.

Example 6-8

Process 1:

```
void main( process_name p ) {
    int x, y, z;
    process_name r;
    ..
    r = create second( p );
    resume r in( x, z );
    ..
    resume r;
    ..
};
```

Process 2:

```
void second( process_name q ) {
    int u, v, w;
    ..
    resume q out(u,v);
    ..
    coreturn q;
};
```

The parameter of main is the name of the process, whereas the parameter of second is the name of its parent process. The name of the process running second is stored in r in the main process during the **create** statement. When main executes its first **resume**, the second process begins the body of second and continues execution until it reaches its **resume** statement, at which point it passes the values it has stored within u and v to x and z in main. Then the execution of main continues forward from the **resume** statement. The second **resume** in main starts the completion of second's execution, which terminates with the **coreturn** that terminates the second process

---

[7]   If the lengths of these lists or the order of object types do not match, the program is erroneous.

and passes control back to main, allowing it to complete its body. During this transition, no values are passed between the processes.

Master–Slave Coroutine Structures. Two interesting program structures utilize remote resumes. The first structure is centered around one "master" process that creates and calls other processes; these "slaves" always return control to the master process; therefore, only the master process need know the global process structure. In particular, under this structure, we can establish the rule that each child process never has to name its parent as it resumes or returns.[8] This is a "safe" interaction mode because the master process structures all interprocess interactions and each slave process can execute a stand-alone algorithm modified slightly to relinquish control (possibly passing data) at appropriate points.[9] The next example illustrates the use of this safe coroutine structure to govern the simultaneous execution of several algorithms that rely on the preservation of stacked state information.

Example 6-9

We want to compare two tree structures to test whether they have the same values in the same order at their leaf nodes, with no concern for the connections among internal nodes of the trees (this "same fringe problem" is taken from [SYMB86]). A "standard" solution uses a tree-to-leaf-list program that traverses a tree in left-to-right order and produces a result list whose components are the values of the atoms at the leaves of the tree being scanned, listed in left-to-right order. The main comparison program calls this tree-to-leaf-list program twice to obtain leaf lists for the two trees being compared. Having both lists, the comparison program simply scans them to check for equality.[10] The tree traversal process used in the tree-to-leaf-list program could be expressed as a recursive process, in such a process implementation, the path down the tree to the current position is stored in the stack.

An alternate solution uses three processes. The tree traversal program runs within two separate processes under the control of a master process that performs the leaf value comparisons. Each child process scans one tree to find its leaf values. Each time a child finds a leaf value, it returns control and the leaf value to the parent, which then asks the other tree traversal process for its next leaf value. The two leaf values are compared in the main program. This approach to the problem requires that the tree traversal programs be separate processes because each uses its own stack to retain the status of its tree traversal. No parameters need be passed when the child processes are **resume**d, but the tree traversal routine must return a leaf value from each call.[11] Here is a skeleton of the (recursive) tree traversal process within one of the scanning processes:

---

[8]   The system must know that the return is always made to the parent—i.e., that the safe interaction mode is being used.

[9]   The flow pattern of this mode occurred in the previous example, but the program expressed things in the general manner.

[10]   Some space could be saved by merging the second tree traversal with list checking, but the program would be harder to understand.

[11]   A special value must be returned to signify reaching the end of the tree.

1. Is the present position a leaf? If so, **resume**, returning the leaf's value (when this process is **resume**d, execute a **return**). If not, call this procedure to traverse the left part of the subtree rooted at the present position, ignoring any returned result value.
2. If the right part exists, call this procedure to traverse the right part.
3. Return the special termination code.

Be sure to notice the difference between **resume**, which gives a leaf value back to the parent, and **return**, which backtracks the recursive scan internal to the child process (except when the end of the tree is reached). The parent (not shown) initiates the two children to perform the tree traversals and then enters a loop checking for the equality of the leaf values and for simultaneous tree termination codes.

Figure 6-7 illustrates snapshots of these processes in the midst of their searches.

General Coroutine Structures. In general, any coroutine can resume any other coroutine whose identity is known. In this loosely structured system (compared to the safe discipline used in the tree scanning example), the structures of the algorithms within all coroutines in the set considered together determine whether any one of them actually completes execution, because it is possible that a suspended coroutine is never reactivated by any other coroutine in the set.

Example 6-10

Consider three processes written as procedures within an enclosing block, where there exists a (global) declaration of the objects holding process names (we have placed this global declaration in the first line of the process set that follows. Assume initially that the object "process_1" has been loaded with the name of the initial process and that it has been initialized to execute procedure e:

```
process_name process_1, process_2, process_3;
                       //the programs assume that these names are global

void e( .. ) {
      ..
m:    process_2 = create f( a, b );        //not C++
      resume process_2;                    //not C++
      ..
n:    resume process_3;                     //not C++
      ..
};

void f( .. ) {
      ..
p:    process_3 = create g( d, e );        //not C++
      resume process_3;                    //not C++
      ..
      coreturn process_3;                          //not C++
};
```

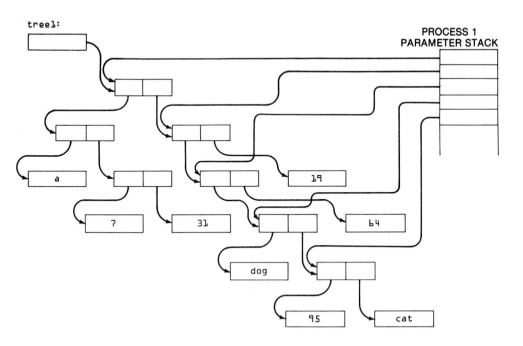

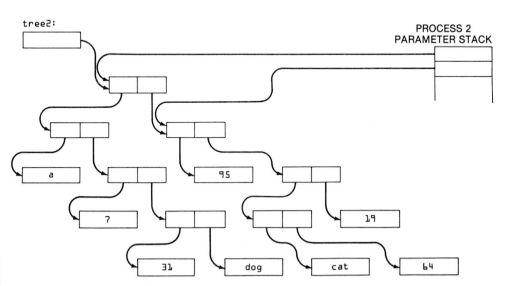

Figure 6-7 Snapshot of the coroutine stacks executing the tree fringe algorithm

```
void g( .. ) {
       ..
q:     resume process_1;              //not C++
       ..
r:     resume process_2;              //not C++
       ..
       coreturn process_1;               //not C++
}
```

The following history is compatible with this three-process program:

1. Start process_1 executing procedure e;
2. Execute process_1 through line m;   //execution of e
3. Create and start process_2;
4. Execute process_2 through line p;   //execution of f
5. Create and start process_3;
6. Execute process_3 through line q;   //execution of g
7. Resume process_1 after line m + 1;
8. Execute process_1 through line n;   //execution of e
9. Resume process_3 after line q;
10. Execute process_3 through line r;   //execution of g
11. Resume process_2 after line p + 1;
12. Execute process_2 to its **coreturn**;   //complete f
13. Resume process_3 after line r;
14. Execute process_3 to its **coreturn**;   //complete g
15. Resume process_1 after line n;
16. Execute process_1 to its **return**;   //complete e

This event sequence is depicted in Figure 6-8, which shows that each process has been completely executed following the statement sequence.

Note the difference between **coreturn** process completion, which transfers control to a member of the parallel set of processes, and **return** process completion, which returns control to an outside procedure. The latter may effectively terminate the coroutine set's cooperative behavior.[12]

Semantics of Coroutine Operations. The semantics of the **call, return, resume,** and **coreturn** operations can be built from common elements, including the following:

1. Saving the state on a stack
2. Restoring a saved state from a stack
3. Creating a new activation block on a stack
4. Destroying an activation block
5. Copying a block of values

---

[12]   See also Problem 6-8.

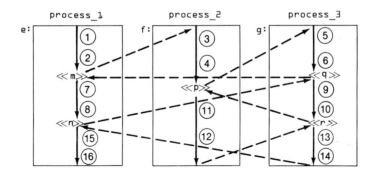

Figure 6-8   An execution sequence with coroutine interactions

The semantics of the control flow operations are suggested by the following "program" (see also Problem 6-9):

```
void resume() {
    save_state_on_stack();
    find_next_stack_and_pointer_to_it();
    if ( there_was_an_out_list )          //in the old process
        push_values_on_new_stack();
    change_to_new_stack();
    if ( there_was_an_in_list )          //in the next process
        pop_values_off_stack();
    restore_state_from_activation_block_on_stack();
}
```

This program does not show any details concerning the object names in the **in** and **out** lists, nor any test for length and type matching between these lists.

The similarities between the coroutine control operations and conventional call/return actions suggest that there would be little cost (in terms of added control mechanisms) to add coroutine support to a system.

Example 6-11

Coroutine structures are supported in the Symbolics 3600 LISP machines [SYMB86]. A special system call instantiates and initializes a new process. One parameter of the process creation primitive is a flag that indicates whether the new process is restricted to the call/return coroutine flow discipline.

Example 6-12

Simple two-module coroutine structures are supported by one option available within the Alpha AXP's jump instruction.

6.3.3 Operations Amenable to Parallel Execution

Some operations on compound objects can be built from repetitive execution of independent operations performed on their component parts. It may be possible to issue the corresponding operation requests simultaneously or to build special-purpose architectures that use parallel execution to implement these operations.

Example 6-13

A vector addition operation $z = x + y$ accesses all components of the operands x and y to add them together. The individual component additions ($z[i] = x[i] + y[i]$) are independent of each other. The vector addition function could include parallelism directives. Matrix addition presents a similar opportunity for parallelism.

The **dosim** (do simultaneously) statement expresses data parallelism:

```
dosim for( .. )        //not C++
    <statement>;       //loop body for possible parallel execution
```

The single statement in the body of a **dosim** statement may be a nested **dosim** loop statement; the combination of loop indexes and ranges in the nest specifies the set of objects to which the innermost loop body can be simultaneously applied. When **dosim** loops are tightly nested (the only statements that are not **dosim** statements being located in the innermost loop), the innermost body can be executed, in parallel, for all combinations of the index quantities consistent with the ranges specified in the nested **dosim** statements. The maximum possible degree of parallelism from these loop bodies is equal to the product of the loop iteration counts for all the **dosim** loops forming the tight nest.

Example 6-14

This program fragment specifies the simultaneous incrementation of 15 elements of the array c:

```
dosim for ( int i = 1, i <= 3, ++i ) {    //not C++
    dosim for ( int k = 1, k <= 5, ++k )
        c[ i, k ] = c[ i, k ] + 1;
};
```

This fragment expands into 15 parallel statements including:

```
c[ 1, 1 ] = c[ 1, 1 ] + 1;
c[ 2, 4 ] = c[ 2, 4 ] + 1;
c[ 3, 3 ] = c[ 3, 3 ] + 1;
c[ 3, 5 ] = c[ 3, 5 ] + 1;
```

This similar program yields less parallelism; it leads to three sequential fragments, each with five loop iterations:

```
dosim for ( int i = 1, i <= 3, ++i ) {
```

```
for ( int k = 1, k <= 5, ++k )
    c[ i, k ] = c[ i, k ] + 1;
};
```

If there are no procedure or function calls inside a conventionally written loop, the **dosim** parallelism can be detected easily by a compiler, despite the absence of the **dosim** keyword to give the clue. But if there are procedure calls in the loop, the compiler cannot be expected to analyze the situation, so the **dosim** keyword is useful. It can be risky to simultaneously call subroutines, because the compiler might assume that the programmer's implicit assertion that the loop bodies can be executed in parallel is correct, but this might not be the case—in this case, we create difficult debugging problems. A deeper analysis of the program's dependencies could check for these complicated interrelationships.

6.3.4 Parallel Statements

Parallelism between dissimilar statements is flexible, yet it may be hard to implement while still improving program execution speed.

The **cobegin** construct specifies statement-level parallelism, permitting the statements within the **cobegin** to be performed in parallel (in general, they may be executed in any order utilizing any degree of parallelism). Execution of the **cobegin** statement is not complete until all of its constituent statements have been completed. Thus, the end of the **cobegin** acts like a barrier within the program; see Problem 6-12.

We use this syntax to express the **cobegin** structure:

```
cobegin {                    //not C++
    <statement_1>;
    ..
    <statement_n>;
};
```

The constituent statements could be compound statements. Alternately, task initiation statements inside a **cobegin** structure could specify the parallel execution of a set of tasks performing called procedures. The **cobegin** synchronizes the tasks with the creating program because all the tasks must finish execution before the calling program completes its **cobegin**.

Example 6-15

```
cobegin {           //not C++
    task p(a,b);
    task g(x,y);
    task h(u,a,b);
};
```

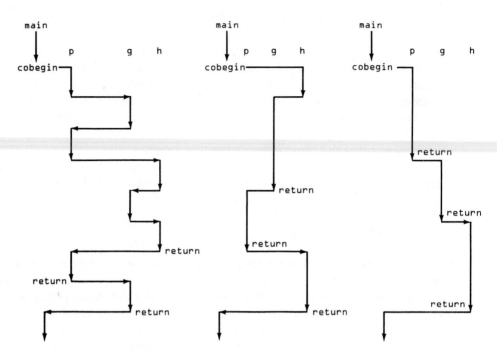

Figure 6-9   Three **cobegin** execution sequences

Figure 6-9 illustrates some execution sequences compatible with the **cobegin** in this program fragment. Note that the keyword "**task**" could be eliminated without introducing any confusion.

6.3.5 Fork/Join Specifications

A **fork** instruction transfers control to a label, whence the system executes the steps as a separate task. The task that initiated the **fork** continues its own execution path. There is no interaction between the two threads until each one executes a **join** instruction. One variation of this protocol adds a count to the **join**; this count is the number of processes that must arrive at the **join** before control can flow beyond the **join**; only one process continues from the **join**. The **join** statement acts as a barrier.

The **fork**/**join** structure can be used to create unstructured parallelism, because no structure defines exactly which program threads will combine at the **join**. The **fork**/**join** structure is used in some operating systems to specify task creation and completion. To produce functional behavior, the independent tasks might have to synchronize their behavior; the techniques discussed in Chapters 7 and 8 can be used for this purpose.

6.3.6 Recovery Blocks

A *recovery block* is a program section that is specified to behave like an atomic action. In other words, all the actions specified within the block are performed or none of them are performed. The block may specify (1) a logical predicate that specifies a completion condition which must evaluate to **true** before storing the results computed in the block and (2) alternative statement sequences that could be executed to satisfy the completion condition. Failure of the block can occur because the program demands failure (by executing a **failure** statement) or because none of the alternatives is able to satisfy the completion condition. At the end of a recovery block, the status of all objects is certain. In some sense, the end of the block acts as a *barrier*, though not implying interprocess synchronization. The recovery block concept is useful in reasoning about the status of objects when parallel activity is used to perform a program.

Recovery blocks were introduced by Randell [RAND75] to permit a programmer to request assurance about the state of the process; therefore, the block syntax is based on the notion of *assurance* that a certain predicate is true upon exit from the block. His syntax (modified slightly to conform to C++ style) is

> **ensure** <predicate>   //not C++
>   **by** <statement_0>;
>   {**else by** <statement_i>;}*
>   {**else error**;}

The semantics of this statement are defined by the execution of the following steps:

1. Create temporary copies of all objects modified by any statement within the **ensure** statement.
2. Choose statement_0.
3. Perform the chosen statement using the temporary object copies. If the statement failed to complete, go to step 5.
4. Evaluate the predicate (using the temporary copies); if true, go to step 7.
5. (The predicate is false or the statement failed to complete.) If there is another alternate (an **else** clause with a statement that is not **error**), continue to step 6. Otherwise, this **ensure** statement has failed.
6. Reset the temporary copies from the original copies, choose the next alternate statement, and go to step 3.
7. Copy the values from the temporary copies to the permanent copies and delete the temporary copies. (The execution of the statement is now complete.)

Because step 4 tests the overall conditions, all actions requested within the statement must have been completed before reaching the predicate testing point, which must be a synchronization point. If parallel operations were used to speed the execution of the **ensure** statement, the predicate testing point would become a barrier beyond which no parallel thread can proceed until all of them have reached that point. The synchronization at this barrier acts in a manner similar to the synchronization at the end of a **cobegin** statement.

When an **ensure** statement fails, it signals this condition, which might then cause the failure of an alternative in a logically enclosing **ensure** statement.

An important special case is an **ensure** statement whose predicate is the logical constant **true**. In this case, the assurance at the completion of the **ensure** is simply that no failure occurred within the constituent statements. This assurance cannot be asserted until all constituent statements have been completed (at least until it is certain that they will not cause fatal exceptions or failures).

6.3.7 Comments

Unless independent parallel execution is very efficiently implemented in the system, **cobegin** structures require high overhead yet give little speed payoff, so there is little point in choosing a parallel realization for **cobegin**, unless the parallel statements are themselves complex. However, the barrier construct implicit within **cobegin** is useful for controlling interprocess synchronization.

The **dosim** construct helps find parallelism, and the resulting semantics define possible parallel executions of the included statements; this structure is similar to the actual execution structure supported directly by an array machine. Frequently, the **dosim** parallelism can be discovered by a compiler analyzing the program text.

The **ensure** construct provides another general barrier specification, testing a programmer-specified predicate, with failure implying restoration of the process state prior to the initiation of the **ensure** statement. Within superscalar processors (and in shared-memory multiprocessor systems), barriers can be used to assure synchronization among instructions that may have been issued out of order. In addition, the state consistency checks within the **ensure** predicate are similar to some data integrity checks used in secure systems; see Section 9.2.4.

Other interprocess synchronization structures connected with message passing and object sharing are discussed in Chapters 7 and 8.

6.4 ENHANCING PARALLELISM OPPORTUNITIES

One can make conceptually simple modifications to the processor and/or program to enhance the chances of finding parallelism within the program (thereby speeding execution), while preserving the illusions and the program's functionality. These techniques include adding functional units to the processor, unrolling loops to make more operands and operations available for scheduling, and adjusting register assignments to make more operands available for use (which has the effect of making more instructions available for issue). These adjustments may move more operations into the enabled set (on the average), so that more instructions can be issued during a given time interval. As we make these modifications, we try to support the illusions, so we must maintain all system behavior, including any side effects of instruction execution, such as exception occurrence.

To simplify the presentation, we restrict our discussion to load/store processor designs, in which all operands and results are in processor registers. It is easy to track operand availability in this environment. Generalizations to processor designs that access operands in memory are straightforward.

6.4.1 Adding Functional Units

With more functional units, it may be possible to increase the number of tasks being executed simultaneously. As technology permits more devices in each chip, the cost of adding a functional unit becomes small. However, the law of diminishing returns does apply, because for every algorithm, there exists a limiting number of functional modules beyond which all opportunities for parallelism will have been exhausted, and providing additional functional modules will not decrease the program's makespan.

Example 6-16

Figure 6-10 illustrates the execution schedule for the tasks from Figure 6-3 if two F_2 modules are available. Adding the second F_2 module reduces the makespan in a list schedule from 12 to 10.

Even if the processor's instruction issue mechanism can reorder instructions, compiler reordering might be used to increase the average number of enabled instructions within each instruction issue window. Reordering can reduce the makespan by shortening a critical path through the execution sequence.

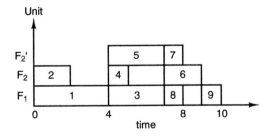

Figure 6-10   A schedule for the tasks of Figure 6-3 utilizing additional functional units

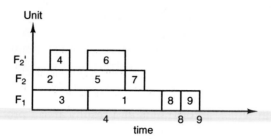

Figure 6-11   A schedule based on task interchange (see
Example 6-17)

Example 6-17

Consider exchanging tasks 1 and 3 in the program order of the task set in Figure
6-3. Then with two copies of the F_2 module and a lookahead window width of 3,
the makespan is reduced to 9 (see Figure 6-11).

This example illustrates that by adjusting the program order, we can obtain
shorter makespans without compromising the system's functionality.

In the absence of other mechanisms to support the illusion of instruction
completion occurring in program order, instruction reordering may alter the
relative order of the completion of an instruction and the detection of exceptions
generated by other instructions (see Section 6.6.8).

6.4.2 Register Assignments

A good register assignment algorithm can reduce the number of antidependen-
cies in the program. Recall that an antidependency is a WAR precedence constraint that is violated if one instruction writes over a value that should have
been read previously by another instruction. Issuing instructions out of order to
enhance parallelism will destroy functionality if the WAR precedence constraint
is violated; this will not happen if the old value is kept intact until all reads
specified in the program have been completed. Thus, we can assign a separate
register to hold the new value, with the old value retained in its register until all
of the necessary reads have been completed (whether they occur in order or not).
Instruction issue can proceed using the new register number to access the new
value and the old register number to access the old value. After the last read of
the old value has been completed, the old register can be freed for other uses.
Static scheduling in this style is straightforward.

Example 6-18

Here is a simple program sequence that illustrates the benifits of register reassignment.

$$v = u * y;$$
$$u = x * y;$$
$$t = x + 7$$
$$x = z + 1;$$
$$y = x + 3;$$
$$z = x + 6;$$

Each line corresponds to a single instruction in a R-R processor. Assume that there is a multiply unit that uses two clock times to form the product and an adder that uses a single time unit. If this program were executed without overlap, the makespan would be 8. Even without renaming, the program could be executed in an overlapped processor by scheduling the operations as suggested in what follows:

Multiplier	Adder
$v = u * y;$	$t = x + 7$
$u = x * y;$	$x = z + 1;$
	$y = x + 3;$
	$z = x + 6;$

This gives a makespan of 5 time units. The second addition cannot be moved up because its result overwrites an operand of the second multiplication.

If the second instance of x (the one that received the sum) were assigned to a different register than the first one (that was loaded before this sequence began), the second addition could be moved up and the makespan reduced to 4.

6.4.3 Unrolling Loops

The concept behind loop unrolling is quite simple—if we know that a loop will be executed n times, we can replace the loop with a sequence of n copies of the loop's body. This transformation accomplishes two important things: (1) it removes (or reduces) loop management instructions (count and test for completion), and (2) it permits more instructions to be considered when reordering a straight-line code segment. Unfortunately, it also increases the program's length. Thus, one can consider combining m (typically, $m = 2$ or 3) iterations into a straight-line loop body to reduce overhead and gain reordering opportunities to reduce the program execution time. For the moment, we focus on the loop bodies and assume that all conditional branches have been handled correctly.

After unrolling a loop, one can schedule interleaved execution of the unrolled set of loop bodies. The execution structure will bear some resemblance to the schedule of a pipelined execution of the loop bodies.

Example 6-19

Suppose that the tasks of Figure 6-3 constitute a loop body, with T_9 the loop termination test. If there is a barrier at T_9, the execution schedule is constructed by repeating the schedules we found earlier. The best schedule for a single execution of the loop body with two copies of each execution module and with an issue window width of 4 gives a makespan of 6 cycles (see Figure 6-12a).

Now unroll the loop and look at schedules interleaving several iterations of the loop body. An interesting overlapping combination for behavior in the steady state fits two executions of the loop body into 9 time units—the irregular template shown in Figure 6-12b can be repeated indefinitely. In the figure, we denote the task executions of consecutive iterations using numeric superscripts. For example, 1^0 denotes the first execution of task T_1, and 1^1 and 1^2 denote its execution for the second and third times. Fitting two iterations into 9 time units suggests an average duration of 4.5 cycles per iteration, but this cannot be achieved as an overall average because the irregular boundaries of the schedule template leave a small amount of idle time in the functional units at the beginning and at the end.

An important antidependency case arises from loop unrolling—suppose that the value of an object that is updated during each iteration is held in a register. For example, an iteration counter could be updated independently of the execution of the loop body. However, if the count is used within the loop body,

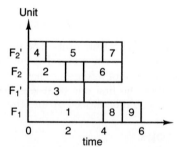

a) Schedule for a single iteration

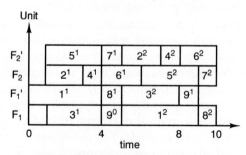

b) Schedule for two interleaved iterations

Figure 6-12   Loop unrolling can speed a loop body schedule

as a subscript, for example, its new value cannot replace the old one until the old
one has been used in its subscript role. The new value, however, could be computed and placed in another register.

Example 6-20

Consider this simple loop:

    for (i = 1 ; i < n ; i++)
        c[i] = b * c[i];

The processor has a multiplier, an adder, and a branch unit that tests for loop completion. There is one port to memory, which (unrealistically) takes only 1 cycle to
access memory. The multiplier uses 2 time units and the other modules use only 1
to complete their operations. Within each iteration, the adder has to be used once
to compute the address of the next component of c and once to increment i. Figure
6-13a gives a simple schedule for the loop as it was written. Unrolling the loop
does not improve the timing much because the register containing the address of

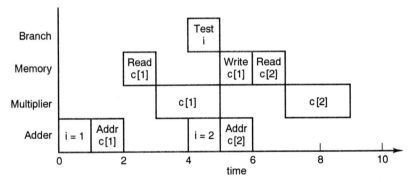

(a) The schedule for the loop body using the same registers during each iteration

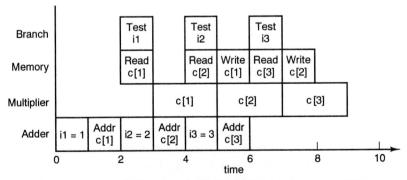

(b) The schedule for the loop with three register versions of each object

Figure 6-13 Multiple register versions can improve loop
unrolling

the current component of c must retain its value until the store is initiated. Thus, the loop body requires 4 time units on the average (with some unrolling).

By unrolling the loop three times and assigning three different registers to hold the address of c[i], we obtain the schedule of Figure 6-13b, which executes the loop body in 2 time units on the average.

The loop unrolling process presents a space–time trade-off. We increase the space occupied by the program (because the loop becomes longer) in order to speed execution. We cannot carry this on indefinitely, because the program can get too long to fit within the processor's instruction buffer or cache; if this occurs, the execution speed will decline dramatically due to the instruction cache misses.

6.4.4 Comments

One can enhance program execution speed by adding hardware or by utilizing compiler optimization techniques. These include renaming registers, providing more places to hold objects during a computation, and finding threads of execution or individual instructions that can be executed independently.[13] In the following section, we study ways that we can build systems to perform statically scheduled parallelism. Additional opportunities arise when dynamic parallelism is possible; Section 6.6 covers designs that exploit opportunities for introducing dynamic parallelism into program execution while still supporting the simple illusions.

6.5 IMPLEMENTING STATICALLY SCHEDULED PARALLEL ACTIVITIES

An efficient system that supports parallel activities requires a special hardware configuration. In this section, we explore several architectures supporting statically scheduled parallelism, including single instruction stream arrays, pipelines, barrels, VLIW processors, and horizontally microprogrammed processors. In the next section, we consider architectures supporting dynamically scheduled parallel activities.

6.5.1 SIMD Arrays

An *array processor* contains an array of *processing elements* interconnected in a regular pattern. In an array with a single instruction stream, the processing elements operate in response to control signals broadcast from a central control unit. A memory module (with its own local address space) is associated with each processing element. Data objects that serve as operands and store results

---

[13]   Many interactions between compiler techniques and system architecture are presented in [LILJ94].

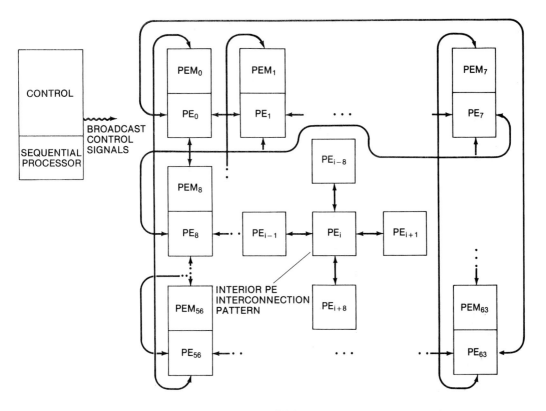

Figure 6-14   ILLIAC IV system structure

are accessed in the local memory. Every attempt to access an object stored in another processor's memory is implemented using local accessing and data communications through the interconnection network. The complete system has multiple data streams, because each processing element accesses its own local memory during each memory access commanded by the central controller. Thus, the array machine is an SIMD (single instruction stream, multiple data stream) system.

Figure 6-14 depicts the array processor structure. It has spatial parallelism with replicated physical modules.[14] A related array architecture, the systolic processor structure that achieves parallelism both by spatial diversity and by overlapped execution, is discussed in Appendix J.

The ILLIAC IV [BOUK72] exemplifies SIMD array machine design. It has a central control unit (that performs some indexing and counting functions) and an array of n (64, in the ILLIAC IV) processing elements (PEs). We number the PEs

---

[14]   This is not the structure of the Massively Parallel Processor (MPP) [POTT85] or various MIMD designs using arrays of independently operating processors, as in Hypercubes and the CM-5 [THIN91].

from 0 to (n - 1). Each PE has its own processor registers and ALU, a trivial control section, and an associated (2048-word) local memory (called PEM—processing element memory). The programmer-visible registers include a 64-bit routing register R and an 8-bit mode register D. The system control unit fetches instructions and distributes control signals and timing pulses to all PEs. Because the same signals arrive at each PE, each PE either performs the common array operation or idles during the operation. The system will efficiently execute any algorithm that simultaneously performs the same useful operation in all PEs.

Example 6-21

Consider this parallel program fragment:

```
int  x[ 8 ][ 8 ], y[ 8 ][ 8 ], z[ 8 ][ 8 ];          //three two-dimensional arrays
..
dosim for ( int i = 0, i <= 7, ++i )
    dosim for ( j = 0, j <= 7, ++j )
        x[ i ][ j ] = y[ i ][  j ] + z[ i ][ j ];
```

Now assign the components of x, y, and z to the PEMs such that the (i, j)th component of each array is in the (i, j)th PEM. The program's effect can be realized by simultaneously executing the statement

```
x = y + z;
```

in every PE. Thus, the computation in the 64-iteration loop is performed by a single execution of the noniterative instructions in the loop's body, and all loop overhead has been eliminated (because the problem size matched the array size).

The control unit (CU) can perform integer arithmetic and conditional tests to support overhead functions, such as loop control and simple global manipulations. Its own registers provide operands and store results from its operations.

The array machine's structure supports the efficient execution of any algorithm in which the same statements process a collection of diverse data sets, such as relaxation techniques to solve partial differential equations (PDEs). In a simple mapping of this type of problem, each processing element is associated with a single grid point in the problem space, with its local memory holding the state of all data objects corresponding to that point in the problem space.

To detail array machine design, we divide the discussion into three major subsections: data accessing, control structures, physical layout, and system performance.

Data Accessing.   A PE can directly access an object stored in its local PEM using a local address. To command such an access, the control unit broadcasts a common base address and addressing mode information that governs an address computation within each PE. The broadcast address comes directly from the instruction stream or was computed within the control unit using the contents of control unit registers. The local address computation may add the broadcast address to the contents of an index register local to the PE. This local indexing option permits simultaneous access to objects at different local addresses in different PEMs. For example, a "diagonal" slice across an array stored in layers across the PEMs can be accessed simultaneously by using local index values based on the positions of the PEs in the array.

Data values to be used in all PEs can be broadcast from the control unit like addresses; like addresses, they can be computed in the central control unit or can be obtained from the instruction stream. A broadcast constant is used exactly like an immediate operand in a uniprocessor program.

Neighboring PEs are connected through bidirectional communication links that attach to a PE-local communication register, called R (for routing). The R register in one PE is connected to the R registers in four neighboring PEs, as follows. There are two sets of paths. One path set interconnects the R registers to form a linear structure, there being a link from R_i to R_j, with $j = (i \pm 1) \bmod 64$. The other path set interconnects an R register to those in the two PEs eight positions away [$j = (i \pm 8) \bmod 64$]. The complete interconnection structure creates a logical 8 x 8 matrix structure, with additional toroidal connections between the top and bottom of each column and from the end of one row to the beginning of the succeeding row, as shown in Figure 6-14. This two-dimensional structure suggests that one refer to the neighbors in terms of geographic directions, as follows:

1. *North (N)*: $(i - 8) \bmod 64$
2. *South (S)*: $(i + 8) \bmod 64$
3. *East (E)*: $(i + 1) \bmod 64$
4. *West (W)*: $(i - 1) \bmod 64$

Special "routing" instructions in ILLIAC IV pass data among the R registers. In a single instruction, a data object can be moved to one neighboring R register. These actions occur simultaneously in all PEs, the overall effect being that the set of R register contents is shifted by one position across the array.

Because there is no conflict among the parallel data transfers, all of them can be executed in parallel. The routing facility is convenient for solving partial differential equations because the discrete version of the PDE requires that the solution satisfy a local relation at each grid point; these relations involve the value at the point and the values at specified neighboring points.

Control Structures. The common control unit fetches all array machine instructions, interprets the instructions, and issues PE control signals to implement PE array instructions.

Two control issues that do not have obvious answers for array machines concern the location of the program itself and the mechanisms provided to conditionally execute instructions.

The *program location* choice could follow either the Harvard or the von Neumann approach. The ILLIAC IV design follows the von Neumann approach; the PEMs store all instructions, including those executed entirely within the control unit. Instructions are fetched from the PEMs in blocks, one block containing 64-bit words (at the same local address) from each PEM in one row of the PE array. For instruction addressing, the address space is organized as though addresses were 64-way interleaved among the 64 PEMs. A naturally aligned block of eight consecutive words comprises a single instruction block. These 512-bit program blocks are buffered in the control unit; an individual instruction occupies 32 bits.

Global condition testing must be able to govern conditional sequencing or conditional execution at both global and local levels. Global control flow is determined within the control unit. Conventional control sequencing instructions define the program's global control structure; these include loop control and subroutine call and return instructions. Global conditional control flow tests made within the control unit can be used to terminate counting loops. However, not all control flow decisions can be confined to the control unit. For example, convergence testing in an iterative calculation requires examining conditions within individual PEs to determine global control flow. Thus, conditions local to each PE must be made visible within the control unit. Some global condition tests are based on condition bits within the D registers of the PEs. An array instruction selects which one of the 8 bits in the D register will be directed to the control unit. The 64-bit vector of these condition values is loaded into one of the control unit's four 64-bit registers, say, A. If PE_i is sending condition bit $C_{i,k}$, then the connection makes $A_i = C_{i,k}$. Conventional control unit instructions then test A's contents.

For local conditional execution, there is only one option: A PE may idle[15] rather than execute the instruction broadcast from the control unit. Let the *mode* M of a PE denote the contents of the PE's D register. The local idle decision compares the local mode against mode information broadcast from the CU to choose whether to execute the broadcast instruction or to idle during its execution. A general design in this style includes within each array instruction a mode condition (MC) field; the MC value determines which local mode values enable instruction execution and which values induce an idle cycle in the PE. Let j_i denote the value of M_i interpreted as a binary integer. With m bits in M_i and 2^m bits in MC, each bit of MC corresponds to one M_i value,[16] so let bit MC_j correspond to mode value j. The local execution rule is that PE_i in mode k performs the broadcast instruction if bit MC_k was set in the instruction. If bit MC_k is clear, the PE idles during the execution of the broadcast instruction.

---

[15] This rule is necessary because only the single (broadcast) control signal stream flows from the common control unit.

[16] In ILLIAC IV, $m = 2$.

Physical Layout. For highest performance, the links between PEs should be as short as possible, because the maximum length among the paths limits the speed of routing instructions. If the designer lays out the system according to the simple matrix view (such as the drawing in Figure 6-14), the connections around the ends of the rows and from the top to the bottom row will be much longer than the interior connections. Figure 6-15 shows a double folding of the array structure that reduces the longest link to the distance between two physical PEs.

Performance. How fast is an array machine? Certainly, an array system will perform well if the application problem matches the array structure defined by the PE interconnection pattern. Let n denote the number of PEs in the array, and let A denote the algorithm to be executed. A linear speedup suggests that the array processor should execute A n times faster than a uniprocessor built using the same technology and having the same PE/CU architecture. After all, the array has n processing elements, all working on the problem. The actual speedup of A executed on the array machine is much less than a factor of n for several reasons, including the following:

1. Not all instructions in A are within loops; the array structure speeds execution of loops but not of straight-line program sections.
2. Some loops in A may not fit exactly into n processors.
3. A large problem will have to be divided into blocks to fit the array machine, and additional operations will be required to coordinate the computations among neighboring blocks.
4. Certain algorithms, such as relaxation methods to solve partial differential equations, converge more slowly (i.e., require more iterations) when performed in parallel than when performed sequentially.

The following simple analysis illustrates the impact of the first limitation. To eliminate all other effects,[17] assume that all loops do fit exactly into the processor array; in other words, when a loop is being executed, every processing element is performing a useful function. Then the program outside the loops consists of sequential steps that cannot be distributed across the PEs in any manner; this implies that the sequential steps are performed in the control unit or in a single PE (while the other PEs idle).

To emphasize the architectural effects and discount technological effects, we compare the speed of the array machine against the speed of a conventional machine implemented with the same technology. Both machines have the same basic instruction execution rate performing the same instruction set. Let f denote the fraction of its time that the hypothetical conventional machine spends processing the iterative loops that were distributed across the array. Due to our generous assumption that everything fits perfectly into the array, this fraction f of

---

[17]   These assumptions give the benefit of the doubt to the array architecture.

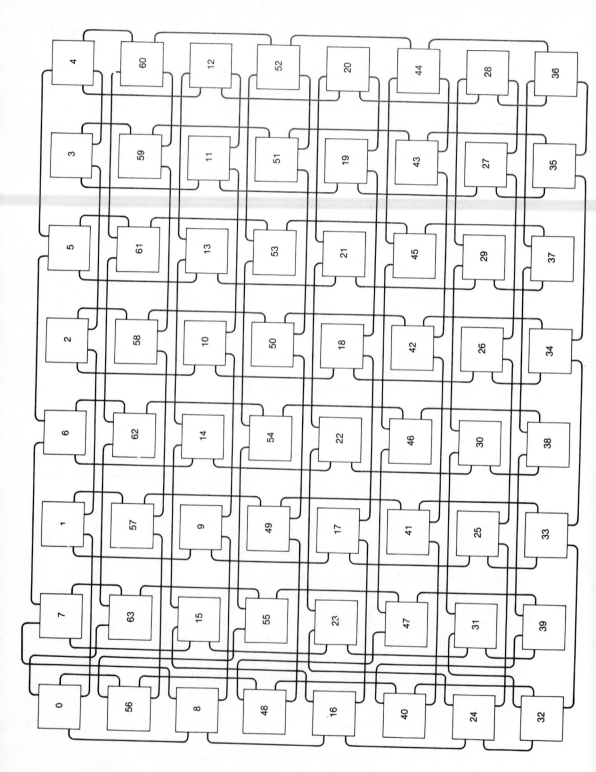

278

the algorithm can be speeded up by a factor of n when it executes on the array machine. But the remaining fraction $(1 - f)$ of the computation must be performed sequentially. During these computations, the array processor operates at the same speed as the conventional machine. Thus, the time T_A spent by the array processor is

$$T_A = T_C(1 - f + f/n) \qquad (6\text{-}2)$$

where T_C is the time spent by the conventional processor. Thus,

$$T_A/T_C = 1 - f[(n - 1)/n] \qquad (6\text{-}3)$$

The minimum limit of the ratio T_A/T_C is $1/n$, but this minimum is rapidly lost as f declines from 1. For example, when $f = n/(n + 1)$, the array will be idle half of the time. For $n = 64$, the array will be idle more than half of the time if the fraction of sequential operations in A is greater than 1.5%. When the array is idle half the time, the speedup factor is only 32.5. As f decreases, the speedup factor declines.

The array machine would fare better in this comparison if all sequential steps could be executed in the control unit and their execution could be overlapped with the execution of the array steps. This overlapping technique reduces the performance degradation due to the need for sequential execution of some instructions. These and related observations concerning the performance limits imposed by sequential regions within programs were originally made by Amdahl [AMDA67];[18] several variations of this are named Amdahl's Law.

The second and third observations on our performance degradation list concern the match between the machine's configuration and the application problem. With significant mismatch, the array PEs cannot be used all the time, and the optimistic speedup factors we just determined can be far off the mark.

Another aspect of the problem-array match issue concerns the time required to communicate values among neighboring points if the problem array is larger than the PE array. By judicious choice of the mapping of problem points onto the PE array, the communication time can be reduced.

A further factor cutting the array's performance benefits arises from the convergence properties of certain numerical algorithms. Numerical analysts have observed that relaxation methods for solving PDEs converge more slowly when the updates of a single array iteration are performed in parallel, rather than by a sequential processor scanning the array of problem grid points. It is difficult to quantify this effect without numerical experiments, but it does reduce the benefits of array processing.

---

[18]   It is important to note that Amdahl's rule is based on using the identical algorithm on both the array and sequential machines. In fact, there are many situations in which the Amdahl limit can be exceeded by modifying the algorithm for execution on the array machine.

Finally, if the loop body includes the evaluation of functions that use conditional execution to evaluate their behavior in different regimes, every PE will be idled during some conditional path; this reduces the speed enhancement.

Discussion. The array processing theme is recurrent in computing history. Early designers proposed interconnecting simple processing elements, each associated with a very small memory. An array architecture was proposed by von Neumann for solving partial differential equations. At that time, high logic costs made array architectures economically unfeasible. Another early parallel array machine design was Unger's paper design for a "Spatial Computer" [UNGE58]. This design included processing logic with each bit in a square array of visual sensors. Although only simple logical operations and counting were supported, the amount of logic per memory bit was too high. Serious thinking about array designs revived as technologies changed and logic costs started decreasing faster than memory costs. When logic is expensive compared to memory, a system configuration with a lot of memory supporting a small amount of logic is attractive. With cheaper logic, one might consider a system architecture with data manipulation logic migrated into the memory structure. With more logical elements per memory element, one could obtain more parallelism.[19] If only all of that parallelism could be used to perform "useful" functions for the application at hand! Then system performance could skyrocket. This is the basic argument for array processing.

Holland [HOLL59] proposed a parallel array architecture that had a simple processor associated with each memory word. Although the multiplicity of processors makes parallel processing possible, each parallel process does require many memory words to hold its data set and its program. If N denotes the average number of memory words required to run a single process (N includes both program and data words), the fraction of Holland machine processors that could be performing useful work must be less than $1/N$. This straightforward argument shows that the Holland design with one memory word per processor cannot be efficient. Furthermore, the system is almost impossible to program. First, because each instruction's successor has to be a physical neighbor of its predecessor, the program's flow structure has to be mapped onto the two-dimensional connectivity provided among the words in memory. This constraint means that every loop has to fit into a physically cyclic structure! Second, to access a data object, a path to the object has to be constructed by executing program steps; also a nontrivial task. Comfort modified Holland's design by moving the processing elements to one edge of the array; this improved the memory/processor ratio, but the programming problems were not significantly alleviated.

---

[19] This argument does not work in the limit, because a memory bit can be realized using simple logic, so having a processor associated with each memory word can never be a good design.

The ILLIAC IV system was the first array system to be implemented; it was used for about 10 years before being dismantled due to maintenance difficulties. Goodyear Aerospace built the Massively Parallel Processor (MPP); that system includes 1024 bit-serial processors in a square array; this machine is designed primarily for image processing [POTT85]. In terms of the internal logical connectivity, MPP is like the ILLIAC IV, but the program can control the connectivity at the edges of the array. The four possible edge configurations are as follows:

1. Open (matrix with no edge connections)
2. Single cycle (like ILLIAC IV)
3. Open cycle (like ILLIAC IV without a connection from PE_{N-1} to PE_0)
4. Cylinder (on each row the opposite ends of the row are connected to each other)

Many contemporary array machines do not fit the SIMD array paradigm, being collections of independent processors interconnected via message pathways or sharing a large memory. These architectures are discussed in Chapters 7 and 8.

6.5.2 Vector Operand Pipelines

Pipelines are efficient structures for implementing certain operations within the single instruction stream paradigm. You know that RISC processors can efficiently execute a processor's instruction stream by dividing the necessary activities into a sequence of substeps that can be performed in parallel on consecutive (independent) instructions. Arithmetic pipelines provide high throughput on arithmetic operations by overlapping the executions of consecutive instructions. In this section, we discuss this type of pipeline, emphasizing its use for processing vector operands.

The SIMD array machine's parallelism is achieved by simultaneously executing identical steps within a set of identical replicated processing elements; we might say that that architecture exploits *parallelism in space*. In a pipeline, different parts of a single operation are executed simultaneously within dissimilar modules connected into a cascade chain. Because each pipeline operand passes through several stages in successive time steps, we say that the pipeline exploits *parallelism in time*.

An array machine can achieve high performance if the problem size matches the machine array structure, but size mismatches greatly reduce system efficiency. A pipeline achieves fast processing by streaming the vector components through the pipeline. The number of cycles required to process an entire vector is linearly related to the length of the vector operand. The management overhead can be amortized across all components of the vector, so the effective

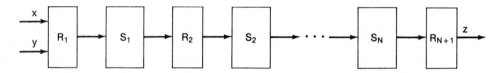

Figure 6-16   Basic pipeline structure (R, interstage register; S, functional stage)

system speed (counting operations on components) will be high if the vectors are long. The efficiency of a pipelined vector machine is limited by its maximum vector size, but it is not affected by vector size as much as the array machine's efficiency.

In this section, we describe the structure of arithmetic pipelines and show how they can be used to process vector operands. In addition, we show how to interface an arithmetic pipeline to the rest of the system; we need mechanisms to "feed" operands to the pipeline and to store results coming from the pipeline. We will describe two (programmer-visible) techniques—one interfaces the pipeline directly to memory,[20] and the other interposes programmer-visible registers between the pipeline and memory.

Pipeline Structures.   The basic pipeline structure depicted in Figure 6-16 performs an operation that has two operands and one result. Two operand vectors (x and y) enter the pipeline and one result vector (z) leaves the pipeline. The arithmetic operation is performed in the N pipeline modules (sometimes called "stages"), $S_1, \ldots, S_N$. Each stage contains only combinational logic. There is a holding register R_j between every pair of adjacent pipeline stages. The input to the logic in stage S_k comes from R_k and the output from S_k goes to R_{k+1}.

The objects that enter the pipeline on the same clock pulse are taken to be the operands for one execution of the pipeline's function (such as addition). Thus, to add two vectors, the machine feeds to an addition pipeline the operand vector components so those components with matching indices arrive during the same clock pulse. The corresponding component of the sum vector appears at the pipeline's output after a delay of N clock periods.

To discuss pipeline design issues, we need precise descriptions of vector operands, pipeline functionality, and pipeline timing.

Vector Operands.   The basic definition is straightforward:

Definition. A *vector operand* is a sequence of *component* data objects having identical type.

---

[20]   This is a comment about the programmer's view; the implementation will require buffer registers to synchronize the memory system to the pipeline.

The components of one vector are grouped together because they are stored in memory locations whose addresses follow a regular addressing pattern. It is tempting to assume that the phrase "regular addressing pattern" implies that all components of one vector must be stored in contiguous memory locations. This restrictive rule has some appeal, but enforcing this limitation would make it impossible to access a matrix (stored as a vector) to obtain one of its rows for one operation, and one of its column vectors for another operation.[21] In general, we want to support a "regular addressing pattern" that takes the contents of every nth memory location to form a vector operand. For example, a vector could constructed from the components of array w[i] by selecting w[5k].

The "stride" of a vector operand describes the relationship between the operand's logical structure and its addressing structure:

> **Definition.** The *stride of a vector operand* is the difference between the memory addresses of successive vector components, measured in units equal to the size of a single component of the vector.[22]

A stride of 1 implies that the vector's components are separated by an amount equal to the component size, so logically contiguous components are contiguous within virtual address space. At the hardware level, a stride of 1 implies using all contiguous information bits exactly once. This special case provides maximum execution efficiency.

The programmer's view of component selection is logically separated from the hardware addressing mechanism by two intervening mappings:

1. The component size separates adjacent components (measured in units of the addressing granularity).
2. The programmer's stride separates adjacent components of a subvector operand (measured in units of the sizes of the components of the underlying vector).

The hardware stride (measuring the difference between the physical addresses of contiguous vector components) is the product of the component size and the programmer's stride, as illustrated in Figure 6-17. The memory's organization and the hardware stride interact to enhance or diminish the effective memory bandwidth. A prime-way memory interleaving scheme can provide very high-speed memory–pipeline communication for almost all values that the programmer's stride might assume.

---

[21] This effect could be achieved by restructuring the matrix (by transposition, for example) between the two vector references. It would be better to have a way to make both types of references without re-copying (or restructuring) the entire vector between the two references. After all, restructuring will consume many memory cycles.

[22] Because the addressing pattern is "regular," and all components have the same type, the difference between the memory addresses of components v_i and v_{i+1} must be the same for all applicable i.

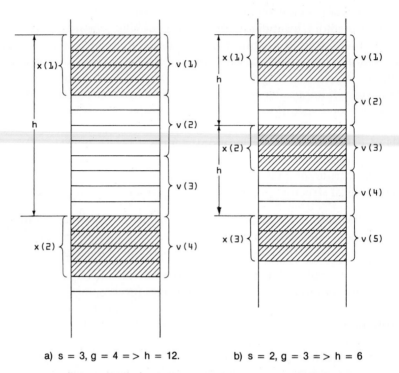

a) s = 3, g = 4 => h = 12.   b) s = 2, g = 3 => h = 6

Figure 6-17 Illustrating combinations of programmer
stride s, addressing granularity g, and hardware stride h.
(v denotes the underlying vector.)

Pipeline Functionality. The pipeline's effect on a set of components can be
expressed as the functional composition of the actions performed by the individual pipeline stages. Let u_i denote the output from stage i and let f_i represent the
function performed by stage i. Let the inputs to the first stage be denoted by x
and y, and the output of the last stage be z. The following relations are a direct
consequence of the pipelined interconnection:

$$u_1 = f_1(x, y) \tag{6-4}$$

$$u_i = f_i(u_{i-1}), \qquad 2 \leq i \leq N \tag{6-5}$$

The overall function can be ascertained by back substitution:

$$z = f_N(f_{N-1}(\cdots f_1(x, y) \cdots)) \tag{6-6}$$

Pipeline Timing. For correct functional behavior, the pipeline's control
logic must synchronize the arrival of operand components at the pipeline's two

inputs. Maximum speed is achieved if successive operand components arrive at the pipeline's input on successive clock pulses; then the processing rate would be one input operand pair per clock pulse. To introduce the pipeline's timing into our functional relationships, add a second subscript (k) on the u's to denote time and a single subscript on x, y, and z to denote components within each vector, as follows:

$$u_{i,k} = u_i(t = k)$$

$$x_i = i\text{th component of } x$$

$$y_i = i\text{th component of } y \tag{6-7}$$

$$z_i = i\text{th component of } z$$

Now define $t = 1$ to be the time when x_1 and y_1 arrive at the pipeline's inputs. Then we have the relations

$$u_{i,k} = f_i(f_{i-1}(\cdots f_1(x_{k-i}, y_{k-i}) \cdots)) \tag{6-8}$$

and

$$u_{N,k} = f_N(f_{N-1}(\cdots f_1(x_{k-N}, y_{k-N}) \cdots)) \tag{6-9}$$

The timing is such that z_k is the same as $u_{N,k+N}$; therefore, the computation of the pipeline is expressed by

$$z_k = f_N(f_{N-1}(\cdots f_1(x_k, y_k) \cdots)) \tag{6-10}$$

The pipeline's timing can be represented in a space–time diagram showing the progression of the vector components. Conventionally, this type of timing diagram uses one row for each vector component, with labels within blocks indicating the function being performed; this convention is similar to the one used to represent pipelined instruction execution, but it differs from the one used in Gantt charts, where each row corresponds to a functional element. Figure 6-18 represents pipelined vector addition using the component per row convention.

Pipelined System Design Issues. The designer must do the following:

1. Choose the programmer's view of vector operations.
2. Choose the vector operations to be pipelined.
3. Define the functions of the pipeline stages.
4. Design the hardware interface between the system memory and the vector-holding parts of the processor.

The Programmer's View of Vectors. A system can be designed to hide vector representation details from the programmer, leaving a high-level view of

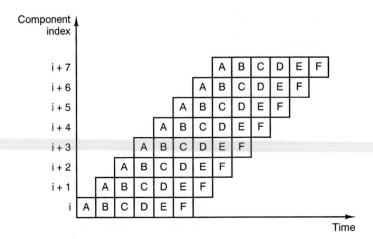

Figure 6-18   A space–time diagram illustrating pipeline
operation

vector objects and operations, much as the internal details of a C++ class definition can be hidden from a programmer using the class as an abstract data type.
Assume for the moment that every vector operation has two vector operands
and one vector result.[23] Some vector operations perform a component-by-
component scalar operation on each pair of corresponding components. Operations of this type include arithmetic (add, subtract, etc.) and logical operations
(and, or, etc.) on vector operands. Some component-by-component operations,
such as divide,[24] might not be considered by a strict mathematician to be a vector
operation, but are included in some vector machines.

The programmer's view of a vector machine's operations is affected by the
designer's choice of the locations from which vector operands interact with the
pipeline. In particular, are vector operands fed to the pipeline from memory locations or from processor registers? In a similar manner, we ask whether vector
results are stored in memory or in registers. The answers to these questions affect programming details, especially the operand specifications. A vector stored
in memory is specified by its origin, its length, and its stride. All three parameters must be provided, although in some designs (for some operations), the
stride is fixed at 1 by the processor design. A vector in a register is specified by
the register number and the vector's length. The vector length is limited by the
size of the vector registers or by the size of the length field within a vector
descriptor.

---

[23]   Minor adjustments will have to be made to the following presentation to apply it to operations for
which this simple assumption does not apply.
[24]   Under the componentwise view of vector operations, the vector machine versions of multiplication and division are $c_i = a_i{}^*b_i$ and $c_i = a_i/b_i$.

TABLE 6-1   FIELD USAGE IN THE CDC STAR FAMILY[a]

| Field Name | Interpretation of the Contents | |
	The Field Contains	The Designated Register Contains
F	Function	
G	Subfunction[b]	
X		Offset for P
A		P's length and base address
Y		Offset for Q
B		Q's length and base address
Z		Control vector base address
C		R's length and base address

[a] In addition, register (C + 1) contains the offset for both the control vector and for R.

[b] For simple operations, such as ADD, the subfunction field determines many things, including whether an operand is taken true or complemented, whether an operand component's magnitude should be used, whether a scalar value should be "broadcast" in place of a vector, and whether register (C + 1) is used (if it is not used, the offset is taken to be zero).

Where are pipeline operand and result specifications for a vector instruction found? Because the specification of a vector located in memory can be large, it probably should not be located in the instruction itself. Thus, we find designs with such specifications in memory or in processor registers. The following examples illustrate the contrasting design choices.

Example 6-22

In CDC STAR-100 machines,[25] vectors are located in memory; the processor takes vector descriptors from processor registers. There are 256 registers, each holding 64 bits. There are no vector registers. Register numbers in each vector instruction specify the locations of the descriptors of the vectors involved in the operation. Each descriptor spans two registers, which need not be contiguous. Figure 6-19 illustrates the vector descriptions, the format of many two-operand instructions, and the memory operands. Table 6-1 describes the roles of the fields in the instruction, where P and Q denote the operand vectors, and R denotes the result vector. For each vector, one register contains the origin of the space holding the vector and the vector's length; another register contains the origin ("offset") of the vector operand within the space.[26] Thus, one register could used to hold a common offset

---

[25]   This class of machines includes the Cyber 203, the Cyber 205, and the ETA10.

[26]   Because the length defines the total space available, the actual vector length is the difference between the length of the space and the offset of the first component.

shared by several vectors. The length field permits each vector to have as many as 65,536 components. The stride of every vector is 1. Every vector in an operation has an independent length. The length of the computed result R is determined by the amount of space allocated for the result. If the operands are not as long as the result, the processor fills them out with zeroes.

The basic vector operations in this processor use an implicit unit stride. To achieve the effect of other strides, the processor supports general vector copy instructions that perform scatter and gather operations; these copy between a unit stride vector and a set of components that have arbitrary positions (specified by a vector of indices) within another vector. For example, the gather operation with X and Y operand vectors and the result vector Z performs this assignment for each i: $Z[i] = X[Y[i]]$.

Example 6-23

The CRAY-1 processor [CRAY75] contains eight vector registers, each able to hold 64 components. Each vector instruction contains register numbers specifying the source and destination vector registers. The vector length for a vector operation is taken from the processor's VL register.[27] The operation

$$x = y + z;$$

with x, y, and z being vectors of length less than 65, can be performed by the instruction sequence[28]

```
LOAD A0,=length;    //get the length from the instruction stream
LOAD VL,A0;   //put the length in VL (it cannot be loaded directly from memory)
LOAD V1,Y;        //load the addend
LOAD V2,Z;        //load the augend
ADD V1,V2,V3;     //perform the addition
STORE V3,X;       //store the result
```

This program fragment includes register–memory transfers. Once the processor's vector registers are loaded, a sequence of operations can be performed on the same vectors; this saves memory accesses, which improves system performance compared to a system with vectors accessed directly from memory.

To make it easy to handle regular nonunit stride patterns, the processor has an instruction that constructs a vector $x[i] = i * p$, where p is a parameter of the instruction. This index vector can be used to control regular scatter and gather operations (see Example 6-27).

What Operations Should Be Pipelined? The second pipeline design issue concerns the selection of the operations to be pipelined. Frequently executed vector operations are prime candidates for pipelined implementation, because their high execution frequency implies the possibility of a large speed improvement. The speed payoff is not the whole story—the designer must consider whether pipelining the operation is feasible. To make this determination, the designer

---

[27]   All vectors participating in a single instruction must have the same length.

[28]   Register names starting with V are vector-related; a V register named with a numeric designation, such as V3, holds a vector value.

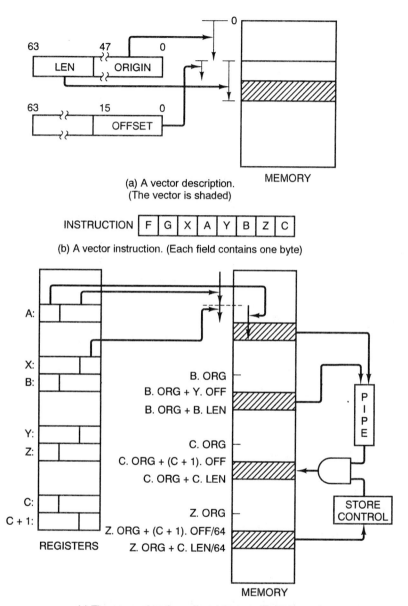

(a) A vector description.
(The vector is shaded)

(b) A vector instruction. (Each field contains one byte)

(c) The operand and result register specifications and
memory spaces

Figure 6-19   Vector operands and instructions in the
CDC STAR series

examines algorithms that can be used to implement each operation. To be pipelined, an operation must be equivalent to a functional composition of a set of
suboperations. In other words, the operation must fit the functional description
in Equation (6-10). An operation that satisfies this functional composition condition may not be pipelined due to its logical complexity or due to inherent delays.

Pipeline Structure Design. The third pipeline design issue concerns the detailed pipeline structure for implementing the selected operations. In addition to
the functional composition requirement, each pipelined operation must meet
several criteria derived from the synchronism implicit in the pipeline structure.
With synchronous timing, the pipeline stage delays cannot be shorter than the
delay of the slowest suboperation. Thus, to avoid serious timing bottlenecks due
to pipeline stage delays, all suboperations should have comparable complexities,
so they can be completed in roughly the same amount of time. It may be feasible
to separate a slow suboperation into several cascaded suboperations to relieve a
speed bottleneck.

The pipeline's synchronism forces the interstage data flow and control flow
structures of the computational algorithm to be independent of the operand data
values. Any value-dependent flow pattern adjustment might disrupt the timing,
forcing the designer to reject an algorithm that might be attractive for nonpipelined computers.

Example 6-24

Booth's multiplication algorithm scans the multiplier's bits, doing nothing unless
two consecutive bits of the multiplier differ, in which case it either adds or sub-
tracts the multiplicand with the partial product. This algorithm is attractive for a
nonpipelined implementation because shifting and testing is faster than addition,
so cycles can be shortened if they do not require any arithmetic operation.[29] But
conditionally shortening the cycle makes the multiplication time depend on the operand values.

Why is a simple implementation of this algorithm inappropriate for a pipeline?
Although the number of additions/subtractions required to form the complete
product cannot be greater than half the number of bits in the multiplier, an addition may be needed at any bit position. Therefore, a straightforward pipelined implementation of the algorithm must permit an addition in every bit position. With
an adder at every bit position, we might as well implement the shift-add algorithm,[30] because the synchronous timing constraints prevent us from reducing the
delays when no additions are required.

Example 6-25

Integer addition can be separated into partial addition and carry propagation.
Floating-point addition contains the same steps, preceded by sign adjustment,[31]

---

[29]   Another way to avoid large delays is to use a carry save adder, as in a Wallace Tree multiplier.
[30]   See Problem 6-24 for another option.
[31]   This is necessary with the sign-magnitude convention (see Section 5.3.2).

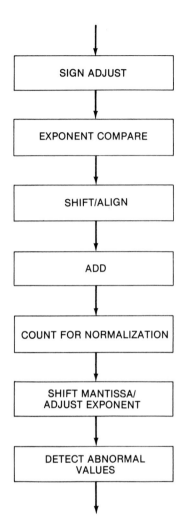

Figure 6-20   A floating-point addition pipeline structure

exponent comparison, and mantissa shifting, and followed by result normalization. This suboperation decomposition is suitable for a pipelined implementation, as illustrated in Figure 6-20.[32]

Example 6-26

Unlike addition, integer division is not easily separated into pipelined stages. The obvious implementation of the pencil-and-paper trial subtraction division algorithm requires a pipeline with a number of stages equal to the length of the operand's mantissa, and each stage has a logical complexity close to the complexity of a nonpipelined division module. A pipelined implementation using this strategy is not likely to be cost-effective, because the hardware cost is likely to be high. Also,

---

[32]   One has to add logic to detect and handle the unusual values (infinity and NaN) in the IEEE standard.

division is infrequently performed. Therefore, speeding division would produce little decrease in the average instruction execution time.

With a good set of suboperations for implementing each vector operation, the pipeline's general structure for implementing the scalar operation can be drawn. If several different operations are performed in the same pipeline, the designer must choose how to integrate them into one comprehensive pipeline structure. Switches placed between the stages, statically set for the duration of the operation being performed, could configure the pipeline for the current operation. Such static switching forces the controller to wait until the last result of an operation to leave the pipeline before a different operation can be initiated. To overcome this delay, one could design a pipeline with the function code passed along with the operand values. A design in this style may have larger stage delays than a design with static switching, but this approach allows more overlap between successive operations.[33]

Most linear pipeline structures have no feedback within the pipeline. By adding feedback around pipeline stages, other vector operations, such as dot product, can be implemented (see Problem 6-30).

Processor–Memory Interfacing. The fourth design issue concerns the interface between the memory and vectors within the processor. This design problem is easy in a load/store architecture becaues the interfaces to vector registers do not pose rigid timing constraints. Therefore, we do not study this version in detail. In contrast, a direct connection between a pipeline and memory poses timing constraints because a new set of components must be fed into the pipeline on each clock pulse. In a similar manner, vector result components must be sent from the pipeline's output to memory, one on each clock pulse. Because the interface problems at the pipeline's input and output are symmetric, it is sufficient to detail the input problem.

To match the arrival and departure of operand and result components to the pipeline's timing, (1) the interface controller must buffer all incoming and outgoing information, (2) the memory requests must be timed to synchronize with the pipeline, or (3) the pipeline must be designed to accommodate "blank" slots that can be inserted whenever an operand is not available at the correct time (and the result writing process must be able to buffer components that cannot be sent directly to memory).

The first of these options is attractive, so consider adding buffers between the pipeline and memory so that the pipeline can always accept and emit vector components during every cycle. The input buffer must be large enough to assure that it can always feed the pipeline, even under a worst-case timing mismatch. A straightforward calculation determines the buffer-size requirements

---

[33] See Problem 6-30.

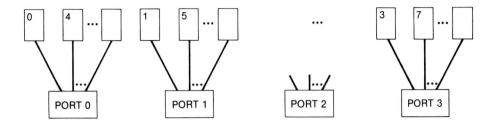

Figure 6-21   Memory port organization in the CRAY2

from the longest memory access delay and the number of component streams (counting both inputs and outputs); see Problem 6-21.

A design with rigid timing may not need buffers; this approach is used in the CRAY-2 when loading and storing vector register contents.

Example 6-27

The CRAY-2 memory is divided into four "quadrants," each containing 32 modules [CRAY85]. Each module holds 2 million words of 64 bits each. Figure 6-21 shows this structure. Four "background" processors can perform vector operations. Each processor has a fixed phase during which it is permitted access to each memory quadrant; these "slots" are allocated according to a four-phase cycle, as illustrated in Figure 6-22. If the module number of a processor's memory request matches its current phase group, the access proceeds without delay. On the other hand, an out-of-phase request must be delayed until the proper slot time arrives.

If the stride is 1, the processor's first component access will synchronize with proper phasing for accessing all vector components during consecutive memory cycles. A stride not equal to 1 can occur in the "gather" processor instruction, which loads a vector register from memory. During this instruction, the memory access control logic slows the processor's memory requests to a rate such that it can be guaranteed that (1) all requests can be satisfied, and (2) the results will arrive at the processor in their proper order.

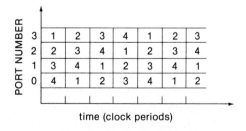

Figure 6-22   The phasing of process-port interactions in the CRAY2. (Each number indicates which processor can access the memory port during the clock period.)

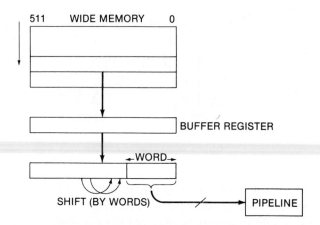

Figure 6-23 Converting super words to a stream of words (CDC STAR-100)

Memory Bandwidth. To make vectors available to the processor, the memory bandwidth may have to be increased, whether the memory is connected to vector registers or to operation pipelines.

Two methods to increase memory bandwidth come to mind—widen the memory so that more bits are accessed in a single memory cycle or interleave the memory so that several memory requests can be handled "simultaneously." If the hardware stride is 1, widening the memory and fetching many contiguous bytes in a single memory cycle results in little waste because we have foreknowledge that the fetched data will really be required to perform the operation.[34]

Example 6-28

In the CDC STAR-100 series, all operand and result vectors for pipelined operations have a stride of 1, except during scatter and gather operations. The STAR-100 memory is organized into 512-bit "super words" (swords) with 16 parity bits apiece. A sword from memory is copied to buffer registers in the processor. Figure 6-23 depicts using a shift register for the (conceptual) conversion of swords into word-serial form to feed a pipeline.

Memory bandwidth can be increased by interleaving. In this case, there is no reason to force the hardware vector stride to be 1. Without loss of generality, we assume that the width of each memory module exactly matches the width of a single vector component. For any uniform component spacing within the memory address space, the memory controller can be designed to sequence the memory requests according to the hardware stride value. The requests will be evenly distributed among the modules if the stride value and the degree of interleave

---

[34] This is not true at the vector's end, but this "edge effect" does not impact performance in a major way.

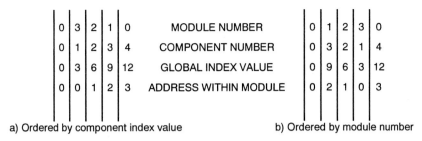

0	3	2	1	0	MODULE NUMBER	0	1	2	3	0
0	1	2	3	4	COMPONENT NUMBER	0	3	2	1	4
0	3	6	9	12	GLOBAL INDEX VALUE	0	9	6	3	12
0	0	1	2	3	ADDRESS WITHIN MODULE	0	2	1	0	3

a) Ordered by component index value   b) Ordered by module number

Figure 6-24 Illustrating how a stride relates to an interleaved memory. (Module width = one address; stride = three addresses.)

are relatively prime.[35] For these reasons, a prime-way interleave might be considered to reduce the number of problematic stride values. This prime-interleave design is used in the BSP system, the interleave being 17 [KUCK82]. Figure 6-24 illustrates the order of requests presented to a four-way interleaved memory when the stride is 3.

Pipeline Speed. How much speedup is achieved by pipelined implementations? The answer depends upon whether the pipeline must be flushed before starting the next operation. Consider a design requiring flushing, and thus forbidding overlap between consecutive pipeline operations. This timing is illustrated in Figure 6-25. The time for a vector operation comprises the elapsed time between its initiation and the initiation of the next operation. There are two components: (1) T_{load}, the time spent feeding operands to the pipeline; and (2) T_{empty}, the time spent emptying the pipeline after the last operand components have been presented. Thus, we have

$$T = T_{load} + T_{empty} \tag{6-11}$$

In all designs, T_{load} depends linearly on the vector length. The flush time (in units of pipeline cycles) is always one less than the number of pipeline stages.

Example 6-29

A pipeline with a delay of three clock pulses can accept a set of operands every clock pulse. For vectors of length L, the execution time T is $L + 2$. The per component execution time decreases as the length of the vectors increases; see Table 6-2.

Design Constraints and Variations. The major pipeline design constraint comes from the synchronous clocking of the interstage registers. All information must move through the pipeline at the same rate. As a consequence, the

---

[35]   The difficulty is easily seen by looking at the situation when the stride equals the degree of interleave. All components of the operand vector are located in the same physical module, and the memory bandwidth equals the bandwidth of a single module. If this bandwidth had been adequate, we would not have been worrying about techniques to improve it!

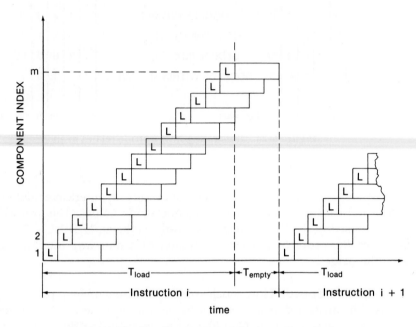

Figure 6-25   Pipeline timing with no overlap. (L denotes
a load cycle.)

interstage register holding information relevant to the operands affecting the
computation of the output vector component c_i must hold *all* such information
that is present in the pipeline. Now it may be true that some of the data in an interstage register may be neither used nor changed by the logic in the next stage.
The information must be gated through this stage to the next interstage register
nevertheless, because otherwise it would lose its synchronism with the other information relevant to its component computation. What would happen if this
clocking constraint were violated for some information I present in stage s?

TABLE 6-2   PIPELINE INSTRUCTION EXECUTION
TIME AS A FUNCTION OF VECTOR LENGTH

Vector Length	Operation Time (clocks)	Time per Component (clocks)
5	7	1.4
10	12	1.2
32	34	1.06
256	258	1.01

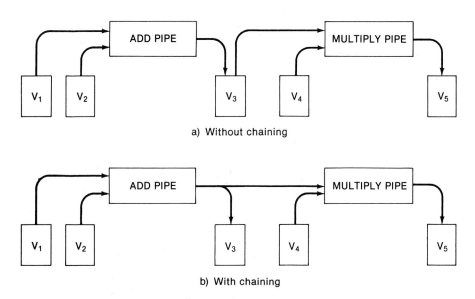

a) Without chaining

b) With chaining

Figure 6-26   Pipeline data flows affected by chaining

Assume that *I* will be needed at stage *k* farther down the pipeline.[36] At stage *k*, we need *I*, which was in stage *s* $(k - s)$ clock cycles ago. How can we find the proper component of *I*'s information? We might put it in a shift register. This design is equivalent to one that shifts *I* through the interstage registers in all intermediate stages, which is the same as synchronously shifting it through all stages.

An important variation on a basic pipelined design synchronizes the activities among multiple pipelines to save time. The CRAY-1 design includes this *chaining* possibility. Chaining can be initiated when the result vector X from one pipeline P_1 is destined to register V_k, which is an input operand for another pipeline P_2. Without chaining, pipeline P_2 would have to wait to read X from register V_k. The read could start after all component values had been written into V_k.[37] With chaining, P_2 accepts X directly from P_1, provided that no delay has to be inserted in the path between the pipelines. Figure 6-26 shows the data paths that correspond to operand chaining. An optimizing compiler could rearrange program steps to ensure that chaining could be used. Figure 6-27 illustrates the pipeline timing with and without chaining.

In some applications, most vectors and matrices contain many components whose values are so small as to be insignificant. A pipeline can save time when operating on such *sparse vectors* by skipping across those components that have

---

[36]   If it were not needed in any succeeding stage, it should not have even been sent to stage *s*.
[37]   The register could be designed so that the only delay corresponds to the time to read a single component after it has been written into V_k; the text describes the CRAY-1 design.

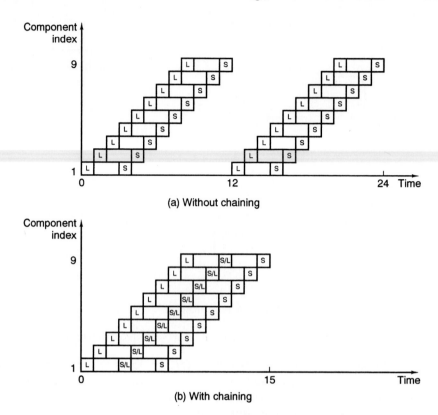

Figure 6-27   Pipeline timing affected by chaining.
(L = load pipe; S = store pipe result.)

insignificant values. The insignificance criterion is problem-dependent; without loss of generality, we suppose that only zero components are insignificant. A more general insignificance criterion could be reduced to this case by replacing insignificant component values with zero values. A special representation scheme for a sparse vector V consists of (1) a vector V_{NZ} containing the values of the nonzero components of V, compressed together, and (2) a *control vector* V_C indicating which components of V are zero and which (the others) should be taken from V_{NZ}. Figure 6-28 illustrates this representation, as used in the CDC STAR computers.

Example 6-30

A basic way to implement sparse vectors is to mask the act of storing result components in memory. In the CDC STAR machines, the mask is in the control vector; this vector contains a 1 in every bit position corresponding to a component that is to be saved. The length of the control vector is equal to the length of the result vector. Masking by the control vector determines whether the result component is

V	3,	0,	0,	6,	0,	−2,	0,	1,	0,	4,	3,	0,	7,	0,	0,	2,	0
V_C	1	0	0	1	0	1	0	1	0	1	1	0	1	0	0	1	0
V_{NZ}	3,			6,		−2,		1,		4,	3,		7,			2	

Figure 6-28   Sparse vector representations
(CDC STAR series)

actually stored or not; the component's value is always computed, but any component not stored cannot signal an exception condition.

For example, suppose we are adding u to v to produce w, using the control vector t. Here are the vector values before the operation

$$u = (2, 3, 7, 1, 4)$$
$$v = (1, 2, 6)$$
$$w = (6, 9, 10, 12, 8)$$
$$t = (1, 1, 0, 1, 0)$$

After the addition, the value of w is

$$w = (3, 5, 10, 1, 8)$$

If the addition of u_2 and v_2[38] had caused a trap, the result in w would have been the same, and no trap would have been signaled.

Operations accepting sparse vector representations[39] and representation-changing operations are provided: The STAR has a componentwise vector compare operation whose component-by-component comparison results are stored as a vector of status bits. The COMPRESS operation compresses a vector to form the sparse representation, the compression process being governed by the bits in a control vector operand. The instruction sequence

```
COMPARE A,B,C      //B = threshold; C is the status vector result
COMPRESS A,C,D
```

converts a complete vector in A to a sparse representation consisting of the control vector C and the compressed vector D containing the significant component values. Another processor operation compresses a vector by comparing its components against a second vector; this saves the need for a separate COMPARE operation because the control vector contents depend only upon the values in the vector.

Comments. By pipelining vector operations, the designer can significantly improve the speed of these operations. Pipelining the implementation of vector operations is the key to the high performance of most "supercomputers." In

---

[38] In the C++ style, we use zero-origin indexing, although the manufacturer uses one-origin indexing.
[39] See Problem 6-35 for the pipeline control logic for sparse operands.

principle, all operands and partial results pass through an assembly-line-like sequence of processing stages separated by clocked interstage holding registers. By careful design, the processor–memory interface can feed components to the pipeline every processor cycle. The timing requirement is less restrictive if the vector pipelines are connected to vector registers, rather than to the system's memory.

Variations on the basic pipeline design have been used to compute vector dot products and other functions that do not exactly match the basic pipeline's straight-line pattern. Two design variations reduce delays between operations: one passes the operation code along with the data, and the other chains together consecutive operations that use different pipelines. Systolic arrays are related to the pipelining scheme, but the identical modules in the systolic array perform complete operations on single components of the problem's vectors; systolic arrays are covered in more detail in Appendix J.

Pipelining of nonvector operations has been used to improve the performance of scalar machines such as the IBM 360 Model 91 [ANDE67] and the CDC 7600, where overlapped execution of the same operation can be performed on different (scalar) operands. Pipelined instruction execution, which is somewhat different from arithmetic pipelineing, is the key to the success of RISC processor designs.

6.5.3 Barrel Processing

The barrel structure is similar to the pipeline structure. In both, processing is divided into subfunctions, each fitting into a fixed time interval. The two structures differ, however, in philosophy and application. A pipeline processes related data quickly for a single process; it contains more hardware than the minimum logically necessary to perform the operations. On the other hand, a barrel design handles unrelated data for several unrelated processes more slowly than a single processor; it is designed with minimum hardware beyond that required to meet its functional requirements. Barrel structures can be effective when one wishes to implement a set of logically independent processors having identical characteristics, with low speed requirements. The basic barrel architecture is shown in Figure 6-29.

In this section, we describe the basic operation of a barrel design, the possibility of overlapped barrel designs, and the performance of barrel systems, including their usefulness for device and channel controllers.

Basic Barrel Operation. An N-stage barrel cycles state information for N independent processes; at each processing step, the processor performs one step of the process whose state is held in the interstage register R_N that feeds the processing logic. On the next clock pulse, the result of the step is placed into R_1, while the other process states are simply passed along the "shift-register" structure.

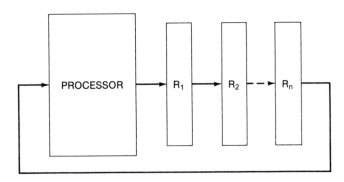

Figure 6-29   Barrel architecture with a single
processing stage

The overall effect is that of N independent processors each running at $1/N$ times the basic speed determined by the clock period. We have virtual parallelism, but there is no real parallelism inside the machine.[40] Rather, there is timeslicing at a fixed low granularity.

The barrel performs different operations on successive cycles, because the operation performed by the processor in the barrel is based on the information held in register R_N. In other words, the barrel's function selection design is similar to the mechanism used in a pipeline in which the function code travels with the data operands.

If the barrel has only one processing stage, the barrel structure can be realized easily using a random-access memory to hold process states (see Figure 6-30). Include a barrel (memory) address register BAR whose contents point to the state ready to be processed (this corresponds to the state stored in R_N in the shift-register realization). During a single step, the following activities occur:

1. Read the state memory at the address in BAR to the barrel data register (BDR).
2. Perform the indicated operation on the information in BDR.
3. Write the resulting state information back to BDR and then to the state memory at the location designated by BAR.
4. Increment BAR (modulo the barrel's length) and loop back to step 1.

Overlapped Barrel Operation.   The preceding execution scenario also applies to an overlapped system implementing a barrel holding N process states. By interleaving the state memory, we can realize overlapped execution. For example, if the state memory were interleaved with an even degree of interleave, the memory accesses in step 1 of cycle $(n + 1)$ and in step 3 of cycle n could be overlapped, because they access states held in different memory modules. With

[40]   If the barrel processing is pipelined, there is real parallelism inside; we discuss this design later.

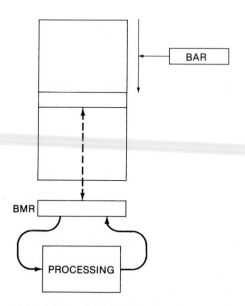

Figure 6-30   A barrel processor using a random-access
memory to hold process status

four-way interleave in the state memory, all the steps can be overlapped (see
Problem 6-36). This design can be generalized to produce a pipelined barrel
processor coupled to an interleaved state memory.

Barrel Performance.   What performance does the barrel structure provide? We discuss the simple barrel system with a single processing stage. On the
basis of overall throughput, we expect the barrel system to be comparable to a
uniprocessor system executing a single process.

How does a barrel system compare against a system containing n slower
processors? The barrel system has less hardware. The barrel system could be
built with a technology compatible with other system logic, even though barrel
processor's instruction rates do not demand fast logic. Technological compatibility among all logic in the system is attractive for design, fabrication, test, and
stocking replacement parts. These considerations lead one to consider barrel
structures to implement slow channel controllers for a system with a fast central
processor. All is not roses, however; one disadvantage of the barrel over the n-
processor design is that the barrel has only one physical processor, so a single
failure in that processor will disable all n virtual processors.

Comments.   How does a barrel system compare against a single, fast
processor multiplexed by a software scheduling algorithm? There seems to be little difference; after all, we could view the barrel processor as a fast processor

```
                              compute condition
                              if true goto a
                              <common>
        if (condition) {    b: <next part of program>
            uncommon}
        else {
            common
        }                   a: <uncommon>
                              goto b
```

        (a) Program   (b) Layout in memory

Figure 6-31   Barrel processing execution schedule.
(Process 2 serving a device requiring a READ every
16 cycles.)

multiplexed on a cycle-by-cycle basis. Is there any difference between the systems? Clearly, the nonbarrel processor is multiplexed over a time interval encompassing the execution of many instructions. Thus, the simple fast processor provides bursty intervals of fast execution for its processes, whereas the barrel provides regular short execution intervals. If the processor controls a peripheral device, during a block transfer, it might have to feed data to the device at a reasonably uniform rate. To accommodate a controller with bursty processing to this environment would require a data buffer between the processor and the device. The barrel processor provides a guaranteed service rate and response time, so it can provide steady service to each device without any hardware buffering.

Example 6-31

A high-level language statement to read an input file will be translated by the compiler into a call to a procedure that constructs a control program to command the device holding the desired file. Within that control program, the compiler uses block read commands to request copying a block of information from the file into a specified memory buffer. The block copy is implemented by the channel controller as a sequence of individual instructions, each one transferring an individual data item from the device to the memory. The time interval between these data transfers (and the interval between the read instructions) must match the device data rate. In a programmed controller, the read timing interval can be adjusted by inserting null operations (NOPs) into the program. If the programmer knows the basic execution speed of the control program, he can insert the proper number of NOPs to match the device speed.

To illustrate this timing with a barrel controller, suppose that the barrel supports four virtual processors. Then the program for a particular device will utilize every fourth cycle (see Figure 6-31). If the device read rate is one-sixteenth of the barrel's instruction execution rate, the program requires three NOPs between every read. For this case, the barrel's execution follows the pattern illustrated in the figure.

A second advantage of the barrel design over the time-multiplexed processor is that the barrel's scheduling decisions can be trivially implemented in hardware. This low-level scheduling defines the base timing on which we can build a program to provide regular interactions. In summary, the barrel design is very effective when the processor must interact with the environment at a steady pace.

Barrel structures have been used in numerous commercial systems. The Honeywell H800 system [HONE60] implemented eight virtual processors using a state memory, although they were scheduled on a priority basis. Historically, the next important use of the barrel architecture was in the CDC 6600 [THOR70] system, where a barrel implemented 10 "peripheral processors," designed primarily to control input/output devices. Many high-performance systems use a barrel processor to implement a set of channel controllers.

6.5.4 VLIW Processors

Each instruction in a very long instruction word (VLIW) processor is sufficiently wide to include more than one instruction to be executed during the same instruction execution cycle. In effect, each instruction includes a separate start list (see Section 6.2.2). The code generator (statically) determines a set of instructions that could be simultaneously executed without violating functionality, and collects them into a single instruction word. No dynamic scheduling decisions are required.

A simple approach to forming long instruction words uses a field within the long instruction word for each functional unit within the processor. For example, with an integer module and a floating-point module, the long instruction word would contain two instructions—one for the integer unit and one for the floating-point unit. The compiler forms the wide instructions. The instruction width depends upon the number of functional units within the processor.

The probability of being able to place useful instructions within all fields of one instruction will diminish as the number of fields increases. In this design approach, one cost of increased parallelism is additional memory space to hold the fixed-format wide instruction words. This space is lost because the amount of added parallelism is not proportional to the increase in instruction width.

This design approach was used in the Multiflow computers [COLW87], but has not proved popular because wide instruction words cannot always be filled with useful operations. Another disadvantage is that the very long instruction can not be completed until all of its component instructions have been completed; this implies that any cache miss will slow the entire system because the next wide instruction cannot be issued until the cache miss has been resolved. Finally, any VLIW instruction format and interpretation is very dependent upon the processor's structure; if this is changed as models are upgraded, all programs must be retranslated to give maximum benefit from the processor's parallelism. This form of static parallelism has been supplanted by the dynamic parallel instruction issue schemes incorporated in superscalar processors (see Sec. 6.6).

6.5.5 Horizontal Microprogramming

Like VLIW processors, horizontally microprogrammed machines utilize wide instruction words that specify simultaneous activities. Here the basic operations are at the register-transfer level. Sequences of these microinstructions are then devised to implement the instruction set of a virtual processor. Compared to vertically microprogrammed processors (in which each microinstruction specifies only a single activity), horizontally microprogrammed processors do provide faster system speeds. For this reason, designers have always used wider microinstructions in higher-performance processor designs, tailoring the design to speed execution of frequently executed processor instructions.

The design decisions at the microprogramming level are unlike those confronted in VLIW and superscalar designs, primarily because the operations are so primitive that the complexity of dynamic issue logic is not balanced by sufficient benefits. Thus, dynamic parallelism decisions are not appropriate at the microprogrammed level. This decision rests upon several facts: First, there are few uncertainties about the course of execution within a microinstruction sequence. Second, microprograms exhibit high degrees of conditional branching while decoding fields or machine conditions, so the program does not contain long fragments without conditional transfers. Third, the time delays added by dynamic instruction issue mechanisms are not compatible with the short execution times of the register-transfer operations used at the microprogram level.

6.5.6 Comments

A spectrum of options is available to support parallel execution beneath a program expressed as a single instruction stream. Important differences between these techniques lie in the granularity of their parallelism. We started with entire arrays and ended with simple microinstructions. The common feature of these techniques is a single control unit that issues a group of instructions that the program translator has collected together for simultaneous (parallel) execution. The system's functionality and support for the illusions is based on correct behavior in the translator's algorithms that add parallelism to the program, because no checking incorporated in the execution engine verifies correct functionality.

6.6 IMPLEMENTING DYNAMIC I-STREAM PARALLELISM

The static parallelism strategy does not provide the same degree of flexibility that can be provided by incorporating dynamic parallelism detectors within the processor's control unit. With vector processing, this flexibility is not helpful, but in most other environments, adding dynamic parallelism can dramatically increase the system's performance. In this section and the next two chapters, we explore dynamic parallelism in various guises.

This section covers the design of superscalar processors, in which logic within the control unit detects possible parallelism within the single instruction stream that is presented for execution. The control logic is designed to support the illusion of a single control point and thereby to support functional behavior. The dynamic parallel execution occurs between functional units that can perform several operations simultaneously (either by being replicated or by having pipelined implementations) or between several different functional units that can operate independently.

Most superscalar designs permit some form of out-of-order instruction issue (e.g., instruction issue that violates program order). Completion out of order is permitted in some designs, though we will see that this option presents problems in supporting the illusion of precise exceptions, which is necessary in the single control point illusion. To discover parallelism within straight-line sequences between conditional branches, one incorporates decisions similar to those used during static code generation, as discussed in Section 6.2. Adding dynamic decision making and buffering (both invisible to the programmer) can increase parallelism possibilities over the parallelism that can be found statically. In addition, speculative execution beyond conditional branches can improve performance, but additional control logic is needed to implement this possibility while supporting the illusions.

In this section, we assume that the processor executes a single program and the processor has a load/store design.[41] Within these constraints (which are not confining), we build a conceptual implementation of parallel activity coordinated by an easily understood mechanism. Then we move to alternate designs whose control mechanisms require less logical complexity.

6.6.1 A Conceptual Value-Tracking Scheme

In the easily understood design, the processor issues all instructions for execution in program order. In terms of our basic parallel execution model, the shared resources are the registers and the tasks are computations involved in the individual instruction. In this design, all memory accesses take place in program

---

[41] The techniques do generalize to other processor designs, but give most benefit in load/store architectures.

order, so the only control problem concerns managing values in the registers. All instructions take operands from registers and store results in registers (the result of a branch, whether conditional or not, is the contents of PC).

All superscalar schemes require a mechanism that tracks register writes and reads, because they might occur in violation of program order. Our goal is to add bookkeeping that tracks this activity and control logic that blocks inappropriate actions to assure that the processor behaves in a functional manner. The bookkeeping is based on the program order of execution. A simple (but unrealistic with respect to implementation) mechanism bases the bookkeeping on a count of the instructions that have been executed (in program order). We use this integer to uniquely identify each instruction. The first instruction executed by the program will be labeled with number 1, and so forth.

To define the functional behavior, consider program execution in which each instruction is performed atomically without overlap. This execution defines the functional behavior of the program. Each register presents a synchronizing problem that is independent of the synchronizing problem regarding any other register. Thus, it is sufficient to devise a scheme that correctly manages the reads and writes of a single register. Therefore, our discussion emphasizes proper control of one register, which we denote by Q (using R would be confusing because R will be used to denote read actions).

The sequence of accesses to Q can be depicted as a sequence of R and W symbols, with the corresponding instruction numbers added as subscripts. If, for example, Q is read by instruction n, we write R_n in the history sequence.

Suppose that Q's history contains R_i. What was the source of the value that should be read? Clearly, it appeared in Q when a write to Q was performed. In particular, it was the write that occurred most recently before instruction i. This suggests a mechanism for generating identifiers of the register contents:

1. Execute the program on a conceptual processor that performs instructions atomically. Add an execution counter EC (*not* the program counter) that increments each time an instruction is performed. Add an identifier field ID to each register.
2. Each instruction copies EC to the ID field of all result destination registers.

This exercise associates a label with each register's contents. When instruction i is executed, the labels of the correct operands are present in the ID fields of the source registers. Similarly, the results of the operation can be labeled with the EC value for this instruction execution.[42] Now form an *internal identifier* (II) of each value by combining the identifier[43] of the register holding the value with the corresponding ID value, as in (2, 35) for the value written into register 2 during

---

[42] Notice that the instruction is not labeled; it is its instance in the execution sequence that is labeled.
[43] In this example, we use integer labels for all registers, even if they cannot be selected using numbers.

the execution of instruction 35. The II identifiers can be combined to describe the
entire program execution, which becomes a list of actions such as

$$(6, 9) = (1, 3)\ OP\ (3, 6)$$

We call this description the *labeled execution description* (*LED*) of the program.

Because there is a single write to each object, the order of these statements
is irrelevant, provided that each value is written before it is read. The foregoing
constraint is one basic limitation on the operation of a superscalar processor.
Other limitations may arise from a desire to provide precise exception handling,
from the size(s) of the temporary holding places and from the choice of the ID encoding scheme in the processor.

The superscalar control mechanism does not need to know the complete
LED; in fact, it only needs to track value identifiers and all instructions that have
been started (which we associate with the instruction decoding phase) and not
completed (meaning that all results have been copied to their eventual destinations). The conceptual design that we study next provides a basis from which we
develop realistic options by changing the locations where processing can stall
and/or the encodings of the II labels.

6.6.2 Conceptual Design

The internal processing of a single instruction can be divided into the following
phases:

1. Decode and issue an execution request packet.
2. Perform the operation.
3. Issue a result store request packet.
4. Store the result.

Although this list suggests four stages of instruction execution,[44] it is actually
used to suggest general flow patterns and not to have any relationship to any
pipelining present in the implementation of the processor or its functional units.

During the *decode* phase, the controller does its identifier bookkeeping.
This phase must be implemented such that the instructions appear to have been
handled in program order. But that does not mean that instructions have to be
issued in program order, if the effects are correct. The term "issue" has several
meanings in various superscalar designs; our interpretation does not conform to
any of the conventional meanings. The format of an execution request packet depends upon other design decisions; see what follows for specifics.

During the *perform* phase, the result values are determined from the oper-
and values. The design might obtain the input values during the decode or

---

[44]   Notice the similarity between this scheme, the stages of a RISC machine's instruction pipeline, and
the data flow implementation described in Section K.2.

perform phases (or both). Until an operand value has been obtained, it is described in the packet by its internal identifier. There may be significant delay during this phase while the functional unit determines the result(s). We assume that this delay is unknown. If we design the mechanism so that its functional behavior does not depend on any timing assumptions, the system will certainly give correct results regardless of any unexpected delays (such as the delay to access memory after finding a cache miss).

During the third phase, the functional unit forms a store request that includes the II of the result along with the corresponding value. This phase is separated from the actual access to store the result because the controller might wait to copy the value to the destination.

In the final phase, the result is copied to its destination and the execution of the instruction is thereby completed.

Next we consider several design options, ignoring the serious question of conditional branching and its effects; we return to those in Section 6.6.8. So for the moment, we assume that the program executes instructions in the order they are fetched from memory addresses. In particular, we assume that the system knows which instructions are going to be executed, and starts their execution as soon as possible subject to the correctness constraints imposed by the chosen control scheme.

For each design option, we discuss the parts of the design that are required for functional behavior, the corresponding control rules, and the tag values that make it all possible. Within each design approach, we try to make the control scheme as simple as possible consistent with functional results.

6.6.3 No Buffering Anywhere

We start from the conceptual design and impose the restriction that there be no buffering in the implementation. An instruction cannot be issued if the operand registers are not valid or if the functional unit is busy. If an instruction cannot be issued, the processor must stall issue because there is no way to buffer the instruction that could not be issued. Thus, in this design, instructions are issued in program order and their execution in functional units is also initiated in program order.

If instructions were executed atomically, the result register would have been loaded with the result of the operation before the instruction is completed and the next one issued. If the instruction $(n + 1)$ needs the result computed in instruction n as an operand, instruction $(n + 1)$ will have to wait for that result. The fact that instruction n has been issued means that the value in its result locations is no longer valid for use as an operand of a future instruction. Thus, when the instruction is issued, the result register(s) must be marked invalid.

The mechanism beneath this design includes the following elements:

1. Flags:
   a.   Each register has a valid flag.
   b.   Each functional unit has a busy flag that is set when it cannot accept a new request.
2. Conditions for instruction issue:
   a.   Previous instruction was issued, *and*
   b.   Valid flags of all operand registers set, *and*
   c.   Busy flag of functional unit is clear.
3. Adjustments upon instruction issue:
   a.   Clear the valid flag for (each) result register(s).
   b.   Functional unit may become busy.
4. Actions upon operation completion:
   a.   Copy result(s) to the destination register(s) and set their valid flags.
   b.   Functional unit may become free.
   c.   If instruction issue is stalled, check whether this frees the stall.

Rules 2a, 2b, 3a, and 4a assure that the set of register values within the system is limited to a single version of each register and that each instruction's operands are read from the correct version of each register (this is why condition 2a was necessary).

These rules do not imply anything about the order of instruction completion, which is fine, because our goal was to develop rules that order events such that the results are functionally correct, and our definition of the results covered only the contents of the registers. If we desire precise exceptions, we have to add more rules to assure a condition that implies that instruction completion will appear to have occurred in order, despite the possibility of exceptions.[45]

6.6.4 Buffering before Functional Units

A variation on this scheme permits buffering decoded instructions that cannot start processing in their functional units, either because the unit is not available or because the operand registers are not yet valid. Figure 6-32 illustrates this design when the buffer is distributed in front of the functional units. The places that hold instructions for the functional units are called *reservation stations*. The performance advantage of this scheme comes from the fact that instructions can be initiated out of program order without affecting the functionality of the results; this might speed program execution.

The mechanism beneath this design includes the following elements:

---

[45]   The rules presented in this section do not consider precise exceptions, unless noted otherwise.

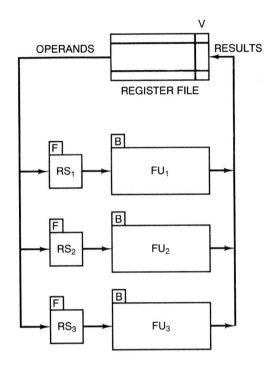

Figure 6-32   A superscalar processor with reservation
stations

1. Flags:
   a.   Each register has a valid flag.
   b.   Each functional unit has a busy flag that is set when it cannot accept a
   new request.
   c.   Each reservation station has a full flag that is set when there is no
   space in the reservation station for another request.
2. Conditions for instruction issue to reservation station or functional unit:
   a.   Previous instruction was issued, *and*
   b.   Valid flags of all operand registers set, *and*
   c.   Reservation station not full.
3. Adjustments upon instruction issue:
   a.   Copy operand values to reservation station entry.
   b.   Clear the valid flag for (each) result register(s).
   c.   Functional unit may become busy.
4. Actions upon operation initiation in the functional unit:
   a.   Clear out the reservation station entry.
5. Actions upon operation completion:
   a.   Copy result(s) to the destination register(s) and set their valid flags.
   b.   If instruction issue is stalled, check whether this frees the stall.

The major differences between these rules and those for the previous design lie in the possibility of out-of-order instruction execution. The register-valid flags guarantee that the results will be functional despite reordering within the execution sequence. After all, there is nothing sacred about initiating execution in order as long as the correct operand values are used. This is the *scoreboard* scheme.

Example 6-32

> The CDC 6600 processor included the original implementation of the "scoreboard" scheme, which incorporates the tests we just described. It has a load/store architecture. Instructions can be issued out of order until the buffers in front of the functional units fill and block further instruction issue.

Another way to achieve a similar effect is to widen the issue window from the instruction buffer; this saves instructions that are not yet issued in a central place and permits arbitrary reordering and may empty arbitrary positions in the instruction buffer. These spaces might have to be compressed out of the buffer to assure in-order execution of instruction pairs that are interdependent. Another difficulty with this option compared to the scoreboard scheme is that it does not include reading available operands for instructions that have not been issued; this effect will reduce performance compared to the schemes we present next.

6.6.5 Buffers at Functional Units Containing Operand Values

To further speed execution without affecting functionality, we could read the values of operands as soon as they are available and issue an instruction to a reservation station even though its operands are not all available. To assure functionality with this design, we need to associate identifiers with the unread operand values and add appropriate control rules to coordinate the operand values. This version retains the restriction that only a single value can be stored for each register within the register portion of the system.

The mechanism beneath this design includes the following elements:

1. Flags:
   a. Each register has a valid flag.
   b. Each functional unit has a busy flag that is set when it cannot accept a new request.
   c. Each reservation station has a full flag that is set when there is no space in the reservation station for another request.
   d. Each reservation station operand entry has a value flag that is set when the operand entry does contain a value (when it is clear the field contains an identifier, which is a register number).
2. Conditions for instruction issue to a reservation station or functional unit:
   a. Previous instruction was issued, *and*

    b. Result register is valid, *and*
    c. Reservation station not full.
  3. Adjustments upon instruction issue:
    a. For every operand whose register's valid flag is set, copy the value to the operand field of the reservation station entry, setting the corresponding value flag.
    b. For every operand whose register's valid flag is clear, copy the register number into the operand field of the reservation station entry, clearing the corresponding value flag.
    c. Clear the valid flag for (each) result register(s).
    d. Functional unit may become busy.
  4. Conditions for operation initiation in a functional unit:
    a. The unit is available, *and*
    b. The value flag for very operand value is set.
  5. Actions upon operation initiation in the functional unit:
    a. Clear out the reservation station entry.
    b. If instruction issue is stalled, check whether this frees the stall.
  6. Actions upon operation completion:
    a. Copy the result(s) to the destination register(s) and set their valid bits.
    b. Functional unit may become free.
    c. Find all operand fields in valid reservation station entries for which the value flag is clear and in which the register number matches the destination register number of this operation; copy the result to all such fields and set their value flags.

The major differences between these rules and those for the previous design lie in (1) the use of result register validity flags to limit instruction issue, and (2) the control of the spaces in reservation station entries that await missing operands. The rule limiting instruction issue until the result register is valid prevents the processor from the need to handle more than one version of each register's value. With respect to the reservation station spaces, when an operand is not yet available, its place is marked with the number of the register whose value should be used for the operand. There are two difficulties in the implementation: (1) the need to associatively find all reservation station fields that contain the register number, and (2) the need to be able to issue instructions out of order from the reservation station for maximum performance.

    In terms of our general scheme, all missing operands could be identified with the number of the instruction whose result is to be used. To make this scheme work correctly, the instruction issue mechanism would have to track the instruction number and also the instruction number that corresponds to the (missing) result that will fill an invalid register.[46]

---

[46] This number could be stored in the invalid register.

A more realistic variation on this design marks missing operands with an identifier of the functional unit that will produce the value that should fill the field. The challenge in this design approach is to correctly identify the results because a functional unit can be working on several instructions at the same time (because it is internally pipelined, for example). We do not detail these modifications here (see Problem 6-41).

Central Window. A different type of variation on the reservation station scheme changes the location of the reservation information, moving it from buffers dedicated to functional units into a single buffer covering the entire processor. The benefit from this change comes from pooling the reservation station resource, making it less likely that instruction issue would have to stall for lack of a reservation station buffer to hold the instruction. The disadvantage of this design is that the logic to initiate activity in a functional unit must examine all entries in a large set to find any that are destined for the unit and have all operands valid.

Of course, increasing the size of the reservation station in front of a functional unit can decrease the chance that instruction issue will have to stall because the buffer is filled. The speed of this scheme is partly limited by the restriction to a single copy of the contents of each register.

6.6.6 Buffering before Registers

The previous scheme limits instruction issue whenever the result register is not valid. This rule has the beneficial effect of guaranteeing that all WAW precedence constraints will be met by the actual schedule. But it has the detrimental effect that instruction issue can be held up despite the fact that the instruction's operands are all available, simply because there is no way to track the result to guarantee satisfying the WAW precedence constraints.

To overcome this limitation, one could propose a drastic change—increase the number of programmer-visible processor registers. There are at least three reasons why this is not the best approach to the problem: (1) One would have to widen all register number fields in instructions; (2) the processor state gets larger, so saving it becomes more difficult; and (3) to build a series of compatible machines of varying performance, even the low performers would have to be designed with the large number of registers, making them expensive.

The approach that we study here is called *register renaming*. The basic idea is that a high-performance machine can place buffers in front of the programmer-visible registers to hold values that have been computed out of order. Allowing several instances of the contents of a register adds to the control mechanism, but it can increase the system performance greatly. Register renaming was first introduced in the IBM 360 Model 91 design [ANDE67].

The mechanism beneath this design includes the following elements:

1. Flags:
   a.   Each register has an associated buffer with a buffer full flag.
   b.   There is a tag associated with each entry in each register buffer.
   c.   There is a valid flag associated with each entry in each register buffer.
   d.   There is a current tag field associated with each register (this is the tag value associated with the last entry in the register's buffer).
   e.   Each functional unit has a busy flag that is set when it cannot accept a new request.
   f.   Each reservation station has a full flag that is set when there is no space in the reservation station for another request.
   g.   Each reservation station operand entry has a value flag that is set when the operand entry does contain a value (when it is clear the field contains an identifier, which is a register number).

2. Conditions for instruction issue to reservation station or functional unit:
   a.   Previous instruction was issued, *and*
   b.   Every destination register has a new tag value available and space in its buffer to hold the result of this operation, *and*
   c.   Reservation station not full.

3. Tag adjustments upon instruction issue:
   a.   For every operand, assign the current tag value associated with the register to this operand.
   b.   For every destination register, assign a new tag value for the result and allocate a space in the buffer for that result.

4. Other actions upon instruction issue:
   a.   For every operand whose register (or its buffer) contains a valid value that is assigned the same tag value, copy the value into the operand field of the reservation station and set field's value flag.
   b.   If the condition of 4a is not satisfied, place register number and associated tag value into the operand field of the reservation station entry, clearing the corresponding value flag.

5. Conditions for operation initiation in a functional unit:
   a.   The unit is available, *and*
   b.   The value flag for very operand value is set.

6. Actions upon operation initiation in the functional unit:
   a.   Clear out reservation station entry.
   b.   If instruction issue is stalled, check whether this frees the stall.

7. Actions upon operation completion:
   a.   Copy result(s) to the destination register(s) or their buffers and set their valid bits
   b.   Find all operand fields in valid reservation station entries for which the value flag is clear and in which the register number and tag

matches the destination register number and tag of this operation; copy the result to all such fields and set their value flags.
8. Tag management actions upon operation completion:
   a. If the current tag value associated with the register is not equal to the tag value of the result, discard the result and its tag.

6.6.7 Store Ordering and Reordering

Processor instructions place results in internal registers or in memory locations. There is no guarantee that instructions complete in program order, which poses the problem of timing the store actions that complete instruction execution. The timings with respect to precedence constraints and with respect to program ordering are important considerations in the design of high-performance processors. In the following, we assume that other mechanisms (such as those we have just discussed) handle precedence constraints correctly, so the system is guaranteed to produce functional results in the absence of exceptions and interprocessor interactions. If the specification requires that the design meet store ordering constraints, additional tags and control mechanisms are required. We consider the two situations separately, because they affect different aspects of the system's behavior.

Register Store Ordering. The ordering of stores internal to the processor affects exception precision. If exceptions must be precise, it would seem that all values to be stored must be buffered so they can be reordered and performed in program order. The buffer and associated control logic that govern the store ordering are called a *reorder buffer*. Actually, the precise exception requirement's reordering constraint is not quite as tight as it seemed, because it would be permissible to store the results of an instruction whenever it could be guaranteed that no predecessor would cause an exception and that the precedence constraints would be satisfied.

To impose precision on these issues, it can be useful to define those combinations of register contents that comprise important views of the processor's state (these definitions follow [JOHN91]):

Definition. The processor's *in-order state* at time t consists of the contents of the registers as they would exist at the completion of the instruction preceding (with respect to program order) the first instruction uncompleted at time t.

Definition. The processor's *architectural state* at time t consists of the contents of the registers as they would exist at the completion of the last instruction that was issued prior to time t.

Definition. The processor's *lookahead state* at time t consists of the contents of the registers at time t, and all register updates that will occur when pending instructions (i.e., those issued prior to time t) complete execution.

Similar definitions replace the time with the identification of an instruction that is in execution (this makes sense for the in-order state) or has just been issued.

Expressed in these terms, to support precise exceptions, the processor must present its in-order state with the instruction that caused the exception in execution when the exception handler is entered. Results that are pending and not in the in-order state must be discarded when the exception handler is initiated; if the instructions are executed after the exception handler, they will be restarted after the exception handler has completed its job.

Memory Ordering. Memory accesses can take many processor cycles, especially if there is a cache miss during the access attempt. There is no need for a program to wait for the completion of a memory write operation, *provided* the system is designed to behave as though it followed the single instruction illusion. Thus, the STORE unit within a processor can buffer write requests and complete them in any convenient order, just so the results correspond to functional behavior. This requirement does not imply that they have to be completed in program order. Rather, it implies two requirements: (1) The result of several writes to the same address should be the result of the last write in program order, and (2) if the processor reads from a location to which it has issued a write, the value returned must be the value stored during the most recent write operation. The first requirement implies that when a new write arrives at the buffer, any pending write (that precedes this one in program order) to that same location should be canceled. Conversely, if the new arrival preceded the one in the buffer (again, with respect to program order), the new write should be canceled. We can easily design control logic to impose the rule that all writes be delivered to the write buffer in program order, which would "solve" the program order requirement with respect to writes to a single memory address. The second requirement implies that the contents of the write buffer must be examined on every read attempt; if there is a match of the addresses, the value in the write buffer (or a value coming from a module internal to the processor) must be returned as the result of the read. The latter implies that the write buffer behaves as a *victim cache*.

Programs in a multiprocessor system expect that each processor will interact with the memory in program order. If this is not the case, major difficulties can arise; they are described in Section 8.2. Therefore each processor, regardless of how it is implemented internally, must present the appearance of executing all memory accesses in program order. The internal implementation of the processor, such as the choice among the speedup options just discussed, is not relevant to this requirement. Victim cache functions have to be implemented to handle coherence operations correctly. This requirement implies that the LOAD and STORE functional units have additional control logic to assure that their memory activity is consistent with execution in program order. At the very least, this implies that LOAD and STORE requests be issued to the memory in program order, even if the values to be written do become available earlier than program order would dictate that they be stored. Further coordination rules are described in Section 8.8; for now, we simply assume that all LOADs and STOREs are coordinated at the processor so that they do occur in program order.

6.6.8 Uncertain Execution Sequencing

The preceding discussion assumed that the actual sequence of instruction execution can be known prior to instruction initiation. After all, this assumption lies behind our strategies of fetching and issuing instructions before their predecessors have completed execution. Unfortunately, this assumption is never completely correct, though it might be correct across long sequences of processor instructions. Three major causes of uncertainties are (1) exceptions, (2) eonditional branches, and (3) interrupts. How does uncertainty affect our techniques for speeding instruction execution? We focus on exceptions and conditional branches, because these are caused by events directly related to instructions being executed in the processor. Interrupts are caused by external events that cannot be controlled by the program, and there is no requirement that the handling of an interrupt be directly related to the execution of any particular instruction(s) in the program. We introduce barriers, which provide a technique for reducing sequencing uncertainties.

Exceptions. A major design decision concerns whether exceptions shall be precise:

> **Definition.** An exception is *precise* if the exception handler is entered with the processor in a state that is consistent with single control point execution. In particular, all instructions that precede the one that caused the exception should appear to have been completed, and all instructions that follow the exception's cause must not appear to have been initiated. An exception that is not precise is *imprecise*.

In most processor designs almost every instruction is a potential cause of an exception. Therefore, demanding precise exceptions imposes tight constraints on the implementation, because the processor state must reflect that precision when the exception handler is entered. However, to achieve higher raw speed, not all designs impose this constraint on their behavior.

Example 6-34

The Alpha AXP processor specifications state that exceptions do not need to be precise.

It is likely to be difficult to write exception handlers for machines with imprecise exceptions, and it is probably true that programs that execute on a processor that does not support precise exceptions should not be programmed to use the occurrence of exceptions as a method to handle nonfatal unusual operand combinations.

Barriers. How can we design a machine that tolerates imprecise exceptions to gain speed, yet gives the programmer the option to coordinate exception handling at specified points in the program order? We include a barrier instruction. Recall that during a barrier instruction, the processor assures that the actions of subsequent instructions are not made visible until it is certain that all instructions preceding the barrier will complete successfully (without causing exceptions, that is). Furthermore, if an exception caused by an instruction preceding the barrier has not been signaled, the control unit must assure that the exception handler is invoked before passing the barrier, and that the handler sees a processor state reflecting the completion of all instructions preceding the barrier, yet no indication that any instruction following the barrier might have been initiated.[47] Only after these conditions have been assured can the barrier instruction be considered completed.

Example 6-35

The Alpha AXP processor has a barrier instruction TRAPB (Trap Barrier). When the instruction issue mechanism encounters this instruction, it stalls instruction issue until it can be certain that no preceding instruction will cause an arithmetic trap.

The Privileged Architecture Library (PAL) in the Alpha AXP is designed to implement useful functions as though they were single instructions. Because they might give incorrect results if an old exception (called a trap in the documentation) were to interrupt its execution, the CALL_PAL instruction itself acts as a barrier with respect to exceptions—the CALL_PAL instruction will not be issued until the controller is certain that no preceding instruction will cause an exception.[48]

Barrier instructions can be used to create the effect of precise exceptions, albeit inefficiently. To achieve this effect, one places a barrier after each instruction that could cause an exception. This strategy is clearly inefficient during program execution, but it could be a useful aid to program debugging.[49]

---

[47] This implies that any exceptions that might be caused by instructions following the barrier are discarded.

[48] If a predecessor does cause an exception, that exception handler will see the CALL_PAL instruction as the next one to be executed upon completion of the handler.

[49] However, one must be careful, because introducing the barrier does change the relative timing of adjacent instructions. This timing might have been the source of the program's difficulties.

The synchronization from a barrier is similar to the synchronization that occurs at the end of a recovery block. It also bears a distant resemblance to the barrier at a **join** instruction. A barrier instruction could be used to coordinate instruction modification with instruction fetch. These problems arise if a program that modifies its own instructions is executed on a processor that buffers instructions within an instruction buffer or an instruction cache.[50] The program's behavior may depend upon whether the writes that modify instructions are performed while the instructions being modified are held within the processor or while they are still in memory (before they have been copied into the instruction buffer). It can be argued that programs written in this style should be discouraged, but there is nothing in the program execution model that states that a program cannot modify itself by writing new instructions. So we seek ways to make the semantics correct (which means that the results behave as though there were no speedup mechanisms and the processor executed its instructions in program order). One way to achieve correctness is to have the instruction cache monitor all memory writes to assure that none of them actually writes into any words stored in the cache. Another method is to include a barrier instruction that assures that subsequent instruction fetches will behave as though they had been made directly from memory.

Example 6-36

> The SPARC processors have a FLUSH instruction. The FLUSH instruction has a memory address; the effect is to flush the instruction buffer within the processor of the contents of that address. It acts as a barrier in that all predecessor instructions must have completed all their memory operations before the FLUSH is executed. By placing a FLUSH instruction between the store instruction modifying an instruction and the execution of that instruction, the appearance of sequential execution is preserved.

Notice that if the FLUSH operation did not have a memory address operand, the system would have to flush the entire instruction buffer, and the program's efficiency could be reduced by the presence of the FLUSH instruction.

Example 6-37

> The PowerPC processors have an "instruction synchronize" instruction (isync). This instruction acts as a barrier; when its predecessors have completed, it flushes all prefetched instructions from the processor's instruction cache.

Conditional Branching.   When a conditional branch instruction is encountered, the control unit cannot determine the instruction's successor until the value of the branch condition is known. As long as the outcome of a conditional branch is uncertain, the value in the program counter is unknown, and the choice of the next instruction is uncertain. Therefore, unless one gambles about

---

[50]   In the following, we use the term *instruction cache* to cover both cases.

the outcome of the branching decision, one must treat each conditional branch as a barrier in order to support the program order illusion. Because conditional branch instructions are a common occurrence, we seek other options that permit the control unit to issue useful instructions. In one, we simply abandon the illusion of execution in program order, relying instead on correct programming to assure functional correctness. In the others, we design the processor so that it behaves as though instruction issue had been suspended until the branch decision became known, while still permitting the issuance of instructions that might be executed.

Abandon the Illusion. In this approach, the controller guesses the outcome of the branch and assumes it to be correct. Instruction issue continues along the assumed path, and any results that are computed are stored in their destinations. No correction is made if the prediction turns out to be incorrect. This approach does not produce desirable results in most cases, but it can be used at the end of a loop, where the processor predicts that the branch will be taken to the top of the loop. In particular, the programmer can have the start of the loop body compute values useful for the next iteration, but the program is written so that these (incorrect) results computed inside the loop are never examined outside the loop after it is exited. Even though the incorrect results are not destroyed, this does not make any difference because those results become *dead* when the loop exit occurs. So the net result is that the dead objects contain values that are inconsistent with the program order illusion, but this makes no difference because they do not affect other results.

A design can give the programmer control over the use of this option by placing a flag within the branch instruction if it is to be predicted without error recovery; this strategy is not helpful in a processor that contains the branch adjustment logic we discuss next, because recovery logic will be included within such a design. It is useful, however, if all other conditional branches are treated as barriers.

Branch Adjustments. Other techniques for removing the need for a barrier at each conditional branch support the program order illusion in different ways. Among the many options (see [CRAG92]) to approach this problem, we discuss these five briefly:

1. Wait for the branch condition value to be determined.
2. Use branch folding.
3. Change conditional branches to anticipatory branches.
4. Follow both branches.
5. Choose one branch and recover if the choice was wrong.

The implementation of these options may be affected by the choice of the source of the branch condition. Usually, either a condition code held in a register or a value held in a general-purpose register is tested during the conditional branch. The precedence relationships related to the register being tested must be honored. If condition codes are used, the WAW precedence constraints at the condition code register can make the condition code register become a bottleneck preventing overlapped execution, because it must be treated like a destination register in many instructions. One simple approach to handle the condition code write bottleneck is not appropriate to control other instruction results—most instructions do not read the condition values; in fact, most condition codes stored in the register are never examined by any instruction. Thus, one can design the control unit to ignore writes to the condition code register when their results have been superseded by another write without an intervening read of the condition code register. The control unit tracks which instruction is the most recent one that will write into the condition code register and it does not stall until it reaches an instruction that reads the condition code register; this has the effect of ignoring the condition code writes whose results will not be used by the program. In this manner, the processor knows the source of condition values that will have be either read or tested, and the dependency can be handled like other register dependencies.[51]

Example 6-38

The IBM System 360 Model 91 processor designers introduced this design option; the control unit tracked the last instruction that will modify the condition codes by keeping a single cc bit associated with each instruction. When an instruction is issued that will write to the condition code register (and there are no intervening reads of the condition code register), all cc bits are cleared, and the cc bit for the new instruction is set. When an instruction whose cc bit was set writes its results, any instruction waiting to read the condition can proceed.

Wait for the Condition. In this approach, the next instruction fetch is delayed until the outcome of the condition test is known. The execution of previous instruction(s) continues during the pause. The delays required to wait for the condition code register to be loaded can hurt system speed.

Branch Folding. This is used in the PowerPC 601 to reduce instruction delays. Each branch instruction is taken from the instruction queue as quickly as possible, and the controller determines whether it is known if the branch will be taken. If it is known that the branch will not be taken, the branch is simply removed from the queue and it never has to be considered for issue. If it can be determined that the branch will be taken, instruction fetching can be adjusted accordingly. If the branch outcome cannot be determined in advance, the branch

---

[51]   This strategy only works if any instruction that writes into the condition code register does force values into all the bits in the register. In other words, no instruction modifies some flag values and leaves the others unchanged (this pattern occurs in the MC68020 design).

instruction advances through the instruction queue and will be issued in the normal manner.

Example 6-39

> The PowerPC 601 processor contains a buffer of prefetched instructions from which it chooses instructions for execution by its various execution units. It has other logic that looks into that buffer for conditional branch instructions whose outcome can be determined in advance of the dispatch of the instruction. Branch outcomes are based on a condition code register, so the control logic might simply look for the absence of intervening instructions that modify the condition codes, or it can use more sophisticated tests that use knowledge of which condition code bits might be modified by each intervening instruction and which will be tested. In any case, if the branch outcome can be known ahead of time, the processor effectively uses no time to execute the branch.

Anticipatory Branches. An anticipatory branch instruction defines a branch to be taken at a future point based on present conditions. One design has a fixed gap between the anticipatory branch instruction and the place where the branch is actually taken, such as two instructions. This design is used in SPARC. Alternately, one could design a processor with a variable gap; the branch is taken when a "take pending branch" instruction is executed. Anticipatory branches can be useful in long loops, and they do not slow the system if they have a fixed gap, provided that useful work can be accomplished in the instructions that are executed (in the *delay slots*) before the branch decision is made.

Branch Prediction. The remaining conditional branch designs attempt to execute instructions (*speculatively*) beyond the branch in *anticipation* of its outcome. When the actual value of the branch condition becomes known, the instructions are either completed or dropped. As long as the controller is following a speculative option, the machine state must be managed so that the option can be dropped easily if the actual branch condition value shows that the choice was incorrect. This means that if a speculative instruction wishes to write a result, its completion must be deferred until the branch outcome is known. Instruction completion can be deferred by holding the results within the functional units or within the reorder buffer in the processor (where it would have to be tagged to indicate that its completion is tentative, pending the outcome of the branch decision). Once the branch decision is known to be correct, the processor's state can be updated (from the results of the instructions on the chosen path) by completing the deferred operations or writing from the write buffer. If the branch decision turns out to be incorrect, the speculative results are discarded, and any speculative instructions that have not completed can be discarded (this option is useful if it frees functional units for useful work). This "hiccough" slows execution, but if there is a high probability that the guesses are "good," this back-out process may not slow system speed appreciably.

Follow Both Paths. In the first design option, the control unit (in parallel) follows the consequences of both taking and not taking the branch. Each speculative result is marked to indicate the branch outcome that makes the result valid.

Follow One Path. In this class of designs, one branch outcome is predicted as most likely and the corresponding execution path is pursued. The key to success lies in the choice of the *branch prediction logic* that makes a decision regarding the likely outcome of a conditional branch. A number of prediction schemes have been proposed and used, including the following:[52]

1. All backwards conditional branches will be taken.
2. The prediction is based on a bit in the instruction that indicates whether the branch is likely to be taken.
3. The branch will be taken this time if the same branch was taken the last time it was executed (if recently).
4. The branch target address will be the same as it was the last time this branch was executed (if recently).
5. The branch target address will be the one that was used most frequently in recent executions of the instruction.
6. The branch instruction itself contains prediction information.

Schemes 3, 4, and 5 are implemented using a branch prediction module with an associative memory searched using a key matching the address of the branch instruction. Under the third scheme, the branch prediction memory contains a bit indicating whether the branch was taken the last time through. Under the fifth scheme, the memory contains the address of the actual successor of the branch the last time it was executed. The design of the fifth scheme is left as an exercise (Problem 6-49). One of the first two prediction schemes can be used when the associative search in the branch prediction memory fails.

This prediction design can be improved in several ways: (1) The buffer search can be based on a few low-order bits of the instruction's address, reducing an associative search to a simple fetch from a definite address. (2) We can eliminate checking whether there is a valid prediction in the buffer because there is little penalty in using the old contents to make a prediction. (3) The prediction history can be enlarged to decrease the penalty that accrues after a missed prediction. Suppose that a branch is almost always taken. Then it will almost always be predicted to be taken. If the prediction is wrong once (and a single prediction bit is used), the error will occur on two consecutive executions of that branch instruction—once when it goes the other way and a second time when it gets back to the common direction. By enlarging the buffer, the history can reflect more recent outcomes and whether they disagreed with the longer-range average prediction. Then add a rule that the prediction shall be based on the recent average.

---

[52]   Other branch prediction schemes and statistical performance models are presented in [CRAG92].

Alternately, the branch instruction and the supporting mechanism can be designed to specify target prediction information.

Example 6-40

The Alpha AXP processor has three basic branch instructions. The conditional branch instructions contain signed offsets that are added to the PC to determine the target address. If the offset is negative, the branch is predicted to be taken.

The unconditional branch instructions also contain an offset value that determined the target address. The address of the successor instruction is loaded into a destination processor register. A bit within the instruction provides a hint for use in future predictions. If the branch is marked as a subroutine call, the next instruction address (the address of the instruction that follows the call—to which control would return after the subroutine has completed its operation) is pushed onto a branch prediction stack. Otherwise, the next instruction address is not passed to prediction logic.

The target address of a jump instruction is taken from a processor register. Two bits within the jump instruction specify the prediction computation and the use of the prediction stack. If bit 15 is set, the prediction is popped from the prediction stack; otherwise, it is found by adding the sign-extended displacement field from the instruction to the program counter. If bit 14 is set, the next instruction address is pushed onto the prediction stack. Thus, with both bits set, (1) the prediction comes from the stack, with the popped jump target predicted to be the next instruction address, and (2) the next instruction address is pushed on the prediction stack. This combination supports a limited form of coroutine resumption (because it manages at most two cooperating processes). Other combinations correspond to simple jumps, to subroutine calls, and to subroutine returns.

All Alpha AXP processor branch instructions include information about how to predict the outcome of the branch. There is a branch prediction stack. The prediction mechanism uses bits and fields in the branch instructions to save prediction information and to make the prediction, as outlined in Table 6-3. It is important to note that all information used to make the branch prediction is available at the time the branch instruction is added to the prefetch buffer; thus, the prediction can be determined without knowing the outcomes of instructions preceding the branch instruction. In this processor, the four instructions that use PC-relative predictions (JMP, JSR, RET, and JSR_COROUTINE) take their successor addresses from a processor register; in fact, all of these instructions perform the same actions, which include saving the next instruction address in a processor register (Ra), but they make different predictions about the branch target.

6.6.9 Instruction Queue Management

The instruction queue provides instructions for issue and must be managed in a manner compatible with the instruction issue rules and the branch prediction policies. If instructions must issue in order, the queue management module only decides when to load more instructions into the queue. If, however, instructions can be issued out of order, the rules governing instruction issue and branch

TABLE 6-3   ALPHA AXP BRANCH PREDICTION

Instruction				Prediction	
Function Code	Branch Type	Actual Target	Prediction Stack Changes	Target Location	Prediction Used If ..
BR	Unconditional	PC-relative	—	PC-relative	True (always)
BSR	Branch to subroutine	PC-relative	Push return address	PC-relative	True (always)
JMP	Jump	Rb	—	PC-relative	True (always)
JSR	Jump to subroutine	Rb	Push return address	PC-relative	True (always)
RET	Return	Rb	Pop return address	Top of stack	True (always)
JSR_ COROUTINE	Jump to coroutine[a]	Rb	1. Pop return address 2. Push next instruction address	Old top of stack	True (always)
Bcc	Conditional	PC-relative	—	Target	Displacement < 0
				Next	Displacement > 0

[a] Coroutine structures are discussed in Section 6.3.2; this instruction's prediction works only in a restricted set of cases.

predictions must be considered. All queue management policies require that any instruction that has been issued must be removed from the instruction queue, which may require shifting part of the queue. The following policy discussion will assume that there is only one copy of each type of functional unit and that each instruction can be performed by only one of these units. Generalizations beyond this simple limitation are straightforward, but are left to the problems.

The memory interface, particularly the width of an instruction fetch from the instruction cache and the behavior after an instruction cache miss, also affects the queue loading policy.

In-Order Instruction Issue.   When instructions are issued in program order, the instruction buffer is advanced one position after every instruction issue. If up to n instructions can be issued in the same processor cycle, the n positions at the head of the instruction queue are all potential sources of instructions to issue. The issue logic examines all instructions in the issue positions for the availability of their operands and their functional units. Any instruction whose operands and unit are available is issued *if* its predecessors are also available for issue. At the end of the cycle, the controller shifts the queue to remove the issued instructions. Because instructions are issued in order, the entire queue can be shifted after each instruction issue.

Multiple instruction issue requires more memory bandwidth for instruction access. A wide data path may be required to balance the rate of instructions leaving the queue with the rate of instructions arriving from memory. The queue will have to be loaded in parallel to meet this bandwidth balance. The controller might wait to load anything until the amount of space at the end of the queue is sufficient to hold all instructions that are accessed during a single memory read from the instruction buffer.

Example 6-41

The DEC Alpha AXP processors fetch instructions in naturally aligned blocks. The controller does not fetch more instructions until the space at the end of the queue is adequate to hold an incoming block of instructions. If the target of a branch instruction is aligned in the same way, all bytes accessed during the instruction fetch will be used during program execution (unless one is a branch that is taken); thus, instruction fetch delays will be reduced (and therefore program speed will be enhanced) by aligning branch targets.

Out-of-Order Instruction Issue. New constraints and the possibility of new limitations arise when instructions can be issued out of order from the instruction queue. It is necessary to obey the data flow precedence constraints, as noted earlier. It may also be necessary to honor a rule that all instructions issued to a single functional unit be issued in order, while still permitting out-of-order issue with respect to instructions performed by different functional units. The Alpha AXP, for example, has the rule that all instructions performed by the integer unit be issued in order, and that no instructions performed by other units can be issued ahead of their integer unit predecessors. Thus, the integer unit instructions act like barriers in the instruction issue process. The window for out-of-order instruction issue might be different for branch instructions, because it is valuable to fold branches whenever the controller knows the outcome of conditional branch instructions; this reduces the need for speculative instruction fetching. In a similar manner, a design could provide different window sizes for different functional units.

Example 6-42

The Alpha AXP processor forces integer instructions to be issued in order because the issue window width is one for instructions using the integer unit. The issue widths for branch and floating-point instructions are wider, because their execution times are longer.

The possibility of issuing instructions out of order complicates the queue manager because the issued instructions to be removed may be interior to the queue. The logic is straightforward, but many data paths are required to speed the shifting process.

Speculative Instruction Queue Loading. When the processor empties the instruction queue but is speculatively fetching instructions, should it fetch more instructions from memory? The answer is not immediately obvious. One might compare the memory fetch delay with the expected wait for a resolution of the actual branch outcome. If the branch outcome will be known before the fetch can be completed, and if the confidence in the guess is low, it seems unwise to attempt a memory fetch for instructions that might never be needed.

6.7 SUMMARY

Single instruction stream parallelism is useful if one wishes to express an algorithm in terms of a single execution point passing among separate modules. Static and dynamic algorithms can detect and take advantage of opportunities for parallel execution. Static parallelism is used in VLIW and microprogrammed designs, whereas dynamic parallelism is used in superscalar processors. Both schemes use list scheduling techniques to determine an execution order compatible with precedence constraints and functionality requirements.

At the hardware level, synchronous parallelism can improve system throughput. It is especially beneficial if the program performs the same operation on all components of a regular structure. Array and vector processors use synchronous parallelism to speed execution of these kinds of problems. By Amdahl's rule, the speedup possible through array and vector processing is limited by the amount of inherently sequential processing in the algorithm.

Superscalar designs incorporate list scheduling into the instruction issue mechanism. Barrier instructions can be used to create the appearance of in-order instruction issue despite the use of out-of-order issue to speed programs. The barrier can also coordinate exception handling with program progress in predictable ways, even if the exceptions are inherently imprecise.

All techniques discussed in this chapter speed the execution of a single program on a processor having a single control section. In the next two chapters, we present design options that support the parallel execution of several instruction streams that logically interact, either by passing messages among themselves or by sharing some resources (usually memory) whose states are visible to several processes.

6.8 TRENDS

Programmer specifications of parallelism opportunities within individual tasks are likely to fade from common usage as compilers use more sophisticated algorithms to find parallelism. However, the additional compilation time required to execute algorithms that detect parallelism tends to restrict their use to large programs that have long execution times. Thus, ultimate speed enhancement comes only at the cost of additional compilation time.[53]

Pipelined processing has become the normal mode for instruction execution, as exemplified in RISC processor designs. This trend will continue, and may supplant vector pipelines, to the extent that they will disappear from almost all architectures.

Processor arrays should continue to be attractive for high-performance systems, but designs with a centralized control unit will disappear, because designers will prefer to use available processor modules that contain independent control units. The delay introduced when passing signals off the processor chip should limit the speed of any system that uses frequent synchronization among processing modules that are located in separate hardware modules.

Because logic in VLSI is inexpensive to replicate, processor complexity is not limited to the same extent that it was in the past. Superscalar execution using sophisticated branch prediction should become the norm, though the degree of parallelism that is possible will be limited by the number of registers and the complexity introduced by trying to predict further ahead than one conditional branch instruction.

Barrier instructions will continue in instruction sets so that programmers can detect errors and so they can synchronize instruction modification with the instruction buffer to assure that the basic illusions are supported by the design.

6.9 CONCEPT LIST

1. Functional correctness
2. Correctness constraints: dependency, antidependency, write ordering
3. Read and write sets
4. Atomic action illusions and atomic instruction completion
5. Schedules; feasible schedules
6. List scheduling algorithms
7. Conditions for linear speedup by adding functional modules
8. Instruction initiation in and out of order
9. Instruction completion in and out of order
10. Remote procedure call program structures
11. Coroutine structures; **create, resume, coreturn** statements
12. Simultaneous execution statements: **dosim, cobegin, fork, join**
13. Recovery blocks; assurance of conditions
14. Adding functional units or registers to enhance parallelism possibilities

---

[53] This can present debugging problems because timing errors might appear when maximum overlapping is introduced into production versions of a program.

15. Software optimization of parallelism: register assignment, loop unrolling
16. Array processors
17. SIMD machines: single instruction stream, multiple data streams
18. Amdahl's rule(s)
19. Vector pipelines
20. Chaining
21. Vector representations: strides, sparse vectors
22. Barrel processing
23. VLIW (very long instruction word) processor design
24. Horizontal microprogramming as VLIW system
25. Superscalar processing: dynamic evaluation of precedence constraints to permit multiple instruction issue
26. Buffering to enhance issue chances: in front of functional units or registers
27. Write buffers
28. Buffering results before writing to assure completion in program order
29. Precise and imprecise exceptions
30. Barrier instructions to synchronize instruction modification
31. Conditional branch prediction
32. Instruction queue management

6.10 PROBLEMS

6-1.   Consider an application process A executed on a set of identical execution units (EUs) that operate under a central controller.[54] In other words, as more EUs are added, A's execution time decreases until there are n units; further expansion does not reduce the execution time. Thus, n denotes the maximum parallelism of the application process. A designer wishing to quantify the trade-off between system speed and the EU multiplicity collects dynamic statistics on the percentages of time that parallelism is used. For each i in the range 1 to n, the designer determines p_i, the probability that the system with n EUs is using at least i of those units at a randomly selected time. The designer wishes to use the p_i data to find $S(k)$, the speedup obtained (relative to $k = 1$) of the system with k EUs. The controller uses this simple execution strategy for a k-EU system ($k < n$):

1. Assume that $k = n$ and then reduce the program to a sequence of maximally wide steps (i.e., in any step as many as n EUs may be used simultaneously). There should be no possibility of simultaneously executing any pair of consecutive n-wide steps.
2. Translate each n-wide step into a sequence of k-wide steps. If p denotes the number of EUs actually used in the n-wide step, replace the n-wide step by a sequence of $\lceil (p/k) \rceil$ steps, with all but the last one using k EUs, and the last one

---

[54]   Each EU either performs an operation or idles during the cycle; some operations can be different from the others that are executed simultaneously.

using the remainder required to complete the p-wide step. Only after this sequence of steps has been completed can the next p-wide step be initiated. Assume that all machine steps and operations take unit time.

(a) Specify an algorithm to convert the p_i data to $S(k)$ data.

(b) Find $S(k)$, $1 < k < 4$, for a system with $n = 4$, $\{p_i\} = (1, 0.75, 0.15, 0.03)$.

6-2. Rewrite the list scheduling algorithm of Section 6.2.2 to include the evaluation of precedence constraints among the tasks being scheduled. You will have to add a data structure to hold the precedence information, and you will have to insert steps that find the tasks that have completed at time t to know how to determine the enabled sets.

6-3. A designer claims that the values of any parameters passed to a process during a **resume** operation cannot be retained at the top of the stack during the execution of the resumed process. The objective is to provide a uniform addressing scheme that accesses both the parameters and local objects of the procedure being **resumed**. Discuss whether this claim is correct. If it is not possible to retain the parameters on the top of the stack, propose an alternate allocation scheme that permits the resumed process to continue to access the parameters.

6-4. Describe the state of the stack of a child process that has been created but not yet resumed. Recall that the **create** operation passes parameters to the new process.

6-5. Comment briefly on the consequences of placing a **create** statement inside a **for** loop. You may assume that the loop's count limit is a constant value known at compile time, if that will help you.

6-6. Write a program for the parent process controlling the tree comparison algorithm described in Example 6-9.

6-7. Write out the tree equality processes and the main program for the second approach to the same fringe problem described in Example 6-9. Define the data structures that you use.

6-8. Discuss the degree of compatibility between these two notions: (1) that a process can be independently specified and (2) that it is easy to adjust the process so it can become a member of a set of processes that cooperates through the coroutine mechanism. Be sure to discuss the consequences of a process not getting a chance to complete its body if its colleagues do not issue a sufficient number of **resume** commands that reactivate the process.

(a) Answer the question under the assumption that all programs perform their steps in a straight-line order.

(b) Now answer the question with procedures that contain looping and conditional execution structures.

6-9. Write program steps to express the semantics of **call**, **return**, and **coreturn**. Use the common elements that appeared in the **resume** program in the text.

6-10. We wish to implement a coroutine structure. Recall that there is only one execution point in the program. Explain why one cannot use a single stack holding activation blocks for all subprocesses cooperating to perform the overall process. (*Hint:* Remember that the individual subprocesses might be calling local procedures.)

6-11. Write a matrix multiply algorithm in a high-level language.   [*Please turn for more.*]

(a) Use the traditional sequential approach to the problem.

(b) Add **dosim** to the language and use it wherever possible to specify parallelism. Try to achieve the maximum amount of parallelism; this may require modifying the algorithm you developed for part (a).

6-12. Show how the termination of a **cobegin** can be implemented using a shared object that operates as an (integer) counter. Assume that the separate statements within the cobegin statement are treated as separate threads sharing access to the process's stack. Be sure that you resume the correct thread of execution.

6-13. A designer proposes to support **cobegin** parallelism using several physically separate functional units. The idea is that each unit could be assigned to execute (in parallel) the separate statements in the **cobegin** construct. The processor whose program contains the **cobegin** acts as a common control unit that issues signals to initiate operations in the functional units. The computer's control unit waits for completion signals from all functional units before moving on to the program statement following the **cobegin**. We wish to have a hardware-supported design that uses only a small set of significant events for control purposes.

(a) Draw a picture of system, showing the functional and control units.

(b) Describe a set of timing rules and ordering constraints sufficient to make the operation of the system correspond to the **cobegin** semantics. At the same time, you wish to maximize the amount of parallel execution when a program is executed.

(c) Are there any restrictions on the contents of the **cobegin** statements? Consider the following questions:

  1. What would happen if there were nested **cobegin**s?

  2. How does each process access memory?

  3. How is the stack of the parent process accessed?

6-14. Consider unrolling the loop that includes the tasks used in Example 6-19. Draw a timing diagram to illustrate how three instances of the unrolled loop could be executed in a machine that has three copies of each of the functional units. Try to minimize the makespan for the three iterations and show how the pattern you develop could be repeated to schedule additional iterations of the loop.

6-15. Develop an ILLIAC IV algorithm structure for the following matrix problem: Test the array to find the first PE whose A register contains a positive data value. Then copy that data value to the first PE by using mode changes and routing instructions. The "first" ordering is based on the PE numbering discussed in Section 6.5.1. If all PEs contain negative numbers, the result should be –1.

Specify the behavior of the algorithm. Be sure to include a logical expression for the PE mode bit setting and logical conditions governing the direction of information routing. Assume that the R register is a master–slave register (therefore, its current contents can be fed to one other PE at the same time that R is being set from another PE). Let $R_{in}(i)$ and $R_{out}(i)$ denote the incoming and outgoing routed information at PE_i, respectively. Assume that conditional statements are executed only in PEs where the mode condition is satisfied and that conditional execution of a routing instruction may disable the reception process, but never affects the transmission process. Thus, data can be sent from PE_i with $M = 0$ to PE_j with $M = 1$ if the execution condition states that $M = 1$ for the routing instruction to be executed.

(a) Specify a scan algorithm that uses linear searching.

(b) Devise a better searching strategy to minimize the average number of routing instructions required to execute the complete algorithm. Compared to linear searching, how much routing time did you save?

6-16. We wish to solve Laplace's equation for the function $V(x, y)$. The algorithm uses overrelaxation on a two-dimensional grid. The values of the potential V are given along the boundaries. The iterative step updates the estimate of the potential V at each interior grid point using these update steps:

$$\text{CORR}(i, j) = (1/4)[V(i+1, j) + V(i-1, j) + V(i, j+1) + V(i, j-1)] - V(i, j)$$
$$V(i, j) = (5/4)[\text{CORR}(i, j)] + V(i, j)$$

These steps are repeatedly executed until $|\text{CORR}(i, j)| < \varepsilon$ at all interior grid points. We wish to solve this problem on an array machine having the ILLIAC IV interconnection structure.

For this problem, consider only the case with a 6×6 array of interior points in an 8×8 grid. The edge PEs of the 8×8 array correspond to the edges of the problem space (where the potentials were specified as the boundary conditions).

(a) Write out a sequence of steps that executes the algorithm, including the routing steps needed to pass neighboring values among the PEs. Assume that the PEs have an unlimited number of mode values.

(b) Specify the actual mode settings required to disable the appropriate PEs to make the algorithm work properly with only two mode bits in each PE.

(c) How many array operations are required to perform one iteration? Include the convergence test in your count.

6-17. Specify the routing instructions required to communicate the grid point values from each nearest neighbor (N, S, E, and W) to a problem grid point in an array machine connected like the ILLIAC IV. Be sure to consider the special cases that arise when either the sending or receiving point is at the boundary of a subarray—a group of modules in which the problem-array correspondence follows the "regular" array connections without folding or remapping.

6-18. An array machine of size $n \times n$ is used to solve a problem of size $n \times 2n$. The algorithm structure requires routing information from the point at position (i, j) to the point at position $(i, j + 2)$. The machine, however, has interconnections like the ILLIAC IV system. Suppose that the problem was mapped onto the array by sliding the right half of the problem array over the left half, so that the PE at location (i, j) holds problem variables for problem grid locations (i, j) and $(i, j + n)$. It is claimed that the desired copying can be performed by two routing instructions moving information in the direction of increasing values of the second coordinate, except that the routing pattern for the information leaving the PEs with $j = n$ or $j = n - 1$ must follow a different path.

(a) Show that the claim is correct. An example is sufficient.

(b) Show that if the programmer uses a folded mapping onto the array [a mirror image of the allocation described before, in which the PE at location (i, j) holds problem values for the problem grid locations (i, j) and $(i, 2n - j)$], the need for special routing from the last two columns does not go away. By showing that there is an advantage to the assignment described in the beginning of the problem, complete an argument that the folded mapping is less desirable than the sliding mapping for this problem.

6-19. Enumerate all special cases for communication with the N, E, S, and W neighbors that might occur at the boundaries of the ILLIAC IV array for the array mappings discussed in Problem 6-18. How many mode bits would you like to have so that you do not have to reload the mode registers between copying operations?

6-20. In an array machine, the performance improvement (compared to a sequential machine) is limited by the bound found from Amdahl's Law. The computation in the text assumed that when the sequentially executed instructions were performed no array operations were taking place. Further performance improvements could be obtained by overlapping execution of control unit instructions with the array instruction execution. To bound the performance improvement that can be obtained in this manner, suppose that all sequential instructions in fact could be moved to the control unit, that all array functions actually use all of the PEs in the array, and that there are no logical conditions that prohibit the sequential instructions being overlapped with array operations.

(a) Find an upper bound (as a function of f, the fraction of sequential instructions in the algorithm) on the speedup obtained from array processing when the control unit instructions are always overlapped with useful PE array operations.

(b) Find the value of f for which the maximum speedup is obtained.

(c) Find the range of values of f for which the system's speed is controlled by the execution time for the sequential instructions alone.

6-21. Amdahl's rule concerning the speedup possible in an array machine states that the performance benefit gained by the array is limited by the amount of time that the system must spend performing essential sequential (nonparallel) instruction sequences. For each of the situations to be outlined, explain whether this argument could be used to place a bound on the system's performance.

(a) A **cobegin** program structure.

(b) A systolic array machine.

6-22. Write a program fragment compatible with[55] the CYBER 205 architecture to perform the vector addition x = y + z. Assume that this program fragment occurs before any context has been established, so that all vector description information must be loaded into processor registers.

6-23. A designer is proposing a pipeline structure for the implementation of componentwise vector multiply-add. The ith component D_i of the result vector D should be $A_i^* B_i + C_i$, where A, B, and C are the operand vectors containing integer components. The multiplication is performed using a carry-save-adder tree.

(a) Assign functions to pipeline stages for performing this function.

(b) Draw a picture of your pipeline design.

(c) Describe the timing of your design. Is there any obvious bottleneck? Explain.

(d) Discuss the usefulness of the design.

---

[55] In other words, load the descriptors in the registers so that a configuration similar to that shown in Figure 6-18 is attained. Assume that the registers can be loaded from immediate operands contained in the program. For simplicity, assume that the vectors are allocated memory space statically (the locations and lengths are all known when the program is written).

6-24. In the text, we argued that Booth's algorithm was not attractive for a pipeline because the number of add/subtract operations depended on the operand bit patterns. In this problem, we develop a multiplication algorithm derived from Booth's algorithm that might be more suitable for a pipeline implementation. Recall that in Booth's algorithm, the values of consecutive pairs of multiplier bits are examined to determine whether to add (subtract) the multiplicand to (from) the partial product. In either case, the multiplier and the partial product are shifted one position after the test (and the addition or subtraction, if required).

    (a) Devise a generalization of Booth's algorithm that examines three consecutive multiplier bits to determine whether (and what) to add to (subtract from) the partial product. A 2-bit shift is made after the test and the chosen arithmetic operation (if any) is completed.

    (b) Would the algorithm you devised in part (a) be suitable for pipelining? If so, how many stages would the pipeline require?

6-25. A pipelined machine has an addition pipeline with a stages and a multiplication pipeline with m stages. Let c denote the number of components of a set of vector operands. The following questions are to be answered with expressions that are functions of a, c, and m. Assume that no delays are introduced outside the pipelines.

    (a) How long does it take to perform a vector multiplication? What is the speed measured in cycles per component?

    (b) The machine is used to perform a multiply-add operation of the form $xy + z$, where x, y, and z are c-component vectors. What is the average speed measured in cycles per component? There is no chaining and the multiplication has to be completed before the addition can be initiated.

    (c) Repeat part (b) if the machine chains the multiply and add operations.

6-26. We consider the design options facing a designer attempting to use one pipeline structure to implement two radically different operations, such as floating-point addition and multiplication.

    (a) Draw pipeline structures for two separate pipelines, each implementing one of the operations. Show the subfunctions that are performed in each stage. Do not try to estimate or balance the stage delays.

    (b) Draw an integrated pipeline for the two operations. Switches between the stages determine the data flow patterns. The switches are set by the function code and remain in the same positions until the operation is completed.

    (c) Draw an integrated pipeline for the two operations in which the function code travels through the pipeline along with the operands.

    (d) Compare the designs from parts (b) and (c). Consider the delays in the operations and the possibility of initiating a new operation while the final stages of the previous operation are being completed. (*Hint:* You may want to draw timing diagrams to study important special situations.)

6-27. A pipelined implementation of floating-point addition follows the pipeline structure shown in Figure 6-20. The floating-point representation allocates 16 bits for the (biased) exponent and 48 bits for the normalized fraction, which is the mantissa encoded using the sign/magnitude convention. All significant mantissa bits are explicitly present in the representation.

(a) Specify what information should be included within each of the interstage registers in the pipeline. Choose the information to minimize the register widths, while retaining functionality.

(b) Specify the width of each interstage registers.

6-28. Draw a sequence of figures showing the flow of data through buffer registers that interface a wide memory system to the input side of a pipeline processing a vector with a stride of 1. Use the following configuration parameters: the memory accesses eight operand components per memory cycle, and there are two pipeline cycles per memory cycle. Show the steady-state operation of the buffer, and restrict your attention to a single vector and its components.

6-29. This problem concerns the sizes of operand buffers between memory and a vector pipeline. The vector pipeline requires a pair of operand component values from memory during each pipe cycle. The two operand buffers are configured as word-shifting serial–parallel and parallel–serial registers (see Figure 6-23). The stride of each vector is 1. We impose some restrictions on the problem. First, all events are timed by the one-phase clock that times pipeline cycles. Second, the vector operation has two vector operands and one vector result. Third, a memory read request cannot be issued until the buffer that is to receive the data is free. Fourth, the memory access time is unpredictable, but is never greater than m pipe cycles. In other words, the data read in response to a read request issued at time t will certainly arrive at the registers by time $t + mc$, where c is the length of a pipe cycle. Each memory read request retrieves p operands in parallel; these can be loaded in parallel into the operand buffers, and on the next cycle, the first operand can be gated from the buffer into the pipeline, if necessary.

Determine the size of the operand buffers necessary to guarantee that operands always will be available for the pipe. Be sure to account for the memory cycles required to store the results coming from the pipeline.

6-30. The discussion in the text emphasized pipelines in which a vector result is produced from one or more vector operands. It is possible to insert registers or feedback paths that accumulate results from the values that pass through. Designing a controller for an accumulating pipeline structure is similar to the problem of designing a controller for the component-by-component pipeline. For example, one could compute the dot product of two integer vectors using a multiply pipeline followed by an addition pipeline with its output connected back to one of its inputs. This problem details that design.

(a) How many partial sums of the desired dot product are circulating in the addition pipeline when the last partial product has exited from the multiply pipeline?

(b) Specify a control sequence for this pipeline to accumulate the partial sums circulating in the addition loop. This addition is performed after all input components have been processed. Remember that you cannot speed up the pipeline, whose structure is fixed.

6-31. The control unit in a CRAY-1 processor detects chaining possibilities. Chaining can be employed when the result from one pipelined vector operation can be directly passed to another pipeline's operand input in exactly the same clock phase that it is passed to its destination register. For this problem, assume that the machine has two pipelines and that the issuance of the second operation can be delayed to the proper cycle to allow this chaining. Assume that all operations have two vector operands and one result vector. Each instruction contains three register numbers, two specifying the two operand locations, and one specifying the result location. In addition to the obvious flow-related timing constraints, there is one constraint on the register numbers between the two chained instructions: the result of the second operation cannot be directed to the same register as the location of either operand of the first instruction. If this constraint is violated, the second instruction will not be issued until the first instruction has been completed (because the source register will have been reserved). This question concerns the design of the logic to control the result/operand streaming and the data paths to be used when the operations are streamed. State the minimum necessary coordination rules to detect when an instruction can be issued in this streaming mode.

6-32. Can the possibility of chaining be detected during compilation? Explain.

6-33. This problem concerns the number of cycles saved by chaining two pipelined vector operations using the Cray chaining scheme. Assume that (1) a result register is reserved until it has been completely filled, and (2) a pipeline cannot be used to initiate an operation until it has been flushed out.
   (a) Determine the quantities that affect the amount of time saved by chaining.
   (b) Write an expression giving the time saved by a single successful chaining, expressed in units of processor cycles.

6-34. The proponents of pipelined and array machines both claim (and rightly so) that their architectures do provide performance benefits. A designer takes these arguments to heart and proposes building an array machine with pipelined processing elements. Can the arguments that supported the pipeline and array structures separately be used to support the proposed combination? Explain.

6-35. Specify pipeline control logic that determines when to feed another component of an operand vector to a pipeline. Suppose that the pipeline's operation has two sparse vector operands and one sparse vector result and that every nonzero component of the result vector must come from the pipeline. Your answer should include a Boolean condition that becomes true when the next (nonzero) component of an operand vector should be delivered to the pipeline from one of the compressed operand vectors.
   (a) Draw a timing diagram to illustrate all the special cases for an addition pipeline. Write a Boolean condition that becomes true when the next component should be delivered to the pipeline from the compressed vector.
   (b) Repeat part (a) for multiplication.
   (c) Repeat part (a) if an operand component may bypass the pipeline and be sent directly to the result vector.
   (d) Repeat part (c) for multiplication.

6-36. Draw a timing diagram illustrating the operation of a barrel processor that uses a state memory that has four-way interleave. The system is emulating eight virtual processors. Discuss the difference between this implementation and an implementation using shift registers in a cyclic path. All processing is performed in a single processing stage.

6-37. In the design for the superscalar processor without any buffering, there was a condition stating that the previous instruction must have been issued before the controller can issue the next instruction. Explain the role of this condition in assuring that the correct values are read from each register during each instruction.

6-38. The Tomasulo algorithm ([ANDE67], [TOMA67]) supports an out-of-order instruction issue like the scoreboard scheme described in Section 6.6. Tomasulo's algorithm differs from the scoreboard scheme in the way that it tracks the sources of operands that are not yet available when instruction issue is attempted. In the scoreboard scheme, the sources are identified with register numbers, whereas in the Tomasulo algorithm, the identifier of the functional unit is used. It is claimed that the Tomasulo algorithm is more flexible than the scoreboard scheme because there exist situations in which it will permit instruction issue when the scoreboard would stall instruction issue.

(a) Show an example of such a situation.

(b) Discuss the general conditions under which there is an advantage to the Tomasulo strategy.

(c) Devise and describe a scheme that extends the Tomasulo algorithm to a system in which results come from pipelined functional units.

(i) Specify the difficulty that arises from using the Tomasulo algorithm with pipelined units.

(ii) Show how your proposed mechanism has eliminated the difficulty.

6-39. This problem concerns the design of a processor with overlapped instruction execution using a scoreboard or Tomasulo's algorithm (see Problem 6-38). Both control strategies define the behavior for functional units performing R-R instructions. In this problem, we wish to add load and store functional units to the design. The load and store operations take the address from an integer register in the processor: The data flowing to and from memory may flow to or from any processor register. What rules govern instruction issue for load and store instructions?

6-40. This problem concerns the management of a processor's result buffer that is supposed to assure that the state changes arising from task execution are performed when possible except that they must be performed in program order. Each task, when it completes, sends its task number along with its results and their destinations to the buffer manager. Assume that the processor has a load/store architecture, so all task inputs and results are associated with processor registers. The buffer manager is supposed to enable the writes of the results to processor registers when possible. If there is an interrupt, all tasks that have been started (or have completed) but that preceded the interrupting task, will be rescheduled for a later time (and any results that were generated will be discarded). The buffer manager maintains the buffer entries in the order of the program steps that generated the corresponding result values.

(a) Describe how the buffer manager determines the position (within the buffer) of a newly arriving task result. Define the structure of the task result packet, in addition to any auxiliary data needed to properly manage the buffer.

(b) Specify a logical condition that will be true when the buffer manager determines that a result packet can be copied to the corresponding registers and removed from the buffer.

6-41. This problem concerns coding schemes to distinguish among the results that are about to be produced by a functional unit so that the unit number can be used in seeking to find all reservation station fields that need the value when it becomes available. One might use result tags that go along with each operation within the functional unit/reservation station.

  (a) Find the minimum number of distinct result tag values associated with a functional unit. Let n denote the maximum number of problems that can be in process in the functional unit. Let m denote the maximum number of requests that can be held in the reservation station associated with the functional unit. In answering the following questions, assume that these tag values are represented by integers 1, .. , min, where min denotes your answer to this question.

  (b) When is a result tag assigned to an operation?

  (c) Diagram the logic that finds where an operation's result should be placed when it leaves the functional unit.

6-42. Consider a design that permits instruction issue out of order but uses write buffers to force instruction completion in order. Instruction completions are chained by keeping with each operation the number of the functional unit whose result must be stored before the associated result can be written. For example, if instruction 3 will be performed in functional unit 2, then the unit number associated with instruction 4 will be 2.

  (a) Describe the chained data structure that is established by this encoding and show why it corresponds to instruction completion in program order.

  (b) Write out all control actions needed to manage register contents and functional unit write buffers.

  (c) Explain why this control design permits functional units to handle more than one operation simultaneously provided that the results from each unit are produced on a first-in-first-out (FIFO) basis.

  (d) Explain why it is necessary (for functionality) that each functional unit behave in a FIFO manner when the scheduling scheme described before is in use. What functionality requirement(s) might be violated if this ordering constraint were not obeyed? Explain.

  (e) Describe how the data structure associates results with the instructions that caused them to be computed.

6-43. The description of the scoreboard indicated that instruction issue will have to stall if the buffer in front of a functional unit is filled up.

  (a) Describe the reason why the controller cannot continue to issue instructions (out of order) after the filled buffer is detected.

  (b) Describe a way to add bookkeeping information to permit continuing instruction issue after the buffer full condition occurs.

  (c) Your design from part (b) probably contains a different limitation on continued instruction issue. Describe that limitation, but do not try to remove it.

6-45. A designer proposes a redesign of a reorder buffer controller. His goal is to permit results to be stored in registers as quickly as possible. The proposal is based on the observation that a result R can be stored in its destination if no results waiting in the buffer for register R also precede the instruction in program order. Assume that the reorder buffer is implemented in a circular queue whose pointers are in registers named queue_head and queue_tail; items enter the queue at queue_tail and leave it at queue_head.

(a) Devise an example to show that this modification can speed program execution. (*Hint*: Which system bottleneck is relieved by the proposed scheme?)

(b) Describe a set of flags that can be used to correctly manage the buffer.

(c) Specify control logic that sets a flag next to a buffer entry when the result in the entry can be copied to its register destination. Assume that the buffer's pointer management is correctly handled, and that the two pointers are not permitted to match.

(d) Does this scheme support precise exceptions? If not, show a modification that does support precise exceptions. Explain your answer.

6-46. For each of the superscalar control schemes described in Section 6.6, identify the location of all information that is included in the three important state sets: (1) the architectural state, (2) the in-order state, and (3) the lookahead state.

6-47. Explain why an instruction to save the condition (or status) register must be treated like a conditional branch instruction when the controller is attempting to issue instructions out of program order.

6-48. Example 6-38 presented a design that monitors condition code sources to correctly handle dependencies through the condition code register. But the design works correctly only if a single instruction can be waiting for those results.

(a) Explain how the design fails if two instructions that want to read the condition code register are both deferred, and between them there is an instruction that sets the condition codes.

(b) Adjust the design by adding a rule that halts instruction issue when the problem identified in part (a) might arise. Specify consistent rules governing both stalling and resuming instruction lookahead.

6-49. We wish to design a branch prediction module for a processor with a condition code register. Suppose that there was a previous processor design (with which we must be compatible) that has some instructions that modify only some of the condition code bits, leaving the others unchanged. Therefore, the logic described in the text that keeps track of the last instruction to write into the condition code register will not support the program order illusion. One way out of this difficulty would be to add barriers to the program. A designer proposes another approach—that the processor be designed with additional logic to track more detailed information about the condition code values used in branch prediction.

(a) Choose (or define) a processor architecture in which some instructions make partial modifications to the condition codes. For example, a load instruction might change a zero flag and leave an overflow flag unmodified. Then create a program for this processor that does not obey the program order illusion if the text's logic is used.

(b) Describe the additional logic needed to determine the earliest time that a branch outcome can be known. Assume that the processor uses a reorder buffer to assure that instructions are completed in program order.

6-50. State the prediction and update rules for a branch prediction buffer that maintains two bits that reflect the last two outcomes of the branch test. The desired behavior is that the prediction is changed only if two consecutive branch outcomes are contrary to the prediction. Devise your answer so that the prediction is based on only one of the buffer bits. Your answer should state the buffer actions for every possible execution of a conditional branch instruction.

6-51. A processor using overlapped execution for speed can perform instructions more quickly than a nonoverlapped processor. Conditional branches cause difficulties because the processor cannot anticipate the actual program flow until the condition for the branch has been determined. We also know that an anticipatory branch instruction can be added to the processor's repertoire to remove this difficulty and allow speedier execution when the processor's execution is overlapped. This problem concerns the utility of this (or similar) schemes at other levels of system design.

(a) Discuss the value of anticipatory GOTOs in a programming language such as FORTRAN or C++. Do not answer the question with an essay on why GOTOs are undesirable; rather, assume that they are going to be used and discuss whether an anticipatory version would speed system performance. Explain your answer.

(b) Repeat (a) for the microcode level of design.

6-52. This problem concerns the design of branch prediction logic using the branch taken frequency of recent executions of the instruction. The frequencies are determined from the value in a counter that indicates the (signed) count of the difference [(#times_taken - #times_not_taken].

(a) Choose a simple piece of information from the buffer that can be used to make the prediction.

(b) How is the buffer information updated when a branch is executed?

7

PARALLELISM BY MESSAGE PASSING

Let me hear from thee by letters.

— *Shakespeare*, Two Gentlemen of Verona

*A letter is an announced visit, and the postman
is the intermediary of impolite purposes.
Every week we ought to have one hour for receiving letters,
and then go and take a bath.*

— *F. Nietzsche*

Delay is preferable to error.

— *Thomas Jefferson*

A designer wishing to improve system performance could design the system to allow many related activities to proceed synchronously, as in the parallelism techniques discussed in Chapter 6. Most of those techniques relied on foreknowledge of the timing or logical relationships among the set of possible parallel activities. A second method is to program a number of simultaneous processes that share memory and whose progress is coordinated by atomic actions and barrier constructs. A third method is to support a number of simultaneous processes, performing somewhat independent computations, the set being coordinated by messages passed among the processes. This strategy matches modularity concepts, as each process can be specified independently of the others. The design

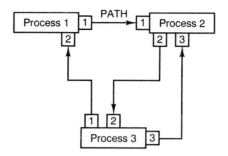

Figure 7-1 A message-passing network

options concerning communications among modules within a processing node are similar to those available for interprocess communication.

Thus, the basic coordination paradigms supporting asynchronous parallelism fall into two categories: shared resources, described in Chapter 8, and messages passed among processes, described in this chapter.

To describe message-passing systems, we add a few illusions concerning the structure and behavior of message-passing links within the system. The structural considerations are as follows: (1) The communicating entities are separate processes, which themselves have designated *ports*. (2) The ports serve as the communications interfaces between the processes and entities outside the process. (3) Messages are passed among the processes on *paths*. (4) Without loss of generality, we assume that each path is unidirectional (i.e., that messages travel only in one direction on a path). (5) Each path connects one port to another port. The system structure is isomorphic to a directed graph whose nodes correspond to processes and whose branches correspond to message paths (see Figure 7-1).

The message-passing illusions are the following

Message Ordering Illusion. Messages that pass through a path arrive at the destination in the same order that they were sent from the source.

Message Integrity Illusion. Messages that pass through a path are not garbled during their passage (they arrive unchanged).

Message Survival Illusion. No messages are lost on any path.

Finite Delay Illusion. All messages sent on a path arrive after a bounded delay.

Process-Message Interaction Illusion. All interactions between a program and messages at its ports are governed by special statements or instructions, as illustrated in this simple example.

Example 7-1

> There are two processes P and Q, each with a single port, named using the process name. The processes could communicate using blocking send and receive commands by executing a program like the following:
>
> Process P   Process Q
>
> m = "Message";   **receive**(n, P);
> **send**(m, Q);
>
> Because **send** and **receive** block, the process that reaches its communication statement first must stop and wait for the other process to reach its matching statement. At that time, the communication transpires. Even though the processes view this interaction as one-way communication, the implementation must include two-way communication to coordinate the process blocking and synchronization.

After you have completed this chapter, you will understand several options for providing message communication between processes and processors. You will learn about the interactions between individual processes and message communication systems and the implementation of these communications. You will understand the application of these techniques in implementing module interconnections and input/output in computer systems. You will appreciate the delays incurred by messages passed through the operating system, and understand the appeal of simple messages that can be easily decoded and handled at both the sending and receiving nodes. You will see that the logical communications structure can be implemented within a physical structure that differs from the logical structure implied by the programmer-visible communication paths. You might wish to expand your understanding of message-passing systems by studying data flow systems, which are based on passing packets that hold values among a network of modules that is structured to reflect the dependencies within a computational algorithm. Appendix K presents this model, its limitations, and one approach toward its implementation. Another related topic concerns functional behavior of a set of communicating processes; this topic is covered in more detail in Appendix L, where we prove the functionality of systems based on a restricted message-passing model.

7.1 BASIC MESSAGE-PASSING SCENARIOS

The message-passing illusions imply that logical paths connect ports to each other. One might assume that each logical path corresponds to a physical path. Some logical connections are actually implemented using message-passing mechanisms within a single processor. Other virtual message paths may utilize hardware links between physically diverse modules. Despite these variations, processes are programmed assuming direct unidirectional paths between ports.

Another important aspect of the illusions concerns the processes in the system and the nature of their interactions with messages. Our model of these interactions is based on the actions of an interrupt or exception handler within the operating system. The important elements of the model concern the processes, their states and their interactions with the message-passing service.

In the basic model, processes are assumed to exist forever, though they might not always be executing a program. Each process may execute commands, such as send and receive, that specify interactions with the message-passing system.

7.1.1 Interprocess Interactions through the Message System

There are many equivalent ways to model interprocess interactions through a message system. We start with one based on an exception processing scenario. In this model whenever a process executes something that causes an exception, a message is sent to the operating system, which must "service" the exception before the process can resume its execution.

This waiting scheme, along with blocking and nonblocking send and receive schemes, give three interaction options that we discuss in this section.

Waiting. The scenario for a waiting interaction is as follows:

1. Process P causes an exception.
2. The exception is communicated as a message to the operating system.
3. The exception handler (EH) is activated and performs its function.
4. EH notifies the operating system that its task is complete.
5. The operating system reactivates P.

Consider the operating system as a message service for the moment. Another view of the same scenario includes process state information, as in the following:

Action	P's State	EH's state
	Running	Waiting
1. P1 causes exception		
	Waiting	Waiting
2. Operating system gets message		
	Waiting	Waiting
3. EH starts function		
	Waiting	Running
4. EH notifies operating system		
	Waiting	Waiting
5. P1 reactivated		
	Running	Waiting

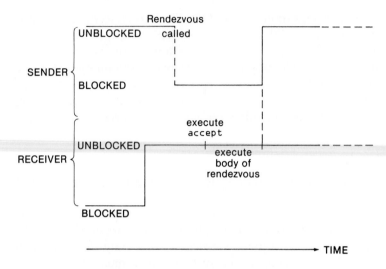

Figure 7-2   The timing of a rendezvous interaction

This does not show the details of the activation and deactivation of the exception handler. In steps 2 and 4, both processes are waiting while the operating system is performing its duties.

Now change the basic scenario by replacing the exception handler with a user process that has been waiting for the message to arrive; in this case, we might view the interaction as a *remote procedure call*, taking the view that the action performed by the receiver is an activation of a procedure defined within that process module. This interaction pattern is called a *rendezvous* in Ada.[1] A representation of the timing of this scenario is shown in Figure 7-2.

We can use this model as a building block for constructing all other models of message-passing interactions. Thus, in the basic interaction, the sender blocks waiting for the receiver to complete some action, and the receiver was waiting for the message to arrive. After the message interaction has been completed, both processes may continue their independent computations.

Blocking.   A blocking message interaction is similar to the waiting interaction pattern, except that the sending process continues its own execution once the receiver has taken the contents of the message. In other words, the waiting for the receiver to execute the body of the rendezvous is eliminated.

Nonblocking.   Under nonblocking message-passing protocols, the sender does not wait for any response from the receiver, including not even waiting to

---

[1]   The pattern actually differs in a detail regarding the choice of the action taken within the receiver.

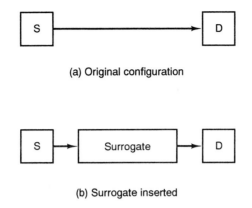

(a) Original configuration

(b) Surrogate inserted

Figure 7-3   Surrograte processes inserted to buffer
messages and change the apparent protocol

know whether the receiver has received the message. The sender can synchronize with the receiver by later receiving an acknowledgment message from the
receiver.

How does this scenario fit with the preceding waiting model? To model
this protocol, we insert a *surrogate process* (see Figure 7-3). The sole purpose of
the surrogate process is to forward every message that it receives. The important
property is that the surrogate responds immediately to the message sender so
that that sending process can continue after the message has been copied into the
surrogate. To perform its function, the surrogate must *buffer* the message, because the receiver to which it sends the message might not be ready to receive
the message. This behavior pattern matches the behavior of a message buffer
within the operating system or the message-passing subsystem.

7.1.2 Process States

In this preceding discussion, we used the notion of process state to connote the
nature and progress of the activity in the process. In general, the combination of
process activity and message interactions describes limits on the process schedule and the interactions between processes and the message-passing system. The
following states model the interactions of processes with the message passing
system:

   1. Running, not interruptible
   2. Running, interruptible (willing to be interrupted if a message arrives)
   3. Blocked while sending (waiting for an acknowledgment)
   4. Blocked while receiving (waiting for a message from a specific source)
   5. Idle (waiting for any message to arrive)

The running states just described do not distinguish whether the process scheduler has actually allocated processor time for the process in question. The term "ready" is used to indicate the state of a process which is simply waiting for the process scheduler to allocate time for its execution. A ready process can be interruptible or noninterruptible. Transitions among these states occur when a process executes a meessage-passing operation or when an event external to the process occurs (such as a message arriving from another process).

7.1.3 Comments

The basic model includes the important elements of all interactions, including the need for the message receiver to react to the message before sending a response back to the initiator of the transaction.

A number of details were suppressed. For example, how are processes named? How do program steps specify message interactions? What can processes know about the state within the message-passing system and their own status within the system? How does the system respond to failures? We discuss these issues and modifications to the basic communication model as we move from the process level down to communication between modules within a processing node.

Processor scheduling issues will be considered within the operating system level of the implementation, because that is where the interactions with the message-passing modules occur. After visiting these levels, we will show how similar design issues and options affect the physical level, where physical communication paths and signaling protocols are used to implement the virtual services that we use at the higher levels of abstraction.

7.2 PROGRAMMING INTERPROCESS MESSAGE COMMUNICATION

Three types of program-level activity imply message passing: (1) direct message passing, (2) synchronization barriers, and (3) input/output. We emphasize programmed message transmission. At this level, specific **send** and **receive** actions activate the message-passing system.

7.2.1 Specific Message-Passing Operations

At the process level the communications operations fall into three general categories:

1. Send
2. Receive
3. Test

A big question concerns whether send operations block the executing process, which cannot continue until the receiver becomes available (of course, if the receiver is available, there is no delay at the blocking operation). A complementary issue concerns blocking within the receive operation.

By straightforward programming using these basic operations one can construct basic message-passing interactions, such as a pair of processes coordinating their activities by exchanging blocking messages. The interactions are straightforward when only two processes "talk" to each other because each one knows the source of every message that it expects to receive. In a general environment, we must be able to specify what should happen if several processes can communicate with a process P. Because P cannot know the actual event sequence within all processes, it cannot know the order of arrival of messages from other processes. If P executed a blocking receive and then waited to resume until the source designated in the receive operation sent a message to P, the responses to messages from the other sources might be delayed for a long interval. To permit specification of the conditions under which the process should be resumed, the program should be able to define a predicate (about the status of messages in the ports) that, when true, causes the process to resume execution. To describe these states, create a logical variable associated with each port of the process and build a resumption predicate from these variables.

What part of the system is going to check the resumption predicates? There are several approaches, including the following:

1. The system checks associated resumption predicates during a receive operation.
2. Add an intervening process that checks the predicate and sends a message to process P only when the condition is met.

Both of these approaches simply pass the problem to somewhere else within the system; including a resumption predicate with the receive request moves the burden to the operating system or its message handling service. Placing an intervening process that evaluates the predicate does remove the predicate from the receiving process, but the original problem remains (albeit in the other process) and several new problems (or limitations) may be introduced. To illustrate the new problems, notice the major difficulty that arises if the receiving process wishes to use different resumption predicates at different times. To make such a change one must reconfigure the interconnecting paths to include the new process that "solves" the predicate evaluation problem. Reconfiguration during system operation introduces other interesting problems, such as the correct way to handle messages that happen to be waiting at an input port of a process that is being deleted from the system.

One way to provide the resumption predicate facility with minimum impact on the system is to provide the capability to read the port status. A simple case in which this capability is needed is a process that should be resumed whenever a message arrives at any of its input ports.

Example 7-2

Process R has several incoming message ports. The process is supposed to respond to each message as it arrives, regardless of the port at which it does arrive. The receiver can execute a loop in which it uses a nonblocking **receive** to test each input port in turn to see whether a message has arrived. When any message arrives, the wait loop is terminated. Here is such an algorithm:

1. $i = 1$;
2. If there is a message at port i, goto step 5;
3. $i = i + 1$;
4. If i = maxi, set i = 1 and goto step 2;
5. Computation;

The continuous cycling (called *busy waiting*) of this algorithm wastes processor time. It is desirable to remove busy waiting from programs wherever possible. With support from lower levels of the system, busy waiting can be replaced by a programming construct that blocks the executing process until a ready condition becomes true. The simplest useful ready condition is the OR of a set of events. We call this construct the *alternative wait*; most programming languages that support message passing provide an alternative wait construct.

The alternative wait construct awakens a process whenever any one of a specified set of (input) ports has received a message. The program can then evaluate its own resumption predicate to decide whether to wait for additional messages or to proceed to further processing. This allocation of functions provides a reasonable compromise, because it imposes only simple requirements on the message-passing system and it permits the processes to wait for message arrival without using processor cycles to execute busy wait loops. Furthermore, arbitrary resumption predicates can be evaluated within individual processes.

In the remainder of this section, we discuss some language designs that include direct support for message handling. Our examples come from occam, PL/1, and Ada. For each language, we show how processes and signaling paths can be specified. We describe basic single-port message passing operations. Finally, we show how alternative wait operations can be specified.

Occam. Occam [MAY83] was created at Inmos, Ltd., for programming the Transputer chip family, a product line designed to support sets of processes interacting through passed messages. Each Transputer chip [WHIT85] contains a processor, some memory, and four pairs of unidirectional communication links. Occam supports message passing with a minimum set of linguistic mechanisms.

Process Declarations. Occam processes are defined by the **PAR** program construct. Each parallel portion within the **PAR** construct becomes a separate process when the **PAR** is executed. The **PAR** therefore functions like a **cobegin**. The **PAR** syntax is

```
PAR
    <statement_1>
    <statement_2>
    ..
    <statement_n>
```

Note the absence of printable statement terminators; the new line character terminates each statement. There also are no **end** statements or braces to group statements; indentation is used to specify statement grouping. A set of parallel processes, with each process executing a separate sequential program, is written

```
PAR
    SEQ
        <statement_list_1>
    SEQ
        <statement_list_2>
    ..
    SEQ
        <statement_list_n>
```

Basic Message Communication. In occam, the operator symbols "!" and "?" denote message sending and reception, respectively.[2] The occam syntax for the send (output) and receive (input) statements is

```
c ! m
c ? m
```

Here c is a channel identifier and m is an object name specifying the memory object that contains the message contents.[3] Because the channel name is global to all communicating processes, each communication path is a many–many entity.

In occam, both "!" and "?" block when used outside the alternative waiting construct. Therefore, the sending and receiving processes are exactly synchronized at the time they exchange a message through simple send and receive actions.

Example 7-3

Two communicating occam processes pass a message as follows:

```
CHAN port              //declare the channel, global to the processes
    ..
```

---

[2]   One mnemonic device for remembering these symbols is that "!" corresponds to making an emphatic statement, whereas "?" corresponds to asking a question (whose answer is the received message).

[3]   Notice the similarity of this syntax to that used in object-oriented programming.

```
PAR                    //start the processes
    SEQ
        ..
        port ! m    //send the message
        ..
    SEQ
        ..
        port ? mm //receive the message
        ..
```

Alternative Waiting. Occam's alternative wait construct **ALT** may contain a number of clauses, each preceded by a condition, called a "guard," which is an input statement. When the **ALT** statement is executed, the system determines whether any of the input operations are enabled (because send is blocking, the receive operation will be enabled only if the corresponding send operation has been initiated already). If none of the receive operations is enabled, the process blocks at the **ALT** until one becomes enabled. If at least one of the receive operations in the **ALT** is enabled, an enabled one is selected and performed. At this point, the corresponding sending process unblocks. After the receiving process completes its receive, the statements in the associated clause are performed to complete the execution of the **ALT** construct.

Example 7-4

```
CHAN one, two, three, four          // channels declared
    ..
    ALT
        one ? x
            four ! x
            n := x
        two ? x
            three ! x
            n := x + 3
            count := count + 1
```

The **ALT** statement in this program fragment has two guards, so the process can receive a message from either channel one or two, forward it to an appropriate output channel, and then store (in n) some information about the contents of the message that was actually received. The following execution histories are compatible with this program structure:

History 1   History 2

one ! <>   two ! <>
one ? x   two ? x
four ! x   three ! x
n := x   n := x + 3
                             count := count + 1

The first statement in each of these histories is performed by some process not shown in the program fragment.

PL/1. PL/1 interprocess communication uses objects of type event. An event object has two components: its completion and its status. These values can be read and written. The completion component is one if the event has occurred, and zero otherwise. The event's status is zero if the state is "normal;" a nonzero value can indicate the nature of the abnormality. An event object can be associated with the invocation of a task or an input/output operation, in which case its completion component becomes true (nonzero) when the task or operation is completed. The following operations on event objects are available:

1. **SIGNAL_CONDITION**(e)   // causes event e to occur;
2. **EVENT**(e)   // associates a task with an event;
3. **ON_CONDITION**(e) <statement>   // establishes a handler for the event;
4. **WAIT**(<e_list>){(<expression>)}   // wait for the occurrence of at least[4]
                                     //<expression> of the events listed in e_list;
5. **COMPLETION**(e)   // access the completion component;
6. **STATUS**(e)   // access the status component.

Execution of an **ON_CONDITION**(e) statement dynamically associates a handler with the event e; the body of that handler is the statement following the **ON_CONDITION** phrase. When e has been signaled, dynamic nesting finds the most recently associated handler that will respond to the signal. A program can use the **WAIT** statement to block until a minimum number of the listed events have occurred; this option allows alternative waiting but does not handle arbitrary predicates. The behavior of an occam **ALT** statement can be emulated by **WAIT**(<list>)(1) followed by a set of conditionally executed statements that together determine which events on the list actually did occur. Because the name of the PL/1 event object may be globally visible, the **EVENT** construct may provide many-to-many signaling, just like the occam channel construct.

Ada. Independent program executions, which we have been calling processes, are called *tasks* in Ada.

Process Declarations. Tasks are declared by headers and bodies written as separate program entities. A task begins execution when the block in which it is instantiated is entered. Thus, the act of object initialization applied to a task object leaves that new task in a ready state with respect to process scheduling. The block whose entry initiated task execution becomes the "parent"[5] block to the

---

[4]   If the expression is omitted, the process waits for all events on the list.
[5]   The Ada terminology is different—the task we are calling the child is called a dependent task of the task we are calling the parent (the role of the parent task does not have a technical name in Ada).

"child" task that was activated on block entry. The parent block cannot be exited until all of its child tasks have completed execution.

Example 7-5

    This Ada program block contains the declaration of a task object:

```
procedure parent .. is
    type message is
        ..;                    --declare structure of messages
    task child is
        entry input1( mess : message );
        entry input2( mess : message );
    end;
    task body child is
        ..                     --declare objects local to child
    begin
        ..                     --body of child
    end;
        ..                     --other declarations for parent
begin
        ..                     --body of parent
end;
```

    Basic Message Communication. Ada interprocess communication is handled through a mechanism called the *rendezvous*. A rendezvous port[6] corresponds to an **entry** interface declaration within a task specification; the entry has a name and a formal parameter list as specified in the declaration. The entry name will be used like a port name to establish a connection between two communicating processes. The parameter list specifies those parameters to be communicated from the sender to the receiver when the rendezvous occurs. To initiate its part of the rendezvous, the sending process executes a statement that looks like a procedure call, except that the "procedure name" is the entry name. To initiate its part of the rendezvous, the receiving process executes an **accept** statement that looks like a procedure specification, followed by the keyword **do**, a statement list that constitutes the body of the rendezvous, and the terminating **end**.

Example 7-6

```
procedure parent is
    type message is char( 29 );
    task child1 is
    end child1;
    task body child1 is
        a, b : message;
```

---

[6]   Ada does not use the term "port," but we do for consistency with our previous discussion.

```
begin
     ..
     channel1( a );              --send message to child2
     ..
end child1;
task child2 is
     entry channel1( mess : message );
end child2;
task body child2 is
     c, d : message;
begin
     ..
     accept channel1( c ) do    --rendezvous channel1
          ..                     --body of rendezvous
     end;                        --end of rendezvous body
end child2;
     ..
end;
begin
     ..                          --body of parent procedure
end parent;
```

In this program, the two child tasks start execution at the same time—when the procedure parent is entered. At the same time, the parent procedure is also activated. There is a single rendezvous (named channel1) between the child processes.

Once the sender executes the rendezvous call, the channel is enabled. Once the receiver executes the **accept** on that channel, the rendezvous is made, and the statements within the rendezvous body are executed by the receiver. Only after the rendezvous body has been completed by the receiver may the sender continue past its rendezvous call. Thus, when the rendezvous in the example occurs, child2 will execute the body of the rendezvous before the system unblocks child1. Figure 7-2 illustrated this timing.

The usual name scope rules apply to the entry call name, which may make the entry name visible to more than one cooperating task. Therefore, the rendezvous structure provides a many-to-one communication path. Only a single task knows about the **entry** declaration, so it is the only task that can accept this event. However, this task can have multiple **accept** statements, and hence many handlers, for the same **entry** name. In this manner, the Ada rendezvous differs from a remote procedure call, in which a single procedure body is associated with each procedure name.

The simple rendezvous described previously used blocking **send** and **receive** operations.[7] The sender blocks until the receiver executes the **accept**

---

[7] More elaborate varieties of sends and receives that support polling will be described in what follows; these varieties allow a process to continue even if its communicating partner is not yet ready to participate in an interaction.

operation to complete the rendezvous, and the receiver blocks at its **accept** if no sender has executed a call to that rendezvous. Information can be conveyed from the sender to the receiver through the parameters passed in the call statement; when the **accept** is executed, the actual parameter values are handled like procedure parameters. Notice the similarity of this structure to the **coreturn** operation (except here there are several control points).

Alternative Waiting. The Ada **select** construct provides alternative waiting; it is similar in spirit to the occam **ALT** construct. In Ada, unlike occam, the "guards" on the alternatives do not have to be **accept** statements; they can contain Boolean conditions involving object values and/or timing conditions.

In the simple case, each **select** alternative contains only a single **accept** statement. When the execution of the **select** statement starts, all **accept** rendezvous names are examined to determine whether any one has been called. If none of them have been called, the process blocks until one of them is called. If, on the other hand, at least one of them has been called, one of those is chosen. The sequence of statements that follows the chosen alternative is then executed.[8] When that sequence is completed, either by reaching the end of the set or by executing a **return**, the receiver has completed the **select** statement and the caller is unblocked to resume execution following its call to the **accept** entry.

Example 7-7

```
select
    accept path1( x : integer; y : out integer ) do
        y := x + 4;
    end;
or
    accept path2;
end select;
```

Notice that the rendezvous entry can have **out** parameters;[9] these can be used to send data or acknowledgments back to the sender. The second **accept** shows that the entry need not have either parameters or a body; the path2 rendezvous forces process synchronization without any data being communicated or any statements being executed within the receiver before the sender can proceed.

The preceding **select** statement will cause the receiving process to block until either path1 or path2 has been initiated from another process; if both had happened before the **select** statement was reached, one of the two would be picked for execution. Figure 7-4 illustrates this sequencing.

An Ada **select** statement can contain one or more **delay** statements as alternatives to message reception.

---

[8]   This sequencing rule is similar to the **one_of** statement discussed in Section 4.2.1.
[9]   In Ada, each procedure parameter has a local copy; if the parameter is specified as an **out** parameter, the contents of the local copy are copied back to the object named in the calling sequence when the procedure returns.

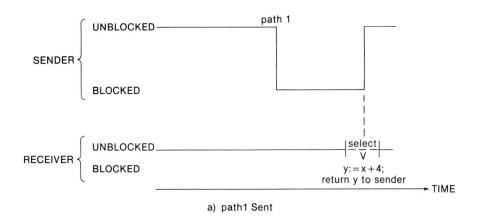

a) path1 Sent

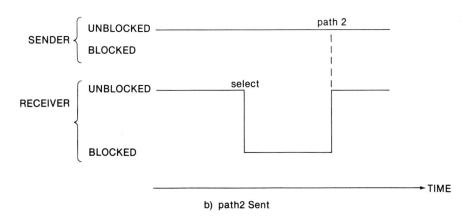

b) path2 Sent

Figure 7-4   Ada rendezvous timing with receiver select—some timing possibilites for Example 7-7

Example 7-8

```
select
    delay 50;
        y := x + 4;
    end;
or
    accept path2;
end select;
```

If 50 units of delay elapse after the **select** is started without the path2 entry being called, the attempt to accept a rendezvous at path2 will be aborted, and the assignment statement will be executed. Figure 7-5 illustrates this possibility.

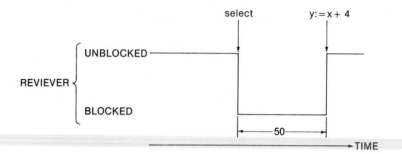

Figure 7-5   Delay in an Ada select statement—a possible
event sequence for Example 7-8

The **delay** predicate becomes true after the specified amount of time has
elapsed, the timer having started when the **accept** statement was initiated. Like
the **accept** alternative, the **delay** alternative can be followed by a sequence of statements that will be executed if the timer times out.

A third option for a **select** statement is an **else** clause, which will be selected
if none of the other guards is true. The **else** option may also contain a statement
list. A **select** statement with a simple rendezvous entry and the **else** option tests
for the presence of a message at an input port, without blocking the process if
the entry has not yet been called.

The following example illustrates a more general **select** option.

Example 7-9

```
select
    when b = 7 => accept path1( x : integer ) do
        a := x;
    end;
or
    when a + b > 10 => accept path2;
else
    miss := true;
end select;
```

The Boolean conditions are evaluated to determine which of the two rendezvous entries will be examined. The **select** condition is true if both the predicate is
true and the associated rendezvous entry has been called. If neither of the
Boolean/entry conditions holds, the assignment to miss will be performed and the
select thereby completed.

The previous discussion of **select** covers its use on the receiver's side of the
rendezvous interaction. The **select** construct can also be used on the sender's
side, preventing the sender from blocking when the rendezvous cannot be completed immediately. Only two of the receiver's option types make sense from the

sender's side: **delay** and **else**. With **delay**, the sender places a limit on the time it is willing to be blocked pending completion of the rendezvous. By using **else**, the programmer can create a nonblocking **send**. Within the sender's version of the **select** statement, the entry call can be followed by a set of statements to be executed if the entry call was selected for execution.

Example 7-10

```
select
        path1( 3 );
        x := x + 3;
else
        y := 7;
end select;
```

In this program fragment, the process does not block if the rendezvous cannot be completed immediately. In the next fragment, the process is willing to be blocked for a limited time waiting on the completion; if the waiting time passes without the rendezvous occurring, a new value will be assigned to y and processing will continue.

```
select
        path1( 3 );
        x := x + 3;
or
        delay 45;
        y := 13;
end select;
```

Summary.   Some high-level languages allow programmers to create independently scheduled processes. These processes can communicate among themselves by passing messages or parameter values. The syntactic structures that express these notions are specific to each language, but the basic semantic features are similar. In particular, basic operations send and receive messages. These operations can be blocking or nonblocking. There may be a way to receive a message if one is available, continuing execution if the message is not available. A receiver may wait for one of a set of messages. There is usually sufficient flexibility in the constructs that a programmer can create arbitrary message-passing protocols. In this way she can create nonfunctional programs. Despite the nofunctionality, at least there is weak synchronization between the communicating processes when messages are passed around.

The other important model of message interactions uses an "event" facility in the language to associate a block of program (the *handler*) with a specific occurrence at an interface from the outside world. The handler is automatically invoked when the corresponding event occurs. A generalization of this model is the activation of a module when a specific combination of events has occurred.

This scheme is used in data flow systems (described in Appendix K), in which a module is activated when a specific activation condition is satisfied by the waiting messages (called "tokens" in data flow systems).

In Appendix L, we prove that a system with blocking **send**s and **receive**s is functional if certain other conditions, which are not too restrictive, are met. The argument works because blocking produces certainty regarding which message will be received at each **receive** statement. Therefore, there is no ambiguity concerning the values propagated among the processes, and the system's functionality can be deduced easily. When one introduces the alternative wait, one cannot determine which message will be received, so one cannot determine with certainty the values that will be processed during each phase within the receiving process. Therefore, one cannot argue that each program fragment will process the same data regardless of the (feasible) schedule. Any functionality arguments regarding such systems must be based on the semantic properties of the steps within the processes.

7.2.2 Operations that Imply Message–Passing

Many sceanrios, viewed from the outside, might not appear to involve message passing, because no explicit message-passing operations appear in the program. However, the internal operation of many interactions can be modeled or implemented using message-passing paradigms. These scenarios include input/output operations and procedure calls within an object-oriented environment.

Input/Output Communication. An input device produces messages directed to the computer system. In a similar manner, an output device accepts messages from the system. These external modules operate asynchronously with respect to the system's timing and execution sequences, so they cannot be modeled within statically scheduled paradigms such as those discussed in Chapter 6. Rather, important events are signaled by messages passed through the system, to which the system responds as though it were dealing with a message from another process. A module (device or channel controller) acts as the other process in the message exchange.

Object-Oriented Procedure Calls. In object-oriented systems, the act of invoking a procedure or function that is associated with a class or an object is considered to be the act of sending a message to that class or object. A message of this type acts like a remote procedure call or a rendezvous. Its destination is the object or the class that corresponds to the first parameter of the procedure, so the destinations are treated as addressable entities obeying visibility and scope rules imposed by the language for normal objects and classes.

7.2.3 Comments

Programming languages include explicit message-passing operations, such as send and receive. Other operations imply message passing within their implementations or can be modeled as interprocess message passing; these include synchronization at barriers and input/output operations. All of these require support from the operating system, because its process scheduler must be made aware of the changes in the process scheduling state that accompany these operations.

7.3 OPERATING SYSTEM SUPPORT FOR MESSAGE PASSING

The message service has to verify that each message can be sent and then correctly deliver it to its destination. It needs to coordinate these activities with the process scheduler. Usually, these services involve operating system software, though some processors support basic mechanisms within their instruction sets.

   The operating system is responsible for managing all system resources, and knows about all processes and their logical interconnections. It also knows the permissions granted to processes to participate in interprocess communication. An operating system's message-passing software assumes responsibility for correctness and for enforcing boundaries. For example, a process cannot provide an arbitrary address as a message destination and then expect that the message will be delivered. The operating system must perform several tests before it can honor a message-related request; for a send request these include the following:

1. Are you allowed to send a message?
2. Are you authorized to send to this destination?
3. What is the current physical location of the logical destination?
4. Where is memory space to buffer the message?

Similar questions have to be answered when servicing a receive request. After the checks have been made and have succeeded, the system moves on to process the message request. It must perform actions such as the following:

1. Notify the communicating processes about the message interactions.
2. Change the scheduling states of the communicating processes, including blocking the requesting process.

   Making these checks and performing these functions can consume significant processor time. The delays arise because the operating system must consult permission information, allocate memory space for message buffers, and record information to notify processes about the occurrence of message-related events. These delays can be significant, compared to the time required to actually communicate the message across a wire.

If the destination of the message is located at a physically distinct node, the message will have to be restructured to fit the format for messages passed along the connecting link(s). We focus on higher-level details and do not detail this level of message processing. These details do not have a significant impact on the system's architecture, unless one wishes to include a message-formatting module (which is likely to be a straightforward change). In the following, we focus on two shortcuts that may be effective, depending upon the system's architecture.

The first shortcut applies to messages within a shared, paged memory system. If one can align each message with a page boundary, the message-passing act can be implemented by moving pages from one virtual address space to another. The system takes the pages holding the message out of the address space of the source process and inserts them into the address space of the destination process. This implementation does not require message copying; only page descriptors are moved between page tables to effect the transfer. Additional actions must be taken to signal the receiver about the availability of the message.

The second shortcut concerns short, fixed-format messages, called *active message* ([VONE92]). The header of an active message contains a selector guiding a receiving procedure. The message transfer is effe ed by low-level programs, which avoids the overhead of invoking the operating system and changing processor state. Because the system does not change processing contexts, the act of moving the message to or from a buffer involves low-level access with high privilege. It is extremely important that this software be correct, because errors here can disrupt the database within the operating system.

The receiving process should be notified about the arrival of the active message; this can be accomplished in several ways. First, the conventional message-passing operation could be included in the program of the receiving process. Second, the active message-handling software could set a flag object that the receiver will examine to find whether the message has arrived. The difficulty with this option is that it returns to busy waiting, which wastes processor cycles.

In general, the operating system's role in message passing can consume many processor cycles, which adds delay to the transaction and can seriously impact system performance if many messages are passed during a computation.

7.4 PROCESSOR SUPPORT FOR MESSAGE PASSING

Some processor designs include specific instructions in support of interprocess message communication. A simple version appears in the Alpha AXP system, where PALcode can send an interrupt to any processor in the system; the number of the processor is the parameter of the PALcode call. In the following, we detail some features of the Intel iAPX 432 and of the IBM AS/400, two processors with more elaborate instructions that support interprocess message passing.

7.4.1 Intel iAPX 432 Message-Passing Support

The Intel iAPX 432 processor directly supports interprocess message passing. The processor "knows" about *port*[10] objects; a port object emulates a message path. A port object can be declared to contain a message queue that can be ordered with respect to time of arrival (i.e., FIFO), priority (with FIFO ordering among messages with the same priority value), or deadline within priority. Every processor operation on an ordered queue leaves each queue in a state satisfying its individual ordering constraint.

In this system, each message-passing operation copies a message between a named memory location and the queue in the port specified as an operand. The sending process is blocked until the message has been copied to the queue in the port. Thus, the fact that a process continues execution does not imply that the process at the other end of the port knows about the message. SEND blocks if queue space to hold the new message is not available. In a similar manner, RECEIVE blocks if the queue within the named port is empty. These instructions automatically adjust the process scheduling queue to block and unblock processes whenever a message cannot be copied as requested; the process will be unblocked automatically when the queue's status changes.

To provide message passing without blocking, the iAPX 432 processor has "conditional" SEND and RECEIVE operations. Each conditional operation has an operand that names a Boolean flag to be set to reflect the operation's success. A conditional SEND or RECEIVE operation will never block; rather, the condition result will be false if the corresponding unconditional operation would have blocked, and true otherwise. The user program is responsible for correctly responding to the returned condition values. In particular, because the processor will continue program execution even if it cannot complete the communication operation, the program must test the returned flag to decide whether to retry the operation. Thus, if one wants to support the message survival illusion, one must rely on correct interactions within each process.

Another pair of message-passing operations, SURROGATE_SEND and SURROGATE_RECEIVE, do not block. One operand of each surrogate operation is the name of an event, call it "DONE". These operations establish a surrogate object to be placed in the port's queue to perform the desired SEND or RECEIVE operation. In effect, this surrogate object holds the operation in a queue of waiting processes managed by the system. To check for completion, the original process

---

[10] We use Intel's terminology, which calls these objects ports even though their behavior is like that of paths.

looks for the event that we called DONE. This event will occur when the surrogate has received the desired service.

These message-passing operations are adequate for implementing high-level language interprocess communication. Because the blocking decision is based on the availability of queue entries and not on the actions of any other process using the port, iAPX 432 blocking is not identical to the high-level language blocking described in Sections 7.1 and 7.2.

7.4.2 AS/400 Message-Passing Support

The IBM AS/400 supports message passing with objects of type event. The AS/400 event object type should not be confused with PL/1's type EVENT, because the two are quite different. For example, an AS/400 event object contains many components, including an event_data field holding message contents. The processor operation to send an interprocess message is called SIGNAL_EVENT; the operations to receive an interprocess message are WAIT_ON_EVENT, TEST_EVENT, MONITOR_EVENT, and RETRIEVE_EVENT_DATA.

The SIGNAL_EVENT operation has two required parameters and one optional parameter. SIGNAL_EVENT(PROC, EV, DATA) signals the event named EV within the process named PROC, and copies the (optional) DATA value to the event_data field of the newly caused event.

We choose four other event operations from this processor to illustrate different ways that a receiving process can discover that an event has occurred. There is no strictly blocking receive operation, because a timeout value must be specified with every operation that might block the executing process. Executing the operation

WAIT_ON_EVENT(data_out, monitor_template, timeout)

causes the executing process to block until either the requested event has occurred or the timeout interval has elapsed. The monitor_template is a data structure that includes the name of the anticipated event and an optional "compare value." If no compare value is specified, any occurrence of the designated event will unblock the process. If a compare value is present, the event_data value of a candidate event must match the compare value in the wait command before the event is considered to have occurred. This matching rule permits a program to choose to respond to an event selected because its event_data value matched a specified value. This test occurs without the process actually receiving the message.

The TEST_EVENT(event_description) operation makes a nonblocking test to see whether an event has occurred. If a specific event is named, then the processor returns[11] a status result indicating whether the event has occurred. In addition,

[11] This "result" may appear as a value in the processor conditions (that can be tested subsequently). Another option asks the processor to take a specified branch based on the condition value; the selection among these options is made by 2 bits in the function code.

data describing the event that was detected are placed into a specified memory object. If the event_description is null, no event is specified, and the processor selects the highest-priority event that has occurred and responds with a description of that event. If no event has occurred, the returned status is false.

The MONITOR_EVENT operation has a single operand, whose value is a record describing the event, the entry point of a handler, the compare value, the priority of the designated event, the event buffer size, and other status flag values. Performing this instruction establishes the designated entry point as the entry to the handler for the event described in the record. The event buffer size determines the number of occurrences of the event that may be queued while the monitor is disabled. If the event is signaled when the queue is full, the new signal is ignored.[12] The event priority selects one among multiple events and controls whether the process can be interrupted by a new event while the handler is reacting to an earlier event. There are 256 priority values. A process' "main program" is not an event handler; it has lowest priority and will execute only if no enabled handlers have unsatisfied signals outstanding.

The RETRIEVE_EVENT_DATA instruction has a single parameter, pointing to the place to which the event's data will be copied. These data include the event identifier, the compare value (if any), the time that the event occurred, the identifier of the process that caused the event, and the number of pending (unsatisfied signals) requests for this event type. This operation has no parameter to specify the event whose data are to be copied; the instruction is designed for use inside a handler invoked after an event occurs. The data are returned for the event whose occurrence invoked the handler.

Other AS/400 instructions are available to enable and disable the event handlers; when they are disabled, the associated events are queued for later handling.

7.4.3 Comments

Some high-level languages, including Ada, explicitly support interprocess message passing, both with and without blocking. A few processor designs support interprocess message passing in their instruction sets; features of the high-level operations may be directly supported by instructions. In other systems, interprocess message passing must be emulated by system support software, but this process can be time-consuming. If message-passing speed is a paramount consideration, one might design a multiprocessor system using only simple message-passing mechanisms that bypass the operating system. Low-level message passing in this style is used inside the implementations of shared memory systems.

---

[12]   If this situation occurs, the message will be lost and the system may behave in a nonfunctional manner.

7.5 PROCESSOR TIME ALLOCATION

In Chapter 6 we discussed scheduling techniques that find parallelism within a single process. Now we consider a related question—scheduling blocks of time during which a processor will be devoted to executing a program for a single user. To make these decisions, the scheduler uses information about the scheduling state of each process, along with priority information. It then chooses the process that will use the processor during the next scheduling interval.

The intimate connection between message passing and scheduling is that processor time can be allocated only to unblocked processes; processes become unblocked when they receive a message or when a rendezvous is completed. Processor interrupts, which govern the processor time allocation at a low granularity, may connote scheduling state changes and thus affect processor scheduling. Other message-related events also affect scheduling. For scheduling purposes, each process is characterized by its scheduling state, of which "running" is one possible value. But running, as described in Section 7.1.2, covers two different states (ready and active), one of which is chosen by the scheduler when it chooses whether to give processor time to the process. The scheduling module chooses a feasible schedule that, we hope, is desirable, in that it supports some nonfunctional goal such as system performance.

7.5.1 Scheduling

Process scheduling within the operating system requires more than the simple list scheduling algorithms described in Chapter 6. Like the instructions being scheduled in Chapter 6, processes may become enabled or disabled when they interact with their environments, in this case, particularly with the message-passing system.

Most operating system scheduling modules are divided into two major parts. The *scheduler* determines which processes are ready and places them into a "ready queue" whose order reflects priority with which the processes will be given access to the processor. The *dispatcher* takes a process from the head of the ready queue and starts the processor executing that process. In this section, we discuss both the scheduling function and related issues concerning the process scheduling state. Important message-passing events may change the scheduling states of processes within the system.

Scheduling States. The *scheduling state* of a process reflects the process' readiness to perform instructions. Three types of scheduling state are important:

1. *Active*. The process is executing instructions.
2. *Ready*. The process could execute instructions if it were permitted access to a processor.

3. *Waiting.* The process cannot proceed until some event external to the process has occurred.

There is only one active state. Several ready states may be defined to distinguish among different process priorities. In a like manner, several waiting states may be defined to specify the event(s) on which the process is waiting.

Models describing interactions between a message-passing system and process states specify the semantics of all statements involving process-message interactions. Under the rendezvous model, the following scenario is possible:

1. P becomes ready;
2. P is scheduled;
3. P is dispatched and starts running;
4. P executes **receive**, and enters a wait state;
5. The scheduler dispatches another process;
6. The awaited message arrives from Q, and P is moved to the ready state;
7. P is scheduled;
8. P is dispatched, and executes the statement following the **receive** statement;
9. Q is moved to the ready state.

In the message-passing model, processes will have to wait for message-related transactions such as message transmission or reception (if the message-passing operations are blocking), and the occurrence of one of these transactions may change the scheduling state of a process. Usually, a process enters a waiting state only when it initiates an operation that cannot be completed until an external event has occurred. For example, a process might attempt a blocking **receive** to read an incoming message. If the message has not arrived when the **receive** operation is initiated, the process must wait until the message does arrive. But it is possible that the message has actually arrived before the process asks to **receive** its contents. In this case, the **receive** operation, which might have initiated waiting, will not require any delay. Thus, in general, we cannot tell by examining a program whether a particular step will cause the process to enter a waiting state. Figure 7-4 illustrated these possibilities.

Example 7-11

Process P wants to read a file from a disk. To perform this operation, P sends a message to a disk read process R, which has been waiting for a command message. After making its request by sending the message to R, P will wait to read a completion message returned from R. The skeleton of the programs for this interaction looks like this:

```
void P() {
    ..
    send( request, read_req );
    receive( complete, read_over );
    ..
}
```

```
void R() {
    while ( true ) {
        receive( req, read_req );
        ..                          //here the request is interpreted and executed
        send( complete, read_over );
    }
}
```

Procedure R acts as a service process to handle disk requests. When it is not servicing a read request, R waits at its **receive** statement. When a message containing a read request arrives at the port named read_req, R awakens.

Now suppose that P is unblocked and R is blocked waiting at its **receive** operation. The history of process interactions and process states may continue:

1. Process P sends a message to R asking for a READ.
2. Process P tries to perform the **receive**, but the message has not yet been sent. Therefore, P enters a wait state until the completion message arrives (from the read server) at the port named read_over.
3. The request message arrives at read_port, so the scheduler moves process R from the wait state to the ready state.
4. Process R performs the read function.
5. Process R sends a completion message to read_over.
6. The completion message arrives at read_over, so process P's state changes from wait to ready.
7. Process R loops around, tries to perform the read at the head of the loop, and enters a wait state, because no message is waiting.

In steps 2, 3, 6, and 7, the scheduling state of at least one process changes.

Without special processor support, every scheduling state change requires a call to the operating system, which can consume a significant amount of time.

The Schedule. The scheduler module maintains a queue of ready processes; when the processor is to be allocated to another process, the process at the head of this *ready queue* is *dispatched*. The actual order in which the processes are given processor cycles is the *actual schedule* followed by the system. The actual system schedule must respect the scheduling states of the processes. Any schedule that satisfies this general condition is called a *feasible schedule*. The major functional requirement is that the scheduler not construct an infeasible schedule.

In addition to the feasibility requirement on the schedule, the scheduler should try to avoid some situations that, though they are undesirable, are feasible. These include the following:

1. Unfairness
2. Starvation
3. Deadlock

A "fair" scheduling policy guarantees that any waiting process will wait for execution for only a finite time after it becomes ready. Starvation occurs when a process waits for an enabling event that never occurs; consequently, it waits forever. A deadlock is more complex because it involves interactions among a set of processes.

Deadlock.   The possibility of a deadlock introduces difficulties. Informally, a deadlock occurs when (1) all processes in a set are waiting, and (2) there is no way that the processes in the set can ever become ready. Deadlock arises if the only actions that would awake the waiting processes could be performed only by processes that must remain inactive because they are also in the waiting set. To make these notions precise, define the wait set for a waiting process, as follows:

> **Definition.** The *wait set* for a waiting process P contains those processes that could act individually in such a way as to move P to the ready state.

The set of processes in P's wait set depends upon the event for which P is waiting. We define a deadlock in terms of the wait sets:

> **Definition.** A set of processes $S = \{P_1, P_2, .. , P_n\}$ is *deadlocked* if
> (1) all members of S are waiting and
> (2) the wait set of each process $P_i \varepsilon S, 1 \leq i \leq n$, contains only
>   processes in S.

Example 7-12

A simple interesting deadlock example involves blocking **send** and **receive** operations.

Our example uses these four processes:[13]

A:	**send**(mes, M1);	B:	**send**(mes, N1);
	send(mes, N1);		**send**(mes, M1);
	receive(mes, N2);		**receive**(mes, N2);
	receive(mes, M2);		**receive**(mes, M2);

C:	**while** (**true**) {	D:	**while** (**true**) {
	receive(mes, M1);		**receive**(mes, N1);
	send(mes, M2);		**send**(mes, N2);
	}		}

A schedule in which A completes execution before B begins avoids deadlock. However, if A sends a message to M1, and then B sends a message to N1 before A sends its message to N1 we reach a deadlock because neither A nor B will be able

---

[13]   We omit all operations that do not involve message passing; their presence has no effect on the deadlock.

to complete its second **send** (because both processes C and D will be waiting to complete their **send**s before becoming ready to receive the messages that would be sent by A and B in their second lines). At the deadlock, all processes will be waiting to complete a **send** operation.

Many deadlocks, such as the one in the example, arise from an unfortunate choice of a feasible schedule. It is important to notice that an application algorithm may be specified such that its scheduling constraints always force the system to a deadlock. In the following, we assume that the inherent program structures do not force a deadlock; therefore, any deadlock that does arise is a consequence of a poor scheduling choice. Within this context, we discuss three important issues concerning deadlocks:

1. Prevention
2. Detection
3. Recovery

Deadlock Prevention. It may be possible to prevent deadlocks by restricting the interprocess communication patterns. Otherwise, deadlock prevention must rely on a scheduler that anticipates the possible future behavior of all processes and then decides whether a deadlock is imminent and could be prevented by appropriate scheduling. Because the scheduler cannot know the future, this strategy cannot remove all deadlocks.

One way to give the scheduler a chance at foretelling the future is to restrict communication patterns. Imposing scheduling constraints sufficiently strong that they remove the possibility of deadlocks may reduce system efficiency because processes will have to remain idle when they must wait, lest they proceed into dangerous deadlock territory. Some designers bypass the assurance of no deadlock and accept a low probability of deadlock in return for increased efficiency. In such a design, one hopes that deadlocks occur infrequently.

Deadlock Detection. A deadlock detection policy may be biased by the system's structure or be based on usage restrictions. General deadlock detection is difficult because a hypothetical deadlock detector must know not only who is waiting for what action (this is easy), but also who might perform the awaited action (this can be very difficult or impossible). The following modification of Example 7-12 illustrates this possibility.

Example 7-13

Divide the program in process_B of Example 7-12 into two procedures, as follows:

```
void x() {
    send( mess, N1 );
    send( mess, M1 );
}
```

```
void y() {
      receive( mess, N2 );
      receive( mess, M2 );
}
```

Next, make two paths P and Q and two processes F and G that call x and y conditionally based on the value of an external shared object t:

```
F:    if ( t < 3 ) {              G:   if ( t >= 3 ) {
            x();   // a call                 x();   // a call
            send( mess, Q );                 send( mess, P );
      }                                }
      else {                           else {
            receive( mess, P );              receive( mess, Q );
            y();   // a call                 y();   // a call
      }                                }
```

Now execute processes F and G along with processes A, C, and D from Example
7-12. One cannot tell (before execution) whether process F or process G will call x or
y. At the deadlock discussed in the previous example, processes C and D are waiting for one of A, F, and G to execute a **receive** operation. One cannot determine from
a static analysis of the programs whether F or G will execute the **receive** that permits
C (or D) to proceed beyond its **send**.

A pragmatic deadlock detection policy states that any process that remains
in the same wait state for longer than T time units must be a member of a deadlocked set. This rule does not account for any characteristics of the environment
or of the processes themselves, but it certainly does detect any deadlock within T
time units after its occurrence. The problem is that it also labels some nondead-
lock situations as deadlocks.

Deadlock Recovery. Unfortunately, there is no "good, simple" way to recover from a deadlock. A naive "solution" terminates one process P in the deadlocked set. If in the deadlock P were waiting for the completion of a
message-passing transaction, terminating P does not permit any other process to
proceed. Another recovery approach is to force completion of a message transaction that is part of the deadlock. But this form of "relief" may leave the process
set in an inconsistent state, which is unacceptable. It also does not work, because
we could construct a deadlock so complex that, for a given n, completing n message transactions does not relieve the deadlock.

Deadlock recovery can be accomplished correctly[14] if the system can reverse the effects of all processes aborted during recovery. To reverse the effects,
one must have a record of all transactions whose results depended on passed
messages. The record must include the process identities, their (value) states,

---

[14]   A "correct" recovery from a deadlock results in a system state that could have arisen had the system followed a different feasible schedule that does not reach any deadlock.

and the contents of the messages passed among the processes. Keeping this history imposes overhead on all message-passing transactions, but is necessary if correct deadlock recovery is required. This approach can be seen to be similar to the transaction approach used in shared memory systems (see Section 8.2.3).

Another way to recover from deadlock uses a history of the "system state" captured at selected "checkpoint" times. The system state at the checkpoint includes the states of all processes and the contents of all messages that are in transit when the checkpoint is taken. If a deadlock is reached, one could restore the system state from the consistent configuration in the checkpoint. Then one tries for a schedule that does not reach the deadlock (this should be possible if our assumption that the processes are programmed such that a feasible schedule without a deadlock does indeed exist).

A deadlock recovery strategy can also be used to recover from errors and failures.

Many basic deadlock issues are discussed in [HOLT72]. Deadlocks can also occur when messages cannot be forwarded through a network of paths, as we discuss in Section 7.6.3.

Livelock. *Livelock* is a deadlock in which one or more of the waiting processes is active (from the view of the operating system), but only because it uses busy waiting to test for the occurrence of the event that will never occur (because the set is deadlocked). In other words, the livelocked process is not doing useful work, yet it gives that impression. It is extremely difficult to detect livelock, because the scheduler cannot know what each process is actually doing.

7.5.2 Processor Support for Scheduling

Processor support for scheduling and dispatching has been incorporated into several systems. We emphasize scheduling support in the following; dispatch support is usually limited to straightforward instructions that save and restore processor state. We explore some related design issues in Section 7.9.

Example 7-14

The Intel iAPX 432 supports port objects (see Section 7.4.1); each port object contains a queue that is automatically ordered according to the criterion (FCFS, priority, and/or priority with deadlines) specified when the port object was declared. The designers included a port for processor scheduling [COX83]. Adding a process to the scheduling port schedules that process; taking a process from the head of the queue in the scheduling port dispatches the process.

Example 7-15

The Honeywell DPS/6 processor contains an instruction LEV with many options [HONE80]. This instruction handles certain priority selection functions. A reserved memory block contains pointers (which may be NULL) to state information about processes that are ready to run. A fixed priority level is associated with each location in the pointer block. The priority level associated with the process in execution is saved in a processor register. One version of LEV checks whether the executing process has the highest priority among the ready processes. If it does, the executing process continues execution. On the other hand, if it does not, the processor is dispatched to the highest-priority process described in the pointer block. There are 64 priority levels.

To assist in the LEV operation, four 16-bit words (at addresses $20 .. 23_{10}$) contain 64 bits set to reflect the presence of non-NULL pointers at each priority level. One common feature of schedulers—the scheduling queue—is not directly supported by the LEV instruction. So the operating system's scheduler module must adjust the contents of the ready priority block so they contain the processes at the heads of the queues within the priority levels.

Other variants of LEV help maintain the priority list, automatically updating the status bit vector when they update the priority list. Thus, LEV quickly finds the highest priority nonempty item in the set of ready processes.

The DPS/6 represents the ready status of the processes at the heads of the queues at the various priority levels in a bit vector. The LEV instruction finds the position of the highest-priority task in the vector and activates the corresponding process. Without hardware support, one can find the position of the rightmost 1 bit within a word using arithmetic and logical operations, and then counting the number of 1 bits within the result (subject to a minor fix): Let BV hold the bit vector. The two's complement of BV matches BV only in its rightmost positions up to and including the position of the rightmost one in BV. Thus, an NXOR operation between BV and –BV produces a string of 1's starting at the right end and continuing to the rightmost 1 of BV.[15] Counting the 1 bits in the NXOR result gives the position of the rightmost one in BV, using one-origin indexing.

Example 7-16

The SPARC-V9 processor population count instruction counts the number of 1 bits in its operand and returns that count in a register. This could be preceded or followed by the zero test to find the position of the rightmost 1. This technique could be coupled with the BV processing described before to implement a rapid dispatcher that initiates the highest-priority ready task.

7.5.3 Comments

Scheduling and dispatching functions are central to processor management. The scheduling algorithm must be chosen carefully to avoid undesirable behavior. Processor support for basic queueing and dispatching operations can speed the execution of these low-level management functions, but operating system software must be invoked to modify process scheduling states, which may change when important message-passing events occur. Unfortunately, calling the

---

[15]   The special case when BV = 0 has to be handled separately.

operating system and having it serve the message-passing request can consume many processor cycles as the operating system saves state, deciphers the request, and then makes the requested changes and modifies the scheduler's database. For example, [VONE92] comments that buffer management at the sending and receiving processors can cost over a thousand instruction times, partly from the complexity of the decisions that have to be made, and partly from the context switching required to move between the application and the system. The designer thus has a great opportunity to simplify or accelerate these actions. One possibility is to program busy waiting if the application programmer knows that the wait for the other part of the message transaction will be short. Another possibility is to design the processor so that the overhead of operating system calls is minimized.

7.6 MESSAGE COMMUNICATION MECHANISMS

The architecture of the underlying message-passing system affects lower levels of system implementation, including message switching and forwarding functions. We examine these schemes in this section before we turn to similar message-passing mechanisms used within the implementation of the system.

7.6.1 Messages

From the software view, a message is a block of related information that travels together. There is no limit to its size or function, because these aspects are determined by how the software utilizes the message contents. The illusion remains that the message system can transmit messages of arbitrary length, limited only by the sizes of the memory spaces available to hold the messages at the sender and receiver.

Despite the illusion of unlimited message length, most message-handling protocols impose an upper limit on the length of each message transmission. These limits can arise from physical considerations, field sizes in the message format, buffer space limits, or other considerations. The fact that there is a limit means that extremely long messages from an application will have to be divided into *packets* that conform to the size limits imposed by the communication subsystem. Within the message-passing system, packets are sent as separate messages, to be reassembled at the destination to form the complete message seen by the application. This strategy supports the illusion that the system can pass a message of arbitrary size.

An analogy can be made between the act of packetizing a message and the act of dividing memory into frames for convenience of the system's memory manager. Dividing a message into packets has no semantic consequences for the communicating processes, but it does simplify the implementation of the message-passing system.

Because packets are independent messages at the transport level, there can be no guarantee that all packets comprising a single message will follow the same route from their source to their destination, that all will successfully arrive at the destination, or that they will arrive in order. To handle these contingencies, the message-passing system includes within each packet information sufficient to permit message reassembly. This includes (at least) a message identifier, a packet sequence number, and some indication of the end of the message (this could be a packet count or a termination code). Message reassembly is straightforward using the packet numbers.

The message header should also convey routing information, which includes the addresses of the source and destination ports (or modules). The forms of module addresses used within the headers are tied to the communication protocol and the network structure. As we look at various interconnection structures, we see how the addresses can be tailored to fit that structure and how message packets can be routed to reach their destinations. The destination information must be visible to all sink nodes, so they can choose whether to receive an arriving message.[16]

7.6.2 Requirements on the Message-Passing System

In principle, one can broadcast messages, which are destined for all receivers in the system. But they confuse many protocols. On the logical level, broadcast messages present many complications because it is difficult to verify that all receivers did indeed receive the message. So in the following, we focus on messages destined to a single port. We want to support the message-passing illusions in the implementation.

To support the *message survival* illusion, the path itself must not lose messages, and the processes at the ends must cooperate with the path so that messages are not lost at the path-port interfaces. If the communication subsystem might lose messages, software at the receiver and sender must detect the omission and cooperate to retransmit any lost messages, thus supporting the illusion of a lossless virtual path. By introducing and checking redundancy within and among the message packets, one can detect message distortion and message loss.

One problem with this scheme concerns the level of trust about message communication. To create a difficult situation, we suppose that both sender and receiver must be absolutely certain that both of them know the status of their acknowledgments. If one never trusts that a message will be received, one gets into a hopeless regression that starts in this manner: (1) I send you a message, but do not know whether you got it. To relieve my concerns, (2) you send me a message

---

[16]   This comment may seem trivial, but it has implications for message encryption schemes.

acknowledging that you did receive the message. But do you know whether I received this acknowledgment? Not unless, (3) I send you an acknowledgment. Now we have the same problem, and we are in a hopeless regression. Eventually, we have to trust that a (last) message was correctly received.

The *message ordering* illusion states that the set of messages passing through a path is transmitted and received in FIFO order. This illusion is trivially supported if the message passes along an error-free path that uses a single switched circuit. If the implementation contains alternate routes for packets to reach the destination, the sender must add sequence numbers to the packets so the receiver can properly order the packets after they have arrived. The receiver uses the sequence numbers to reorder the packets to form the message.

The *message integrity* illusion states that messages not be garbled. By adding redundancy to the messages and defining protocols for error detection and recovery, any virtual path can be made to support this illusion to a specified degree of accuracy. These coding techniques lie outside computer architecture.

7.6.3 Physical Interconnections

At the physical level, every message-passing structure is composed of sending modules, paths, switches, and receiving modules. The choice of the interconnection structure affects message delays, the choice of algorithms that make message routing decisions, and the system's capacity, bandwidth and reliability.

Modules. There are three different types of modules in a message-passing system: (1) sources, (2) destinations, and (3) switches. With a simple interconnection topology, such as a bus, the path is connected directly to all modules, so every message can be received directly from the path by its intended destination. The destination module recognizes its messages by sensing a match between its own address and the destination address within the message on the path.

In most topologies, a message passes through message switch modules and along intermediate paths to reach its intended destination. A *switch module* is an intermediate module that directs incoming messages to appropriate outgoing paths; the switch examines the header to determine how to route the message toward its destination. In some interconnection schemes, the message-switching function is handled by software within the same physical modules that send or receive messages. In order to reduce confusion, we view the message-switching software as a separate switch module.

Paths. Paths connect one or more message sources with one or more message sinks. A path may introduce errors or may fail (meaning that it cannot transmit any messages to the sinks). Thus, we assume that a path delivers all messages to their destinations and does not corrupt those messages.

If a path has only one source module, the source can initiate transmissions at any time. If the path has several source modules, some scheme must determine when each source is permitted to initiate a message transmission. The schedule can be statically fixed, by adopting a fixed timing rule. To handle uneven demands, a dynamic mechanism using an *arbitration protocol* should be devised. The details depend on the topology.

Topologies. Several interesting topological structures have been used or proposed for interconnecting modules within a (multiprocessor) system or a local network, including the following:

1. Complete interconnection
2. Bus
3. Multiple buses
4. Crossbar
5. *n*-cube
6. Tree
7. Ring
8. Multistage interconnection network
9. Hierarchical structure

The first four topologies permit messages to pass from source to sink with no need to be held within and later forwarded from an intermediate switch node. The others include intermediate switches that might delay or store and forward message packets.

Complete Interconnection. In a complete interconnection (see Figure 7-6), each message source has a private path to each message sink. Very high bandwidths can be supplied, because each virtual path corresponds to a physical path. The obvious disadvantage is that each source module requires a port for a path to each sink module. This crowds the nodes with interfaces and makes it difficult to expand the system. Each sink must be able to receive multiple messages or to reject messages in case too many arrive simultaneously. Message routing is performed when the source module selects the output port.

Bus. The bus structure permits many message sources and many message sinks to be connected to a single communications path, usually configured to pass data bits in parallel along parallel paths. An arbitration scheme governs access to the bus; it usually operates by passing a "GRANT" signal along a daisy-chain structure starting from the bus controller module. The daisy chain passes through all source modules. A source module that receives the GRANT signal and wishes to transmit a message does not forward the GRANT signal to its successors in the chain; it then transmits its message during the next transmission

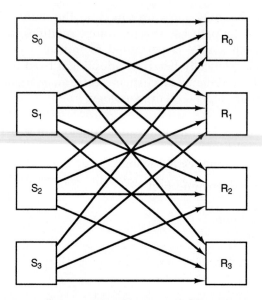

Figure 7-6   Complete interconnection topology

slot. Figure 7-7 shows a bus with its daisy chain passing the GRANT signal down the bus.

All modules connected to the bus can observe all messages that pass along the bus. This property is important in implementing snooping protocols to support the single memory illusion in shared-memory multiprocessor systems (see Section 8.7.1). Because all messages are visible to every module on the bus, it can be difficult to provide security against interlopers observing messages that they are not authorized to see. Encrypting messages can provide one level of protection, but the destination module number must be visible so that each message can be correctly routed to its destination.

One advantage of the bus connection is that each module requires only a single bus interface unit (BIU). One disadvantage is that the system's total bandwidth is limited by the capacity of the bus. Some bus bandwidth is consumed by arbitration among the senders, unless that function can be overlapped with data

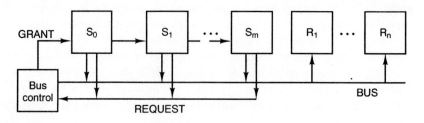

Figure 7-7   Bus topology

transmission. This problem can be remedied by (1) using arbitration protocols that can be overlapped with data transmission, or (2) using special bus protocols that permit the sender to make a "burst" transmission, effectively giving it exclusive access to the bus for the duration of the message packet. The disadvantage is that other senders are locked out during burst transmissions; they may experience delays that degrade their responses to external events. Overlapped arbitration is used on memory buses.

CSMA. The carrier-sense/multiple-access (CSMA) scheme is similar to the bus scheme in that there is a shared communications medium; the major difference lies in the protocol used to determine which sender is permitted to transmit information. An important difference is that whereas buses have many signal and control paths, a CSMA link usually has only a single (serial) path. With CSMA, there is no separate arbitration mechanism, rather, each sender that wishes to transmit listens to the traffic and waits until no message is passing by. Then it starts to transmit. If another sender also decided to transmit during the same dead time, there will be a collision, and no message will be received correctly. After a collision, both senders wait and try again later. They cannot try immediately because it is guaranteed that they will collide again. Various waiting protocols have been used, the most common being a random interval chosen within an increasing delay window for each colliding sender. The CSMA protocol was developed for Ethernet systems, and is used in local-area networks. Its details do not affect system architecture, because it is not used to pass messages within a single processing node. We mention it only to distinguish it from the bus interconnection scheme.

Multiple Buses. The bandwidth limitation of the single bus structure can be alleviated by adding more buses. Systems have been proposed utilizing either complete connections (in which all modules are connected to all buses) or partial connections (only subsets of the modules are connected). Each bus still needs arbitration to control access. Examples of multiple bus systems with both complete and partial interconnections are shown in Figure 7-8. The multiple bus scheme introduces another difficulty: The sinks must be able to receive several messages or to arbitrate among the buses, because several buses might be transmitting messages to the same sink module.

Comparing this scheme to the single bus system, we see several disadvantages: (1) Each module requires several BIUs, (2) each source module must choose a bus for each message it emits, and (3) messages are not seen by all modules. The major advantage of this scheme is the increased bandwidth.

A special class of multiple bus designs has two buses: one for processor–memory interactions and a separate one for input/output–memory interactions. The separate input/output bus provides high data bandwidth to high-speed peripherals, such as disk systems. The input/output data traffic

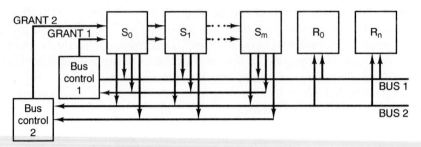

(a) Every module connected to every bus

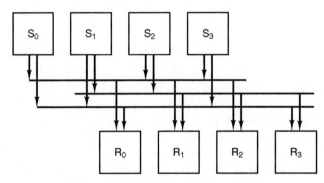

(b) Some module-bus connections missing

Figure 7-8 Two topologies with several buses

using the I/O bus between memory and peripherals does not affect the processor, which does not have to be connected to this bus. However, it is still true that the processor initiates communication by passing commands to the device controllers that do access this bus. With a second bus, each memory module must be able to arbitrate among conflicting requests; because high-speed I/O was the problem being solved, the preference is to give preference to access requests arriving on the I/O bus.

Crossbar. In a crossbar switch, there is a bus from each source and from each sink, with a switch at each intersection (see Figure 7-9). In some other schemes, the sink modules must arbitrate among several requests, but in the crossbar, this problem is hidden in the switch modules, because only one switch can be sending a message to one sink at one time. The big disadvantage of the crossbar structure is the large number of switch modules to cover all bus intersections.

n-Cube. The connections in the *n*-cube structure are based on the node numbers. Suppose, for simplicity, that the number of nodes is r^m, with m the dimensionality of the cube. A module number D is divided into n fields $D_1 .. D_n$

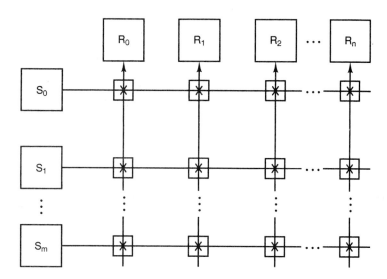

Figure 7-9　A crossbar switch system

(numbered from left to right), each containing one base-r digit. Each field corresponds to a *dimension* of the n-cube. Each module is connected to n paths. There is a linear path connecting the set of r modules that share identical values in $n-1$ address digits.

In an n-cube, a message is moved from its source in module S to its destination in module D by progressive routing that moves the message closer and closer to its destination by matching address digits. Suppose that the message progresses by matching the address from left to right.[17] The first move is to the module numbered $D_1 S_2 S_3 .. S_n$, from which it moves to the module numbered $D_1 D_2 S_3 .. S_n$, and so forth until the destination is reached. A system using a routing strategy like this, with a fixed order for matching address digits will not experience delays. On the other hand, any system that does not order things in this way is open to deadlocks.

Tree. We describe a full binary tree having n levels with all source and sink modules at the leaves. The nodes internal to the tree are message switches with no processing capability. To describe the interconnection structure, we name the switch nodes using the symbols 0, 1, and x in the names. Each switch has two paths toward the leaves and one path toward the root. The names associated with the daughters of the switch are found from the name of the switch by replacing the leftmost x with 0 or 1. The root is named with a string of n x's. For example, the daughters of the switch at position 010xxx are named 0100xx and

---

[17]　This is certainly not the only possibility, but it is attractive for wormhole routing, because it reduces the probability of deadlocks within the routing mechanism.

0101xx. In this code, all x's in a switch name will be clustered at the right end of the name; therefore, if one is willing to deal with variable-length names, one can remove the x's from the names.

A message passes through the tree by moving upwards (toward the root) until it reaches a switch node whose name matches the destination's node name in all positions that are not x. Then it travels downwards (toward the leaves) along a path selected by the next bit of the destination name.

A network structured as a tree can be partitioned into separate subtrees by blocking messages from the paths interconnecting the subtrees. A disadvantage of the tree structure is message congestion close to the tree's root. The following simple calculation illustrates the problem. Suppose that message destinations are chosen at random. Then half of all messages have a destination number that differs from the source number in the first position. Any message meeting this condition must pass through the switch at the root of the tree. With random addresses, half of all messages pass through the root node.

The message congestion toward the root can be alleviated by intelligent allocation of processes to the nodes or by adding paths to the tree. One simple approach is to provide more paths upwards from each switch node. This strategy constructs a *fat tree* structure, which is used in the CM-5 machine ([THIN91]). In a fat tree, there is a much higher probability of finding a path for an outgoing message, but there are many more paths than in a conventional tree.

Ring. In a ring structure, all source and sink modules are connected to switch modules that themselves are connected cyclically (using unidirectional links) to form the ring (see Figure 7-10). Each message is passed around the ring until it reaches its destination. Each switch module checks each arriving message

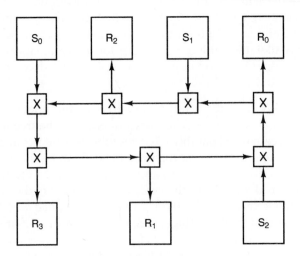

Figure 7-10   A ring network

to see whether it is being sent to the associated module. The test examines the destination address in the header field. There is no need to correlate node naming with ring position.

The disadvantages of this structure include (1) bandwidth limited to the path bandwidth, (2) the average message transit time takes the message halfway around the ring, (3) the entire ring fails if any path fails, (4) every message is delayed at each switch to permit the switch to determine the message routing, and (5) it is difficult to add or delete nodes from the system, because these changes break the ring structure. The transit time problem can be alleviated by adding paths that skip across switch nodes; see Figure 7-11. The failure problem can be alleviated by wiring the ring with two rings, passing messages in opposite directions. One advantage of the ring structure is the simplicity of the interconnections and the fact that each node requires only a small number of connection points—two for the simple ring. Furthermore, it can be built from unidirectional links, each with one source and one sink, which is ideal for optical interconnections.

Multistage Interconnection Network. This name is associated with the particular style of interconnection described here and should not be confused with the fact that a message passing through some other networks also pass through several switch modules. The switch modules in a multistage network have two inputs and two outputs; each switch can connect each input to each output. For convenience, number the switch levels starting from the destination end, which we call level zero. At level i, the packet routing is determined by bit i of the destination address; if the bit is zero, the upper output is selected. When two messages arrive that desire the same output path, one is blocked by the

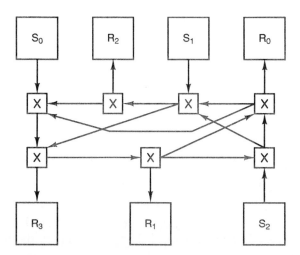

Figure 7-11   A ring network with skip paths added

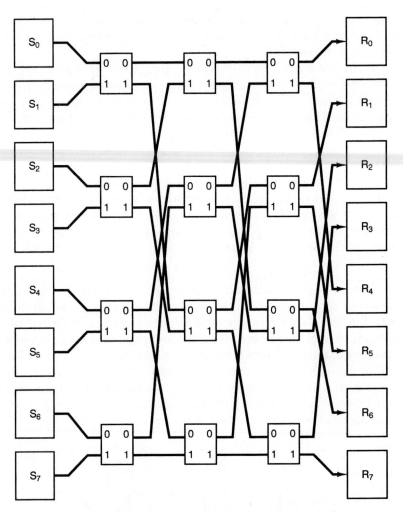

Figure 7-12   A multistage interconnection network
with eight sources and eight sinks

switch. In a symmetric configuration with n sources and n sinks, there are $\log_2 n$ levels of switches; each level has $n/2$ switches. The connection structure for eight modules is pictured in Figure 7-12.

The multistage network is convenient when one set of modules acts as message sources and another set acts as message sinks. For example, when connecting processors to a shared set of memory modules, the processors act as sources (of memory access requests) and the memory modules act as sinks.[18]

---

[18]   For the moment we ignore the return traffic comprising values read from the memory.

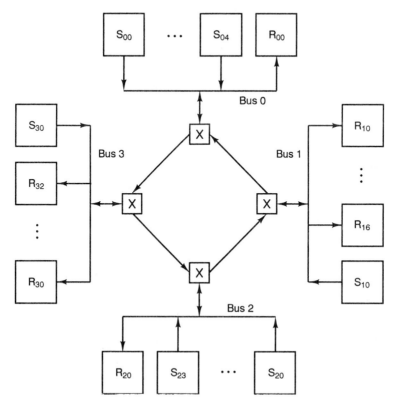

Figure 7-13   A hierarchical ring—bus system

Hierarchical Structures.   A hierarchical interconnection structure can be constructed from almost any combination of the structures described before, but not all combinations are useful. Interlevel switch modules pass messages among the levels. For example, Figure 7-13 illustrates a hierarchical system with a ring at the root of the hierarchy and bus interconnections at the second level. For easy routing, each node address includes a prefix indicating the bus to which the module is connected. The routing policy is trivial: When a module on bus A sends a message to a module on bus B, the interlevel switch on bus A forwards the message to the ring because the bus prefix part of the destination address does not match the name of this ring. Then the interlevel switch connecting the ring to bus B picks up the message and forwards it to bus B, whence it is picked up by its destination node. Similar policies are used in other hierarchical interconnection structures.

7.6.4 Wormhole Routing

In the previous discussion, we assumed that long messages were divided into packets that were independently routed through the network and reassembled at the destination. This strategy has advantages and disadvantages. A different scheme, the wormhole routing scheme, can be useful for some local interconnections. The basic idea behind wormhole routing is that a message is divided into very small quanta, called *flow units*, or *flits*, that follow their leader (the header) from source to sink. Flits are unlike message packets, because a flit does not include any control information, and therefore must follow its header's trail through the network. Message flow is limited by the fact that each switch node is able to store only a single flit for each message. The impediments occur only for the header flit, because the followers replace their predecessors in the switch buffers. A message header might be blocked from further progress because a path is busy or because there is no free flit buffer in the next switch node. If the header flit is blocked, a trail of flits will be blocked in the modules backwards along the path. This pattern might extend back to the source, which may have to stop transmitting further flits until the header finds a way forward. In addition, this pattern may produce a deadlock within the network.

One advantage of this scheme is that only one set of routing decisions need be made to send a complete message. Furthermore, all message information arrives in order, so message reassembly at the sink is trivial. Another advantage of this scheme is that the bandwidth is reduced because there is only one header for each complete message.

There is a significant disadvantage to wormhole routing because a set of messages deadlock within the flit buffers. At such a deadlock, there will exist a cyclic pattern of flits (of different messages) waiting for a flit buffer to become available at the next node so they can progress. The cyclic nature of the waiting implies that none are able to progress because no buffer will become available until the deadlock is resolved. One might try to relieve the deadlock by canceling a message and retransmitting it later. It has been proved that if there are four or more nodes in the network and there is only one flit buffer in each node, it is not possible to devise a static wormhole routing scheme that avoids deadlocks.

7.6.5 Comments

There are many useful interconnection network topologies. Each has its application in a particular environment. Protocols for message transmission, identification, and reconstruction can be built on top of the network to assure reliable message transmission supporting the message-passing illusions. We now focus on low-level interactions within a single processing node; while these lie beneath the picture for many users, they share common features with the network level.

7.7 INTERMODULE MESSAGE PROTOCOLS

Many operations within a computer involve a master module and a slave module communicating data and control information amongst themselves. These interactions are similar to the remote procedure call model. Interactions of this type support memory accesses, input/output requests, and coprocessor–processor interactions. We will show how calls to an asynchronously operating coprocessor module can be activated from the processor. Similar interactions are used to initiate input/output operations. A universal question concerns one's view of which module controls the intermodule interactions. Even though the processor initiates these types of interactions, the other module can assume control once it has been activated.

7.7.1 Input/Output Transactions

A request for an input or output action is initiated by an intermodule message from the processor to a controller. Once the transfer is initiated, the remaining events have unpredictable timings because the input/output device and channel controllers must respect the timing of the external device(s) to which they are connected. Three communication questions arise: (1) how does the processor specify an input/output device, (2) how does the device controller obtain memory access, and (3) how is the processor notified that the operation is complete?

Device Addressing. Whether I/O is viewed as part of the memory address space or in a separate address space does not affect many issues, but it does affect the processor's interfaces and the choice of control lines on the processor's bus. A device placed into memory address space is designed with interface logic that makes it appear to the bus as though it were a memory module that responds to certain memory addresses. The devices are usually placed at the top of the address space. A device that is not in memory address space is relegated to a special address space containing controllers, and special processor instructions are used to communicate with the device. The bus includes a signal that distinguishes bus cycles that access memory from those that access devices.

Example 7-17

> The Intel ix86 processors have INPUT and OUTPUT operations that copy information between device controllers and either memory or a processor register. A control line on the bus distinguishes the two types of cycles. The Power PC601 has a similar strategy for distinguishing input/output cycles from memory cycles.

In the following, we assume, without loss of generality, that all input/output devices and controllers are addressed within memory address space.

Command Interface. Controller commands are usually passed as data directed to specific addresses to which the controllers respond. A casual observer of watching the memory bus would not be able to distinguish data copying from command initiation and status sensing. This loose coupling between control and data passing is common to module interfaces mapped into memory addresses, whether with input/output modules or with coprocessors.

Controller Access to Memory. Most input/output transactions transfer a block of data between the device and memory. The device or channel controller initiates memory access requests, which means that it contends with the processor and other controllers for bus cycles. The input/output controller and the processor share access to memory, which can introduce synchronization problems. Ignoring these issues for the moment, the controller performs a simple copying algorithm without any assistance from the processor. In effect, it operates as an independent processor.

Processor Notification. How does the processor track the progress of the activities in the input/output controller? The two common possibilities are (1) have the controller send an interrupt signal when a critical point has been reached, or (2) have the processor poll the status of the module when it needs to know whether the module is available to start another operation.

7.7.2 Block Transfers

A block-transfer bus cycle permits the same controller to retain control of the bus for more than one data transfer. By permitting block transfers, a design amortizes the arbitration overhead associated with the transfer across several transfers. This can improve average system performance.

7.7.3 Coprocessor Calls

Adding a coprocessor module may improve system performance by enhancing the processor's capabilities. In other words, the coprocessor performs functions that seem to be extensions of the processor's instruction set. Likely candidates for coprocessor functions include (1) specialized functions requiring complex computations that could be performed in parallel with other processor activity and (2) functions requiring tight encapsulation (strict isolation) from outside influences.

A coprocessor may be connected to the processor through a special port or to the system's bus in a manner similar to an inoput/output device. Without loss of generality, we detail designs in which the coprocessor is connected to the memory bus.

Coprocessor activity is initiated by the execution of processor instructions. The basic interactions that initiate and signal termination of the coprocessor's actions are similar to the interactions that support basic input/output actions. Differences arise concerning how the coprocessor gets operands and commands and how it performs its functions. For example, one could ask whether the coprocessor has any specific control over the processor.

Coprocessor Control Interactions. The actions of the processor and the coprocessor must be coordinated and support each other. The global view of the interaction is that the processor sends a remote procedure call request to the coprocessor, which then performs its function. Two issues deserve some attention: (1) How are the two synchronized? (2) How do they arrange cooperation? Both questions can be answered with designs that impose fixed rules, but a design permitting flexible interactions offers more options though it may impose a performance penalty.

There are two basically different approaches to controlling a coprocessor. The first, exemplified by the 80287, incorporates knowledge of coprocessor-specific details within the processor's implementation. One cannot change the coprocessor's interface because the processor must know all details of the coprocessor's activity. The coprocessor executes in parallel with the processor; it enters a busy state while it is computing its function. To synchronize its progress with the coprocessor, the processor executes the WAIT instruction.

The flexible approach starts with a general interface between the coprocessor and the processor in which the two become partners and either can request help from the other. In one mode, the coprocessor takes control of the processor for as long as it requires control in order to implement its function; this permits the coprocessor to perform its function using general support functions designed into the processor.

The SPARC-V8 architecture supports a limited coprocessor interface, including instructions to load and store the contents of coprocessor registers, to conditionally branch based on condition codes within a coprocessor, and to request that the coprocessor perform a general operation. The format of the coprocessor operate command is similar to the R-R operate class format, which includes three register numbers and an operation field. This design is similar to designs for channel controllers that give the processor control over the contents of registers within a module connected to the system's memory bus. All of these features were eliminated in version 9 (SPARC-V9 [WEAV94]), because the SPARC organization was not aware of any implementations of coprocessors other than an optional coprocessor chip implementing standard floating-point instructions. Thus, the SPARC-V9 designers removed two instructions in SPARC-V8 that invoked the coprocessor and replaced them with two "implementation-dependent" operations. These instructions might be used to

TABLE 7-1   MC68020 GENERIC COPROCESSOR INSTRUCTIONS

Processor Operation	Operand(s)[a]	Coprocessor Operation
General	Command word	General
Branch on condition	Condition code; branch target	Show condition
Write condition to byte	Condition code; destination address	Show condition
DBcc on coprocessor	Condition code; branch target	Show condition
Trap if condition true	Condition code; operand address	Show condition
Save	Destination address	Save
Restore	Source address	Restore

[a] All these have an unlisted operand, which is the coprocessor number.

build a coprocessor interface, but this requires special processor features to implement the implemetation-dependent instructions. They also removed some state copying and conditional branching instructions that based their decisions on the state within the coprocessor module. To replace conditional branch instructions one needs to copy the coprocessor's status information and then test that flag.

The MC68020's Coprocessor Interface.   To illustrate the flexibility that is possible within the coprocessor paradigm, we study the MC68020's coprocessor support; it illustrates how a wide variety of coprocessor functions can be integrated with ordinary processor functions. After the processor initiates coprocessor activity, the coprocessor responds by leaving information for the processor to examine. The important guarantee is that the processor responds as though it has received a remote procedure call, based on the contents of a status register. Any coprocessor command asks the processor to perform a supporting operation. Any command passed from the coprocessor to the processor can be chained to a successor command. Thus the processor can be asked to execute a sequence of rendezvous-style commands to support the coprocessor-defined interaction.

The MC68020 can support up to eight coprocessors. All coprocessor activity is initiated by the processor asking the coprocessor to perform an operation.

Seven coprocessor instructions are implemented by the processor; they fall into three groups. The first group contains only one general-purpose instruction. The second group contains four operations in which the processor reacts to coprocessor conditions. Finally, the third group comprises two operations that save and restore the coprocessor's state. Table 7-1 lists the seven processor instructions, their operands, and the relevant coprocessor commands.

To be compatible with the processor, each coprocessor design must satisfy some simple interface requirements. The coprocessor should appear to have 10 word-size processor-visible locations (16 bits each), and the design may use six

TABLE 7-2 COPROCESSOR INTERFACE REGISTERS FOR THE MC68020

Name	Address	Size (bytes)	Role
Command	A	2	Processor writes here to _start_ general instruction
Condition	E	2	Processor writes here to _start_ conditional operation
Save	4	2	Processor writes here to _start_ coprocessor save
Restore	6	2	Processor writes here to _start_ coprocessor restore
Response	0	2	Processor reads this for command/status
Control	2	2	Processor writes here while processing exception
Operation	8	2	Processor writes operation here on request
Operand	10	2	Processor writes operand value(s) here
Register Select	14	2	Processor reads this during some register transfers
Op address	1C	4	(Read/write) operand address here
I address	18	4	(Read/write) instruction address here; trace uses this
—	16	2	(reserved)
—	C	2	(reserved)

more. For descriptive purposes, we call these locations "registers," although the coprocessor implementation may not use a register for every one. The processor-visible coprocessor registers have addresses constructed by putting the register number in the low end of the address, and the coprocessor number in bits 15, 14, and 13.[19] The coprocessor registers are addressed according to the list in Table 7-2. The table also gives a brief description of the role of each register. The roles will be amplified as we describe how some simple interactions are achieved.

**Initiating Coprocessor Instructions.** All coprocessor instructions start execution when the processor writes into one of the four coprocessor registers listed at the beginning of Table 7-2. The choice of the register indicates which of the four coprocessor operations (listed in Table 7-1) is to start execution. This initiates an interaction in the rendezvous style; the processor cannot proceed beyond the coprocessor instruction until the coprocessor gives permission. The coprocessor communicates back to the processor by indicating its status in the response register, which the processor is required to monitor. In effect, the coprocessor takes control from the processor for as long as it wishes. During this interval, the roles reverse: The processor becomes a slave to the coprocessor, which can send it commands, also in the remote procedure call style. We will detail the general and conditional coprocessor instruction interactions, ignoring the save and restore operations that have obvious implementations.

---

[19] This space is selected based on the FC codes on the memory bus.

First, consider the execution of a general coprocessor instruction. The instruction word contains a coprocessor number and specifies an effective operand address. The extension word specifies the coprocessor instruction (see Figure 7-14). The coprocessor activity starts when the processor writes the extension word to address 0xA in the coprocessor. When the coprocessor detects its number on the address line and the designated FC code on the status lines, it activates itself and copies the data word to the chosen register. In this case, it goes to the operation register from which it will be interpreted as a (coprocessor) command. The interpretation of this command word is entirely at the discretion of the coprocessor designer.

The coprocessor conditional operations follow a similar scenario, except that the processor writes to the coprocessor's condition register (at address 0xE). The 6-bit condition code written into that register is taken from the instruction stream, but its interpretation is strictly determined by the design of the coprocessor. Up to 64 different conditions can be evaluated by the coprocessor. For example, the condition code might be interpreted by a list processing coprocessor to indicate whether a list is empty. The coprocessor evaluates the condition (which may require processor assistance) and leaves the result in its response register. The processor reads this result and then responds to the value in accordance with the operation. The coprocessor behaves exactly the same way for all of four of these processor instructions; the instructions differ only in the way the processor responds to the condition values.

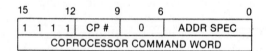

15			12		9		6		0
1	1	1	1	CP #		0		ADDR SPEC	
COPROCESSOR COMMAND WORD									

Figure 7-14   The general coprocessor instruction in the MC68020 (from [MOTO84]; courtesy of Motorola, Inc.)

Requests from the Coprocessor. Processor assistance for the coprocessor's functions is provided through a very flexible interface. Once the coprocessor initiates its operation, the processor is committed to reading the coprocessor's response register and performing the command found there. The coprocessor may ask the processor to perform any of a number of generic operations by placing a command request in the response register. Notice the way that was stated—the processor is committed.

With a few exceptions for exception handling, responses from the coprocessor contain two control bits with universal interpretation: a CA ("come along") bit which, if set, tells the processor whether there will be a subsequent response containing a command before this instruction is complete, and a PC bit that asks the processor to write its program counter into the I address register in the coprocessor (the value copied there is the location of the function code byte of the coprocessor instruction). A value of CA = 0 indicates that the coprocessor has completed the communications required for it to finish the instruction it is processing; the processor may proceed with its instruction stream at this point. The coprocessor might continue executing its instruction in parallel with the processor's continuation of program execution. The remaining bits (excluding CA and PC) of the response contain a function code and an operand field as required; the format is not fixed. Table 7-3 lists the functions that the coprocessor can request of the processor to support the execution of an operation or show condition coprocessor instruction. Additional processor responses that copy data are permitted when the general coprocessor instruction initiated the processor-coprocessor interaction; these additional operations are listed in Table 7-4.

The operations that the coprocessor can request of the processor are quite general; they allow the coprocessor to obtain complete control over the operation of the processor. For example, the coprocessor can read additional extension words from the main instruction stream by using the transfer instruction stream operation. This operation updates the scanPC within the processor. The coprocessor instructions can be arbitrarily complex and can utilize many operand specifications. Figure 7-15 illustrates a possible command format for a list coprocessor operation that combines two lists to form a third. In fact, the coprocessor is even

TABLE 7-3   OPERATIONS THAT AN MC68020 COPROCESSOR CAN REQUEST OF THE PROCESSOR

Response	Meaning/Operand(s)
Busy state	Not finished with previous operation
Status	May give permission to handle interrupts; tells whether the coprocessor has completed its instruction; gives condition value
Transfer operation word	Copy the instruction word to register 8
Transfer instruction stream	Copy block of instruction words to register 10
Supervisor status check	Respond whether the processor is in supervisor mode
Take exception	(Three varieties—beginning, middle, or end of the coprocessor instruction) the processor should take an exception; operand value is the exception number
Transfer to/from top of stack	Copy n words to/from register 10
Take address and transfer data	Copy n words to/from register 10 starting at the address in register 1C
Transfer processor register	Copy specified processor register to/from register 10
Transfer processor control register	Like preceding, except with control register

TABLE 7-4   OPERATIONS THAT AN MC68020 COPROCESSOR CAN REQUEST OF THE
PROCESSOR WHILE PERFORMING A GENERAL COPROCESSOR INSTRUCTION

Operation	Meaning/Operand(s)
Evaluate address and transfer the address	Evaluate the effective address of the instruction and copy it to register 1C
Evaluate address and transfer data	Evaluate the effective address of the instruction and copy n words of data (the direction is a parameter) to/from register 10; another parameter is the type of effective address calculation allowed
Write to previously evaluated effective address	Copy n words of data from register 10
Transfer n processor registers	Use mask from register 14 to choose which registers to transfer; copies them to/from register 10
Transfer n coprocessor registers	Obtains mask from register 14 and copies to/from the instruction's effective address location
Transfer status register and PC	Allows a coprocessor to force a branch in the processor and to change processor status

able to take control of the processor, because it can load all of the processor's
registers, including its program counter.

Example 7-18

A new MC68020 coprocessor instruction in the "general" category has been implemented. During its execution, the coprocessor makes three requests of the processor. The first request asks the processor to read 2 bytes from the program (the
request is "transfer instruction stream"). The second request asks the processor to
"evaluate address and transfer data." The final request is another "transfer instruction stream" request, but for 4 bytes this time. Based on this interaction order, we
can ascertain that the processor instruction is followed by 2 bytes containing the
first information requested by the coprocessor, followed by the bytes required for
the effective address computation specified in the coprocessor instruction, and
completed by 4 bytes of data passed directly to the coprocessor. This format is
shown in Figure 7-16a.

If the order of the last two coprocessor requests were reversed, the effective address bytes (if any) would appear after the rest of the instruction bytes (Figure
7-16b).

The very general coprocessor interface supported by the MC68020 permits
the implementation of very elaborate coprocessor functions without changing
the processor in any way whatsoever. Thus, the coprocessor can become a natural extension of the processor's functionality. The interaction pattern parallels the
rendezvous pattern in many respects, even within the interactions when the
coprocessor asks the processor to perform a supporting function (here the roles
reverse).

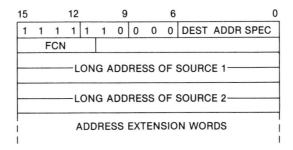

Figure 7-15 Format of a hypothetical operation for a list coprocessor

Replacing Coprocessor Functions. Because the coprocessor has a simple interface with the rest of the system, it would be easy to collect all coprocessor activities into a software module. This implementation would not be as speedy as one with separate hardware for the coprocessor functions. But it would easily fit into the system, being activated by the operating system when it receives an interrupt signaling an attempt to execute an instruction that requires an absent device. This design approach is used to replace the coprocessor functions when the coprocessor is absent.

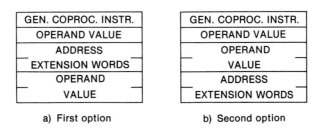

Figure 7-16 Illustrating some operand locations for a general coprocessor instruction

7.7.4 Comments

Commands from the processor to I/O channel and device controllers are like messages to independent processes—you do not know whether the recipient will respond or when it will become available. Coprocessor support is quite different; but the interaction is still like message passing. With many messages passing around the system, it is important that the modules be designed so they can respond quickly to the message when required. This requirement is our next topic.

7.8 PROCESSOR FEATURES SUPPORTING FAST MESSAGE RECEPTION

At low levels, the processor design can expedite message reception, primarily by quickly responding to external interrupts caused by the message-reception hardware.

7.8.1 Fast Interrupt Decoding

At the hardware level, the arrival of a message at a processor is heralded by the occurrence of an interrupt sent from the interface module receiving the message. This module must have immediate access to a buffer space to hold the incoming information. A preallocation of a buffer space can be achieved by setting a pointer within the interface module. Some interrupt sources require speedy responses, which depend upon the source of the interrupt and the contents of the message that accompanies the interrupt. Hardware assistance for decoding the interrupt cause and for selecting the appropriate response will speed the system's response to the interruption or message.

Responding to a general interrupt may require all of the following steps:

1. All instructions in the executing process that were issued prior to the interrupt's occurrence must be completed, at least to the point of being certain that they themselves will not cause interrupts.
2. All instructions that have been issued out of order must be canceled.
3. The vector entry holding the entry point address must be read.
4. The state of the interrupted program must be saved.[20]
5. The processor state must be changed to reflect the occurrence of the interrupt; this may mean changing to system or supervisor mode.
6. The address found in step 3 must be loaded into the program counter.
7. The first instruction is fetched from the address in the program counter.

Step 2 is necessary only if the processor is able to issue instructions out of order. Step 3 involves a memory access only if the interrupt vector holds entry points rather than instructions from the interrupt handler (we discuss this option in what follows). Step 4 makes registers available for the interrupt handler; this step can be trivial if the processor state change in step 5 automatically makes registers available.

The delay before performing the first instruction of the interrupt handler is dominated by memory access delays. Without hardware assistance in decoding the cause of the interrupt, additional time will be spent inside the interrupt handler simply deciding how to process the actual interrupt that did occur—this requires a structure akin to a C++ **switch** statement. The delay between the occurrence of the interrupt and the execution of the first instruction that is

---

[20] The amount of saving depends upon the convention regarding returns from interrupts.

specific to the cause of the interrupt is the important measure of the interrupt handling design. Designers can reduce the delay by reducing the number of memory accesses and selecting the addressing patterns used within the interrupt handler itself. The following techniques can be used:

1. Provide hardware decoding of the interrupt cause.
2. Minimize the number of registers that have to be saved in memory.
3. Place interrupt handler instructions inside the interrupt vector, rather than just entry point addresses, to which control must be transferred.
4. Increase the stride between interrupt entry addresses within the interrupt vector so that complete handlers can be included within the interrupt vector itself.

Example 7-19

The MC68020 interrupt decoding scheme includes simple decoding; the vector base register (VBR) points to the beginning of a 1024-byte block that contains a list of entry points. To find the entry point for the handler associated with interrupt J, look at the address in location (VBR + 4*J). The 4 bytes in the vector hold a single address. The interrupt decoding also handles up to 16 interrupts initiated by the execution of the TRAP processor instruction.

Two memory accesses are required to fetch the first instruction of the interrupt handler under any scheme in which a vector holds a list of entry points; the first simply finds the address for the instruction fetch. With pipelined instruction execution, there can be a significant delay before the first instruction of the handler is executed.

An important option defines the contents of the interrupt vector to be the instructions of the handler (rather than the entry point address). By adjusting the spacing between the entry points in such an interrupt vector, a pipelined machine can execute the handler quickly without performing extra branches.

Example 7-20

The Alpha AXP processors execute PALcode operations that are selected by the address portion of the CALL_PAL instruction. After waiting to ensure that this cannot be interrupted by an exception caused by a previously issued instruction, the processor takes a trap to a location in the PAL entry space.

7.8.2 Fast Context Switching

Every program needs some workspace, including an interrupt handler. In a register-based, machine the workspace includes processor registers. When an interrupt occurs, we need to establish an environment for the execution of the interrupt handler. Because the interrupted program is not related to the interrupt, its workspace should not be disrupted by interrupt processing.

We desire a fast mechanism that switches the processor's context to provide the interrupt handler with register workspace. The simple option is to provide a separate complete set of processor registers for use by the interrupt handler.

Another simple option provides a separate stack pointer for the interrupt handler. If general processor instructions can use the stack for temporary workspace, this option does not restrict the functions that can be performed in a simple handler. If the handler has to perform complex operation sequences, the registers will be desirable, and must be saved.

A third option, like the previous one, relies on the observation that most interrupt handlers are short and do not need much workspace. Thus, this design style provides a partial register set for exclusive use by interrupt handlers.

Example 7-21

The SPARC-V9 processor has a second set of eight global registers for use by interrupt handlers. Thus, an interrupt handler that uses only the first eight registers does not have to save (or restore) any processor registers. However, the stack format must include space to save other registers in case the interrupt handler requires such space or in case the process is going to be moved to the ready state so the processor can execute another process.

Example 7-22

B 5700 obtains workspace for all programs, including interrupt handlers, on the stack of the executing process. When an interrupt occurs, the state of the executing process is saved and then the handler is initiated in a new activation block on top of the stack. If the stack runs out of the space within its segment, the interrupt is handled on a separate system stack.

If the operating system decides to schedule another process, it executes a special instruction that changes the active stack in a single instruction. Thus, the processor always thinks that it is operating on a stack.

The disadvantage of this design is that every procedure call involves saving a lot of state information. Because entering an interrupt handler is like calling a procedure, this activity can consume many memory cycles, which delays the system's response to the interrupt.

7.8.3 Barrier Implementations

An *interprocess synchronization barrier* is a (conceptual) point at which the members of a specified set of *cooperating processes* coordinate their progress by waiting for each other. In other words, none of the cooperating processes can proceed beyond the barrier until a *progress predicate* has been satisfied. The common predicate is the all_here predicate that becomes **true** when every cooperating process has reached the barrier. For example, an interprocess synchronization barrier with an all_here predicate occurs at the completion of a **cobegin** structure. Another important version of the all_here barrier occurs at memory barriers that are used to synchronize the usage of shared objects (see Section 8.8.1).

A simple implementation of a synchronization barrier designates one process as the *coordinator*; this process checks for satisfaction of the barrier's progress predicate and notifies the processes that they are permitted to proceed beyond the barrier. One can view the synchronization barrier as a point at which messages are exchanged to notify the coordinator about the status of each cooperating process, though shared-memory objects can also be used for this purpose. Interprocess barriers can be used to coordinate the use of shared-memory objects—these barriers are implemented by sending low-level messages among processors.

A global barrier synchronizes a number of component processes that have to wait for their compatriots to reach the barrier before they can proceed. A counter or an AND gate can be used in the implementation of a global barrier. If a central counter is used, it becomes a bottleneck; so one could organize the processes into a tree, placing a local barrier at each node of the tree, with each barrier using a private counter. When the local barrier is passed, that fact is propagated to the next level of the barrier tree. Processes cannot resume execution until the barrier at the root of the tree has been passed; this requires that messages be passed down the tree structure. Of course, the local switch nodes cannot issue permission to proceed until the barrier condition has been resolved at the root of the appropriate subtree.

Example 7-23

> The T3D processor is organized as a tree structure for barrier coordination; a tree of fast AND gates propagates completion information to the root of the subtree to which the application has been assigned. A tree of OR gates is also provided to implement the Eureka! coordination mode, which can be used to signal that one member of a team of processes has succeeded by finding a way to satisfy a global goal.

We discuss local barrier synchronization in Section 8.8.1.

7.8.4 Comments

The delays inherent in interprocessor signaling mechanisms can present a system performance problem. If one could devise techniques that reduce the overhead and could overlap the communication and processing activities, one might be able to pass messages efficiently. Speedups for interprocessor barriers and short message passing can be effective ways to improve system performance in many applications.

In Chapter 8, we study synchronization techniques for coordinating accesses to objects in a shared memory space. The implementation of the coordination mechanisms might require passing messages among memory controllers and/or processors within the system. These messages are generated at low levels of the system's implementation and do not have to be checked by any software. Therefore, they are not expensive to transmit, unlike messages developed within user-level programs, which do have to be checked by the operating system before they can be sent out.

7.9 SUMMARY

In this chapter we explored the message-passing model, which is compatible with loose coupling among interacting processes. We described basic process–message interactions and showed how they are specified and implemented in a few high-level languages. The distinction between blocking and nonblocking send and receive primitives becomes important in modeling the process–message interaction, because the ability not to block allows more programming flexibility, at the cost of greater system complexity. By requiring blocking in message interactions, the system's functionality is easily shown. Some basic processor support for message passing is provided by all processors in their interrupt and trap handling mechanisms. Increased efficiency can be provided by incorporating hardware interrupt decoding, space within the interrupt vector, and extra registers for use during interrupt processing.

Message passing is used in the implementation of some coherence protocols supporting shared-memory models, but in those designs, the messages are simple and generated by the underlying mechanism, so the checking overhead is reduced to a minimum, as we see in the next chapter. An important special case is active messages, with fast receivers and special decoding vectors that support very efficient implementations.

7.10 TRENDS

Within local multiprocessor systems that support loosely coupled process interactions, interprocess coordination is usually handled through shared-memory schemes (see Chapter 8). However, multiprocessor systems designed to perform tightly coupled algorithms can use interprocessor messages effectively, because the delays from blocking within message-passing operations can become insignificant because the processors are all executing similar algorithms, arriving at their communication points in close synchronization.

Both blocking and nonblocking message-passing operations should continue to exist in programming languages. Their use is likely to diminish, as the shared-memory model is used more widely. Message passing will continue to be important within the implementation of shared-memory systems and for distributed database systems. (These applications are discussed in Chapter 9.)

General coprocessor interfaces seem to be disappearing, because many details have to be handled to serve a small market segment unless very common operations are supported (as with float operations). In high-performance systems, these operations are moving into processor chips. The logical requirements regarding synchronization between the processor and the coprocessor remain, even if they describe interactions within the processor device. Also, the delays incurred in passing signals off the processor chip can hurt performance.

The data flow model, a special case of message passing described in Appendix K, uses message passing among a set of modules interconnected according to the structure of the algorithm that performs a task. This model has some intuitive appeal, but its overhead is likely to overwhelm its benefits, unless it is used to schedule complex processes, in which case it simply provides guidance about scheduling, and the same functions can be performed efficiently in software. Therefore, this model seems likely to fade as a way to build message-passing systems. It does remain useful for modeling logical dependencies, as we studied in Chapter 6.

It is indisputable that messaging services, such as the Internet, will expand in the future, but this trend is not likely to have a significant effect on the architectures of the processors within the network.

7.11 CONCEPT LIST

1. Message illusions: ordering, integrity, survival, and finite delay
2. Message queueing in paths
3. Process states
4. Remote procedure call model
5. Rendezvous interactions
6. Process blocking to wait for message interactions
7. Busy waiting
8. Programming constructs: send, receive, and alternate wait
9. Delay conditions
10. Resumption predicates
11. Processor instructions to support message passing and scheduling
12. Surrogate modules
13. Event values
14. Process scheduling and message passing are similar
15. Process dispatching versus scheduling
16. Deadlocks and process scheduling
17. Processor instructions can assist with scheduling
18. Message packets
19. Interconnection topologies: complete, buses, crossbar, n-cube, and ring

20. Packet routing strategies
21. Wormhole routing; deadlock possibilities
22. Input/output commands
23. Coprocessor protocols
24. Fast interrupt decoding
25. Extra processor registers aid fast context switching
26. Barrier implementations
27. Active messages: quick buffering or complete handling

7.12 PROBLEMS

7-1. Three attributes of a message communication path that ensure system functionality are
1. All messages are delivered.
2. Message order is preserved.
3. Message contents are not garbled.
   Construct three simple examples to show that each of these properties is necessary for system functionality. (You need to construct a nonfunctional example for a system in which two of these properties are satisfied and the third is violated. This will be required for each of the three possible violations.)

7-2. Write out generalizations of the message-passing illusions for a system that permits broadcast messages, for each of the following two options. Discuss the possibility that the composition of the system (its set of processes) changes dynamically.
(a) Each broadcast is directed to all modules within the system.
(b) All modules are identified with a module number (which is unique within the system) and a set of "group numbers." Each broadcast is directed to every module having the specified group number within its set of group numbers.

7-3. Consider a single arc of a message-passing system and the ports at its two ends. Draw a state diagram (or a state transition table) showing the overall state of the arc and its ports, including states of the arc and its ports. You may assume that the system starts in a dormant state and restrict your analysis to the states reachable from that initial condition. Show all possible transitions among these states. Label each transition to indicate its cause.

7-4. Consider a system design in which path–port associations can be dynamically changed. To change this association, a processor can execute a command

change(<path>, <port>);

The effect of this statement is to change the destination of the named path to the named port (assume that there is some global scheme for naming ports). Abide by the rule that a path can have only one input port and one output port at one time. If an attempted change violates this rule, the executing process will be suspended until the path–port assignment changes and that the single port assumption is satisfied. Answer the following questions twice—once for paths that do not incorporate queues and once for a system in which the paths incorporate FIFO queues.

(a) Specify the event on which process P should wait if it has executed change(path x, y) and is blocked as a result of this attempt to change the assignment.

(b) Construct an example system that obeys the rules above but is nonfunctional. Try to make an example in which no process changes the path–port association for any other process. (In other words, each port change is initiated by the process attached to the source port on the path.)

(c) Construct an argument that you cannot construct such an example if there is a synchronization constraint between message reception activities and path–port association changes. In other words, the system will be functional if there exist adequate constraints synchronizing the processes.

7-5. Write Ada processes using the rendezvous mechanism and selective reception to mirror the programs in Examples 7-12 and 7-13. Try to minimize the number of contexts where each rendezvous name must be known.

7-6. Write an occam program for a set of tasks that includes one target task that receives, in any order, two messages across channel_1 plus three messages across channel_2, placing them in the arrays input_1[2] and input_2[3]. After the five messages have been received, the task proceeds to call a function named doit, which has five parameters comprising the five messages. If any additional messages happen to arrive on the channels while these necessary inputs are being collected, they are not to be received, but are to be left with their sources blocked.

7-7. Show how one could implement the Ada **select** using simple remote procedure call with the procedure name, supplemented with flags internal to the receiver that indicate when the receiver activated the wait for reception and then what action should be taken if the procedure is called by an arriving message. (The process is disabled otherwise.) Your answer should detail how we do this.

7-8. Discuss the possibility and desirability of using timeouts to detect failures in a message-passing mechanism. Discuss the sensitivity of a timeout design to the system's environment. You choose appropriate parameters to describe significant properties of the environment. State the types of system environments for which timeouts work well, and those for which they would be undesirable.

7-9. Show how the IBM AS/400 EVENT operations could be used to emulate the semantics of Ada exception handling.

7-10. Discuss the relationship between low-level interrupt handling and high-level message-passing structures. Two high-level message reception models use (1) specific receive operations and (2) on-condition handlers. Which of these matches closely with the structure of the low-level interrupt system? Explain.

7-11. Detail an argument that a FIFO scheduling policy is a fair scheduling policy.

7-12. Construct a diagram illustrating the interprocess message flow and the changes in process scheduling state for the set of processes described in Example 7-12.

(a) Follow a schedule in which process A terminates before process B begins.

(b) Follow a schedule leading to a deadlock, such as the one(s) described in the example.

7-13. The text claimed that an NXOR operation between BV and –BV will give a bit pattern with 1's only at the right end and the number of 1's equal to the position of the rightmost bit in BV that was one (counting the rightmost bit position as position 1). Show that this is indeed the case by computing the bit patterns in BV NXOR (–BV) for the following values:
   (a) BV = 0xA454
   (b) BV = 0x8000
   (c) BV = 0

7-14. Construct an example showing that the loss of a message can cause a deadlock among a set of communicating processes.

7-15. Consider the Honeywell DPS6 dispatching scheme. Write a sequence of operations (at the register-transfer level) to find and dispatch to the highest-priority ready process. Use the encoding with level zero having first priority for the processor. Suppose that the process presently executing in the processor remains ready to execute after the LEV instruction has been completed.

7-16. A designer's interesting argument goes as follows: Some coprocessor operations take a "long time." Even if the coprocessor were able to operate "off-line" while the processor continued to execute its program, there could be a significant probability that the coprocessor would be busy when the processor wanted to initiate a new coprocessor instruction. Therefore the designer proposes implementing the coprocessor as a barrel, with synchronous slot timing in which every process is given an equal number of execution slots.

  The claim is that the barrel design would lower the probability of the coprocessor being busy and therefore causing the processor to wait. Formulate a condition on the execution times of the coprocessor and the processor whose truth implies the correctness of the designer's argument. Explain the reasoning behind your condition and explain why the designer's argument falls apart if your condition is false.

7-17. A coprocessor to be attached to an MC68020 system is designed to implement a NEWCALL instruction: "call this procedure using these parameters, but perform it on a new stack whose origin is specified." The instruction's operands specifying the number of parameter words and the address of the entry point are taken from long words in the program stream following the NEWCALL instruction word. The actual parameters (for the call) were placed on the execution stack before this instruction was initiated. For example, NEWCALL P,3,S creates a new stack whose origin is at S, pops three words from the top of the current stack, pushes the old stack pointer value, copies the parameter words to the S stack, and then pushes the program counter onto the new stack before setting the program counter to P. Figure 7-17 illustrates the effects of this operation, and should be used as a reference to define the format of the new stack. You are asked to find a sequence of coprocessor–processor and coprocessor–memory interactions that are sufficient to implement this NEWCALL instruction. Use the MC68020 coprocessor interface described in the text.

7-18. Consider a coprocessor designed to interface with the MC68020 processor. It is designed to implement operations on doubly-linked list structures stored in memory. The list beads contain three longwords (32 bits in each one). The first

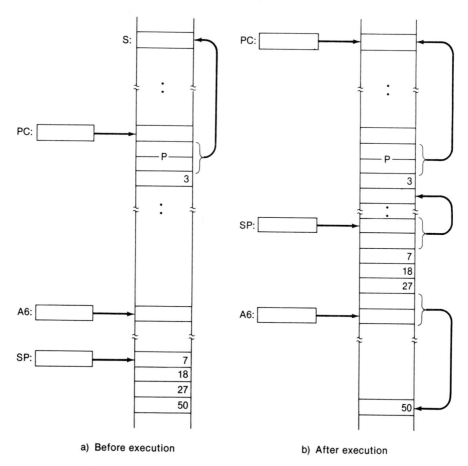

a) Before execution   b) After execution

Figure 7-17   The effect of the NEWCALL 3,S instruction
introduced in Problem 7-17

longword in a bead contains the address of the (first byte of the) successor bead,
the second, the address of the (first byte of the) predecessor bead, and the third
contains a value. In this problem, we investigate the interactions between the
coprocessor and other modules on the bus, including the processor and memory.
For this problem, you will study the implementation of a list compare operation
that should return true to the processor if the two list operands contain identical
values in the same order. The two lists are described by pointers to the first beads;
each pointer occupies a pair of extension words following the coprocessor
compare instruction. List the sequence of bus writes and reads that occur when the
coprocessor performs the list compare instruction. Annotate the list to indicate the
activities taking place within the coprocessor. Make such a list for each of the two
following conditions:

(a) The coprocessor can make DMA requests to access memory directly.

(b) The coprocessor cannot make DMA requests and has to ask the processor to make memory accesses on its behalf.

7-19. A message-passing system is designed to "post" the arrival of a message, which means that when the message arrives, the system simply changes the value(s) in process-local objects to indicate the message arrival. Here are three possible ways that the state could be changed upon message arrival:

    1. A Boolean value is set.

    2. A Boolean value is set and a descriptor of the memory space holding the new message is placed into a designated (process-local) message pointer object.

    3. The message is simply added to a (process-local) queue, whose pointers are updated by the system.

    (a) For each design, indicate the division of responsibility of assuring that the message-passing illusions are supported by the implementation.

    (b) For each design, discuss how error checking and requests for retransmission would be incorporated into the design. Assume that the sender adds redundancy to each outgoing message and that there is a checking function **boolean** validate(message m) that returns **true** if the message meets the redundancy check.

7-20. Repeat Problem 7-19 at the system level where it is visible that the system is using packet-level redundancy. However, user programs wish to know about complete messages only. Assume that the first words in each packet contain the following control information:

    1. A unique identifier of the message of which this packet is a part

    2. The position number of the packet within the message (one-origin indexing used)

    3. The total number of packets within the message

Assume that error correction has been handled at a lower level, so that all message packets can be assumed to be correct.

    (a) Describe the activities initiated by packet arrival. Write an algorithm to handle this event.

    (b) When does the packet manager inform the application about the arrival of a message?

7-21. The wiring in a daisy-chain implicitly associates a priority with each module sharing access to a common communication link. The priority order reflects the order of connection along the daisy chain. A designer wishes to change this scheme so the following conditions apply:

    1. A "logical address" is associated with each module along the communication link.

    2. The module priorities are ordered based on the logical module addresses, such that the module with the highest address has the highest priority.

    You are asked to design a bus access control system that delivers a grant signal to the highest-priority module that is making a transmission request. The priority resolution activity is initiated by an (external) P_start signal. Your solution may introduce special control messages or connections on the bus. Your design should be complete within itself; that is, it should not rely on the use of any bus connections that you do not specify. If you need to add special signals to effect your access control scheme, just specify new bus leads for the desired information. Try to design your protocol so that a minimum number of extra leads are required.

(a) Specify your access control protocol.

(b) Describe the signals that the modules will use to communicate bus grant information among themselves.

(c) Describe how a module decides whether to accept the grant signal when it arrives.

7-22. Consider the following argument: Source and destination modules appear to be symmetric in a message-passing protocol. Therefore, it should be reasonable to design a bus system in which the priorities for message transmission are based on the values of the message destinations rather than on the values of their sources, as described in the text.

(a) Sketch a bus allocation policy based on this philosophy.

(b) Compare this allocation scheme with one using priorities based on source module numbers.

(c) This scheme could be generalized to using the pair of source and destination names in each message to reference a table that holds the corresponding message priority value. Could you design a reasonable allocation policy using this scheme for determining message priority? Explain.

7-23. A designer wishes to handle access arbitration among several priority classes through a daisy-chain interconnection. She proposes a hierarchical structure in which there is a separate daisy chain for each priority class. A control unit called the "priority class controller" (PCC) is placed at the head of each daisy chain. The PCCs are themselves interconnected to the system processor through a separate daisy-chain network. Figure 7-18 illustrates this structure.

(a) Describe the functions performed by each PCC.

(b) Compare this design against one in which there is a single daisy chain interconnecting all requesting modules.

7-24. The interconnection topology of this system uses a two-level hierarchy. Let p_1 denote the probability that an arbitrary message is directed to a node within the local level of the connection structure. Assume that the probability of choosing a node within a level is the same for all nodes within that level. For each configuration specified, determine the average and maximum numbers of switches that handle a single message. Choose (and define) the appropriate configuration parameters that affect your answers.

(a) Both levels use crossbar switches.

(b) The local level uses a bus and the global level uses a ring.

(c) The local level uses an n-cube and the global level uses a ring.

7-25. The processor whose address is $s_2 s_1 s_0$ sends a message to the destination whose address is $d_2 d_1 d_0$ through the multistage interconnection network shown in Figure 7-11. Make a list of the source–estination paths that are blocked by this transaction. To simplify your answers and- show the conflict patterns, use x in bit positions where either a one or a zero would cause a conflict.

7-26. A simple unidirectional ring interconnection network is modified by the addition of a path from node i to node $i + 3$ (the nodes are numbered in order of their position in the ring, modulo the ring size). What routing rules should the switch modules use to minimize the number of links across which a message must pass?

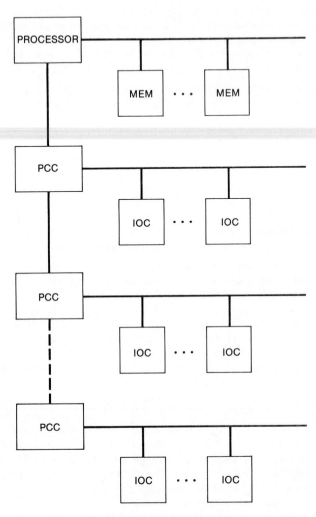

Figure 7-18   The priority class network

What configuration information must reside in each switch to permit your algorithm to work? Explain your answers.

7-27. Write a specification of a consistent set of policies for naming nodes within a hierarchical bus or ring system such that message routing is simplified. Then specify how each switch determines how to forward an arriving message.

7-28. Illustrate each of the following difficulties that may arise in a bus system using messages broadcast to processes. Each broadcast message is to be acknowledged by each recipient before the sender can conclude that the broadcast has been completed.

(a) Acknowledgment messages from two destinations can conflict and corrupt each other.

(b) The source cannot know the identities of all destinations if processes can be dynamically created and destroyed.

(c) The time to poll all destinations for their acknowledgments may be comparable to the time it would have taken to transmit the message individually to each destination.

8

SHARED-RESOURCE SYSTEMS

Friends share all things.

— Pythagoras

The state held in a shared resource can be used to communicate information among a set of cooperating processes, much as messages can be used. It is easy to see that a shared-memory object (or other resource that retains some state) can be used as a mailbox for message communication. It is easy to see that proper coordination between the sending and receiving processes will be required to make the shared mailbox operate correctly. The basic difficulty is that the simple memory and atomic action illusions do not apply to systems in which state can be shared among the processes (within a shared memory, in particular). Any process can change the contents of any memory location, and this change might be visible to any other process sharing the memory. In fact, any change due to the action of one process could occur in the midst of an action initiated by another process. This presents serious problems if the second process wishes to view its action as an atomic action.

In this chapter we study general ways that shared resources can be used for interprocess communication. Our theme has four parts: (1) the memory illusion must be revised for systems containing shared memory; (2) process specifications must state their usage of shared resources at all levels, which redefines

410

the illusion and the notion of process correctness; (3) low-level support is required for an efficient implementation of resource sharing and synchronization; and (4) similar scheduling/timing techniques can be used at most levels of the hierarchy. For example, the philosophy of the transaction model, originally designed to describe interactions between the high-level programs governing sharing processes as they access one or more resources, tinges processor instruction sets and memory models. At the instruction set level, a single MC68020 instruction can be used to update a shared list structure. This instruction's logic reflects a specialized transaction like view of certain (basic) interprocess interactions.

If the implementation or use of accessing and synchronization mechanisms is improper, the system is at risk—it might exhibit nonfunctional behavior if the synchronization features are improperly used, because schedule feasibility will have to be defined in terms of compliance with the synchronization mechanisms.

Despite these possible difficulties, resource sharing can be desirable. Sharing can enhance modularity among virtual machines, especially if the virtual machines are loosely coupled. Many applications can be mapped into a set of parallel processes accessing a common memory space. Shared global memory undergirds the basic structure of massively parallel systems. Coordination through sharing can be easier to program than coordination through message passing and also might entail less overhead. However sharing introduces new opportunities for specification and implementation errors.

To deal with these situations coherently, we start with specification techniques, trying to provide a convenient environment within which one can specify the behavior of interacting processes sharing memory objects. Functionality and correctness definitions are based on sharing models that are, in turn, based on coordination techniques. Correct sharing, then, is defined in terms of correct program coordination. The system's implementation should conform to the model of coordinated sharing underlying the program's structure. Most coordination models are based on generalizations of the simple memory and atomic action illusions, which work correctly if the system really does have a common memory that supports atomic transactions. Unfortunately, this simple view does not directly describe contemporary and future high-performance system designs.

One potential source of coordination errors within an implementation lies in the fact that most high-performance designs that speed memory accesses create multiple copies of memory objects. For example, cache memories hold local (*surrogate*) copies of objects that are visualized as being located in a shared main memory. Without special design features, a processor cannot assume that the state within its surrogate copy of a shared object always represents a faithful copy of the state of the shared object as it might be viewed from another process. In general, each processor has its own *local view* of the contents of shared memory (provided by its surrogate copy), but the programmer does not want to have to know about such implementation details (that should be encapsulated within a virtual machine that has shared memory). In particular, he would like to think that there is a consistent *global view*, describing the state of the shared memory's contents, reflected in all views seen by sharing processes, as shown by their accesses, whether those reach local surrogate copies or the global object.

Another class of potential problems arises because each processor's implementation may reorder instruction execution (either instruction issue or instruction completion) to speed its execution. This strategy, described in Section 6.6, seems innocent, because the processor design can include tests to ensure that, despite instruction reordering, the program will exhibit functional behavior if executed on a single processor. The problem is that some speedup techniques guaranteed to produce functional behavior in a single-process system may introduce risks of nonfunctional behavior in a multiprocess system even though each process, acting alone, would exhibit functional behavior.

Our quick overview identified several requirements for the implementation of a shared-memory system, which can be phrased in terms of the *risks* of the following: (1) unfortunate timing of actions by processes sharing a consistent global view of shared resources; (2) unfortunate buffering of objects between processors and memory; (3) unfortunate interruptions of single memory transactions; and (4) unfortunate reordering of the actions initiated by a single process. To remove these risks requires special attention within the system's implementation.

In this chapter, you will learn about several viewpoints for structuring a set of programs utilizing shared objects and about how these structures can be implemented, including assistance required from the system's implementation.

We start with the basic single-memory illusion under which all processes see a consistent (global) memory. We demonstrate synchronization problems arising from interleaving of atomic read and write actions. Then we find basic principles and techniques that can remove these difficulties at software and hardware levels. Our abstract structural models contain multiple processes whose activities utilize shared resources and whose activities are synchronized through the states within shared objects. We present specification and implementation techniques for systems using shared resources. We also show how these techniques can be used to coordinate the use of multiple resources within a processor's implementation.

When we turn to the implementation details, we revisit the risk issues because we must face the fact that many design techniques that speed execution do introduce new risks. Although one can design the system to give the appearance of a globally consistent memory at all surrogate copies, imposing this tight constraint may impair performance. Most prefer to insert low-level programming steps that identify those portions of the program within which certain risks are acceptable. We discuss special implementation techniques that assure that such boundaries are honored.

After you have read this chapter, you will understand the risks inherent in the use of shared memory for interprocess coordination. You will know several ways to coordinate the use of shared resources, ranging from high-level programming constructs to low-level hardware techniques. You will know how to incorporate shared resources in the illusions. You will know how a design can correctly support these illusions. After you understand these issues and design techniques, you should study Chapter 9 to learn about the remaining problems arising with resource sharing—building boundaries between virtual machines and preventing unauthorized accesses across those virtual machine boundaries.

8.1 SYNCHRONIZATION IN SHARED SINGLE-MEMORY SYSTEMS

A computer system sharing a single memory can be modeled as a set of independent processors, a set of memory modules, and an interconnection network that permits processors to access memory modules. In the first part of the chapter, we stay within this context and illustrate some basic benefits and problems associated with shared resource designs. The additional problems arising from high-performance processor and cache designs are covered later in the chapter. In essence, we start with systems that do support the single memory illusion, showing how they can violate the atomic action illusion and how that illusion can be revised to become applicable to these systems. Later, we introduce the problems arising within systems that do not support the single memory and program order illusions.

A simple shared-memory system (Figure 8-1), with two processors and one memory module that can be accessed from either processor, is sufficient to illustrate the basic synchronization problems. The single memory module has two *ports* through which requests may arrive. Low-level conflicts are not germane to the synchronization problem, so we insert an *arbitration unit* within the memory module. The arbitration unit *serializes* incoming requests, passing chosen requests to the memory itself. The memory module is placed in the *busy state* while a request is being serviced. If the arbitration unit receives two requests, it selects one and passes it to the memory controller. It also sends a *wait signal* to

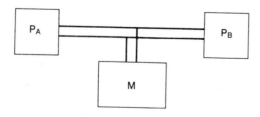

Figure 8-1   A simple shared-memory system

the processor whose request was not forwarded. Finally, if the memory is busy servicing a previous request when another request arrives, the memory module sends a *wait signal* to the processor making the new request. When the arbitration unit sends a wait signal, either it buffers the second request or it relies on the processor to continue making its request until the memory is able to service it.

An arbitration unit might seem to be adequate for coordinating memory usage by the two processors. Certainly, the arbitration unit insulates the memory from confusing duplicate requests. Thus, the memory does support the illusion of atomic actions. And each processor gets the service it expects, because each read or write request does access the appropriate location and the requested action is performed. If the system did not provide at least this level of structure, it would be extremely difficult to understand and program. It is reasonable that any functionality definition would assume that this level of noninterference is provided. If we extend this notion to the process level of abstraction, we get the notion that a set of processes sharing memory should exhibit the same results as those that would have been obtained if each process were executed atomically (without any interruption from any other process). Many, but not all, programs can be executed in this manner and still be consistent with their algorithms. This version of functionality is expressed in the following definition, due to Lamport [LAMP86].

> **Definition.** A system is *sequentially consistent* if and only if its results match those that would have been observed if the system followed a schedule in which all processes are executed without interleaving and the steps of each process are performed in program order.

It is inefficient to demand that a system's actual schedule follow the sequentially consistent definition, because the definition removes the possibility of parallel execution in independent processing modules. So one might desire that the system's behavior appear as though a sequentially consistent schedule had been followed. Unfortunately, even if all processes execute their instructions atomically in program order, the system can be nonfunctional.

Example 8-1

Two processes share the integer object S, with initial contents x. We represent the timing of each process' execution as the progression down a vertical column. The following execution sequence represents sequentially consistent behavior, because there is no interleaving and each program is executed in program order.

```
        PROCESS A           PROCESS B
        A = S;
        A = A + 1;
        S = A;
```

```
        PROCESS A              PROCESS B
                               B = S;
                               B = B + 1;
                               S = B;
```

Upon completion, S contains $x + 2$, which is the "correct" result because there is no interleaving in the schedule.

The individual steps of the two processes could have been interleaved in many ways, while maintaining program order for each process. The interleaved access pattern in the following schedule preserves program order for both processes.

```
        PROCESS A              PROCESS B
        A = S;
                               B = S;
        A = A + 1;
                               B = B + 1;
        S = A;
                               S = B;
```

After this schedule is completed, S contains $x + 1$! The final contents of S are different in the two schedules even though the same program steps were executed in program sequence in each process and the memory behaved correctly.

The *nonfunctional behavior* in the example is due to a timing risk rearing its ugly head. A system satisfying the basic single memory illusion with atomic read and write operations is not able to assure functional behavior when two processes share access to the same memory object. The designer of a system with shared resources wants to remove any possibility of nonfunctional behavior. Now we discuss methods for specifying other requirements to obtain a guarantee of functional behavior.

8.2 BASIC ISSUES, CONCEPTS, AND APPROACHES

Our simple example uncovered the need to synchronize accesses to shared resources so that the system's results do not depend on timing choices permitted within the bounds of the program specifications. In other words, we need to limit the ordering of the events in the interaction. We need to implement the controls efficiently. And we need to be able to convince ourselves (and others!) that indeed we have accomplished these ends. We discuss these issues in this section.

8.2.1 Issues

We use shared memory systems to illustrate our points, realizing that the same issues apply to all shared-resource systems in which the states of shared

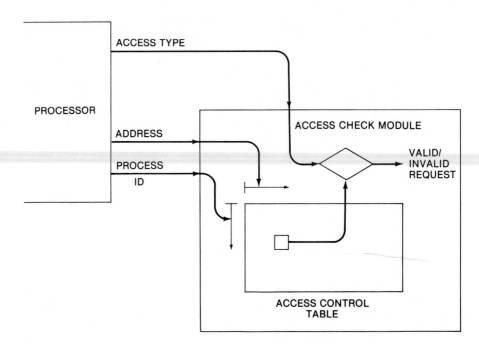

Figure 8-2   Using an access control table to check the
validity of an access request

resources can be changed and sensed by programs. Four basic issues in the design of shared-memory systems are as follows:

1. Access control
2. Synchronization
3. Protection
4. Security

Access control determines which processes may access which resources. Although this sounds negative, the important aspect is positive—the basic goal of
access control is to *permit access* to resources whenever possible. An access control module can be interposed between the processors and the shared resources
to check every access request against the contents of a (conceptual) access control table (ACT) whose contents define the legality of each potential access attempt (Figure 8-2). Disallowed access attempts are intercepted and the offending
process may be terminated or delayed until the desired access can be completed.
If the system can never complete the access, the process becomes permanently
blocked and will be terminated by the scheduler. The contents of ACT are *dynamic* during process execution. Any process may request changes to the ACT,
but such requests must pass validity checks. Overall, the values in ACT together

with the synchronization rules limit the interactions and thus determine the system's functionality.

Synchronization constraints limit the relative timing of accesses to shared resources from sharing processes. Proper synchronization ensures legitimate information flow and system functionality. Synchronization constraints can be modeled in various ways. These constraints are the major topic of this chapter.

Protection, which prevents processes from making arbitrary access to resources belonging to other processes, is an important system feature. The basic goal of a protection scheme is to *prevent* access to shared resources that are physically shared, yet logically separated. Protection enforces *static* boundaries between processes, in contrast to access control, which enforces *dynamic* boundaries. Sharing and protection are basically incompatible, for sharing gives access permission whereas protection restricts it. Designers must strike a balance among these conflicting desires to produce a "reasonable" system that supports functional process behavior. Protection will be covered in the next chapter.

Security, another important concern in resource-sharing systems, imposes access restrictions based on external security attributes; see Chapter 9.

8.2.2 What Is Correct?

A system should exhibit functional behavior, which we define to be *correct*. A detailed definition of correctness depends upon the programming model. Some simple system structures or properties of applications give obviously correct behavior for all feasible execution sequences. Defining correctness in terms of sequentially consistent behavior is commonplace because it is easily understood and its consequences are easily determined. With realistic complex systems, there may be no obvious way to know what constitutes correct behavior. Clearly, we need programmer specifications concerning functionality and correctness (these may be implicit in how the program is written). More details concerning correctness and the structure of proofs showing the correctness of shared resource system models are presented in Appendix L.

To discuss the activities in a system with shared resources, we must find a way to distinguish among the various write accesses to each shared object. For this purpose we introduce *version numbers*; a new version number is associated with each write to an object, just as we associated version numbers with the contents of processor registers in describing superscalar designs. The version numbers associated with an object should vary monotonically (usually increasing). A simple version numbering scheme assigns version number i to the ith write to an object. Version numbering is important for proofs and is used within the management algorithms supporting correct sharing in certain distributed architectures (see Section 8.7.2).

8.2.3 Programming Models

Several different approaches can be used to specify the use of shared objects by cooperating processes.[1] We discuss commutative steps, the transaction model, the use of passed access permissions, and the use of monitor program modules. The choice of the model affects the system's structure, its implementation, how it is programmed, and the proofs of its logical properties.

The Sharing Supervisor. For pedagogical reasons, we introduce the notion of a *sharing supervisor*, a mechanism that supervises the progress of the system's processes in such a manner that all sharing protocols are obeyed. For the moment, we assume that there is a centralized sharing supervisor, even though this implementation strategy might not be wise. We assume that every sharing supervisor is designed so that (1) it does not introduce logical inconsistencies or nonfunctionality, (2) it does not introduce deadlocks, and (3) it does schedule tasks in a fair manner.

Later, we show that one can devise a distributed sharing supervisor that will support certain sharing schemes; other sharing schemes may require centralized support.

Commutative Steps. Sometimes one can prove functionality by working from the semantic properties of the computational modules within the system. For example, suppose that two modules perform computations that, if executed atomically, are commutative. If one starts with a functional schedule and interchanges the steps that activate those commutative modules without introducing any interleaving between them, one produces a different feasible schedule that gives functional behavior. Interchange arguments can help one understand the operation of some shared-resource coordination schemes. In particular, they help one understand the functionality of the transaction model that follows.

Example 8-2

Here are two commutative functions:

$$f_1(x) = x + 17 \tag{8-1}$$

$$f_2(x) = x - 100 \tag{8-2}$$

For any x, the result of performing these functions in either f_1f_2 or f_2f_1 order[2] is

$$x - 83.$$

---

[1] The use of a set of copies of an object is presented in Sec. 8.7.2.

[2] One must be careful about the interpretation of the ordering of the functions. Here we wrote the execution sequence, so that f_1f_2 means that f_1 is performed before f_2. But if the symbols were being used to express the mathematical use of the result of one functional computation as an argument of the other function, the order would be reversed: then f_1f_2 means $f_1(f_2)$, so that f_2 is performed first.

Atomic Actions. Example 8-1 contains some basic elements:

1. A shared object whose state can be read and written
2. Two processes executing programs that require reading and later rewriting a shared object, whose new state depends on information derived from the previous state of that shared object

It should be clear that the example's problems would disappear if each process could request exclusive access to S during its read–modify–write sequence. In other words, functional behavior could be achieved if each sharing process were able to perform certain critical operations (or operation sequences) in a transaction *atomically*, that is, without interference from any other process. In other words, it would be helpful to extend the notion of atomic actions from individual instructions to instruction sequences, or transactions. Conversely, after these boundaries are stated, the sharing supervisor should be free to schedule all statements (operations) outside transactions in any interleaved manner that is consistent with the other programming illusions.

Because there is no algorithmic way to determine transaction boundaries, linguistic structures and/or processor instructions that declare these boundaries must be supported within the system:

> **Declaration Requirement.** Every sharing program must specify the start and termination of each transaction that the program expects to behave as though it had been executed atomically (i.e., without interference from other processes).

Functional behavior is defined in terms of conformance with the information provided in the transaction declarations and the processor instructions that support these declarations. This information conveys the scope of the sharing and the intervals during which access to the shared objects should be restricted.

If a transaction specification is incorrect, the program may be nonfunctional, but that difficulty is not the responsibility of the implementation. The implementation is, however, responsible for supporting the transaction semantics. Transactions occur at many levels of system activity, ranging from complex transactions involving distributed databases to simple ones involving binary lock objects.

Under the transaction model, the execution history of each sharing process can be broken into time intervals, each either a transaction or an introverted sequence.

> **Definition.** A *transaction* by process P_1 includes access to one or more shared objects. During the transaction, no other process may change the state of any of the shared objects accessed by P_1 during its transaction.

If we want functional behavior, all actions that change the state of any shared object must be included within some transaction, because otherwise the schedule could include unprotected reads and writes, leading to interprocess interference that results in nonfunctional behavior. Outside specified transactions, processes are free to perform arbitrary actions that do not access the state of any shared objects; this behavior cannot affect system functionality. These intervals are also important in our discussion, so we name them:

> **Definition.** An *introverted sequence* is a block (contiguous in program order) of a program that is not within a transaction and during which the process does not access or modify the state of any shared object.

Because a program executing an introverted sequence does not access shared objects, interprocess interactions are not at issue during an introverted sequence. By contrast, the results obtained from a computation performed within a transaction may depend on the values in shared objects. Our goal is to design and implement the system so that every transaction executed by P appears to have been performed atomically. Thus, transaction boundaries specify limits on interprocess interactions and on accesses to shared objects, and they correspond to boundaries of noninterference between processes.

Transaction Specification Schemes.   The following schemes illustrate various ways to specify the transaction structure within a program. The way we talk about transactions may be influenced by the way that we view the underlying implementation.

Under the *first transaction scheme*, the implementation guarantees that no sharing process other than P_1 will access any shared object during the execution of a transaction being performed by P_1. In a program under this scheme, each transaction is bracketed with special delimiters or marked with a keyword; our syntax will be

```
transaction {      //not C++
      ..
};
```

The sharing supervisor must prevent any transaction interleaving by forcing a process to wait if it is about to start a transaction while another transaction is being processed. If all transactions are commutative, it should be clear that the system will behave in a functional manner if this exclusion condition is satisfied. The major difficulty with this scheme is that the exclusion imposes a very tight constraint on the schedule because it prevents simultaneous progress of two or more transactions even if they do not access the same or related shared objects.

The *second transaction scheme* permits more parallel activity. This scheme is based on the observation that two transactions in different processes can execute in parallel if no shared object is accessed by both transactions. Under the second scheme, a program's transaction specification lists the shared objects that will be accessed during the transaction; we use the following syntax:

transaction(<shared_name_list>) {   //not C++

       ..

};

During program execution, the sharing supervisor can determine whether a new transaction can be initiated by comparing its shared name list against the shared name lists of all transactions in process at the time.

In the *third transaction scheme*, the transaction declaration specifies the type of access that the program desires to make to each shared object. If shared object S is only read during transaction T_1, then there is no reason why another transaction T_2, that only reads S, should not be allowed to execute in parallel with T_1. After all, reading the value does not change the contents, so it does not interfere with the other process. However, if T_2 is going to write a new value into S, then T_2 cannot be permitted to execute while T_1 is in progress, for otherwise S's value, as seen by T_1, changes. Under this scheme, the program's transaction specification lists the shared objects and the type of access desired to each object, as in

transaction(x : **read**; y : **write**; z : **read**, **write**) {   //Not C++

       ..

};

This specification defines the *read set* and the *write set* of the transaction. The empty intersection condition (see Sec. 6.1) determines whether two transactions interfere with each other. The sharing supervisor can permit a process to enter a transaction if the empty intersection condition is satisfied between the new transaction and (individually) every other transaction that is being processed.

Example 8-3

Table 8-1 specifies the read and write sets of six transactions. The following pairs of transactions can execute simultaneously because they satisfy the empty intersection condition: (A, B), (C, D), (D, F), and (E, F). Note that the relation "can execute simultaneously" is not transitive.

Figure 8-3 illustrates several different execution histories of the processes executing the transactions. The histories in Figures 8-3a and 8-3b are serializable, whereas the history in Figure 8-3c is not serializable. For functional behavior, the schedule of Figure 8-3c must be prohibited.

Passed Capabilities.   Our second object-sharing model uses *capability passing* to control and coordinate accesses to shared objects. A capability C_i describes a resource R_i and specifies a set of access rights AR_i governing whether

TABLE 8-1　SOME TRANSACTIONS AND THEIR
READ AND WRITE SETS (see Example 8-3)

Transaction	Read Set	Write Set
A	P, Q, R	T
B	P, Q	S
C	Q, S	T
D	R	P
E	S, T	P
F	S, T	Q

the possessor of the capability is permitted to make an access of a specific type to the object described by the capability. If process P_k possesses C_i, it may access R_i subject to the access limits specified by AR_i. If P_k does not possess C_i, it cannot access R_i. For the moment, assume that capabilities cannot be duplicated. Then two processes share R_i by passing C_i among themselves. Two actions are required to completely pass C_i from P_j to P_k: (1) P_j grants C_i to P_k and (2) P_k takes C_i. Because these take and grant operations are the basis for interprocess coordination in this scheme, it is called a "take–grant" scheme. Ways to reason about take–grant schemes are presented in Appendix L.

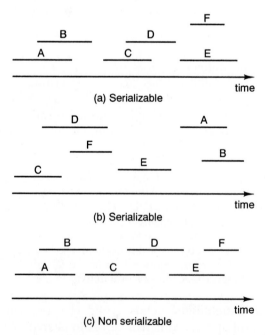

(a) Serializable

(b) Serializable

(c) Non serializable

Figure 8-3　Some transaction schedules

Monitors. Our third model of resource sharing encapsulates each shared resource within a monitor,[3] which is a software module that hides the contents of a shared object and coordinates all accesses to that object. One could implement a monitor as a C++ class that both performs operations on the value in the object and properly coordinates accesses from the sharing processes. Procedures within the monitor determine the semantics of interprocess interactions through the particular shared object managed by the monitor. To reason about a system using monitors, we must prove some properties of the monitors themselves. As an aside, note that if a monitor may determine the identity of the process that called it, the monitor can be programmed to behave like a take–grant system.

8.2.4 Comments

The models we presented in this section typify most high-level models of object sharing. We illustrate their implementation and use in this chapter.

8.3 SHARING IN HIGH-LEVEL LANGUAGES

We need ways to express shared-resource coordination rules if the language's resource naming rules may make a resource accessible from several tasks (and thus make it shared). In this section, we see how a resource might become accessible from several different processes; understanding these possibilities leads to an understanding of implementation options. Then we will explore some techniques used to specify coordination of shared-resource usage.

8.3.1 How Several Processes May Have Access to a Shared Resource

Here are three ways that two processes may come to have access to a common resource:

1. Common nested blocks
2. Parameters passed by reference
3. Common external objects

Common Nested Blocks. Two processes executing in the same nested execution environment share memory objects instantiated in a common encompassing block.

---

[3]   Monitors were introduced in [HOAR74].

Example 8-4

```
procedure f( .. ) is
    a, b, c : integer;
    T : task;                            //Not Ada or C++
    procedure g( w, x : integer ) is     //g is statically nested inside f
        d, e : integer;
    begin
        ..
    end g;
    procedure h( u, v : integer ) is     //h is statically nested inside f
    begin
        ..
    end h;
begin
    ..
    g( b, c + 4 ) task( T );             //Not Ada or C++
    ..
    h( b, c );
    ..
end f;
```

In this PL/1-style program routine g is called for execution as a child task[4] from the task executing f. The child task will be managed by the operating system as an independent process. If the system has several processors, both the "parent" process (executing f) and the "child" process (executing g) could be running simultaneously. In this program, after g is called as a separate task, the calling instantiation of f and the new instantiation of g share the objects a, b, c, and T as a consequence of static nesting rules. The data objects visible when the parent has called h are illustrated in Figure 8-4.

Parameters by Reference. A parent process P and its child process Q share memory object M through a reference parameter if a parameter reference from Q can access M and P can directly name M. This situation may arise if Q's parameters are passed from process P by reference or by name.

Example 8-5

```
void f( int x ) {
    int a, b, c,    *d, *e;
    task T;                              //Not Ada or C++
    d = new int;
    e = new int;
    ..
    T = create g( d, e );                //Not Ada or C++
    fork T;                              //start T as an independent process
    ..
}
```

---

[4]   This tasking is specified by the appearance of the word "task" in the call statement.

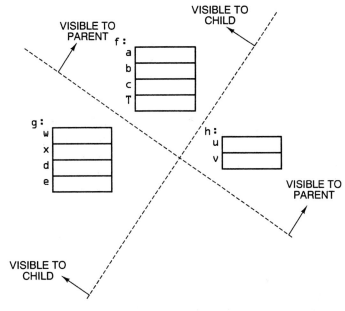

Figure 8-4   Data shared by nesting

```
void g( int *u, *v ) {
    ..
}
```

In this program, the same memory object is accessed as d from the parent process executing f and as u from the child process executing g. This shared object has different names when referenced from the two processes. The data structures are shown in Figure 8-5.

An object may be shared through parameter passing even though the processes do not share any activation records. Thus, a static analysis of the program's behavior cannot detect this condition.

Common External Objects.   The third method for sharing resources is through access to common external objects, such as files in the file system. It may seem that this sharing technique is really identical to sharing through block nesting, using the view that all external objects are included in an outer block that surrounds all programs active in the system. Although this view is technically correct, it is not very useful—common global objects are declared together and comprise a known set, and linguistic rules can be devised to require that those variables that are going to be shared be so declared. On the other hand, an

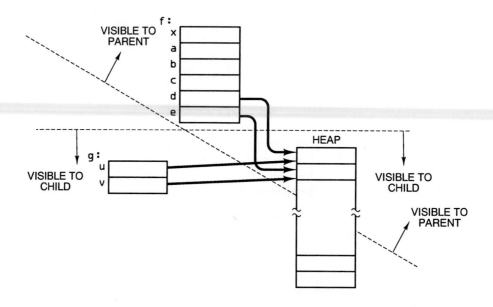

Figure 8-5   Operand sharing caused by parameters
passed by reference

external object may be accessible to any program in the system, and there is no
realistic way to force programmers to make a declaration of the sharing limits on
the object. Because two programs may share a file because their users happened
to designate the same file as a run-time parameter, it is impossible to determine
before program execution whether two processes do, in fact, share an external
object.

8.3.2 Synchronization Specifications

The processes that share access to a resource must coordinate their use of the resource to ensure functional system behavior. In this section, we review several
techniques that have been used or proposed for such specifications.

There are two basic approaches—access limitation and transaction validation.[5] Under either approach, every sharing process is divided into a set of

---

[5]   This use of the term "transaction" is not consistent with our previous use of the term. This ambiguity is present in the literature on these subjects. In this context, we define a transaction in terms of the
behavior of the program executing the transaction. In the previous interpretation, the word
"transaction" identified a program block that is to be executed under a guarantee that certain interactions with other processes would not occur.

transactions. Within each transaction, some data value consistency may be demanded or ensured. Each transaction is designed so that it performs correctly if the system limits access to shared resources in accordance with the specifications for the duration of the transaction.

Here are five specification techniques based on access limitation:

1. Region constructs
2. ACQUIRE and FREE operations
3. Semaphore objects
4. Capability access control
5. Monitors

Each of these techniques can be adapted to specify both the objects being shared and the access limitations required for "correct" program behavior. The access limitation may be as follows:

1. No other process may make any access to the object.
2. Other processes can read, but not write, the object.
3. Other processes can either read or write the object.

Under the first limitation, the process imposing the limitation obtains exclusive use of the object and may write into the object. The second limitation is appropriate if the process wishes to read the object and demands consistency in the value held there—thus, no other process may write to the object. In the third limitation, the executing process wishes merely to read the value at one time instant and does not require that the value be maintained for any time afterwards.[6]

Transaction validation is the second basic approach to synchronization. Under this approach, a transaction is initiated without any assurance that the executing process does have the desired access rights or that any mechanism has excluded accesses from other processes to the shared resource(s). Under the optimistic assumption that it is unlikely that another process will interfere with the transaction, the process attempts to execute the transaction without prior checking or locking. It does check for consistency at the conclusion of the transaction, and stores the results of the transaction's actions only if the consistency check succeeds. The implementation of this version of a transaction requires a short validation protocol on entry to the transaction and a longer consistency check upon transaction completion. Because the transaction validation approach amounts to taking a gamble, there is some chance that the transaction will experience interference—in this case, it will have to be restarted and tried again. The optimistic transaction approach is similar to branch prediction schemes; all try to guess the outcome. They will provide benefits if the gamble wins frequently. But in case the gamble loses, the system must compensate for any activity that took place after the incorrect guess was chosen. The transaction view can be applied

---

[6]   The third case can cause difficulty for functionality proofs, but does permit implementation flexibility.

to region constructs, the first among the methods for specifying access imita-
tions. The difference between transactions and regions will become apparent
when we discuss their implementations in Section 8.4.

Region Constructs.   The **region** construct permits limited compile-time
checking for correct shared resource usage. Limited compile-time checking is not
possible with other synchronization specification techniques, because they do
not impose sufficiently structured usage patterns.

The simple **region** statement contains a body (which is a statement list)
and a list of all shared resources to which access will be required during the execution of the **region**'s body. A possible syntax is

```
region ( <shared_resource_list> ) {        //not C++
       <statement_list>;
};
```

The semantics require that the executing process P obtain exclusive access
to all listed resources during the execution of the statements within the region. If
the requested exclusive accesses cannot be granted at the beginning of the **region,** P will be blocked until some other process has freed resources that it has
been using, thus permitting process P to enter its **region.**

Example 8-6

This program fragment specifies exclusive use of the object mailbox into which this
process will insert a message.

```
region ( mailbox ) {                        //Not C++
       mailbox.message = message_to_send;
};
```

Some useful variations on the **region** construct allow the programmer to
state the types of access required within the region; such variations were introduced in Section 8.2.

An important variation of the **region** construct is the *conditional critical region.* A conditional critical region behaves just like a **region,** except that there is a
Boolean condition specified in the **region** statement that must be true before the region can be entered. If the condition is not met when process P attempts to enter
the region, P is blocked. Process P can be unblocked after some other process has
accessed one or more objects whose state affects the Boolean condition. When
the process is awakened, it tests the Boolean condition again. If the condition is
satisfied, the region is entered. If the condition remains unsatisfied, P is blocked
again. Here is a syntax for the conditional critical region:

```
region ( <name_list> ) when ( <boolean> ) {     //Not C++
       ..
};
```

Regions may be nested. By using nesting, the program can be written to minimize the time that a process holds access to each shared resource while remaining consistent with functional system behavior. If nesting were not allowed, all shared resources used anywhere in the **region** must be acquired at the beginning of the **region**. The block structure requires that all resources acquired at the beginning of a **region** be held until the end of the **region**. If **region** nesting is allowed, a **region** can be nested to establish a shorter duration of restricted access, thereby reducing the number of scheduling constraints. The major logical difficulty with **region** nesting is that nesting permits deadlocks.

Example 8-7

Process A	Process B
region(a, b) {	**region**(c, d) {
..	..
region(c) {	**region**(b, e) {
..	..
};	};
..	..
};	};

The processes will deadlock if the execution sequence is

1. A locks a and b.
2. B locks c and d.

Now neither process can enter its nested **region**.

One way to remove the deadlock possibility is to restrict the order in which resources can be locked. Placing the shared resources in an ordered hierarchy will avoid all deadlocks. In the hierarchy scheme, every shared resource is assigned a level number; we use 1 to denote the level containing resources that can be locked for the longest intervals. Resources with higher level numbers are lockable for progressively shorter intervals. Here is the basic hierarchy rule:

> **Region Hierarchy Rule.** A **region** cannot be entered if the executing process holds any locked resource whose level number is equal to or greater than the lowest level number assigned to any resource on the list associated with the **region** being entered.

This hierarchy rule is sufficient to avoid all deadlocks and yet does permit flexible operation. Note that one must know about all shared resources and their usage patterns to assign each resource to a level in such a manner as to satisfy the hierarchy rule while minimizing scheduling constraints.

Some terminology is useful to help us discuss the behavior of systems with resource hierarchies concisely. We say that process P is *operating at locking level j* if it has locked some resource at level j but has not locked any resource at any

TABLE 8-2 ASSIGNMENT OF
LEVELS TO OBJECTS

Name	Locking Level
a	1
b	2
c .	3
d	4

level $k > j$. The region hierarchy rule states that a process P operating at locking level j cannot lock any resource at any level less than or equal to j. If process P attempts to lock any resource at level k and is placed in a wait state, we say that P is *waiting at level k*.

Example 8-8

To prevent deadlocks in the programs presented in Example 8-7, we assign resource levels. We choose the assignment shown in Table 8-2. With this assignment and the previous versions of the processes, the attempt by process B to lock object b is illegal, because when process B reaches that lock statement, it will be executing at locking level 4, and object b is assigned to level 2. Therefore, B's program will have to be changed to be consistent with the resource hierarchy rule. A simple change extends the interval during which B holds access to b, as in the following:

Process A	Process B
region(a, b) {	**region**(b, c, d) {
..	..
region(c) {	**region**(e) {
..	..
};	};
..	..
};	};

We can prove that a resource hierarchy rule guarantees the absence of deadlocks by using a "waiting graph" $W(t)$ that depicts the waiting state of the system at time t. The nodes of the waiting graph correspond to processes, and its branches correspond to waiting relationships among processes. There is a node for every process that exists at time t. There is a branch from node P to node Q if and only if process P is waiting for process Q at time t. If the system has a deadlocked set of processes, the waiting graph must contain a cycle.

Example 8-9

Figure 8-6 illustrates the waiting graph for the processes of Example 8-7 when their deadlock is reached.

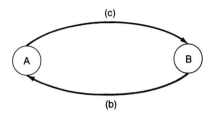

Figure 8-6   A cyclic waiting graph implies a deadlock

Now we argue that there cannot be any cycles in the waiting graph if re-source hierarchy locking is enforced. Consider the relationship between the lock-ing levels of the processes at the endpoints of a branch in the waiting graph. In particular, consider a waiting graph path leading from node P to node Q to node R (see Figure 8-7). The branches in the path indicate that P is waiting for some re-source X that is held by Q. In turn, Q is waiting for another resource Y that is held by R. Let k be the locking level of Y. Because Q is waiting for Y, it is waiting at level k, and any objects it holds are at levels lower than k. Because Q holds X, the level of X must be less than the level of Y. Thus, the waiting level of P is less than k, the waiting level of Q. We see that the waiting levels must increase along any branch in the waiting graph, and, therefore, along any path of any length. Because levels must increase along a path, and a cycle is a closed path, there can-not exist a cycle in the waiting graph, and therefore there cannot be a deadlock in the system. QED.

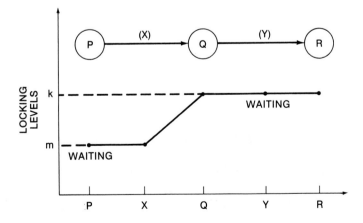

Figure 8-7   Levels along a path in the waiting graph

Separate ACQUIRE and FREE. The **region** construct allows nesting and permits static checking of program correctness (to check whether a shared resource is only accessed from within a **region**). Additionally, the **region** construct can be implemented efficiently and gives freedom from deadlock if hierarchical resource numbering is used. One disadvantage of the **region** construct is that the block structuring forces the process to retain an object to the end of the **region** in which it was acquired. This interval may be longer than absolutely necessary. Thus, even though the programmer may know that the process will not access some resource, he cannot make the resource available to other processes until the end of the **region**'s block.

To separate control over acquisition from control over relinquishment, ACQUIRE and FREE statements can be introduced. The ACQUIRE statement's single argument is a list of the resources to be acquired.[7] The implementation guarantees that all resources on the list will be available to the process when the ACQUIRE is completed. If any one is not available, the process waits until all become available. The FREE statement's single argument is a resource list; all the named resources are FREEd. Notice that an ACQUIRE-FREE pair with matching lists is *almost* equivalent to a **region**; the difference lies in the program-structuring implications of the **region** construct.

Separating the ACQUIRE and FREE statements provides more flexibility than the **region** construct and might reduce the probability of a process having to wait to obtain access to shared resources. This flexibility comes at a cost. One is that a compiler no longer can provide any guarantees concerning the use of shared resources. In fact, no algorithmic test can guarantee even that a resource that has been ACQUIREd will eventually be FREEd. The difficulty is that the process' execution sequence may be data-dependent, and either pass through or around a FREE operation. In contrast, the **region**'s block structure always guarantees this important property for objects accessed directly from the body of the block. Other process properties might be checked automatically when **region** specifications are used, but become difficult, if not impossible, to check if the unstructured ACQUIRE-FREE pair is used to specify access limitations. Among these properties are the following:

1. Is a set of sharing processes free from deadlock?
2. Is every attempt to access a shared object preceded by acquisition of the proper access rights?

Note that whereas checking these properties with ACQUIRE-FREE is impossible, checking them with **region**s is not trivial, due to the possibility of calling a subroutine from within the **region**.

---

[7]   An alternate design including a specification of the access modes could be used.

Two-Phase Locking. Two-phase locking (2PL) is often claimed to be the solution to many problems related to shared objects. The two phases are the locking and releasing aspects of a transaction. In two-phase locking, all locking precedes all FREEing. Although this discipline is not sufficient to guarantee all desirable properties of a locking scheme, it does reduce the deadlock problems. Certainly, combining 2PL with a lock hierarchy will remove any possibility of deadlock from the system.

Semaphore Objects. A semaphore is a flag object used to limit the progress of processes past certain checkpoints in the program. The program correctness relies on correct programming. In particular, a process desiring to access a shared resource R must obtain access permission by successfully performing certain prescribed semaphore operations before accessing R. Then the process must perform other semaphore operations when the access is complete.

The two basic operations on a semaphore S are P(S) and V(S).[8] The P(S) call is used to obtain permission to proceed, and V(S) is called to relinquish this permission, permitting another process to pass the P(S) test. The functions P and V are defined to assure that only one process can be executing in any block bracketed by P(S) and V(S), for the same S. The effects of P(S) and V(S) are identical to ACQUIRE(R) and FREE(R), respectively, except for the interpretation of the operand; a shared resource (R) is directly named in the ACQUIRE call, and a semaphore (S) is named in the P call. The association between S and the set of resources to which it controls access is a programming convention; the compiler cannot verify correct semaphore usage unless it knows the S–R association used by the programmer.

Two semaphore generalizations can be useful. The first extends the P operation to a set of semaphores, and the second extends the resources controlled by a semaphore to include a set of interchangeable resources.

The *set-extended* P operation has a list of semaphore names as its operand; the system ensures that all of the specified (set of) semaphore tests succeed before the executing process may proceed. A set version of V is not logically necessary, because the effect is the same as the effect of a sequence of calls to a version of V that frees a single resource on each call.

A *generalized semaphore* coordinates shared accesses to a set of functionally interchangeable resources. Whereas the basic semaphore permits at most one process to be executing within the set of controlled program segments, the generalized semaphore permits up to n processes to be executing within the controlled segments, where n is the initial value within the semaphore object. Disk drives on which user disk packs can be mounted are logically equivalent because any drive can handle any user disk. Therefore, the system could allow users to

---

[8]   The names are initials for the Dutch words meaning "pass" and "free;" semaphores were invented by Dijkstra, a Dutchman [DIJK68b].

lock disk drives interchangeably until all drives are allocated. A simple sema-phore cannot directly handle the allocation, because it can represent the status of only one copy of the resource.[9]

Capability Access Control.   In this access control scheme, cooperating processes pass around one or several capabilities that contain permission to ac-cess a shared resource.

> **Definition.** A *capability* is an object that contains both a description
> of another object and information limiting the operations permitted
> upon the object.

A simple coherent capability-based system uses the following two rules: (1) The fact that process P possesses C, a capability describing resource R, means that P has permission to access R in accordance with the access rights in C; and (2) a "correctly programmed" process does not retain a copy of capability C after it passes C to another process. Only one process at a time can access the resource described by C; the processes use **send** and **receive** to move a capability from one process to another in the same manner that a message can be passed.

A more practical capability-based design uses these rules: (1) Process P cannot use capability C to access R until after P has issued a specific "load C" com-mand; and (2) P's permission to use C to access R terminates when P issues a "remove C" command. Under these rules, several processes may hold simultane-ously unloaded capabilities for R; the important operations are load/unload plus copy and restrict_access_rights. Figure 8-8 illustrates one way under this scheme to build data structures leading from a virtual address to an object. We return to this model in Section 9.5.1.

Monitors.   A monitor encapsulates a set of shared resources within a mod-ule similar to a C++ class. We make the shared resource invisible outside the class, so all direct accesses to the resource must originate from instructions within the monitor class. Therefore, the monitor routines can be designed to con-trol and synchronize all accesses to the shared resource. Although this construct is fine for accesses to single shared resources, it must be modified to support transactions involving sets of shared resources.

To impose a monitor structure on a transaction-based design, one must make an a priori assignment of shared resource sets to monitors.[10] Otherwise, the monitor must allow a process to acquire access rights and hold them, while

---

[9]   A single semaphore could be used to control access to a data structure that itself contains a list of status information about the set of resources.

[10]   This might not be possible, since each resource must be confined to a single monitor; if this were not the case, the single monitor would not be able to control all accesses to the object, except by insert-ing an artificial flag and a monitor at each individual resource.

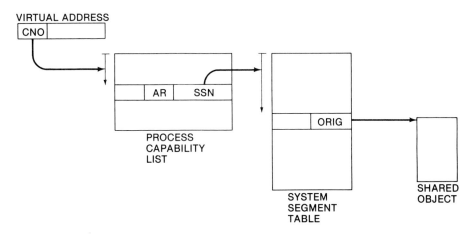

Figure 8-8   Access rights from a process capability list

excluding other interfering transactions. This behavior is analogous to the behavior of a monitor structure handling locklike objects.

8.3.3 Comments

We have seen several ways that processes may share access to common resources and several ways that the programmer may specify the access restrictions and/or checks that will guarantee proper coordination. A general question that influences the choices among different synchronization techniques concerns the number of low-level implementation details that are made visible at higher specification levels. If more structure is required (by hiding lower-level primitive operations), flexibility is reduced, but so is the possibility of making errors by misusing the primitives. However, the structural requirements may force shared objects to be locked for longer intervals than would be required if lower-level primitives were made available. Deadlocks can be reduced or removed from the scheme by imposing additional structural constraints. Finally, the choice of the specification primitives also determines the location of the responsibility and trust for logically correct behavior.

Notice the strong parallels between the high-level specifications and the general specification methods discussed in Section 8.2. In the next two sections we present some alternative methods for implementing the access restrictions and/or checks that we have been discussing.

It is important to note that there are two complementary sides to this: an *optimistic* one and a *pessimistic* one. Under the optimistic view the sharing processes use some prescribed method to coordinate their resource usage under the assumption that other processes will not interfere with the choreographed coordination. This view is consistent with the "everything correct" design approach; it emphasizes the *access rights* needed by the sharing processes. On the other hand, the pessimistic view is that every program is suspicious, so everything must be checked. The pessimistic view emphasizes *access exclusion*.

8.4 SHARING AMONG COOPERATING PROCESSES

How does one implement the programming mechanisms that specify and support correct sharing? We cover four sharing mechanisms:

1. Semaphores
2. Monitors
3. Regions
4. Transactions

Certain sharing features must appear in correctly programmed processes that share objects; we discuss building these implementations using semaphores, which therefore assume the role of a synchronization primitive. Thus, we discuss the implementation of semaphores first.

8.4.1 Semaphore Implementations

In writing programs, we use the keyword **atomic** to designate an indivisible (compound) statement. While a process is executing the **atomic** statement, no other process can manipulate any objects accessed within the statement.

Our first implementation of the semaphore class uses an integer[11] variable (L) that is zero when the semaphore is locked and 1 when it is free. Because the initial semaphore is free, L is initialized to 1. The P and V procedures lock and free the semaphore. Here is the semaphore class definition:

```
class semaphore {
public:
    void P( semaphore S ) {
        wait: atomic {                    //uses busy waiting
            if ( S.L <= 0 ) goto wait;
            S.L = S.L - 1;
        };
    }
    void V( semaphore S ) { S.L = S.L + 1 }
private:
    int L = 1;          //the counter inside – initialized to "free"
};
```

---

[11] In this usage, the variable acts like a Boolean, but later we generalize the semaphore, making a design that requires an integer in this role.

If the indivisibility requirement covering the statements within the atomic statement is violated, more than one process may be able to pass through P(S). This scenario results in several processes all behaving as though each one has exclusive access to the objects controlled by the semaphore object.

The waiting loop within the body of P cannot be placed inside the atomic statement, because while one process is waiting for the V operation, other processes must be allowed to execute and thus eventually to call V(S), freeing the semaphore. The implementation is written so that once in each cycle through the wait loop, the waiting process comes to the point labeled "wait," which is outside the atomic region; there the waiting process can be interrupted and another process can access S.

The loop within P wastes processor time and memory accesses in *busy waiting*. The busy waiting can be eliminated by changing the implementation so that the semaphore object interacts with the system's process scheduler. We simply block any process waiting for a semaphore to be freed. The process can be moved back to the ready list once the semaphore is freed. A blocked process can be "parked" on a queue of waiting processes within the representation of the semaphore object. Here is a second implementation of the semaphore class, using process queueing to eliminate busy waiting:

```
class semaphore {
public:
        void P( semaphore S ) {
                goto test;
                wait: queue_self( que );
                test: atomic {
                        if ( S.lock <= 0 ) goto wait;
                        S.lock = S.lock - 1;
                }
        }
        void V( semaphore S ) {
                S.lock = S.lock + 1;
                make_ready( unqueue( que ) );
        }
private:
        int lock = 1;
        queue_of_processes que;
};
```

The procedures queue_self, unqueue, and make_ready are system scheduler functions. The first changes the scheduling state of the executing process, removing it from the ready state and placing it on the queue specified in its parameter. The second function removes one process description from the waiting queue specified in its parameter, returning the process description as the result. If the

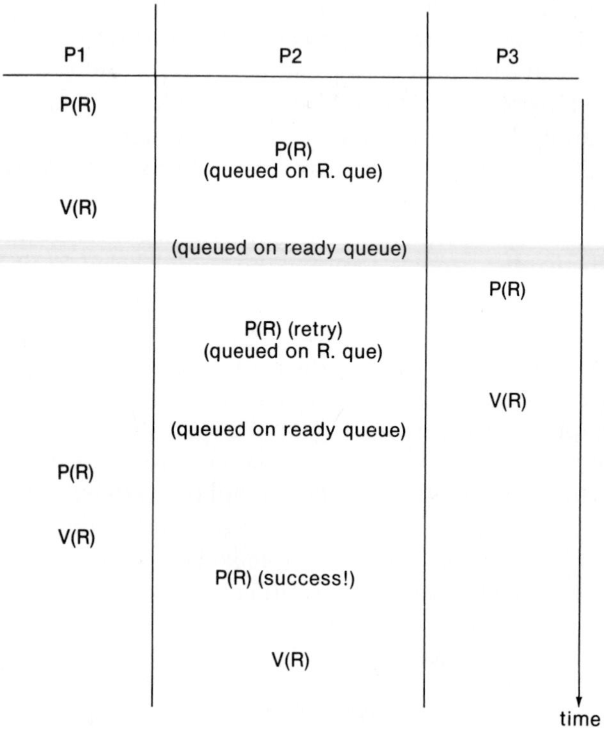

P1	P2	P3
P(R)		
	P(R) (queued on R. que)	
V(R)		
	(queued on ready queue)	
		P(R)
	P(R) (retry) (queued on R. que)	
		V(R)
	(queued on ready queue)	
P(R)		
V(R)		
	P(R) (success!)	
	V(R)	

time

Figure 8-9   An event scenario with semaphores

waiting queue is empty, no process description is returned. The third procedure takes its argument process and adds it to the ready queue.[12]

In either semaphore implementation, the requesting process does not see the waiting, whether it is busy waiting or sitting on the scheduling queue.

It is possible that a process be denied a pass through the P operation due to unfortunate timing. Consider this example of unfair system behavior.

Example 8-10

Three processes, P1, P2, and P3, share access to resources covered by the single semaphore R. The chart in Figure 8-9 illustrates one possible event sequence, with the scheduling states for process P2 are described in parentheses. The other processes are running (or ready) continuously.

The scenario of Figure 8-9 is unfair in that P2 requested the semaphore before P3, but was not allowed to pass until after P3 has completed its access to the controlled region. The scenario shown in Figure 8-10 illustrates a more serious effect, causing P2 to be foiled at all of its attempts to successfully pass P(R).

---

[12]   This action does not have to cause process suspension; the decision whether to suspend the executing process in favor of the newly ready one depends on the scheduling policy, the priorities of the processes, and other scheduling parameters.

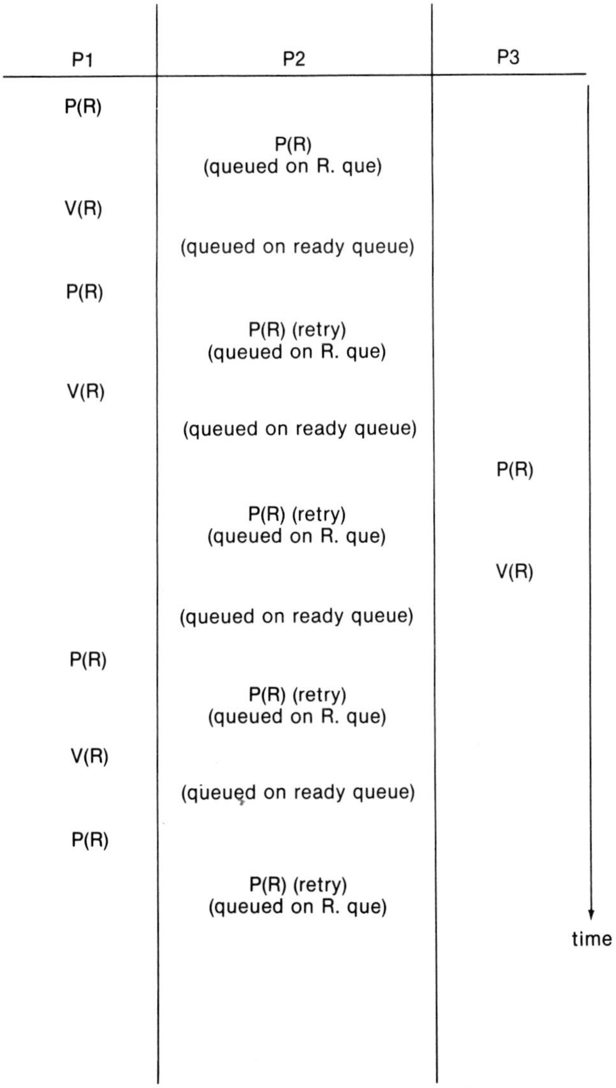

P1	P2	P3
P(R)		
	P(R) (queued on R. que)	
V(R)		
	(queued on ready queue)	
P(R)		
	P(R) (retry) (queued on R. que)	
V(R)		
	(queued on ready queue)	
		P(R)
	P(R) (retry) (queued on R. que)	
		V(R)
	(queued on ready queue)	
P(R)		
	P(R) (retry) (queued on R. que)	
V(R)		
	(queued on ready queue)	
P(R)		
	P(R) (retry) (queued on R. que)	

time

Figure 8-10   A second event scenario with semaphores

It may seem that this example shows that the implementation of P(R) is unfair. Actually, the problem in the scenario arises from interactions between the process queues inside the semaphore and inside the scheduler. Neither the scheduler nor the semaphore is, by itself, unfair.

List Semaphores. Now consider the implementation of generalized semaphore operations that handle a list of resources. The basic requirement for this type of generalized semaphore is that all resources on the list should be locked before the process passes through the P operation. Notice that the P operation with a list argument cannot be implemented by an algorithm that goes through the resource list, executing a P operation with a single operand for each resource on the operand list. The difficulty with this strategy is that any of the indivisible P operations might queue the executing process if the semaphore associated with the resource cannot be passed. If this combination occurs, the attempt to pass the list semaphore will succeed in locking part of the list before encountering a locked semaphore that queues the executing process. Then some resources on the list are locked while the process waits. This can lead to a deadlock. The following program fragment illustrates the (almost) correct semantics of the P operation (see Problem 8-13).

```
class semaphore {
public:
      int lock  = 1;
      queue_of_processes que;
};
void P( semaphore *X, int n ) {
      int k;
again: for ( int i = 0, i < n, ++i ) {
            atomic {
                  if ( X[ i ].lock == 0 ) {
                        k = i;
                        goto unloop;
                  }
                  else
                        X[ i ].lock = 0;
            };                    //end of the atomic block
      }
      return;                //it all got locked here!
unloop:    for ( int j = 0, j < k - 1, ++j ) {
      V( X[ j ] );         //this may free other processes
      queue_self( X[ k ].que );    //wait on the one that was locked
      goto again;          //back to try again
}
```

Counting Semaphores. The counting semaphore permits up to a preset (maximum) number of processes to pass into the critical regions based on the same semaphore at the same time. We simply represent the semaphore's state with a counter whose value denotes the number of free instances of the resource. The detailed programs are almost identical to the programs for the simple semaphore, except that the semaphore class has to be parameterized by the initial value of the resource count.

8.4.2 Monitor Implementations

The implementation of a monitor must assure that at most one process is executing within the monitor at any time. Within the implementation we use a simple semaphore to control access to the externally visible functions within the monitor. The following example illustrates this technique.

Example 8-11

The following class structure behaves as a monitor.

```
class mon {
private:
    semaphore mon_semaphore;
public:
    void f( int x, y, z ) {
        P( mon_semaphore );
        ..                        //functional part of f in here
        V( mon_semaphore );
    }
    void g( int x, z ) {
        P( mon_semaphore );
        ..                        //functional part of g in here
        V( mon_semaphore );
    }
    void h( int x, y ) {
        P( mon_semaphore );
        ..                        //functional part of h in here
        V( mon_semaphore );
    }
}
```

The monitor's synchronization control is independent of the functions being performed within the monitor. A well-formed monitor will conform to this structure, which will leave its internal state such that all later procedure calls can proceed normally.

8.4.3 Region Implementations

A simple **region** can be implemented in a manner similar to the implementation of the list variety of the P operation on semaphores.

Implementing a conditional critical region is more difficult; like the list version of the P semaphore operation, the entire set of objects on the region's list will have to be unlocked if any of them are found to be locked by other processes or if the region's entry condition is not met. How do we specify or choose the variable object on which the process should wait if the region's entry condition is not met. Because the system cannot predict which object's state will change to make it possible to meet the region's entry condition, we require that the programmer name (as a parameter of P) the object (or semaphore) on which the process should be queued in the event the region's entry condition is not met.

Here is the structure of a simple implementation of the guard for entering a conditional region with two locked objects; it uses list semaphore operations.

```
void guard( semaphore x, y ; boolean_function e ) {
again:      P( x, y )
        if ( e( ) ) return;        //items locked, evaluate condition, return if condition met
        V( x, y );
        queue_self( x.que );  //assumes that first variable is the one to wait on
        goto again;
    }
```

Exiting a conditional critical region is just like exiting a critical region.

Consider the following scenario involving a conditional critical region CCR(aa), with an implementation in which a process is queued on the object if the region cannot be entered. There are two processes, named R and S:

1. R attempts to enter CCR(aa) and fails (the entry condition is false).
2. R queues itself on aa.
3. S locks aa.
4. S unlocks aa without modifying it.
5. R is made ready (because S unlocked aa).
6. R attempts to enter CCR(aa) and fails (the condition is still false).

Notice two important things about this history: (1) When R queues itself on aa in step 2, the waiting queue for aa is empty, and aa is free; (2) the check at step 6 is bound to fail because the value of aa has not been changed. The first observation shows that even if an object is free, it may contain processes waiting for a state change. The second observation shows that unnecessary steps are executed if R is awakened but S has not modified aa.

To improve execution speed, it is helpful to know whether a process exiting the region did modify the controlled object.[13] If it did not, then it is certain that the condition has not changed, so any process waiting for a state change should remain queued. On the other hand, if the exiting process did modify the object, all processes waiting for their entry conditions to become true should be awakened.

---

[13]   We cannot know whether a write actually changed the contents, but we presume that any write did make a modification, and therefore awaken other waiting processes after a write has been performed within the region.

8.4.4 Transaction Implementations

Transactions are significantly different from semaphore or monitor implementations because before they initiate their activities, they do not check to assure that they can be executed without difficulty. The checks occur at the end, and the entire transaction will be restarted if the checks fail.

A typical approach to transaction implementation is the optimistic implementation of [KUNG81], which divides each transaction into four phases:

1. Read
2. Compute
3. Validate
4. Write (this is also called *commit*)

At the beginning of the *read phase*, the process obtains global synchronization information (used later to validate the transaction) and then makes local copies of all global (and local) objects that will be written during the transaction. One can write the new values into the global and local objects only after the transaction has been validated, so during the read phase, the process sets up a local shadow copy of all objects to which it might make write accesses during the transaction.

During the *compute phase*, the transaction performs its usual algorithm using the local object copies.

The *validate phase* checks whether the empty intersection property does hold between the transaction being completed and those that did complete during the execution of this transaction.

During the *write (or commit) phase*, the transaction stores the results of its computations and updates the validation information. To ensure that the writes and validation are synchronized, we use a global semaphore to encapsulate the validate and commit phases into a smaller (atomic) transaction. The global semaphore serializes the (atomic) commit phases of all transactions.

The validation scheme relies on a monotonically increasing global transaction number GTN, which records the progress of transaction completion. When transaction T is initiated, it records the current value of GTN; this value indicates which transactions have previously committed and therefore cannot have dependence relationships with T. As each transaction commits, it changes GTN and records (in a global list) the members of its write set (containing the names of the objects whose state was changed during the commit phase). Later, when T enters its validation phase, it locks the global semaphore that serializes execution of validation phases among all the transactions. Then T obtains the current GTN. If the transaction is validated, during its commit phase, it will take the next GTN as its number. Therefore, used GTNs correspond to completed transactions (that have performed their commits). Now the range of GTN values between T's

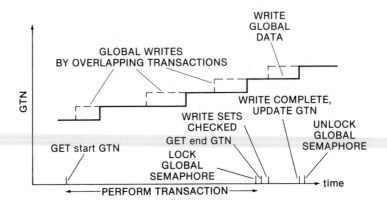

Figure 8-11   Illustrating the execution of a transaction
when global transaction numbers are used for
coordination

starting GTN and T's validation GTN corresponds to the set of transactions that
have written global data since T started its computation and before it entered its
validation and commit phases (see Figure 8-11). The system maintains a list of
GTNs and the corresponding write sets. The validation process checks for a null
intersection between T's read set and the write set of each transaction that wrote
data while T was in process. If all these intersections are null, T has been validated because it is known that no objects that T read were written to between the
time that T started its transaction (which is before it read them) and the time that
T wishes to commit its results to the global database. Once it has been validated,
the executing process can update the global state and then proceed beyond its
transaction. On the other hand, if any intersection is not null, T cannot be committed and must be retried at a later time.

This program fragment illustrates this strategy:

```
T:   start_trans_no = global_trans_no;      //start read phase; get GTN
     make_local_replicas_of_global_objects();
     make_local_replicas_of_local_objects(); //end read phase


        ..                                   //transaction body here; compute phase


     P(global_semaphore);                    //start validation phase
     end_trans_no = global_trans_no;         //get current GTN
     for ( int i = start_trans_no + 1, i <= end_trans_no, ++i ) {
         if ( intersection( T.read_set, write(i) ) != null )
             abort(T);                       //might count here; see text
     }                                       //end validate phase
```

```
update_data_base_from_shadow();    //start commit phase
update_local_objects_from_shadow();
this_trans_no = global_trans_no + 1;
global_trans_no = this_trans_no;
write(this_trans_no) = T.write_set;
V(global_semaphore);                        //end commit phase
```

The order of the object updates and the change to the global transaction number is critical to the success of the implementation strategy; this correctness relies on the ordering of the actions during the (unlocked) read phase. Another essential ingredient for the success of this implementation strategy is that the global transaction number is monotonically increasing, so it totally orders the validations and commit phases of all transactions.

If a transaction has to be aborted because the values read by the transaction have been modified by another intervening transaction, the process releases the global semaphore and branches to statement T to retry the complete transaction from the beginning. If there is a lot of activity accessing the same shared objects, this looping may continue indefinitely, effectively starving the process. If this occurrence is commonplace, the transaction model is not appropriate to the situation—in fact, the model was introduced to coordinate concurrent activity for environments in which there is infrequent overlap between transactions.

One could design the implementation to detect when a transaction is starved and to lock out all competing transactions while a process S that has been "snubbed" completes its entire transaction. To assure completion without interference, the global semaphore can be locked to prevent other processes from completing their transactions while S executes its transaction. To decide whether a process has been snubbed, the implementation could count the number of times that S has been forced to abort the same transaction. To implement this feature, one must add counter initialization before the transaction is entered (at statement T) and counter incrementation and testing where the abort is taken.

How does one reason about the properties of a system that uses this transaction model? The checking that validates the transaction verifies that there has been no change in the values of the objects in the read set of the transaction between the time that they were read and the time that the transaction is validated. Thus, the action of the transaction is the same as it would have been if it had been entirely executed within the validate–commit phases, when the global semaphore is locked. Thus, we can argue that the actual schedule is equivalent to a schedule in which all transactions are performed serially in the order of the global transaction numbers they obtained during their commit phases. So the system's behavior is equivalent to the behavior under a serialized schedule. Whether this produces correct behavior depends on the transaction's semantics (do they commute?). In addition, it depends on the correctness of the assumption that no process accessed the shared objects without obeying the transaction scenario.

8.4.5 Comments

All of the implementations that we showed rely on the ability to perform the P operation on a semaphore object. It appears that we have circularity—we can implement synchronization among a set of cooperating processes if we can implement synchronization among a set of cooperating processes (to perform P on a semaphore or to impose atomicity on an operation sequence)! There are two ways out of this bind—we can design the hardware to support uninterruptible operations or we can use complex software algorithms that are usually considered only for distributed computer systems (see [KOHL81] for a survey of these techniques). Dijkstra's original semaphore paper [DIJK68b] presented a software implementation that does not require any hardware support; unfortunately this software implementation used busy waiting. Thus, it is mainly of academic interest. An improved version of Dijkstra's algorithm can be found in [DORA80].

We move down to the implementation of atomic processor instructions that support functional behavior in distributed systems.

8.5 ATOMIC PROCESSOR INSTRUCTIONS

To properly coordinate the use of shared resources, the sharing processes must be able to perform atomic operations and transactions. In principle, all sharing can be coordinated by software schemes, but these are so inefficient that special processor instructions that support process synchronization and execute atomically are needed to support resource sharing. Efficient implementations of these instructions require hardware support to guarantee atomicity. Techniques used to effect such guarantees at the hardware level are discussed in the next section.

8.5.1 Simple Semaphore Support

A simple processor instruction for atomic synchronization performs the P operation on a simple semaphore object. This basic support must be coupled with correct software that manages process blocking and retry. The details depend on what the processor does if the semaphore cannot be locked. This choice affects the structure of the software that blocks a process when it is unable to lock the semaphore.

The simplest synchronization operation performs a P(S)-style operation on a bit in memory; this operation, often called "test and set," is available in many processors.

Example 8-12

The IBM 370 TESTANDSET operation sets the (memory) operand byte to all ones; the previous value of the operand's most significant bit is placed in the condition code register. With this design, the locking process is responsible for checking the previous lock value (from the condition code register) and not proceeding into the transaction if the lock was previously set.

Example 8-13

The HP 3000 atomic instruction has the usual memory operand X and a mask value M taken from the top of its stack. The result in the memory location is M OR X, and the result left on the top of the stack is M AND X. The net effect is that any of the bit positions selected by the mask will serve as a flag to signal that a lock has been set.

Example 8-14

The VAX processors include several atomic operations. The BBSSI and BBCCI instructions test a single bit in an operand. The BBSSI instruction sets the selected bit and branches to the location specified by a signed branch displacement if the bit was set beforehand. (Thus the branch occurs when the lock cannot be set.) The BBCCI instruction works similarly, but clears the bit.

An alternate design maintains control in the system by forcing an interrupt whenever the flag is set. Therefore, it is possible to correctly support simple semaphores at the system level. This approach runs into difficulties because the interpretation of the semaphore is coupled with the implementation buried within the operating system. For example, if a list locking attempt fails part way through the list, it is difficult to know how to correctly recover the semaphores from the list that were already locked.

Atomic operations with more complex semantics may be supported.

Example 8-15

The MC68020 supports two types of atomic operations—testandset and compare. Testandset is a byte operation using the sign bit as the lock. The previous value of the sign bit is left in the N and Z condition bits for later checking.

One (uninterruptible) compare operation has three operands: a memory location M, a compare value C, and an update value U. The processor first compares the (old) contents of M with C; the subtraction used to make that comparison determines the condition code settings. Then some value, selected by the truth of the predicate $c(M) = C$, is updated. If the predicate is true, U is stored in location M. If the predicate is false, the contents of M replace C. The application software is responsible for correctly testing the condition code or dealing with the updated values left by the compare instruction.

8.5.2 General Semaphore Support

One could support general atomic semaphore operations with an uninterruptible operation that adds an integer to the (integer) contents of a memory location.

The result is returned to the program for further checking. The atomic add operation corresponds to the P operation on generalized semaphores.

Example 8-16

> The VAX processors support uninterruptible adds to memory with the ADAWI (add aligned word, interlocked) instruction that performs an atomic add of one operand to the other, leaving the result's status in the processor's condition codes. The prior value of the sum operand is not available or checked.

Example 8-17

> The Ultracomputer design [GOTT83] includes an atomic add to memory that acts like the ADAWI VAX instruction. We cover its implementation later.

8.5.3 Load Locked/Store Conditional

This pair of instructions is designed to behave in a manner similar to the actions required at the beginning and end of a transaction. At the beginning of a transaction, the processor executes the load locked (LOADL) instruction, which copies a value from a memory location into a register and marks the memory region (see what follows) for this process, and sets its lock bit. Every other processor in the system should become aware of the marked memory region and notify the locking processor if its program writes to the locked region (such writes are permitted). The locking processor clears its lock bit when it hears that another processor has written to the locked block. When the locking processor reaches the end of its transaction region, it executes the store conditional (STOREC) instruction, which attempts to write into the same location (or region). The STOREC instruction is blocked if the lock flag is clear (because another processor has written into the region since the LOADL instruction completed). To make this operate correctly, at least the STOREC instruction must act as a barrier. A bit indicating whether the store succeeded is placed in a processor register.

Example 8-18

> The MIPS processors [KANE92] provide one of the first implementations of this construct; in these machines, the locked block comprises only the word that was written during the load instruction. The two instructions are called load linked (LL) and store conditional (SC). The bit indicating the success/failure of the store attempt replaces the operand in the register being stored during SC.

Example 8-19

> In the Alpha AXP processors, the operands for the locked load and store conditional are either longwords or quadwords. The size of the locked block is implementation dependent, but it must lie in the range from 8 words up to the size of a physical page of memory. The matching store does not have to access the same object as the initiating load instruction. The store instruction places the lock bit into the operand register. The varying (and therefore uncertain) granularity of the

locked blocks imposes space allocation constraints, which are described in advice that hardware designers should limit the range to not more than 128 bytes, and the software should leave a space of at least 128 bytes between any pair of locked locations that are supposed to behave as though they are noninteracting lock objects.

Due to the branch prediction schemes used in this processor, one should not place a backward conditional branch after the conditional store instruction, because the processor will predict that the backward branch will be taken, which is hopefully not the case (after all, we are being optimistic in this design). If the processor performs a memory operation other than the expected conditional store while the lock_flag is set, the test in the conditional store might always fail, so this pattern of instructions should not be used.

The conditional store operations are barriers. Because the addresses in the load and store operations might not exactly match, if you want to have the blocking be based on the set of locations, you must insert a memory barrier instruction to assure that memory coherence has been achieved before the store instruction can be allowed to proceed (see Section 8.8).

Most processors using locked/conditional pairs for synchronization restrict the actions that can be taken while the locked flag is set. In particular, system calls and interrupts usually clear out the flag when they are recognized. The Alpha AXP manual contains a specific warning about this—a timer interrupt will reset the locked flag, so that any program with a long processing time between the lock and store will fail.

Any implementation of this pair of operations must involve passing the effective physical address out of the processor module so it can be seen by other processors; this attribute can be used to achieve other purposes.

Example 8-20

The CRAY T3D system [KOEN94] is an array of DEC Alpha processors with local memories. The interconnection constructs a central memory from the contents of the local memories. The fact that Alpha's load_locked and store_conditional operations cause the processor to emit the effective memory address makes it possible to implement another operation, which is a block move between the local memory of the processor executing the instruction and the global memory.

8.5.4 Other Synchronization Operations

Some processor instructions support special synchronization situations. We illustrate a few of these in the following examples.

Example 8-21

The MC68020 supports a double compare and swap operation (CAS2) that has two memory operands, two update values, and two comparison operands. Both of the memory operands are compared against the corresponding comparison operands. Both destinations or both compare operand memory locations are updated depending on the outcome of the comparison. Both comparisons must succeed (the

TABLE 8-3   IBM SYSTEM/38 LOCKING OPTIONS

	Rules about Operations			
	Executing Program		Other Programs	
Lock Value[a]	Allowed	Allowed	Prohibited	
LSRD	read	read, write	destroy	
LSRO	read	read	write, destroy	
LSUP	read, write	read, write	destroy	
LEAR	read, write	read	write, destroy	
LENR	read, write, destroy	—	read, write, destroy	

[a] L = locked; S = shared; E = exclusive; RD = read; RO = read-only; UP = update; AR = allow read; NR = no read.

compared values must match) for both destinations to be updated; otherwise, both compare values are updated. This instruction directly supports the transaction view of interactions on a shared list structure. This instruction can be used to coherently update list pointers.

The next two examples exhibit instructions that "lock" objects by changing access rights in descriptors that point to the objects. This technique provides an indirect way that a process can prohibit accesses by other processes while the process performs its atomic transaction.

Example 8-22

The IBM System/38 supports five different locking/sharing modes. The lock mode is stored in lock field within each data descriptor. The five possible values of a lock are shown in Table 8-3. Several processes can set their own lock values on the same shared data object, provided that the lock values that are simultaneously set by different processes on the same object do not impose contradictory access permissions or restrictions. When attempting to set the lock, the processor checks whether an inconsistent lock status might arise if the instruction were completed; if so, the processor will suspend the executing process until the lock can be set as desired. Locks are enforced by the "data management" system, which manages database files containing records. The enforcement is achieved by controlling and checking the pointers along any paths accessing the file. Information not included in the file system is not subject to such access mode checks.

Example 8-23

The Intel iAPX 432 processor places lock information in segment descriptors. The segment descriptor of a general object contains three access mode control bits that are available for interpretation by type-manager software, and four other access modes have built-in interpretations: read, write, delete, and "unchecked copy." The last permits a process to override a built-in mechanism that limits descriptor copying to prevent dangling references. The default mechanism checks whether the

TABLE 8-4   LOCK STATES IN THE INTEL iAPX 432

Lock State[a]	When Set	When Cleared	Set/Cleared By	Comments
Unlocked	—	—	—	—
H/w locked	Start of cycle	End of cycle	Processor	Used within an instruction execution
S/w short-term locked	Start of instruction	End of instruction	Processor	Used for complete atomic instruction
S/w long-term locked	Start of critical region	End of critical region	Instruction execution	Used for transaction

[a] H/w = hardware; S/w = software.

descriptor can be copied, comparing the levels (of procedure nesting) between the declaration of an object and the destination of the copied descriptor. The copy is prevented if the descriptor would be copied to a nesting level that statically encloses the level of the objects declaration. It can be dangerous to give out unchecked copy permission.

Processor-interpreted locks are found at location 0 in the data parts of some system-type objects. Locks for data objects are declared and named through programming conventions; they must reside in the data part of the object.

Each lock object contains two fields. One contains the number of the process or processor that set the lock. The other specifies the state of the lock; there are four possibilities, listed in Table 8-4. While performing a lock instruction, the processor attempts to set the lock to the long-term software state. This succeeds only if the lock was previously unlocked. By examining the lock state after an unsuccessful lock attempt, the process can decide whether to wait for the lock to become free rather than blocking itself. If the state is not a long-term software lock, the process can idle until the lock becomes free. This choice avoids the overhead of process blocking and rescheduling. Because the long-term software lock is set only when the processor is engaged in a transaction (whose length might be unpredictable), the process can decide to suspend itself when this situation is detected. If a delay estimate were available, the choice could be made wisely (see Problem 8-29).

8.5.5 Comments

Because software solutions to synchronization problems are so inefficient, it is essential to design synchronization support into the processor's instruction set. We have shown several optional ways that this support can be provided, ranging upward from a simple uninterruptible semaphore operation. All are sufficient for the task; the more elaborate versions provide better protection against programming errors. All of these operations require support at the hardware level.

8.6 IMPLEMENTING ATOMIC ACTIONS

Realistic implementations of atomic operations can be supported by mechanisms built into the processor, the memory, or the processor–memory interconnection network. Any implementation involves three steps: (1) read, (2) modify, and (3) write. This sequence is called an RMW sequence. The choice of a realistic implementation depends partly upon the choice of the processor–memory interconnection structure. We discuss four techniques that work when there is a single copy of the shared object:

1. The pocessor holds the bus during the entire atomic instruction.
2. The memory interlocks during the atomic instruction.
3. The memory executes the atomic instruction.
4. The processor detects conflicting writes during the atomic sequence.

8.6.1 Bus Holding

If a single bus passes all memory access requests, the processor can prevent interference by holding onto the bus during the entire execution of an atomic operation.

This technique fails logically if there is more than one bus for memory accesses. It fails in performance if the speed loss caused by locking up the bus is considered significant. Another drawback is that each module's bus control logic must sense whether the bus is locked.

Example 8-24

The MC68020 implements its atomic instructions by holding onto the bus during the complete instruction. In particular, the processor will not issue a bus grant signal during the read–modify–write cycle. In addition, the processor pulls low the RMC' signal to indicate to all bus modules that an uninterruptible sequence is taking place. A designer of add-on modules should be aware of this interlock signal. The uninterruptibility requirement lengthens the period when the bus is locked and nothing else can be communicated across the bus. The amount of this delay affects the interrupt response time. In the worst case, the atomic operation may consume eight bus cycles (assuming no additional delays within the memory).

8.6.2 Memory Interlocks

Under this scheme, the memory is notified when an RMW sequence begins, and the selected memory module interlocks further requests until the write portion of the RMW sequence is completed. This protocol includes these steps:

1. The processor requests a read access for an RMW sequence.
2. The memory locks up the addressed location and returns its contents.

3. The processor stores that value and determines its replacement.
4. The processor requests a write operation for the RMW sequence.
5. The memory performs the write and releases the interlock.

Under this design, the processor modifies the data that was read to produce the data written back, so the memory need not know which atomic operation is being performed. After step 1, the memory module is interlocked so that no other request can be handled. The interlock persists until the lock value is updated in step 5. During the interval between steps 2 and 4, the bus is available for other operations which do not reference the interlocked memory locations. The possibility of overlapping unrelated memory accesses with the RMW sequence is one advantage of this scheme over the bus locking scheme.

8.6.3 Memory Performs the Operation

In this option, the entire RMW sequence is performed by the memory module, which is designed not to accept another request while any RMW sequence is underway. A typical sequence of events follows:
1. The processor requests an RMW cycle, sending the operand value.
2. The memory reads the selected location, saving the value.
3. The memory writes the processor data into the location.
4. The memory returns the data read to the processor.

The sequence uses the same elementary steps as for "normal" read and write operations, with two data transfers across the bus. Notice that four bus cycles with two data transfers would be required if the processor performed the modify part of the operation. It would be possible to design an intervening module (see Figure 8-12) to perform the operation.

In a system in which the processor does not perform the modification, special modules must be designed to support every atomic processor instruction. This requirement may rule out this implementation option. Another drawback is that an indivisible operation involving several different memory modules (such as the MC68020 CAS2 operation) may be difficult to implement in this manner. The same problem arises if the accessed object spans the boundary between two memory modules.

When an interconnection network with significant delays is interposed between processors and memory, the atomic operation must be performed within the memory system to avoid significant delays and memory holding times. The interconnection network can participate in performing the operation, at the cost of additional functionality in the switch modules.

Example 8-25

The NYU Ultracomputer [EDLE85] contains 2^n processors connected to 2^n memory modules through an Omega interconnection network [LAWR75]. Figure 8-13

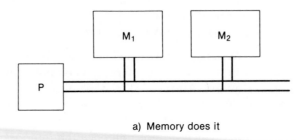

a) Memory does it

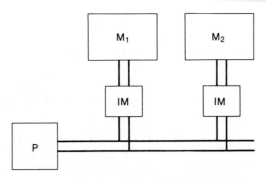

b) Intervening module (IM) does it

Figure 8-12   Two ways to have "memory" perform an atomic operation

illustrates the structure of the interconnection network for $n = 3$. The interconnection network routes memory access requests in packets using successive address bits (from the left end of the address if there is no interleaving) to direct each request packet. Each intermediate module has two inputs and two outputs. Let i denote the level (measured as the number of switch modules traversed from the signal's entry into the switch network) of switch module S. This module uses bit i of the memory module number part of the address to direct the flow within S. If only one module input has a request, that request is directed to the output whose number matches the value of bit i in the module number part of the address in the access request. If both inputs have a request and if they do not conflict, each request is directed by S to its outputs according to the same rule. If they do conflict (which happens if they agree in bit position i of the module number) and one or both of them does not ask for the add-to-memory operation, one of the requests is forwarded, and the other is suspended (i.e., not acknowledged). The same thing occurs if both are add-to-memory requests to different addresses.

The remaining case is the interesting one. In this case, both requests are directed to exactly the same address and both request add-to-memory. Let v_0 and v_1 denote the two operand values (presented on the data lines at inputs 0 and 1), and let m denote the value stored in the addressed location when the cycle begins.

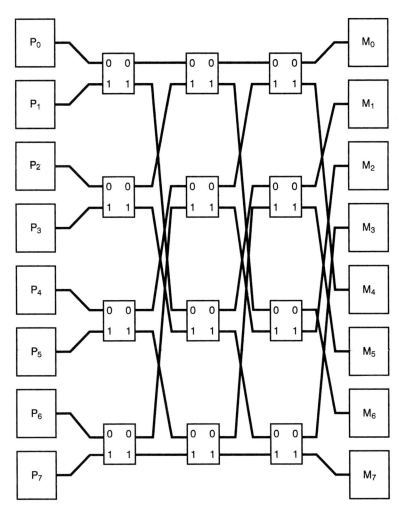

Figure 8-13   An eight-element Omega network—the style of NYU Ultracomputer processor–memory interconnections (after [GOTT83]; © 1983 IEEE)

Module S forwards a single add-to-memory operation with $v_0 + v_1$ as the operand value.[14] While the memory is responding to the unified request, S determines (randomly) which of its input requests will appear to have been served first. Suppose that the request at input 1 was selected to have priority. Then when the memory returns m (the previous value held in the location) as its response, the module returns $(m + v_1)$ and m to inputs 0 and 1, respectively. These responses are those that would have been obtained had the request at input 1 been performed during one

_____

[14]   As far as memory is concerned, this single request produces the same effect as the conflicting requests would had they been presented serially.

memory cycle and the request at input 0 during the next memory cycle. The added logic in *S*, which detects the conflicting requests, forwards the composite request, and creates these results, has an effect equivalent to serializing the two requests. It accomplishes this feat within a single memory access cycle. The network is known as a "combining network" due to its capability to combine conflicting requests into a single composite request.

One might question whether the Ultracomputer switch design solves an important problem—this argument centers on whether the probability of conflicting requests is so great that the additional connection node logic gives a worthwhile increase in system performance. In addition, one might ask whether both programs can proceed if a conflict is detected. In other words, one might ask how many algorithms can do useful parallel work after encountering conflicting requests to a common LOCK object. Then one might ask whether this number is sufficiently high to justify the complexity of the intermediate node.

8.6.4 Detect Conflicting Write Accesses

One could implement the effect of having atomic actions by designs in which interfering writes are detected and the atomic sequence is retried if there was interference. This design style is similar to that used to assure coherence among surrogate copies of memory objects, which we discuss in what follows.

8.6.5 Comments

Two general approaches can be used to implement atomic actions: (1) prohibit interfering writes, and (2) notify others so they will notify you if they interfere, in which case you retry the operation later. Both techniques are supported in processor instructions, and both styles can be used to implement those operations, though the notification scheme can introduce long delays that may impact system performance.

There are important similarities between the implementation of RMW sequences and the design of systems that copy objects to improve speed, but wish to give the illusion of a single object to support understandable semantics.

8.7 IMPLEMENTING A SINGLE COPY VIEW

Up to this point, we assumed that there was a single copy of each object within the memory system. This illusion permitted the system to coordinate the actions of independent processes through the single copies of the lock objects. Creating the appearance that there is a single copy of each shared object is an important part of implementing functional object sharing. Unfortunately, this assumption is not valid at low levels due to caches, local memories, global memories, and the possibility of memory requests being stalled within the network interconnecting processors and memory. Thus, we must implement protocols that correctly manage sharing among several copies of a shared object.

There are two significantly different approaches based on one's view of the multiple copies—in the first view, there is a single *master copy* of the object, the others being *surrogate objects* whose contents reflect the contents of the master copy. In the second view, there is a cooperating set of objects, with democratic voting determining the current contents of the "object." In this section, we explore both views. We start with the master object approach, which is the approach used to achieve cache coherence in multiprocessor systems.

8.7.1 Coherence with a Master Object

The problem of maintaining coherence with a master object is often phrased in terms of caches. Any mechanism supporting the single object illusion should assure that all caches appear to contain the same contents within each memory location. In other words, we design for cache coherence. Often one thinks that the master object is in main memory and the surrogate copies reside in cache memories. But in fact there are two possible relationships between the main memory copy and the cached copies: (1) The main memory copy is the master copy, or (2) the cached copy can become the master copy, without concern for updating the main memory copy.

We introduce some terminology covering the general problem before we return to the cache coherence version.

> **Definition.** A system exhibits *complete consistency* if all surrogate copies of a master object contain the same value at all times. The set of objects is said to be *coherent* if the system exhibits complete consistency.

> **Definition.** The logic that controls the object state to assure coherence is called a *coherence manager*.

Because the act of reading an object does not change the value therein, reading does not create any coherence problems. System functionality requires that every read operation accesses one of the coherent copies of the object. However, the act of writing to an object does change its contents, and thus may cause a coherence problem—after the write is completed, all valid surrogate copies should contain the same (new) value. ,Thus all surrogate copies that remain valid after the write must have been updated during the write operation.

There are two different approaches to the cache coherence problem:

1. Do not make surrogate copies of shared information.
2. Notify all surrogates upon any write to the object.

There are two options under the second approach, depending upon whether the surrogates are invalidated or are updated when the write occurs. We return to this choice after examining the first option.

Cache Only Unshared Objects. This "solution" will provide functionality and retain most of the speed benefits of caching if the system knows which objects are shared and if shared objects are not accessed frequently. In this scheme, we trust programmers to identify all shared objects, just as we trusted them to declare all transactions. Once we know which objects are shared, we can build a mechanism that marks all shared things and keeps them out of caches. Any other (unmarked) object could be in any cache. This approach relies on correct program declarations and thus falls under the "everything correct" approach.

In principle, a system designer could adopt the "anything goes" position with respect to the coherence problem, but then the design must be based on a conservative assumption—that every memory access reaches something that might be shared (so we had better be careful with it!). Unfortunately this assumption, coupled with the limited caching approach, leads to the conclusion that we cannot cache any object. Thus, a system with truly independent cache memories cannot be consistent with the "anything goes" approach.

Example 8-26

In the PowerPC 601, each page table entry contains 3 bits governing the relationships between the cache contents (if any) and the master (main memory) copy of information within the page. The three bits are as follows:

1. W (write through)
2. I (inhibit caching)
3. M (force memory consistency)

The I bit marks those pages that contain shared objects, which are always accessed from main memory, because they cannot be cached. Functional behavior requires consistency between the setting in these bits and the use of the objects within the page. In particular, any object that is supposed to maintain the single copy illusion and is shared (so that several processes might write to it) must be marked with $I = 1$ or $M = 1$, but if there exist alias descriptors of the same page, the bit settings in those descriptors must be consistent. Table 8-5 summarizes important combinations of values within these page control bits. An entry marked "global writes" indicates that the writes can initiated within any processor sharing the page.

Setting $M = 1$ demands that a cache coherency protocol be used to update or invalidate a cache line whenever it is written to by another processor, as discussed under cache notification. When $M = 0$, writes by other processors do not affect the contents of the local cache. The write throughs that are initiated from the local processor when $W = 1$ do not achieve cache coherence, both because the write requests might be buffered locally, and because these writes are not sensed by any other caches within the system.

TABLE 8-5   POWERPC 601 PAGE CONSISTENCY BITS

WIM Value	Coherent?	The Order of these Actions Determines the State of the Copy in the Following	
		In Memory	In Cache
000	No	Write backs	Local writes
010	Yes[a]	Writes	—
001	Yes	Coherent writes	Global writes
100	No	Writes	Local writes
101	Yes	Coherent writes	Global writes

[a] This provides coherence by default, because ince there is only one copy of the object.

Cache Notification.   To maintain coherence among multiple copies of a shared object, every write to the object must either update or invalidate every surrogate copy of the object, and these actions must be considered part of the write operation. So all cached copies must be notified about the occurrence of the write, which can delay the write considerably, because it is not finished until these actions are completed.

If we distinguish writes to separate those that demand coherence from those that do not, we save checking for and updating objects that are known not to be shared. We assume that coherent writes are distinguished, which leaves two problems to be solved: (1) How are the copies notified? (2) How are the copies modified? There are two different notification schemes:

1. Snooping
2. Directed messages

In a hierarchical system, different notification schemes can be used at different levels. There are two different copy-modification schemes

1. Invalidation
2. Update

In the following, we discuss notification options that work with the invalidation approach to the modification problem; the changes to form protocols that work with updating (rather than invalidation) add logically simple extensions to most invalidation protocols.[15]

Snooping.   In the snooping protocol, each cache observes all memory access requests. Each cache checks whether each write is a coherent write and, if so, the cache examines its directory and looks for a surrogate copy of the write's

---

[15]   The MESI protocol relies on invalidation and thus does not easily extend to an updating option.

target object. The standard snooping design operates on a common memory bus monitored by all caches.

Snooping designs can be costly, because (1) every coherent write requires searching every cache directory, which becomes unavailable to the local processor during the search, and (2) memory bus bandwidth is consumed with snooping transactions. Design modifications can reduce the performance impact of these two problems. In the first design enhancement, the cache maintains two directories or supports two simultaneous searches. With two directories, one handles the snooping searches; the other assists with local accesses, and is not involved with snooping actions unless a surrogate copy of the write's target object exists in the local cache. Thus, the amount of interference with the local processor is proportional to the fraction of the snoop searches that find a match. A second design enhancement expands the cache control logic so that while the cache modifies its entry, the local processor can still access the cache. A third design enhancement adds a separate snooping bus dedicated to snooping transactions, thus reducing bus contention delays, which increases the effective memory bandwidth.

The broadcast operations must complete successfully to assure that the snooping activity has achieved coherence before a coherent write instruction can be considered complete. One method is to provide a "completed" bus line with wired-NOR connections to the modules. The line will be low if any coherence manager pulls it low, which will happen while the manager is completing its part of the coherence protocol. When the line rises, all managers have completed, and the coherent write operation can be considered complete.

The MESI Protocol.   This snooping protocol permits the main memory copy of a shared object to become obsolete (without any marks in memory indicating that this has occurred). The protocol name is an acronym built from the cached object states used in the protocol. Here are the states:

1. M(odified): The current value of the object is located in this cache and nowhere else within the system. In particular, the value in main memory is not the current value in the object.
2. E(xclusive): The value in this cache matches the value in main memory, but there are no valid copies in other caches. In other words, this is an *exclusive* copy of the object. No other caches need to be notified if an exclusive object is modified.
3. S(hared): The value in the cache matches the value in main memory, and there may be (valid) shared copies in other caches. Shared values can be read from the local copies, but an attempt to write an object that is in the S state requires a state change.
4. I(nvalid): The value in the cache is invalid and should not be used.

TABLE 8-6   LOCAL ACTIONS UNDER THE MESI COHERENCY PROTOCOL

| State | Type of Request from Local Processor | |
	Read	Write
Modified	—	—
Exclusive	—	Change to M state
Shared	—	1. Broadcast "write" message 2. Change to M state
Invalid	1. Broadcast "read" message 2. Change to state E if no "shared" response arrives; else to state S 3. Fill the cache line	1. Broadcast "write" message 2. Change to M state 3. Fill the cache line

If a write buffer is included in a processor, that buffer must be considered as a victim cache and therefore must participate in the protocol. In, fact, an object in the victim cache must be considered to be in state M. Why?

To determine the activities and state transitions necessary to support this protocol, first consider the coherence activities initiated by the local processor's actions. To isolate the actions within one processor, assume that no snooping messages arrive at this cache. The local processor may request a read, a write, or a read that starts an RMW sequence. In Table 8-6, we summarize the local responses to all possible processor-initiated local actions. The broadcast messages mentioned in the table initiate snooping checks at all other caches, which respond as described in what follows. All actions listed in an entry must be concluded before the local operation can be considered complete.

The second part of the MESI protocol specification details local actions in response to snoop messages received from other caches. Table 8-7 lists these

TABLE 8-7   SNOOP INTERACTIONS IN THE MESI PROTOCOL

| State | Type of Snoop Message that "Hits" a Cache Entry | |
	Read	Write
Modified	1. Emit value and "shared" message 2. Change to S state	1. Emit value[a] 2. Change to I state
Exclusive	1. Emit "shared" message 2. Change to S state	Change to I state
Shared	Emit "shared" message	Change to I state
Invalid	—	—

[a] This condition occurs if a nonfunctional program is being executed or if there is "false sharing" (see Problem 8-41).

actions; they assure global consistency among the states of the cache lines. In particular, at most one cache can have the same line in the M state.

It is easy to convince oneself that the MESI protocol keeps consistent records about the existence of multiple object copies, and prevents any process from reading an old copy of the contents of a shared object that might have been replicated elsewhere in the system. Thus, a system following the MESI protocol supports the illusion that the system contains only a single copy of each object.

Directed Messages. Directed message protocols replace broadcast snoop messages with messages directed to the caches that are known to hold copies of the object being accessed. There are several advantages to this option, including the fact that the snooping protocol requires that all shared writes be broadcast to all caches that might hold the object being written. The broadcast requirement implies that the bus must carry traffic for every cache within the system, which makes system expansion difficult due to the bus bandwidth limitations. Thus knowing where copies exist that must be invalidated or modified can reduce the communication overhead. All message-based protocols have a minimum overhead amounting to two messages for each cache that holds a copy of the object. The scheme can be designed to be scaleable, meaning that the cost of updating and of representing the sharing information is linearly proportional to the system size.

Now we present the basic invalidation strategy, assuming that the locations of all cached copies are known. Then we turn to the representation of the directory information (that indicates the locations of the copies within the system). The details of each protocol can be inferred from these two pieces of information.

The basic message-based coherency protocol uses these steps:

1. Obtain update permission.
2. Update or invalidate the copies.
3. Write the new value to the object.
4. Release write access to the object.

In step 1 the process obtains exclusive rights to invalidate all cached copies of X. If another process is also attempting to write to X at the same time, this step will resolve their conflict, leaving one in charge of X; the other process will have to await its turn after the first has completed its update. While the winner retains control, the system state will be set so that any write request from another node will receive a "busy" signal in return, which will force it to retry its request. Another result of the first step is that an *invalidation node* is identified; this node will retain control of the invalidation procedure, returning control to the writing step to complete step 3 of this algorithm.

During step 2, the invalidation node sends messages to each cache holding a copy of X, asking that the copy be invalidated. When its copy has been invalidated, a cache returns a success message to the invalidation node. After all copies have been invalidated, the step is complete, and the invalidation process returns control to the writing node.

In step 3, the writing node updates its (cached) copy of X. This is a safe action, because all other processes have been locked out, and no node has another copy of X. (Whether this change is sent to the memory is not relevant for the consistency protocol, though it does affect the state of the copy in central memory.)

In the final step. the writing node releases the exclusive access to X that it held during the previous steps. Then another node may attempt to write to X.

It should be clear that this protocol will ensure that at most one process can write to X at one time, which provides the illusion of atomic memory writes.

To complete the description of the protocols, one must examine the representation of the directory that describes the copies of each cached object.[16] In the simplest situation the system has no virtual memory mapping, one level of interconnection, and one level of directories. Furthermore, the system uses an invalidation protocol. So, we discuss the design options for a single level directory that covers cache line copies within a cluster of nodes. It should be obvious how to generalize the following from the cluster level to hierarchical structures.

The directory system designer must make several decisions:

1. How is the directory found?
2. How is the directory organized?
3. What information is placed in each directory entry?

The directory must be logically associated with the memory space that holds X, so that it can be found during the process of accessing X. One option uses a data structure, akin to a page table, but describing the cache lines within a memory space. This structure can be found by a simple computation from the memory address of X. Nodes that have cached copies of X can find the directory by executing the same protocol used to find X in the first place, or by retaining a pointer to the directory within their management information. Thus, the directory can be found easily using existing protocols. The state of the cache line is kept within the directory entry.

The possible state values depend upon the protocol being used, but must include one that prevents other processes to initiate writes to the object (we indicate this state with "W").

The directory designer specifies how the identities of the sharing nodes are contained in the directory entry. Each node is assigned a unique identifying number, which we call its *cache number*. Several ways to include location information within the coherence directory follow:

---

[16]   Actually the directory describes cache lines, but talking about them as objects connects the discussion to the objects being manipulated, so we retain the object labels.

1. Bit vector
2. Fixed set of location fields
3. Location fields with an overflow list
4. Linked list

We illustrate the schemes using the simple sharing pattern exhibited in Figure 8-14a.

Under the *bit vector* scheme, the location information is contained in a bit vector whose length equals the number of caches. One bit corresponds to each sharing node; see Figure 8-14b. This scheme is also called a *fully mapped directory*.

A scheme using a *fixed set of location fields* allocates, in each coherence database entry, several fields that hold node numbers or an invalid code.[17] Managing these fields is straightforward until all fields contain valid entries and a new copy must be created. Now either a previously valid entry must be invalidated or we create an *overflow location list*. Figure 8-14c illustrates this option, which is also called a *limited mapped directory*.

Finally, *linked-list* representations spanning the sharing nodes provide a flexible, scaleable[18] representation. Each node that contains a valid copy of the cache line is on the list. When a write occurs, all copies are removed from the list, except the list entry corresponding to the copy that is being updated. To complete the write invalidation, the manager passes a message containing both the line identifier to a node on the sharing list; each node responds with an acknowledgment message that contains the identifier of its successor. This particular structure is not, however, useful because the structure imposes a high cost for updating the list when a cache line is removed from a cache; see Problem 8-45.

The IEEE scaleable coherent interface [JAME90] uses a doubly linked list to chain together the names of the sharing caches; see Figure 8-14e. This structure makes it easier to maintain correct cache copy information than the singly linked list data structure.

Under all designs, the state of the memory entry is contained in the directory entry along with the information about the locations of the copies. The choice of states to be represented within the directory entry depends upon the protocols being followed. It is necessary to have a state that locks out writes while one is in progress; it may be useful to have states to indicate whether there are any cached copies and whether the memory copy is dirty. In Figure 8-15 we show, for various representations of the sharing information, the status during the write invalidation process that was inititated because cache 4 wrote a new value to the shared object named X.

With the linked-list representations of the sharing information, it may be useful to mark the link in each cache to indicate whether that entry is at the

---

[17]   In our example we represent the invalid code using a zero.
[18]   This means that the space allocated in any node does not expand when more nodes are added to the system.

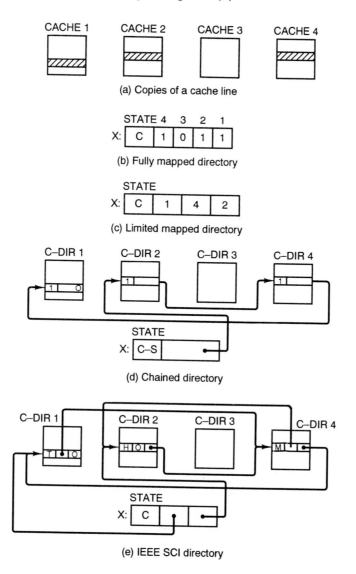

Figure 8-14   Cache directories during read sharing

head, tail, or in the middle of the list structure. The head mark (represented in the figures with H, in contrast to M for middle and T for tail) is useful if the head is delegated the authority to complete the invalidation protocol. Of course, marking the head requires changing that mark when the update moves the head role to another cache.

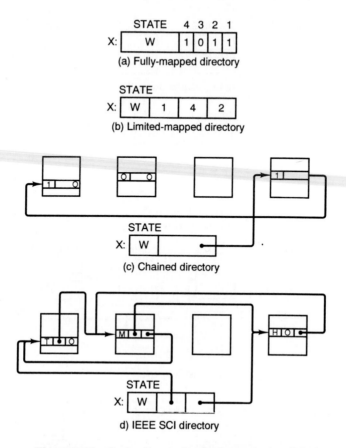

STATE   4 3 2 1

X: | W | 1 | 0 | 1 | 1 |

(a) Fully-mapped directory

STATE

X: | W | 1 | 4 | 2 |

(b) Limited-mapped directory

STATE

X: | W | |

(c) Chained directory

STATE

X: | W | | |

d) IEEE SCI directory

Figure 8-15   Cache directories during write invalidation
for cache 4

Hierarchical Coherency Protocols. How do we modify single-domain
coherency protocols to handle more complex hierarchical domains?

Figure 8-16 shows a system with a coherence directory (CD) between each
cache and the system bus. The domain of each CD contains just the single cache
memory directly connected below the CD module. When a processor desires coherence, the CD module asks the other CD modules to make surrogate checks
and invalidate cache entries if appropriate. Because each CD checks for surrogates, the cache does not have to do anything unless the CD's surrogate search
finds a match against the address being modified. This structure removes snooping checks from the local caches, leaving them available to serve requests from
their local processor. This structure is logically identical to a design with two
cache directories in each node.

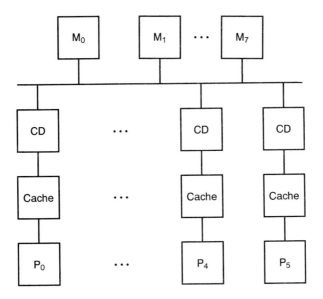

Figure 8-16   Cache directory domains

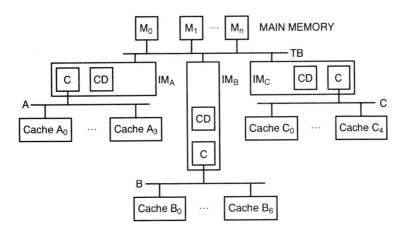

Figure 8-17   A hierarchical system with caches on
local buses

We can extend this approach to other hierarchical structures. Figure 8-17 shows a system with a hierarchy of memory buses. The cache memories associated with processor nodes are at the bottom of the figure. These caches are grouped according to the bus (A, B, or C) to which they are connected. These buses are interconnected along the topmost bus TB, where the main memory is attached.[19] Each interface module (IM) contains the coherence manager and a co-herence directory describing the collective contents of all caches connected to the corresponding lower bus (A, B, or C). Every coherence request that originated at any node connected to the local bus is forwarded by the coherence manager to the TB bus. A coherence protocol is used on this bus.[20] If none of the CDs has an entry matching the coherence request, coherence has been achieved, and the re-questing processor can continue. If a CD does match the request address, it re-lays the coherence request to its local bus. Several local caches on that bus might have to perform invalidations. When all matching caches on the local bus have completed their invalidations, the coherence request has been completed there, and the CD can signal completion to the TB level.

The hierarchical coherence directory structure isolates local subsystems from coherence requests that will not require local attention. A straightforward hierarchical approach to the coherence problem will be sufficient in any hierar-chical system structure.

Example 8-27

> The KSR-1 processor [KSR92] is structured with two levels of ring interconnec-tions, with coherence controllers at each switch node on the ring. Coherence re-quests are passed around the rings.

Summary. A multiprocessor system can be designed so that whenever a write is made to a coherent object, all surrogate copies of that object are either updated or invalidated. The processor initiating the coherence request has to wait for a completion signal from the coherence manager before it can continue instruction execution; the completion signals can be implemented by wired-OR connections or by message passing. The requests can be distributed by broad-casting or by passing messages to those caches known (from directory informa-tion) to hold surrogate copies of the coherent object. Compared to snooping, directing a message to each copy can be efficient if the system has an efficient message-passing mechanism and if there are many caches with few surrogate copies in the system.

The coherence protocols used in a system with a hierarchical structure can be different at each interconnection within the system; each subtree must assure coherence within its domain; the completion message is passed up the hierarchy only after this coherence has been assured. When the top of the hierarchy be-lieves that coherence has been achieved, the completion signal travels back down to the initiating processor, which can continue its program with assurance about the state of the shared memory.

Alternatively, one can design a system in which multiple object copies are permitted to have different contents, provided that the incoherence does not

---

[19]   The position of the main memory is not important to the coherence protocol.
[20]   It can be different from the protocol used on the local buses.

become too extreme. This approach adds fault tolerance and reduces the need to obtain responses from all copies when updating a "coherent" object.

8.7.2 Democratic Coherency Protocols

To improve failure resilience, a system might allocate and maintain several copies of each shared object. In this section, we discuss voting protocols that assure consistent behavior without relying on a designated "correct" copy of the updated object. In fact, there is no need for the copies to contain identical values, but we will require that a majority[21] of the copies contain the same value.

This scheme, originally proposed in [THOM79], associates a coherence controller with each node containing a copy of the database. In the high-level model of the system's behavior, each coherent update occurs as the result of a transaction, with a read set and a write set, modeled as in Section 8.4.4. The read and compute steps of the transaction are performed at the originating node.

The validate decision is based on a vote taken among the coherence controllers. Each controller's vote compares the status of the database at the node against information within the validate request. Recall that a transaction T operating on a centralized database can commit if the values read by the transaction are still current when the commit is attempted. If all the values are still current, we know that no other transaction has interfered with T by writing new values to any member of T's read set. In the centralized database commit decision, we used a centralized counter called GTN (global transaction number). We first show how that validation scheme could be used in a distributed system, and then we show how the effect of a centralized numbering scheme can be achieved in a distributed fashion. Each object contains both its value and a version identifier, a number that increases monotonically during program execution.

In the following, we assume that the coherence controllers communicate along a logical ring structure—that is, each node's coherence controller has a designated successor to which all voting requests are forwarded. Without loss of generality, we assume that the N nodes are numbered in order around the ring such that the successor of node i is node $(i + 1)$ mod N. Assuming this particular communication structure does not restrict the system's logical behavior, but it simplifies vote counting.

Voting with a Centralized Counter. Our first voting scheme uses a centralized counter holding the GTN value. To simplify this discussion, we also assume that an interlock prevents a second transaction from obtaining a potential

---

[21]   The nodes might be given unequal numbers of votes; a majority is defined in terms of the maximum vote count.

new GTN value and asking for a vote while any other vote is taken.[22] The version identifier for an object X is the GTN value obtained during the commit phase of the transaction that last wrote a new value into X.

To determine whether a transaction can be validated, each node votes to express its opinion as to whether the proposed commit would preserve consistency. If no node rejects the commit and a majority of the nodes approve it, it is performed; otherwise, the transaction must be retried. The transaction's timing is described by the value held in GTN when the transaction read its input values.

Transaction Structure. A node performs a transaction by executing these steps:

1. Obtain the current GTN value
2. Read the transaction's inputs and perform the computation using local shadow copies of all objects that are written during the transaction.
3. Send out a validation vote message (described in what follows).
4. Receive the vote outcome and decide whether to commit or abort.
5. Send out a commit/abort message.
6. Receive a confirmation that the commit/abort has been completed.

Notice the similarity between these steps and the steps used in the software implementation of a transaction. The major difference is that the commit decision is made by a vote taken among the nodes that hold copies of the objects involved in the transaction. The following voting scheme covers the simple protocol in which the control messages are passed around the nodes following a ring structure and each node has a copy of the entire database.

Validation Voting. The validation vote message includes the following:

1. The "please_vote" identifier of the request type
2. The GTN corresponding to the time the transaction began execution
3. The transaction's read set
4. The transaction's write set
5. A field to hold the count of OK votes
6. A field to hold the count of PASS votes (see what follows)
7. The node number of this (originating) node

Each node votes based on whether it thinks that the values that the transaction read from the objects in its read set are still current. This decision checks each member of the read set of the transaction; it compares the version identifier of the node's copy of the input object against the version identifier current when this transaction started (from the second field listed before). A simple inequality test is sufficient; if the local copy of any member of the read set is newer than the proposed transaction, the node votes to reject the transaction.

---

[22] Later, we modify the design to eliminate these restrictive assumptions.

In the base case, only one validation vote request can pass through the system at one time (an unrealistic assumption), and each node votes either to approve the transaction (by voting OK) or to reject the transaction.

A node votes OK only if the GTN in the message is greater than the version identifier associated with every local copy of an object listed in the read set specified in the message. If the local vote is OK, the node modifies the cumulative vote and forwards the please_vote message to the next node in the ring. If the node votes OK, it also records the information about the write set of the transaction, along with the GTN number, and marks this transaction as "pending."

A node votes to reject the transaction if it contains a copy of any input object whose identifier is larger than the GTN in the message. If the validation is rejected, the node forwards a reject message in place of the please_vote message. A node receiving a reject message for a transaction that it did not initiate simply passes that message along the ring.

Vote Resolution. The transaction's originating node knows that the validation checks are complete when it receives a vote message or reject message that contains its node identifier.[23] If the outcome is a majority OK vote, the node initiates a commit message that contains the transaction number, a list of the locations written to, and their new values.

If the outcome is a NO vote, the node initiates an abort message that contains the GTN of the transaction. (Later it can retry the entire transaction, rereading the objects in the read set and performing the computation anew.) The abort message is required because nodes that have voted to approve a proposed transaction must be told to ignore the transaction.

Commit Actions. A node receiving a commit message obtains the transaction's GTN from the commit message. This information, along with the write set and write values, is used to determine how to update the local object copies. If not more than one transaction can be active in the system at the same time, it is adequate to perform an update and to assign the transaction's GTN to the new copies of the objects. If, on the other hand, the node receives an abort message, it cancels the pending transaction and forgets the possible update information.

Handling Simultaneous Transactions. One way to "handle" simultaneous transactions is to prohibit them, requiring global approval to initiate a transaction. This strategy presents a circular problem: A node has to pass a message around the network to determine whether it can initiate a transaction! Furthermore, because transactions are based on optimism about conflicts, the chance of interference between two simultaneous transactions is supposed to be small.

Thus, we want to modify the transaction protocol to avoid the need for internode synchronization before initiating a transaction. In effect, the system must

---

[23]   The GTN value could have been used here.

be able to correctly respond to vote requests even though several vote requests might be pending simultaneously.

The basic interference problem is that nonfunctional behavior may result if one vote request asks to update an object that was an input for a transaction being handled at another node. The voting algorithm must assume a conservative position, which means that it must check any incoming request against all previous requests that it is holding in the pending status. If there is no conflict (because the empty intersection condition is satisfied) between the incoming request and the pending requests, or if the node would have rejected the transaction, the node votes as before. If the new transaction would have received an OK vote except that it conflicts with a higher-priority transaction that is pending, the node votes PASS and increments the PASS count in the circulating message before forwarding it. Finally, if the conflict is with a lower-priority transaction, the node defers its decision about the new transaction; it reconsiders when the conflicting transition is removed from the pending status. This rule allows the second (higher-priority) transaction to avoid a retry if that is possible.

The rules concerning vote outcomes have to account for PASS votes. If two transactions were receiving PASS votes and neither one could reach a majority of OK votes, one (or both) would be aborted. Thus, once a node finds that the number of PASS votes is high enough to guarantee that the system will never vote to validate the transaction, the node should change the outcome to reject.

Node Failure. If a node fails and does not forward a please_vote message, the transaction originator will never obtain any response to its vote request. To detect this situation, the originator uses a timer. If the timeout expires, the originator assumes that the transaction cannot be committed, and it retries the whole thing later. Just as with an actual NO vote outcome, the originator must emit an abort message to notify the voters that they can forget the previous attempt. The foregoing steps guarantee system integrity if one of the voting nodes fails.

What if the node originating the transaction fails between the time that it sends a vote request and the time that it can send a commit or abort message to the other nodes? Clearly, each participating node requires a timer measuring the time since it sent an OK vote; if this timer fires to indicate that there is no timely response from the initiator, the vote is canceled, and the object copy is made available once again.

8.7.3 Voting without a Centralized Counter

One simplifying assumption in the previous discussion was that there was a central source of global transaction numbers. Although having such a source makes the protocol a bit simpler, a truly distributed version of this protocol must obtain unique, monotonic version identifiers without resort to any common data objects. One approach uses a local counter (like a clock), concatenated with the node number (in the least significant portion of the value).

Synchronized Clocks. Suppose that all local clocks are synchronized. Then the clock value can serve as a unique monotonic identifier. If two nodes initiate a request at the same time, their version identifiers will appear different because the node number portions will not match. Thus, any two version identifiers will be unequal. The node numbers were placed into the least significant part so that the clock time dominates the decision, and the node numbers only break ties in the time field.

No Clocks. To assure that all global requests are properly ordered, the requesting nodes must assure that their proposed version numbers are consistent with monotonic numbering as seen from the database. This condition can be met by checking (and revising, if necessary) the local version number counter whenever a write is attempted. The basic requirement is that all actions appear to have occurred in order as viewed from the local processor. In particular, in every transaction, the version number of the result must exceed the version numbers of all operands and the version numbers of all previous writes that were initiated from the node. Thus, we can set the local version number as follows:

$$\text{version\_number} = 1 + \max_i(\text{version\_number}, \{\, V\_N[\,i\,]\,\})$$

Here V_N[i] is the version number of the ith member of the read set for the transaction. The one is added to assure that numbers are not duplicated. It is proved in [THOM79] that this rule is sufficient to assure serializable behavior.

8.7.4 Comments

We have explored some implementation options to produce the effect of logically correct memory sharing. The approaches range from shutting down part of the system during a critical operation to allowing conflicting access requests to appear to have been handled serially. The simplest solutions use the least amount of support logic but incur the greatest time overhead. A designer has to choose between a simple, slow solution and one of the more elegant, faster solutions.

Two special situations require note. The first, called *false sharing*, involves two processes that share access to one cache line but are running beneath separate caches. Assume that a cache line represents the granularity of the surrogate management system. Now suppose that each process writes to that same line, but to different parts of the cache line. At the granularity of the cache line, it appears that these accesses conflict, and any coherence protocol that handles true sharing correctly will initiate object invalidation and copying for each write to the cache line. If the sharing in the cache line is false, these steps incur unnecessary overhead. The same comments apply to the blocks implicitly defined by an implementation of the load locked/store conditional synchronization scheme.

The second special situation involves *write races*, which occur if two processes try to modify the same object in an overlapped manner (one process initiates the write access while a second process was in the process of writing to the same object). If that object is not a synchronization object, there is a programming error. But coherence managers do not know the programmer's intentions. They will see this as a problem, and will have rules to handle these conflicts. Write races are one type of event-ordering problem. Next we turn to event-ordering issues.

8.8 IMPLEMENTING A PROGRAM ORDER VIEW

Processors designed to optimize performance (when used in a uniprocessor system) may reorder events such that the end result matches the effect of strict execution in program order. The problem is that the reordering may be based on tests that consider only the potential effects of the reordering on the local program. In particular, the processor can interchange two memory writes that access different objects without changing the behavior of the algorithm, provided that it is executed in a uniprocessor system without interference. In a multiprocessor system with shared memory, such tests are not sufficient to assure functional behavior.

To illustrate the problems that can arise, consider this example.

Example 8-28

Process P1 wants to send a message that is stored locally in a location named M to process P2. Under their communication protocol, P1 will copy M into a shared buffer named mailbox and then set the flag mailbox_full to indicate that the mailbox is full. When P2 sees that mailbox_full is set, it will copy M from the mailbox into its receiver space R. Then P2 notifies P1 that its message has been received. A synchronization problem occurs if the process simply sends the first message in mailbox.

Consider this attempt at the first part of the protocol:

Process P1	Process P2
mailbox = M;	**while** (! mailbox_full); //busy waiting
mailbox_full = **true**;	R = mailbox;

Without other restrictions, each processor can reorder its memory accesses, provided that the appearance of execution in program order is maintained in the view of the executing process. This rule permits the two statements in each program to be reordered, because all memory accesses attempted within each individual program reach separate objects. However, if both processes reordered the statements,

P2 could think that the mailbox was full and read it before the write from P1 became visible to P2. Consider this event sequence (viewed from a global perspective):

Process P1	Process P2
write(mailbox_full, **true**);	
	read(mailbox_full); //seeing "true"
	read(mailbox);
write(mailbox);	

The net effect is that P2 receives the old value from the mailbox, even though each processor's local logic thinks that the system's behavior must be logically correct because the processor did not detect any conflicting accesses.

This example shows that the local appearance of execution in program order is not adequate to obtain sequential consistency, because the behavior obtained from the second interleaving is not consistent with any interleaving of the process' steps in program order. We need a coherence mechanism that assures understandable program behavior.

Recall our division of each process into intervals during which they interact with shared things and introverted intervals (which do not involve shared objects). Local reordering during an introverted sequence cannot affect sharing, because shared objects are not accessed during those intervals. We hope to add synchronization mechanisms such that during a transaction, a process can assume that it has exclusive access to the objects used in the transaction. The critical coordination points occur at transaction boundaries; in these neighborhoods, local reordering can cause great difficulties.

Example 8-29

Consider placing the interactions of Example 8-28 within transactions synchronized by TEST_AND_SET operations on a lock object:

Process P1	Process P2
testandset lockit;	testandset lockit;
write(mailbox_full, **true**);	read(mailbox_full); //seeing **true**
write(mailbox);	read(mailbox);
clear lockit;	clear lockit;

These fragments do not reflect the complete picture, because both processes must check whether mailbox_full contains the proper value before they can proceed with the sequence outlined above. Therefore, the programs in both processes must include loops that cover the situation when the flag contains the "incorrect" value. (The same concern will apply to succeeding examples that elaborate on this situation.) This issue aside, it may appear that the locks solve the problem.

However, despite the common lock object, each processor is free to reorder operations that locally appear to be without conflict. Thus, P1 could write to mailbox_full before its testandset has been completed. The following history becomes possible:

```
          Process P1                  Process P2
    write( mailbox_full, true );

                                testandset lockit;
                                read( mailbox_full );   //seeing true
                                read( mailbox ) ;
                                clear lockit;

    testandset lockit;
    write( mailbox );
    clear lockit;
```

In this history, P2 reads the old value in mailbox, so it is not functionally correct. Complementary difficulties appear exist at the termination of the transaction.

To prohibit the problematic histories, the system needs a way to prohibit a processor from moving instructions across transaction boundaries. Fortunately, this can be implemented using only local operations, because the local reordering of memory accesses caused the difficulty, so local constraints are adequate to resolve the problem.

8.8.1 Memory Barrier Instructions

A complete memory barrier (MB) instruction prevents the processor from reordering memory accesses across the barrier. In other words, all memory accesses for the execution of instructions that appeared prior to the MB instruction in program order must appear to have completed prior to the initiation of any accesses for instructions that follow the MB in program order.

The memory reordering problems can be removed from our example by placing MB instructions at the boundaries of each transaction, because this is the critical place.

Example 8-30

The difficulties displayed in Example 8-28 can be removed by inserting MB instructions into the sending processes:

```
          Process P1                  Process P2

    testandset lockit;          testandset lockit;
    MB;                         MB;
    write( mailbox_full, true ); read( mailbox_full );   //seeing true
    write( mailbox );           read( mailbox );
    MB;                         MB;
    clear lockit;               clear lockit;
```

The first MB in P1 prevents the appearance of mailbox_full being set before the message has been copied into the mailbox.

TABLE 8-8   SPARC-V9 MEMBAR SEQUENCING CONSTRAINTS

Name	These Must Occur before MEMBAR	These Must Occur after MEMBAR
StoreStore	Stores	Stores
LoadStore	Loads	Stores
StoreLoad	Stores	Loads
LoadLoad	Loads	Loads

One can define more flexible memory barrier instructions that specify more specific restrictions on program reordering.

Example 8-31

The SPARC-V9 processor includes a general memory barrier instruction, MEMBAR. Two fields in the instruction encode the reordering restrictions. The code in the first field specifies the relative sequencing of the loads and stores issued by this processor; there is a separate bit for each possible combination; see Table 8-8. The constraints mentioned in the table relate to the behavior of instructions issued by the processor executing the MEMBAR instruction.

The stores must complete to the point that all other processors are guaranteed to see their effects; this is equivalent to stating that they must leave any surrogates of a shared object in a coherent state before the MEMBAR instruction is completed.

Additional instruction sequencing constraints are specified by the contents of the cmask field in the MEMBAR instruction; the three bits in this field indicate restrictions on instruction completion ordering, as summarized in Table 8-9.

Example 8-32

Two PowerPC instructions implement different memory barrier functions. The first, sync, acts like a memory barrier with respect to all loads and stores, and the

TABLE 8-9   POSSIBLE INSTRUCTION COMPLETION
RESTRICTIONS FROM THE SPARC-V9 MEMBAR INSTRUCTION

Barrier Type	Sequencing Constraint
Synchronization	All predecessor instructions (in program order) must complete before any successors can be issued
Memory issue	All preceding memory operations (in program order) must complete before any successor memory operations can be issued
Lookaside	A preceding store operation must complete before a succeeding load to the same address can be initiated

previous instructions executed by this processor will appear (to all other processors) to have completed their memory accesses and to have modified the global memory object. The second instruction, eieio,[24] creates a barrier with respect to input/output devices, but other processors or modules accessing memory may not see the completion of the instructions preceding the eieio instruction; thus, it cannot be used to coordinate accesses to shared objects from separate processors.

8.8.2 Instruction Barriers

A related difficulty can arise with programs that rewrite themselves. Most processor designs do not include checks to find whether a memory write operation affects instruction stream information that happens to be present in an instruction buffer (or cache) within the processor. This design decision is made because most programs do not modify themselves and the checks would add control logic to the processor. This is not efficient if it is infrequently used.

To support the illusions of a single memory and instruction execution in program order, it is necessary to add a special barrier operation to a program that modifies information that might be present in an instruction buffer. A special instruction is used for several reasons:

1. Invalidating the entire instruction buffer can cause many misses when fetching instructions, so invalidations can slow program execution.
2. If each MEMBAR instruction invalidated the instruction buffer, instruction cache misses would be frequent.
3. Programmers are discouraged from writing programs that modify themselves, so most programs will not exhibit the problem, and will not need to use the instruction to synchronize the instruction buffer.

Even though the instruction buffer synchronization problem is local to a single process, it is logically identical to the problems of maintaining a consistent memory view in the presence of surrogate copies of memory information.

Example 8-33

The PowerPC architecture specifies an icbi (instruction cache block invalidate) instruction, but it is not supported in the PowerPC 601, which treats it as a NOP. The instruction forces reads from memory to the instruction cache block B that contains the effective address from the icbi instruction. If block B is supposed to be forced to be coherent across all processors (due to the contents of the WIM field in the page descriptor), then the processor executing the icbi instruction invalidates block B in all processor instruction caches in the entire system. On the other hand, if block B is not forced to be coherent, the icbi instruction simply forces the executing processor's instruction cache to be invalidated.

The PowerPC instruction isynch is related to icbi; isync causes the processor to wait for all previous instructions to complete and then to discard all prefetched

---

[24]   The mnemonic is an acronym for "enforce in-order execution of I/O."

instructions, which forces memory fetches to get subsequent instructions. This instruction has no effect on other processors. Unlike icbi, this instruction does not have any address specification, so it deals with all instructions indiscriminately. The cache invalidations will cause many more I-cache misses after isynch than after icbi, because more entries are invalidated when isynch is executed.

Example 8-34

The FLUSH instruction in SPARC processors has a memory address operand; the processor will guarantee that the double word that includes the specified address will behave coherently with respect to instruction buffering within the complete system.

Example 8-35

The Alpha AXP supports instruction buffer synchronization with a PALcode procedure. Thus, the executing process is responsible for calling that PAL procedure after it has written to a location that might be interpreted as a portion of the instruction stream yet before it reads that location for interpretation within the instruction stream. This synchronization is also required after any change in the virtual $\rightarrow$ physical address mapping that affects the program's memory locations. The PAL call has no address specification, so it handles all of the instruction cache in the same manner. Placing this function in PALcode rather than in the processor's instruction set simplifies the implementation of the processor, but increases overhead incurred when the procedure does have to be called. This PAL call is one of only three that must be supported in all implementations of the Alpha architecture.

All instruction buffer barrier operations that make the entire buffer coherent will significantly slow program execution, because the instruction buffer or cache is effectively empty upon the completion of the instruction, so that the next instruction fetches will all cause buffer or cache misses.

8.8.3 Comments

Improving processor performance by permitting execution out of sequential order is an important technique. But we need to support the single control point illusion. Unfortunately, the only way that functionality can be assured is by making execution out of order be conditional on passing local tests for compatibility between the effect of execution in program order and the effect of the actual (out-of-order) execution. Therefore, processors in a multiprocessor system must support interprocessor synchronization.

The communication times within the system and the possible reordering of instruction execution within each processor may introduce variations between the program's perception of the execution order, the processor's perception of that order, and the actual activity. In fact, the actual orders might appear to be different at different points within the system. In particular, the order of reads and writes of a shared object can be uncertain. Barrier instructions can be inserted into programs to assure correct synchronization. From the point of view of the processor executing the barrier instruction, it guarantees the relative ordering between the execution of the instructions prior to the barrier (in program order) and the instructions following the barrier. In particular, all instructions prior to the barrier must be completed before any of those that follow can be initiated.[25]

8.9 SUMMARY

In this chapter, we discussed how to design mechanisms to assure that shared objects will be correctly utilized by a set of cooperating processes. We explored alternative specification techniques and related programming specifications. The essential requirement is to define the execution intervals during which a process requires that certain noninterference constraints be met in order that that process perform its function properly. These specifications translate directly into lower-level constructs, leading to both processor instructions and to hardware-level constructs that support atomic (indivisible) operations. We have seen that indivisibility, while not logically required, is required if the system is to operate efficiently. Finally, we see that these same techniques can be used at the hardware level to coordinate the operation of a set of functional units sharing access to processor registers.

The synchronization methods range from highly pessimistic to highly optimistic protocols. Optimistic protocols are faster than pessimistic ones, but they do entail a risk of having to retry the transaction or operation if the optimistic assumption (that no others will interfere with the transaction) turns out to be incorrect. All logically correct protocols, whether optimistic or pessimistic, are equivalent in the sense that the semantics of each one can be implemented using any of the others.

We also studied the important problem of providing coherence among multiple copies of a logically single object. Updates to these objects have to be performed atomically, which suggests that protocols similar to those supporting atomic sequences can be used. We showed hierarchical extensions of snooping and directory-based protocols that solve this problem.

In the next chapter, we explore one other important aspect of object sharing—the secure protection of information from unauthorized access. The issues addressed in this chapter dealt with coordinating potentially overlapping accesses to shared objects without regard for whether such accesses should be allowed at all. The designer of a secure system is concerned with limiting accesses

---

[25]   But within the SPARC-V9, the programmer can specify the types of memory operations that are to be synchronized at the barrier.

based on the rules in a specified security policy. The issue of providing security is orthogonal to the issue of synchronizing permitted accesses that we have been studying in this chapter.

8.10 TRENDS

Specifications concerning the use of shared objects should follow the transaction style to define the regions within which processes assume that they have exclusive access to the shared object. Programmers should continue to believe in the single copy illusion despite efficient implementations that really use surrogate objects to provide fast access from many processors. The lock/conditional store instruction pair supporting an optimistic transaction style at the processor level should continue to be attractive.

The shared-resource model should continue to be extremely important for defining interactions in high-performance multiprocessor systems. In particular, distributed systems with local caches will continue as an important problem area. It seems probable that designs relying on programmers to specify the degree of coherence required in different objects will remain popular, because these structures have the potential for maximum flexibility (and, therefore, for the least additional execution delay) while providing coherence when required.

Distributed databases are logically similar to shared main memories, but larger access delays to reach stored objects and the need for protection against node failures make object replication and voting schemes attractive for implementing distributed databases.

Recent descriptions of shared-memory systems and their coherency requirements in bottom–up terms should disappear; designers will change emphasis from implementation details to logical requirements from applications. In this chapter, we assumed that this change will occur (we did not use some terminology that we think should disappear) when we discussed memory models.

Security and protection concerns will have an increasing impact on the design of multiprogrammed systems.

8.11 CONCEPT LIST

1. Functional behavior
2. Sequential consistency
3. Nonfunctionality may arise from arbitrary interleaving of operations
4. Access control table
5. Synchronization constraints must appear in programs and within atomic processor instructions

6. Atomic actions
7. The single copy illusion simplifies synchronization designs
8. Version numbering
9. Atomically executed transactions (or regions)
10. Capabilities pass access permissions among a set of sharing processes
11. Sharing through parameters passed by reference
12. Semaphores, simple and general
13. Separating ACQUIRE and FREE operations—a risk of deadlock
14. Two-phase locking or hierarchical numbering to prevent deadlocks
15. Monitor software structures
16. Transactions—an optimistic view of execution possibilities
17. TEST_AND_SET operations
18. LOAD_LOCKED, STORE_CONDITIONAL instruction pairs
19. Master and surrogate object copies
20. Interprocessor communication to synchronize surrogate object copies
21. Cache coherence
22. Snooping protocols
23. Cache directories
24. Write invalidate protocols
25. MESI protocols
26. Hierarchical coherence protocols
27. Voting protocols for coherence and transaction coordination
28. Version numbers
29. Memory barrier instructions
30. Instruction barrier instructions

8.12 PROBLEMS

8-1. Construct an example that shows the nonfunctionality of a system constructed in the following manner: Start with two processes, each executing a few commutative transactions. Add the following connection between two successive transactions within one (or both) process(es). The logical connection is that the process saves a value stored during the first transaction and uses it to affect a value stored during the second transaction.

8-2. A data object that is structured as a doubly linked list is shared between two processes. They desire to coordinate exclusive accesses to the list to perform the following two operations:

    1. Find the list entry whose value field meets a search criterion and delete it from the list.

    2. Insert a new list entry in the position that maintains the entries in a logical order based on increasing values in the field named SEQUENTIAL.

(a) Describe a monitor-style design that solves the logical requirement.

(b) Describe a different locking protocol that maximizes the chance that the two processes can access simultaneously entries in the list, while still providing the illusion that the two accesses were managed by a scheme such as the one you designed in part (a).

8-3.   It has been claimed that in order to share a program object among several processes, each should have an independent address space that is logically organized as a segmented address space.

(a) Why would one wish to have segmentation?

(b) Could the logical independence requirement be met by allocating the program to a designated set of pages within a paged, but not segmented, address space? Explain the advantages and drawbacks of the paging option (compared to the segmentation option).

8-4.   We study the relationship between **region** synchronization with a list and the use of lock objects to implement the **region**'s semantics.

(a) The header for a general **region** construct contains a list of resources to be acquired, as in the following

region(x, y, z) { .. }

Show that this construct cannot be implemented correctly if the operating system automatically queues a process immediately when it fails in an attempt to lock an object.

(b) Show that the issue in part (a) disappears if one can define a shared-resource hierarchy with exactly one object at each level. Define the order in which objects listed in the **region** header must be locked.

8-5.   Write complete send and receive procedures for inserting and removing messages from a mailbox object. Use the **region** construct to synchronize accesses. You may wish to base your answer on the send fragment developed in Example 8-6.

8-6.   Present a brief argument that shows that if a system shares memory among all processors in the system, an implementation of a set of cooperating processes based on the message-passing model could be replaced by an equivalent set of processes whose cooperation is based on the shared-memory model. In your answer, you can use critical regions wherever you need to specify points at which interprocess coordination/synchronization is needed. Your answer should show how a set of processes programmed using message passing can be converted into a set of processes communicating through shared memory. You may use conditional critical regions if you like, but you may not have to.

8-7.   The text claimed that a process that is attempting to **ACQUIRE** a list of resources and fails part of the way through the list has to relinquish its hold on the resources that it had locked before the failure was discovered. Construct an example to show that a deadlock can occur if this policy is not followed.

8-8.   In this problem, we explore the use of semaphores such that each semaphore governs access to a specified set of shared objects. The program may have several semaphores, each one controlling access to a different set of shared objects. The association between an object and a semaphore is defined in the shared object's declaration; for example:

      int A lock s1;   //Not C++

This statement declares the integer A and states that locking s1 will prevent another process from accessing the integer A. Notice that this declaration does not declare s1; it merely establishes the fact that s1 will control access to a set that includes A. The same semaphore can be associated with several shared objects, in which case all the objects are locked together when the lock is set. The list in a **region** header states the semaphores to be set during execution of the **region**.

(a) Is this structure more or less general than the **region** construct defined in Section 8.3.2? Explain.

(b) State one important reason why this structure might be preferred over the **region** construct.

(c) Design a data structure for accessing objects and locks to permit hardware checking for lock setting during every access attempt. Make your structure consistent with the proposed scheme for declaring object–semaphore associations.

(d) Could a compiler automatically generate the semaphore lists to be checked upon entry to critical regions that have been bracketed in the program? Could the compiler check for illegal accesses to shared objects? Explain.

(e) Discuss the effect of permitting one object to be locked by any one of several semaphore objects. In this variant, the object declaration could list more than one lock object.

8-9. This problem concerns the design of a semaphore structure to control accesses to a set of interchangeable resources.

(a) A designer proposes that the count that would have been the state of a generalized semaphore be moved into an integer variable to which access is controlled by a simple semaphore. Could you use this proposed solution as the basis for a solution that solves the problem?

(b) A second designer proposes that the design of part (a) be modified by adding another lock object to which a using process will make an access attempt only if the count reveals that no resources are available. The program for a using process might look like the following:

```
again:    P( biglock );
          if ( count == 0 )
              flag = true;
          else {
              count = count – 1;
              if ( count == 0 ) {
                  flag2 = true;
                  P( waitlock );
              };
          };
          V( biglock );
          if ( flag ) {
              P( waitlock );
              V( waitlock );
```

```
            goto again;
    };
    ..                          //critical region in here
    P( biglock );
    count = count + 1;
    if ( flag2 ) {
            V( waitlock );
            flag2 = false;
    };
    V( biglock );
```

Explain why the flag2 tests are required. Does this proposal solve the problem? Explain.

8-10. Show how bad timing can result in message loss or message duplication if the buffer has a message vector and a full flag. The system does not use a lock to limit access to the buffer. Consider both the interleaving of the low-level memory operations and the order of events in the sending and receiving programs. [*Hint:* For sending (receiving), the critical events are setting/testing the flag and filling (emptying) the buffer.]

8-11. Repeat Problem 8-10 if the flag can assume three values to denote these three states of the buffer: full, in_use, and empty. Enumerate the types of nonfunctionality that may arise and relate each one to the structure of the interleaving.

8-12. The major advantage of object sharing using a common descriptor is that object relocation is simplified.

(a) What drawbacks are inherent in this design? Explain them.

(b) Devise a scheme to transfer ownership of the common descriptor from one process to another. The solution to this problem may need interlocks and timing constraints to assure correct access from other processes during the transfer process. Design your solution to minimize the amount of time that accesses from other processes would be delayed. Assume that the descriptor contains a status field that can be used by the mechanism that delays accesses during the transfer. Your solution should specify the state of this control field and its effect on other accesses.

(c) Within the structure of your solution to part (b), show how an access to the object is achieved. Include all required checks.

8-13. The unfairness of the P and V implementations shown in the text can be fixed to remove the possibility of unfair system behavior. This problem concerns such fixes.

(a) Show that the problem may arise when there is a process in the waiting queue in the lock and some other process executes P(R).

(b) Rewrite the P and V procedures so that they do not exhibit the problem you identified in part (a).

(c) Show that the problem that was exhibited in Example 8-10 still exists. Discuss how you might change the P procedure to overcome this difficulty.

(d) Show that a similar difficulty lurks in the implementation of the list_P operation given in the text.

8-14. Consider a system in which sharing processes have a common descriptor table and every descriptor contains the lock on the segment it describes. There are two options: (1) The lock contains a single bit to indicate whether the segment is locked, and (2) the lock contains both a lock bit and the process number of the process that locked the segment.

    (a) For each option, describe the actions on the lock in the descriptor while LOCK-ing a segment. State where the responsibility for correct locking lies.

    (b) For each option, describe the actions on the lock in the descriptor while FREE-ing a segment.

    (c) For each option, describe how run-time checks for access validity are made. State where the responsibility for correct access checking lies.

    (d) If the shared segment is read-only for all sharing processes, can the design be changed to permit more than one process to access the segment simultaneously? Explain.

8-15. In this problem, you will consider the implementation of the monitor construct in a multiprocessor system.

    (a) Show that if the same monitor module can be executed on more than one processor, correct implementation does require an underlying atomic synchronization operation.

    (b) Show that if each distinct monitor is statically assigned to a specific processor, processor scheduling techniques can be devised to provide correct synchronization.

8-16. Write out the details of a monitor with two entry points lock(controlled_type x) and free(controlled_type x) that are supposed to behave like P(S) and V(S) with respect to the objects controlled within the monitor. Pay careful attention to the states of the locks and semaphores when lock(x) causes the executing process to become blocked.

8-17. This problem is concerned with the design of a locking scheme that permits a process to lock the same object multiple times without deleterious effects. It is easy to argue that this situation requires the use of a counter within the lock.

    (a) Briefly describe why the counter is required.

    (b) Briefly describe why the procedure requesting the lock operation should be identified to the program handling the lock operations.

    (c) Write out the implementation of P(L, proc) and V(L, proc), where L is the name of the lock and proc is a process identifier (guaranteed by the system to be both correct and unique).

8-18. To shorten the access time to shared objects, a designer proposes that although in memory there is a single descriptor of the object (indirect pointers being used to reach the descriptor from the sharing processes), a process be allowed to obtain a copy of the unique descriptor during the time that process is executing within a **region** in which it locks the object. The copy of the descriptor would be unlocked, while the unique descriptor would be locked during the **region**.

    (a) Describe the actions on **region** entry and exit, especially actions referencing the descriptor. Assume that the lock is kept in the unique descriptor. Pay attention to the problem of finding the unique descriptor if the process wishes to lock the same segment a second time.

    (b) Prove that this scheme preserves system functionality. In other words, if the system using shared descriptors is functional, prove that this system also is functional. Note that you do not have to argue about the functionality of the system based on shared descriptors.

8-19. This problem concerns process queueing after a process tries to enter a conditional critical region and finds that the entry condition is false. The issue here is the selection of the object on which the process will be queued.

(a) One option is to queue the process on the first shared object that is both listed in the **region** header and used in the entry condition. Discuss this option and show how it is possible that the process be starved even though the entry condition may become true.

(b) Another option is to queue the process on all objects listed in the **region** header that appear in the entry condition. Show data structures to implement this option. Specify which operations must access or modify these data structures. Remember that you must update the queues so that the process is activated whenever a value has been changed in one of the objects used in the expression. Would it be better to allow the coder to specify which object's queue should be used when the process cannot enter the **region**? Explain.

8-20. Discuss this claim: A system uses critical **region**s to coordinate the use of shared objects and allows nested critical **region**s. If a subroutine may access shared objects, region nesting can be a problem, especially if the subroutine may be passed shared objects after they have been locked. Suppose that each lock object contains the (Boolean) state of the lock and the queue of processes waiting on the lock. The claim is that either the system may deadlock or else the programmer must write different versions of the subroutines that may access shared objects, based on whether the object was locked before the call or not.

These programs differ in whether the passed parameter is already locked:

```
        Program 1                        Program 2

a: shared int;                   a: shared int;   ..    ..
procedure f( x : shared int ) is procedure f( x : shared int) is
begin                            begin
    .. --body of f                   .. --body of f
end;                             end;
..                               ..
begin      --calling program     begin --calling program
    lock( a );                       ..
    f( a ); --a is locked;           f( a ); --a is not locked;
    ..                               ..
end;                             end;
```

If the claim is true, show how problems arise and how a program should be written to avoid them. If the claim is false, show how the program should be written so that a single copy of the subroutine is adequate. In addition, if the claim is false, can you find a simple modification of the design using process numbers in locks to allow region nesting?

8-21. Amend the transaction program of Section 8.4.4 to check whether the executing process has been snubbed and should be allowed to complete its entire transaction under the protection of a global lock.

8-22. Consider a processor design that contains completion buffers to order transaction completion. These buffers operate in a manner analogous to those that handle in-order instruction completion in a superscalar processor. The designers claim that this approach reduces the need to retry transactions that fail the intersection tests. Comment on this claim.

8-23. A shared procedure rewrites some of its own instructions when in a loop. The programmer defines a "code transaction" to be any region (within the program) in which the process requires exclusive access to the program object itself. The possibility that the program itself could be modified makes sharing difficult. One proposed design locks the entire procedure segment while a process is executing within the code transaction.

(a) Show how this design could be implemented in a system with several processors.

(b) Can you devise a simple way to relax the rule so that it keeps other processes from making conflicting accesses within the code transaction? In this context, do you need a special definition of an access conflict? Explain.

8-24. In this problem, we consider the following design proposal. It is claimed that the design simplifies guarantees that locking operations, say, TESTANDSET, will operate correctly even in the presence of caches associated with processors. Following is the design proposal: The addresses of all objects that can be operands of TESTANDSET are limited to a distinguished set of addresses (such as those with their first eight address bits equal to 0xFF). Further, any object with such an address cannot be loaded into any cache.

(a) What system modules (regardless of whether implemented in hardware, firmware, or software) are affected by the design change?

(b) Where are the checks that ensure correct locking in the proposed system design?

(c) Compare the proposed design against a conventional design.

8-25. One approach to implementing uninterruptible operations on lock objects (L1, L2, etc.) is to place a single global lock (GL) at a designated location, such as location 0, and adopt the convention that any lock operation that should be atomic be, in fact, preceded by an atomic LOCK operation accessing GL. After the lock interaction has been completed, GL is FREEd. This question is based on the observation that because GL is locked only while another lock is being locked, it will be locked for shorter intervals than other locks in the system.

(a) How would queues containing processes waiting for locks to become free be organized? In particular, where would they be located? Where in the operation execution sequence would a process be queued?

(b) Would it be effective simply to have processes busy wait for GL? Explain.

(c) What information about the environment would you desire if you had to evaluate the performance of this design style?

8-26. Discuss the interprocessor communications required to implement the Alpha APX locked read and conditional store instructions correctly.

(a) Compare the interprocessor communications required under this scheme with those required under snooping cache coherence protocols.

(b) Discuss why the question in part (a) is interesting.

8-27. In this problem, we consider a processor that uses instruction lookahead to improve speed and that it predicts branch outcomes based on the direction of the branch. In particular, conditional backwards branches are predicted as being taken, whereas forward branches are predicted as not being taken. Further assume that the processor synchronizes accesses to shared objects with a pair of instructions that do not always succeed; a conditional branch is used to initiate a retry when the attempt actually fails. Under these conditions, a processor-level instruction sequence that performs an atomic update might have a structure like this:

```
tryagain:  synch1 x;         //read the contents in x
           <compute_new x>;
           synch2 x;         //write new value into x
           if_fail_goto tryagain;
```

  (a) Describe the operation of this atomic update fragment if the synch instructions are LOADL and STOREC.
  (b) Explain why the fragment is based on inconsistent assumptions about system behavior.
  (c) Fix the fragment to produce a version that is based on consistent assumptions about system behavior.

8-28. Devise an implementation of the Load_Locked, and Store_conditional instructions using messages broadcast to all processors. Each message that initiates the instruction contains the number of the processor executing the Load_Locked or Store_conditional instruction, along with the effective address of the instruction's memory operand.
  (a) Describe the conditions under which additional messages must be passed among the processors to implement the semantics of these instructions.
  (b) Specify the information in each of the messages you identified in part (a).

8-29. In Example 8-23, we commented that providing a time estimate for the duration of a long-term software lock would help decide whether a process that has just missed setting the lock should idle until the lock is freed, the alternative being to suspend the process and swap to another process.
  (a) Suppose that the system clock could be copied quickly. Show how the clock reading could be used to determine the time remaining before the lock will be freed. How do you arrange to know the region's execution time (the duration of the locked interval) and the time the lock was set?
  (b) Write out the actions of a process setting this lock, and at the same time saving enough information to enable the idle/suspend decision to be made by a later process if it finds the lock set.
  (c) What information would you need to determine whether the design developed in this problem is worthwhile? Explain any criteria you use to make your selections.

8-30. Consider the LOCK states that the System/38 can apply to objects (see Table 8-3). When an object is not locked and a lock request is made, there is no problem in changing the lock accordingly. But when the lock is set, it is possible that a new request could ask that the lock be placed in a state that is not consistent with the present state of the lock. Take the position that the lock states that give permission to processes that do not set the lock are permissive (so the permissions can be removed without penalty). But the permissions that a process gains for itself by setting the lock cannot be removed except by the process that set the lock in the first place. Answer the following questions using this rule concerning conflicts in setting the locks.

(a) Process P2 wishes to set lock L1 to LEAR. For which previous states of the lock can this instruction complete without waiting for P1 to clear the lock?

(b) Complete Table 8-10. The row labels indicate the state of the lock as set by process P1, and the column labels indicate the lock state desired by process P2. In each entry, write the state of the lock after P2's instruction is completed, or the word "WAIT" to indicate that P2 must wait for P1 to change the lock's state before P2's instruction can be completed.

TABLE 8-10   IBM SYSTEM/38 LOCK STATE CHANGES (SEE PROBLEM 8-30)

State Previously Set by P1	State Desired by P2				
	LSRD	LSRO	LSUP	LEAR	LENR
(None)					
LSRD					
LSRO					
LSUP					
LEAR					
LENR					

8-31. A designer proposes two schemes to help a system implement atomic operations. Both schemes are supposed to allow the system to be configured with memory modules that were not designed to handle special semantics for the atomic operation. You are to evaluate the two schemes, making some preliminary design decisions and discussing their comparative features. Both schemes are based on having memory modules that support an atomic memory operation that swaps the contents of the addressed memory location with a processor register.

In scheme A, the object value of all 1's is reserved to indicate that the object containing all 1's is locked for processing by some process. The processor's control unit would not allow the atomic instruction to proceed if the previous value swapped into the processor turned out to be all 1's. The object is "unlocked" when the processor performs another swap with the locked location. Answer questions (a) through (d) for this design.

(a) Detail the sequence of operations required to perform an atomic increment operation on a shared integer value in a memory location.

(b) Are there restrictions on the values that may be assumed by the shared object? (Does your answer depend on the representation conventions for integers?)

(c) Will your design guarantee functional system operation based only on the sequencing rule, or does it rely upon the "correct" implementation of system or application software? If the answer is "yes," define the dependencies. If your answer is "no," show how functionality is provided.

(d) Can user processes be interrupted while performing the atomic operation? Explain.

In scheme B, the value of all 1's is used in the same manner as in scheme A, but the operand value is located in the location following the lock flag location. [In this design, if the operand address is A, then location A holds the lock, and location (A + 1) holds the integer quantity.] Answer questions (a) through (d) for scheme B.

(e) Compare schemes A and B and recommend one of them. Defend your selection.

8-32. A designer tries to provide atomic operations with minimum effect on memory module design. He proposes that a memory module be designed so that it could be locked and unlocked by sending specific memory access codes. The proposed sequence of operations to implement an atomic operation is as follows:

1. Memory is accessed for a "start uninterruptible operation" cycle.
2. The addressed memory module locks up and returns the previous contents of the addressed location.
3. The addressed module is unlocked by another access attempt.

There are three design options concerning when the addressed module decides to unlock itself:

1. A write cycle to the same address.
2. An "unlock" memory operation is requested.
3. The processor that locked the module makes any other access request to the module.

(a) Compare these designs for generality and protection.

(b) Describe the memory module control logic for each design.

(c) Are there any limitations on the operations that could be performed on operands within the module in a single operation?

8-33. How important is it that the priority resolution in the NYU Ultracomputer be fair? What would be the consequences of fixing the request priorities based on the ports where the requests arrive? In your answer, consider both the logic in the switch modules and the system's functional and performance characteristics.

8-34. This problem concerns the use of a cache to speed access to shared objects. Each cache is associated with a processor. Object addresses are segmented. Under design A, the cache holds (segment_number, physical_origin) pairs, and is searched using the segment number. Under design B, the cache holds (process_number, segment_number, physical_origin) triples, and is searched using the (process_number, segment_number) pair. Note that design A requires cache invalidation on process switching.

(a) If there is one processor, describe how all copies of the physical location of a segment can be updated when the segment is relocated. If your solution requires searching for some entry in a cache, specify what search field is used, what value is being found, and what the search criterion should be.

(b) Repeat part (a) if there are several processors. Describe the interprocessor communication required to perform the relocation and update function. Show the timing of all events that are important to a correct implementation of your solution.   [*Turn the page for part* (c).]

(c) Introduce a "reference count" that contains the number of caches that hold copies of a descriptor. Show how the relocation difficulty in a multiprocessor system could be alleviated by adding the rule that a segment cannot be relocated while it is described in some cache. Are there any drawbacks to this design? If so, what are they?

8-35. This problem concerns the design of a cache that participates in a snooping coherence protocol. The text comments that during cache updates driven by the snoop logic, normal cache accesses from the local processor would have to be delayed; furthermore, it proposes a solution using a duplicated cache directory. A designer proposes that this problem be alleviated by building the cache as a set of interleaved modules. Let c denote the degree of cache interleaving, s the probability of receiving a snooping coherence request during an arbitrary cache cycle, and h the snooping hit ratio (the fraction of snoop requests that actually match an entry in the local cache).

(a) What is the probability that a processor access will encounter interference from a snooping request?

(b) Describe the cache design strategy, specifying those portions that are affected by the interleaving.

8-36. This problem concerns a hierarchical implementation of the MESI cache coherence protocol. The system is structured as a tree, with a coherency controller at each node of the tree, all processors at the leaves of the tree, and the common global memory at the root of the tree. Assume that all child nodes of one parent and their parent are connected together through a private (i.e., not shared with other nodes) snooping bus. We wish to argue that all the coherency controllers can use the same states and interaction protocol.

(a) State adjusted meanings of the MESI states so they can be applied to entries within a coherence manager at an intermediate node.

(b) Show that the state transitions and interactions defined in the text for the single-level coherency system can be used in this design. In particular, argue that the same transitions can be described in a manner consistent with the state interpretations you developed in part (a).

8-37. Describe the four states of the MESI coherence protocol in terms of the master/surrogate copy distinction. Outline an argument that the master copy is always coherent and correct if the MESI protocol is followed during all writes.

8-38. The system contains a bus using a snooping protocol to invalidate surrogates upon a write access by one of the processors. Draw a timing diagram showing the coordination signals on the bus. Describe the differences between the signals in this system design and the signals in a bus-based system using the MESI protocol to invalidate cache entries.

8-39. In this problem you will modify the MESI protocol. The objective is to reduce the number of snoop requests required to implement an RMW instruction.

(a) Find the snoop requests emitted from a processor that is performing a TEST_AND_SET instruction under the MESI protocol operating as specified in the text.

(b) It is proposed to change the protocol by adding a snoop request "Start RMW operation." Specify modifications to the MESI protocol to support this change.

(c) Repeat part (a) for the modified MESI protocol you developed in part (b).

8-40. Specify how to modify the MESI coherence protocol to behave correctly if the processor that initiated a coherent write operation fails before all responses have arrived from all caches.

8-41. A cached system can exhibit "false sharing" if two different processor caches hold the same cache line, which is wide enough to hold two separate shared objects.

(a) Construct an example that shows how a pair of processes can exhibit false sharing and still be functional, provided that one can assign separate dirty bits to parts of the cache line. (*Hint*: Add in the capability to store data blocks smaller than a cache line.)

(b) Define the behavior of the cache that is trying to write an object when it discovers that another cache is emitting a value for that entry (look at the combination leading to the footnote in Table 8-7).

(c) By tracing the state sequence of the MESI protocol for your example from part (a), show that the correct answers are obtained by following your rule from part (b).

8-42. Consider a system with cached shared objects. It is claimed that to provide a correct write operation that is synchronized among all sharing nodes, the number of directed messages that must be transmitted cannot be less than twice the number of copies of the shared object being written. Please exclude the possibility of broadcast messages for the purposes of this argument.

(a) Discuss why this claim is correct if you use a bit vector representation of the directory information.

(b) Justify your answer to part (a) by showing the problems that could occur if fewer messages were used.

(c) What is the bound on the number of messages if a singly linked list is used instead of a bit vector?

(d) Revise your answer to part (a) if each message can contain a copy of the bit vector.

8-43. The data structures that hold information regarding the locations of cached object copies must be updated when that information changes. For each of the designs described in Figure 8-14, describe the messages that must pass between nodes to update the caches and the information about the locations of the surrogate copies when write invalidation is in use.

(a) A processor performs an RMW access to an object present in its local cache.

(b) A processor performs an RMW access to an object that is not present in the local cache.

8-44. The doubly linked list of cached copies used in the IEEE SCI design has the advantage that it takes only a few messages to update the data structure, even when the object is being removed from the cache. In this problem you are asked to develop an update algorithm that uses the minimum number of messages to unlink an item from the list, yet works correctly under all possible circumstances.

(a) What is the minimum number of messages that would have to be sent to other cache directories to unlink an entry from the list, ignoring any coordination problems? Explain the uses of the messages that you identify.

(b) Using an example, describe the difficulty that can arise if two caches that occupy adjacent places in the list attempt to unlink themselves at about the same time. Assume that they did not recognize that there was a problem, and that they simply used the design of part (a).

(c) Revise the design of part (a) so that the situation described in part (b) cannot arise. Explain the need for any messages and/or states that you add to the protocol.

8-45. Choosing to use a singly linked list of cached copies increases the number of messages required to remove a cache from the list when its line is overwritten. Describe the messages used to remove an list entry under the representation scheme of Figure 8-14d. Strive for the minimum number of messages as you design the protocol.

8-46. Describe the meanings of the messages used to update a sharing list under the IEEE SCI design within a two-level hierarchical system. Is your answer changed if the type of connection at either level is changed? Explain.

8-47. Consider the system shown in Figure 8-17. The text discussed the implementation of a cache invalidation protocol to achieve cache coherence. In this problem, you modify this design to support the MESI protocol.

(a) What state information is needed in the coherence directories participating in the MESI protocol? Describe the relationship between the states of the surrogates of X in the local caches and the state of the CD entry related to X. Your answer should specify the valid combinations of states and the transitions among these composite states that are induced by both local and remote activity.

(b) A processor connected to local bus A executes an instruction to write to the object named X. Describe the consequent state changes within the CD for bus A and the caches connected to bus A.

(c) For the situation of part (b), describe the actions within local bus B when there is an entry in the CD for bus B that matches X. Be sure to cover all possible states in the system.

8-48. A correct implementation of multiprocessor cache coordination requires policies for cache invalidation and updating values in the memory. Assume that all caches are associated with processors. Policy options include invalidating the entire cache when any entry must be invalidated and invalidating single entries as required. Another dimension requiring attention concerns the timing of processor operations relative to any intercache signaling that may be necessary. Design a signaling and invalidation scheme to handle TESTANDSET operations correctly. Specify the processor timing.

8-49. This problem contrasts and compares the techniques used to build software monitors in cached multiprocessor systems with the techniques used to coordinate accesses to multiple copies of objects in distributed databases. Assume that every cache is associated with a single processor.

(a) Can the distributed voting scheme used for database synchronization be used to coordinate monitors?

(b) Can monitor techniques be used to synchronize accesses to database copies distributed across a network? If the answer is "no," explain how the monitors could be enhanced to change the answer to "yes."

8-50. This problem concerns the voting rules for approving a transaction commit in a distributed database. The claim is that the rule for voting OK on a new incoming approval request must include a check against the transaction commit times of any variable that will be written by a transaction for which the node has previously voted OK, *if* that proposed commit has not been canceled.

    (a) Construct a scenario that produces nonfunctional behavior if this check is not made.

    (b) Describe the contents of each vote request message to make it possible for each node to make all necessary checks when it votes.

    (c) Contrast this situation with proper handling of write buffers in cache coherence protocols.

8-51. Specify the types of barriers (in the style of the SPARC-V9 processor described in Example 8-31) that should be used in the transaction implementation of Example 8-30. Your answer should declare the minimum number of constraints that still assure functional system behavior.

8-52. Explain the need for each of the MB instructions in the processes of Example 8-30. Show how nonfunctional behavior will result if each MB instruction is removed, with the other three being retained. (*Hint:* The first case was discussed in the example.)

9

PROTECTION AND SECURITY

*Three may keep a secret if
two of them are dead.*

— B. Franklin

*Many a man is saved from being a thief
by finding everything locked up.*

— E. W. Howe

Our illusions about computer systems are based on the view that the processes within the computer system are logically separate entities that do not interact, except in the controlled manner discussed in the last two chapters. A key question concerns the locus of responsibility for supporting these boundaries. *Protection* and *security* are two aspects of this issue. Protection separates processes according to self-declared boundaries between processes and objects. Security also establishes and enforces boundaries between processes and objects, but these boundaries must conform to an externally defined security policy, typically, using externally defined attributes associated with processes and objects to determine permissible accesses by those processes to those objects.

Protection schemes establish boundaries within the computer system, but they do not attempt to verify that particular people are using the computer or that the processes or objects have externally defined properties that affect the access permissions accorded to the processes within the system. Both security and protection systems require checks that validate each access attempt, at some level of granularity. At a high level of granularity, files are checked for access permission when they are opened, and the system limits each process to the access modes that had been requested when the file was opened. Such checks can be built into the file system software. If one is concerned about limiting access to objects located within the memory, process boundaries become important, and each access attempt must be checked, by the MMU, for example.

In this chapter we formalize the security and protection requirements and show several approaches to the implementation of computer systems that protect information. We discuss an approach to secure system design based on using simple conceptual structures realized mostly in hardware. This approach should produce a design with provable security properties.

What will we trust as we build a computer system to protect information and provide security? At the lowest level, only two things: hardware and encryption. We trust that the hardware works correctly and is tamperproof. We trust that any encryption used within the system cannot be reversed by an attacker and that it cannot be bypassed (this is easily argued if the hardware is tamperproof).[1] Upon these two basic trusts, we construct a secure system.

A number of system designs have been created to address the security problem; most use a large proportion of software and a small amount of specialized hardware to ensure the system's security properties. Although it may be possible to implement a secure system in this manner, it may be extremely difficult to convince people outside the implementation team that the system does indeed possess the desired security properties. On the other hand, moving a larger fraction of the solution into hardware and retaining a smaller fraction of the solution in software can make the system more easily understood; this may even make it possible to prove that the system does possess desirable security properties. Once the desired intellectual feeling of security has been achieved, an alternate implementation migrating the hardware support to software might be considered because this kind of design can be based on commodity parts. However, shifting the implementation from hardware to software makes it more difficult to convince people that the desired access limitations have been provided.

After you have read this chapter, you will understand the problem of controlling information access, whether for simple protection or tighter security, and you will know several methods for securely restricting information access through software and hardware kernel designs. In addition, you will understand some potential attacks against secure systems and you will see the difficulty of thwarting these attacks.

---

[1]   Of course, our basic position remains: that within a reasonable system encryption cannot be a complete solution to the problem because it will slow execution too much.

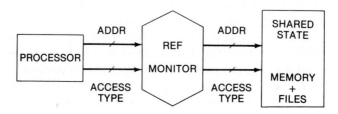

Figure 9-1   The reference monitor

9.1 PROTECTION

Proper synchronization among processes sharing resources requires proper coordination algorithms within the sharing processes themselves. The complete implementation of a sharing system requires either that all processes in the system behave "correctly" with respect to the shared objects or that the system checks that other processes do not access the shared resources. In this section, we show how a system can be designed to handle access authorization information and to use that information to detect unauthorized access attempts.

All access checking mechanisms that provide effective protection or security use checking mechanisms placed between the processor and the memory, as depicted in Figure 9-1. The checker is usually called a *memory management unit* (MMU). Most MMU designs rely on a data structure containing space descriptors holding access permission bits. For example, page-based access permissions are determined from page descriptors originally fetched from tables in memory. A limited version of protection applies to files. The operating system verifies permissions when a process attempts to obtain access to the file.

9.1.1 Checks During Visibility Changes

The visibility of a resource changes when a process attempts to "open" (or close) a file, an object, or a device. The act of opening the resource effectively makes the resource visible because it places the resource within the set of resources accessible to the process. One way to prevent unauthorized access to a shared resource R by nonsharing processes is to prevent them from opening R. If the process cannot open the resource, it cannot either read or write to the object. The second level of control governs whether a process is permitted to write to a file. Controlling access based on the type of access can be enforced by file system software because this software is always encountered on any access to the file itself. To prevent unauthorized accesses, the file system software checks whether the requesting process is permitted to make the requested access to the file before performing the function on behalf of the process.

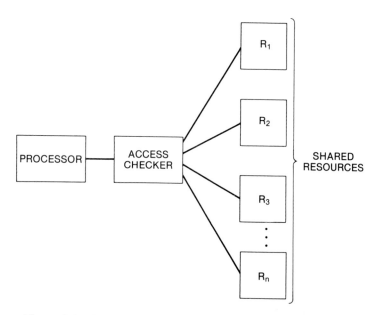

Figure 9-2   Access checker placed between the processor
and the shared resources

Some secure systems handle *dynamic changes* in access rights by determining the proper access rights for each object (or segment) whenever the segment is loaded into the address space. This provides correct behavior even if the permissions might be changing during program execution, but it does consume extra effort to make the checks on demand rather than as a batch upon process initiation.

9.1.2 Checks During Access Attempts

For stricter verification that an executing process does not overstep the boundaries that have been imposed from outside, the system can check every access attempt to verify that it is authorized. Such a check can be performed by a monitor, a device driver, or the memory management unit. To work correctly, these checkers must be encountered during every access attempt. Furthermore, the access rights seen by the checking mechanism must be set properly.

The checker is placed between the executing process and the resources, as shown in Figure 9-2. In the context of secure system design, the checker interposed between the processor and the shared resources is called a *reference monitor*.

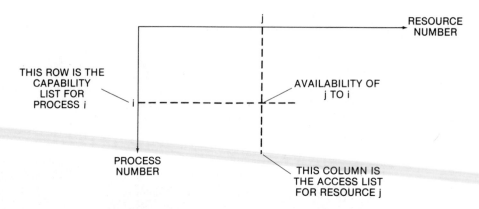

Figure 9-3   The access control matrix (ACM)

9.1.3 Representations of Access Control Information

We present four ways to represent access permissions, starting with the most flexible and ending with the least flexible. They are as follows:

1. Access control matrix
2. Capabilities
3. Key access control
4. Ring numbers

Access Control Matrix and Capabilities. Two general representations of access rights are *capabilities* and the *access control matrix* (ACM). Both representations allow all access rights to all objects for all processes in the system to be specified independently. Capabilities represent this information using a set of independent objects (that could be distributed within the system's memory), the ACM collects it all in a single matrix, illustrated in Figure 9-3. Each row of the access control matrix corresponds to a "subject," an active entity that can issue requests to access resources. In the present context, processes are the only subjects. Each column of the matrix corresponds to a resource (which we call an "object"). The matrix entry ACM(s, j) contains the access rights of subject s for object j.

Usually, the access control matrix is "sparse," because most processes will be denied access to most objects. Then one can compress the information by removing the "null" entries. For example, we could replace the matrix with a set of lists containing the nonnull access entries. The capability list and access control list representations collect the rows and columns of the ACM, respectively.

Definition. The *capability list* for subject s is a list of all shared resources that may be accessed by the subject; each entry in the list contains the name of a shared object accessible from subject s and an access rights field specifying the types of access allowed to that object.

Definition. The *access list* for object j is a list of all subjects that may access that object; each entry in the list contains the name of a subject that may access object j and an access rights field specifying the types of access allowed from that subject.

The capability list for a process bears a striking similarity with a segment descriptor table (SDT); the major difference is that the SDT defines both access rights and object addresses, whereas the capability list defines access rights without fixing the addressing. The difference is apparent in a system with capability registers in the processor. With each access attempt, the instruction specifies a capability register to name the object to be accessed. One cannot permit the capability register to be used for checking unless it also determines the addressing, because the association between the capability and the contents of the object must be maintained at all times.

The capability list for process P does not need to be accessed unless P is in execution. Thus, the capability list may be swapped to secondary memory if P is not ready for execution.

Each access list is logically associated with the resource whose access rights it describes. Because searching the list to find the rights for an executing process is tedious, the access list structure is not used to control memory accesses. It is, however, perfectly suited for monitoring file accesses and is used in this manner in many systems. Like the capability list, the access list can be swapped out if the resource is not likely to be accessed.

Example 9-1

The IBM System/38 (and therefore, the AS/400) supports access permission control using a mechanism similar to a capability list. Access authorizations are associated with files and other "system objects." Each process may have a private set of authorizations. In addition, it may inherit authorizations from other processes and it always inherits the "public" authorizations associated with the object in question. The combination of authorizations for a particular access attempt is determined by the "OR" of the permissions obtained from these three types of sources. An access is permitted if it is compatible with the cumulative authorization determined from the environment, as described above.

The System/38 processor rights checking mechanism monitors not only simple read and write accesses, but also accesses that control the existence of and authorizations for the object. Table 9-1 lists the types of access that are separately controlled by the system; notice that the monitored operations suggest file operations.

With space authorization permission, the process can obtain a pointer to the contents of an object, with no further checking during a later access attempt. A process with the authorized pointer permission can obtain a copy of the pointer in

TABLE 9-1   IBM AS/400 ACCESS TYPES AND PERMITTED OPERATIONS

Access Type	Typical Operations Permitted
Object control	Transfer ownership; destroy
Object management	Grant authority; rename
Authorized pointer	Store permissions in pointer
Space	Get pointer to contents— accesses not checked later
Retrieve	Read contents
Insert	Put a new entry in the object
Delete	Remove an entry in the object
Update	Overwrite an entry in the object

which the access rights are based on the current system state. Thus, the access rights in the pointer are bound when the copy is obtained. As a result, the program with the pointer copy might hold more permissions than would be allowed if the access permissions were checked when the actual access was attempted. The discrepancy can arise because a program holding object management permission might have changed the access rights during the intervening time.

Access Keys. Under this scheme, the system validates an access request if there is a match between a key value associated with the executing process and one or more key values associated with the object to which access is being attempted. The basic check is illustrated in Figure 9-4. A general key-based access control scheme allows one to associate with each resource a separate set of key values controlling each type of access; furthermore, a process may be associated with an arbitrary number of key values. The access check examines the resource's key value(s) associated with the type of access attempted, looking for a match between any key in that set and any key possessed by the process. Note that under this scheme, two processes accessing the same resource will examine the identical sets of resource keys (there being only one per resource) when making an access attempt to that resource. In effect, the resource's key set is a global entity. This fact makes the process of assigning key values difficult (the problem of finding a good assignment of key values is closely related to the covering problems discussed in logic design).

Given that resource keys (and therefore the access rights) are public, how can one set the keys so that different processes have different access rights? One could just create new key values to distinguish all necessary combinations of (access right, resource). If there is no limit to the number of key values, this scheme is perfectly general. If the number of different key values is limited or if the number of key values that can be associated with a process or with a resource is

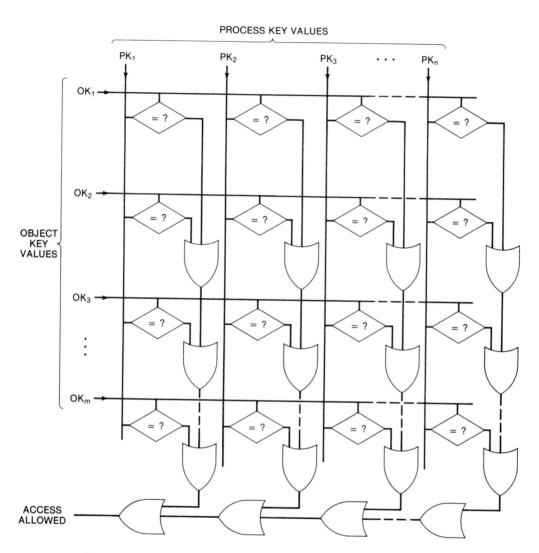

Figure 9-4 Key checking logic—multiple keys and no override values

limited, the key access control scheme cannot provide general sharing relationships. For example, it can become overloaded if a large set of complex constraints are required.

Example 9-2

The IBM 370 uses a page key scheme. Each process has one (4-bit) "access key" A; each page has a "storage key" S and a "fetch protection bit" F. The system does not distinguish between execute and read accesses, so every access attempt is treated

TABLE 9-2   IBM 370 PAGE ACCESS
CHECKS

Access Key, A	Fetch Protection Bit	Permissible Access Modes
0	0, 1	Write, read
S	0, 1	Write, read
$\neq 0, \neq S$	0	Read
$\neq 0, \neq S$	1	(None)

as a read or a write. Table 9-2 describes the checks and the corresponding permissions. Setting $A = 0$ allows the process access to everything in memory; this mode should be reserved for the operating system. When the processor is executing a user program, $A \neq 0$ and the page can be accessed by any process whose access key matches the page's storage key; the F bit defines whether write access is allowed.

If the storage key is a static property of the page, all processes that can obtain some access to the page are allowed to use exactly the same set of access modes to that page and also to all other pages in the system.

Ring Numbers.   This protection scheme ([SCHR72] and [ORGA72]) assigns a "ring number" to each process and a set of ring numbers to each resource. Arithmetic comparisons between the process' ring number and the resource's ring number(s) associated with the desired access type determine the validity of the access. The basic notions are as follows:

1. Each process executes at any time in a ring number p.
2. Each segment has a range of ring numbers for each type of access.
3. Access attempts are checked by comparing the ring numbers of the segment and the process.
4. Processes may change ring numbers during procedure call and return.

The conventional interpretation of ring numbers associates higher ring numbers with more access limitations, and thus with fewer access possibilities. Thus, under this interpretation, the core of the operating system runs in ring 0.

The legality of an access attempt in a ring protection system is determined by the type of the access desired. For each type of access, one or two integer limits may be defined; we use i_1 and i_2 to denote the limits. The semantics of the one-limit scheme are identical to those of the two-limit scheme with $i_1 = 0$. The general rule is that an access attempt is permitted if p lies within the access limits associated with the mode of the attempted access:

$$i_1 \leq p \leq i_2$$

Let r_1, r_2, w_1, w_2, e_1, and e_2, respectively, denote the limits for read, write, and execute accesses, respectively. The conditions that permit an access to proceed are as follows:

$$r_1 \leq p \leq r_2 \qquad \text{for read}$$
$$w_1 \leq p \leq w_2 \qquad \text{for write}$$
$$e_1 \leq p \leq e_2 \qquad \text{for execute}$$

We could base a ring protection scheme on one limit by setting the lower[2] limits to zero and dropping the subscripts. This scheme makes sense if the ring limits are ordered, such as $w < r < e$. With this ordering, decreasing a process' ring number increases its access rights. The following discussion uses this assumption.

Suppose that ring numbering is used to control accesses at a segment granularity to objects in main memory. Further, suppose that process P is executing instructions (from segment C) in ring p. Because P is executing instructions, C's execute ring numbers must include p. As long as the program's execution point lies within C, the program will not fault while fetching instructions. What happens if the control point tries to move to another segment S? Another set of ring brackets governs accesses to segment S, and p may or may not satisfy the conditions for execute access to S. If it does, there is no problem and program execution can proceed in the new segment without a hitch.

Two mismatch cases need to be considered. First, suppose the attempt to access an instruction fails because $e_2(S) < p$. This situation could arise when P calls a service procedure within the system that must execute within the system's context. It is easy to convince oneself that this type of call should be allowed to proceed, and that it would make sense to change the process's ring number while it executes the server procedure. Under this scheme, P's ring number would change to $e_2(S)$, which is the maximum value of the ring number permitting execute access to S. This scheme does permit indirect subversion of the ring protection mechanism. For example, if the procedure in S reads information and then returns it back to the calling program in C, the net effect is that the C program has read the value within a protected segment whose contents were supposed to be invisible from C. This subversion works because the called procedure is allowed access to the referenced object based on the ring controls that apply during execution within C; because the process' ring number was reduced upon call, those rights are more comprehensive than the caller's.

How can we install a check to eliminate this type of subversion? One way is to automatically determine the address space from which the pointer (in the parameter) came, and then use the ring numbers associated with that environment to make the access rights check. Another technique is to install a "gatekeeper" procedure that checks the validity of all parameters before allowing the

---

[2]   We could reverse this encoding, but there is no logical advantage (see Problem 9-4).

called procedure to commence execution. To make such checks accurately, the person creating the checker must be aware of exactly how each parameter is used within the called procedure. This observation leads to the conclusion that the person who wrote the procedure segment is *uniquely qualified* to write its gatekeeper(s).

To complete a gatekeeper design, we need to devise a mechanism that checks whether a call is calling a gatekeeper (which is all right) or another procedure in the segment (which is not all right). This check is necessary because we are distinguishing between gates (which can be externally visible) and procedures used in the (hidden) implementation (which should be encapsulated within the module). We can organize the link vector information so that a gate check can be based on the index of the entry point within the link vector—we could establish an index limit that separates gate procedure entries from entries to other procedure entries; if a call constitutes a ring crossing that requires that the process' ring number be reduced before the procedure can be executed, then the call must be to a gate entry. Another option distinguishes gate entries in the link vector by virtue of some special marking (see Example 9-3).

Continuing the scenario, suppose that the procedure call did reach a gate entry point. What is the appropriate ring number for the process while it executes the procedure? In general, there is no reason why we should accord the process more privilege than necessary to do its job. This observation has been codified as the *principle of least privilege*:

> **Definition.** The *principle of least privilege* states that a process should not be accorded more privilege that the minimum necessary to perform its function.

Returning to our scenario, by least privilege, the calling process should execute in ring $e_2(S)$, where it has the least privilege that is compatible with fetching instructions from S. When the process returns to the caller, its ring number must revert to its previous value.

A special case involves calling a procedure whose function is innocuous, so that it could perform its function correctly while executing within any privilege category without harming the protection of the system. With strict ring number protection, this can be achieved by permitting execute access to the procedure's segment from any ring number.

The other situation causing access difficulties upon call, in which the caller has too much privilege to call the procedure, is not symmetric to the previous situation. We could make an argument that the call should be allowed and should run at ring e_1, arguing that we should make the least change of privilege required to perform the procedure. We could argue that the call should not be allowed at all—why is a trusted procedure needing to call a procedure with less trust? We refer the interested reader to [ORGA72] for a complete discussion of these points and a complete description of the Multics implementation of these mechanisms.

Example 9-3

In the Multics system, ring number protection controls access to memory segments. There are eight ring numbers. Each data segment has two ring numbers, w and r, with $w \leq r$. These numbers are used for the one-limit scheme discussed before. Thus, if $w < r$, there exists a range of ring numbers from which the segment is read-only. Each procedure segment has three ring numbers, $e_1 \leq e_2 \leq e_3$. A process has all access permissions to the segment if $p \leq e_2$, but if $p < e_1$, a ring crossing trap will occur. If $e_2 \leq p \leq e_3$, the situation is interpreted as an inward call that is permitted if the call reaches to a gate entry point and denied otherwise; after the call, the process will be executing with $p = e_2$. Finally, if $e_3 < p$, all access is denied. The gate entry point is distinguished because its representation is different from a "normal" entry point. The interested reader should study [ORGA72] for more details.

Example 9-4

Ring number protection in the Honeywell DPS/6 minicomputers is applied to memory pages. There are four possible ring values. Each page descriptor contains three ring numbers, denoting the ring of lowest privilege at which the operations of read, write, or instruction fetch ("execute") can be performed on objects within the page. The comparison is based on the ring number of the executing process (held in the processor's state), unless the space had been accessed by indirection, in which case the test uses the ring number associated with write privilege from the space where the indirect address accessing the item was found. The latter case checks parameters passed to the process; by accessing indirectly the spaces described by the parameters, the system checks the caller's access rights for the parameters.

Example 9-5

The Intel 386 processor supports a "protected mode" in which protection based on ring numbering is applied. There are three types of segment descriptors:

1. Data segment descriptors
2. Code segment descriptors
3. System segment descriptors

We listed the types of segment descriptors *and not the types of segments*, because the same memory space can be described by several descriptors, with each one claiming to be a different type of descriptor. Every descriptor contains a code indicating its descriptor type.

Every segment descriptor contains a 2-bit ring number. There are bits in each descriptor limiting the accessing mode that can be used with the corresponding segment (when accessed through this descriptor). Table 9-3 lists the types of access permitted through data and code segment descriptors (indicating whether specific permission is required from the descriptor to make the access).

Every memory address specification contains the name of a "segment register." Before a program can access an object, it must load a segment register with a

TABLE 9-3   INTEL 386 ACCESS TYPES

	Automatic	Conditional
Data segment	READ	WRITE
Code segment	EXECUTE	READ
System segment	— see text —	

descriptor of the segment. The ring number legality checks are made when the segment descriptor is loaded into a segment register. Three ring numbers enter into the decision to permit the move operation to load the segment register:

1. CPL, the ring number of the executing process (from its code segment descriptor)
2. RPL, the ring number of the segment from which the descriptor was read
3. DPL, the ring number within the segment descriptor being loaded

For the move to succeed, the following predicate must be true:

$$DPL \geq \max(CPL, RPL)$$

Once the descriptor is loaded into the register, data accesses of the type automatically permitted (listed in the automatic type column of the table) are enabled. The conditionally permitted accesses are allowed only if the permission bit is set in the loaded descriptor.

Control transfers are checked using different rules. A jump instruction can transfer control from one code segment to another only if either (1) the DPL of the target segment matches the current CPL or (2) the target is a conforming segment and its DPL is less than the current CPL. The second rule permits a transfer to a service routine; in that case, the CPL does not change, so the new program runs at the old privilege level.

Sixteen type code values can be represented within segment descriptors. We discuss only the call gate, trap gate, interrupt gate, and task gate types, because those directly influence the CPL value in the processor. To complete a CALL through a call gate, the following predicate must be true:

$$\{DPL_{gate} \geq \max(CPL, RPL)\} \text{ AND } \{DPL_{code} \leq CPL\}$$

When a gate is used, the gate contains the address of the next instruction. In all CALLs, the target of the instruction is specified by a segment number and an offset. The two cases are distinguished by the nature of the object accessed by the segment number. For a "normal" CALL, a code segment is designated; when a gate is used, the gate object is designated by the segment number, and the gate object contains both the segment number and offset of the next instruction (the offset part of the original object designation is ignored); it also contains a count indicating the size of the parameter space that should be copied to the new stack.

There is a separate stack for each privilege level; when the privilege level does change from executing a CALL or a RETURN, the stack is changed accordingly. A call to a more privileged level causes the creation of a new stack for that execution, and the subroutine parameter words (the number of such words was included within the gate descriptor) are copied onto the new stack, along with appropriate control information so that conditions can be restored when the new privilege level is exited.

Inside the new procedure, the parameters can be verified to be correct. In particular, it may be necessary to check whether the procedure will be able to read and/or write to spaces described by the parameters. These access rights can be checked by executing VERR (VERW) to verify whether a read (write) will be permitted to the operand location. Other instructions (1) copy the access rights from a segment descriptor to a register or (2) obtain the length of a segment. These instructions permit further checking before attempting accesses that might fail.

Upon return[3] from a procedure, the privilege of the descriptors left in the registers is checked, because they might be residues left by the more privileged CALLed procedure, and therefore might permit illegal accesses if used from within the calling program. Any that are invalid are replaced with null descriptors.

9.1.4 Comments

All schemes that seek to intercept unauthorized access attempts have to make run-time checks. Correct access permission information must be available to the checking mechanism, and there must be assurance that this information cannot be corrupted by unauthorized processes within the system.

There is a significant variation in generality among the representation schemes presented in this section. An ACM is totally general, permitting accessing patterns without any overriding structure. Using a set of capability objects to define access rights is another general scheme. Access key schemes can be general within limited contexts, because limits on the sizes of key values and on the number of keys that can be assigned to individual processes and object do limit the flexibility. A ring numbering scheme imposes a linear ordering upon the classes of processes and objects; this is quite useful for separating users from system programs, but is not adequate to distinguish among general classes of users and objects. Secure systems try to provide high degrees of assurance about access controls and conformance between the checks and system security policies; these requirements and designs are covered now.

9.2 SECURITY REQUIREMENTS

Every secure system design is based on a formal requirement that unauthorized users not be allowed to access information in unauthorized ways and that the system be designed in such a manner that one can be convinced that this requirement has been met. We emphasize certain military security requirements, not because they apply to all situations, but rather because they have been explicitly codified. Some other security models are mentioned in Section 9.2.3. In Section

---

[3]   These comments apply to a far return (in which the code segment can be changed).

9.2.4, we present integrity models, which are related to security models, but are not well understood. It seems difficult to form a coherent model covering integrity for both the system and the data within the system.

There are two important aspects to the computer security problem. First, one wishes to restrict access to the system to those persons who are authorized to have access to the system. This problem is the *system access limitation problem.* Passwords can be used to deter illegal access attempts; however, bitter experience shows that password protection is not airtight. The second security problem is to limit access to each piece of information stored within the system to only those users who are authorized to access that piece of information. This problem is the *data access limitation problem.* This security problem can be approached by appropriate system design. In the following, we use the shorter term "security problem" for the problem of restricting information access to individuals authorized for access to the information.

Many people naturally associate encryption with information security. Encryption protects information that can be surreptitiously observed, by making it extremely difficult to correctly interpret the information. This method protects information being communicated across public channels from being observed by unauthorized individuals. Information within a processor should not be encrypted so that it can be processed by efficient algorithms. Thus, encryption cannot be used to protect information within the system.

9.2.1 Access Control

Before we move into the meat of the security problem, we comment on the system access limitation problem. First, physical security methods are always adequate—if you keep all unauthorized people from physical access to anything connected to the machine, there is no way for them to obtain access to information within the system. But physical security can impose too many limits for many applications. Second, plaintext passwords are not adequate. Any scheme that involves a fixed response to a request ("type your password now") is subject to attack by eavesdropping on the authentication interaction. The attacker simply listens to the password and replays it to obtain access to the system.

Some authentication schemes both check some information from the individual and also require possession of a device that performs some transformation on a piece of data. The authentication interaction under such a system can be difficult, if not impossible, to duplicate. One scenario goes this way [WONG85]:

1. The user presents her name and requests login.
2. The system responds with a challenge integer C.
3. The user enables her transformation unit (TU) by presenting her password to the TU.

4. The user gives C to TU and requests the result TU(C).

5. The user presents TU(C) to the system.

To check authorization, the system also computes TU(C) from its stored information. If this value matches the user's response, the login succeeds. Several features are essential for the success of this scheme. First, the TU transformation must be complex and not easily determined by experiment. Second, the challenges C must not repeat. Third, the TU must appear to operate even if presented with the wrong password; this deters off-line attempts to determine the correct password. The TU described in [WONG85] uses the DES (Data Encryption Standard) algorithm in a box holding a key that can be set only when the battery is first connected to the TU. If the battery is disconnected, the password and the transformation key are immediately lost.

It may appear that this approach clearly "solves" the access control problem. But what if an attacker inserts a relay box along the path to the system, permitting the login interaction to proceed and then diverting the subsequent interaction with the system to another terminal? We certainly would have a problem!

There is also a problem in knowing that a user is really talking to the system when she attempts to login. If the user were talking to an impostor, the impostor could determine how we log in and then follow our procedure. These simple examples illustrate that every protection scheme at best suppresses a presumed attack or set of attacks. A good way to devise and debug protection schemes is to attempt to attack the system in novel ways.

Now we return to the major topic of the remainder of the chapter—the security problem—controlling access to information within the system itself. At the same time, we wish to provide a reliable computer system that faithfully executes instructions for trusted users. If we do not require the ability to perform instructions, we could conclude that a brick is a secure computer system—it does not reveal any inappropriate information!

9.2.2 Military Security Policies

Military security policies define standards for controlling information access. In addition, techniques that check a system design against the requirements at different levels of assurance have been established [DOD85]. It is certainly true that these military requirements do not apply in detail to civilian systems. Nevertheless, similar system design approaches might be used to build civilian systems.

Security Attributes. The military security requirements concerning information located in paper documents handled by human beings have evolved over a long period of time and are well understood. They are based on assigning security attributes to both persons and information containers. To determine whether a person is allowed to read a document one compares that person's security attributes with those of the document. Generally, a person is allowed to read the document if her security clearance is at least as high as the security level of the document in question.

What is really happening? For each individual, the security authorities determine the level of trust that they are willing to assign to that person. Similarly, the security authorities determine the importance of the information stored in each document and then assign it a security level that reflects the consequences of that information falling into unauthorized hands. The information container is then labeled with a code name representing the security classification assigned to the information. If the document is a paper copy, the code name(s) is written in large letters at the top and bottom of each page, on the covers, and in other designated places.

The military system uses one set of labels to describe security attributes of both information and humans. For example, a person having a "top secret" clearance is allowing to read documents that are labeled top secret. In general, an inequality comparison determines whether the read should be allowed, because the top secret person can read unclassified documents. A further screening is used in military environments—does the proposed reader of the document "need to know" the information contained within the document? This decision could be based on one or more category labels, which are further security attributes assigned to users and documents. A category is assigned to a document if its contents should be needed by persons working in the corresponding area. In a similar manner, a set of categories is assigned to each person based on her function and assignment; together these determine her need to know the contents of documents assigned to the category.

We discuss the labels and the relationships among the levels before we turn to the policies. As we pointed out, document sensitivities and trust levels are usually described using the same terms. Each sensitivity label includes both a hierarchical level and a set of categories.[4]

All access control decisions are based on a dominance relation:

Definition. If security level L_1 *dominates* level L_2, we write $L_1 \geq L_2$, and we sometimes say that L_1 is *higher* than L_2 or that L_2 is *lower* than L_1. The dominance relation is reflexive ($L_1 \geq L_1$ always), but the members of some pair of levels might not dominate each other in either direction (then we say that they are *incomparable*). The dominance relationship among security levels imposes a partial ordering.

In general, the dominance relation defines a partially ordered set (POset). In simple situations, a linear ordering may be sufficient. In other cases, the POset may be a lattice (in a lattice, there exists both a least upper bound and a greatest

---

[4]   Later, we generalize this structure.

lower bound for every pair of objects). In many environments, there is no least upper bound over all levels because no individual is authorized to access all objects in the system.

Example 9-6

The United States military security scheme has four hierarchical levels:

1. Top Secret	(TS)	(highest)
2. Secret	(S)	
3. Confidential	(C)	
4. Unclassified	(U)	(lowest)

The dominance relationship among these hierarchical levels is a simple linear ordering, in the order of their appearance in the list.

The dominance relation among category sets is based on set inclusion: category set C_1 dominates category set C_2 if set C_1 includes set C_2. Suppose that F, G, and H denote separate categories. Then the category sets $\{F, G\}$ and $\{F, H\}$ dominate the simple set $\{F\}$. Because domination implies more restricted access, access to a document with the category set $\{F, G\}$ is more restrictive than access to a document with the category set $\{F\}$.[5] An intuitive interpretation that the set in the label implies an "OR" operation among the categories is therefore not correct; the proper relationship among the separate categories in a document category set is "AND." In other words, information assigned to the category set $\{F, G\}$ belongs to both categories, and an individual wishing access to such information must be authorized for both categories F and G in order to be permitted access.

Access decisions are based on composite dominance relationships involving both the level and category checks. Thus, $(L_1, C_1) \geq (L_2, C_2)$ if and only if $L_1 \geq L_2$ and $C_1 \geq C_2$. Because the dominance relation is transitive, all dominance relationships can be developed from a set of "simple" dominance relationships —those that are not derivable by using the transitive property of the dominance relation. We can represent a POset as a picture in which we place dominating entities toward the top of the picture, and place an arc between two entities that are related by simple dominance. A security POset with two categories and the set of US military hierarchical levels is illustrated in Figure 9-5. This set forms a lattice because all (H, C) combinations exist as levels in the system.

The previous definition of security-level dominance amounts to using disjoint rules: one about levels and the other about categories. This "complete" structure contains more combinations than required in most realistic environments. It is hard, for example, to argue that unclassified information should be separated into categories, because the unclassified level suggests free access for all. Thus, the general specification of the relationships between trust levels and information sensitivities should be viewed as a general POset and not as a pair of

---

[5]   Thus, $\{F, G\} \geq \{F\}$.

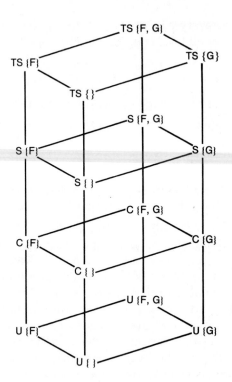

Figure 9-5 A security dominance POset for four levels
and two categories

separate rules covering levels and categories. In subsequent discussions, we take
this general viewpoint, describing dominance relationships without reference to
the (level, category) model. We use the general term "level" to denote the complete set of security attributes associated with people and documents (whatever
they may represent). The basic dominance relation is defined by the POset of
these security levels.

An implicit assumption in all designs and discussions is that the information within processor registers is accessible to the user. Therefore, the processor
serves as an information container having security attributes inherited from the
process in execution at the time. In most discussions, the process inherits its security attributes from the individual who initiated its execution; there will be exceptions to cover processes that require varying security attributes to perform
special services.

Access Rules. Two types of policies limit access to objects:

1. Mandatory security
2. Discretionary security

Mandatory Security. The mandatory security requirements limit the direct visibility of information based on the level of sensitivity assigned to a document and the level of trust assigned to each individual who is trusted to handle any document. The mandatory security policy limits both read and write permissions for accesses by a user's process P to an information container X.

Read access rights decisions are compatible with a simple intuitive interpretation of security. A person is allowed to read any information container whose classification is lower than or equal to the level of trust assigned to the person. Formalizing, we see that the read access right is based on dominance: A person can read a document if her trust level dominates the sensitivity level of the document and not otherwise. This property concerning read access rights, extended from the individual to the process working on behalf of the individual, is called the simple security property [BELL75].

> **Definition.** A system that obeys the *simple security property* gives process P read access to object X if and only if $L_p \geq L_x$.

Under what conditions should P be permitted to write to an information container? In the human–paper system, documents are written and then released into the system; once released, a document's contents are fixed—dynamic document modification does not occur. A computer system is not so simple: It may be possible to write over portions of a block of information. We need a rule that constrains the *flow of information*. A basic requirement is that the system should be designed so that the read limitations imposed by the simple security property cannot be violated in spirit through inadvertent information copying. For example, if a TS user could read information from a TS document and then write that same information into a U document, the information has, in effect, been declassified. After this write had been completed, any user would be able to read the copied information. It should be clear that the flow occurred when the information was placed into the U container. Thus, we need to prohibit writing information into a container lower than the level at which the program is executing. This property concerning write access rights is known as the *-property, pronounced "star-property" [BELL75].

> **Definition.** A system that obeys the *-property gives process P write access to object X if and only if $L_x \geq L_p$.

Certainly, we trust the people using the system; in particular, we believe that they would not downgrade information—after all, when they received their clearances, they were told not to "leak" or downgrade any information to which they were entrusted access. Why, then, have the *-property? Well, part of the problem is that actions in computers are performed by programs, not by people. There is always a chance that someone inadvertently chooses the wrong program or misuses a procedure. This would not be a big problem—in fact, if this were the worst security problem that we had to face, we'd be extremely lucky (compared to reality, that is)! But in general, we do not have any assurance about the programs being executed. An attacker could insert a new "wonderful" program that is a really good word processor, but in addition to helping with word processing, it also puts a copy of everything that is typed into an unclassified container that the attacker could peruse at her leisure. A program like this is called a *Trojan Horse* (you cannot tell what is inside the gift, but it certainly is not good for you). Enforcing the *-property prevents Trojan Horse attacks. General Trojan Horse attacks, in principle, could be prevented in several ways, including these two: (1) We could assert that nothing incorrect would ever be executed as a program; guaranteeing this property requires either having a compiler that never produces anything that breaches security or checking for security breaches in each program that is entered into the system. (2) We could trust nothing and check everything. This is what the *-property requirement really does. The second option represents the only realistic approach to system security because the "nothing illegal" approach is clearly unrealistic.

The preceding access control rules—the simple security property and the *-property—together comprise the *mandatory security requirements* [DOD85]. A system meets the mandatory security requirements if its read and write access controls do not permit accesses that would violate either the simple security property or the *-property.

Discretionary Security. *Discretionary access controls* add access limitations to those imposed by the mandatory rules. The additional restrictions are based on the identity of the user on whose behalf the access request is being made. The discretionary controls can be codified as a list of user's names attached to each information container C. Associated with each name on the list are special declarations about limits on the named individual's ability to access the document in question. In general, a list entry contains a pair (U, AR), where U is a user name and AR denotes the access rights permitted for or denied to U for C. In the computer model, this list is called an *access control list* (acl); an acl may exist for each object in the system. The discretionary access rule states that no access should be permitted that violates the access controls imposed by the access control list; in particular, this means that an access denied by the access control list should not be permitted.

It is very easy to subvert discretionary access limitations to allow user U to read information I that not supposed to read. The subversion is accomplished with the assistance of another user (our friend, whom we call "F"). Our friend F is allowed to read I. Because F can read I, she can copy it into another container, say, J, upon which no acl access limitations have been imposed. Now U simply reads J, because F did not forbid U from reading J.

Thus, we see that at best, discretionary access controls provide a very weak limitation against reading information. In contrast, mandatory access controls are tight and consistent. The weakness of discretionary controls arises because the access limitations are not intimately associated with the information they govern. If one needs to say something positive about discretionary access controls, one can state the following fact: If user U has never been permitted access to a container I, then the discretionary controls guarantee that U never accessed the information in I directly from container I. Notice that this statement makes no claims regarding whether U accessed the information in I indirectly. As a consequence, the statement is quite weak, and it seems difficult to strengthen it.

Example 9-7

Object O is at hierarchical level S and in categories A, B, and D. The acl for O contains an entry permitting user J to read, but not write, O. The access rights that a process P, executing on behalf of J, will obtain depends on the hierarchical level and categories in P's security context. Table 9-4 illustrates some process security contexts for P along with the corresponding access rights granted P for O.

TABLE 9-4   ACCESS RIGHTS ACCORDED A PROCESS

Process Attributes		Maximum Rights to an S Object in {A, B, D}:		
Hierarchical Level	Categories	Mandatory	Discretionary	Composite Rights
S	A, B, D	Read, write	Read	Read
TS	A, B, C, D	Read	None	None
S	A, B	Write	Read, write	Write
TS	A, B	None	Read	None
C	A, B, D	Write	Read	None

Security State. To enforce the security policy, the system must retain information describing the security attributes of all users that access the system and of all information contained within the system. It must also store information defining the security policy being enforced (such as the security POset). The set of all such security management information is collectively called the *system's security state*.

Other Military Security Requirements. Additional military security requirements [DOD85] include a "trusted path" requirement, a labeling requirement, an auditing requirement, and a requirement that a system design be analyzed to detect and limit covert channels.[6] The *trusted path* is a secure

---

[6]   A covert channel is a means of communication not intended for communication by the system designers. Banging on the jail cell wall is a covert communication channel.

communication link from a human user at a terminal to the computer. All inter-actions across the trusted path must be initiated by the user from the terminal;[7] this path must be used to initiate or authenticate certain actions that change the system's security state. The *labeling requirement* states that all human-readable outputs produced by the system should be labeled with the security levels of the information contained within the visible output. The *auditing requirement* states that all activities that change the system's security state and actions that might indicate a threat to the system's integrity should be recorded so that the record can be analyzed later if the system's security does become compromised. Finally, the *covert channel analysis requirement* states that the designers should produce an argument to the effect that the amount of information that can flow in violation of the constraints is strictly limited to an acceptable bandwidth.

Covert Channels. A *covert channel* is an information path that was not in-tended by the system designers and that subverts the system's security policy. Covert channels are usually based on the ability of one procedure to indirectly change some system attribute that can be observed indirectly from another proc-ess at a different security level. Object state, temporary access restrictions, and timing patterns are potential communication routes that might be used to estab-lish covert channels.

The following example shows a simple design that contains a covert chan-nel and how that channel could be utilized to bypass the access control limits.

Example 9-8

Our system has a single processor with cache memory. Two processes are running; one (called HIGH) runs at a high level from which it is trying to convey informa-tion to another process (called LOW) operating at a low level. Any information flow from HIGH to LOW violates the *-property.

We convey the information 1 bit at a time. The HIGH procedure forces cache misses to signal a "1" value and permits fast cache accesses to signal a "0" bit. To force a cache miss, HIGH simply makes many read accesses to diverse addresses to fill the cache memory. Suppose the LOW process can determine its execution speed by reading a reliable clock. Therefore, it can determine the bit sent by HIGH. Once it has determined the bit, it can write up to HIGH's level both the bit it ob-served and the fact that it has seen a bit value. After HIGH reads this information, it sends the next bit. Because HIGH can see the bit that LOW thought it received, it can correct errors. Alternately, a redundant coding scheme can be chosen to im-prove the reliability of the communication through the covert channel.[8]

---

[7]   This prevents a Trojan Horse from subverting the identification requirement.

[8]   Such encoding schemes are not important here; the important point is that information is conveyed from HIGH to LOW.

Certification Levels. The military security evaluation document [DOD85] specifies several levels of "certification" that may be attributed to a computer system based on its ability to enforce the military information flow requirements. Each certification label consists of a letter followed by a numeral. A lower letter signifies more confidence in the system's security properties. A higher number (within the certification set having the same letter designation) signifies more confidence. Thus, B2 is better than C3 or B1. At level B2, all of these five functional requirements must be met:

1. Mandatory access constraints must be obeyed.
2. Discretionary access controls must be obeyed.
3. Human-readable outputs must be labeled.
4. Significant events must be audited.
5. Covert channels must be analyzed.

At level B2, a formal model of the system's security policy must be provided. At level B3, the designers must prove the consistency of the security policy with its axioms and they must provide a descriptive top-level specification (DTLS) of the implementation. Furthermore, they must present a "convincing argument"[9] that the DTLS is consistent with the policy model. At level A1, a formal top-level specification (FTLS) must be provided. "A combination of formal and informal techniques shall be used to show that the FTLS is consistent with the model" and a mapping of the FTLS to the source code of the trusted portion of the system software must be provided as "evidence of correct implementation."

9.2.3 Other Security Policies

Many security policies map into the hierarchical model embodied in the military system, but other applications do not operate within a hierarchical environment. Some environments have categories without levels, such as a business with categories that correspond to departments within the organization.

A completely nonhierarchical security requirement arises within the investment community. A security analyst in a brokerage house may be permitted to know the intimate details of the operation of a single company within a business sector. Suppose that she may choose which company to study. Once the company is chosen, all other companies in the same business sector become unavailable to the analyst. But once the financial information that was visible becomes public, the analyst should be free to choose another company. This environment is not hierarchical and not static, both attributes of the military system.

---

[9]   The quotations in this paragraph are taken from [DOD85].

9.2.4 Integrity Specifications

Information integrity is an elusive concept. Intuitively it is quite simple—any information that was obtained from a reliable source and that has been processed by reliable programs is assigned high integrity because we have good reason to believe it correct. In contrast, information from unreliable sources or processed by unreliable programs is assigned a lower amount of integrity. It is intuitively reasonable that the result produced by a reliable program becomes unreliable if any of the inputs is unreliable, even if some of the inputs had high reliability.

Hierarchical Integrity Models. Could one construct a POset of integrity levels, attaching programs and information containers to the integrity levels therein? We discuss one such model based on [BIBA77]. There are two important differences from the security model based on level POsets. First, in the integrity model, the permissible information flows are reversed from the security POset structure—during usual unassured processing, information cannot gain integrity, so "permissible" information flows permit moves toward the bottom of the integrity POset. Second, there is no basis for restricting reading information based on its integrity level, so any program can read information from any integrity level. This makes it impossible to predict the integrity level of the program's results, because that integrity level must be lower than the integrity level of any object read during the computation. Thus, the result's integrity depends upon the integrity levels of all information that happened to be read while the result was being computed.

Models Using Integrity Checkers. Clark and Wilson ([CLAR87]) present an interesting integrity model that emphasizes the integrity of certain designated items within the system and clarifies the relationship between the integrity of an object and the procedures that are used to modify the object. The key concepts in this model are the following:

> **Definition.** A *constrained data item* (CDI) is an item within the system whose contents enter into the evaluation of an integrity predicate.

> **Definition.**[10] An *integral system state* is a system state that satisfies all of the system's integrity predicates.

> **Definition.** An *integrity verification procedure* (IVP) evaluates one or more integrity predicates to determine whether the current contents of the CDIs do satisfy the integrity constraints specified in those predicates.

---

[10]   This terminology is not presented in the Clark and Wilson paper.

Notice the implicit assumption in this approach and these definitions that the integrity of an object or set of objects can be deduced algorithmically by examining the contents of the objects. In many real-world situations, the term "integrity" connotes conformance between the information within the object and the status of something external to the system (did the reporter quote the politician accurately?); this type of integrity cannot be checked by any algorithm within a proposed IVP. The IVPs in this model are similar to the **ensure** predicates used in recovery blocks (Section 6.3.6).

Clearly, the individual actions performed by a process might not maintain system integrity unless they are collected together to form a higher-level module that does maintain integrity. These observations lead one toward the following:

> **Definition.** A *transformation procedure* (TP) effects a change in the state of the system's objects.[11]

> **Definition.** A *well-formed transaction* is a sequence of actions that leaves the system in an integral state if the system was in an integral state before the transaction was initiated.

This model does not include hierarchical levels of integrity—a system state is either integral or not. Therefore, it does not conform to the Biba model, but it does have a different intuitive appeal. A well-formed transaction could be composed from a sequence of procedure executions, each of which is not (by itself) a well-formed transaction. To handle these transaction structures, it may be desirable to impose a mechanism that requires that the complete sequence be executed before the system state is changed. A mechanism to build assured pipelines (see Section 9.5.2) might be applied to this transaction model problem.

The IVPs of the Clark and Wilson model could be added to a system designed along the lines of the Biba model. The idea is that if the IVP assures integrity, probably it is reasonable to elevate the object within the integrity POset.

Because integrity does not fit neatly into a hierarchical model, we leave the subject; the interested reader can investigate current literature.

9.2.5 Comments

Hierarchical military security schemes fit into a POset level structure, with read and write accesses limited by the mandatory policy that compares the security levels of the procedure and the object being accessed. Other models of security and integrity do not fit the POset model. In the following, we emphasize system designs to enforce information access limitations imposed by POset-based security policies.

---

[11]   A transaction accessing shared objects is a TP under this definition.

9.3 ATTACKS ON SECURE COMPUTER SYSTEMS

To understand security requirements and the problems that might arise in designing a system to meet security or integrity requirements, we present a few ways that a system that is claimed to be secure might be attacked. We also exhibit a scenario demonstrating an important implementation difficulty arising from a strict interpretation of the discretionary security requirement. We start with some definitions:

> **Definition.** An *attack* is an attempt to access information to which access should be denied if the system were enforcing the security requirements.

> **Definition.** An attack *succeeds* if the attempted (illegal) information flow does occur.

> **Definition.** A *security flaw* is a defect in the design or implementation of a secure system that permits an attack on the system to succeed.

A system could be subjected to a physical or a logical attack. At the outset, we rule out *physical attacks*—we will not attempt to protect the system against a person who can open the cabinet and attach oscilloscopes or logic analyzers to internal electrical connectors or who can remove, modify, or replace system hardware. After all, a person with internal access can see all information passing through the system, including all information passing between memory and the processor. After recording all traffic on the memory bus, a simple analysis could reconstruct the entire contents of memory, thereby revealing all "secrets."

We concentrate on *logical attacks* made by executing one or more programs. Because we assume that the system access problem has been solved, we require that the user executing an attack program must be an authorized user of the system. Because any program might be a Trojan Horse (TH), we have to look for any way that the user's (TH) program could attack the system. The simplest kind of security breach occurs if the program can read information to which the user is not authorized to have access.

Figure 9-6 introduces the diagrammatic symbols that we will use to describe processes, objects, and their security attributes. Figure 9-6a shows a data object depicted by a vertical rectangle; its security attributes are shown in a smaller horizontal rectangle divided into three rows. The name of the data object is written above the value rectangle. The first security attribute is the level, whose value is indicated by a word. The term "hierarchical level" will be used whenever the security state contains both the level and a category list, whereas the term "security level" will be used when the level information has a general

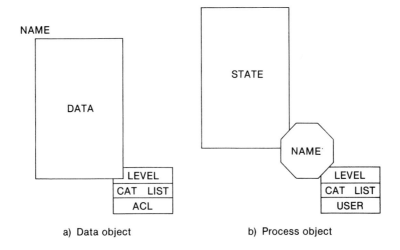

NAME

DATA

| LEVEL |
| CAT   LIST |
| ACL |

STATE

NAME·

| LEVEL |
| CAT LIST |
| USER |

a) Data object   b) Process object

Figure 9-6   Diagrammatic representations of data and
process objects and their security attributes

interpretation and consequently there is no category list.[12] The second security
attribute is the category list, whose value is indicated by a name list.[13] The third
security attribute of the data item is the access control list (acl), whose value
would be indicated by a list of pairs of the form (user, rights). Figure 9-6b shows a
process depicted by an octagon containing the name of the process. Its security
attributes are depicted in a horizontal rectangle similar to the one used for a data
object. The only difference between the two security attribute sets is that the
third process attribute is a user name. Each process has an associated internal
state, depicted as a data object extending upward from the octagon. The internal
state includes the processor register contents. Other information may be included in the internal state, depending on the implementation of processes in the
system; for reasoning about the system's security properties, it is adequate to include in the internal process state all items that are not accessible to other
processes.

9.3.1 Attacks Based on Unauthorized Reads

The simplest attack on a secure computer system executes a program that tries to
read information from a sensitive object (we name this object INTERESTING)
within the system. If the system's access controls are not tight, the read might be

---

[12]   The dominance relationship among hierarchical levels is a totally ordered relationship. The dominance relationship among security levels defines a POset; in general, the POset is not equivalent to a
totally ordered set.
[13]   For the moment, we continue showing the c-list, which is not required, because with the c-list, we
can illustrate level dominance without drawing the POset diagram required if we used security levels.

allowed even though the information should not be visible to the user whose program makes this read request. It is simple to design access controls that block this type of attack.

9.3.2 Attacks Based on Unauthorized Writes

Two programs can collude to compromise information if the *-property is not enforced by the system's access control mechanisms. This attack requires two programs operating at two different security levels chosen so that one level dominates the other. To be specific, suppose that the colluding programs P_1 and P_2 execute at security levels L_1 and L_2, respectively, and that $L_1 > L_2$. The object INTERESTING at security level L_1 contains information desired at security level L_2. Figure 9-7 illustrates this situation. The attack follows this scenario: First, P_1 reads INTERESTING and writes its contents into another object LEAK at security level L_2. Note that P_1 is allowed to read INTERESTING by the simple security property. The program is allowed to write into LEAK only because the *-property is not enforced. Second, P_2 reads LEAK, which is at security level L_2, the security level of P_2. This read is legal because the security level of the program matches the security level of the object being read. But this read obtains a copy of the information originally contained in INTERESTING.

Another type of attack involves planting a malicious Trojan Horse program TH that is claimed to provide a service for system users. It may mask its subversive nature by actually providing the claimed service. But at the same time, it copies information in violation of the security policy. This copying will be permitted if TH executes in the security context of the user who requests TH's service. To obtain the contents of INTERESTING, TH simply copies information from INTERESTING into a dummy object LEAK, at security level L_2, from which P_2 can later read the information that was contained in INTERESTING. The attack succeeds if the *-property is not enforced, because TH can write to LEAK, which compromises the system's security. This attack may appear similar to the previous attack, but there is an important difference in that the user whose information is compromised is totally unaware that the information has been compromised. In fact, the TH attack will work even though no human attacker is permitted access at security level L_1. Furthermore, this attack succeeds even if the attacker is not logged onto the system at the time the prohibited action is attempted.

The first two attacks show that enforcing the *-property is an important element in providing security. Our next attack shows that any attempt to provide discretionary access controls is doomed to failure. Again we use a Trojan Horse program THD (making a discretionary attack). To make the attack, THD executing on behalf of user U_1 at security level L_1 reads the object LIMITED whose access control list is set so that only U_1 is allowed to read LIMITED, and then THD writes LIMITED's information into a new object PUBLIC at security level L_1. Because

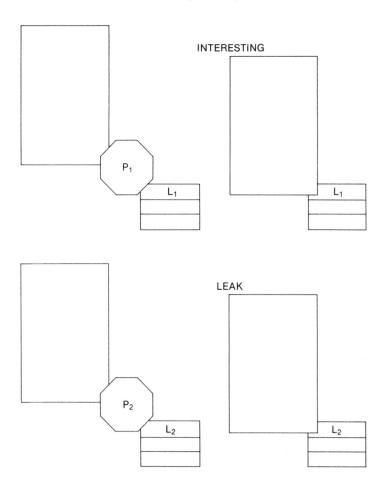

Figure 9-7   A security breach occurs if the *-property is not enforced: P_1 reads INTERESTING and writes its contents into LEAK, which P_2 then reads. This is a security breach if $L_1 > L_2$

THD created PUBLIC, it can give all users read access for PUBLIC. Any user who has clearance to security level L_1 can read PUBLIC and thus read the contents of LIMITED, which were supposed to be inaccessible to everyone but U_1. As before, because this is a Trojan Horse, the attack will work even if no attacker is authorized to access the information that will be compromised, and the attacker does not have to be logged on to the system at the time of the attack.

These Trojan Horse attacks do not depend on how the system is implemented; they simply use the ability to insert an arbitrary program into the system to subvert the (inadequate) security guards implicit in the system's specification or implementation. Another interpretation of these attacks is that they show that the system's access control specifications are inadequate to provide the expected protection against unauthorized use of the information within the system.

Another problem with discretionary access controls concerns the timing of the effects of a dynamic change in an access control list. In particular, an acl change may revoke a previously granted access permission [GLIG79]. The following scenario illustrates this situation; it is phrased in terms of a discretionary access model:

1. P_1 creates OBJ and obtains all rights to it.
2. P_1 adds user U to OBJ's acl, granting *read* rights to U.
3. P_1 loses trust in user U and removes U from OBJ's acl.

Step 3 is legal because P_1 "owns" OBJ and therefore may control the contents of its acl.

The revocation scenario presents a semantic problem if user U's access rights to OBJ were granted at time t_g and (later) revoked at time t_r. While U had access to OBJ, it could have copied (and retained) a capability C_{OK} for OBJ. After t_r, U could use C_{OK} to obtain access to OBJ, even though P_1 had revoked U's access to OBJ at t_r. Look at this modification of the previous scenario:

1. P_1 creates OBJ and obtains all rights to it.
2. P_1 adds user U to OBJ's acl, granting *read* rights to U.
3. P_2, executing on behalf of U, obtains capability C_{OK} to OBJ and stores it in a local object LOCAL.
4. P_1 loses trust in U and removes U from OBJ's acl.
5. P_2 retrieves its copy of C_{OK} from LOCAL.
6. P_1 attempts to read information from OBJ using C_{OK}; this (disallowed) access is permitted by C_{OK}.

The capability acquired in step 3 will contain read access permission, because U has read access to OBJ when step 3 is performed, according to U's acl. As a result, the access rights loaded during step 5 will contain read permission. It should be clear that the activities of both steps 3 and 5 are legal. The problem is that step 6 should be disallowed, because P_1 revoked U's access to OBJ in step 4. An abstract statement of this difficulty is that the *binding* between the access rights and the object description occurs too soon if the system requires immediate revocation of previously granted access rights upon a change to an acl. It may be reasonable to make a "strict" interpretation of the discretionary access rule, stating that the ability to access the object should be governed by the contents of the acl when the access is attempted. This strict interpretation means that the system must make the discretionary access check exactly when the access is attempted. Another option is to change access rights in the MMU table immediately upon any revocation request, but this plan requires having a data structure that permits the system to easily find all descriptors that contain relevant access rights. If one of these schemes is not used, the intended revocation will not take effect immediately. The requirement for immediate revocation reduces system efficiency so much that an alternate interpretation of the discretionary security requirement is desirable.

9.3.3 Other Attacks

Other attacks on a "secure" system can be based on knowledge of its design and/or implementation. For example, a system whose security relies on capability objects that contain access rights can be subverted by copying access rights to an improper context. It is also possible to attack a capability-based implementation by changing the access control information in a capability to grant read access to the (unauthorized) user holding the modified capability.

Another possible attack uses covert channels, such as the one in Example 9-9. And, of course, other attacks might succeed if the system's behavior does not conform to its specifications. The details of an attack that exploits implementation errors depend on the specific implementation.

As we study design options, we must be alert for all possible attacks, attempting to design the system to foil those attacks.

9.4 SOME SECURE SYSTEM DESIGN OPTIONS

Now we discuss briefly some design approaches that can provide total or partial system security. Partial security is provided by a system that either does not address or does not solve the general problem. In the absence of good designs that meet all security requirements, some partial approaches have been chosen for implementable systems. We consider these approaches:

1. Employ single-level operation.
2. Verify all programs.
3. Verify critical programs.
4. Monitor all access attempts.
5. Support objects containing access permissions.

9.4.1 Single-Level Operation

One can *operate the system at a single security level.* This approach has been used in many operational military computer systems. At any time, the system is operating at a single designated security level. When the system's level is being changed (if that is permitted), all information within the system is securely erased (perhaps by overwriting the information several times). The secure erasure ensures that there is no flow of information from the machine's previous security level to its new security level. It should be clear that there can be no flows of information in violation of the mandatory access constraints in a single-level system, because all information and users are confined to the single level. To enforce discretionary access controls in the system, add acl checks to the file system's access control mechanisms.

A single-level system does not provide multilevel security, so this approach gives a partial solution to the system security problem. This approach is, at best, an awkward and inconvenient way to provide computing resources to human users; the range of permissible activities is always constrained by the system's security level at the time.

9.4.2 Verify All Programs

A second approach to system security relies on *verifying all programs*. Clearly, complete verification represents an onerous task. If all programs were verified to obey the system's security policies, we would know that there could be no illegal flows, and the system would meet the access constraints. The obvious disadvantage of this design approach is that programs cannot be changed without reverification, an expensive and time-consuming process, at best! The verification hurdle would push the managers of a totally verified system toward remaining static and not to be upgraded or modified. This design strategy falls under the "nothing illegal" approach. Because a verified system can provide secure operation for a predefined application, we categorize this approach as a partial solution to the secure computer design problem. The required verification induces rigidity and providing verification may be extremely expensive, or impossible.

9.4.3 Verify Critical Programs

Under this approach, all programs in the system are examined to determine whether their behavior might affect the system's security. All programs that have been identified as "critical" are then verified to behave properly. This approach falls into the partial category because verification alone is not adequate for a total solution to the security problem. Also, one can raise questions about the choice of the programs that are assigned to the critical category and therefore are subject to verification. The scheme collapses if a program that is really critical escapes the screening and is not verified.

This approach can be used to show that critical system software does perform proper functions without compromising security requirements. The set of critical programs comprises the *security kernel* of the operating system. For this approach to provide a completely secure system, all unverified programs must be confined so that they cannot perform unauthorized actions that would compromise the system. A supporting mechanism may be required to assure this conformance; combining verified kernel programs with an access checking mechanism can comprise a total solution to the security problem.

The monitor method for controlling access to shared information (Section 8.4.2) can be the basis for a partial solution to the security problem. Recall that a monitor is a software module that controls all accesses to a shared object. To see how this approach works, first recognize that information private to a process (i.e., unshared information) cannot be used to compromise security *if* its privacy is maintained. Second, recognize that proper accesses to shared objects cannot compromise security. Thus, if we introduce a monitor for each shared object such that the monitor "properly" limits accesses to the shared object, the security problem will have been solved. To perform its function, the monitor must accurately know the identity of the program that initiates each request. Thus, the monitor acts like the MMU for accesses to the shared object whose access it controls. And it is no accident that Figure 9-2, that illustrated the monitor's gate-keeping role, looks much like Figure 3-20, that illustrated the MMU's role. The major difference concerns the scope of the space over which access is controlled. The MMU monitors and limits accesses to all of memory, and the monitor software monitors and limits accesses to shared objects. It is easy to see that an MMU-like access controller will be required to prohibit all accesses to shared objects whose access is not controlled through the monitor.

Can we eliminate the need for specialized hardware modules, such as the MMU-like access checker? First, notice the similarity between the encapsulation required to make monitors work properly and C++ class encapsulation. A C++ class effectively hides all objects declared within its realm. Only the names declared to be visible publicly are available for general use. Thus, if we encapsulated within C++ classes all objects that should be not accessible to all users, any program would have to call a procedure defined for the class before it could access the encapsulated object. The basic difficulty with this approach is the simple truth that we have no guarantee that the C++ class construct is enforced at lower levels within the system. Thus we do need hardware checkers that are encountered on every access attempt.

9.4.4 Monitor Every Access Attempt

In this basic approach to system security, the system *checks every access attempt* to verify its conformance with the security policy in effect. The composite mechanism checking all accesses is called the *reference monitor*. We emphasize the reference monitor approach in the remainder of the chapter.

The reference monitor approach is consistent with the "everything checked" design approach. It should be clear that any approach to system security requires limiting object access at a fine granularity. All access attempts must be checked. The MMU is the logical site for these checks. But for efficient MMU operation, it cannot execute, on each access attempt, a complex algorithm to determine the proper access rights starting from the security attributes of the executing program and the object to which access is desired. Thus the MMU must be loaded with access control information that conforms to the security policy being enforced. Thus the system must include software that sets the access control information within the MMU and that has been proven correct.

We see that a realistic design includes one module that sets access control information and another module that checks every access for conformance with the access control information. To verify the system's security properties, only these modules need to be verified. The argument follows this train of thought: The MMU can enforce the security properties *provided* that the access control information it uses is set in accordance with the security policy being enforced *and* provided that the MMU does correctly enforce the access rights it has been given. The system enforces security policy S only if the system software that sets the access control bits does so in accordance with S. Therefore, a verification of the correctness of the system's software for setting the access control bits should be tantamount to a verification of the system's security properties. However, there is another link—we must also show that the system properly maintains the state of its users. In particular, we must somehow guarantee that the access control information passed to the MMU is appropriate for the program in execution. This added requirement implies that the system module(s) that maintains and swaps program state must also be verified to be correct.

9.4.5 Use Objects Containing Access Rights

To monitor every access attempt, the system must determine the permitted access rights prior to checking the legality of an access attempt. Determining the access rights is a complex process. Although the system would perform properly (satisfying the security requirements) if these calculations were made at the time of each access, system speed would be greatly improved if the access-rights determinations were made before any access attempt was initiated.

The system makes a *commitment* or a *binding* when it determines the access rights to be accorded for a process to an object. When the commitment is made, the access right information is placed into a system object. Thus, this design approach requires that the security attributes of programs and objects not change between the time that the access rights are bound to the object and the time that those rights are used to rule on the legality of an access attempt.[14] Furthermore, the access rights placed in a holding object *must* have been determined for a particular program–object combination, because this pairing assumes a critical role

---

[14] The *tranquillity principle*, which asserts the constancy of an object's security attributes, formalizes this important requirement.

in defining the access rights under the security policy. It follows that an object containing access rights cannot be used to check accesses attempted by any program other than the one for which the rights were determined. If these rules are obeyed, this approach can provide the total security that we seek.

9.5 THE REFERENCE MONITOR APPROACH

The reference monitor in a secure computer system checks every attempted memory access. The reference monitor's checking mechanism is interposed between the processor and the system's memory (actually including all program-visible state that might be shared between two or more processes), as shown in Figure 9-2, so no memory access can be made without the reference monitor having the opportunity to check its legality. If an attempted access violates the permitted rights, the attempt is intercepted by the reference monitor.

      To enforce properly the security policy, the reference monitor must retain the security relevant attributes of all processes and all objects within the system. To validate an access attempt, the reference monitor uses the security attributes of the subject and the object to determine the access rights. The system would be incredibly slow if making these checks required accessing the saved security states during a memory access (i.e., between the time the processor generates an address and the time the memory access is made). To speed up the system, some security state references could be made beforehand and the results retained within the reference monitor. We discuss two different approaches to prechecking and show why one scheme does not work and the other does. The first, which does not work, uses capabilities. The second, which does not use capabilities, provides a better approach to secure system design.

9.5.1 Capability-Based Secure System Designs

Early secure system proposals used capabilities to support access controls ([FABR74], [LAMP71], [NEED77], and [NEUM80]). In this section, we present several capability-based designs, showing how they work, why it is difficult to implement secure systems in this manner, and why it is difficult to prove that such designs do indeed enforce the desired security policy.

      A capability contains two important fields: an object identifier and a set of access rights. The identifier field must be large enough to uniquely distinguish the object among all objects in the system, including all files. Therefore, a capability can be large. Without loss of generality, assume that the access right information in a capability covers each access type that will be checked. The access types include read and write, and may include execute and other operations for capability manipulation.

The basic access control rule in a capability-based design is as follows:

Access Rule. A process possessing a capability can access the described object in accordance with the rights contained within the capability.

In this section, we illustrate this class of designs using features of the Intel iAPX 432 system. Other designs incorporate variations on the basic capability scheme ([ENGL72], [ENGL74], [LEVY84], [NEED77], and [WISE86]).

Example 9-9

In the Intel iAPX 432 documentation, those objects that behave like capabilities are called "access descriptors;" for consistency, we will call them "capabilities." The basic access rights supported in an Intel iAPX 432 capability are as follows:

1. Read
2. Write
3. Unchecked copy
4. Delete

In addition, several capability bits control access rights whose interpretation depends on the type of the object described by the capability.

The *unchecked copy* access right allows a program to copy a capability object even though the copy operation might result in a dangling reference. Without this permission, the program may copy a capability only if the nesting level[15] of the destination location (of the copy operation) is higher than the nesting level of the source location. This rule prevents dangling references, because it forces capabilities to stay in containers whose lifetimes must be nested within (or be identical to) the lifetime of the space allocation. If the unchecked copy permission is granted, no check is made during capability copying, so a capability C could be copied to a global activation block that lives after the object described in C has been deallocated.

The *delete* right confers not only the right to delete the capability itself, but also the right to change the access rights stored in the capability. If the delete rights bit is not set, the capability cannot be overwritten by any memory write operation.

Three bits in an iAPX 432 capability are reserved for system interpretation; they control access rights for special "system" object types and can be interpreted to control access rights to representations of objects having some user-defined object type. The interpretation of these "type rights" (TR) bits depends on the type of the object being described. For example, a programmer may create a new object type and write type management software. This module may use the 3 TR bits to specify limits on the ability of the process holding the capability to perform operations on the object. In Section 5.3.1, we saw that in this system, a type control object (TCO) defines a new data type. One TR bit in the TCO governs the "create rights;" this bit governs whether this TCO can be used to create an object that is an instance of the type described by this TCO. Another TR bit governs the "amplify rights;" if set, the

---

[15]   The level check here is not the security level (in any sense), but rather the nesting depth level (in the program structure).

AMPLIFY_RIGHTS instruction can be used in the type definition programs to obtain added rights to permit the type definition software to access and manipulate the object's representation. The two input operands for the AMPLIFY_RIGHTS operation are the object descriptor and the TCO. When the instruction is executed, the TCO's read, write, and delete rights bits are ORed with the corresponding rights bits in the descriptor of the representation of the object to determine the rights bits giving access to the representation object. This expansion permits the type manager to access the representation even though the user program may not be able to access the representation at all.

Object Accessing Using Capabilities.   A capability plays an important role related to the existence and usage of an object. First, the capability was created when the object was created, and it will be deleted when the object is deleted.[16] Second, the capability must be presented to make an access to the object.

The act of object creation not only creates the object and an associated capability, it also initializes the contents of the object, its capability, and the portion of the system's security state related to the object. During initialization, the system may give "ownership" of the new object to the process that performed the create operation; object deletion and other operations could be restricted to the object's owner.

The reference monitor uses addresses for access-rights determination and caching, so it needs a way to associate a capability with the address presented for each access attempt. There are two ways to establish such an association:

1. Include a capability within each effective address.
2. Specify an association between address A (in the process's virtual address space) and capability C prior to the use of address A.

Under option 1, the processor presents a capability on every access attempt. Because a capability is large, each access attempt requires a large address specification. Clearly, this option requires a wide address bandwidth and cannot be used to build an efficient system.

To speed access and to reduce the system's memory bandwidth, option 2 should be selected. In designs using this option, the act of accessing is divided into two steps: The first step establishes the capability-address association and the second step attempts the actual access. The capability-address associations for a process are contained in the process object table (POT) for that process. A POT entry is selected by the segment (object) number in the high-order bits of the virtual address, as illustrated in Figure 9-8. The access rights in the POT entry were placed there when the POT entry was loaded, and are used to mediate the access attempt, as indicated in Figure 9-9. We discuss three generic instructions that establish a capability-address association in the POT:

---

[16]   Actually, capability deletion is not logically necessary if the system is designed so that a dangling capability cannot be used to access anything.

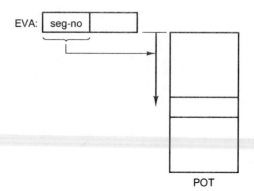

Figure 9-8   Accessing a POT entry using the segment number

1. Load POT.
2. Append to POT.
3. Add block to POT.

The load POT (LPOT) instruction has two arguments—the capability C for segment S and the segment number n to be used in an address that references an item within S. During LPOT, the access rights assigned to the executing process for S are placed into the POT entry at index n. These rights are taken directly from C. Addressing information may be placed in the POT entry during LPOT; the address must be correct so that the accessing mechanism can be guaranteed to always reach the corresponding object and to enforce the proper access rights. Figure 9-10 illustrates the LPOT operation.

The append to POT (APOT) instruction is a variation of the LPOT operation; it has only one operand: a capability C. The operation adds C to the POT at an empty position within the table. The result of APOT is the segment number n to which C was assigned.

The add block to POT (ABPOT) instruction is the third way to add capabilities to the POT. One ABPOT instruction associates a block of capabilities with a block of segment numbers. The ABPOT operands are a block of capabilities and a range of segment numbers. The system loads the entire set of capabilities into the POT during this operation.

Example 9-10

The Intel iAPX 432 address space is divided into four parts, called environments. Each environment is defined by a list of capabilities stored in a segment. Each environment can contain 16,384 capabilities, so the total address space comprises 65,536 segments. Environment 0, the "context access segment," defines the domain of the context, including the instruction segments. Therefore, environment 0 cannot be changed dynamically except by transferring control to another context (by CALL or RETURN).

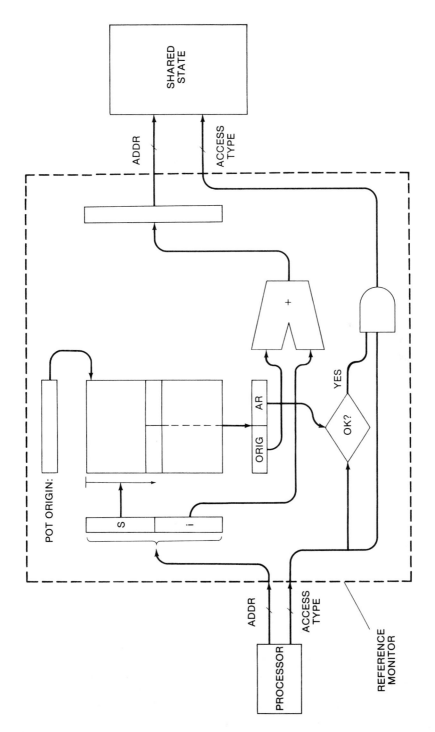

Figure 9-9 Using POT to check an attempted access

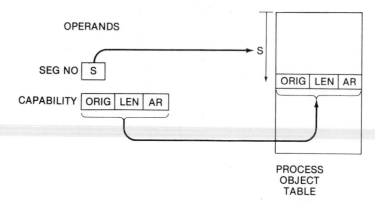

Figure 9-10   Loading the process object table (POT)

A program can redefine its address space by loading any other environment by executing one of the six operators "Enter Environment[17] n" or "Enter Globals as Environment n," with n = 1, 2, or 3. The act of loading an environment places the entire set of capabilities described in a segment into the POT; thus, these instructions are in the ABPOT class. A simple Enter Environment instruction takes a segment full of capabilities as its single operand. The Enter Globals instructions get the segment full of capabilities from a designated place called the "process globals," found from a descriptor in the process object; this descriptor is accessible from all domains within the process.

The LPOT operation illustrates all important logical requirements that must be imposed on operations that load the POT; the APOT and ABPOT operations add convenience but do not add logical features. Therefore, without loss of generality, in the following, we discuss LPOT only.

An effective capability-based system must use some variant of LPOT to establish an address-capability correspondence that is guaranteed correct. Even with this correctness guarantee, capability-based designs have weak points.

The Limits of Capability-Based Systems. The design just outlined is adequate in the sense that no access can be made that is contrary to the rights permitted in some capability. However, an implementation problem and several serious logical problems exist within the capability design approach. In this section, we present these topics related to the integrity of capability-based systems:

1. Capability integrity
2. Access right control
3. Security policy enforcement

---

[17]   In early iAPX 432 documents, these operations were called "Enter Access Segment n."

Capability Integrity. It is critically important that the contents of all capabilities be protected from alteration. Suppose, on the contrary, that such controls were not imposed. There are several attacks on this loose design. To make the first attack, a program simply changes the access rights within a capability it holds and thereby grants itself any desired access rights to the described object. For example, consider an unclassified process P that possesses a capability C permitting write access to the object INTERESTING whose contents are classified secret (see Figure 9-11). The rights in this capability are compatible with the mandatory access policy. If P were able to write read rights into C, then P would be permitted to use C to read information stored in INTERESTING. But reading information from INTERESTING to P violates the simple security property and therefore violates the mandatory access constraints. This scenario clearly subverts the intent of the capability, which was to limit P's access to INTERESTING by permitting write access only.

Another type of attack is possible if the capability system does not guarantee capability integrity. This attack starts with a capability C_1 that is accessible to process P_1. Capability C_1 contains both read and write access rights to object F_1 at the same level as the executing process P_1. For example, an unclassified process P may possess a capability C permitting read and write access to the object CLEAR, whose contents are unclassified (see Figure 9-12).[18] In the next step of the attack, process P writes a new object identifier into C so that it describes another object INTERESTING, whose contents are secret. Then P can use C to read the contents of INTERESTING, thereby violating the simple security property.

From these attacks we can see that it is imperative that a capability-based secure system be designed to ensure the integrity of all information in each capability. It is sufficient to protect all capabilities from uncontrolled alteration. Two different design approaches can protect capabilities from alteration. In the first approach, each capability is "tagged"[19] with a distinguishing mark (usually, in an added bit attached to the capability). A tag value must be associated with every item in memory—the tag must have at least two possible values to distinguish capabilities from other stored items. The system must be designed so that no processor operations can modify the contents of any memory word that is tagged; if this condition were met, the capability contents would be protected against alteration (except by special capability instructions performed in a special way) and the system could not be attacked by a program that constructs bogus capabilities.

Under the second design approach for capability protection, all capabilities are placed in distinguished memory segments (or portions thereof) to which no

---

[18]   These access rights are compatible with the mandatory access policy.

[19]   In casual usage, the term "tagged" denotes an object whose tag is set to indicate that it is a special type of object. This usage is deceptive because it may suggest that other objects (sometimes described as being "untagged") do not actually have tag bits. In fact, a tag field is required to designate the status of every accessible object!

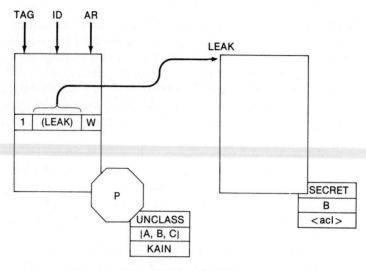

a) A proper configuration

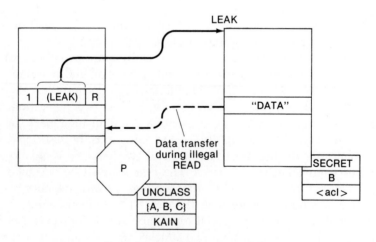

b) An illegal configuration and the
illegal READ that it permits

Figure 9-11   A security breach by changing access rights
within a legally held capability

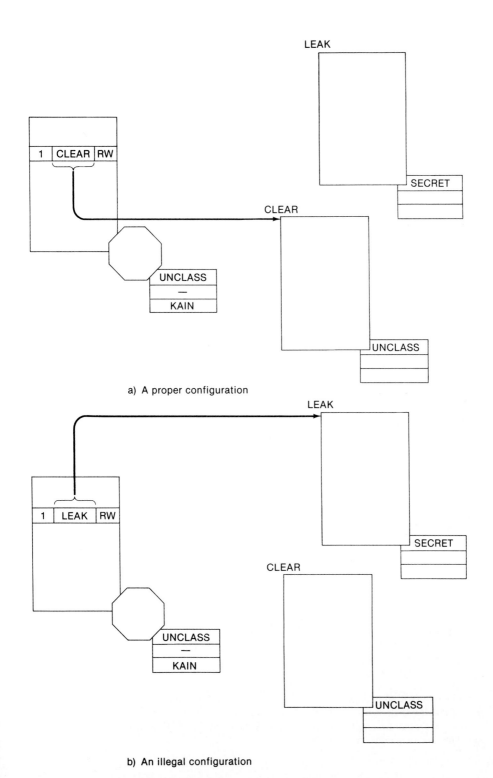

a) A proper configuration

b) An illegal configuration

Figure 9-12   Reaching an illegal configuration by overwriting an object identifier in a capability

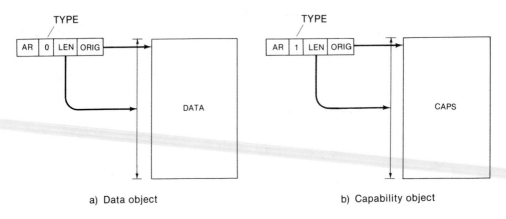

a) Data object   b) Capability object

Figure 9-13 Descriptors and objects when capabilities are segregated into segments

process can make uncontrolled write accesses. Each space descriptor contains a type field to distinguish a capability space from a noncapability space (herein called a data space, for simplicity[20]). Figure 9-13 illustrates the space descriptor for this design and the type information contained therein.

From the preceding discussion, the reader may conclude that data and capability objects *must* be tagged or else separated into different segments in order to obtain the desired capability integrity. In a general sense, this conclusion is correct, but semantic variations may change the rule in small ways. Observe the Intel iAPX 432 design:

Example 9-11

Each iAPX 432 object contains two regions—a data region and a capability region. Either of these regions may be empty.[21] The descriptor of the object contains a "fence" value, defining the separation between the two regions (see Figure 9-14). Addressing within the segment is relative to the fence location; capabilities are accessed by subtractive indexing and data are accessed by additive indexing. From an instruction's function code the processor can determine whether each particular operand is a capability or a data object, and can choose the proper address calculation to make the appropriate memory access.

The iAPX 432 scheme is similar to the separate space scheme—in fact, one may wonder what difference there really is between the two schemes. The iAPX 432 scheme permits the same name to be used for two distinct spaces, one holding data and the other, capabilities.

---

[20] Calling noncapability objects "data" does not mean that capabilities themselves are not data; they certainly are data in the sense that they are manipulated to perform useful algorithms.
[21] If one of these were empty for every segment, the system's allocation would effectively separate capabilities and data into separate segments.

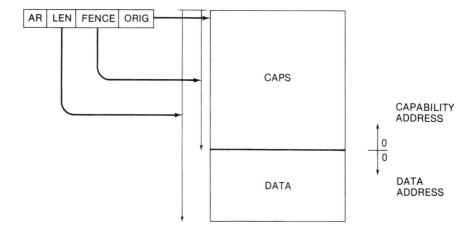

Figure 9-14   A segment in the iAPX 432—data and
capabilities separated by a fence

Example 9-12

The CAP computer [NEED77] restricts capabilities to the instruction segment,
where they are separated from the instructions by a "fence" value. This design has
the advantage that all objects that users cannot modify (instructions and capabilities) are collected together.

We have two basic schemes for distinguishing capabilities from data: by
using tags or by having capabilities define the contents of the spaces they describe. On the surface, it may seem that the two schemes are identical—in each,
there are space descriptors, and these space descriptors contain type information. There are two major differences, however:

1. In scheme 2, type information need not be added to all data objects.
2. In scheme 1, the tag type information describes the object to which the
   type information is attached, and in scheme 2, the type information in the
   capability describes the contents of the space described by the capability.

It may seem that the second scheme appears to be better on all counts—it
does not require that a tag bit be added to all objects in memory, and it still provides the desired capability protection. However, there is one disadvantage—space descriptors and data must be completely separated from each other;
they cannot be intermixed in memory. This rule prevents one from writing subroutines that expect a parameter list with a mixture of data and capability objects. This rule also limits data structures that mix data and capabilities.

Once capabilities have been distinguished from data objects, the operations
manipulating capabilities must similarly be separated from the operations that
manipulate data objects. General data manipulation operations should not be

permitted to operate on or produce capabilities because these operations could be used to create bogus capabilities and can defeat the system's security. What capability operations are required? The list includes the following:

1. Capability copying
2. Object management
3. Access rights manipulation

An operation allowing the creation of a capability describing a portion of another object can be useful, but is not logically necessary.[22]

There are several ways to implement capability copying:

1. Include a special memory-to-memory operation.
2. Add tags to processor registers.
3. Provide special capability registers.

The first option does not provide any way for a capability to reside in a programmer-visible processor register. Therefore, all capability operations must take capability operands from memory and leave their capability results in memory.

Example 9-13

> The Intel iAPX 432 instruction COPY_AD copies one "access descriptor" (AD) in a memory-to-memory operation. All of the source capability (AD) is copied directly to the destination, except for one AD bit that indicates whether it has been copied; this bit is set in the source object and cleared in the destination object. The copied bit is used by memory garbage-collection algorithms.

In the second option, a capability can be copied to a processor register, but it is tagged; the processor prohibits modifications to tagged objects in its registers. One difficulty with this scheme is the length of a capability; a single capability may be large, exceeding "normal" register size limits.

The third option includes special capability registers, possibly in a special capability coprocessor. Logically, this is like adding a tag bit to mark capabilities that reside in other registers.

After the designer has selected a technique to assure capability integrity, she must pay close attention to access rights propagation within and among capabilities; after all, the capabilities are there to control object access in a manner consistent with the security policy being enforced by the system.

Access Right Control. The second design problem is to control access rights propagation, because proper rights bit values are essential to system integrity. It is difficult to assure that all rights are consistent with the security policy, because by simple capability copying, one process may propagate all its access

---

[22]   Introducing descriptors of portions of objects complicates modules managing space allocations and modules managing access rights.

permissions to any other process. Therefore, we face a dilemma: If a capability can be copied, its access rights can be passed to an unauthorized program, but if no capabilities can be copied, there is no way to share objects. Because it is difficult to argue that capability copying should be prohibited, it is necessary to provide some means for restricting access rights in conjunction with capability copying. One could consider restricting all capability copying to programs running in special "type manager" domains; this scheme was the basis of the PSOS design [NEUM80].

Access rights restrictions can be imposed by using an explicit operation that limits the rights or by restricting the setting of the rights bits based on the context in which the capability exists [KAIN86]. We call the explicit instruction RESTRICTACCESSRIGHTS (RAR).[23] The operands for RAR are a capability and a mask that defines the access privileges to be deleted. If rights are encoded so that a "1" denotes the right to make an access, and if a "0" mask value means "delete this right," then the rights are restricted when the mask is ANDed with the AR field of the capability operand. Figure 9-15 illustrates the RAR operation.

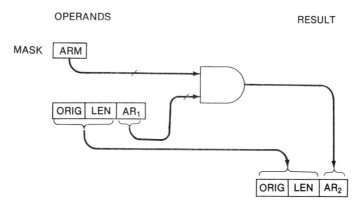

Figure 9-15   Restricting access rights ($AR_2 = AR_1 \wedge ARM$)

Example 9-14

The iAPX 432 operation RESTRICT_RIGHTS changes the access rights fields of its access descriptor operand (located in memory) by clearing those bit positions specified by the other operand. Clearing an access right bit removes the corresponding right.

The second method for imposing access rights restrictions is based on rules that limit the values of the rights bits. One might use a comparison between the security properties of the object R described by the capability C and the security

---

[23]   We "restrict" the rights because it can be argued that a process should not be able to pass on rights that it itself does not possess. (We will read more about this argument later.)

properties of the segment S within which C is stored to limit the AR values. A simple version states that the rights within C cannot exceed those that could be permitted to a process P *if* P were executing in a security context matching the security attributes of S. To implement reasonable security controls, additional rules must be imposed to assure that the rights are used in a manner compatible with the context within which they were set.[24] Enforcing all of these rules may require more mechanism than a design that does not copy access rights.

Security Policy Enforcement. All secure systems must maintain conformance between the security policy and the system state. In a capability-based system, this conformance relies on correct interactions between capability copying (including any rights changes made while copying), RAR operations, and the patterns of object sharing (the last determines how capabilities can be propagated among processes). It is difficult to reason about this (complex) set of relationships and interactions and then to prove the system's conformance to any given security policy. Because the access rights in propagated capabilities must be masked in accordance with the security attributes of both the sending and receiving processes, a portion of each process will have to be trusted to correctly use these attributes to limit the copied access rights.

The following example illustrates a simple capability copying action that can compromise system security.

Example 9-15

This scenario [BOEB84] illustrates the ease with which incorrect access rights can be propagated. The players are two processes P_1 and P_2 operating at levels L_1 and L_2, with $L_1 > L_2$. There are two segments S_1 and S_2, containing information at levels L_1 and L_2, respectively. As a consequence of these level assignments it is appropriate for P_1 and P_2, respectively, to have access to capabilities C_1 and C_2 permitting both read and write accesses to S_1 and S_2, respectively. It is also permissible for P_2 to have access to a capability C_3 describing S_1, giving only write rights. Similarly, P_1 may have a capability C_4 describing S_2, with read rights permitted. This situation is depicted in Figure 9-16a.

An illegal access can be obtained by following this scenario:

1. P_2 copies C_2 to S_1 (using C_3 to obtain access to S_1).
2. P_1 uses the copy of C_2 to write into S_2.

The arrangement after step 1 has been performed is shown in Figure 9-16b. Because the copy of C_2 permits writing to S_2, the second operation is permitted by the access rights in C_2, but it violates the *-property.

Some design approaches that prohibit the compromise exhibited in this example are presented and categorized in [KAIN86].

---

[24]   See Problem 9-15 and [KAIN86] for further details.

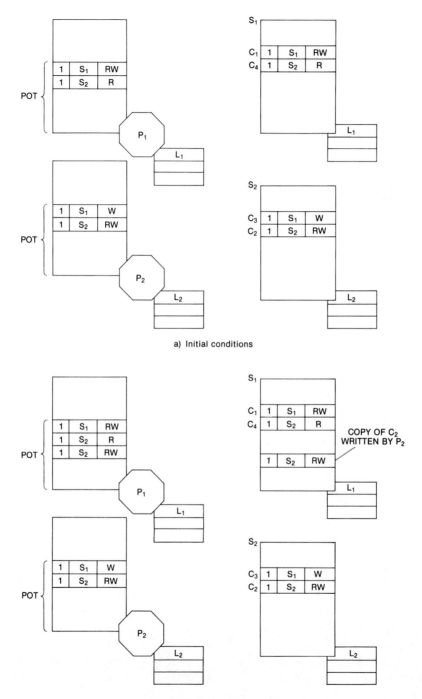

a) Initial conditions

b) With dangerons capability in POT (P₁)

Figure 9-16 Capability copying can violate the
*-property (L₁ > L₂)

Comments. Important difficulties inherent in capability-based systems center around the integrity of the capabilities and the access rights contained therein. Because it is difficult to maintain consistency between the system's security policy, the access rights in capabilities, and the eventual use of those capabilities, a capability-based design claiming to support security must be approached with great caution and skepticism.

9.5.2 Context-Based Access Rights Determination

The capability-based designs just discussed suffer because the association between an object's description and the access rights it contains for a process is established when the access rights are put into the capability. This binding of access rights to an access descriptor occurs too soon and in the wrong context to obviously assure conformance with the system's security policy. The context difficulty arises because the access rights are set by the "issuer" of the capability and it is difficult for the capability issuer to know with certainty which process (or processes) will use the capability to access memory.

An alternative approach defers all access-rights determination until an object is loaded into a process's POT. The access rights are determined using information about both the object (for which access will be granted) and about the process (to which the access will be granted). In this section, we detail secure system design approaches in which the access rights are determined during LPOT. We will show how this design corrects most of the problems inherent in capability-based designs. We hope that moving the rights determination step closer to the time of use will also alleviate the revocation timing problem.

In a system using LPOT, the reference monitor can be divided into two pieces. The first piece (ARS—access rights setting) determines the access rights to place in the new POT entry. The second piece (ARC—access rights checking) checks each memory access attempt against the rights stored in the POT. All ARC checks can be performed by the MMU (Section 3.8.1); we concentrate on ARS in the remainder of this section. To perform its function, ARS examines the appropriate context and object information and determines access rights based on the security attributes of both process P (performing the LPOT) and the object.

The acl state is examined when LPOT is executed; this timing implies more prompt revocation than the standard capability design. Nevertheless, if a permitted access is revoked while process P holds the revoked right within its POT, process P continues to hold permission to make the newly prohibited accesses until its POT is discarded or until its POT entry is overwritten, because the act of revocation changes the acl but does not change any POT entry for any process.

The Multics system and the SAT and LOCK system designs use this approach to rights determination, with important terminology and implementation differences.

Multics. The Multics system associates a known segment table (KST) with each process in the system; an entry is placed in this table when the process attempts to access an object that has not been entered into the KST. The KST plays the role of the POT in our earlier general discussion. In Multics, objects are called segments and are equivalent to files.

When file F is added to process P's KST, the access rights of P to F are determined. The file's acl is examined to see whether the user is allowed access to the object or if her rights have been restricted in any manner. A ring numbering system (see Section 9.1.3) is used to impose further access restrictions.[25] The rights determination step compares the process's ring value and the ring values in the acl entries giving the user access to the file. There is no check based directly on the hierarchical levels and categories that may be associated with the user or with the file's contents.

Example 9-16

A Multics file's acl has a separate entry for each access mode for a particular user.[26] An acl entry contains both a user name and a pair of ring numbers defining the ring range from which that user may access the described file in the described access mode. The access rights are determined when F is loaded into P's KST. Suppose that file F is being loaded for process P, executing on behalf of user U, and executing in ring R. To determine the access permissions, the following algorithm is repeated for each possible access mode m (read, execute, or write):

1. Search the acl for an entry matching (U, m);
2. Let r_1 and r_2 ($r_1 \leq r_2$) be the two ring numbers in the acl entry;
3. Set the access permission for mode m if $r_1 \leq R \leq r_2$;

SAT (Secure Ada Target). In the SAT system [BOEB85], each program is executed within a security context consisting of a hierarchical level, a category list, the identity of the user, and a domain. The program executing with such a context is called a *subject*, and each subject has an associated name space table (NST) containing segments located within the subject's address space; the subject's access rights for an addressable segment are contained in the NST entry for that segment. A segment is loaded into the NST when the processor executes a load NST (LNST) or an append to NST (ANST) instruction. The NST plays the role of the POT, with the LNST and ANST operations corresponding to LPOT and APOT, respectively. The object descriptors are called *tagged objects*; they are similar to

---

[25]   Recall that the ring numbering scheme was developed as a way to insulate trusted programs and information from untrusted programs by using a clever (linear) encoding scheme. This does not quite apply to the mandated (level, category) structure, because the security-level dominance relation defines a general POset, not a linear ordering.

[26]   The actual scheme for describing users in a Multics acl utilizes several attributes of users, including the user's name and the user's group. To simplify our discussion, we assume that the acl entry contains only a user name and that there is only a single matching entry for each (user_name, access_mode) pair. The interested reader is referred to [ORGA72] for details of the general design used in Multics.

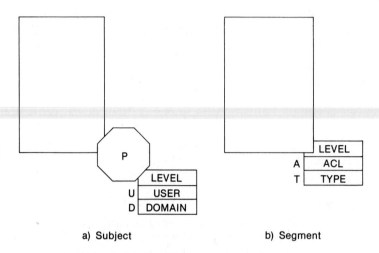

a) Subject   b) Segment

Figure 9-17   SAT/LOCK security attributes

capabilities, but contain only object identifiers, without any access rights information.

The SAT system's security state is held within a global object table (GOT). Every object, subject, security level, domain, and type is described in the GOT; all security-relevant object attributes are stored in the GOT. These include the level dominance relations, the object acls, and the domain definition and transition tables (see what follows), in addition to the security attributes assigned to objects and subjects.

In SAT, each subject's security attributes form a triple {subject_level, user, domain}.[27] Similarly, each SAT object's security attributes form a related triple {object_level, acl, type}. In figures we label the three security attributes to conform to this terminology (see Figure 9-17). As the SAT system adds a segment to a subject's NST, it determines the proper access rights consistent with the system's security state at that moment. The attribute components of the subject and the object are used to determine the access rights placed in the NST entry. The access rights determination is defined by three (conceptual) data structures:

1. Basic access matrix (BAM)
2. Discretionary overlay matrix (DOM)
3. Domain definition table (DDT)

---

[27]   We will conform to the published SAT terminology and use the simple word "level" to denote a node in the POset describing the dominance relation among security levels.

Each of these data structures is accessed using different parts of the subject's security attributes and the object's security attributes to limit the access rights placed in the new NST entry.

The BAM specifies the mandatory limits on the access rights; a BAM entry is found (conceptually) by the selector (subject_level, object_level). This matrix can be initialized so that its contents are equivalent to the information in the level dominance POset.

The discretionary overlay matrix (DOM) is the collection of access control lists (acls); it is used to enforce the discretionary security policy. The DOM entry found by the selector (user, object_name) contains the acl entry for the user for the named object.

Notice the correspondence between the security model and the first two parts of the access-rights determination. Because the system is implemented so that the rights determined on loading the NST must be encountered while making any memory access, the SAT system must enforce the mandatory and discretionary security policies. To satisfy the complete security requirements, the system must meet the additional requirements, such as the labeling requirement. We will see that the DDT check can be used to support many of the additional system security requirements.

The DDT restricts access rights based on the selector (domain, object_type); the entry found by this selector specifies the maximum rights permitted from the subject's domain to any object of the type object_type.

The domain construct can be used to enforce required data flows through "assured pipelines." Object types and program domains can be set to be consistent with read and write restrictions compatible with data flowing through the pipeline. For example, the labeling requirement [YOUN86] states that all printed output should be labeled with appropriate labels that should reflect the sensitivity of the contents of the document. A structured modular labeling function might be isolated within a single procedure that inserts labels. The printed output will be properly labeled if the (correct) labeling procedure processes all output before it is printed or displayed. How can we guarantee that the labeling procedure is unavoidably encountered between the act of reading an object and the act of printing its contents? One must be able to argue that the labeling program must have been used, and also that the labeler's output could not have been corrupted by another procedure, by programming errors, or by a subversive program placed in the system by an attacker.

Example 9-17

We use the DDT access restrictions to construct an assured pipeline containing the labeler module and the module that controls the output device (see Figure 9-18a). In addition to the types and domains used elsewhere in the system, we use two domains, two types of instruction segments, and one type of data object to define the pipeline's data flow path. The labeler's domain will be called LAB; the labeler

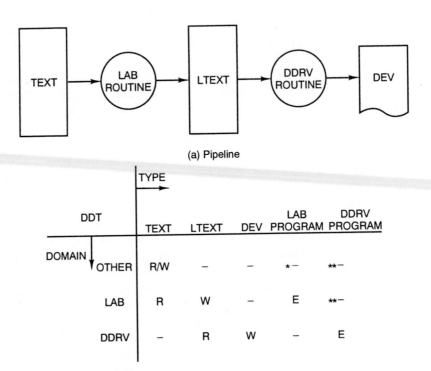

(a) Pipeline

DDT	TYPE				
DOMAIN ↓	TEXT	LTEXT	DEV	LAB PROGRAM	DDRV PROGRAM
OTHER	R/W	–	–	*–	**–
LAB	R	W	–	E	**–
DDRV	–	R	W	–	E

* (CHANGE TO DOMAIN LAB)
** (CHANGE TO DOMAIN DDRV)

(b) DDT access rights

Figure 9-18   Using DDT to enforce labeling flows

program is placed in an instruction segment of type LPROG. The DDT is set to permit the execute access to segments of type LPROG *only* from the LAB domain. The
labeled text will be stored in an object of type LTEXT. The DDT will be set to permit
a program executing in the domain LAB to write into objects of type LTEXT. Further,
objects of type LTEXT can be neither read nor written by any program executing in
a user domain; this restriction isolates items in the pipeline from external interference.[28] To guarantee that the device cannot display or print any information that
has not been properly labeled, we create a separate DDRV domain for the device
driver program, and set the DDT to permit read access to objects of type LTEXT
from this DDRV domain. Furthermore, the DDT is set so that no other data object
types can be read by a program executing in the DDRV domain; this limitation ensures that the device driver cannot read unlabeled data and thereby move that information to the output device. Figure 9-18b illustrates these restrictions and the
relevant DDT entries.

---

[28] In particular, this restriction prevents unauthorized modification of outgoing (labeled)
information.

To complete the design, we need a mechanism that determines (and switches) the execution domain for each subject. First, assume that the initial execution domain for a subject has been set correctly by the system; then we need to consider only domain changes during program execution. Proper modularity dictates that domain changes can occur during CALL and RETURN and not at other times. Consider domain changes during CALL. The need for a domain change could be detected by the normal access checking mechanisms because the first instruction of the called procedure will not be accessible from the old domain (as a consequence of the DDT settings). The MMU will detect this illegal access attempt. The system will be activated, will discover that a CALL was just made, and will consult the domain transition table (DTT), using the selector (domain, type). A nonnull entry signifies that a domain change should be made; the DTT entry contains the identity of the next domain to be used. To complete the domain change, the system software creates a new subject initialized for the procedure's execution. When the called procedure RETURNs, the saved state within the completed subject will be consulted to find the subject that initiated the CALL; control returns to this subject, thereby restoring the calling procedure's domain.

Observe how the desired information flow has been enforced—a user program operating in a general domain may create arbitrary text and place it in a segment. The user program calls the labeler to request that this text be labeled. The call to the labeler causes a switch to a subject operating in the LAB domain. The labeler places its labeled text in an object of type LTEXT. The DDT restrictions insulate the labeled text from programs executing in the user domain (irrespective of the mandatory and discretionary policy restrictions). Once the labeler has completed, execution returns to the original subject, operating in the user domain. At some later time, the user program can call the device driver, passing a pointer to the labeled text object as a parameter. The device driver program causes the (labeled) information to be displayed. To complete the design, place verified labeling and device driver procedures in the LAB and DDRV domains, respectively. The domain restrictions guarantee that these procedures must have been called before the output was displayed. To prove that the system does meet the labeling requirement, we only have to prove that the LAB program properly inserts labels and that the DDRV program properly displays everything within the segment presented for printing.

The SAT domain mechanism is a generalization from earlier domain designs (summarized in [LIND76]) in which domain access restrictions were based on the name, rather than the type, of the accessed object. By using type (rather than name), it is possible to create and destroy temporary objects for use in the pipeline; this change promotes more efficient memory usage. The change also simplifies proofs of system properties, because an abstract property (of object type), rather than a specific object name, determines access rights.

Figure 9-19 illustrates the complete access rights checks using the BAM, DOM, and DDT matrices. An AND combination of the BAM, DOM, and DDT access permissions obtains the actual access rights for security enforcement. In Section 9.8, we introduce the need for policy exceptions; in SAT, these cases are folded into the domain concept—certain domains may be given expanded access rights (in violation of the *-property) to permit essential operations.

LOCK. The LOCK system [SAYD87] is an outgrowth of the SAT design. Numerous details were changed, but the underlying approach of determining access rights when an object enters the address space of a process remains unchanged. One important difference is that in LOCK, the notion of a tagged object disappears. Eliminating tagged objects greatly simplifies the system, since special tagging operations and manipulations are not required. This change is permitted because no security problem can be introduced if an arbitrary process adds an arbitrary object to its address space; if the object is not to be visible, the system simply sets its access rights to null. Furthermore, a process cannot see its access rights for any object, since that information is not stored in any object visible to the process. Note that if a process were able to view (or otherwise determine) its rights to an object, a covert channel could use a receiver that examines POT entries for null access rights. This particular covert channel can be removed by hiding the actual access rights from each process.

The second LOCK change concerns write access permissions; subjects are not permitted to write an object whose security level dominates the level of the subject. This change is driven not by security concerns, but by the perennial desire to build systems from available components. The underlying problem is that all MMU designers have made the "reasonable" decision that it is unreasonable to grant write access to a program if the program is not permitted to read an object. Therefore, the underlying hardware permits reads to any object that can be written. This implies that the system cannot permit a write to an object that is not at the same security level as the executing subject. Thus, any writes that move information upward in security levels must be handled by privileged software that must reside inside the trusted computer base.

9.6 SOFTWARE SUPPORT FOR SYSTEM SECURITY

Some security features require software support, whereas others may utilize a combination of software and hardware support. In this section, we describe software support for system security, including features that could have been supported with either software or hardware. After reading this section, you will appreciate the difficulty of designing and implementing a largely software approach to providing system security.

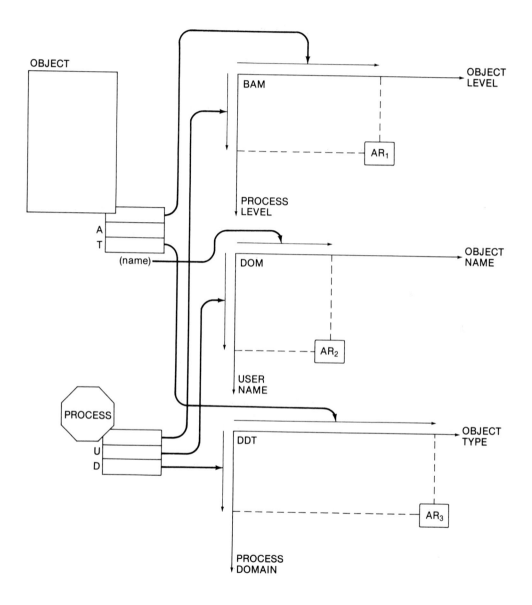

Figure 9-19 Using BAM, DOM, and DDT to determine access rights
$(AR = AR_1 \wedge AR_2 \wedge AR_3)$

9.6.1 System Security State

All information relevant to access controls is part of the system's security state. The security state specifies the security attributes of all objects, users, and processes within the system. The contents of the security state determine the access rights that will be accorded to each program in the system. If the security state always contains the "correct" information, and if all access attempts are checked against that state, the system can be easily shown to conform to its security policy. Therefore, security state maintenance is perhaps the most important function of a secure system's software. In this section, we detail the security state and show how software might be used to maintain and utilize this state to set access rights.

Security State Information.   In an abstract sense, the complete security state is defined by a general access control matrix like the one described in Figure 9-3. This general unconstrained specification does not have sufficient structure to reason easily about the system's security properties.

The security state contains all security attributes of all objects in the system. The security attributes associated with an object may depend on the type of the object itself. For example, a process has a user identifier among its attributes, whereas a storage object has an access control list. It is convenient to consider every security-relevant item as an object. The logical security attributes of all object types necessary to implement the mandatory and discretionary security policies are summarized in Table 9-5. In the table, we do not distinguish all object types such as integer versus real; rather, we distinguish all object types that have an important role with respect to the system's security.

The secure system must regulate three activities regarding its security state. First, it must protect the security state information against unauthorized access, including modification and viewing. Second, it must be able to update the security state to reflect changing conditions. Third, it must correctly use the security state to determine the access rights of processes to segments.

TABLE 9-5   OBJECT TYPES AND THEIR
SECURITY ATTRIBUTES

Object Type	Security Attributes
Segment	Level, acl, type
Process	Level, user, domain
User	Level
Device	Level

The security state protection issue may seem circular: We need to protect the security state, whose function is to protect objects against unauthorized access. But the security state itself is an object (or a collection of objects). The cycle can be broken by asserting that when the system is initialized, the security state is correctly configured; thenceforth the security state will be protected properly. After correct initialization, security state protection can be achieved by denying access to its memory space except when the security state manager within the system is in execution.

The security state must be available to receive change notifications whenever conditions change. Because such changes could be used to subvert the system, it is important to limit the use of operations that change the security state carefully, restricting their use only to authorized personnel. Conceptually, this protection could be achieved by preventing access to the procedures that modify the security state except when a specially authorized user makes a special request.

Finally, the security state must be available for inspection when a program requests access rights for an object. At that point, the system must access the security attributes of the object and the process and then apply the proper tests to set the access rights. The result must be delivered reliably to the MMU that checks all access attempts.

Associate Access Rights with Proper Entities. The secure system must ensure that the access rights allocated for a particular objects be used only to access that object. To complete an access, the system must have a memory address and an associated access rights field, which, for convenience in this discussion, we will call a descriptor of the object, though a descriptor might not be used for this purpose.

Because the MMU is performing the access validity checks, the object's descriptor must be placed into the MMU's state before the object can be accessed. An illegal access using descriptor D could be forced in several ways:

1. Tampering with the access rights field in D
2. Exchanging D's AR field with the AR field from another descriptor
3. Using D to access a memory location outside the bounds of the object described by D[29]
4. Tampering with the location information within D
5. Using the MMU table for process P_i to check an access on behalf of process P_j $(\neq P_i)$

Another form of access violation could occur if the system moves information within memory and does not properly update the segment origin pointers.

---

[29]   A related attack uses a dangling descriptor reference to access a memory location that has been assigned to another object.

For example, suppose the descriptor D points to unclassified information whose origin is location 3000. Now suppose that the memory manager reallocates memory and places another segment of information, that happened to be classified secret, at location 3000. Then an access attempt using descriptor D would access the secret information. But the access attempt would have been checked on the basis that the information being accessed was unclassified (as described in D). This type of security violation could be prevented only if the memory management function were contained within the system's security kernel. A similar argument shows that input and output device control must also reside within the security kernel (see Problem 9-20).

The origin of the MMU table used to translate and mediate memory access attempts for a process is part of that process's security state, thus, the association of an MMU table origin with a process must be maintained properly. This requirement means that the process dispatcher, which issues the new MMU table location to the MMU, must be implemented correctly. Furthermore, the process states saved by the scheduler/dispatcher must be protected from tampering.

9.6.2 The Software Kernel Approach to Secure System Design

Several secure system projects have adopted a software approach to the implementation of system security, the only hardware support being the MMU that makes the usual access checks. Software implementers desire a good modular decomposition of the job to be performed, making a separate module for each functional partition of the job. When security requirements are imposed, it becomes desirable for the software that performs security-relevant functions to execute with the minimum security privilege required to perform the job. This approach minimizes the number of module interactions that must be considered when reasoning about the system's security properties. We are back to "the principle of least privilege."

One might consider providing system security by inserting a security kernel beneath an existing operating system. A hierarchical design in this style places the security kernel just above the hardware[30] (see Figure 9-20). The difficulty hiding in this attractive picture is that the security kernel must manage the system's physical resources. Taking these functions out of a complete operating system and reimplementing them in the kernel introduces a large performance degradation. For example, the KVM/370 secure system [GOLD79] operated at approximately 25% of the performance of the insecure 370 system [LAND83].

Thus, experience suggests that it is essential to provide some hardware support for the security aspects of the system. Even with hardware support, a small software kernel that dispatches processes and handles interrupts and traps will be required.

---

[30]   See [BERS79] and [NEUM80] for details of this design style.

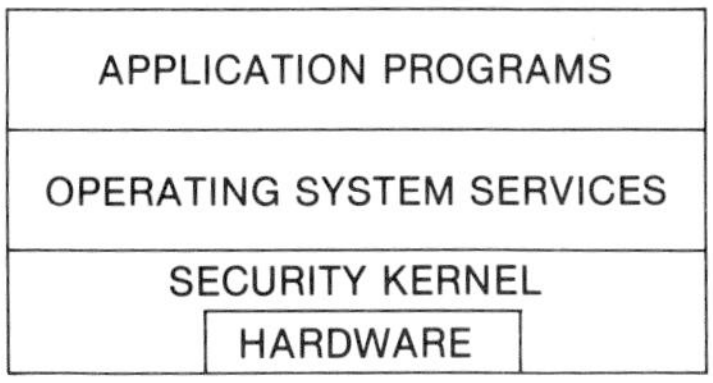

```
┌─────────────────────────────────┐
│     APPLICATION PROGRAMS         │
├─────────────────────────────────┤
│   OPERATING SYSTEM SERVICES      │
├─────────────────────────────────┤
│       SECURITY KERNEL            │
│    ┌───────────────────┐         │
│    │     HARDWARE      │         │
│    └───────────────────┘         │
└─────────────────────────────────┘
```

Figure 9-20   The implementation hierarchy when using a software security kernel

9.7 HARDWARE SUPPORT FOR SECURE SYSTEM IMPLEMENTATION

A secure system implemented by software executed on an unmodified insecure system performs poorly. Hardware support for security enhancements separates the security kernel software from the application software, which can enhance system performance and simplify reasoning about the system's security properties. In this section, we explore some design options that provide some hardware support.

We survey some systems that contain facilities to support secure access checking and thus a secure system implementation. The Multics system, originated at MIT and later supported by Honeywell, had hardware "hooks" to support security features. The MC68020 has some hooks also; it may be possible to add a security coprocessor module to the MC68020's bus to enhance the security of that system. We also cover (1) the SAT system, designed at Honeywell as an adaptation of the DPS 6/96 computer to meet or exceed the Department of Defense requirements for level A1 security certification, and (2) the LOCK system, an outgrowth of the SAT system; LOCK was designed at Secure Computing Corporation.

9.7.1 Multics Security Features

The Multics system was based on hardware modifications added to a "standard" computer design of the late 1950s; the unmodified machine was the GE 635 system, largely patterned after the IBM 709. Access checking mechanisms were added, using ring numbers to define access rights. We have seen that the ring number scheme does not directly support a general security POset structure. Multics system software controls which memory descriptors each process can see, thereby controlling the rights accorded that process. An MMU makes all access validity determinations.

9.7.2 MC68020 Security Features

The MC68020 processor supports security checks through its MMU interface and its module call/return instructions. First, consider the MMU checks. Three "FC" control signals from the processor indicate the type of information being accessed and whether the access is being made from user or supervisor mode; Table 9-6 specifies the encodings for the supported combinations. The FC values do not have to specify the type of access being requested; that information is present on the read/write bus line. Type FC7 (CPU space) is issued during any bus cycle that does not reference memory for instructions, their operands, or their results. Type FC3 may be used by a system designer to implement special features, but types FC0 and FC4 are reserved by Motorola for future expansion. Because the processor will not generate the type FC3 signal, special hardware would have to issue the FC3 signal code.

TABLE 9-6 MC68020 ADDRESS SPACE INFORMATION

FC Value	Mode	Information Type
0	(Reserved)	
1	User	Data
2	User	Instruction
3	(Not used by the processor)	
4	(Reserved)	
5	Supervisor	Data
6	Supervisor	Instruction
7	CPU Space	

Source: From [MOTO84]; courtesy of Motorola, Inc.

The MC68020 processor instruction CALLM, used to call a "module," can assist the design of secure systems. The module descriptor (Figure 9-21) contains an access level field, which specifies the "level" of execution for the module. The processor holds the level of the executing program. The desired level (specified in the CALLM operand) is examined by the processor during CALLM. The processor determines whether a level increase has been requested, and, if so, emits a bus request to external hardware added to control the use of CALLM. The level control hardware can initiate bus read cycles (referencing within the CPU) to read the current access level and the requested increase in access level. Having assessed the legality of the proposed change, the external hardware can use bus cycles to write into the CPU address space and thereby to authorize the change.

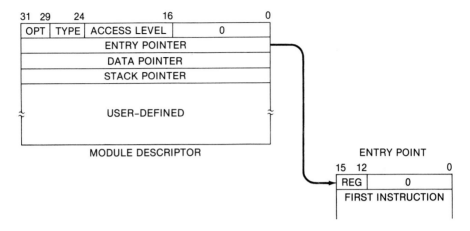

Figure 9-21   MC68020 module descriptor and entry
point (after [MOTO84]; courtesy of Motorola, Inc.)

Alternatively, the hardware can signal denial of the requested change. In addition to this authorization check, the external hardware may request a new stack for the execution of the called procedure, and the processor, in response to this request (still within the CALLM instruction), copies either the parameters or a pointer to the parameters onto the new stack. A pointer to the new stack, if requested, is contained in the module descriptor.

Because the external hardware can make an arbitrary determination of the access rights validity, it may appear that an arbitrary security policy can be implemented by suitable level number encoding. However, the processor does use an implicit one-dimensional ordering of the levels to decide whether to ask the external hardware to check the attempted CALL. Level changes are permitted only upon module call (and return) and then only when the call would increase the access level.[31]

The MC68020 also supports a complementary RTM (return from module) operation that exits a module and returns to the calling environment. During this instruction the processor checks whether the return would lower the level of execution, in which case the external (CALLM) hardware is consulted to check the validity of the requested change.

Although the basic MC68020 is not a secure system, a few important hooks are provided for a designer who wishes to add modules to the system to implement a higher level of security than could be provided under the simple native user/supervisor mode dichotomy. But it seems that it would be difficult to use this feature to implement a general secure system.

---

[31]   This type of call cannot violate the security policy; see Problem 9-14.

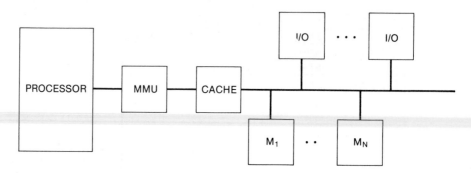

Figure 9-22   Base configuration of the Honeywell DPS6/96

9.7.3 ix86 Security Features

Like the MC68020, the features within Intel processors do not support a general secure system, but the i386 and i486 do support ring number protection that can be used to separate user programs from the operating system, which would protect the operating system from inadvertent or malicious user actions. This feature could be used to separate a security kernel (trusted computing base) from the remainder of the operating system and from the user. But the inherent linear hierarchy within any ring-based scheme does not permit any distinction based on any nonlinear relationships, such as POset relationships among military security levels. To use read and write access checks based on ring numbers to implement a general secure system, it would be necessary for the trusted computing base to create data segment descriptors whose access bits are customized for the security level of the executing process.

9.7.4 SAT Security Features

The SAT system prototype design was designed as a modification of an existing minicomputer system, the Honeywell DPS 6/96, to form a complete secure system that meets the A1 requirements [DOD85]. The system design does not really depend upon the architecture of any particular processor. This system's base configuration is depicted in Figure 9-22. In the base system, the memory management unit (MMU) translates virtual addresses to physical addresses and makes access rights checks. The processor notifies the MMU of the type of each access attempt. The MMU obtains the access rights for this subject from a table stored in main memory (but not accessible to the executing subject). Each process has a separate memory map with independent access rights information. The security properties of the system rely on the integrity of the access rights tables.

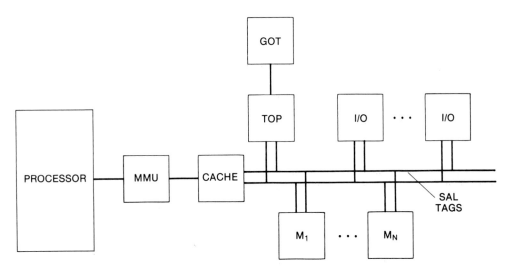

Figure 9-23   SAT/LOCK prototype configuration

In the SAT system, the contents of the memory access tables (and thus of the access rights accorded to executing processes) are carefully controlled by a combination of system software and hardware.

To enforce the security policy in a provably correct manner, several modifications are made to the base system hardware:

1. Add tagging to memory.
2. Add tagged object control lines to the bus.
3. Add a tagged object processor (TOP).

Figure 9-23 illustrates the prototype SAT configuration. In addition to the hardware changes shown in the figure, low-level software must be changed to handle interrupts securely.

Memory tagging guarantees the integrity of tagged objects (TOs) stored in memory modules. All memory modules are modified to store the tag values, always to access the proper tag and to restrict the propagation of the contents of any tagged memory words. The propagation restrictions are enforced based on the control signal on the secure access line on the bus.

The secure access line (SAL) on the bus can be asserted by a module making a memory read request if that module is designed to handle tagged objects. Any module (such as the processor) not designed to handle TOs is not permitted to assert the SAL signal. The memory is designed to not respond (with meaningful data) to read requests if the addressed location is tagged and the SAL signal was not asserted with the read request.

The reference monitor mechanism is centered in the MMU, which makes all per-reference access rights checks, and the tagged object processor (TOP), which performs all operations that manipulate tagged objects.[32] The TOP operations are extensions to the processor's instruction set. The TOP operations that change the reference monitor's security state change the memory tables defining the subject's access rights. Some TOP operations affect other parts of the system's security state. Other TOP operations simply copy TOs. (The processor cannot be used to copy TOs because TOs are not permitted in processor registers.)

SAT Security State. The security state of the SAT system is governed entirely by the TOP, which manipulates tagged objects. The global object table (GOT), which holds the descriptions of all objects known to the system, is managed by the TOP. We show how the TOP design and function guarantee the integrity of the system's security properties.

The TOP module performs all operations on tagged objects and maintains the security state of the system. It also performs functions on behalf of the system security officer, who controls the system state by governing the importation of objects and the assignment of security attributes to such objects and to users. Because TOs cannot be handled within the processor, TO operands for TOP operations must be taken either from memory or from TOP registers. The SAT design team decided that all TOP operations should be memory-to-memory operations, so that the TOP retains no state and does not require saving and restoration on process switch. Therefore, all TO operands and user-visible results for TOP operations are located in the memory accessible to the executing subject.

The GOT contains all the security attributes of all objects known to the system. These objects include files, users, levels, subjects, domains, and many objects of many other types, including the type type, which is included to permit the creation of new types of objects and the instantiation of objects of these new types. A GOT entry contains at least the following attributes of each object:

1. Unique identifier (UID)
2. Type
3. Owner
4. Security level
5. Access control list (acl)
6. Location
7. Length

[32] LOCK's security coprocessor is called the SIDEARM; it controls the system security state in ways similar to those used in SAT's TOP. SIDEARM does not have to copy tagged objects, because there are no such distinguished objects in a LOCK-style system.

The *UID* value is used to identify this particular object among all objects in the system; it can be considered as the "key" for searching the GOT to find the attributes of the designated object.

The *type* of the object describes how it can be used and the interpretation of its contents. The type could be denoted by the UID of the appropriate type object. Certain types must be built in to the system, because they have security-critical roles; these types include user, memory container, device, type, level, program, and domain.

The *owner* of the object is that user who is authorized to delete the object and to control the contents of its acl. The owner could be denoted by a UID.

The *security level* of the object reflects the sensitivity of its contents. Again, a UID could be used to denote this information.

The *access control list* contains a list of all users whose access to the object have been permitted or limited by the object's owner.

The *location* and *length* specify the space holding the object's contents.

Other object attributes may be stored in the GOT entry for an object, depending on the type of the described object.

The SAT's TOP. SAT's tagged object processor (TOP) performs all operations that involve tagged objects as operands, results, or both. The TOP is implemented as a separate module controlled through an interface like a coprocessor interface. The system's security state cannot be changed except by executing a TOP operation. We give an overview of the set of TOP operations, which can be conveniently grouped into six categories:

1. Object existence control
2. Tagged object copying
3. Subject state modification
4. System security state modifications
5. Status query operations
6. System security officer operations

The basic *object existence* operations create and destroy objects. These operations are called CGEN and DGEN (create and destroy GOT entry). DGEN is simpler; its single operand is a tagged object describing the object to be destroyed, and its effect is to delete that object from the system. There are several details, however, connected with the validity of the operation request. For example, the executing subject must be executing on behalf of the user who owns the object. The operand must be a legitimate tagged object. The security level and domain of that subject must be such that (in effect) the subject has both read and write access to the object. Any exceptions arising from a violation of these conditions must be handled in such a manner that the executing subject cannot use the responses as the receiving end of a covert channel. (These details are not covered here.)

An object is created by the CGEN TOP operation, whose arguments include a TO for the type of the object to be created and type-dependent parameters required for the object instantiation process, such as the size of a memory space (or file) to hold the object. The result of the CGEN operation is that a new object is created having the specified type, with the following security attributes:

1. Security level, from the executing subject
2. Type as specified in the argument
3. Access control list, giving all access rights to the creator and none to anyone else
4. Owner, from the user associated with the executing subject

After creating the object, the TOP places a TO for the new object in a memory location specified (in an operand) to receive this result.

The final object existence TOP operation allows the user to create an image of a memory object; the image is a "window" into a contiguous subset of the object's representation.[33] The result of this operation is a TO (and a GOT entry) that describes the window (which is treated somewhat like a separate object).

TOP operations in the second category support *tagged object copying*. Special operations are required because there are no TO registers that can be loaded and saved to effect copying. Two operations are supported; the first copies a single TO, and the second copies a block of memory that is allowed to contain TOs. Because the TO alignment restrictions require only alignment to word boundaries, tagged objects may overlap; special rules cover situations in which the operation actually reads or overwrites part of a tagged object.

The third category of TOP operations support *subject state modifications*, which means that the execution of an operation in this set changes the view of the system as seen by an executing subject. The primary operations in this set are the LNST and ANST operations, analogous to the LPOT and APOT operations discussed earlier. These instructions modify the image of virtual memory as seen by the executing process. A similar operation modifies the virtual device set seen by the process; it is called LVDT (load virtual device table); it assigns a device to a virtual device number. Its operands are a TO describing a device and an integer that defines the number by which the device will be known. The final operation that modifies the subject's view of the system assigns temporary nonsharable memory space to the executing process. Although this operation is not logically necessary, it enhances system performance by reducing the number of GOT references that the TOP must make (because the temporary space need not have any specific security attributes—these are inherited from those of the executing subject). Its parameters are a segment number and a length.

---

[33]   There are no windows in LOCK.

TOP operations in the fourth category *modify the system's security state.* There are many ways that the system security state can be modified by authorized users, such as system operators and the system security officer. A few operations (related to object ownership and the privileges associated with ownership) are available to nontrusted programs. The first of these operations allows a user to change the acl of an owned object. The parameters of this SDAC (set discretionary access controls) operation are an object descriptor, a user TO, and a bit vector describing the new state of the acl for the described object. This operation may either expand or contract (revoke) access rights accorded to another user. The other two operations that affect the system security state are involved in transferring the ownership of an object. The SAT view of object ownership changes is that the act of changing ownership is like sending a message from the old owner to the new one. (It is necessary that the new owner explicitly receive ownership in order that there be a cognizant owner who can control the object's existence and the contents of its acl.) To assure that the ownership of an object does not "get lost," the SAT system maintains three ownership-related lists associated with each user; the contents of these lists affect the effect of several TOP operations, and may be visible to programs executing on behalf of the owning user. The three lists contain:

1. All owned objects
2. Objects whose ownership has been sent to this user, but that has not yet been received
3. Objects whose ownership has been sent by this user to another user, but that has not yet been received

A single object can be on at most one of the lists of a single user. However, an object whose ownership is in transit is present on list 2 of the receiving user and on list 3 of the sending user.[34] An entry on list 2 or 3 describes an object whose ownership is being transferred, plus the identity of the other user involved in the transaction. Figure 9-24 illustrates the list configuration when the object MOVING is being sent from SENDER to RECEIVER (these being user names).

The two ownership changing operations are GOWN (Give OWNership) and TOWN (Take OWNership). GOWN can be executed for any object owned by the executing (sending) user. The operands of GOWN are a descriptor of the object to be given away and a descriptor of the user to whom the object is to be given. GOWN removes the sent object from the sender's list 1 and places it on both the sender's list 3 and the receiver's list 2.[35] TOWN can be executed for any object on either list 2 or list 3 of the executing user. Executing TOWN removes the object from list 2 of the receiver and list 3 of the sender and places the object on list 1 of

[34]   This is the only situation in which an object may appear on the ownership lists of more than one user.
[35]   As noted before, user identities are also placed into these list entries.

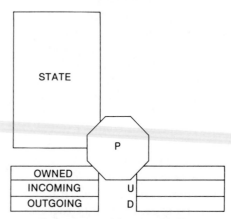

a) A process with ownership lists

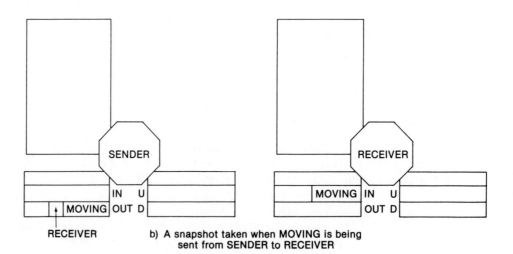

b) A snapshot taken when MOVING is being
sent from SENDER to RECEIVER

Figure 9-24   Ownership list state

the executing (receiving) user. Figure 9-25 shows the ownership lists before, during, and after the GOWN-TOWN ownership transfer of object M.

Common sense suggests that it may not make sense for a user to be considered as the owner of an object if that user cannot both read and write the object.
If this constraint is to be honored by the system, a user can be considered to be
the owner of the object only when she is executing a program in a security context that permits both reading and writing the object. In particular, the subject's
security level must match the security level of the contents of the owned object.

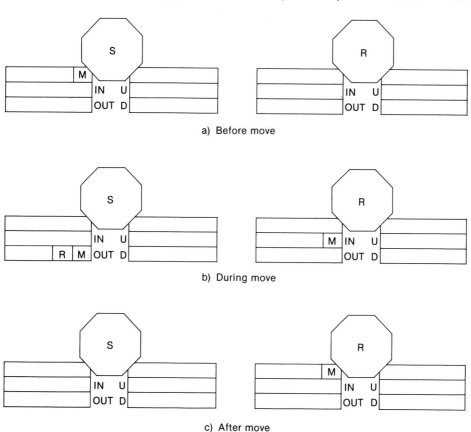

c) After move

Figure 9-25   Ownership list states encompassing an ownership transfer.
(The process state object is irrelevant and not shown to simplify the pictures.)

This reasoning leads one to the conclusion that the visible contents of the owner-ship lists must change as the security context of the executing subject changes. The changing visibility of the ownership list entries implies a changing ability to pass and receive objects as the level of the executing subject changes.

The TOP *status query operations* allow a subject to learn limited information about the system's security state, as it pertains to the subject or to visible objects. A subject, for example, can find the security level of an object that it is able to read (this permits labelers to perform their function). A subject can find what objects are listed on the incoming and outgoing ownership lists. A subject can find its own security level.

The final set of TOP operations support special operations allowed only to the *system security officer* (SSO). These operations assign security levels and types to objects entering the system from the outside. New users can be added to the authorized set and assigned security attributes. Operations supporting system installation, checkpointing, and restart are also provided.

An important privileged TOP operation, TWO (trusted write override) writes information in memory, even if prohibited by the mandatory policy restrictions. This operation can be executed only by subjects that operate in domains for which trusted write privilege has been extended to the subject by virtue of the DDT entry. It probably seems that the ordinary write operation would be adequate for this operation; however, the A1 requirements [DOD85] imply that all downgrade operations must be audited—having a separate operation for these cases facilitates implementing this audit requirement.

Interrupt Handlers. Low-level interrupt handlers play an essential role in maintaining the system's security, because they operate in supervisor mode and have access to the state of the entire memory (except for the access restrictions imposed by the inability of the processor to access a tagged word). In the SAT system, these handlers are written to make appropriate tests and to dispatch TOP operations when necessary to effect the proper operational semantics. For example, when a program requests access to a segment for which it has improper access rights, the MMU causes a trap, and the interrupt handler invokes the TOP to see whether the subject in fact has special privileges that make the operation permissible. One important situation of this type concerns calling a procedure defined to execute in a domain different from that of the calling program. An attempt to enter the procedure causes an interrupt, and the handler invokes the TOP, which consults the DTT and finds out whether a new subject should be entered to change domains. The TOP and the interrupt handler cooperate to set up the proper subject, pass the parameters, and transfer control to the new subject. (A similar scenario applies to the return from that subject.)

9.7.5 LOCK Security Features

We describe LOCK's features by comparing them against SAT's features. The major changes affect the hardware and tagged object support. LOCK is designed to support various system processors using conventional MMUs to perform the access checking for the reference monitor role. The absence of tagged objects in LOCK removes the need for the features within SAT that handle tagged objects. The security coprocessor within LOCK is called the SIDEARM; it handles requests to change domains and to add objects to the memory map for a process; the latter operation implies determining access rights from information in the system's security state. A third change is the elimination of window objects. Having windows complicates many management details; in most applications, there is little penalty incurred by copying into a separate object the smaller portion of a large object to which a process desires access.

9.7.6 Comments

The SAT/LOCK design illustrates how designers can use high-level system requirements to affect the hardware-level system implementation. By using hardware separation and a special module (the TOP or SIDEARM) for capability manipulation, designers can isolate security features in such a manner as to simplify reasoning about the system's security properties. It is important to note that the SAT design implements important mechanisms at low levels, but because the mechanisms are general, all policy details can be defined by tables contained within the system's security state. Thus, the same hardware and low-level software can be used to support applications with differing security requirements. The LOCK design reduces the need for special hardware compared to the SAT design. All secure systems will require some special software within the trusted computing base, which comprises all security-critical software.

9.8 POLICY EXCEPTIONS

A realistic complete application system cannot operate strictly in accordance with the mandatory and discretionary policies, for a number of reasons. First, information is downgraded from time to time. Second, some documents and databases contain portions with different security attributes. Third, the system operations staff must perform system maintenance functions. Finally, the system security officer must be able to change the system's security state to modify the security POset, to register new users, and to update user security clearances. In this section we explore these needs.

9.8.1 Downgrading

The act of downgrading changes some information from one security level to another, lower, level. Information that is no longer sensitive could be downgraded by a user copying it to paper and reentering it at a lower level. It would be efficient to allow a distinguished set of users to assume the downgrader role, in which they acquire permission to move information in violation of the *-property restrictions.

In the SAT system, a DDT entry can grant the downgrade privilege to programs executing within a specified domain D. This privilege is restricted to objects of a specified type T. Giving downgrade privilege expands the access rights otherwise granted to a subject accessing the object in question. To restrict the downgrade privilege to a distinguished set of SAT users, access to the

SECTIONS

	1	2	3	4
a	Secret	Top secret	Unclass	Secret
PARTS b	Unclass	Secret	Top secret	Top secret
c	Secret	Top secret	Unclass	Secret

Figure 9-26   Logical structure of a composite
multilevel object

instruction segment containing the downgrading program could be restricted
(by the discretionary access control mechanism).[36]

One could provide downgrading by permitting a trusted process write access to objects at lower levels (in violation of the *-property). This simple design
could be made type-specific by defining the domain of execution for the downgrader to limit its read access to certain object types.

9.8.2 Composite Documents and Multilevel Databases

In the paper world, there exist composite documents and databases, both containing portions[37] having different security attributes. The complete object must
be assigned to a security level that dominates the levels of all of the object's constituent portions. In a level-category scheme, this means that the composite object's hierarchical level must equal the highest hierarchical level associated with
any portion of the object, and its category set must encompass all categories associated with any portion of the object. Figure 9-26 illustrates the logical security
structure of a multilevel composite object. Difficult design issues arise when handling composite objects. After looking into their representations, we show some
covert channel problems arising from attempts to permit the use of general database accessing methods to access multilevel databases.

---

[36]   One might think that the DTT could limit the access. This view is correct in terms of the type of
check that may fail on an attempt to access the downgrading program itself. But the DDT check failed
because the subject was in the wrong domain when it tried to call the downgrader. The logical extension of such reasoning in reverse in time leads to the conclusion that somewhere along the path the
user must have made her way through a "gate" controlled by a discretionary access check.

[37]   We use the word "portion" to denote a contiguous piece of the document containing information
having the same security attributes. Without loss of generality, we assume that the division of a document into portions is made so that each neighbor of a portion S has different security attributes from
those of S. Document portions, as defined in this manner (and as used here) for security purposes, have
no necessary relationship to the document sections created by the document's author to reflect the semantic structure of the document's contents.

Representations of Composite Objects. There are two basic options:

1. Store the compound object as a single object.
2. Store the compound object as a set of objects, along with a rule for combining the objects to form the composite document.

Under either scheme, an "index" describes the portional structure of the composite document, including the security attributes of each portion of the document. Under the first option, the index governs the decomposition of the document into its visible portions based on the level from which it is to be viewed. Under the second option, in contrast, the index governs the combination of portions to form a *view object*, which is specially constructed so that all portions are readable from the level assigned to the view object. To satisfy the simple security property, the level of the view object must dominate the levels of all portions included in the view object.

Example 9-18

Consider the document "complex" whose structure is described by the following "declaration," in which we have interjected security attributes into an Ada record description of the object:

```
type sectype ( level1, level2: sec_level ) is
record
    portiona : text( level1 );    //Not Ada due to level specifications
    portionb : text( level2 );
    portionc : text( level1 );
end record;

type composite_complex is
record
    section1 : sectype( secret, unclass );
    section2 : sectype( top_secret, secret );
    section3 : sectype( unclass, top_secret );
    section4 : sectype( secret, top_secret );
end record;

complex : composite_complex;
```

The storage allocation for the object under each of the two representations is shown in Figure 9-27. In the figure, we use shorter names such as "s1" for section1 and "pb" for portionb. The associated index object is also shown in the figure; it is identical in structure for the two representations, but the internal index information gluing the structure together is slightly different for the two representations.

One way that a program could deal with one of these object representations is through calls to a **package** that is the type manager for the type class multilevel_object (of which the type composite_complex is a member). The **package** would operate in its

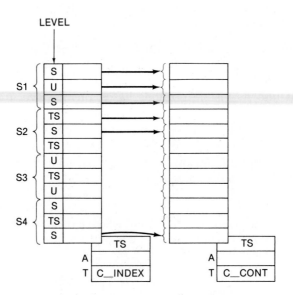

a) Contents in a single object.
(The contents sections are larger than the
index entries.)

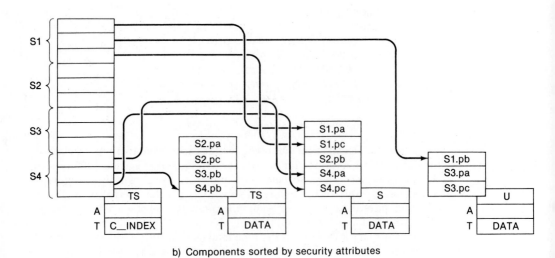

b) Components sorted by security attributes

Figure 9-27   Representation options for a composite object

own domain. The functions that such a **package** should provide are discussed in Problem 9-26. A **package** encapsulation of the composite objects effectively hides the chosen representation scheme.

Under all options for composite object management, the object manager software may have to be verified to be correct, especially if it does respond to an access request by coalescing portions having different security attributes to form a single object. Thus, the composite object manager lies within the "trusted" part of the system. It is difficult to see how to design efficient systems to meet the requirements.

One method for limiting access to a piece of a composite object is to create a *window* into the object; a subset of the document's contents can be accessed through the window. Figure 9-28 illustrates a window descriptor and the related logical object structures. If the underlying system design supports windows, the result from the multilevel_object type manager could be a descriptor of a window to the portions of the document visible to the calling program. The Intel iAPX 432 system supports windows; they are called "refinements" in that system.

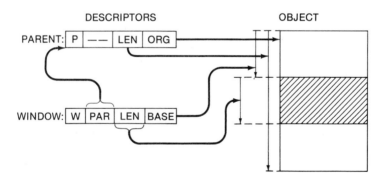

Figure 9-28   A window and its descriptor

In what security context should the multilevel_object type manager be executed? For it to properly establish the window, it must consult the document's index. The information in the complete index should have a high classification, because knowledge of the structure may itself convey information to a user. There are at least two ways to limit access to the index object: one way is to associate a high security classification with the index; the other way is to associate a distinct type with the index, using the DDT to prohibit access from programs not in the multilevel_object type manager's domain.[38]

---

[38]   A third technique using fragmentary indices is described in Problem 9-24.

If we choose the option that associates a high security level with the index, the level of the index should dominate the level of the entire composite document. One problem with placing the index at a high security level is that an executing program cannot access the index unless it has a security level that dominates the level of the index. There are two approaches to this problem—we could build a mechanism to allow a program's level of execution to depend on the level of the object that it is manipulating or we could make a structured or fragmentary version of the index, with more document portions being visible at higher security levels. Many dangers may lurk (in the form of covert channels) in the former approach.

Multilevel Databases. Two new problems arise with multilevel databases—the need to use some fields to select the result of a query, and the need to write information to the composite object that is the database. Additional difficulties arise if the security level of an object or field can depend upon the value contained within the field. We emphasize the problems arising from writing to a field whose contents affect the security level assigned to (1) the field or (2) the record containing the field in question.

Example 9-19

Consider an employee database within a military system. The nature of the individual's assignment might raise the level of trust required to see the information. For example, Liz Jones might be reassigned from "courier" to "secret agent," in which case the fact that she is now a secret agent should be hidden from individuals who do not possess a sufficiently high clearance. In addition, the fact that Liz is no longer a courier should not be visible to people without high clearances. Specifically, assume that courier information is classified secret and secret agent information is classified top secret.

What do these constraints imply about the system's access rules and the views seen by the system's users? First, the subject that rewrites the assignment field must possess top secret clearance. This is easily assured and checked. Second, secret subjects who attempt to view the assignment field in Liz's record should not see the new value. This can be assured if access checking operates at field granularity, but it is not simple, because the field's security level is not a property of the field itself (in other words, the security level of the assignment field is not the same for all instances of the assignment field object). Assume that this problem has been solved. Now the third problem arises—what should happen when a secret subject acting on behalf of Martha (who is cleared to the secret level) queries the database about Liz? Two possibilities appear: (1) Information about Liz's assignment is not presented to Martha, and (2) to Martha, it still appears that Liz is a courier.

The generalizations of the two options illustrated in the example are (1) information that has been upgraded by rewriting disappears from view, and (2) information that has been upgraded by rewriting appears to remain unchanged when viewed from lower levels. A system using the first option contains a covert channel: A high-level Trojan Horse subject can encode and downgrade information by selecting a record and then upgrading the contents of its field F whose security properties depend upon F's contents. Suppose that the Trojan Horse writes records in a set S. Clearly, the choice of the record within S that contains an upgraded F field constitutes information that is visible at lower security levels. In particular, a receiving subject can examine the records within S and look at the contents of field F to find which one has disappeared.

Due to the covert channel within the first option, it is necessary for a secure multilevel database to somehow guarantee that writes that upgrade information do not cause side effects visible at lower levels. This implies that several versions of the field contents must be preserved within the database. One implementation possibility is that the database contains a copy of the complete record that is compatible with being viewed from every possible subject level. This results in keeping a separate copy of the record corresponding to each combination of security attributes of the fields within the record. Each copy is assigned a security level that dominates the levels of all fields within that particular instantiation of the record. This scheme stores correct information, but it uses a lot of space. Another design possibility keeps separate copies of each field for each level at which the field appears to hold different values. To perform some operations, these fields may have to be handled as components of a single record, despite the dispersed structure holding their contents.

Any implementation requires keeping multiple instances of rewritten fields within the database. So we have to handle several objects that have the same name; this is not the same as replicating objects for easy access or failure resiliency, because in those cases, all copies contain identical information. Having multiple copies containing different information to be viewed by different subjects is called *polyinstantiation* [DENN88].

A difficult question is: How should the contents of a polyinstantiated record be presented to a user? There is no consensus on this important question; one possibility is to include a list of all the different instances that are readable (according to the simple security policy) by the executing subject, leaving the subject and/or user the nontrivial task of discovering which combinations of field values are meaningful. An interesting problem is to devise a representation of a polyinstantiated database so that all readable instances can be seen, and at the same time, all access attempts are compatible with the underlying security policy. If the subject is permitted to know its own security level and to know the structure of the level POset, placing the security level of a field within the database keys makes it possible for the query processor to ask for all instances that have readable contents. The reader is referred to recent papers for the latest thinking on this thorny issue.

9.8.3 System Administration

System administrators require special access privileges; they must be able to communicate with all system users to notify them of system status changes, such as imminent shutdown. In the SAT system design, these designated roles can be associated with designated user names, known to the login responder. Access to the programs supporting these roles can be limited by discretionary access controls.

9.8.4 System Security Officer

The system security officer (SSO) is responsible for the security of the entire system. This person must register new users and assign them security properties. She must maintain the integrity of the level POset. In short, she is the critical person in the system, for she has the power to change the security properties of every entity in the system. The system implementation must assure that all SSO actions are indeed requested by a person authorized to serve as the SSO.

9.9 SUMMARY

We explored the requirements for protection, security, and integrity. While integrity is difficult to define and quantify, the other requirements can be met using a combination of hardware checking mechanisms (usually, the memory management unit) and assured software that sets the access permissions used by the checker.

A number of protection schemes were presented, including general access control matrices, capability lists, access control lists, and ring numbering.

The SAT/LOCK design uses a combination of hardware and software to meet those requirements. Capability-based designs may also meet the requirements, but their software will have to be proven to possess many properties. Many design features presented in other contexts are used in the SAT design, including virtual segmented memory, virtual devices, coprocessing, memory management units, and hardware implementation of essential features.

9.10 TRENDS

All MMUs perform access validity checks on all access attempts, though the details differ. Schemes using basic access permission bits in page descriptors will continue to be used. Ring number protection is likely to continue to be used to isolate the operating system from other programs, though general protection mechanisms can do this job better. Segment-based protection is likely to disappear, being supplanted by page-based schemes. This will probably occur even though segment-based protection has great logical appeal, based on the assumption that programmers will group objects together based on the similarity of their usage. Some designers have assumed (incorrectly) that they can save access control bits by removing certain important combinations of protection, such as execute without read, which is necessary to protect against people writing arbitrary objects and then executing those objects as programs. This trend must stop; we now have limited protection, and it is unwise to dilute what protection we already do enjoy.

Many operating systems provide "C2-level" security, which only provides simple discretionary access control. Although this has human appeal, it does not protect data within the system's internal memory and it may be easy to insert Trojan Horse programs into such systems. The need for tight security has been underestimated in the past, and many customers continue using an insecure system until a dramatic event awakens them. For example, the many publicized cases in which unauthorized users access systems has heightened the awareness of both system operators and system users to at least use better passwords, but it will remain true that password schemes are vulnerable unless password encryption schemes, such as Kerberos, are used.

Let us hope that the dramatic events that awaken people to the need for security do not disrupt too many organizations and people before the need for security is taken to heart.

9.11 CONCEPT LIST

1. Protection
2. Access control information
3. Access control matrix (ACM)
4. Key access control
5. Capability lists
6. Access control lists
7. Ring number protection
8. Reference monitor protection
9. Security versus integrity
10. Encryption
11. Military security requirements; certification levels
12. Attacks on systems
13. Trojan Horses
14. Covert channels
15. Tagged objects
16. System security state

17. Policy exceptions, such as downgrading
18. System security officer
19. Multilevel documents
20. Multilevel databases

9.12 PROBLEMS

9-1. Consider a system design using dynamic changes in page keys to effect general sharing and access control. Page keys are assigned to memory pages and system processes, with no limit on the number of keys associated with a single process or with a single page. The granularity of sharing and access control is on the segment basis. The basic mechanism detects when an access attempt fails; when this occurs, the processor is interrupted, and the interrupt handler then attempts to make the desired segment available by changing the key values associated with its pages. Whether the process should be allowed access to the segment is determined by a software-accessed table within the operating system.

    (a) Describe the key-changing policy, and compare it to a scheme in which each page has a process number rather than a key for validity checking.

    (b) Define the data structures required to support this scheme.

    (c) Contrast this scheme with using segment locks for access control.

    (d) Contrast this scheme with using static page keys for access control.

9-2. Page key protection schemes have one important disadvantage: each process sees the same set of key values associated with a given page. A designer proposes to overcome this limitation by allowing a distinct table containing page descriptors to be associated with each process in the system. Comment on the viability of this proposal. What are the perceived advantages and disadvantages?

9-3. Show that using page keys to control access could cause a program to be processor dependent, given a series of processors that are compatible in all respects, except that they have different page sizes. (Recall that paging is used for the convenience of the memory manager's design, and should be transparent to a user program.)

    (a) Show how processor dependency can arise.

    (b) Show how to "fix" the problem by using a "common" page size.

    (c) Are there any adverse consequences of the scheme you proposed in part (b)? Explain.

9-4. In the text, we discussed the design of a ring numbering scheme with a single ring number using zero as the lower limit and the privilege level as the higher limit. Discuss the possibility of using a high fixed upper limit with the lower limit representing the privilege level.

9-5. A designer argues as follows: Ring numbers can be interpreted as hierarchical properties of objects. A resource hierarchy with numbered **region**s is a hierarchical structure. Therefore, there is a form of equivalence between the two notions.

    Discuss this argument, pointing out which of the following properties taken from one hierarchical situation applies to the other one:

    (a) There is no deadlock if the scheme is used; the hierarchy proves this property.

(b) The implementation of one can be used to realize the other.

(c) An arbitrary program formulated using one structuring technique can be converted easily into an equivalent program using the other technique.

9-6. Find all security-level dominance relationships, if any exist, between the following sets of (hierarchical_level, category_set) pairs.

(a) (secret, {a, b}), (top_secret, {a, b}), and (top_secret, {a}).

(b) (unclass, {}) and (secret, {b, c}).

(c) (secret, {c, d}) and (secret, {b, c}).

9-7. Draw the complete security POset diagram for a system using the four military security levels and three categories named A, B, and C.

9-8. Complete Table 9-7 by placing the access rights allowed by the mandatory security policy in each entry within the array. The entry at location (i, j) contains the access rights for process j to object i. The security attributes of the processes and objects are listed in Table 9-8.

TABLE 9-7 MANDATORY ACCESS RIGHTS FOR THE (PROCESS, OBJECT) PAIRS WHOSE ATTRIBUTES ARE LISTED IN TABLE 9-8

		Objects					
Processes		Q1	Q2	Q3	Q4	Q5	Q6
P1							
P2							
P3							
P4							
P5							
P6							

TABLE 9-8 PROCESS AND OBJECT SECURITY ATTRIBUTES

Processes			Objects		
Name	H-level	C-set	Name	H-level	C-set
P1	U		Q1	S	{A, C}
P2	S	{A, B, D}	Q2	TS	{A}
P3	TS	{C}	Q3	U	{B}
P4	S	{B, D}	Q4	S	{B, D}
P5	TS	{A, C}	Q5	TS	{A, B, D}
P6	TS	{A, B, C, D}	Q6	S	{C, D}

9-9. Show that permitting a CALL that decreases the security level of the executing process may violate the mandatory security policy. What type of violation occurs in this situation? Explain your answer.

9-10. A designer makes the following argument: The logical problems associated with revocation of access rights in a secure system are like the logical problems associated with the coordination of proper use of shared resources, as described in Chapter 8, because the shared state varies dynamically under control of user programs.

Comment briefly on this argument. In particular, consider whether the argument has merit and whether the observation, if true, affects the hardware support for the two features under discussion.

9-11. In this problem, we explore the possibility of designing a secure system in which a subject's level is changed dynamically to reflect the security levels of all the information that has been read.

(a) Why does this design trivially satisfy the simple security property?

(b) When an object is read, the system will discover either that (1) the read is permitted according to the simple security property or (2) the read is not allowed. In the latter case, the process must change its level. Describe how the new security level for the process should be determined.

(c) When the process's security level must be changed (see part (b)), what other security-related changes must be made? Explain what they are, why they are necessary, and how the new system state is determined.

(d) How would you show that the your system design does satisfy the *-property? (Do not try to construct a complete proof, but do explain the basis for the reasoning that would be used in a proof.)

9-12. Discuss why the UNIX scheme for limiting file access does not fit with the military security requirements. (The UNIX scheme places each user into a group. The user who owns a file can define the permitted modes of access to that file that shall be permitted to the user, her group, or everyone.)

9-13. In this problem, we devise system rules to support integrity classifications. Assume that there is a POset of integrity levels $\{I_1 .. I_n\}$. Each program and data object has an integrity, in addition to each system user. The goal of this exercise is to devise rules that determine the integrity level of any objects written by a program. We certainly wish that all outputs be labeled with the highest possible integrity level consistent with reasonable rules. To meet this goal, we will need dynamically changing integrities of both process and output objects.

(a) Specify a rule that determines the initial integrity level of a process based on the integrity of the procedure and the user.

(b) Specify how the integrity level of a process changes as the process reads information from objects that have integrity levels.

(c) Specify how the integrity level of an object is adjusted during a write to the object.

(d) Suppose that one wished to "freeze" the integrity level of a particular object. Discuss how you would modify the rules you just developed to handle this need.

9-14. Show that having a capability that is a dangling reference constitutes a security breach.

9-15. Here is a proposed design for a secure system to meet the mandatory and discretionary requirements: Process P may load capability C into its POT if C is readable from P. The access rights in C are copied into the POT when P loads S into its POT. A capability itself may be copied from a readable source segment S to a writeable destination segment D, but the enclosed access rights are modified, as follows: Let AR_S and AR_D denote the access rights in the operand and result capabilities, respectively. Furthermore, let L_D, L_S, and L_C denote the levels of segments D, S, and of the segment described by C, respectively. We always have $AR_D \subseteq AR_S$, because AR_D will be restricted (but never expanded) from AR_S. The AR decrease imposed during the copy operation is made to be consistent with the security policy if a process Q executing at the level of D loaded C_D into its POT and obtained the access rights within C_D. In particular, if $L_D > L_S$, write access is denied in C_D.
   Show that this policy violates the *-property.

9-16. To overcome problems arising from the possibility of transferring access rights improperly while copying capabilities, a designer proposes adding a new access right called *propagate rights*. The basic idea is that a capability without this right set cannot be copied. When the right is present, the capability can be copied to any place to which the executing process has write permission.
   (a) Show that a system using this design as the only limit on capability copying cannot satisfy the mandatory and discretionary access limitations.
   (b) Now add a rule stating that when a capability is copied, the propagate rights bit is automatically cleared. Does this modification improve our ability to construct a secure system obeying the mandatory and discretionary access constraints? Explain.

9-17. The iAPX 432 system supports memory segments with both capability and data parts; it is claimed that the number of different objects that has to be known to the program can be reduced by using this representation technique. To quantify this claim, suppose that p is the percentage of objects that actually contain both access and data information. Find a function (of p) that gives the number of objects saved compared to a design in which an object can either contain data or capabilities, but not both. Assume that the basic separation of information into different logical objects is not to be changed; in other words, two objects that are originally separated (by virtue of being in different segments) remain in different segments in the other design.

9-18. The MMU in Multics uses ring numbers to validate access. Answer the following questions assuming that this ring numbering scheme is used for access checking and that the security model involves a general POset of security levels.
   (a) Show that the system will have to use more than one memory map table for each process.
   (b) Can you use a separate memory map table for each security context in which the process can exist and thereby conform to the security policy requirements?

9-19. This problem explores the possibility of using Ada **packages** to build a secure system.

(a) Complete the reasoning that starts with a system that correctly supports the package concept (thereby guaranteeing isolation of the information private to the package) and then uses a monitor scheme to guarantee that the system's security properties can be enforced.

(b) Can this reasoning be used to argue that using a capability package is adequate to ensure system security?

(c) Can this reasoning be used to prove the enforcement of security by the LOCK design? Try an analogy between TO manipulation by the TOP and an Ada package hiding the type TO.

9-20. Provide a complete argument showing why control of input/output devices must reside within the trusted computer base.

9-21. Here are the basic dominance relations between security levels K, . . . , Q:

$$K < L < M < N < Q$$
$$L < P < R < Q$$

The system's DDT is that shown in Figure 9-18. Ignore the discretionary access controls in this problem. The executing process is operating at level M. Fill in Table 9-9, listing in each entry all possible combinations of (level, type) that could be associated with a segment such that the process executing in the indicated domain has the type of access listed at the head of the column. List a (level, type) combination in the table under access type A if the segment with that combination of attributes has access type A among its access types. For example, if the process executing in domain LAB would have execute access to a segment whose level was M and whose type is LBUF, write (M, LBUF) in the second row, third column of the table. Include all possibilities in your answer.

**TABLE 9-9   (LEVEL, TYPE) COMBINATIONS ON A
SEGMENT THAT PERMIT CERTAIN ACCESS RIGHTS**

Domain of Execution	Access Right Desired		
	Read	Write	Execute
—			
LAB			
DDRV			

9-22. Suppose that we generalize the SAT design to permit additional TOPs and processors. Devise a scenario to show how the lack of synchronization between two TOPs in such a generalized SAT machine could lead to a system security state in which two different users both believe that she owns the same object.

9-23. Draw a detailed diagram showing the structure of the directory object required to describe the composite object complex (of Example 9-18), where the directory is to be structured so that the root is unclassified, and successively higher levels are further out toward the leaves of the structure. Outline how an implementation of the composite_object class would access this structure to construct the description of the object named section3.

9-24. One proposed approach to the problem of providing a visible directory of a composite object uses a set of object indices. The contents of the visible index entries varies according to the level at which the index is being viewed. Let S_i denote the security level of section i of the document. Now suppose that the security levels of all sections satisfy this dominance relationship with levels L_{HIGH} and L_{LOW}:

$$L_{HIGH} \geq S_i \geq L_{LOW}$$

Then there will be a different index for each level L_j satisfying

$$L_{HIGH} \geq L_j \geq L_{LOW}$$

The index at level L_j will indicate all portions readable from level L_j. Figure 9-29 illustrates this structure for a simple case.

Show that this index structure works well if all accesses are read accesses. In particular, show how the index would be used to scan the readable information in the document. Use the name "index" to denote the index object.

9-25. Consider the representation of a composite document. Two representation options were presented in the text. In the first, the complete document was stored in a single container, and the composite_object package delivered window descriptors to a program requesting access to the object. In the second, the document was represented by using a set of containers for the different levels associated with sections of the document. Suppose that the object offsets are visible to the programs using the composite object. Show that there is a covert channel within the offset information used to support the first representation. Therefore, argue that the first representation is not acceptable if the offsets are visible.

9-26. List the operations that you think should be made available for a class that manages composite objects. For each operation, provide a brief description of the intention of the operation and also of its operands. For example, the read operation would accept a pointer to the object, an offset value, and a byte count as operands, and would return that number of bytes starting at the offset location, where only the bytes visible to the requesting subject are counted.

9-27. Discuss this question: Is there a helpful analogy between attempting to write to a higher security level and trying to write into a multilevel database? Does your analogy suggest any implementation techniques for either problem?

9-28. In Section 9.5.1, we mentioned some limitations on the representation of composite documents that contain mixtures of data and capability objects. The limitations derive from restrictions on the locations of data and capabilities, in particular, whether they can be mixed together in the same data objects. This problem explores another design approach in which the program maintains three parallel data structures, each mirroring the logical structure of the composite object. The first data structure holds copies of all the data objects in the structure, in their proper positions within the overall structure. The second data structure is similar, holding copies of all capability objects in their proper positions. Finally, the third data structure holds a single bit for each object in the structure; if the bit is set, the

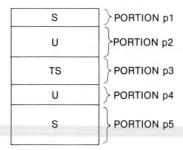

a) The logical file divided into portions

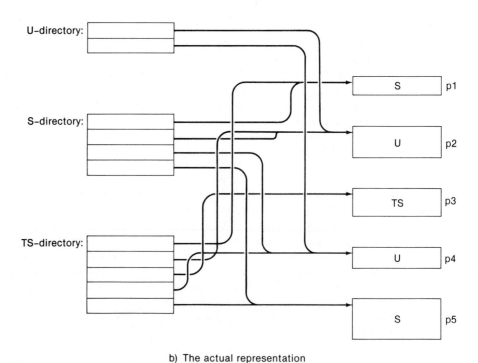

b) The actual representation

Figure 9-29   The level-sensitive directory representation
of a multilevel file

object in the corresponding position is a capability, and otherwise the bit is clear
and the corresponding object is a data object.

(a) Draw a picture illustrating the structure, showing a tree using pointers to link
the structure together. Note that pointers are data objects. Each node within the
tree can hold an object, which can be a data or capability object.

(b) Compare this design with the design in which capabilities in memory are
tagged and can be mixed with data objects in the same segments.

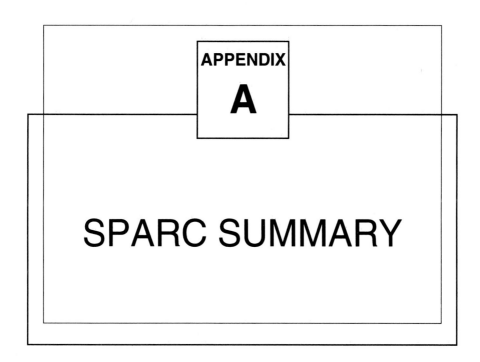

SPARC SUMMARY

Reduced instruction set computers (RISCs) have been proposed because, by providing a carefully selected instruction set and utilizing pipeline structures, the instruction execution process can be made efficient.

Practical implementations of RISC designs use a number of architectural techniques discussed elsewhere in the book; here we present the essential features of the RISC architecture seen from the programmer's viewpoint, using the SPARC design (our specifics are based on the Version 8 architecture in [SPAR92] and the Version 9 architecture in [WEAV94]).[1] The SPARC design has many features similar to those in the Berkeley RISC designs ([PATT82] and [SHER84]), from which it was evolved. The Alpha AXP architecture, discussed in Appendix B, is a different architecture designed in the RISC style.

A.1 SPARC PROCESSOR STATE

A SPARC processor has a basic set of integer operations, implemented within an integer unit integral within the processor, and it may contain an optional floating-point unit and a coprocessor (the coprocessor option is available directly in Version 8, but in Version 9, any access to a coprocessor must be made through

---

[1]   The two designs are called SPARC-V8 and SPARC-V9.

an instruction in the category called "implementation-dependent"). From the programmer's viewpoint, there are 32 integer registers in the processor; each can hold one value comprising 32 bits in Version 8 and 64 bits in Version 9. The integer register numbered zero always contains zero, so only 31 alterable integer registers are available during a computation. Following the conventions used in SPARC documentation, we denote the ith integer register by r[i] or we can use %ri when i is an integer constant.[2]

The remaining programmer-visible registers include two program counters (PC and nPC)[3] and the processor state register (PSR), that includes a 4-bit integer condition code field (*icc*), containing these four condition bits:

1. N (negative)
2. Z (zero)
3. V (overflow)
4. C (carry)

These bits have the familiar obvious interpretations. The values in *icc* reflect the result of the last operation that demanded (as specified by a bit being set in the instruction) that *icc* be written. The extension to 64-bit operands in Version 9 necessitated adding another set of integer condition code bits to reflect the conditions at the left end of 64-bit operands (the *icc* values still relate to 32-bit operands); the new set of condition codes is referenced as the *xcc* integer condition code register). When checking conditions, as in a conditional branch instruction, the Version 9 instructions do contain a field that selects either *icc* or *xcc*; we refer to the choice by using *iccr* in the descriptions that follow.

The SPARC processor organizes its registers into two sets—a set of eight registers (%r0 .. %r7) that is always visible, and the remaining 24 programmer-visible registers, which are implemented within a larger memory internal to the processor. The origin of the locations within the register memory that correspond to registers %r8 .. %r31 is contained in a pointer that can be adjusted by the programmer. The instructions SAVE and RESTORE change this pointer by 64 bytes, thereby changing the register numbering by 16. On SAVE, the pointer is decreased (modulo the size of the register memory), so that the objects that were located in %r8 .. %r15 are accessed through registers %r24 .. %r31 after the SAVE. RESTORE performs the opposite pointer adjustment. In this way, the processor implements a set of register *windows*, whose use can be controlled by the program in execution. There is an internal mask (controlled by the system) that defines which window pointer values are valid.[4]

---

[2]   Thus, r[10] can be represented as %r10, but r[k] has no other representation.
[3]   The reason for two program counter registers is discussed later.
[4]   An attempt to use an invalid window pointer produces an interrupt, after which the system can adjust the contents of the register memory so that the system will appear to have a stack of register windows.

A.2 SPARC MEMORY STRUCTURE

SPARC-V8 memory addresses are 32 bits long, whereas they contain 64 bits in Version 9; the memory addresses designate individual bytes. There are SPARC instructions to handle bytes, halfwords, words, doublewords, and quadwords; the addresses of all items in memory must be naturally aligned (see Section 2.3).

SPARC memory access instructions have only one addressing mode, in which an address is specified by the values in the *imm*, *rs1*, *simm13*, and *rs2* instruction fields (see formats D and E in Table A-2). The effective virtual memory address EVA is computed as follows:

> **If** (*imm* == 0)
>   SPOFF = r[*rs2*];
> **else**
>   SPOFF = sign_ext(*simm13*);
> EVA = r[*rs1*] + SPOFF;

In the first step, the offset is determined; either the sign-extended contents of the *simm13*[5] field or the contents of the register specified in that field are used, with the immediate bit *imm* denoting which option is to be used. In the second step, the offset is added to the "index" value, taken from the register specified in the *rs1* field. Some simple address computations can be specified by choosing r[0], which always contains zero. Every SPARC memory address can be expressed as the result of adding a register's contents to the contents of another register or a (signed) constant.

To express memory addresses in SPARC assembly programs, one writes an expression within square brackets, such as [%r2 + %r6] or [364].

The SPARC instruction format limits the constant part of an address, and hence an absolute address, to 12 bits; a similar restriction applies to literal operands of arithmetic instructions. Therefore, the SPARC designers provided a special method for loading larger constants into registers.[6] The SETHI instruction meets this need; it loads a 22-bit constant (taken from the instruction field *imm22* in format B, which follows) into the uppermost 22 bits of the destination register r[*rd*], clearing the 10 rightmost bits of r[*rd*]. So a 32-bit constant can be loaded in two instructions—a SETHI followed by an ADD. Once a large constant address has been loaded into a register, that constant can be used as the origin of a table of long addresses, so the SETHI instruction does not have to be used frequently. This technique is discussed in Section E.4.2.

SPARC processors have a load/store architecture.

In SPARC, the integer LOAD and STORE class operations support byte (b—8-bit), half (h—16-bit), word (w—32-bit) and doubleword (d or x—64-bit)

---

[5] With its sign extended—which means that $SPOFF_{31} = SPOFF_{30} = SPOFF_{29} = .. = SPOFF_{12} = simm13_{12}$.
[6] A long constant can be loaded by a sequence of shifts and ORs, or by the text's method.

TABLE A-1   SPARC INTEGER LOAD AND STORE INSTRUCTIONS (VERSIONS 8 AND 9)

Mnemonic	Version(s)	Name	Effect[a]
LDSB	8, 9	Load signed byte	$r[rd]_{RW\text{-}8} = M_7$; $r[rd]_{7\text{-}0} = M_{7\text{-}0}$
LDUB	8, 9	Load unsigned byte	$r[rd]_{RW\text{-}8} = 0$; $r[rd]_{7\text{-}0} = M_{7\text{-}0}$
LDSH	8, 9	Load signed halfword	$r[rd]_{RW\text{-}16} = M_{15}$; $r[rd]_{15\text{-}0} = M_{15\text{-}0}$
LDUH	8, 9	Load unsigned halfword	$r[rd]_{RW\text{-}16} = 0$; $r[rd]_{15\text{-}0} = M_{15\text{-}0}$
LDSW	9	Load signed word	$r[rd]_{RW\text{-}32} = M_{31}$; $r[rd]_{31\text{-}0} = M_{31\text{-}0}$
LD (or LDUW)	8, 9	Load (unsigned) word	$r[rd]_{RW\text{-}32} = 0$; $r[rd] = M_{31\text{-}0}$
LDX	9	Load extended word	$r[rd] = M_{63\text{-}0}$
LDD	8, 9	Load doubleword	$r[rd] = M_{63\text{-}32}$; $r[rd+1] = M_{31\text{-}0}{}^b$
STB	8, 9	Store byte	$M_{7\text{-}0} = r[rd]_{7\text{-}0}$
STH	8, 9	Store halfword	$M_{15\text{-}0} = r[rd]_{15\text{-}0}$
ST	8, 9	Store word	$M_{31\text{-}0} = r[rd]_{31\text{-}0}$
STX	9	Store extended	$M_{63\text{-}0} = r[rd]_{63\text{-}0}$
STD	8, 9	Store doubleword	$M_{63\text{-}32} = r[rd]_{31\text{-}0}$; $M_{31\text{-}0} = r[rd+1]_{31\text{-}0}{}^b$

[a] "M" denotes the memory bits accessed during the instruction, starting at the address determined by the EVA computation.
[b] The register number for doubleword operations should be an even integer. These instructions should not be used in new programs for Version 9 machines.

operand widths.[7] On copying word operands, the complete destination is filled with the designated value. On copying to memory operands whose widths are less than the register widths, the rightmost portion of the designated register is copied to the specified memory locations. When copying operands smaller than a register to a register, the bytes from memory are placed at the right end of the destination register, and the programmer must specify whether the leftmost register bits are to be copies of the sign (leftmost) bit from memory or are all to be cleared (in the first case, the operand is considered to be *signed*, whereas the second type is considered to be *unsigned*). The construction of wide items from bytes follows the big-endian convention in Version 8, but in Version 9, a status bit in the process state word chooses the default convention to be used for data accesses, and the user can use the alternate address space options to choose the other option for a particular LOAD or STORE operation.

Table A-1 lists all the user-mode SPARC integer LOAD and STORE instructions. There are additional LOAD and STORE class instructions that

---

[7]   The meaning of a doubleword is changed in Version 9; the 64-bit operand size is called an "extended word" in Version 9 and the doubleword term now applies to 128-bit operands. For compatibility, the Version 8 instruction that loads two 32-bit pieces into consecutive registers has been retained, but its use is not recommended.

interpret the addresses within "alternate" address spaces, whose numbers are included in the *asi* instruction field; these addresses cannot be computed with immediate constants (see format D in Table A-2). The alternate spaces are all privileged in Version 8, but in Version 9, half of them are available to users; the space identifier codes permit the user to choose either endian mode for data accesses to memory.

A.3 SPARC INSTRUCTION FORMATS

Table A-2 defines the SPARC-V8 instruction formats; notice that each instruction bit is used in only a small number of different ways, which simplifies instruction interpretation. The function to be performed in specified by bits 31 and 30, plus the contents of the *op2*, *op3*, *opf*, and *cond* fields. The modifications in Version 9 include the addition of instruction formats to handle additional condition code selectors and other information, producing a total of 23 instruction formats, which we do not detail here. General issues of instruction format design are presented in Chapter 4.

TABLE A-2   SPARC-V8 INSTRUCTION FORMATS

Format[a]	Bit Positions									Functions
	31, 30	29	28–25	24–22	21–19	18–14	13	12–5	4–0	
A	0, 1	disp30								CALL
B	0, 0		rd	op2	imm22					SETHI, Branches
C	0, 0	a	cond	op2	disp22					
D	1, x		rd	op3		rs1	i = 0	asi	rs2	Others
E	1, x		rd	op3		rs1	i = 1	simm13		
F	1, x		rd	op3		rs1	opf		rs2	

[a] These labels are not the same as those used in the SPARC documentation.

A.4 SPARC CONTROL INSTRUCTIONS

All SPARC load, store, and arithmetic instructions advance the PC to the next word, which contains the next instruction. Control instructions provide exceptions to such "normal" sequencing.

All SPARC control instructions implement a *delayed branch*; the instruction immediately following the control instruction is always[8] executed, but the

---

[8]   Unless it is annulled under the control of the annul bit in the instruction; see Chapter 6.

successor of that instruction will be taken from the address determined by the control instruction. This rule is a consequence of the pipelining within the processor. To keep track of progress, even in the presence of interrupts and traps, the processor actually keeps two program counters, called PC and nPC (the latter is an acronym for "next PC"). During sequential execution, nPC = PC + 4, because all instructions occupy 4 bytes. Normally nPC is incremented by 4 when an instruction is initiated, and is copied into PC when the instruction is completed.

Example A-1

> Consider a program executing sequentially that starts at location A0.[9] The consecutive instructions are taken from locations A0, A4, A8, AC, B0, B4, B8, BC, ... If the instruction in location A8 contains a jump to location BC, and the other instructions contain no control transfers, then the consecutive instructions are taken from locations A0, A4, A8, AC, BC, C0, C4, ... The effect of the delayed branching is that the instruction (at location AC) after the branch (at location A8) is executed after the branch instruction and before the branch is taken. This sequencing is counterintuitive, because when the branch is taken, the next instruction does not come from the location specified in its destination. In many algorithms, it is possible to rearrange the program to place a useful instruction immediately after the branch, but if that is not possible, a no-operation (NOP) instruction will have to be placed there. The addition of the annul bit (which was not present in the Berkeley designs) makes it more likely that the delay slot can be filled with a useful instruction.

In the user mode, the SPARC control instruction set contains six types of instructions, comprising three types of jump instructions (one each for testing the integer, floating-point, and coprocessor condition codes), two call instructions, and a software trap instruction (conditional on the *iccr* status), as listed in Table A-3. The codes cc, icc, fcc, and ccc are placeholders for condition codes that are described in what follows. The {, a} option indicates that a comma followed by the letter "a" can be added to the end of the conditional branch instructions to specify annulment of the delay slot instruction when the branch is not taken.

The CALL instruction saves the PC into %r15, so one must exercise care in using that register in environments where the CALL instruction might be used.

In Version 8 the only conditional branch instructions test the condition code values in either the integer or float condition code bits. To execute a conditional branch instruction the processor examines the condition bits from the appropriate condition register (integer, floating-point, or coprocessor, as determined from the *op2* field) and the *cond* field in the instruction to determine whether to branch. The condition codes for integer conditions are listed in Table A-4; similar identical logical expressions are evaluated using the condition bits from the same bit positions of other condition registers during the FBfcc and

---

[9]   In this example, all addresses are expressed in hexadecimal notation.

TABLE A-3   SPARC CONTROL INSTRUCTIONS AVAILABLE IN THE USER MODE

Mnemonic	Version(s)	Format	Name
Bicc{, a}	8, 9[b]	C	Branch on (integer) condition {, annul}
BPcc{, a}	9		Branch on (integer) condition (prediction) {, annul}
BRcc{,a}	9		Branch on (integer) register condition (prediction) {, annul}
FBfcc{,a}	8, 9	C	Branch on (floating-point) condition {, annul}
FBPfcc{,a}	9		Branch on (floating-point) condition (prediction) {, annul}
CBccc{,a}	8	C	Branch on (coprocessor) condition {, annul}
CALL	8, 9	A	Call subroutine (save PC in r[15])
JMPL	8, 9	D,E	Jump and link (save PC in r[rd])
Tcc	8, 9[b]	D,E	Trap on (integer) condition

[a] We use curly brackets {} to enclose optional portions.
[b] These V9 instructions contain a field to choose whether to use the *icc* or *xcc* condition code values. Otherwise, they match the V8 instructions.

CBccc instructions, though the semantic interpretations of the branch conditions will differ from the integer interpretations listed in the table. If a branch is taken, the processor loads nPC with the specified address, which makes it effective for fetching the instruction *after* the one that follows the branch instruction. This timing produces a delayed jump. The Version 9 enhancements of the conditional branch instructions add testing of any of the four float condition codes[10] and of the two integer condition codes, plus tests of register contents (the basic tests are for all zero bits and for sign values. These instructions include prediction, which is discussed in Section 6.6.3.

The destination address specifications in SPARC jump and call instructions have different formats in different instructions. The *disp30* offset in the CALL instruction is a 32-bit offset with the two rightmost bits omitted; these address bits are always zero because instructions are always word-aligned. This (implicitly signed) offset (computed by shifting *disp30* left twice) is added to the PC value.[11] In the 32-bit address space of Version 8, any desired instruction address can be specified in this manner. In the 64-bit address space of Version 9, the choice of instruction locations is limited, though the scope of possibilities is quite wide. The second address specification technique uses a sign-extended displacement value (in the *disp22* field of format C for Version 8, and in various formats having between 16 and 22 bits within the Version 9 design), which is added to the PC; this format is used in branch instructions. Finally, the JUMPL (JUMP and Link) instruction uses formats D and E and computes its destination address in

---

[10]   Four float condition code registers are provided to decrease bottlenecks arising from having to set the condition codes in the same order as the order of the instructions in the program.
[11]   The PC contains the address of the CALL instruction.

TABLE A-4   SPARC INTEGER BRANCH INSTRUCTION CONDITIONS

Condition 1 (C_1)			Complementary Condition (C_1')	
Mnemonic	Name	Logical Condition	Mnemonic	Name
A	Always	1	N	Never
E	Equal	Z	NE	Not equal
LE	Less or equal	Z + (N XOR V)	G	Greater
L	Less	N XOR V	GE	Greater or equal
LEU	Less or equal unsigned	C + Z	GU	Greater
CS	Carry set	C	CC	Carry clear
NEG	Negative	N	POS	Positive
VS	Overflow set	V	VC	Overflow clear

the same manner as the load and store instructions discussed previously; this works the same way in Versions 8 and 9.

In SPARC machines, a subroutine call uses the CALL instruction and a subroutine return uses the JUMPL instruction, relying on an offset added to the contents of the register in which the saved PC value was stored on CALL. For a return to the instruction immediately following the CALL (logically, that is), the offset should be 8, because that displacement skips over both the CALL instruction and the instruction that occupied its delay slot. The register number used in the JUMPL instruction depends upon whether there was a RESTORE operation in the subroutine and, if so, whether it was located before the JUMPL or in its delay slot (see Problem A-6).

A.5   DATA TYPES IN SPARC

SPARC processors support operations on Boolean, integer, and floating-point operands, including format conversions between integer and floating-point representations of numeric values. Integers are represented using two's complement notation. Floating-point operand encodings follow the IEEE standard, in any of four lengths. The representation of data in memory can follow either endian option, depending on the setting of a bit in the processor status register and on the choice of the alternate address space identifier when one is used; the default is the big-endian representation. The processor status register cannot be controlled by user programs, but users can select little-endian operation by using appropriate address space identifiers. Instructions always use the big-endian format.

A.6 OBJECT MANIPULATION IN SPARC

In SPARC processors, like other RISC processors, operand manipulation instructions are RR operations. These instructions use the D and E formats; the three roles in two-operand instructions (the operands and the result) may be assumed by three different registers, or one immediate value can be taken from the instruction itself. The contents of the *rs1* and *rs2* instruction fields designate the register numbers of the source operands, and the *rd* field designates the register number for the result's destination. The second operand value is determined just like an address offset would be determined within a memory address computation (permitting the use of short immediate constants), so we use *SPOFF* to denote the value of the second operand in our descriptions. The effect of each operation is r[*rd*] = r[*r1*] <op> *SPOFF*.

TABLE A-5   SPARC INTEGER MANIPULATION INSTRUCTIONS

Mnemonic[a]	Version[b]	Name
ADD{X}{cc}[c]	8, 9	Add {with C} {rewrite *iccr*}
SUB{X}{cc}[c]	8, 9	Subtract {with C} {rewrite *iccr*}
MULScc	8, 9D	Multiply step (*always* rewrite *iccr*)
S[L∣R]L	8, 9	Shift [left ∣ right] logical value
SRA	8, 9	Shift right arithmetic value
MULX	9	Multiply (64-bit product) (*never* change *ccr*)
[U∣S]DIVX	9	[Un]signed divide (*never* change *ccr*)
[U∣S]MUL{cc}	8, 9D	[Un]signed multiply {rewrite *iccr*}
[U∣S]DIV{cc}	8, 9D	[Un]signed divide {rewrite *iccr*}

[a]We use square brackets [] to enclose a set of options of which one must be selected and vertical bars to separate options in a field.
[b]In Version 9, all condition code rewriting affects both the normal (*iccr*) and extended (*xccr*) condition code bits. A "D" in this column indicates that use of the instruction is discouraged.
[c]In Version 9, the "X" designation is changed to a "C" designation, because ince an "X" generally indicates 64-bit operands in this processor.

Both integer and Boolean operations are provided in SPARC. The basic integer operations include the four arithmetic operations.[12] The add and subtract operations have four variants, based on whether the carry bit C (from *iccr*) is used as an operand[13] and whether the condition codes are modified (see Table A-5). The second operand of these operations is *SPOFF*. Formats D and E are used for all of these instructions.

---

[12]   Instructions for multiply and divide are specified in Version 8, but are not implemented in hardware in many realizations of these machines.
[13]   The carry is used as an operand to implement multiple-precision operations.

Example A-1

Here is a SPARC-V8 program for double-precision integer addition. Each value is located in a pair of consecutive memory words, with the operands in (aligned) memory locations whose addresses are contained in registers r[2] and r[3], and the (aligned) result location specified in register r[4]:

```
LDD      [%r2],%r6      ! load operands
LDD      [%r3],%r8
ADDcc    %r7,%r9,%r11   ! perform the least sig. addition
ADDX     %r6,%r8,%r10   ! note use of the C bit left from the first addition
STD      %r10,[%r4]     ! store the (double) result
```

After this program fragment completes execution, the value in the Z condition code bit will not reflect the nature of the result, but the other condition code bits will be correct, because they can be determined from the most significant bits of the operands and the result.

The SPARC Boolean operations are AND, OR, and Exclusive-OR and the negations of those operations. Finally, there are three shift operations that take the shift count from *SPOFF* and shift the *rs1* operand left, logically right, or arithmetically right, placing the result in *rd;* see Table A-6. Formats D and E are used to specify all of these instructions.

TABLE A-6   SPARC BOOLEAN INSTRUCTIONS

Mnemonic[a]	Name
AND{N}{cc}	AND {negated} {rewrite *iccr*}
OR{N}{cc}	OR {negated} {rewrite *iccr*}
XOR{N}{cc}	Exclusive-OR {negated} {rewrite *iccr*}

[a] Curly brackets {} indicate optional portions.

The SPARC processor also supports floating-point operations, including the four arithmetic operations and square root, on operands of three lengths: 32, 64, and 128 bits. These instructions are represented in format F. They do not affect the float condition code bits. The float condition code values, of which there is a single set in Version 8 and four sets in Version 9, are set by execution of the float compare operations.

Conditional move instructions were added in Version 9; these conditionally copy the contents of one register to another based on tests of processor state. For example, the contents of register %r5 can be copied to %r7 only if the extended condition codes indicate a nonzero condition. Conditions in the condition code registers and in the integer registers (using the sign and all-zero conditions) can be tested. The conditional moves can be made between float registers (in any of the three possible lengths) or from *SPOFF* to an integer register. This rich set of possibilities is provided to reduce the need for conditional branches.

In Version 8, coprocessor operations use format F, and the programmer can control whether the coprocessor condition code register is rewritten with new status information. Version 9 does not have specific coprocessor instructions, but two instructions are reserved for "implementation-dependent" instructions, which can be implemented to utilize an external coprocessor device.

A.7 SUMMARY

We have not covered all SPARC processor instructions in this section; other important instructions are discussed where their uses relate to the topic at hand. For example, some SPARC synchronization instructions supporting multiple processing based on a shared-memory model are covered in Chapter 8.

Register windows are an interesting concept, but the invisibility of old windows makes it difficult to chain pointers through registers to implement static name resolution logic (see Sections 3.6 and D.1). Also, the complexity of the process of invoking management software that handles window overflow and underflow (and of that software itself) makes a programmer want to handle register saving in the traditional manner.

The SPARC specifications specifically mention the possibility that a processor implementation might utilize system software to emulate the behavior of certain instructions, such as multiply and divide in Version 8 and float operations in all versions. The use of interrupts to initiate this activity and then calling system-level software procedures is a common technique for providing compatibility without implementing all features in hardware. If the instructions whose implementation is really in software are used only infrequently, a system with soft implementations will execute programs almost as quickly as the system with a hardware implementation of the instructions.

The SPARC architecture exhibits some useful orthogonality, which contributes to a speedy implementation, because, for example, the SPOFF value can be computed before the instruction has been decoded (if decoding shows that SPOFF is not needed, it is discarded). Many architectures have far less orthogonality in their processor instruction sets than SPARC.

A.8 TRENDS

The changes made in moving to Version 9 reflect some trends in computer architecture. First, notice the change to wider operands. Second, notice the use of vacant space in the instruction encoding space to add new instructions. Third, notice the provision of four condition code registers to hold float comparison results, reducing certain bottlenecks.

A.9 CONCEPT LIST

1. Register windows
2. SAVE and RESTORE operations
3. RISC pipelined instruction execution
4. Delayed branch instructions producing delay slots
5. Annul control over the execution of delay slot instructions
6. Simple addressing modes
7. Condition code saving controlled by instruction fields
8. Multiple float condition registers
9. Move on condition instructions

A.10 PROBLEMS

A-1. Write a SPARC instruction sequence that performs each of the following integer additions:
 (a) %r6 = %r6 + Memory[#0x38] (32-bit objects).
 (b) %r12 = %r3 + %r5 (8-bit objects).
 (c) Memory[#0x2C0E] = Memory[#0x347] + Memory[#0x214] (16-bit objects).

A-2. Write a SPARC program that uses an iterative loop to sum the integers from 1 to n, where n is the integer in register 3.

A-3. The SPARC assembler contains two important built-in functions %hi(<address>) and %lo(<address>), whose values are the leftmost 22 and the rightmost 10 bits of the indicated address. Explain why these functions are needed, why the linker has to be involved in their evaluation, and how they should be handled by the linker.

A-4. Contrast the big-endian memory ordering against the small-endian ordering by comparing the order of memory accesses required to perform (i) sign testing and (ii) subtraction. You should support extended-precision operands (those longer than the longest operand width handled by processor instructions). Assume that two's complement representations are used in both cases.

A-5. Write a SPARC instruction sequence that loads a 32-bit constant 0xC32 into register %r4. Do the job without using SETHI.

A-6. Compute the correct register number to use in the SPARC subroutine return instruction for each of the following cases:
 (a) There are no SAVE and RESTORE instructions in the subroutine.
 (b) There is a SAVE/RESTORE pair in the subroutine, with RESTORE just before the return instruction.
 (c) There is a SAVE/RESTORE pair in the subroutine, with RESTORE just after the return instruction.

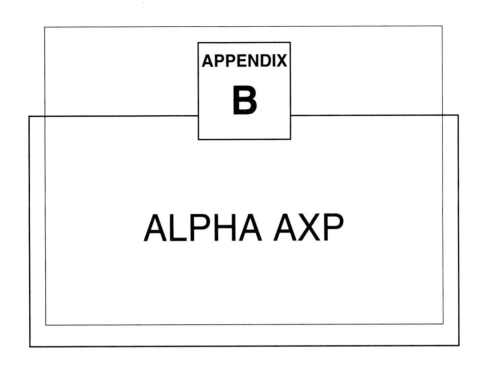

APPENDIX

B

ALPHA AXP

The Alpha AXP processor [SITE92] was designed at Digital Equipment Corporation as a successor to the VAX computer line. During the design process, careful attention was paid to choosing the instruction set to permit maximum parallelism in present and future implementations, anticipating the possibility of having up to eight instructions in execution at the same time. At the same time, they wished to provide compatibility with many aspects of the VAX processor architecture and the operating systems written for that architecture. In this section we view the instruction set of this processor.

B.1 ALPHA AXP PROCESSOR STATE

The Alpha AXP processor has 32 integer registers of 64 bits each and 32 floating-point registers of 64 bits each. Some operations utilize register pairs to accommodate 128-bit operands and results. Register 31 in both register sets always contains zero.[1] The registers are named R0 .. R31 and F0 .. F31.

There is no condition code register; conditional branch instructions can only test (1) the contents of an integer or floating-point register for sign or equality to zero, or (2) the least significant bit of an integer register.

---

[1]   The last register is used, rather than the first one, for compatibility with the VAX.

A single program counter tracks instruction execution; each instruction occupies 4 bytes and must be aligned, so the program counter does not need to track the two least significant address bits, which are always zero.

B.2 ALPHA AXP MEMORY STRUCTURE

Memory addresses are byte addresses. Because naturally aligned accesses are so efficient, they should be used whenever possible. Each virtual memory address contains 64 bits, though the physical memory addresses may be restricted to 48 bits. Each data address is generated by adding the contents of an integer register to the (sign-extended) 16-bit displacement from the instruction. The construction of wide items from bytes follows the little-endian convention.[2]

Each instruction comprises exactly 32 bits that are naturally aligned. The program counter (PC) therefore contains only 62 bits, because the last two address bits of each instruction always contain zero.

Alpha AXP processors have a load/store architecture; LOAD and STORE class instructions support only 32-bit and 64-bit operand accesses, so accesses to items with other widths must be emulated in software.

The Alpha AXP processor is designed so that it behaves as though it references memory in program order, despite the possibility of simultaneous instruction execution. In a system with multiple processors and shared memory, this logical ordering will be preserved, but there is no guarantee about the relative ordering of memory accesses among programs executing on different processors, unless special synchronization instructions are executed by the programs.[3]

B.3 ALPHA AXP INSTRUCTION FORMATS

Table B-1 defines the Alpha AXP instruction formats. As in SPARC, each instruction bit has only a few different uses across the set of all instruction formats. We discuss the uses of the fields as we discuss the instructions themselves. The function to be performed is specified in the *Opcode*, *Fcn*, and *Function* instruction fields.

B.4 ALPHA AXP CONTROL INSTRUCTIONS

The goals of simplicity and the ability to issue many instructions simultaneously had a strong influence on the selection of the control instruction set of the Alpha

---

[2] This is a VAX compatibility feature.
[3] These instructions are discussed in Section 8.9.

TABLE B-1   ALPHA AXP INSTRUCTION FORMATS

Format[a]	Bit Positions							Functions
	31– 26	25–21	20–16	15–13	12	11–5	4–0	
A	Opcode	Ra	Rb	Memory_disp				Memory reference
B	Opcode	Ra	Rb	Function				
C	Opcode	Ra	Branch_disp					Branch
D	Opcode	Ra	Rb	0	i = 0	Fcn	Rc	Operate
E	Opcode	Ra	LIT		i = 1	Fcn	Rc	
F	Opcode	Fa	Fb	Function			Fc	FP operate
G	Opcode	PAL_code_function						PAL call

[a] These labels are not the same as those used in the Alpha AXP documentation.

AXP processors. There is no condition code register, because it would have been a bottleneck restricting instruction issue. Therefore, the conditional branch instructions make condition decisions based on simple tests of register contents. There is a flexible set of instructions to support subroutine structures.

Conditional branch instructions have format C, with register Ra (Fa, if it is a floating-point condition) being tested against the condition specified in the Opcode. A branch instruction target is determined by adding the sign-extended (and shifted left two places) 21-bit Branch_disp field from the instruction to the updated PC (which points to the instruction succeeding the branch instruction):

$$\text{BAddress} = \text{sign\_ext}(4*\text{Branch\_disp}) + \text{updatedPC} \qquad \text{(B-1)}$$

The conditional branch instructions use three basic tests (and their negations) applied to the examined register:

1. Is it zero?
2. Is it positive?
3. Is its low-order bit zero?

The first two can be combined, along with their complements, producing six arithmetic conditional branch conditions. The two conditions testing the rightmost bit of the register can be applied to integer registers, so there are eight possibilities for integer branch conditions. The six arithmetic conditions are available to test the value of a floating-point register. There are two unconditional branch instructions that store the address of its successor in register Ra; they differ in their branch predictions[4]—one is used for subroutine calling.

The four (unconditional) jump instructions use format A; each takes its target address from register Rb (with the two least significant bits forced to zero)

---

[4]   See Section 6.6.3 for a discussion of branch prediction designs and the accompanying strategies.

and stores the address of the instruction following the branch in register Ra. As with the unconditional branch instructions, the four jump instructions differ in their branch prediction activities. These instructions are used for ordinary jumps, subroutine call, subroutine return and (restricted) coroutine activity (see Chapter 8). The Memory_disp field is not used in computing the destination of the jump, but it is used to compute a branch prediction so that speculative instruction fetching can proceed beyond the jump.

There are five integer and three (for each format) floating-point arithmetic instructions that compare the contents of registers Ra and Rb (or Fa and Fb) and place either a nonzero true_value (1 if integer, 0.5 if VAX floating, and 2.0 if IEEE floating) or a zero in register Rc (or Fc) depending upon the outcome of the comparison. These actions can be outlined as

```
if (op1 <relation> op2)      //the operands are contents of Ra and Rb or Fa and Fb
        dest = true_value;    //the destination is Rc or Fc
else
        dest = 0;
```

A special control instruction invokes soft implementations of extensions to the hardwired instruction set. This instruction is called CALL_PAL (PAL denotes the Privileged Architecture Library); it is discussed further in Section 5.3. During the execution of a PAL routine, the processor's interrupts are turned off and the (PAL) program has access to implementation-dependent[5] instructions that, for example, give access to hardware registers that are not visible to the non-PAL Alpha AXP programmer. This approach to extending the instruction set has a historical precedent described in Section 5.3.

B.5 DATA TYPES IN ALPHA AXP

The Alpha AXP processor supports operations on 64-bit integers, bytes (taken from registers), and floating-point numbers, the latter in four different formats.[6] Due to the many formats, there are a large number of floating-point operations; we will not discuss them here.

B.6 OBJECT MANIPULATION IN ALPHA AXP

As in SPARC, all object manipulation operations are RR operations with two or three register number operand specifications; one or two register numbers (or a register and an immediate value) define the operand sources (designated by Ra

---

[5] This means that these instructions can be different in different implementations of this architecture.

[6] These formats are VAX- and IEEE-compatible single (32-bit) and double (64-bit) precision variants.

and Rb for integer operands and by Fa and Fb for floating-point operands), and the final register number specifies which register (Fc) receives the result. Because registers 31 contain zero, simpler variants can be included easily.

Integer operations are specified using formats D and E; their operands are either 32-bit (longword[7]) or 64-bit (quadword) quantities. The operands for integer operations are R[Ra] and *ALOFF*, computed by

> **If** (i == 0)
>   ALOFF = R[Rb];
> **else**
>   ALOFF = zero_ext(LIT);

The literal field *LIT* contains a single byte interpreted as a positive integer (and therefore zero extended to form a complete operand).[8]

Logical operations (AND, OR, and XOR) and their complements can be applied to two integer registers with the result destined for a third integer register. Logical and arithmetic shifts of integer values are provided, with the shift counts taken from the low-order 6 bits of *ALOFF*.

Traditional integer arithmetic operations, *except DIV for integers*, are provided. The data type is specified by the function code. A version of subtraction is used in the compare instructions (see the preceding) to choose a value to be placed in a destination register. The processor detects integer and floating-point overflow and floating-point underflow conditions and causes an exception when either occurs. Because there is no condition code register, other result status information must be developed by instruction sequences that examine register contents. Compare instructions are provided to support this requirement; they leave either zero or a nonzero value in a register based on the outcome of a subtraction to find whether the values are equal, less than, or less than or equal.

Integer arithmetic operations that support index computations are provided; these scaled addition and subtraction operations shift the second operand two or three places left before performing the operation. Such operations can be used to convert item indices (within vectors) into byte offsets.

Conditional move instructions (one for integers and two[9] for floating-point values) are provided to permit certain operation sequences to be implemented without a conditional branch, which would slow instruction issue; the six zero/sign tests available in the conditional branch instructions can be applied to test the integer in *Ra* to choose whether to copy *ALOFF* to *Rc* or to test the floating-point value in *Fa* to choose whether to copy *Fb* to *Fc*. Additionally, one can test the least significant digit in an integer register within a condition integer

---

[7]   This wording derives from VAX terminology, which, in turn, comes from PDP-11 terminology, in which a word is a 16-bit quantity.
[8]   Compare this with the similar SPARC design.
[9]   Two different floating-point formats are supported.

move instruction. Conditional move instructions can be used to determine the largest or smallest of two values in two sequential instructions (see Problem B-3).

Byte instructions operate on bytes within integer registers. Using these instructions, a program can extract 1, 2, 4, or 8 bytes from one operand, can compare bytes against specified values to set a byte mask, or can use the byte mask to select bytes to be cleared to zero in a register.

B.7 OTHER OPERATIONS IN ALPHA AXP

Among the miscellaneous operations in Alpha AXP, one is important in coordinating arithmetic traps with instruction sequencing. Ordinarily, arithmetic operations might be executed in parallel, so that if one of a set of instructions executed in parallel causes a trap, it can be ambiguous as to which of the instructions actually caused the trap. The trap barrier instruction (TRAPB) will stall instruction issue until the processor can determine that none of the preceding arithmetic instructions can possibly incur an arithmetic trap. This feature can be used to guarantee consistency between the current status of trap handlers that are being changed and the program's progress, or to guarantee that the arithmetic traps will be unambiguous.[10]

Integer division and other complex operations have to be provided by software routines; these and other complex operations can be included through the CALL_PAL mechanism, which effectively calls the system's support library. A few basic PAL functions are required of all implementations of Alpha AXP; these assure that basic operating system and programming support will be available. These basic PAL operations are listed in Table B-2. Other PAL functions are provided to support particular operating system environments, such as VMS and OSF;[11] their details depend upon the environment being supported; some are described in later chapters. The CALL_PAL operation supports the implementation of functions that require access to the details of the processor's implementation. We discuss the PAL code strategy further in Chapter 6.

B.8 SUMMARY

The Alpha AXP design reflects decisions influenced by the desire for large degrees of parallelism in instruction execution. The parallelism goal suggested eliminating a condition code register, fixing the instruction width, including branch prediction information in instructions, and limiting memory access

---

[10]   But using TRAPB in this manner will incur a significant performance penalty. See Problem B-2 for details of how to use TRAPB to make all traps unambiguous.
[11]   Four additional PAL calls must be supported in any operating system environment; they support debugging and the generation and management of unique values.

TABLE B-2   REQUIRED PAL FUNCTIONS IN ALPHA AXP SYSTEMS

Mnemonic	Privilege	Explanation
HALT	Privileged	Stop processing after all memory accesses are coherent
IMB	Unprivileged	Fetch more instructions only after being certain that the effects of all previous memory writes will be reflected in what is read
DRAINA	Privileged	(Drain aborts) Stop instruction issue until certain that all possible aborts from previous instructions are certain to be able to complete without aborts

instructions to a small set of operand widths. Alpha's conditional move instructions are more limiting than those in the SPARC; the added flexibility of testing registers of one type to move the other type might be introduced in the future.

The processor manual is more useful than many because it includes comments about the intended usage of certain processor features, and because it includes comments telling programmers and the writers of compiler code generators and optimizers how to use the processor's features to best advantage in gaining execution speed.

B.9 TRENDS

The Alpha architecture includes many techniques that speed execution and that might make possible implementations that issue many instructions in the same processor cycle. These features should continue to be attractive to architects, though the elimination of condition code register(s) does force the program to use longer instruction sequences to implement certain tests. Soon the register count will become the limiting factor, and architects will be forced to use register renaming to make the processor perform as though it has more registers than the programmer can designate in instructions. One might think that the elimination of an integer divide instruction, although a popular move at certain times, might haunt the design, because a subroutine implementation of the operation using the shift and conditional subtract is not amenable to much speedup. The Alpha manual suggests (wisely) that table lookups can obtain approximations to the reciprocal of the divisor and that as few as four iterations based on a table of approximately 1000 entries can produce an accurate result. These techniques that trade space for time do produce efficient implementations of infrequently executed instructions. Similar techniques can be used to approximate other useful operations such as square root (see Chapter 5).

B.10 CONCEPT LIST

1. Limit memory operand widths
2. Eliminate condition code register(s)
3. Use implementation-dependent programs to extend operation set
4. Branch prediction information in instructions
5. Branch prediction stack for subroutine linkage
6. Limited coroutine support
7. Memory barrier instructions
8. Advice to compiler writers and programmers regarding execution speedups

B.11 PROBLEMS

B-1.   Write an Alpha AXP loop to compute the sum of the integers from 1 to n, where n is located in register R3. (Do not evaluate the sum using the arithmetic series formulas.)

B-2.   The Alpha TRAPB instruction coordinates trap handler invocation with progress in the instruction stream.

(a) Describe a strategy for inserting TRAPB instructions into an Alpha AXP program to assure that the trap handler is always certain which instruction caused an arithmetic trap.

(b) Describe how you could insert selectively TRAPB instructions into a program to debug it and determine the location of a trapping instruction by examining separate executions of the program processing the same input data, but with TRAPB instructions in different places.

B-3.   Write a short instruction sequence for the Alpha AXP processor that places the largest of the integers in R3 and R7 into R7.

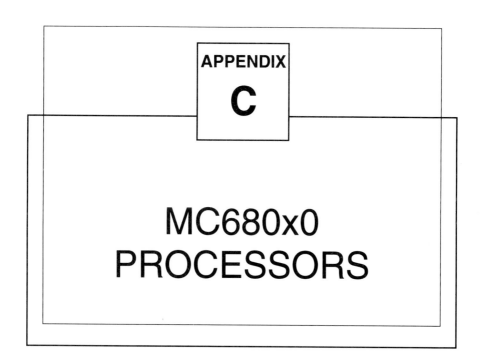

APPENDIX

C

MC680x0
PROCESSORS

The Motorola MC680x0 processor series represents a typical CISC design; it contains several sophisticated features that support the implementation of high-level languages. The MC68020 processor ([MOTO84]) supports complex intermodule control structures; unfortunately (from an architectural interest point of view), successor designs eliminated some of these interesting features. We use this processor as the major example and point out the few variations in the other models in the series, whose members can be described by the values of x that range from 0 through 4.

This appendix should give you an appreciation for the instruction set and certain instruction representations used in the MC680x0 series. You will observe the complexity of instruction representations and the consequent impact on the design's orthogonality.

C.1 MC680x0 PROCESSOR STATE

A MC680x0 processor handles 32-bit operands and addresses, and its data and address registers contain 32 bits. Despite processor registers containing 32 bits, historical evolution dictates that MC680x0 documentation use the term "word" to denote a 16-bit quantity. The term "long word" is used to denote a 32-bit quantity. For consistency with the available documentation, we use the foregoing terminology.

The processor contains eight data registers, called D0 .. D7, and eight address registers, called A0 .. A7. Register A7 has a special role as a stack pointer, so it should not be used wantonly. In addition, the user-mode[1] programmer sees a 32-bit program counter (PC) and a 16-bit condition code register (CCR), of which the leftmost 11 bits are always zero in user mode.

There are five CCR bits: the C, N, V, and Z bits are interpreted as in SPARC processors (see Appendix A). The X bit supports extended-precision operations. The X bit is not modified during the execution of most instructions; in fact, it is modified only during addition, subtraction, negation, certain rotate, and certain shift instructions. The state of the X bit cannot be determined directly through conditional branching, but it serves as an additional operand in specific addition, subtraction, negation, and rotate instructions that can be used to implement extended-precision arithmetic operations.

Whether CCR is affected by the execution of a particular instruction in the MC680x0 is determined by the function code of the instruction; the processor design does not give the programmer an option to selectively override the built-in rules concerning CCR modification.

C.2 MC680x0 MEMORY STRUCTURE

The MC680x0's memory is viewed as a set of bytes. Memory addresses select individual bytes. Conceptually, the memory access instructions may access a byte, a word, or a long word in a single memory cycle, and any of these items may begin at any (byte) address. The construction of wide items from memory bytes follows the big-endian convention.

All MC680x0 instructions are composed of one or more words. Each instruction word must be naturally aligned; thus, its memory address is an even number. The function code and/or addressing information in the first word of an instruction determines whether a single word is adequate to specify the instruction. Sequential decisions may be used to determine the actual instruction length based on the values of fields from the following (*"extension"*) words. For most instructions that require a memory operand, the rightmost 6 bits of the first instruction word specify the addressing mode (the way that the address is to be determined) and the register to be used, if any. For certain combinations of function code, addressing modes, and register numbers, the addressing algorithm uses the contents of succeeding extension word(s).

The implementation of an MC680x0 processor includes a scanPC register that always points to the first program word that has not been interpreted (as an instruction or as an extension word). A general statement of this behavior is as follows:

---

[1]   We describe supervisor mode in Section 4.3.

PC Scan Property. The scanPC register always points to the next program word to be interpreted.

Every MC680x0 processor actually maintains two program counters: the scanPC that obeys the PC Scan Property, and one simply called PC that holds the address of the first byte of the instruction being executed; it is used for instruction retry. Upon instruction completion, scanPC is copied into PC.

In MC680x0 processors instruction lengths vary from 1 to 11 words. The actual length of an instruction is determined by its function code and by the addressing information (both modes and field lengths). The MC680x0 processor advances its scanPC as a side effect of the effective address computations; this is easily accomplished while the required extension words are interpreted.

The MC680x0 addressing modes can be divided into two classes: general addressing modes and branch addressing modes. The *general addressing modes* are used to access operand values and to determine destinations of jump class instructions. We use the term *general operand* to denote an operand whose location or value is determined by a general addressing mode specification. The specification of a general operand is made in 6 bits, of which three define the addressing *mode* and the other three designate a register (in most modes). Mode 6 supports further refinement of the addressing mode; additional information is taken from control fields in extension words. In mode 7, the register numbers serve as extensions of the mode specification. The location of a general operand and the addressing mode used to specify it define limits on the actions that can be performed on the operand.[2]

A *branch addressing mode* can be used only to determine the destination for a branch class instruction.

Now we present a few operand addressing techniques from the MC680x0.

Direct Register Addressing. Addressing modes 0 and 1 specify that the operand is the contents of a processor register. The mode number determines the class of register; mode 0 selects a D register, and mode 1 selects an A register.

Absolute Addressing. Absolute addressing with a 16-bit address is specified in assembly language by "<address>.W" (here ".W" indicates that the address is 1 word long[3]). In the encoded MC680x0 instruction, this general addressing mode is specified by mode 7 and register 0, and uses one extension word for the address; the contents of that word are sign-extended to complete the 32-bit address. This addressing mode is similar to that achieved in SPARC with a short address in *simm13*, using the specification [<address>].

---

[2]   For example, an operand that is an immediate value cannot be the destination of a write action.

[3]   This specification technique is described in [MOTO84] and is clearly not necessary, because a smart assembler/linker combination could determine the minimum length required to represent the address; see Problem C-6.

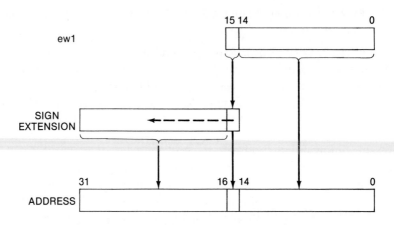

Figure C-1   Address determination for short absolute addressing

For this mode, the address generation process uses the following steps:

```
ew1 = read_2_bytes( scanPC );          //read the extension word
EVA = sign_ext( ew1 );
scanPC = scanPC + 2;                   //move beyond the extension word
```

Here ew1 denotes the first extension word's contents and the function read_2_bytes reads memory at the designated address. This addressing mode can be decsribed by the flows shown in Figure C-1.

Finally, the same address computation can be described by an equation:

$$EVA = sign\_ext(ew1) \tag{C-1}$$

Long Absolute Addressing. Long absolute addressing with a 32-bit address is specified in a processor instruction by mode 7 and register 1, and uses a long word extension for the address. The computation of the operand address is

```
elong1 = read_4_bytes( scanPC );    //read the extension long word
EVA = elong1;
scanPC = scanPC + 4;                //move beyond the extension words
```

This general addressing mode is similar to the previous mode, but with a wider address. Here we have the equation

$$EVA = elong1 \tag{C-2}$$

where elong denotes a long extension word.

TABLE C-1   MC680X0 OPERAND ADDRESSING OPTIONS

Specification in Program	Models	Address Computation
Dn	All	{Data Register n}[a]
An	All	{Address Register n}[a]
(An)	All	EVA = An
xxx.W	All	EVA = sign_ext(xxx)
xxx.L	All	EVA = xxx
(An)+	All	EVA = An; An = An + SIZE
−(An)	All	An = An − SIZE; EVA = An
(d16,{An|PC})[b]	All	EVA = {An|PC} + d16
(d,{An|PC},Xn.SIZE*SCALE)[b]	All	EVA = {An|PC} + d + Xn*SCALE
([bd,{An|PC}],Xn.SIZE*SCALE,od)	2, 3, 4	EVA = Memory[bd + {An|PC}] + Xn*SCALE + od[b]
([bd,{An|PC},Xn.SIZE*SCALE],od)	2, 3, 4	EVA = Memory[bd + {An|PC} + Xn*SCALE] + od[b]

[a] These curly braces indicate that the register's contents are the operand.
[b] Here the curly braces enclose options showing that the address can be based on the PC or an A register. Any address computed using PC will be made to program space; all others use data space.

Simple Indexed Addressing. Indexed addressing with a displacement (the displacement serves the same role as the "offset" in SPARC) is specified in assembly language by "(<disp>,A<n>)", where disp and n are the parameters of the address computation. This general addressing mode is specified in a processor instruction by mode 5 and a register number (n). The single extension word contains the displacement, which is sign-extended and added to the contents of A(n) to find the address. The address computation is

```
EW = read_2_bytes( scanPC );      //read the extension word (the displacement)
scanPC = scanPC + 2;
A = A( n ) + sign_ext( EW );      //add the index
```

Figure C-2 depicts this computation.

Other Operand Addressing Modes. Table C-1 specifies all the MC680x0 operand addressing modes, showing their assembly-language notation and also specifying the computation of the effective address using SPARC notation ([] for a memory read), with size denoting the operand size. The set of modes on the last two lines of the table, which use an "outer displacement" (od), was introduced in the MC68020. Otherwise, all modes are supported in all processors in the family.

610

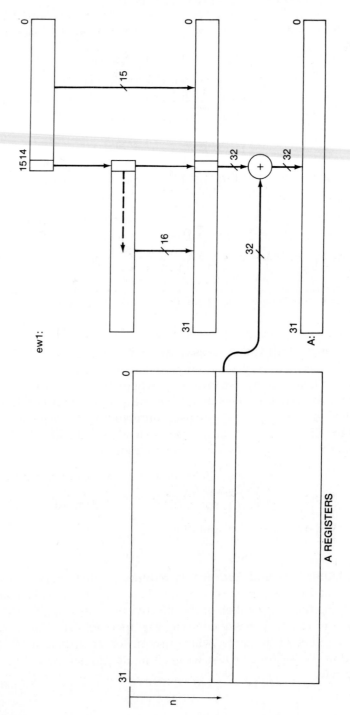

Figure C-2 Simple indexed addressing

Branch Addressing. The MC680x0 processors use PC-relative address-ing[4] in branch class instructions. In a branch instruction that needs only a small PC-relative displacement, the first instruction word contains a signed 8-bit dis-placement, which is added to scanPC to determine the destination of the branch.[5] A 16-bit signed displacement can be specified—when the 8-bit displacement is zero, the contents of the next extension word is taken for the 16-bit displacement. Similarly, a 32-bit signed displacement can be placed in two extension words fol-lowing the branch instruction; this case is indicated by the 8-bit displacement in the first instruction word being 0xFF:

```
D = disp;
if ( D == 0 ) {                          //16-bit displacement follows
        D = read_2_bytes( scanPC );
        scanPC = scanPC + 2;
}
else
        if ( D == 0xFF ) {               //32-bit displacement follows
        D = read_4_bytes( scanPC );
        scanPC = scanPC + 4;
}
EVA = scanPC + D;
```

The need to detect special values in the displacement field of the instruction to determine whether to read extension words to find the displacement shows that sequential decisions[6] have to be made to implement this processor.

C.3 MC680x0 INSTRUCTION FORMATS

The MC680x0 has at least 42 instruction formats; more than would fit in a page-sized table, so we note this complexity and pass over the details. We do, how-ever, wish to show the complexity of the implementation: Just look at a single bit: bit 11 within the first instruction word is used in 9 fields having different names, depending on the function code.

---

[4]   This form of PC-relative addressing, used for branch instructions, is similar to certain PC-relative general addressing modes for operands, but the details are different.
[5]   Note that scanPC is used in this address computation; it contains the address of the instruction fol-lowing the branch instruction, which, therefore, becomes the origin for the address arithmetic.
[6]   The sequence of decisions could be implemented by a combinational logic circuit examining a wider span from the instruction stream (see Problem C-2).

C.4 MC680x0 CONTROL INSTRUCTIONS

The MC680x0 has a large variety of control instructions. Some of them support special features that we discuss elsewhere; here we concentrate on three simple types available in the user mode:

1. Transfer instructions
2. Loop support instructions
3. Subroutine support instructions

Transfer Instructions. The MC680x0 processor has two classes of control transfer instructions—branch and jump—that differ in how the destination address is computed. Conditional transfers are available in the branch instruction class, but not in the jump class.

In assembly language, the condition to be tested is specified within the function code mnemonic, which is constructed from the letter "B" followed by the condition's mnemonic. The least significant bit of the condition code signifies testing the complementary condition. The false condition is not available for conditional branching (because it causes the conditional branch to be never taken, and, therefore, the instruction has no effect); the bit combination corresponding to the false condition is used to specify the subroutine call instruction BSR, which uses branch addressing modes to find the entry address of the called subroutine.[7]

Loop Support. A class of MC680x0 control instructions supports counting loops. Instructions in the DBcc group use a designated data register as a counter and the condition code designated by the function code as a completion condition. Executing the instruction does not change CCR. The codes for conditional branching are used to specify the condition to be checked. The execution of a DBcc instruction proceeds through these detail steps:

D1. Fetch the instruction;
D2. Decode the instruction;
D3. scanPC = scanPC + 2;
D4. If the condition is true, PC = scanPC; start next instruction;
D5. Subtract 1 from the rightmost 16 bits of the counting register;
D6. If the result of the subtraction is -1, PC = scanPC; start next instruction;
D7. ew1 = read_2_bytes(scanPC);
D8. PC = scanPC + sign_ext(ew1);
D9. Start next instruction;

The DBcc instruction is intended for the end of a loop body. The loop can terminate either because the condition was met (see step D4) or because the loop

---

[7]   Here is another example of a complex decision required within the implementation.

counter was exhausted (step D6). If the specified branch condition in a DBcc instruction is met, control flows from DBcc to the next sequential instruction (as occurs at the end of step D4); this action corresponds to terminating the loop. Otherwise, the branch is taken, going back to the start of the loop to initiate another iteration (step D8).

Example C-1

Here is the skeleton for a counting loop that exits only when the count value reaches its limit:

```
        MOVEQ #0xD,D6    --copy the constant D (hexadecimal) to register D6
    L:  ..               --loop body in here
        DBF D6,L
```

The false condition guarantees that the loop will terminate only when the count has reached –1, which occurs after the loop body has been executed 14 times.

A single DBcc instruction performs several functions that match the needs of the common looping program control structure. Correspondences like this are the deliberate consequence of a processor design that takes into account the needs of programs to be executed on the system. It is especially effective to move frequently used functions, such as loop count, test, and branch, to the processor's instruction set level. In a similar manner, frequently used features of programming languages or operating systems might be supported at lower levels. By providing supporting processor instructions, the designer can reduce the number of instructions required to implement commonly used program structures.

Subroutine Support. Subroutine calling in the MC680x0 uses a memory stack that grows toward lower memory addresses. The address in register A7 is the address of the byte most recently pushed on the stack, so whenever an item is pushed on the stack, register A7 is decremented (by the item size) before storing the item at the address in A7. Similarly, to pop data from the stack, A7 must be increased (by the item size) after reading the data.

The MC680x0 supports subroutine calling with several call instructions in which the processor saves PC on the top of the stack before jumping to the specified entry point.

The destination address (dest_address) of a call instruction is determined by using either a general addressing mode (if the instruction was JSR—jump to subroutine) or the PC-relative computation (if the instruction was BSR—branch to subroutine).

On subroutine completion, the saved PC is retrieved from the stack (where it was saved) and the stack status is restored by incrementing register A7. In the MC680x0, the return instruction RTS pops the saved PC from the memory stack and adjusts A7 accordingly. The RTR instruction restores the condition code

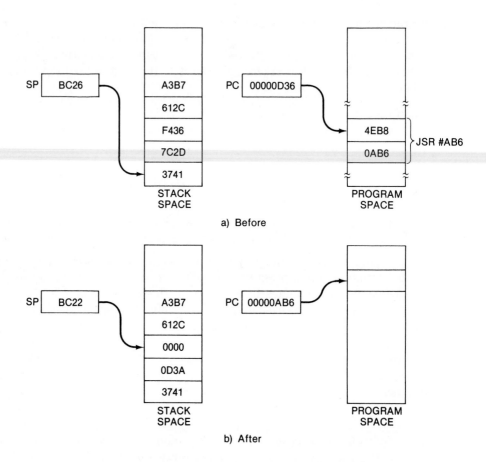

a) Before

b) After

Figure C-3   Illustrating the execution of the subroutine
call instruction JSR 0xAB6

register from the top of the stack before performing the RTS functions; this is
helpful for exiting a subroutine that saved the condition code register immediately upon entry.

Example C-2

Figure C-3 illustrates the contents of memory in the region of the top of the stack
along with the stack pointer and the PC. These are shown both before and after the
execution of the instruction

JSR #0xAB6

located at byte 0xD36 (the instruction is 4 bytes in length, because it uses short absolute addressing).

C.5 DATA TYPES IN THE MC680x0

In addition to integers, other data types that can be manipulated by MC680x0 processor instructions are as follows:

    1. Binary-coded decimal character strings
    2. Bit fields
    3. Indicator bits
    4. Status words
    5. Stack pointers

Notice that there is no support for float objects.

C.6 OBJECT MANIPULATION IN THE MC680x0

The MC680x0 operand manipulation instruction set includes only integer arithmetic[8] is supported, but all four arithmetic operations are provided, and most have variants supporting several operand widths. Logical and shifting operations are also supported. Compare operations test data values and set CCR but discard the difference computed to make the test.

    Operand Specifications. We discuss the specification of the operands of object manipulation instructions before we turn to the semantics of the operations themselves. The operand specification options depend on the number of operands, which, in turn, depends on the function code. Many instructions provide an option called a "general operand," which indicates the possibility of specifying any data or address register in the processor or any memory location; the general operand specifications include those listed in Table C-1.

    In the MC680x0, *two-operand instructions*, such as ADD, take one operand from a processor data register[9] and the other from a general operand. The destination of the result is specified by the value in bit 8 of the instruction. The result always replaces one of the operands, and may be placed in the data register (if bit8 = 0), or in the general operand's location (that location must be writeable).

    For many operations in the MC680x0, the same operation code is used to specify the same operation applied to data of several different widths. The actual operand width is specified by bits 7 and 6 of the instruction, according to the codes listed in Table C-2. The fourth code value is illegal for a width specification, so that bit combination can be used to specify another processor operation code. Although this coding scheme allows the processor to have more functions within a given instruction size, it complicates instruction decoding in the control

---

[8]   But you can add both binary and BCD values in single MC680x0 instructions.
[9]   The processor also has ADD and SUB instructions using A register operands.

TABLE C-2 OPERAND WIDTH
ENCODING FOR MANY MC680x0
TWO-OPERAND INSTRUCTIONS

Value of Bits 7, 6	Width
0	Byte
1	Word
2	Long

unit, and makes the instruction representation (and possibly the functionality)
depend on the function being performed—compromising orthogonality.

Example C-3

Figure C-4 shows the encoding of two ADD instructions with different register
specifications. Examining bit 8, which determines the direction, we see that in case
(a), the destination is the data register, whereas in case (b), the destination is the
general operand's location. Both instructions add exactly the same data in exactly
the same way. In this case, long words are added, because bits <7, 6> contain 2.

Example C-4

Figure C-5 contrasts the encoding of an ADD instruction with the encoding of an
ADDA instruction. (The ADDA instruction adds the contents of a general operand to a
specified A register, leaving the result in the A register.[10]) Notice that the width
code of 3 in the ADDA instruction distinguishes ADDA from ADD, the function code
value being common. The value of bit 8 determines the operand width for ADDA: 0
specifies a word width and 1 specifies a long-word width.

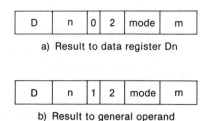

a) Result to data register Dn

Figure C-4 The encoding
of destination variations in
ADD instructions

b) Result to general operand

In the representation of *single-operand operations* (e.g., negation), bits 7 .. 0
specify the operand width and addressing, using the same encoding as for two-
operand operations. The result always replaces the operand, so the addressing
mode must specify a writeable location.

---

[10]   No destination choice is available with ADDA.

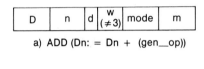

a) ADD (Dn: = Dn + (gen_op))

b) ADDA (An: = An + (gen_op))

Figure C-5 Illustrating the use of illegal width codes to specify other functions

Data Movement Operations. The MC680x0 does not have specific load and store instructions. Rather, it has a general MOVE operation, which permits data copying between general operand locations. In other words, in a single instruction a data value can be copied from one register to another, from a register to memory, from memory to a register, or from one memory location to another memory location. Of course, the destination must be a writeable location.

Figure C-6 shows the format of the MOVE instruction. The size encoding in this instruction does not follow the coding shown in Table C-2, but rather uses the codes shown in Table C-3.[11] The size code 0 selects other operations.

```
 15  13  11      8     5     2     0
┌────┬──┬──────────────┬───────────────┐
│    │  │ DESTINATION  │    SOURCE     │
│ 00 │S ├──────┬───────┼───────┬───────┤
│    │  │  n   │ mode  │ mode  │   m   │
└────┴──┴──────┴───────┴───────┴───────┘
```

Figure C-6 MOVE instruction format. Adapted from [MOTO84]; courtesy of Motorola, Inc.

TABLE C-3 OPERAND WIDTH ENCODING FOR MC680X0 MOVE INSTRUCTIONS

Value of Bits 13,	Width
1	Byte
2	Long
3	Word

---

[11] Notice the apparent violation of orthogonality between the function code and the width code. Actually because the width code is placed within the field usually considered as the function code field, one might view the MOVE width codes are part of the function code. By taking this latter viewpoint, there are three MOVE class instructions with three different function codes. The fact that the assembler does not treat these as three different instructions should not affect our view of orthogonality.

TABLE C-4   COMMON FIELDS IN SOME MC680x0 TWO-OPERAND INSTRUCTIONS

Bit Positions	Mnemonic	Field Specifies
15 .. 12	F	Function code
11 .. 9	n	Register number
8 .. 6	dow	Direction/operation/width
5 .. 3	mode	Addressing mode
2 .. 0	m	Register number for addressing

Two-Operand Operations. Many two-operand data manipulation operations share the common instruction format depicted in Figure C-7. The common elements in these instruction representations serve the roles listed in Table C-4. The two operands are the contents of processor register Dn[12] and the general operand specified by the mode and m fields; the result may be directed to either operand location in many of the operations, as specified in Table C-5. The interpretation of the dow field also depends on the function code, as specified in Table C-5. Notice the diversity of the MC680x0 processor operations. Also note how common encodings have been chosen to make the implementation simpler. However, the dow field has to be interpreted to determine the function, which adds complexity to the implementation.

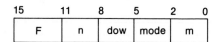

15	11	8	5	2	0
F	n	dow	mode	m	

Figure C-7   A two-operand instruction format

Single-Operand Operations. By looking at a few single-operand instructions, one can see both the common features and the functional diversity provided in these processors. These instructions fit into the format of two-operand instructions (Figure C-7), with F = 4 and bit 8 = 0. The single-operand is a writeable general operand, specified by mode and m. The operand width is specified in the w field. Table C-6 lists three useful instructions in this class.

Other Operations. The MC680x0 supports many other operations not mentioned before; some operations support commonly used system programming functions.

---

[12]   An A register is selected for the register operand if the function mnemonic ends in "A"; see the table for details.

TABLE C-5   ENCODING SIMILARITIES AND DIFFERENCES AMONG SOME MC680x0
TWO-OPERAND INSTRUCTIONS

		dow Bit Values[a]			
Mnemonic	F	8	7	6	Comments
ADD	D	d		w	Add operands; use Dn
ADDA	D	k	1	1	Add operands; use An
SUB	9	d		w	Source – destination; use Dn
SUBA	9	k	1	1	Source – destination; use An
MUL[S I U]	C	s	1	1	Word operands and long result
DIV[S I U]	8	s	1	1	Long operands and word results
AND	C	d		w	Bitwise AND
OR	8	d		w	Bitwise OR
EOR	B	1		w	Bitwise Exclusive-OR, result to general operand only
CMP	B	0		w	Dn - \<gen_op>; set CCR, discard difference
CMPA	B	k	1	1	An - \<gen_op>; set CCR, discard difference

[a]The symbols in these columns are interpreted as follows:
  w is the width encoded according to Table 2-11
  d is the direction—0⇒to Dn; 1⇒to general operand
  s signifies sign interpretation—0⇒unsigned; 1⇒signed
  k is the width for A-register operations—0⇒word; 1⇒long

TABLE C-6   SOME MC680x0 SINGLE-OPERAND INSTRUCTIONS

Mnemonic	Value in Bits 10, 9	Comment
CLR	1	Clear destination
NEG	2	Take the two's complement
NOT	3	Take the bitwise logical complement

C.7 COMMENTS

The MC680x0 processor instruction set design represents a middle ground in orthogonality—there are many orthogonal features in the instruction set, such as the independence of the general operand addressing encodings from the function code. However, there are many dependencies between the other instruction fields and the function code. It seems that these dependencies arise from the limitation of instruction words to 16 bits and the need for compatibility with previous processor models.

We have reviewed many features of the basic operations and addressing modes in the Motorola MC680x0 processors. This processor series contains many instructions useful in supporting operating systems, other functions, and system expansions. We do not discuss these extensions here; rather, we introduce some of these additional features in other places to illustrate how a unified design can support a complete system architecture.

C.8 TRENDS

This processor presents a good example of a CISC design. Unfortunately, its instruction set is too complex for an efficient pipelined implementation, so the processor series is not being continued. It has served very well as the basis of the Macintosh series and in many real-time control applications.

C.9 CONCEPT LIST

1. Extension words
2. ScanPC tracks use of extension words
3. General operands
4. General MOVE instruction
5. Width fields in instructions

C.10 PROBLEMS

C-1. This problem asks you to specify the computation of the effective address of an MC680x0 branch instruction. Recall that there are several possible displacement lengths.
(a) Write a register-transfer sequence that implements the computation.
(b) Suppose that one could obtain a special hardware module that produces a "1" output if all its input bits are identical and a "0" otherwise (ignore any fan-in limitations that this module may have). Discuss the possibility of using one of these modules to assist in the computation of the effective address using the algorithm of part (a). Rephrase the algorithm for use with this module as part of your answer to this question.

C-2. In this problem, you will design a combinational logic circuit to determine the actual destination of a branch instruction in the MC680x0.

(a) Specify all bits in the instruction and the extension word(s) that might have to be examined or used in the determination of the branch target address. Do not include any decoding of the operation code or of the branch condition.

(b) Draw a logic diagram showing the information flows and control logic for this activity.

C-3. Find the hexadecimal representations of the MC680x0 instruction(s) required to implement the following manipulations:

(a) Add the contents of memory location 0x38A5 to register D7, placing the result in the register. All operand values are single words.

(b) Add the contents of memory location 0x38A5 to memory location 632_{16}, where the result should be placed. All operand values are long words.

(c) Add the contents of memory location 0x38A5 and register A4, placing the result in register D2. Again, the operand sizes are long words.

C-4. Write a program for an MC680x0 processor that uses an iterative loop to sum the integers from 1 to n, where n is the contents of register D3.

C-5. A designer proposes the following technique for enforcing a separation among virtual machines that run on a MC680x0 system. Assume that the separation of memory spaces is the only concern. To attack this problem, the designer proposes restricting the formation of addresses by restricting the use of the addressing modes of the MC680x0. The proposed restriction would be enforced by restricting the system so that it is able to run only programs produced by "certified" assemblers and compilers. The following questions ask about important parts of this argument.

(a) Assume that the proposed enforcement mechanism guarantees that the prohibited addressing modes are never used. Can you then certify that two programs will always be separated in memory? In other words, is it possible to select a few addressing modes, restrict address generation to these modes, and then guarantee that certain addresses cannot be generated? Remember that the assembler does know the address information that is placed in the program when it is written.

(b) Now ignore the question of whether the mode restriction really guarantees the desired separation and consider whether the assemblers and compilers can check for the nonuse of the prohibited modes. Can this checking mechanism work properly? Explain.

C-6. The MC680x0 assembler requires that the length of an absolute address be specified by the programmer. Clearly, it is always sufficient to allocate space for a "long" address, but this consumes both space and time if the address is actually short enough to fit within a single word. In a footnote, we explained that it would take a smart combination of assembler and linker to efficiently allocate space for addresses by using word-length addresses when possible. Detail the reasoning behind this comment. Be sure to consider the effect of relocation by the linker, its possible effect on the address format, and therefore the effects on the length of the program itself. Construct an example that illustrates different types of addresses that might have to be adjusted once the program's location has been fixed by the linker, yet could not be fixed during the assembly process.

STACK-ORIENTED SYSTEMS

In this appendix, we summarize important features of two stack-based architectures that were designed to support the efficient implementation of languages with static block-structured naming environments. The Burroughs B 5700 processor supports stacked space allocation and compressed names for all automatic objects visible from each execution context. The HP 3000 processors support stack allocations and some similar features, without the Burroughs level of support for accessing objects that are nonlocal but visible by nesting rules.

These processor designs incorporate logical structures that are essential for efficient implementation of block-structured languages, whether the implementation uses software or hardware support mechanisms. Thus, they represent an important lesson in the implementation of these languages, and state challenges and present options to the software-based implementations of these languages. In current technology, all of these features are implemented by software resting atop processors whose designs contain only a small number of instructions that really assist with the task at hand.

D.1 B 5700 SYSTEM ARCHITECTURE

The essential features of this system are based on the software implementation of ALGOL 60 originally proposed by Randell and Russell in [RAND64]. In the Burroughs B 5700 machines ([HAUC68] and [ORGA73]), a single stack is used for saving procedure call state, for procedure parameters, for activation blocks, and for storing temporary operand values and the results of operand manipulations. Every memory word (of 48 bits) has an additional 3-bit tag whose value distinguishes data objects and control words of various types.[1] Memory addresses select words.

D.1.1 Processor Registers

The B 5700 systems are stack-based in the sense that all operations take operands off the stack or from the instruction stream. Processor registers play an important role in the implementation, and in our description of the system's behavior. Some roles of the processor registers are the following:

1. Pointing to significant places within the stack
2. Holding the topmost stack entries
3. Holding control information

Tables D-1, D-2, and D-3 summarize these registers (and one memory location) according to their roles; we detail their roles in the following sections.

TABLE D-1   B 5700 REGISTERS POINTING TO THE STACK

Register	Role
BOS	Bottom of the stack
S	Top of the stack
LOS	Stack limit (if S reaches this, interrupt)
F	Topmost MSCW in the stack
D[2] .. D[31]	Display registers (see text)

TABLE D-2   B 5700 REGISTERS HOLDING TOPMOST STACK ENTRIES

Register	Contents (If Valid)
A	Word from top of stack
X	Extension of A word if double-precision
B	Stack word just beneath A (and X)
Y	Extension of B word if double-precision

---

[1]   In figures we depict the tag value to the left of the accompanying word.

TABLE D-3   B 5700 CONTROL QUANTITIES

Register	Role
SNR	Number of the executing process (and its stack)
PC	Program counter (divided into segment, word, byte numbers)
D[0]	Pointer to system segment
Memory[D[0] + 2]	Pointer to stack vector (see Section D.1.5)
D[1]	Pointer to user's segment table

D.1.2 Stack Allocation

Each process in the B 5700 is allocated a separate segment; the set of process stack segments is listed in a system segment known as the "stack vector," which starts at the memory address Memory(D[0] + 2); the fixed addressing algorithm that reaches this origin is built into the processor's addressing mechanisms. Space on the current stack is allocated by pushing and popping values during processing, and by performing arithmetic on the S pointer that describes the top of the stack. Activation blocks on the stack are marked with "mark stack control words" (MSCWs) that occupy the first word of each activation record. These marks are inserted by executing a special processor instruction described in Section D.1.6.

D.1.3 Object Representations

Each word within the B 5700 system contains 48 bits (6 bytes) plus a 3-bit tag whose value indicates the type of information contained within the word. Some of the important object types and the corresponding tag values are indicated in Table D-4. Tag values are checked during program execution and memory accessing to validate the appropriate usage of the object or to control the object's role within the operation being performed. We discuss some important tag checks and the roles of various object types in succeeding sections.

Float and integer values share a tag value because the float encoding is compatible with conventional integer representations. Notice that some different types of control words share the same tag code; they are distinguished by the time that they are encountered during processing.

The instruction granularity is a byte; many frequently executed instructions occupy only a single byte, but load instructions occupy 2 bytes, as do some less frequent instructions. Immediate values occupy 1, 2, or 6 bytes; a complete word that is an immediate value has to be word-aligned in memory, so an instruction with a word-size immediate value could occupy up to 12 bytes.

Table D-5 specifies important fields in some control words; many of these fields will be used in the following discussion.

TABLE D-4   SOME B 5700 OBJECT TYPES AND TAG VALUES

Object Type	Tag	Role
Single precision	000	Float or integer value
Double precision	010	Double-width float value
Segment descriptor	011	Descriptor of a program segment
Data descriptor	101	Descriptor of a data segment
Indexed descriptor	101	Point to an individual word within a segment
Indirect reference word	001	Point to another object
Program control word	111	Point to a procedure's entry point
Return control word	011	Hold procedure return address and state
Mark stack control word	011	Mark bottom of activation block

D.1.4 Object Manipulation

The B 5700 is a load/store architecture, but there are no programmer-visible registers, and all arithmetic operations (such as ADD, SUB) pop their operands from the stack and push a result at the top of the stack. The two load operations load either a pointer or a value; the address specification is contained within the instruction. We detail the load operations in the next section. Store operations expect to find both the object and its destination address at the top of the stack.

Almost all instructions (other than load and store operations) behave as stack–stack or memory–memory operations. Arithmetic operations, for example, take their operands from the top of the stack and leave their results there. String operations[2] take descriptors of the (memory locations of) operand and result strings from the top of the stack and then access memory to perform the operation; thus these are memory–memory operations. A few operations perform memory–memory string operations using byte values taken from the stack.

D.1.5 Object Addressing

A (virtual) object address from the instruction stream has two components: a level number L and an object offset i, using the coding described in Section E.3.2. We represent such an address as (L, i). Other addressing possibilities include a pointer in an IRW, an indexed descriptor, and a function call. We start with direct addressing.

Direct Addressing. Direct addressing can be used to access any object within an activation block visible from the current execution point according to

---

[2]   Vector operations, which, like string operators, take descriptors from the stack, were added in the B 7700 system.

TABLE D-5   FIELDS IN IMPORTANT B 5700 CONTROL WORDS

Type	Field Name/Use
IRW	Indirect reference word
	Stuffed flag (= 0)
	L: Lexical level (These are represented in the 14-bit
	I: Index to item compressed format from an instruction)
SIRW	Stuffed indirect reference word
	Stuffed flag (= 1)
	S: Stack number
	B: Displacement (to the MSCW of the activation record)
	I: Index to item
PCW	Program control word
	Stack number (of stack holding this PCW)
	Lexical level
	Pointer to first instruction (segment, word and byte numbers)
	System mode (Run in user or system mode?)
RCW	Return control word
	Machine flag values
	Lexical level (to return to)
	Pointer to next instruction (segment, word and byte numbers)
	System mode (Return in user or system mode?)
MSCW	Mark stack control word
	Active?
	Different stack (DS = 1 if the static link points to a different stack)
	Static link (stack number, displacement)
	Lexical level (of called program)
	Dynamic link (relative offset from here)
	Value (1 if this call is evaluating a name for memory accessing)

the static nesting rules described in Section E.2.3. Each visible directly accessible object has an address represented by an (L, i) combination.

The processor contains 32 display registers, named D[0] .. D[31], that are used to translate (L, i) addresses. Register D[L] contains the address of the MSCW at the bottom of the activation block for the visible nested block at level L. If the

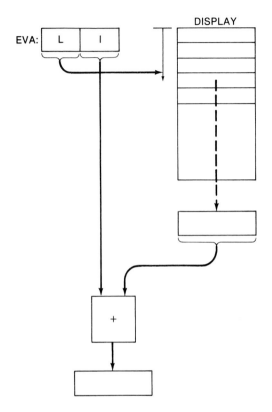

Figure D-1   The B 5700 address computation for an
object in an activation block

processor is executing a program at level j, the contents of D[k] are irrelevant for
values k > j. The translation of the virtual address (L, i) to an effective address EA
is

$$EA = D[L] + i;$$

This address mapping process is depicted in Figure D-1.

Consider the level number field. We know that any address used in a block
at level k cannot contain a level number greater than k. So addresses in blocks at
level k require only $\lceil \log_2 k \rceil$ bits for block numbers. These observations suggest
using a context-dependent field assignment in block-structured names.

In the B 5700 series machines, the executing procedure's level determines
the bit assignments to level number and object index, as shown in Table D-6. A
variant on the obvious encoding reduces the number of different paths for address bits: level numbers are reverse encoded, with their least significant bits on
the left end. Then every address bit may be used in only one or two different

TABLE D-6   ADDRESS FIELD SIZES IN B 5700 MACHINES

	Address Bit Allocation	
Level of Executing Procedure	For Level Number	For Object Index
0–1	1	13
2–3	2	12
4–7	3	11
8–15	4	10
16–31	5	9

ways. For example, the leftmost address bit is always the least significant bit of the block number, and the next bit is either the most significant bit of the object index or the second least significant bit of the level number (see Problem D-2).

Table D-7 summarizes the addressing specifications for all addressing in the B 5700 system. The corresponding address computation paths are shown in Figure D-2.

Simple Indirection.   Tag values distinguish objects holding values from objects holding addresses and control information. The Burroughs B 5700 processors have two load class instructions that push an object on the top of the stack. The VALUECALL instruction chooses the object chosen by the direct address in the instruction. Indirection might occur when the NAMECALL instruction is executed. Then the processor performs a tag-directed process using indirection to

TABLE D-7   ADDRESS FORMS USED IN THE B 5700 SERIES

Address[a]	Address Translation to Make Access	Use
L, I	D[L] + I	Instruction
L, I	D[L] + I	IRW
S, B, I, (DS)	if (DS = 0) then BOS+B+I else Memory[Memory[D[0]+2]+S]+B+I	SIRW
S, B, (DS)	if (DS = 0) then BOS+B else Memory[Memory[D[0]+2]+S]+B	SLINK[b]
E, W, Y, (SU)	WORD ADDRESS: Memory[D[SU]+E]+W BYTE NUMBER: Y	PCW

[a] The (DS) component represents a single bit used to guide the translation process.
[b] This form is used to locate the bottom of an activation block; it is used in the linked pointer structure defining the addressing environment.

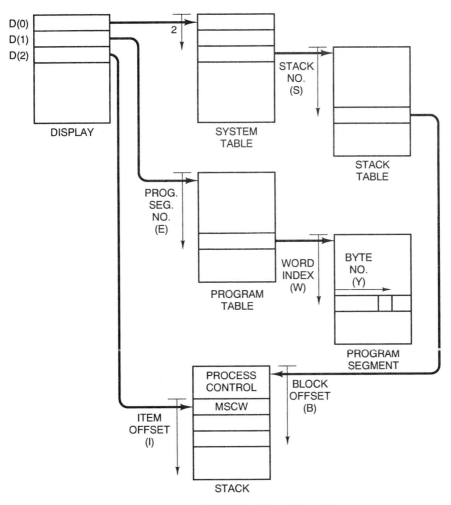

Figure D-2   All B 5700 addressing path structures

search for an object that is not an address specifier. This object is pushed on the stack. In the simple case, this process finds object descriptors along the path to the object. As it accesses each object, it examines the associated tag to determine whether the indirection process has been completed. If not, it uses the pointer to access the next object in the chain.

The processor supports descriptors of both compound objects and their components; the "data" descriptor (of a compound object) differs from a descriptor of a component by the contents of a flag bit contained within the descriptor. An indexed address contains both the origin of the compound object and the index of the component. There is a processor instruction (index_descriptor) that

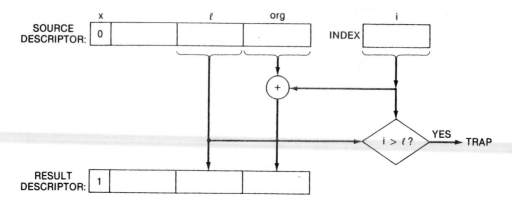

Figure D-3   The INDEX operation in the B 5700 processor

indexes a descriptor of a compound object. While executing this instruction, the processor checks the index value against the limit in the descriptor, replaces the limit with the index quantity, and sets the indexed bit within the descriptor; all of this is conditional on the index value being within the range limit specified in the initial descriptor. The indexing operation is depicted in Figure D-3.

Complex Indirection.   Complex indirection occurs when the indirection process encounters a program control word (PCW) rather than a value-holding object, an indexed descriptor, or an indirect reference word. When the PCW is encountered during the indirection process, the processor performs an automatic call to the function (which has no parameters), expecting that the function will leave the next element in the indirect chain at the top of the stack. Then the indirection continues, using that returned pointer or descriptor to find the next object in the access chain. This scheme supports the ALGOL call-by-name parameter passing convention, as described in Section E.2.3.

Context Changes.   Two types of operations related to context changes have to be considered, though both are related to the need to change the address translation information when the execution point moves from one naming context to another one. The naming context changes upon procedure call and return. The first context change operation alters the contents of the display registers, which must be updated so that the objects that are directly accessible from the new context will be reached through the direct addressing mechanism. The second context change operation arises because addresses that use display registers above number 1 are context-dependent, so any objects that contain context-sensitive addresses must be modified so that they will be interpreted correctly from within a different context. An address is made context-insensitive by replacing its level number with a pointer to the bottom of the corresponding activation record; this pointer contains a stack number and an offset value. The replacement is made by executing the instruction STUFF_ENVIRONMENT.

D.1.6 Calling Procedures

To discuss the process of calling procedures and establishing the addressing information in the display registers, one has to understand the basic stack structure in the B 5700 system. The beginning of the stack segment contains process control information for use by the operating system; this information is not important during the execution of user programs. The remainder of the stack is a stack of activation blocks that are created during procedure calls.

The bottom of each activation block is marked by a mark stack control word (MSCW). During execution of the called procedure, the MSCW, along with the RCW in the next word, holds saved processor state and stack status information. Immediately above this state information are the called procedure's parameters. The local objects used during the execution of the called procedure are located above the parameters. This structure is illustrated in Figure D-4.

Basic Procedure Calls. The steps in the procedure calling sequence have to establish the block's control word structure and load the display registers with appropriate pointers for accessing objects visible according to the static nesting rules (see Section E.2.3). The procedure calling steps that establish this stack structure are

1. Save the TOS;
2. Push the actual parameters;
3. Perform the CALL;

If there is one parameter passed by value, the processor-level calling sequence looks like

```
MARKSTACK
NAMECALL <entry point identifier>
VALUECALL <parameter identifier>        //repeat to load more parameters
ENTER
```

Now look at the activities during these four instructions:

Step 1: The instruction MARKSTACK places a (tagged) mark stack control word (MSCW) on the top of the stack. The new MSCW is loaded with the difference between the present top of the stack and the previous value stored in the F register.[3] This difference is the dynamic link that will be used to restore F on return from the procedure. The F register is set to point to the new MSCW. Thus,

---

[3]   Recall that this register points to the topmost MSCW on the stack.

the F register is the head of a list of all MSCWs on the stack.[4] The new MSCW is marked "inactive," meaning that it is ready for a procedure call that has not occurred.

Step 2: The NAMECALL instruction pushes on the stack an indirect reference word (IRW) pointing to a program control word (PCW) that itself contains a pointer to the entry point of the called procedure. This data structure (see Figure D-4b) will be used to establish the naming environment for the called procedure. In the figure, XX denotes the PCW describing the entry point.

Step 3: Push the actual parameters on the stack. A parameter is passed by value (reference) by using the VALUECALL (NAMECALL) instruction to push the actual parameter. This step includes any processor instructions used evaluate the actual parameter values;[5] these details do not affect allocation or the stack configuration. Figure D-4b illustrates the stack structure after the parameters have been pushed.

Step 4: During the ENTER instruction, the processor performs many actions to support the allocation, accessing, and naming of local objects, in addition to several control actions. The important allocation activity is the creation of a new activation block, which is effected by activating the topmost MSCW (found through the pointer in the F register). The accessing control structures and the naming environment are updated; this activity is discussed in the succeeding paragraphs, though not necessarily in the order that they occur in the implementation.

Step 4a: Use the pointer at the top of the stack to find (1) B: the base of the activation block containing the PCW and (2) E: the descriptor of the entry point from the PCW.

Step 4b: Saves the return program counter and the (nesting) level of the calling program in the word above the MSCW, changing this word into an RCW.

Step 4c: The (new) level number of the called program (NL) is retrieved from the PCW.

Step 4d: A pointer to the topmost MSCW (found from the F register's pointer) is placed in display register D[NL]. The display update procedure (see what follows) is activated with pointer B found in step 4a and the level number (NL − 1) as the actual parameters.

Step 4e: Pointer B is saved in the topmost MSCW, which is set "active."

Step 4f: Finally, the program counter is set to the first instruction of the called procedure (found in E, which was retrieved in step 4a).

Reloading the Display Registers. The reloading process starts with a pointer to the head of the list structure defining the new mapping and the level of the program block corresponding to the first list element. The display updating algorithm proceeds according to these steps:

---

[4]   Because the list is chained using relative locations, it can survive stack relocation.
[5]   In fact, parameter evaluation may itself require procedure calls.

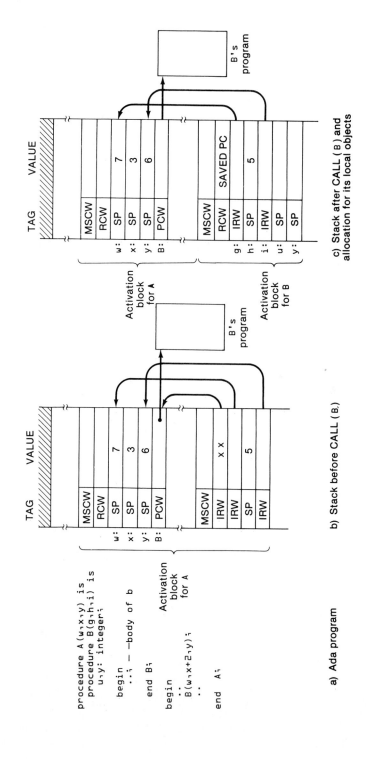

a) Ada program

```
procedure A(w,x,y) is
  procedure B(g,h,i) is
    u,y: integer;
  begin
    .. ; --body of b
  end B;
begin                    Activation
  ..                      block
  B(w,x+2,y);              for A
  ..
end A;
```

b) Stack before CALL (B,)

c) Stack after CALL (B) and allocation for its local objects

Figure D-4 Passing parameters in the B 5700

```
class list_bead {
public:
        list_bead *next;
        address org;
}
register display[32];

void update_display( level L, list_bead *context ) {
        list_bead *here = context;
        for ( int level = L; level >=0; level-- ) {
            display[level] = here.org;
            here = here.next;          //move to the next bead
        }
}
```

Because the naming environment structure mirrors the nested program structure, it is unlikely that this update procedure will actually modify the contents of display registers with low numbers. Thus, the display register reloading process could be shortened if the algorithm were modified to detect when a register update does not actually change the register's contents. The reloading process can terminate when the no-change condition is detected.

D.1.7 Program Linking

The B 5700's linker builds the user-level segment table and modifies information in program segments to make the appropriate logical connections between the program and data segments. The steps that connect program segments together illustrate the linking process, so we concentrate on them here. Program segments are connected together by placing pointers to each other in immediate values that will become PCWs.

As the collector constructs the user-level vector of descriptors, it does the following:

1. Adds a segment descriptor of the space to the user-level object list.
2. Builds either a *space descriptor* for each (static) ED data object or a *program control word* (PCW) for each ED entry point.

Each PCW describes a single entry point, giving the level of the program segment containing the entry point (0 or 1), the segment number (the position of the descriptor within the object lost at the appropriate level), the word offset of the first instruction of the procedure, and the byte offset of that instruction. In the previous section, we saw that a PCW for each procedure nested within the block being entered is located onto the stack. During the execution of the procedure's prologue, the processor instruction MAKEPCW is executed to push a word-length immediate constant from the program stream onto the stack, tagging it as a PCW. The constant was determined by the linker/collector, which places it into the calling procedure's instruction stream. Because a procedure body can be accessed only through level 0 or level 1, 1 bit suffices for the level number in the PCW (see Figure D-5a).

In the figure, we show the execution of a process as task number 0x47, executing a program with the following (Pascal) structure:

```
procedure main is
    procedure sub is
        ..
        aa := sin(v);           //an external call
    end sub;
    ..
end main;
```

The stack vector's index within the list of stack vectors is the same as the process number; thus, it is found in word 0x47 of the stack vector, which is found from the descriptor at offset 2 in the segment pointed to from D(0).[6] While the process is in execution, D(1) points to the user-list segment. For our example, the first entry in this segment describes the previous program, and the second entry describes the segment of library programs where the sin function was found by the linker. Suppose that the entry for the sin function is at byte 3 of word 0x214 within the library program segment. This location information, and the level at which the function should be executed (level 2, because it is externally visible from the library), is stuffed into the constant (whose value is 0x00062140A001) in the prologue of main, as illustrated in the insert in part (c) of the figure. When the MAKEPCW instruction is executed (in the prologue of main), the constant is completed with the stack number to form the constant 0x04762140A001 that is pushed on the stack in the level 2 block; we assume that it had a block offset of 6. Just before the ENTER calling the sin function is executed, the top of stack contains the parameter value (v) above a pointer (2, 6) to the PCW that describes the entry to sin. This structure permits the calling program to construct the address translation environment for the sin function when it is called.

D.1.8 Other Features

Immediate numeric operands can be pushed on the top of the stack using short instructions; the immediate values encompass 8, 16, or 48 bits within the program stream.

Registers within the processor can hold the top two objects on the stack; a validity bit is associated with each one to indicate its status. Arithmetic operations can be performed from these registers; the execution of an operation that has two operands and one result would include the following steps:

---

[6]   This accessing path is built into the processor's architecture.

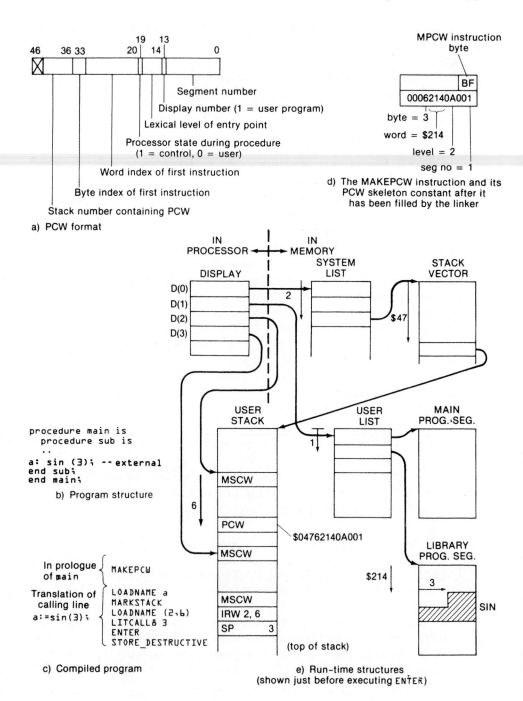

a) PCW format

d) The MAKEPCW instruction and its
   PCW skeleton constant after it
   has been filled by the linker

```
procedure main is
  procedure sub is
  ..
a: sin (3); -- external
end sub;
end main;
```

b) Program structure

```
In prologue   { MAKEPCW
of main

Translation of   { LOADNAME a
calling line       MARKSTACK
a:=sin(3);         LOADNAME (2,6)
                   LITCALL8 3
                   ENTER
                   STORE_DESTRUCTIVE
```

c) Compiled program

e) Run-time structures
(shown just before executing ENTER)

Figure D-5   Linkage data structures in the B 5700

1. Make register A valid (this may require shifting from B or loading from memory).
2. Make register B valid.
3. Perform the addition, leaving the result in A.
4. Mark B invalid.

The processor supports searches through linked lists, as described in Example F-15. This operation assists with bead insertion and bead deletion, in addition to searching. Its use in the implementation of memory allocators is discussed in Section F.6.2.

To allow efficient access to common subexpressions and other reusable temporary objects, the processor contains a DUPLICATE instruction that replicates the object at the top of the stack. Also, a ROTATE instruction cycles the topmost three stack entries by removing the third stack entry and then pushing it on the stack. This is easily implemented by using the A and B registers, and one temporary register (see Problem D-10).

D.1.9 Comments

The B 5700 design is based on a stack. Built-in addressing and allocation mechanisms support the implementation of block-structured programming languages that use static nesting for name resolution. Short address forms are used in the program. Tagged objects in memory automatically specify indirection and can also specify the computation of an address by a function returning a pointer result; this feature simplifies the implementation of call-by-name parameters. Whenever the context changes, the processor may have to make many memory accesses to update the display registers used for accessing automatic objects located on the stack.

D.2 HP 3000 SYSTEM ARCHITECTURE

The HP 3000 system architecture ([HEWL73]) is similar to the B 5700 in (1) the use of a stack to contain activation records, (2) the state saved upon procedure call, and (3) the links that hold the structures together. There are important differences, however, in addressing specifications, in the stack format, and in the list searching instruction.

D.2.1 Object Addressing

Three registers in the HP 3000 processor point to the stack space; they are DB, which points to a space at the bottom of the stack segment that is the base of the stack (but not necessarily the beginning of the segment containing the stack), S, which points to the top of the stack,[7] and Q, which points to the top of the control region of the activation block. The HP 3000 stack grows toward higher addresses, and procedure parameters are placed on the stack before the control words that start the activation block. This means that the parameters are found at addresses beneath that designated by Q, whereas the local objects are stored in locations above that in Q. Because there are likely to be more local objects than parameters, the addressing mode encoding is designed to permit longer displacements going positively from Q (toward local objects) than going negatively (toward parameters).

The particulars of the HP 3000 addressing modes are summarized in Table D-8 and Figure D-6. The P-relative[8] modes are used to access objects within the program segment; these are used in control transfer instructions and for access to constant values. The DB-relative mode is used to access process static objects allocated at the base of the stack space. The Q-relative modes are the subject of our present discussion, and the S-relative mode is used to access intermediate results stored near the top of the stack. From the table, you can see that the design permits direct access to up to 63 parameter words and up to 127 automatic object words for the current procedure. The compiler has sufficient information so that it can translate a name into an address using the appropriate addressing mode.

The HP 3000 addressing modes do not support direct access to objects declared in immediately enclosing blocks, there being no addressing options corresponding to the use of the display registers of the B 5700 processor. Global data can be referenced by using indirect addresses relative to the bottom of the stack (whose location is held in DB). In this processor, every indirect data address is interpreted as a distance beyond the location described in the DB register. Indexing can be used with any of these modes to obtain access to other areas in memory. Indexing is always applied after indirection, if any, and the index quantity is always added to the address, even if the addressing mode specified subtraction from the processor register used in the indexing process. The index register is a processor register separate from the stack mechanism; the index value is saved on the stack during the PCAL instruction and restored during return. Problem D-12 describes one way that these address modes could be used to achieve the effect of two-level addressing.

---

[7]   Actually, there is a register SM that points to the top of the stack in memory and a register SR that counts the number of stack words held in processor registers. Ignoring the effects of buffering, the stack contents in processor registers, SM and SR together define the logical top of the stack, which is the basis for addressing. We proceed as though all stacked objects are located in a memory stack, whose top is in register S.

[8]   The P register is the program counter.

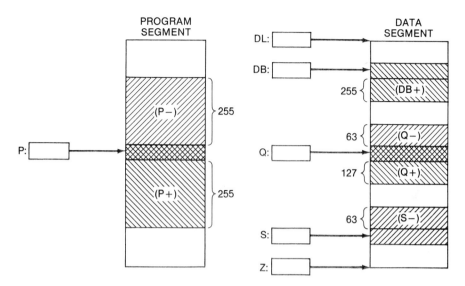

Figure D-6   Addressible spaces in the HP 3000 system.
From [HEWL73]. © Copyright 1973 Hewlett-Packard
Company. Reproduced with permission.

TABLE D-8   ADDRESSING MODES FOR THE HP 3000

Addressing Mode	Address Field Bits						Address Computation
	6	7	8	9	10	11..15	
P+	0	0	d	d	d	d..d	P + d
P-	0	1	d	d	d	d..d	P − d
DB+	1	0	d	d	d	d..d	DB + d
Q+	1	1	0	d	d	d..d	Q + d
Q-	1	1	1	0	d	d..d	Q − d
S-	1	1	1	1	d	d..d	S − d

Source: [HEWL73]; © Copyright 1973 Hewlett-Packard Company. Reproduced with
permission.

D.2.2 Procedure Calling

The HP 3000 activation block format separates a procedure's parameters from its
automatic objects, with the parameters stacked beneath the new activation block
(see Figure D-7). Therefore, the procedure calling steps have to be ordered differently from the B 5700; for the HP 3000 they are

1. Copy the actual parameters to the stack;
2. CALL the procedure, saving the processor's state and the stack block pointer and then updating the stack block pointer from the TOS;
3. Allocate space for the automatic objects;
4. Execute the called procedure;
5. On return, restore the TOS to the beginning of the parameter block.

Step 2 is performed by executing the processor instruction PCAL fentry (the operand fentry is the address of the instruction at the entry point). During the PCAL instruction the processor state is saved and a pointer to the location holding the saved state is captured in a processor register.

The HP 9000 Series 500 system [OSEC84] uses a similar allocation strategy.

Because the process of allocating space on the stack and updating the frame and stack pointers takes time, the HP 3000 design provides a simple call instruction (SCAL) for short routines; this instruction saves the program counter, but does not otherwise modify the stack and associated pointers.

The linkage to find procedure entry points is provided differently for local and global procedures. Local procedures have their code in the same segment as their calling instruction; these are located by specifying their offsets with respect to the value in the PB (program base) register in the processor, which holds the origin of the current procedure segment. External calls reach procedures whose program bodies are located in other segments; these segments are found through a linkage table that is located at the end of each program segment. The location of the end of the current procedure segment is kept in the PL (program limit) register within the processor. The last object in the procedure segment is a count of the number of external segments listed in the link vector part of the procedure segment; this count is used to check the validity of each procedure entry specification. Thus, each entry address in the program is given by (s, e), where s is the number of the link vector entry for the segment holding the procedure's body (the value of s is used as a negative offset from the PL value), and e is the word offset of the entry point within that segment. Figure D-8 illustrates these structures. Each segment descriptor in the link table has an "uncallable" bit that is tested to determine whether it contains entry points. The processor causes a trap to the operating system if the uncallable bit is set in the segment descriptor for a proposed entry point. More details are given in Example 3-13.

D.2.3 Object Manipulation

Object manipulation in the HP 3000 is different from the B 5700 scheme in that the operations are not strictly stack-based. A few exceptions to the stack paradigm support addition and subtraction with the result going to memory locations, or the index register, or the entry next to the top of the stack (referred to as register B). In most other cases, the result of an arithmetic operation is left at the

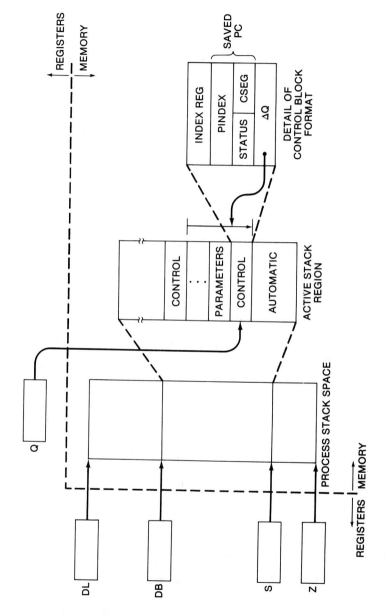

Figure D-7 HP 3000 stack format. After [HEWL73] © Copyright 1973 Hewlett-Packard Company. Reproduced with permission.

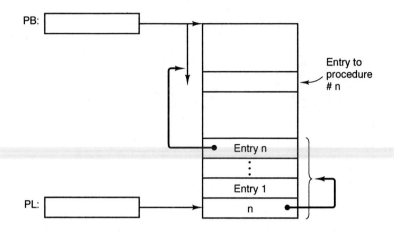

Figure D-8   The linkage list in a code segment in the HP 3000 system

top of the stack. For most arithmetic operations, one operand comes from the stack; either the top of the stack (referred to as register A) or the next entry on the stack can be used as the single stack operand in many operations. Operands from memory can participate in arithmetic operations with the top of the stack operand, the result replacing the A entry at the top of the stack.

Arithmetic operations for double-length integers are all stack-based; the operands are all popped from the stack, and the result is pushed onto the stack.

Float operations are supported with three formats of varying precision; this processor predates the IEEE standard, so the encoding is not compatible.

D.2.4 Other Instructions

Immediate operands in this processor are limited to 1 byte; they can be operands in arithmetic instructions, be loaded into a register or be pushed on the stack.

The ROTATE instruction behaves like the B 5700 instruction. There are several DUPLICATE instructions, which differ according to the operand sizes.

A set of instructions related to the index register support simple loop structures. The index register can be incremented (decremented) by an amount that comes from the stack; then a branch conditional on whether the new index value is zero can be taken to a nearby location in the program (there are only 5 bits to specify this signed displacement). This structure supports short counting loops.

The list search instruction in the HP 3000 processor offers more flexibility with respect to the list format than the list search instruction in the B 5700. In particular, the locations of the value and the successor pointer do not have to have a fixed relationship to each other. The pointers contain the addresses of the

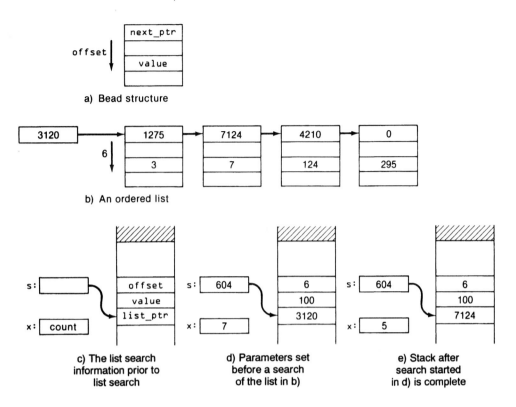

Figure D-9   HP 3000 list searching

pointer words in list beads, which therefore form the linked list structure themselves. There are four operands of the list search instruction; the first two, like
those in the B 5700, are a pointer to the head of the list and the search value. The
third operand specifies the number of words beyond the pointer where bead's
value is stored. These three operands are at the top of the stack. A final operand
is a count that limits the length of the search; this operand is in the index register
named X. The result of the search (left at the top of the stack) is a pointer to the
node where the completion test succeeded, and not to its predecessor, as in the B
5700. Figure D-9 illustrates the data structures, including the result of a search
through the list used in Example F-16.

D.2.5 Comments

The HP 3000 processor uses interesting access modes, chosen considering both
the language needs and the stack allocations used to implement block-structured
languages with static nesting for object name resolution. It supports both indexing and indirection in its addressing scheme. It differs from the B 5700 design in

that accesses to nonlocal visible objects require software assistance to trace the activation record pointer chain. It also differs in that it includes instructions that perform operations on the next to top entry on the stack. The separate index register provides simplicity for certain loop structures. Another interesting feature is the distribution of linkage information among the code segments and the processor support for linking by double indirection, as discussed in Section 3.5.2.

D.3 SUMMARY

Stack-based architectures support three important functions needed in the implementation of many programming languages: (1) allocating space for activation blocks, (2) saving state for procedure call/return in a recursive environment, and (3) allocating space for procedure parameters. Although the logical structure of the stack reflects the semantics of these features, its implementation in a processor presents many problems for accelerating performance by pipelining the processor's instruction execution. The Burroughs designs represent the first attempt to move these logical mechanisms into the processor's instruction set. Other designers have continued this trend, even to the extent of placing system functions within the processor's architecture. These more elaborate schemes have faltered because they have moved policy into the mechanism, rather than providing a mechanism to support a policy, as in the stack-based designs presented in this appendix.

D.4 TRENDS

The use of stack-oriented architectures for holding operands and results for simple processor instructions has passed from the scene because it is difficult to speed execution of such a processor because the stack pointer manipulations become a bottleneck. Complex bookkeeping might be used, but designers prefer simple register structures for which dependence detection (see Section 6.1) is much simpler.

Languages that have nested block structures require stacks in their implementations to hold activation records, including procedure parameters, processor registers, and local objects. So though the implementation of this mechanism in hardware, as seen in the B 5700, might not be attractive, the design is important because it points out the logical requirements arising from the properties of the programming language. Modern processors do provide limited support for related requirements by including instructions that effectively build linked chains of activation block (or "frame") pointers.

List searching instructions, although attractive for memory management (see Section F.6.2), are not provided in modern processor designs for several reasons: (1) They require an indeterminate number of memory references, (2) these references cannot be predicted and thus must be performed in sequential order, and (3) the execution of the instruction cannot be overlapped with its neighbors in any simple manner.

Many features supporting stack allocation and frame pointers are provided in contemporary processor designs; these features provide basic mechanisms for language implementation and should continue to be supported.

D.5 CONCEPT LIST

1. Activation block markers (frame pointers)
2. Context-dependent object names in instructions
3. Instructions to remove context dependency from pointers
4. Processor mechanisms to maintain frame pointers
5. Display registers reflect the static nest structure
6. Tag-based indirect addressing
7. "Thunks" to access parameters called by name
8. List searching operations
9. Addressing modes keyed to important pointers into the stack space
10. Simple call instructions avoid overhead on some calls
11. Program linking is simple when a descriptor table is provided
12. Minor violations of the strict stack discipline
13. Linking by double indirection

D.6 PROBLEMS

D-1. Here is a program using static nesting. Assume that procedure a is nested at the outermost level. We also have an execution history:

```
procedure a is
    procedure b is
        procedure c is          HISTORY:
            ..                      call a;
        begin                       call b;
            ..                      call c;
            d();                    call d;
            ..                      return;
        end c;                      return;
            ..                      return;
    begin                           return;
```

```
                                ..
                            c();
                                ..
                        end b;
                        procedure d is

                                ..
                        begin

                                ..
                        end d;
                                ..
                    begin
                                ..
                        b();
                                ..
                    end a;
```

Draw pictures of the MSCW linked data structures in a B 5700 implementation and execution of this program. Show the linked structures after each call, including both static and dynamic link pointers.

D-2. The address in a B 5700 instruction contains both a level number and an index, encoded according to the level of the executing procedure (as specified in Figure D-1). This problem is concerned with the logic that separates the fields. Let PL denote the register that contains the level of the currently executing procedure. Assume that the address information from an instruction is placed in the 14-bit register ADDR before interpretation. The separated address should reside in registers L and J, with the level number in L and the index in J (both values should conform to the customary integer representation conventions).

(a) How wide is register L? Register J?

(b) Draw a diagram illustrating the data paths to load the L and J registers.

(c) Specify the control logic used to determine the logical values to be placed on the selector lines that control loading bits into L and J.

D-3. This problem is concerned with a designer's choices regarding the implementation of the display vector to support the execution of programs written in a language that uses static nesting for name resolution.

(a) Identify factors that influence a designer's decision whether to automatically store the old display vector in an activation block when calling a new context. Assume that all display entries contain absolute addresses.

(b) Repeat part (a) if the display entries contain addresses relative to the origin of the stack object.

D-4. Here is a proposal related to the retention of the display information across a procedure call. Recall that the B 5700 scheme recomputes the display each time that a new context is entered. A speedup is achieved by adding a check about whether a currently valid display register is actually changed or not. The scheme to be considered in this problem saves all display information on the stack when a new context is created (as in procedure call), and restores the saved information to the display registers when the new context is exited (as on procedure return). A designer proposes saving the following information for each display register:

1. The offset of the base of the block (relative to the bottom of the stack)

2. A different stack flag (DS), true if the block is located in a different stack

3. If DS = true, the stack number of the other stack

The first two items are stored in the same memory word and the third item (if needed) is stored in a second word. These words are pushed on the stack immediately following procedure entry.

(a) How many words are occupied by the saved display registers? How does your answer affect the assignment of names to local objects? Explain.

(b) Would this scheme work properly if the stack origin were relocated in memory space (with the stack number remaining constant) while some display information is present on the stack? (The program is not active while its stack is being moved.)

(c) Draw a picture illustrating the saved display information while a subroutine at level 3 is in execution, having been called from a procedure at level 4. Use the program (with static nesting) and history from Problem D-1 as a specific example. Your diagram should show all saved display information on the stack during the execution of d; this may include previously saved display information.

(d) Does the proposed scheme offer any savings over the Burroughs scheme? Explain; be sure to consider the number of memory accesses required in each scheme.

D-5. A designer proposes that the context dependency of addresses be automatically removed by stuffing the environment into an address whenever it is loaded into a register. Discuss the advantages and disadvantages of this proposal. Consider two cases:

(a) The environment is specified by the absolute address of the activation block base.

(b) The environment is specified by the pair (stack_no, index), where the index specifies the position of the activation block's base relative to the base of the stack object.

D-6. A designer proposes using (level, index) addresses (as in the B 5700) and passing them to the cache memory. This means that the address matched during the cache search process would be the (level, index) address of the object desired.

(a) If this argument were accepted, when would the cache have to be invalidated? Explain.

(b) Would you recommend this strategy? Explain.

D-7. The B 5700 stuffed indirect reference word contains a stack number and a different stack (DS) bit, which can be used to shorten address translation.

(a) Describe why the bit can be used to shorten address translation.

(b) Describe the danger(s) that might arise when copying a SIRW from one stack to another. Does this problem ever arise in "real" programs?

(c) Describe rules for modifying an IRW/SIRW that is being copied so that the problem(s) you identified cannot arise.

D-8. We wish to consider changing the assignment of stack numbers to processes while the B 5700 system is in operation. Because the system is in operation, you must assume that there do exist within the system processes whose execution has not been completed. Two situations that might change stack numbers for processes are

(1) a process runs out of stack space and is given an additional stack that is logically on top of the previous stack, and (2) stack numbers are reassigned, even though the stack contents remain the same (without copying the stack itself). This problem concerns the second situation. Assume that the stack whose number is being changed is not in use by the (system) program being executed when the stack number is being changed (i.e., no processor registers point to the stack whose number is being changed).

(a) What information in memory would have to be modified to change the stack number assignment? Try to make your answer as general as possible, so that it specifies all things that have to be changed. (A general answer would be "All PCWs have to be changed.")

(b) Discuss the desirability and usefulness of changing stack number assignments during system operation.

D-9. A designer proposes using one set of registers to serve both the display register and data register functions. Her basic idea is that the registers could be used for computational purposes if they were not needed for making global references. Her design and supporting arguments are summarized in the following paragraphs:

Design. The CALL instruction automatically fills the processor registers with complete display information, with register R_i holding the pointer to the activation block for level i.[9] During program execution within the called program, registers that were loaded with display information may be overwritten with data. (The compiler will keep track of which registers are holding display information and which are available for data.) The register allocation module of the compiler decides (for each context) which registers should be used for nondisplay information.

Rationale. The processor will use fewer cycles to fill the display registers if it does that automatically during the CALL instruction (fewer cycles than would be required if the same operation were performed by a sequence of instructions in a user program). If the called procedure does access a global object, the new design might run faster than a "conventional" machine design. If the program does not access any global objects at a certain level P, the register allocator would be given this information and it could then use register R_P for data; therefore there does not have to be any loss of efficiency due to register allocation for data unless the usage patterns suggest that the display information would be useful.

(a) Is the claim justified that the processor can fill the registers faster when it does this automatically? Explain.

(b) Presuming that the scheme does provide correct behavior, how does the register allocator decide whether to take another register from the display set and use it for data? Specify what characteristics of the program would affect this decision.

(c) Under this proposal, what would happen during the execution of a return instruction?

(d) Comment on the overall feasibility of the proposed design.

(e) Would your answer be affected if you had to handle indirect object references efficiently? If so, how? If not, why?

D-10. Describe a series of actions involving the A and B registers in the B 5700 that will implement its ROTATE instruction.

---

[9]   Use the B 5700 scheme for numbering levels.

D-11. Describe the steps needed to evaluate the expression x[i] + x[j], where i, j, and the x array are local to the procedure in execution.

   (a) Do this on a B 5700-style processor.

   (b) Do this on an HP 3000-style processor.

D-12. A compiler designer for the HP 3000 Pascal compiler proposes to allocate the first word of each local space to a pointer that describes the value of Q (relative to DB) for the statically enclosing activation block. In this manner, the activation blocks would be linked together to form the tree structure required for global references. Further, she proposes that locations DB through DB + 31 be allocated to hold the display information for an executing procedure, with DB + i holding the location of Q for the block of lexical level i.

   (a) Show how a nonlocal object at location j within the activation block at level s would be accessed from the processor.

   (b) Write an algorithm that updates the display information in the DB block.

D-13. The HP 3000 linked list search instruction leaves as its result a pointer to the list bead that satisfies the matching criterion, rather than to its predecessor, as does the B 5700 linked list lookup instruction. This difference can be significant because the processor does have to find the predecessor bead in order to insert a bead before the one found or to delete the found bead. A software designer proposes that this limitation could be alleviated by redesigning the list structure to place the search value associated with a bead B in B's predecessor in the list. Each bead's format is specified in the following record declaration:

```
class list_bead {
public:
    list_bead *next_pointer;
    int next_size;        //this field contains the search value (for the next bead)
    int present_value;
}
```

   (a) Devise an algorithm to insert a bead into the list having this modified format. At the start of your algorithm, the desired place has just been found by executing the HP 3000 list lookup instruction, so you have a pointer to the first bead whose value meets the search criterion.

   (b) Show an algorithm to delete a bead from the list having this modified format. As in part (a), you start with a pointer to the first bead whose value meets the search criterion.

   (c) Compare the number of accesses to list entries required for the two list formats and make a recommendation for or against the proposed change in the list format.

D-14. One disadvantage of the HP 3000 linked list search instruction was that the result pointed to the bead where the condition was met, and not to its predecessor (which is useful for insertion and/or deletion). Show how a program can obtain a pointer to the predecessor by manipulating the count in the index register (X). Illustrate the operation of your program fragment as it performs the list search depicted in Figure D-9.

NAMING MEMORY OBJECTS

"Of course they answer to their names?"
the Gnat remarked carelessly.
"I never knew them to do it."
"What's the use of their having names,"
the Gnat said, "if they won't answer to them?"

— *Lewis Carroll*

What's in a name? That which we call a rose,
By any other name would smell as sweet.

— *Shakespeare,* Romeo and Juliet

Under the simple memory illusion, we view the memory system as a set of places that hold objects coupled with a scheme for naming those places. Within the implementation, we need an addressing mechanism that, when given a name, selects the corresponding place. The addressing mechanism is the link by which the contents of a place are associated with the name of that place. These names are arbitrary, as Shakespeare poetically points out. Used consistently, object naming provides a basis for communication and understanding. Although none of us were alive when Shakespeare wrote his words, we all know exactly what he was talking about. I could show you a rose, and I believe that it would be the same type of object that Shakespeare was writing about. This understanding is possible because the name "rose" has been used consistently since Shakespeare's time. Names in computer systems are more transitory!

In this appendix, we discuss the naming issues associated with the simple memory illusion. How does a name in a C++ program, such as this_name, become converted into a bit pattern that can be sent as an address to memory when the named item is to be accessed? The first phase of system activity that affects and influences memory system design is *translation*, the term we use not only for the compilation of a high-level language program into a lower-level representation, but also for the translation of symbolic assembly-language programs. Translation reduces a program containing symbolic names to a program in which the only symbolic names are those necessary for linking. The second activity is *linking*, the act of combining several separately translated programs to form a single larger program for execution. The third activity is *execution*, the running of the linked program. We cover naming issues in this appendix, allocation issues in the next appendix, and accessing issues in Chapter 3.

The designer's selection of allocation and accessing methods is affected by her selection of naming methods, but the design options and selection criteria related to object naming are largely independent of the design decisions concerning memory allocation and accessing. In this appendix, you will learn the semantics of names and the structures of objects that can be named. You will review high-level-language naming rules, you will see how processor operand specifications can be treated as names and how they are interpreted, and you will see how data structures used to hold object states can be specified and their components accessed. You will see how some processor designs have incorporated support for and taken advantage of high-level features or requirements. Finally, you will learn some criteria used to compare naming schemes.

One wants to produce a processor and system design that supports the naming illusions supported in high-level languages. A direct implementation of these semantics may require complex computations to determine effective addresses; some of these find direct support in CISC processors. In contrast, RISC processor designs reduce naming options to increase execution speed for basic instructions; this RISC approach may sacrifice speed when complex addressing algorithms are required to match language semantics.[1] Like RISC designs, early processor designs were limited to simple addressing modes. But in the intervening years, several interesting approaches to object naming were developed to support programming language semantics. After studying this appendix, you will be familiar with some of these logically important designs.

Before we start with details of object naming issues and options, we point out that there do exist *associative* memory systems wherein objects are selected based on their contents, rather than their names;[2] the naming discussion in this

---

[1]   Compiler optimization may eliminate or significantly reduce this penalty in many programs.
[2]   We discuss some uses and implementations of associative memory systems in Appendix G.

appendix and the succeeding one are based on the design of *location addressed* memories, in which every object is identified in some unique manner; we call the unique specification the "name" or "address" of the object. A name's interpretation may depend on its usage context, but within each context, each name must have a unique interpretation. Associative memories are useful tools for translating names within the implementation of memory accessing mechanisms; we discuss their implementation in Appendix G.

E.1 GENERAL CONCEPTS

The simple memory illusion holds that after the computer's memory system is presented with a name, it should provide access to the corresponding location.[3] A name might appear in a high-level language statement, a processor instruction, or be taken from a memory-resident object that holds an address of (or a *pointer* to) another object. We want to design the memory system so that accesses will be speedy and so that the system will efficiently utilize the memory space.

The general naming issue concerns name construction and naming semantics. At most levels, a name is either a character string or an integer value. However, a name also may be represented as an algorithm that accesses the location of interest. Or, alternatively, a name may be a set of parameters for a system algorithm that will access the location of interest. A fourth name option includes a selector specifying an addressing algorithm and the parameters of that algorithm. The latter description applies to the MC68020 processor's operand addressing, the address mode specification being the selector. A fifth name option specifies the entry point of a procedure that computes a pointer to the desired address; under this option one can emulate arbitrarily complex addressing modes, particularly ALGOL's call-by-name parameter passing mode.

In this discussion, we divide the naming problem into two parts, based on the complexity of our illusion of the object's role in other objects. A *simple name* denotes a simple object whose internal representation is not visible. In contrast, a *component name* denotes a portion of a compound object; it is possible (or legal) to name a component only if that component's visibility is consistent with our illusion about the type of the compound object. We start with simple names that describe single objects.

The interpretation of the term "single object" depends on the level of abstraction;[4] a matrix may be considered to be a single object when calling matrix manipulation routines, but when writing the routines themselves, a matrix is a compound object, its elements being simple objects. A matrix element might be

---

[3]   At this point, we are not concerned with the choice of the memory operation (READ or WRITE).
[4]   Object-oriented approaches to program structuring develop high-level type or class abstractions like these.

viewed as a compound object at the level of the processor program that does manipulate the elements; an element could be a complex number, for example. And the real and imaginary parts of the complex number might themselves be floating-point numbers that are viewed as compound objects from the hardware level—if the processor directly manipulates floating-point numbers. Clearly, there is no precise definition of a "simple" object; we must be satisfied to use the term intuitively in a context-dependent manner, which should be consistent with the object type illusion supported by the virtual machine.

The rules governing simple name construction vary with the level of abstraction—in a high-level language program, a single character string is a simple name, and in a processor-level program, a bit pattern in a register or an instruction field can be a simple name.

Whatever the form of the names, the set of names forms a name space:

> **Definition.** A *name space* is a set containing all possible names of memory places.

In many high-level programming languages, the names of all objects that are declared or used in a particular program block are specified in object declarations placed at the head of the program block. Each object declaration defines the name of the object, how space should be allocated to hold the object, and how the object's contents may be manipulated.

Example E-1

> C++ declarations occur within a program block, and an object's declaration must appear before the object's name is used in any other statement; if no initialization is specified, each declaration takes the form[5]

>   <type> <name>;

The type information in an object declaration defines the space required to hold the object and also the operations that may be performed on the object. An important illusion is that of strong typing:

> **Strong Typing Illusion.** Each object has a type, and the declaration of that type defines the representation of the object and the operations that can be performed on the object. There is no way that these restrictions can be violated.

Enforcement of strong typing frees the program from any possibility that the results depend upon the internal representations used to encode object values.

An element within a compound object is described by a *component name* that is constructed from several simple names or from a simple name conjoined

---

[5]   A name in angle brackets denotes a syntactic element of the syntactic type named within the brackets.

with an element selector. The structure of a component name depends on the organization of the compound object whose component is being named.

Example E-2

In C++, a component of an array is named by the array name plus a sequence of integer object selectors compatible with the number of dimensions in the array object. The following are legal C++ names for array components.

```
vect[8]
r[x+3][5][v]
```

In C++, a component of an object whose class has been defined within the program can be named by a *qualified* name, constructed from the name of the compound object followed by a period and then the name of the component. The name is legal only in contexts where the component is visible (either because the reference is within the class definition or because the component's existence was declared to be **public**). Here are some component names that might be legal in a C++ program:

```
rec.first
second.first
first.second
```

The naming scheme should support and encourage the use of separate contexts in a program or a system, because complex programs and systems are constructed by combining modules that may have been created by separate individuals. Blocks are the first-level contexts; blocks are collected to form programs; programs are collected to form processes; and processes may cooperate while they use the same system. For simplicity, we might like to separate the naming contexts from each other, but we also might like to permit controlled sharing of objects among contexts, as sharing can speed execution and save space while avoiding needless object copying. Although sharing in this sense is necessary and useful, sharing can cause difficulties, especially when programmers expect the simple memory and atomic action illusions to provide isolation of their programs from other modules. This consideration becomes important when the goals are protection or security, topics discussed in Chapter 9.

E.2 NAMING IN HIGH-LEVEL LANGUAGES

You are already familiar with naming at the high-level language level, so we simply survey naming rules typical of such languages. Later, we see how processor-level designs can support the naming and visibility structures of block-structured high-level languages.

The general requirements regarding the programmer's name space are as follows:

1. Ability to create arbitrary names
2. Ability to name components of compound objects
3. Ability to name objects shared among modules

The first two are familiar and the second one affects processor design issues related to address computation structures, which we discuss in Chapter 3.

The third requirement, the *ability to name objects declared in other program modules,* is important when connecting modules to form a federation that will cooperate to realize the program's application. This aspect of naming system design is important, because relationships among modules determine the program's structure. The naming design must permit the programmer to be able to limit the visibility of some objects (and their names) and also to permit sharing of other objects (and their names); the shared objects connect cooperating modules that comprise a single process.

E.2.1 Names within a Single Context

A program operating within a single naming context includes the definition and all uses of each object name that appears in the program. Every unique name refers to a single object, and for each object, there is a single declaration defining all attributes of that object, such as its type or class.[6] In general, we have the following:

> **Definition.** A *naming context* is a region of a program within which
> the interpretation of names does not change, and each name denotes
> a unique object within that context.

A large program may reference many objects, and the programmer may choose to divide the program into different naming contexts. For example, associating a naming context with a function, a class, or a phase of the program's execution enhances program understandability. In succeeding subsections, we briefly survey the possibilities concerning the interrelationships among naming contexts and the consequences of these interrelationships. We start with the single-context situation.

---

[6]   In some strongly typed languages two objects can have the same symbolic name if they can be distinguished because they have different type attributes that the translator can use to distinguish each object amongst the set of those whose names are otherwise similar. This option is used in C++ and Ada to distinguish among *overloaded* procedures and functions that have the same names but differ in the types of their parameters (the order of the parameter types is also considered). Procedure or function name overloading is more useful than object name overloading; it can be used to define a set of procedures that perform the same high-level function on a related set of parameter types, which can assist a person reading the program in understanding its semantics.

Four pieces of the name construction design are

1. Name construction
2. Declaration syntax
3. Aliasing
4. Component naming

Name construction rules and the *declaration syntax* do not affect system architecture, though they do have implications for the compiler writer.

Aliasing occurs when a single object has two different names. It is logically necessary that there be only a single declaration for each object, but there is no logical necessity for the rule that "there can be only one name that refers to a single object." In other words, there is no logical reason to prohibit aliasing.

Finally, *component naming* must be supported in a programming language.

Aliasing. A language requires special declarations to specify *static aliasing* wherein a memory location has two different names. *Dynamic aliasing* can be introduced into programs due to coincidences among values computed during program execution.

The FORTRAN EQUIVALENCE statement, the Ada **renames** statement, and the **union** construct in C++ define static aliasing.

Example E-3

Both FORTRAN and Ada include specific statements to specify aliasing; the statements

          EQUIVALENCE (X, Y)   /*FORTRAN*/
          x : real **renames** y;   /*Ada*/

declare that the objects named X and Y are to be located at the same memory address. Therefore, X and Y are aliases for the same object. Strong typing rules in Ada limit aliasing possibilities, because both aliases must describe an object of the same type.

In C++, the **union** structure declares a single object that can have several names, with each one having a different object type; this has the same effect as creating an alias, though it does so in a more structured manner, because the alias names all appear together in the program text. For example, the declaration

```
union Example3 {
    char first;
    int second;
};
```

declares a union that can hold either a character occupying a single byte or an integer occupying a single word. The compiler will allocate a word to be certain that the value will not overlap any other object. The problem is not the allocation, but the fact that the following program fragment is legal, even though it stores a character and then retrieves it as an integer, thereby creating representation-dependent behavior.

```
Example3 thing;          //declare an instance of an Example3 named thing
char result;
thing.second = 17;       //store an integer in the object named thing
result = thing.first;    //read it out as a character
```

The same object has two aliases with different type attributes: "thing.first" and "thing.second".

Dynamic aliases can be created through the use of locator objects, through parameter passing, or through computed object selectors, such as array indices.

Example E-4

Aliases can be easily created by using pointers, especially if there is an "address of" operator (such as "&" in C++). This C++ fragment exemplifies these possibilities:

```
int a, *b, *c, d; //The * precedes the name of a pointer to an object of the given type
b = &a;            //Now b points to a, even though
                   //a was innocently declared (without using a pointer)
c = b;             //Now c is in on the act! It also aliases to a pointer to a
a = 6;
d = *b + *c;       //doubles the value in a and places the result in d
```

Aliasing may also occur as a result of parameter passing, which can complicate reasoning about program properties.

Example E-5

Consider this (poorly written) sumdiff procedure:

```
void sumdiff( int *x, *y ) {
    *x = *x + *y;
    *y = *x - 2*(*y);
}
```

It seems that the pointers x and y denote different objects. If that is correct, we can prove that the sumdiff procedure does leave the sum of the operands in x and their difference in y. However, when sumdiff is called by this program fragment

```
int *A;
A = new int;       //Allocate an integer object and set A to point to it
*A = 3;            //Set the integer object to 3
sumdiff( A, A );
```

the formal parameter names x and y are actually aliases for the same object, and the result left in *A is neither 6 (the correct sum) nor 0 (the correct difference), but rather −6! We see that any reasoning about sumdiff that relied on x and y denoting different objects could not be applied to an invocation of sumdiff that introduces aliasing through the actual parameter specifications.

Aliasing can also arise from names of components of an array; if their index values match, they reference the same object, but if their index values are different, they denote different objects. Hence, one cannot tell before program execution whether A[X] and A[Y] refer to the same object. This difficulty arises within register assignment problems, because one cannot assign the same object to two different registers, but one must also assure that the same object is handled consistently. Solving this problem requires additional run-time mechanisms or additional load/store operations to assure that the registers always mirror the memory objects. This problem is discussed in more detail in Section 5.3.3.

Aliasing within programs affects program readability and understandability, but does not have a serious impact on system architecture issues. However, errors in program logic or reasoning about the program can arise more easily when aliasing is present. One must be wary because aliasing can be used to violate the strong typing illusion.

Component Naming. The rules for naming a component of a compound object depend on the object's structure; we survey these rules now.

The set of compound object structures can be divided into four categories, based on whether the structure is static and whether all components within the compound object are themselves of the same type. It is useful to distinguish these cases because the nature of the structure may restrict the naming options within the implementation. Here are the four interesting cases:

1. Static structure, homogeneous component types
2. Static structure, heterogeneous component types
3. Dynamic structure, homogeneous component types
4. Dynamic structure, heterogeneous component types

The archetypal static structure with homogeneous components is the array. Let d denote the number of dimensions of the array. A component within the array is designated by the array's name and a d-dimensional vector of index values. The array's declaration specifies the type and allowable range of the index value for each "dimension." The "space" occupied by the array is a d-dimensional rectangular volume, because any index value can vary through its complete range independent of the particular values of the other indices. In C++, an array is declared in statements like

     int a[10];   int b[5][4];

The components of each of these arrays have names like

     a[3]   b[2][1]

Compound objects in the second class have a static structure with heterogeneous components. In Ada and Pascal this kind of structure is called a "record," in C and PL/1 it is called a "structure," and in C++ it is called a class object.

Example E-6

Here is a C++ class declaration and a reference to one of its components.

```
class structurea {
public:          //this keyword makes the following parts externally visible
    int apart1;
    float apart2;
}
structurea b, c;
..
b.apart1 = c.apart1;
```

Compound objects in the third class have dynamic structures with homogeneous component types. One simple case is an array whose dynamic feature is its dimension, which will not be known until the containing procedure is called.

Example E-7

In ALGOL, the dimension of an array local to a procedure can be specified in terms of the procedure's parameter values. The following fragment exemplifies this capability:

```
function f( n, x : integer ) return integer;  //ALGOL, not C++!
    integer y( n );        //An ALGOL vector declaration
```

Because n, the dimension specified for the array named y, is a parameter of the function f, the dimension of y cannot be known during compilation; it must be determined when the function is called and the actual value of the parameter n is available. Thus, the y array must be dynamically dimensioned.

Example E-8

A C++ programmer can create an array with dynamic dimensions by using the **new** operator,[7] as in this program fragment

```
void Example3_8( int n ) {
    int* xpoint = new int[ n ];
    ..
}
```

Dynamic dimensioning does present allocation difficulties during program execution; in particular, the compiler cannot know how to allocate space for the array or where to locate that space. However, the addresses of the elements relative to the origin of the space can be computed by a simple algorithm that makes few memory references.[8]

Compound objects in the fourth type class have dynamic structures containing components of heterogeneous types. One example is an object whose type is a

---

[7]   The **new** operator is discussed in Section F.3.
[8]   We cover this topic in Chapter 3.

record with variant forms; such types are allowed in Pascal and Ada. A record with variants is similar to a procedure with parameters; the variant used in an instance of the record is selected by the value(s) of one or more *discriminants* (which have roles like parameters). All discriminant objects must themselves be of a type that can assume only discrete values (i.e., a discriminant of type float is not allowed).[9] The actual value of each discriminant must be included in the representation of the record, but is not declared like a record component. All discriminant values have to be constant for the life of the record instance, because they determine the object's structure (see Problem E-2).

Example E-9

In Ada, a discriminant value may be used to specify a subscript range within an array or it may specify which components are to be included in the record. A discriminant-based subscript-range specification is made by placing the formal discriminant name in the range specification. A discriminant-based record structure selection is specified by a **case** structure in which the selector is the formal name of a single discriminant and the selected statement(s) are component declarations. The **case** statement must include a specific clause for every possible value that could be assigned to an object of the type of the discriminant. When the program passes a type that has variants as the parameter to the **new** operator, the actual discriminant value(s) must be specified as parameter(s) of the type appearing in the call of **new**.

Once the allocation of the structure object has been made, the record structure for the new instance is fixed and cannot be changed. When the allocator creates the object, it inserts the actual discriminant value(s) in the record. The allocator places a pointer to the new record in an access variable that then points to the new record.

This Ada program fragment contains a declaration of an object type with two variants and exhibits statements requesting new instances of this type:

```
type place is ( house, apartment );        --An enumerated type is declared
type place_name is string( 1..30 );        --A character string object is declared
type address( ptype : place ) is           --Define a type with a discriminant
record                                          --It is really a record
    street_number : string( 1..30 );
    street_name : place_name;
    case place is                          --The selects the structure based on the
        when apartment =>                       --value of the discriminant
            apt_number : string( 1..6 );
        when house =>
            null;                          --There is no additional component
    end case;                                   --in this case
    city : string( 1..30 );
    state : string( 1..20 );
    country : string( 1..25 );
end record;
```

[9]   If the discriminant is used to select among structural options, its type must be such that there are only a finite number of possible values that the discriminant can assume.

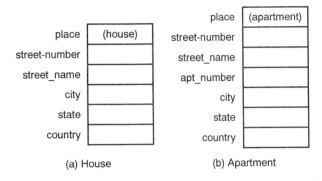

Figure E-1   Forms of variant records for Example E-9

```
type addrpoint is access address;      --Declare a type that points to address objects
ppoint, qpoint : addrpoint;            --Pointers to objects of type address

..

ppoint := new address( house );        --Allocate a house instance of the record
qpoint := new address( apartment );       --Allocate an apartment instance
```

The amount of information in a record of type address depends on the type of the residence being described. When the residence is a house, the record has only six[10] components. On the other hand, when the residence is an apartment, the record has seven components (see Figure E-1). The allocation made in the next-to-last statement of the program creates an instance of the "house" version with six components, placing the value "house" in the discriminant. The last statement allocates another instance of type "apartment." Because the set of components within the record depends upon the discriminant, certain combinations that may seem legal might specify nonexistent components. Here the name ppoint.apt_number is illegal, whereas the name qpoint.apt_number is legal.

E.2.2 Locators

A *locator* object contains an object's name, in the sense that the "value" of a locator tells the present location of another object (the locator's *target*). Accessing an object through a locator at the high-level-language level corresponds to accessing an object through an indirect address at the processor level. The design problem presented by the use of locators concerns whether to support indirection through a memory object within the processor's addressing modes. Because indirection requires an access to the locator object itself to determine the location of its target, a memory access might be required to determine the address of the target object. RISC designers eschew indirection because any additional memory access would complicate the instruction execution pipeline. A RISC machine can give

---

[10]   We are counting the (hidden) discriminant value (named place).

the illusion of memory indirection by copying the pointer into a register and then using that register's contents to specify the base address for a memory access.

Locators may be used to properly describe addressing algorithms, in particular to access dynamic objects or procedure parameters, or to traverse data structures. In C and C++, locators are identified by asterisks in their declarations, as in

      int *intptr;

If we wish to support the illusion of strong typing, the type of a pointer should include the type of the object to which it can point. In C++, it is possible to violate strong typing by declaring a pointer to point to **void** (which effectively eliminates the specification of the type of its target object); the use of such constructs can lead to confusion, but also can be used to overload definitions in a useful manner if care is taken to use the possibility correctly.

How freely can a locator value be copied within a program? The usual answer is that a locator value may be freely passed around a program as long as the interpretation of its contents is not changed by the act of passing it to another context.

The copying allowed by the rule above must be consistent with strong typing if the language demands strong typing.[11] This restriction could be violated if the pointer within the locator object has a context-dependent interpretation or if it is declared to be of type **void**, because that interpretation might change the type of the described object.[12]

E.2.3 Relationships among Naming Contexts

To construct a large (or even a modest, but well-structured) application, a set of separately written program modules is combined (linked) to constitute a larger program. One wants to create separate contexts for separate modules so that programmers do not have to know about all names declared in every program. How are the modules combined? What naming environments are created? Naming contexts are created to limit name visibility as the modules are combined.

Most programming languages support modular separation by providing visibility-limiting (or scope-defining) naming rules. Visibility refers to the programmer's ability to use the object's name outside the context where it was declared. Scope refers to the totality of parts of the program within which the name has the same interpretation. Formally, we have the following:

---

[11]   This amounts to saying that the value of a locator cannot be copied to another locator object unless the types of both are identical, where the locator's type contains the type of the target object.

[12]   Of course, this is just another way to write bad programs, but we mention the problem here because a logically identical problem will show up at the processor level shortly.

Definition. An object name N declared in module M_1, where it denotes entity E_1, is *visible* in module M_2 if N can be used within M_2 to refer to entity E_1.

Definition. The *scope* of a name is the set of modules within which that name is visible.

Flexible name scope rules should make it possible (1) to declare that certain names shall remain *private* to the module, and (2) to declare names that can be used to establish links among modules. Links among modules may be defined by sharing declarations and uses of procedure names, function names, or object names.

Visibility constraints and scope rules imply that a name's interpretation depends on the context of its use. A related issue—object lifetime—is discussed in Appendix F. Visibility, scope, and lifetime issues affect the system's architecture, because they define the requirements for accessibility and continued existence of the objects referenced by the programs; the architect must support these requirements somewhere within the system, and might even exploit these structures in designing the system. If there is little support for these concepts within the processor design, the software must be designed to support the requirements; the software designer faces the same design options to those faced by the processor designer.

A program module that could be linked to other modules may contain three classes of name declarations:

1. Private (P)
2. Externally visible (EV), and internally defined
3. Externally defined (ED), yet internally used

An entity with a private name is not visible in a context outside the one that includes its declaration. Therefore, P names cannot be used to establish links, and P names can be ignored in any discussion of name sharing.

A link from module M_1 to another module M_2 can be established by declaring a name N in M_1 as an EV name and declaring N in M_2 as an ED name. The declaration inside M_2 defines both the name N and the attributes of the object named N. The compiler and the linker cooperate to associate the two declarations and to establish proper addressing information such that the linked interpretation is supported.

Naming rules define how a name is associated with one of these categories. A related rule defines the relationships among object names and entities. We emphasize naming rules in a structured naming environment here.

In a *structured naming environment*, both the distinction between P and EV names and the linkage rules are implied either by the program's textual structure or by the program's execution sequence. The basic structural entity for these distinctions is a "context." As a basis for the rules, we must agree on the following points:

1. How a context is defined
2. How names are declared within a context
3. How contexts are related for naming purposes

The resolution of the first two issues does not affect system architecture; we assume familiarity with at least one method for declaring contexts and objects.

In the next subsections we explore two options for defining the name-entity correspondences: nested naming rules and explicit export/import rules.

Nested Name Resolution. Nesting is a common basis for defining inter-context name visibility. With nesting, if a name is used in a block but not declared there, it is equivalent to having an implicit ED object declaration of that object in the block. The visibility rules are easily phrased in terms of the search strategy used to resolve each name:

> **Nested Name Resolution Rule**. To find the entity corresponding to the name N used in module A, first search A's local declarations for the name N. If A does not contain a declaration of N, search the declarations in the module within which A is nested. If this fails, the search moves to the module within which that one was nested. The search continues in this manner through the module nest until either a declaration of N is found or the outermost (root) module fails to have the desired declaration.

The nested search fails if the name was not declared anywhere along the search path. In this case, the program may simply be in error. One could introduce a rule stating that a name not declared along the search path is actually an ED name to be resolved during linking. This rule is not entirely satisfactory, however, because the translator cannot produce instructions to access N correctly, as N's attributes are not known. The uncertainty could be resolved by delaying some code generation details until link time.[13]

The general nested naming rule does not specify the meaning of module nesting. Two options for defining module nesting are embodied in the static and dynamic rules discussed in the following.

Static Nesting. Under static nesting, the module nesting is based on the format of the program text.

> **Definition.** *Static module nesting* is declared by explicit (textual) or implicit (structural) inclusion; module B is nested within module A if

---

[13] This delay is required by Ada semantics!

the text describing module B is included within the text describing module A or if module B inherits from module A.

The static nest structure is independent of program flow; in particular, the program's execution pattern never affects the static nest structure. Thus, every name can be associated with the proper declaration prior to program execution. Compile-time resolution of static nesting can be used with C++ and Ada programs.

Example E-10

```
void a( int j ) {
    int i;
    void b( int k ) {
        int i;
        void c( int j ) {
            int k;
                ..      //body of c
        }
                ..      //body of b
        }               //end of b
    void d( int k ) {
        int j;
                ..      //body of d
        }               //end of d
                ..      //body of a
    }                   //end of a
```

In this program only three different object names (i, j, and k) are used, but eight objects are declared. Table E-1 shows how each name that might appear in the program would be interpreted if it were used in each procedure body. To distinguish the different declarations from each other, we generate a unique name for each object by combining its simple object name with the block (procedure) name. The table shows which actual object would be designated by each possible name, for each procedure context where the name could appear.

Procedure names are resolved in the same manner as object names.

TABLE E-1   NAME-OBJECT CORRESPONDENCES IN EXAMPLE E-10

Name	Used in Procedure Block			
	a	b	c	d
i	a.i	b.i	b.i	a.i
j	a.j	a.j	c.j	d.j
k	illegal	b.k	c.k	d.k

Inheritance in object-oriented languages provides implicit static nesting. For example, if the class named class2 inherits from the class named class1, then the names declared **public** within the body of class1 automatically become available for use within the body of class2 (or, if appropriate, for use with objects of class class2), unless superseded by an intervening declaration in the body of class2.

Example E-11

This C++ skeleton has two class declarations nested by inheritance:

```
class class1 {
public:
    int inherited();        //A function to be inherited
        ..
}
class class2 : public class1 {
        ..
}
    ..
class2 sample;              //An object of class class2
    ..
sample.inherited();         //A call to the inherited function
```

Static nesting rules can be enforced by the translation program. The details of the name representation depend on the system's allocation and accessing policies and mechanisms (see Chapter 3). Correct name interpretation is guaranteed by the correctness of the program generated by the translator (with respect to addressing, the translated program follows the "nothing illegal" approach described in Chapter 1). In a naming environment using static nesting, processor-level address specification conventions can be devised to save instruction address bits (see Section E.4.1).

Dynamic Nesting. Unlike static nesting, dynamic nesting is based on the actual program execution sequence; the nest structure is defined from the history of entries and exits from program contexts. In most programming languages, procedure and function bodies correspond to contexts, so context changes occur on calls and returns from procedures and functions:

> **Definition.** The *act of invoking a module* is the act of performing a call to the module.

> **Definition.** The *act of completing a module* is the act of executing a return from that module.

> **Definition.** A module is *alive* during the time interval between its invocation and its completion.

Definition. Module m is *dynamically nested within module* n at time t if modules m and n are alive at time t and if the act of invoking n preceded the act of invoking m.

Because the dynamic nest structure that governs the interpretation of name N depends on the execution history up to the time that name N is used, the entity corresponding to name N used in block B cannot be uniquely determined for all executions of block B. The compiler cannot create a static addressing path for the object program and cannot assure access to the proper dynamically nested entity, *unless* the space allocation for each entity is changed dynamically.

Example E-12

Consider this procedure and declaration structure, along with an execution history:

```
void a() {
    int i, j;
        ..                //body of a
}
void b() {
    int i, k;
        ..                //body of b
}
void c() {
    int j, k;
        ..                //body of c
}
void d() {
    int j, k;
        ..                //body of d
}


call a;
call c;
call b;
return;
call d;
call a;
call b;
return;
return;
return;
return;
return;
```

Table E-2 lists the entity corresponding to each possible name used within each procedure consistent with the given history.

TABLE E-2   ACTUAL OBJECTS[a] REFERENCED IN A DYNAMIC NESTING EXAMPLE

			Corresponding Entity			
Name	First Call of a	c	First Call of b	d	Second Call of a	Second Call of b
i	a.i<1>	a.i<1>	b.i<1>	a.i<1>	a.i<2>	b.i<2>
j	a.j<1>	c.j	c.j	d.j	a.j<2>	a.j<2>
k	—	c.k	b.k<1>	d.k	d.k	b.k<2>

[a]Here x<m> denotes the *m*th instance of the object named x. In this table, qualified names based on block names are used to denote the allocated entities.

Dynamic nesting may appear complex, but a look at one implementation may make it understandable. In this implementation, the translator allocates one visible entity corresponding to each distinct name appearing anywhere in the entire program. By properly saving and restoring the values held in the visible entities, it will be true that in every context the entity denoted by name N is found at the visible location corresponding to the name N. Two activities are required to maintain this condition:

1. When entering a new context, the value stored in each place that corresponds to a name redeclared in the new context is saved on a stack. After stacking the old value, a new (initialized) value is assigned to each visible location whose local redeclaration specifies initialization. Only after the stacking and reinitialization will the new context's program body be started.
2. When leaving a context, the values that were stacked on entry are restored to the visible entities. The stacked values are not accessible from within the nested block and the locally declared entities can be accessed because their values are stored in the visible locations.

Notice how the use of dynamic space allocation and value copying permits the use of static addressing.

Example E-13

Figure E-2 shows both the contents of each visible named location and the contents of the stack holding their old values for the execution history of Example E-12. The lifetimes of the activation records and the corresponding contexts are indicated in part (a) of the figure. Figure E-2b shows the current values stored in the common entities i, j, and k in each context. Figure E-2c shows the contents of the stack if each saved set is stacked in alphabetical order (with i on top and k on the bottom).

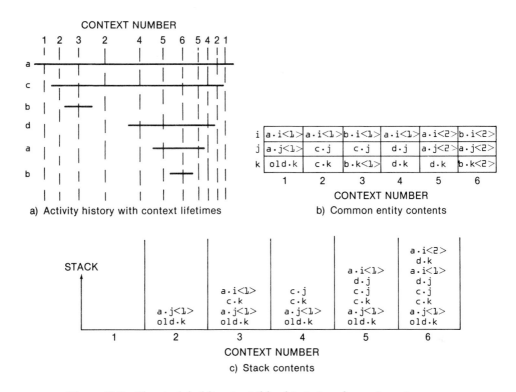

CONTEXT NUMBER
1 2 3 2 4 5 6 5 4 2 1

a) Activity history with context lifetimes

	a.i<1>	a.i<1>	b.i<1>	a.i<1>	a.i<2>	b.i<2>
i	a.i<1>	a.i<1>	b.i<1>	a.i<1>	a.i<2>	b.i<2>
j	a.j<1>	c.j	c.j	d.j	a.j<2>	a.j<2>
k	old.k	c.k	b.k<1>	d.k	d.k	b.k<2>
	1	2	3	4	5	6

CONTEXT NUMBER

b) Common entity contents

c) Stack contents

Figure E-2   The stack holding invisible objects in a dynamic nest (Example E-12)

The preceding scheme works if all objects require the same amount of memory space. If the object sizes differ, additional steps are required; see Problem E-11.

Dynamic nesting is used for all object names in a few languages, such as APL, Snobol, and database programs. Ada, PL/1, and C++ use dynamic nesting rules to find exception handlers; more details are presented in Section 4.2.1.

Naming Objects Not in the Nest. The nested visibility constructs provide simply understood rules determining the set of objects directly visible from any naming context. Occasionally, one may wish to reference objects not accessible according to the nesting rule. These exceptions are most important when static nesting is used; we concentrate on static nesting here. We consider two cases: (1) objects in the same translation unit, discussed in this section, and (2) objects outside the translation unit. The latter objects can be used to create links between separate translation units, as discussed in the next section.

Some objects that are not directly visible according to the module nesting rules have visible names if they are components of visible compound objects.

Example E-14

In C++, one can construct a qualified name to name an EV object declared within a visible class object. Some of its components can be named in the same manner.

```
class t_record {
public:
        int t_first;
        float t_second;
}
class c {
public:
        int d;
        t_record e;
}
void e() {
        int i;
        c *cpoint = new c;
        ..
        i = cpoint->e.t_first;   //the first component of the structure declared in class c
        ..
}
```

These naming rules automatically make an object visible within a large context. A C++ programmer can completely hide an object by declaring it **private** within a class body:

Example E-15

```
class c {
public:
        int d;              //an internal object declared within the class
        ..
        private:            //the following objects are visible only within the class definition
        int hidden;
}
```

The object named hidden is hidden from all but the functions declared in class c.

In a conventional programming language, the programmer has limited ways to control object visibility. In particular, there is no way to specifically name one or more outside naming context(s) within which an object should be visible. Now we present some language design options that give the programmer this type of fine control over object visibility.[14] We use the terms *using context* and *declaration context* to describe the obvious regions. Consider these simple

---

14   These unconventional features are not implemented in most languages.

visibility statements, three by the object's declarer (D) and three by the object's user (U):

D1: **export** E **to** C; *or* "I, the declarer, allow you, the user in context C, to know about object E, which I have just declared."

D2: **hide** E **from** C; *or* "I, the declarer, prohibit you, the user in context C, from knowing about object E, which I have just declared."

D3: **force** E **to** C; *or* "I, the declarer, force you, the user in context C, to know about object E, which I have just declared."

U1: **demand** E **from** D; *or* "I, the user demand the use of object E, which you, the declarer, have created."

U2: **no_see** E **from** D; *or* "I, the user, promise that I will not use object E, which you, the declarer, have created."

U3: **import** E **from** D; *or* "I, the user, wish to know about object E, which you, the declarer, have created."

Some combinations of these declarer/user statements are incompatible; D2 and U1 do not make sense together, because the declarer prohibits something that the user demands. Other combinations make logical sense; D1 and U3 reflect a polite interchange that results in the user knowing about E with the permission of the declarer. Problem E-17 asks you to analyze the combinations that have a consistent interpretation.

By combining renaming, exportation, and importation, a programmer can create an arbitrarily complex naming environment within each translation unit. These translation units can be combined to form the complete program.

Naming Objects Not in the Translation Unit. Two types of objects that are not created in a translation unit may nevertheless become visible within the unit: files and objects declared externally (in another translation unit, that is). One needs conventions such that the programmer can specify these objects and, where necessary, can specify their types.

Because the program accessing any object must be aware of that object's type, any externally declared object that is to be accessed in the translation unit must appear in a declaration, along with some indication that this particular declaration refers to an ED object. In C++, the reserved word **"extern"** preceding a declaration states that the definition of the entity is to be found in another module that will be linked together to form the program.

The second class of objects not within the naming nest includes files in the file system. Interpretation rules for file names are determined by the operating system design. File systems are organized as tree structures. The leaf nodes of this structure are files and the internal nodes are directories and subdirectories.

The tree structure is based on the relation "directory A is on the list of objects in directory B." When this relation holds, directory B is the parent of directory A. In most languages and systems, objects within external files cannot be individually named within procedures that access the file (unless the files are all within the programmer's name space, as in Multics or the AS/400 system). In most systems, in order to access an object internal to an external file, the object must be copied between the file and a locally visible object, which may require copying the entire file to an object.

Naming Procedure Parameters. A procedure parameter may convey a simple value or it may convey a name from one portion of the name space to another. The relationship between naming considerations and the interpretation of procedure parameters has an important influence on some system designs.

A *formal parameter* describes a parameter from within the procedure's body; it is named in the procedure's header. There is an object internal to the procedure corresponding to each formal parameter. The parameter-passing options define the interpretation of the contents of this local object during the procedure's execution, and thus how it can be used. When a procedure is invoked, both the procedure's name and the list of *actual parameter* values are specified. Usually, the order in which the actual parameters are given is the same as the order in which they will be associated with the formal parameters. In addition to the ordering, we have to define how the bits within each actual parameter are going to be interpreted within the procedure's body. Three options are listed in Table E-3.

TABLE E-3   PROCEDURE PARAMETER INTERPRETATION OPTIONS

Method of Parameter Interpretation	Conventional Name for the Option
Value	Passed by value
Address	Passed by reference
Addressing algorithm	Passed by name

The programmer does not have explicit control over the interpretation option associated with each passed parameter because implicit (usage-dependent) parameter interpretations are defined by the programming language. For example, in C, every actual parameter (that is not an array) is passed by copying its value and an expression is also passed as a value. This rule defines the correct semantics of the procedure parameter, but an optimizing compiler might choose another implementation to enhance speed, provided that the correct semantics are obeyed.

In strongly typed languages, such as Ada and C++, the act of value passing may include a conversion from the type of the actual parameter to the type of the formal parameter, if the two types were different and there are defined semantics for the type conversion (these may be implicit from the numeric interpretation of certain types, but in C++ and Ada type conversion algorithms can be specified as type-specific functions).[15]

How is a parameter that is not passed by value to be interpreted? Here programming languages differ; the parameter could be interpreted as an address or as the specification of an algorithm that should be executed to compute the address. If the actual parameter is the symbolic name of a simple object, there is no semantic difference between the two options. After all, either interpretation results in access to the named object. However, if the actual parameter contains a variable part that selects a component from a compound object, that variable part could be evaluated either before calling the procedure or during the procedure's execution. Consider passing the name of the array element x[i]. In most languages, the parameter interpretation rule states that the calling program should convert the actual parameter to the address of the array element and pass that address as the actual parameter (this is called *call-by-reference*). But it is also possible to interpret x[i] as an addressing algorithm to be evaluated whenever the procedure attempts to access the object (this is called *call-by-name*). In this case, the calling program passes an algorithm that constructs the address of the memory location containing the actual parameter. The value of i would be read and interpreted *within the called procedure* as a component selector whenever the called procedure p tried to access its formal parameter.[16] The functional effect would be the same as if the parameter had been passed by reference if the value of i had not been changed during the execution of p. However, if the value of i had been changed during p's execution, there is a significant difference between call-by-reference and call-by-name.

Example E-16

Here is a program using ALGOL call-by-name, expressed in syntax like that used in Ada:

```
procedure f( a, b : integer ) is
    c, d : integer;
    type ar10int is array( 1..10 ) of integer;
    e : ar10int;
    procedure g( x, y : integer ) is
        //the parameters are passed by name because there is no specification to
```

---

[15]   If the type conversion algorithm is not specified, the program is in error (this error can be detected before program execution).

[16]   This rule arises from taking the position that the semantics of calling a function should be identical to the semantics of a program in which the function's body replaces its calling statement, with the formal parameters replaced by their actual counterparts.

```
            //the contrary. This is an ALGOL convention that does not apply to other
            //programming languages.
        begin
                c := 4;
                x := 3;              //usage of x

                ..

        end g;
    begin

            ..

        c := 2;
        g( 4, d );  //call-by-value - usage is illegal  - cannot assign to a constant
        g( c, d );  //call-by-name - usage is c := 3;
        g( e( 3 ), d );    //call-by-name - usage is e( 3 ) := 3;
        g( e( c ), d );    //call-by-name - usage is e( 4 ) := 3;
    end f;
```

If the last call of g were a call-by-reference, the assignment to x would assign a value to e(2), because the value of c was 2 when g was called. On the other hand, if the call were a call-by-name, the assignment would be made to e(4), because c has the value 4 when the assignment to x is performed. Some simpler situations are depicted in previous lines of the program.

Ada's parameter interpretation rules have a different basis. In Ada, the interpretations of a formal parameter are controlled by the presence or absence of the reserved words **in** and **out** associated with the formal parameter in the procedure specification. Rather than specifying parameter interpretations in terms of name resolution rules, the language semantics describe value-copying operations that implement the parameter semantics. The reserved word **in** signifies that the actual value of the parameter shall be copied to the formal parameter when the procedure is called. The reserved word **out** signifies that the actual value of the formal parameter on completion of the procedure will be copied to the location named as the actual parameter. If the actual parameter was an expression and the formal parameter's mode included **out**, the program is erroneous. Furthermore, it is an error for a function to have any parameter with the **out** attribute.[17] A literal interpretation of these rules would impose a large overhead if the parameter were a vector or an array that needed to be copied. The Ada designers realized this fact and left the implementation of these cases at the discretion of the implementer. The wording from the Ada standard is: "For a parameter whose type is an array, . . . , an implementation may likewise achieve the above effects by copy, ... Alternatively, an implementation may achieve these effects by reference, ... The execution of a program is erroneous if its effect depends on which mechanism is selected . . . ."[18] A similar situation applies to C++ parameters that are actually pointers to arrays; these are not passed by value, but

---

[17]   This rule reduces the opportunity to create side effects—unexpected value modifications, thereby enhancing program correctness and understandability.
[18]   See Problem E-9.

rather each one is passed as a pointer to the first element in the corresponding array; this choice avoids the overhead of array copying when passing an array as a parameter.

Under the Ada rules, a scalar object that is an **in** parameter behaves like a call-by-value. However, the **out** semantics do not match either call-by-name or call-by-reference; one significant difference is that in an Ada program, the value of an **out** object seen from the calling context will not be changed unless the procedure successfully exits. The net result is that in an Ada program each module either performs its complete function or else its visible effect on the rest of the program is limited to control flow changes.[19] By contrast, an ALGOL parameter passed by name will be modified in the calling context whenever the procedure writes to the address in the formal parameter.

In Section 3.6 we see how these naming issues influence processor design.

E.2.4 Connecting Modules to Form Programs

A *program address space* is created when a set of program modules is combined to form a complete program. The linker finds declarations that correspond to the names of ED objects; to complete the process, the linker may have to add a module to the program, thus expanding the address space. The program address space encompasses the complete context for name resolution during program execution.[20] Actually, the act of linking translation units to form the complete program can be performed before or during program execution.

The process that finds the declaration corresponding to an ED name is called "resolving" the ED name. Each unresolved ED name must be matched with an EV definition. The matching process scans the lists of EV names associated with files in a list given by the user. This list of file names constitutes the search path, which is specified as a parameter of the link or run command.[21] The system's structure is not affected by the choice of rules for specifying the search path, but it can be affected by the need for linking.

To define the object denoted by a reference to an external object E, the linker must find the externally visible definition of the corresponding object. Usually, the corresponding object was declared to have the same name (E) and to have the same type.[22] Two data structures per module are required to perform

---

[19] This difference is important for a procedure that uses exceptions for abnormal exit (see Section 4.2.1) and for reasoning about program properties; it isolates the problem of determining the procedure's correctness from the problem of determining the effects that errors in the procedure may inflict on its caller.

[20] Although this statement may make it seem as though name resolution must be performed during program execution, this is not the situation in most languages.

[21] The choice of link versus run depends on the timing of the linking process.

[22] Type matching is required in a strongly typed language, but may not be part of the check in other situations.

the linking process: a list of all ED names used in the module and a list of all EV names defined in the module. If we wish to enforce strong typing, each entry on the EV list must specify both the declared name and the declared type.[23] We learn more about these lists in Section 3.5.2.

It should be obvious how the name-matching process can be generalized to require type matching and thereby to enforce strong typing. Notice that when overloading is used, the same procedure name can have several interpretations depending on the types of the actual parameters passed to the procedure.

When is linking performed? Two quite different scenarios are possible. In the first, all linking is performed *before* the program is started; the sequence following this scenario is called *static linking*. In the second scenario, program execution can begin before all linking has been completed, and the linker is invoked if an unlinked reference is encountered during execution. A system following this scenario uses *dynamic linking*. A low-level mechanism is required to detect unlinked references during program execution.

E.2.5 Summary

Numerous naming conventions are used in high-level programming languages. Some of these conventions, such as static nested naming, suggest certain implementation structures that can be supported at lower levels of the system. Other semantic choices, such as the provision of dynamic linking, require support from lower levels of the system. A designer can choose processor addressing modes so they support easy access through linked references to ED objects. In addition, the designer has the option to support context-dependent address interpretation at the processor level; this selection may be used to shorten processor programs. We explore these issues and options in the next section and in Chapter 3.

E.3 PROCESSOR-LEVEL NAMES

Processor-level names are found in assembly-language programs, in data and programs produced by language translators, and in algorithms produced by either compilers or high-level-language programmers. The detailed nature of these names and algorithms depends heavily on the processor's innate addressing mechanisms. Early computers had only simple addressing options; the conventional (CISC) architectures of the 1960s through the 1980s provided many complex addressing modes to support high-level-language semantics and easy access to components within certain data structures; now, to increase instruction execution rates, RISC architectures provide only simple addressing modes. Here we

---

[23] The type specification associated with a C++ procedure includes the types of the parameters, but not the type of any returned result.

emphasize complex addressing mode designs to illustrate how they meet needs derived from high-level-language semantics. We review some conventional (CISC) addressing mechanisms (used in the MC68020) in Appendix C; here we introduce other design options that support processor-level names closely related to the names and naming structures used in high-level programming languages.

After we present several optional interpretations of "one-dimensional" (single-integer) addresses, we turn to "two-dimensional addressing." We cover designs that support efficient naming for block-structured languages, and that support the implementation of systems constructed from sets of cooperating but separated modules.

In this section, you will learn about the addressing modes and address interpretation mechanisms used in diverse processor architectures. You will see the connection between the designs at this level and those at higher levels. Then you will be prepared for our implementation option discussion.

E.3.1 One-Dimensional Processor Addressing

Our elaboration of processor-level address construction modes starts from basic addressing modes that format an address as a single integer. An address resulting from a processor-level name mapping is called an "effective virtual address." It is "effective" because it is an actual address used during object access. It is, at the same time, "virtual," because further translations under control of the operating system (discussed in Section 3.7) may be used to map a virtual address into a physical address that can be handled directly by the logic within the memory system.

The processor computes an effective memory address (denoted in this text by "EA") by executing a sequence of instructions or by using a built-in addressing mode. Some key questions concerning the selection of addressing modes are the following:

1. Must the program be modified to access an object?
2. How quickly can a data structure component be accessed?
3. How easily can a programming error be detected?
4. How quickly can a procedure parameter be accessed?
5. How much address computation hardware must be provided?
6. How many different objects can be accessed?
7. How does the address computation delay affect the processor's speed?

Designers of RISC machines typically place great weight on the last question. Thus, they provide only a single quite simple addressing mode whose address computation can be performed efficiently and can be overlapped with other activities.

Program Modification.   Because every instruction is a bit pattern and can be manipulated as a numeric quantity, a program can compute any bit pattern and attempt to execute it as an instruction. Thus, the program could attempt to access any memory location in this manner. The use of instruction modification to modify operand addresses within a program loop was first suggested by von Neumann. Although this observation was important at the time (because other addressing modes had not been devised yet), it is undesirable to modify instructions to compute object addresses because of the following:

1. The program will be difficult to read.
2. The program will not be reentrant.
3. There is no protection against an access beyond the bounds of a data structure.
4. The instruction manipulations themselves take many instructions and can be slow.
5. If the processor has separate instruction and data caches, additional instructions and/or mechanisms will be required to guarantee functional behavior.

For these reasons, one uses other ways to modify addresses during program execution. Addressing modes in contemporary designs use register contents.

Processor Addressing Modes.   Because it is unwise to manipulate instructions as data, the processor must be designed to support other types of address computations. This requirement leads to the introduction of *indexing* and *indirection*. Indexed addressing was first introduced in the English Manchester MADM computer [WILK56].[24] In a functional sense, either indexing or indirection alone is adequate to provide general accessing to memory. However, providing only one of these addressing modes may not give the most efficient program execution. Contemporary CISC processors support many varied addressing modes that correspond closely to address computation algorithms used to access constituents of composite data objects. The Alpha and RISC designs provide only simple indexed or base-displacement addressing, preferring fast individual instructions over reducing the number of instructions needed for address computations.

If the processor supports more than one address determination method, each address specification must include information regarding the means by which the effective virtual address (EVA) will be determined.

Definition. An *addressing mode specification* (usually contained within an instruction) determines how the processor should use instruction

---

[24]   Index registers were called "B-tubes" in this system; later English designs called index registers "B-lines."

bits and other information to compute an effective address for a memory access.

Seven basic operations are used in effective address computations:

1. Select (a value from a register or a program element)
2. Base (add another value)
3. Scale (shift a value to multiply it by an operand width)
4. Index (add a scaled integer)
5. Indirect (read a value from a memory location specified by an address)
6. Increment (add a constant to) a register or memory location
7. Decrement (subtract a constant from) a register or memory location

It is important to distinguish indexed addressing from base-displacement addressing, because the two have different architectural implications, even though both of them perform an addition of a constant C from the instruction's address specification with the contents of a selected processor register X. The difference lies in the relative sizes of the two addends—in base-displacement addressing, the instruction contains a (small) displacement value to be added to the (base) value found within X.

The reader should be able to use the seven basic address computation operations to devise algorithms that implement the addressing modes of any contemporary CISC processor. RISC architectures provide only indexing, and some address scaling, such as in SPARC control transfer instructions and the scaled add instructions in the Alpha AXP.[25]

Because one-dimensional addressing is straightforward and easily understood, we emphasize two-dimensional addressing and its architectural possibilities and implications.

E.3.2 Two-Dimensional Processor Addressing

Two-dimensional virtual addressing can support the implementation of a block-structured language, can ease the difficulty of combining separately compiled programs to form a single larger program, and can assist in providing program protection and data security. The basic distinction between one-dimensional and two-dimensional addressing lies in the effective address computation. If arithmetic performed during address computations can affect all address bits, the addressing scheme is one-dimensional. If the carry chain is broken between two bit positions, this break defines the separation between the segment number and the index portion of the two-dimensional address.[26]

---

[25]   These four instructions shift the first operand (always from a register) two (three) places to the left before performing the longword (quadword) addition.

[26]   This terminology does not agree with all writers or manufacturers; we choose these definitions so that there is a functional difference between segmented (two-dimensional) addresses and conventional (one-dimensional) addressing.

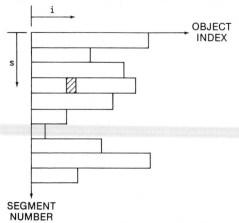

a) The two-dimensional space view

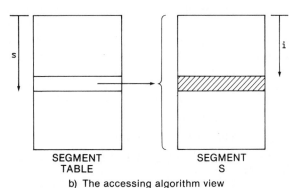

b) The accessing algorithm view

Figure E-3 Two views of two-dimensional addressing under segmentation. [The address is (s, i).]

The segmented address of a simple object contains two integers : a segment number s and an index i, measured relative to the segment's origin. We denote the segmented address by (s, i).

Definition. A *segmented address* contains two integer components that are independently specified and computed.

According to this definition, a segmented address is not the same as a one-dimensional address, because the act of indexing cannot change the segment number in a segmented address. Figure E-3 illustrates the structure of the segmented address space; the shaded element in Figure E-3a is selected by the address (s, i). Figure E-3b illustrates the process of accessing an object within a segment.

In this section, we explore the use of two-dimensional addressing for naming objects declared in statically nested environments and for combining translation units to form programs. The use of two-dimensional addresses to support security and protection is described in Chapter 9.

Statically Nested Naming. The first processor-level implementation of two-dimensional addressing appeared in the Burroughs B 5000 processor [BURR61]. A run-time allocation and addressing scheme had been suggested by Randell and Russell [RAND64] for a soft implementation of ALGOL60 name nesting semantics; this scheme formed the basis for the addressing design used in subsequent large Burroughs systems (B 5700, B 6700, etc.) [BURR69]. We review the Randell and Russell design and then turn to the processor-level details. Remember that this design implements correct semantics in a virtual machine; if it is not easily supported by the processor's address specification options, the compiler will have the responsibility to insert processor instructions that maintain data structures and address computations analogous to those developed in these designs.

Randell and Russell realized that within any single nested program block, unique object names could be created by specifying two independent items:

1. The block in which the referenced object was declared
2. The position of that object among those allocated in the same block

Furthermore, Randell and Russell noted that the static nesting rules imply that only one block is visible at each nesting level from any particular usage context C_U. Thus, from C_U, each visible block is uniquely identified by its level in the static nest. Therefore, the name N of a visible object can be mapped into a two-dimensional address of the form (level_number, index), where index identifies the entity N within the set of objects declared at its level.

In the B 5700 system, the levels are numbered (in user programs) in increasing order starting with 2 at the outermost program block (levels 0 and 1 are used to name system-level and user global objects). Objects within each block are numbered in order of appearance, starting with 2 for the first parameter or local object (if there are no parameters). The second 2 arises from the need to store control information at the first two locations within the block.

Example E-17

We use the following skeleton of a Pascal program (that shows all procedure and object declarations) to illustrate the B 5700 naming conventions. We will suppose that procedure parameters are assigned to the first locations within each block of objects. The B 5700 addresses of the items declared in this program are listed in Table E-4. Every visible name, including procedure names, is assigned an address.

```
procedure main is
a, b : integer;
     procedure g( x, y : integer ) is
     c, d : integer;
          procedure h( u, v : integer ) is
                e, f : integer;
          begin
               ..
          end h;
     begin
          ..
     end g;
     procedure k( r : integer ) is
          u, v : integer;
     begin
          ..
     end k;
begin
     ..
end main;
```

TABLE E-4   TWO-DIMENSIONAL NAMES FOR
THE OBJECTS DECLARED IN EXAMPLE E-17

Object	Address
main.a	(2,2)
main.b	(2,3)
main.g	(2,4)
main.k	(2,5)
g.x	(3,2)
g.y	(3,3)
g.c	(3,4)
g.d	(3,5)
g.h	(3,6)
h.u	(4,2)
h.v	(4,3)
h.e	(4,4)
h.f	(4,5)
k.r	(3,2)
k.u	(3,3)
k.v	(3,4)

TABLE E-5   OBJECTS CORRESPONDING TO CERTAIN NAMES
IN BLOCKS H AND K FOR THE PROGRAM IN EXAMPLE E-17

Address	Object Denoted by Address from	
	Block h	Block k
(2,2)	main.a	main.a
(2,3)	main.b	main.b
(2,4)	main.g	main.g
(2,5)	main.k	main.k
(3,2)	g.x	k.r
(3,3)	g.y	k.u
(3,4)	g.c	k.v
(3,5)	g.d	illegal
(3,6)	g.h	illegal
(4,2)	h.u	illegal
(4,3)	h.v	illegal
(4,4)	h.e	illegal
(4,5)	h.f	illegal

Note that the same address describes different objects; for example, (3, 3) names both g.y and k.u. However, under the static nesting rule, these two objects are never simultaneously visible. Thus the fact that their names have the same representation does not introduce ambiguity. This can be seen clearly by examining the sets of objects visible from the using contexts k and h (see Table E-5).

This use of two-dimensional addressing for the implementation of a statically nested language shows that high-level semantics can be reflected in a processor-level design. The address bit savings made possible by this technique are discussed in Section E.5. Note that this encoding technique produces context-dependent addresses; this fact imposes further requirements on the processor-level design, as we shall see in the following section.

Combining Translation Units. It is a simple matter to combine a number of separate translation units to form a program if the addressing within each translation unit is one-dimensional, and the processor's addressing is two-dimensional. All that is required is to assign a segment for each translation unit. This merging process can be used to combine separately translated modules.

Moving Addresses and Objects between Contexts. No difficulty arises from moving address A from context C_1 to context C_2 if A has the same

interpretation in both contexts. However, difficulties can arise if A's interpretation is context-dependent, so if the interpretation of the address is context-
dependent, the address itself will have to be changed as it is moved to a new
context. Where might this problem arise? How can we fix addresses as they are
moved? These issues are not just academic issues; among several important
situations in which a name may be moved between two contexts, we find the
following:

1. Locator sharing
2. Parameter passing
3. Result returning

Locator sharing naming problems may arise if an access object is declared at
nesting level L_1 and then is assigned an address from a nesting level $L_2 > L_1$. This
pattern is illustrated in the following example.

Example E-18

To illustrate the problems of passing context-dependent pointer representations
around in a program, we need both static nesting and pointer variables. Thus, we
use Ada; the following program[27] illustrates the naming problems arising from
passing a context-dependent address between two contexts.

```
procedure b is           --This overall program is not legal Ada!
    type accinteger is access integer;   --Define a pointer type
    d : accinteger;                      --Declare a pointer object
    procedure c is
        e : accinteger;
        ..
    begin
        e := new integer;     --create new integer and get a pointer to it
        ..
        d := e;
    end c;
    procedure s is
    begin
        d.all := 4;       --The reference in question; the ".all" part designates
        ..                --the object to which d points
    end s;
    begin
        ..    --Body of b
    end b;
```

Suppose that the new object (to which e points) is located in the block associated with the call to c, which executes at level 3 in the program. Suppose,

---

[27] Although this program appears to make sense, in fact it is not a legal Ada program; the illegality is
a consequence of certain Ada allocation rules that have an indirect connection with the naming issues
we are discussing here.

therefore, that the address of the allocated object is (3, 5). When the assignment "d := e;" is executed, the address (3, 5) is placed in location d. Then suppose that s is called, and proceeds to make the assignment of "4" to the location whose address is in d. The address within d is still (3, 5), but now the program is executing in s, where level 3 corresponds to space within s. So the assignment will be made to location 5 within s's space. We have a problem, because this action is not what was intended.

Parameter passing naming problems may arise if an access variable is passed as a procedure parameter. As with sharing, the problem occurs if the parameter value contains an address that moves upward in the naming nest and contains an address with a higher level number. To illustrate this situation, modify the program in the previous example so that s is called from c, with e as an actual parameter. Then when s is called, the contents of e, which have a context-dependent interpretation, are moved into s's context, where they are subject to a different (context-dependent) interpretation.

Result returning naming problems may arise if a locator value is passed from a subroutine to a calling module. This action may occur when a parameter is called by name or reference, when a procedure parameter has Ada's **out** attribute or when the function returns a locator result.

So in a system using context-dependent addresses, one has to modify an address before sending it into an unknown context. In Section D.1.5, we present the B 5700 processor's name representation and its instruction that fixes context-dependent addresses to remove their context dependency.

E.3.3 Systems with Tagged Objects

The code in a *tag* associated with an object can describe important attributes of the associated object. For example, the codes shown in Table E-6 distinguish instructions from integers from floats. For addressing and naming purposes, it helps to distinguish objects with contents relevant to address computations from objects that play no part in address computations. Further distinctions may specify each object's possible role in address computations. We will see that introducing tagging into a design may remove some responsibility from the translator or

TABLE E-6   TAG VALUES TO
DISTINGUISH PROGRAMS FROM DATA

Code	Meaning
0	Instruction
1	Integer
2	Float
3	Pointer

the executable program, because the run-time mechanism that interprets tag values and handles address computations can automatically initiate the necessary actions.

One essential constraint underlies all tagging schemes:

> **Tagging Constraint.** Neither the system nor a programmer may tamper with the association between a tag value and the object it describes.

Without this constraint, a program could substitute an arbitrary tag value for a correct tag, which could change the interpretation of the associated object, and thereby sidestep all implied interpretations, usage constraints, or protection mechanisms.

In this section we explore ways that tagging can be used to simplify address specifications, such as indirection, call-by-name parameter passing, and indexing. In addition, capabilities, which must be tagged to protect themselves against unauthorized modification, can describe memory objects and memory spaces within secure systems.

Tag-Based Indirection. To assist with indirection, we mark each pointer object with a specific tag value.[28] In addition, we design the system so that it knows, for each operand of each instruction, whether the operand must be a value or could be a pointer. For example, an integer multiply operation should not have a pointer as an operand. So if an MPY operand is being accessed and a pointer object is encountered, the processor can determine that the type of the accessed object is incompatible with the operation. If the operand is a pointer, rather than data, the processor uses the object as an indirect address.[29]

One advantage of tag-directed indirection is that a system could be designed so that a called procedure does not have to know whether a parameter was passed by value, name, or reference. To make this possible, the tag-based distinctions must mark addresses and data[30] differently. Then if the procedure wishes to read a parameter's value, it simply performs a memory READ to obtain the value.[31] If the actual parameter had been passed by reference, the READ of the actual parameter's contents will return a tag indicating an indirect address; the processor, upon seeing this tag value, will initiate an indirection, and the

---

[28]   This design does not support strong typing, but it could be enhanced to provide such support (see Problem E-18).

[29]   Note that it is possible to construct a loop of tagged indirect words; a counter or a timer could be used to terminate such a loop. For example, the B 5700 uses a timer that causes an interrupt if a new instruction has not been started within the allotted time interval.

[30]   Here the word "data" does not encompass address objects, even though the value of an address is often considered as data, because it certainly is not an instruction.

[31]   For the following to work correctly, the processor instructions must distinguish whether they desire a value or will accept an object of any type.

proper parameter value will be provided to the processor. On the other hand, if the first READ returns a tag indicating a value (which would occur if the actual parameter had been passed by value), that value is provided.

This tag-based indirection scheme can be extended to assist accessing parameters passed by name. In ALGOL, the semantics of call-by-name require that the value of the subscripts in the parameter's specification be reinterpreted on every access to the parameter from within the called procedure. The addressing design problem is to choose a representation for the parameters of the call-by-name and a way to distinguish the call-by-name from direct and indirect accesses to data values.

One design option assigns special tag values to identify call-by-name parameters. One possible design uses two parameters to represent a single call-by-name parameter: (1) a pointer to the data structure's origin, and (2) a pointer to the object holding the current value of the index quantity. There are two problems with this scheme, which does work well for a one-dimensional vector component passed by name. First, it does not generalize easily to multidimensional arrays, because its (implicit) fixed format limits the number of parameters that can be specified. Second, the indexing granularity is not specified in the parameters.

Another design option uses tagging to mark a pointer to a procedure entry point. A procedure designated and used in this manner must have no parameters (why?) and must return the address of the desired object (defined by the actual call-by-name parameter) as its (single) result. When the processor encounters the tag indicating an entry point pointer while seeking a data object, it simply calls the procedure and uses the (tagged) result as an indirect address. The address interpretation process starts anew. In principle, the procedure could return another indirect object specifier, such as a pointer to another object or to a procedure entry point (see Problem E-15).

Example E-19

We use Ada syntax to emphasize that the following semantics do not apply to C++ programs (not all of the semantics apply to Ada, either!).

```
type ai is access integer;        --Declare a pointer type
procedure g( d : ai ) is          --d is passed by name
    e : integer;                  --the call-by-name is not legal within Ada
begin
    e := d + 6;                   --need to evaluate d here
    ..
end g;
```

Consider the use object tagging in the processor executing this program. Now we impose various parameter passing disciplines on the program. First, consider a *call-by-reference discipline*. In this case, the actual parameter passed can be a tagged pointer indicating the location holding the value to be used. Suppose that procedure g were called from this program:

```
procedure h is
    k : array ( 1..10 ) of integer;
    m : integer;
    ..
begin
    ..
    m = 4;
    g( k( m ) );
    ..
end h;
```

The actual parameter passed will be a tagged pointer to the object k(4). When the addition inside g is performed, the processor knows that it is looking for a value; when it reads the parameter, it finds the tagged pointer and performs the indirection to find the value.

Now consider the *call-by-name discipline*. In this case, the passed entity is not a pointer to the array k, but rather a tagged pointer to the entry point of a procedure to compute a pointer to k(m). When the processor reads the parameter and finds a tagged entry point descriptor, it calls the procedure and uses its result as an operand. Because the returned result will be tagged as a pointer, the processor will initiate indirection to find the correct value.

How would one specify the semantics of address evaluation with this tagging scheme? Consider an access that is trying to read a numeric value. Let the function value(x) be the one that returns the desired numeric value. Then when the processor expects a numeric operand it calls value(x), with x the address from the instruction. The body of value(x) can be expressed recursively as

```
void *value( void *x ) {
    if ( x.tag == numeric_tag ) return x;
    else if ( x.tag == indirect_tag ) return value( x.value );
        else if ( x.tag == entry_tag ) return( value( call( x.value ) ) );
}
```

There is a problem with typing the parameter and the result here; we made them pointers to **void** to make it clear that the parameter and the result are not strongly typed (any value type can be passed in or returned). This approach applied in this program does not produce legal C++.

It may appear at first glance that indirection using tagged objects is the same as indirection without tags, but there is a subtle, yet important difference. A conventional processor design with an indirect addressing mode uses indirection bits in instructions (or in their addressing mode specifications), with the result that each instruction unequivocally specifies the interpretation of each item it might access. With tagging, on the other hand, the accessed item is self-describing and the instruction does not have to anticipate the type of object that will be found at the operand location. This difference is significant when the operand is a procedure parameter. If the language were ALGOL, a parameter could be either passed by name or by value, and the compiler of the called procedure cannot tell which case applies. In fact, any call of the procedure could be either of these cases! There are several approaches to solving this dilemma, which we discuss more fully in Chapter 3. We have seen one approach that uses tagging to distinguish pointers, numeric quantities, entry points, and other addressing specifications from each other. Because the processor can examine the tag to determine which case applies during execution of the procedure, all cases of parameter passing options can be handled easily with a single version of the called procedure that does not need any extra parameters to indicate which case applies.

Tag-Based Indexing.   Several different tagging designs can support indexing. We discuss two options:

1. Generalizing indirection to permit indexing
2. Tagging indexed and unindexed descriptors differently.

The *first option* is similar to the tag-based indirection scheme discussed above. There the indirect word was interpreted as an origin; here the tagged indirect word contains both an index specification and a base value to be added together. When the tagged word is accessed during an attempt to access a value, the indexing is performed and the resulting effective address is used to find the object.

Under the *second option*, the tagged object may contain either the descriptor of a compound object or a pointer to a component of a compound object. The tag (or a flag in the value) indicates which format applies. The descriptor of a compound object contains the origin of the object and the limiting index value. Alternatively, the tagged object may contain the location of a component within the compound object. By performing a processor instruction to index the descriptor, the descriptor of the compound object can be changed to a descriptor of one of its components. A component's location could be represented by the origin of the compound object, together with a separate index value, or by a single value pointing directly to the component's location.

Example E-20

The Burroughs B 5700 processors support descriptors of both compound objects and their components; they distinguish the descriptor of a compound object from a descriptor of a component using a flag bit contained within the descriptor. An indexed address contains both the origin of the compound object and the index of the component. There is a processor instruction (index_descriptor) that indexes a descriptor of a compound object. While executing this instruction, the processor

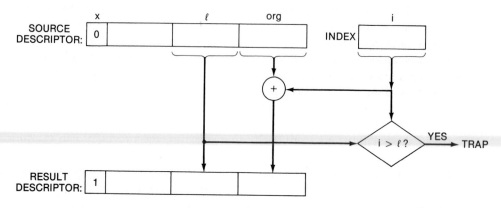

Figure E-4   Descriptor indexing in the B 5700

checks the index value against the limit in the descriptor, replaces the limit with the index quantity, and sets the indexed bit within the descriptor; all of this is conditional on the index value being within the range limit specified in the initial descriptor. The indexing operation is depicted in Figure E-4.

Capability Addressing.   A capability is a tagged object that contains a description of a compound object along with a field specifying access rights. The access rights information specifies the types of memory accesses[32] that the possessor of the capability is permitted to make to the object described by the capability. If the capability is to effectively limit access to the object it describes, it must be protected against unauthorized modification. One method for protecting a capability from modification is to mark each one with a special tag value and then restrict the operations that can be performed on (tagged) capabilities. This design uses tags not to specify automatic indexing or indirection during accessing, but to restrict processing that could modify the capability's contents in an undesirable manner. We study capabilities in detail in Chapter 9, where we discuss their roles in support of multiprocessing and system security.

E.3.4 Instructions that Support Processor Addressing

A fourth processor design option related to object addressing includes processor instructions that compute an object's address without actually accessing the object. This supports parameters passed by reference and the "address_of" operation ("&" in C++). Other processor instructions that support object addressing include those in RISC machines that are designed for loading large constants (that might be interpreted as addresses) into processor registers.

---

[32]   The types of access might include READ, WRITE, and EXECUTE (read for interpretation as an instruction).

Many non-RISC machines have "load effective address" (LEA) instructions to support call-by-reference. By executing an LEA instruction, the program can determine the address of an object and pass it as a call-by-reference parameter. Other instructions related to addressing perform useful index arithmetic.

We look at some examples of these instructions. First consider determining an effective address.

Example E-21

The MC680x0 [MOTO84] instruction LEA (load effective address) places the effective address[33] in a designated address register.

The processor can support address computations with an instruction that performs useful address computations. One such computation finds the address of an element within a multidimensional array:

Example E-22

The VAX11/750 [DIGI77] has three address-related instructions. Two—push address and move address—use a regular addressing mode to compute an address that is either copied into a specified destination or pushed onto the stack. INDEX, the third address instruction, performs the computation

outindex = (inindex + insubscript) * object_size

which is useful in translating a subscript vector into a component address. All of the parameters on the right side of the assignment are instruction operands, as are both the lower and upper limits on the subscript value. A violation of these range constraints produces a processor trap. Multidimensional subscripts can be handled by repeated use of the INDEX instruction.

Example E-23

The IBM System/38 [IBM80] instruction CAI (compute array index) performs a multiply–add that reduces a two-dimensional subscript to a one-dimensional subscript. There is no limit checking. The instruction

CAI w, x, y, z

performs the following assignment:

$x = y + (z - 1)^* w$

Here w, x, y, and z are the names of memory locations. A sequence of these instructions can reduce any multidimensional subscript to a simple index value.

If the processor addressing modes use only addition to generate effective addresses, specific instructions that save effective addresses do not help, because the subscripting (without scaling) can be achieved by integer addition.

---

[33]   This address can be determined by any mode that both produces an address and does not increment or decrement the address register used in the effective address calculation. Addressing modes that violate these conditions are illegal with an LEA instruction.

Example E-24

The PowerPC architecture includes load and store instructions that not only compute their addresses by adding the contents of an (integer) instruction field to the contents of a register, but also replace that register's contents with the effective address that was used. The saving assists sequencing through a regular data structure, such as a vector or a matrix, without requiring additional instructions to compute the next element's location. Notice that the implementation of this option requires only an extra register store, which can be fit into the clock interval when memory is being accessed to perform the READ or WRITE that is also required.

E.3.5 Summary of Processor-Level Addressing

We started with the basic notion that an instruction could be treated like an integer and therefore could be manipulated so that its address specification would directly specify any desired operand. Thus, the basic ability to access any object can be easily attained (in a logical sense), but at a great loss in program understandability and execution speed. So processor designers insert features to assist object addressing. Conventional CISC designs support various modes of address computation that can be chosen for use with many instructions. In contrast, RISC designs reduce all address computations to a single addition of the contents of two registers or of a register and a constant taken from an instruction field.

Two-dimensional addressing can be used in several ways to support language semantics. Context-dependent addresses can be formed to name all entities visible within a statically nested program structure; this technique can reduce size of each address specification (see Section E.4.1). If a set of translation units that have been translated separately into one-dimensional address spaces now need to be linked together to form a complete program, the second dimension can be used to identify the translation unit, simplifying the linking process. But a problem may arise while passing a context-dependent address among contexts; we left its solution open for the moment.

We showed a tagging option that permits a subroutine to be specified and translated independently of the actual form of each parameter passed to it; tags can be used in other ways, such as marking capabilities that support system security (see Chapter 9).

Finally, we have seen that the processor designer can provide instructions that compute addresses or address-related quantities, thereby speeding execution of programs that either pass parameters by reference or make irregular accesses to components of multidimensional arrays.

Now we turn to details of address formation and interpretation, showing how the designer can be clever and save program space. Other aspects of processor-level interactions with the system's memory are covered in Chapters 4 and 5.

E.4 ADDRESS REPRESENTATIONS AND SEMANTICS

Address encoding schemes can be designed to save bits in program representations and consequently reduce the memory bandwidth required to fetch instructions. Other encoding schemes can be designed to produce long addresses despite the length limitations imposed by instruction formats. It is important that the size of an effective memory address, an important processor design decision, be large enough that programs are not unduly constrained by address size limits. It has been observed [BELL76] that the choice of size of an effective address is one of the most important system design decisions, because the address size imposes an ultimate limit to system expansion. If a designer chooses to decrease the size of addresses within instructions, she has to provide a means for generating addresses larger than those that can be represented directly in an instruction.[34] With such an escape route, the address space limitation no longer logically confines the programmer, though constructing longer addresses may be cumbersome and consume processing cycles. However, note that any alternative means for address generation, which may include wide address registers or special registers for address generation, must be visible to the processor-level programmer, who may have the responsibility for controlling the contents and use of these special registers. Contemporary designers are moving toward 64-bit addresses, which would appear to be adequate for a long time into the future.

However an address may have been compressed, it must be expanded to form a complete effective virtual address. How large should these addresses be? And how much memory space should each addressable object span? The answers to these questions define the system's address size and granularity.

In this section we will discuss these issues. You will learn several techniques for reducing the number of program bits consumed for operand addresses. You will see the relationship between address compression techniques and high-level-language structures. You will learn some consequences of each option in the programming domain. You will learn some issues related to address size and the granularity of memory addresses. Further implications of these choices at the hardware level are discussed in Chapter 3.

E.4.1 Address Compression

Because compressed addresses are shorter than uncompressed addresses, a program with compressed addresses will be shorter than one using uncompressed addresses, and will require fewer memory accesses to read its instructions. Therefore, if memory bandwidth is a performance bottleneck, address compression may ease that bottleneck. This form of compression to reduce the sizes of particular fields is not related to the type of compression that recodes the

---

[34]   In RISC designs, this problem is handled by using wide registers in all address computations.

information in a file to save memory space; the latter type of compression is not useful within instructions, because the control unit would be slowed significantly if it also had to decompress the program it was executing.

Compressing addresses within programs reduces bandwidth demands within the processor-memory address path. The processor passes a compressed (virtual) address to memory, where it is expanded into a full memory address. One "cost" of this change is that the address translation function must be moved from the processor complex to the memory subsystem. This technique is important only if the processor chip pin-bandwidth is a performance bottleneck.

We know that compressed addresses can be used to alleviate some performance bottlenecks. We will examine the following "reasonable" techniques for encoding addresses in programs:

1. Using context-dependent addressing
2. Using processor registers
3. Encoding to minimize useless bits

Context-dependent addressing was used in the Randell and Russell naming scheme for nested block structures discussed in Section E.3.2. In this scheme each address consists of a level number and an index. The level number field must be large enough to represent an integer corresponding to the depth of the program's nesting. And the index field must be large enough to represent the maximum number of objects that can be referenced at one level of the nest. Clever encoding can be used here (see Example E-25).

The designer can use *registers more and memory less* by providing addressing modes in which register contents are used to generate wide addresses, as in base-displacement addressing. An important variation on this technique relies on memory tables containing addresses; first, the program loads one register to point to the table; subsequent memory addresses can be loaded to registers by using offsets from the table origin register. Thus, the long addresses can be loaded using one instruction and one memory reference to get the address into a register; the second instruction uses the register's contents for the address and the next data memory reference accesses the desired object. Contrast this approach with that in which the long address is constructed from fragments that are constants from instruction fields, which requires several instructions to construct a single address in a register.

Another technique generates a wide address using a "field" register whose contents serve as the most significant address bits; see Figure E-5.

Several *clever encoding* approaches reduce the address field width. Three encoding options will be covered:

1. Field width depends on nest depth.
2. Field width depends on a static program property.
3. Field contents optimally encoded.

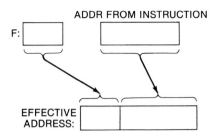

Figure E-5   Field register addressing

If the *field width* can depend on the program's nesting depth, at low levels, only a few bits are needed to represent the level number, and more bits can be allocated for object indices. At higher levels, more bits are required to represent the level number, but it can be argued that fewer bits are needed for the object index; the basic argument is that blocks deeper in the nest perform simpler algorithms and access fewer objects than blocks farther out in the nest.

Example E-25

In the B 5700 series machines, the executing procedure's level determines the bit assignments to level number and object index, as shown in Table E-7. Level numbers are reverse-encoded, with their least significant bits on the left end; this simplifies the logic because every address bit may be used in only one or two different ways. More details of this scheme are presented in Section D.1.5 and Problem D-2.

A simplified context-dependent addressing scheme might be considered—suppose that one dedicates a single bit to distinguish a local address from a global one. Under this scheme, any easily accessible object must be in either the local block or a single global block; this restriction comes from the processor-

TABLE E-7   ADDRESS FIELD SIZES IN B 5700 MACHINES

Level of Executing Procedure	Address Bit Allocation	
	For Level Number	For Object Index
0–1	1	13
2–3	2	12
4–7	3	11
8–15	4	10
16–31	5	9

level design and is not present in the language, so the software must circumvent this limitation.

Example E-26

The B 5000 processor address encoding[35] includes a single bit L to distinguish levels, along with an index field i. The value in L designates whether the index is to be used with respect to the outermost block or with respect to the (innermost) local block. We use the encoding $L = 1$ for a local block address.

To access an object that is not local and is not in the outermost block, the program must manipulate locators. This Pascal program skeleton illustrates the difficulty:

```
procedure main is
    b : integer;
    procedure f is
        c : integer;
        procedure g is
            d : integer;
        begin
            d = b;
            d = c;
        end g;
    begin
        ..
    end f;
begin
    ..
end main;
```

The source location in the first assignment statement is declared in the outermost block; it can be directly named as (0, 2). The destination is local, and is directly addressed as (1, 2). The source location for the second assignment statement (c) is neither local nor in the outermost block; it can be accessed only after manipulating some access variables.

The single bit L encoding saves address bits, but the example showed that it is difficult to reference global objects from within a nested block that is not at the outermost level. How could we modify the processor so that the limitation is circumvented but two-level addressing is preserved? One way is to allow the program to (dynamically) change the identity of the single nonlocal block that is accessible. The pointer to the visible nonlocal block would be in a processor register, so we just permit the program to load the register, which is therefore used like a base register when an effective address is computed. Problem E-13 covers these details.

A second way to reduce address bits is to *redefine field sizes based on a static program property*. Within a single naming context or program, we could count the

---

[35]   This was changed in the B 5700 and succeeding machines.

number of visible objects and assign just enough address bits to be able to specify any of those visible objects. Then the address width for each program module could be determined by the translator. The designer would add a new processor instruction to set the address field width; the translator would insert that instruction each time the naming context changes (see Problem E-21).

A third way to use encoding to save address bits is to choose *optimal encoding* for addresses.[36] All optimal encoding is based on usage statistics. Once the usage statistics are known, address encodings can be selected to reduce the average address length. Huffman coding [HUFF52] produces the minimum average length. The disadvantage of Huffman encoding is that every encoded value may have a different width. Thus, with this coding, the processor would have to determine dynamically the locations of both field boundaries within instructions and boundaries between instructions.

A fourth way to save address bits is to *use a fixed set of address lengths*. Each address contains a code specifying its actual width. By right-justifying the addresses and stuffing zeroes on the left end, a short address will be interpreted to designate an object located near the beginning of the address space. Or one could use sign extension of the short addresses to make the top of the address space accessible.[37] This technique makes a large address space available, but permits that use of short addresses for frequently referenced objects. In many situations, this technique can produce near-optimum space usage without too much decoding complexity.

E.4.2 Address Sizes

The selection of an address compression scheme may determine some address field lengths. Another important address size question concerns the size of a complete virtual address—the one obtained from the effective address computation. This size determines the maximum number of objects that can be visible to a program without resorting to the file system, because the size fixes the number of address bits. Bell and Strecker [BELL76] emphasize the importance of a correct choice: "There is only one mistake . . . in a computer design that is difficult to recover from—not providing enough address bits . . . ."

A designer must choose what shall be included in the virtual address space. An important, relevant question is: "How will the virtual address space be managed?" In the IBM System/38 [IBM81a], for example, all information within the system, including files on removable media, is included within a single virtual address space. Furthermore, virtual addresses are not reused by the

---

[36]   This is not the same as coding for file compression, frequently used to give the appearance of expanded space in secondary memory devices.

[37]   Sign extension is important for generating addresses of device controllers mapped into high memory addresses (to get them out of the way of other allocations, leaving a contiguous free space for the others).

memory allocator. Thus, the virtual space size determines not only how many objects can be accessed, but also how long the system can operate before running out of space. The timeout is inversely proportional to the rate at which space is acquired for objects. In the IBM System/38, 16 megabytes are allocated on each allocation request,[38] and each virtual address contains 48 bits. As a consequence, 2^{23} allocations can be made before the system runs out of virtual space. If a system does not include files in the same virtual address space as main memory, main memory virtual addresses can be much smaller, yet still provide a sufficient number of different addresses.

If virtual addresses are wide, it would be folly to provide enough bits in the address field within each instruction so that the address field in the instruction is as large as a complete virtual memory address. Therefore, the instruction's address field will be shorter than a complete virtual address, and, in order to be general, a scheme to obtain additional address bits must be devised. We discuss five options:

1. Use indirection.
2. Use the contents of a selected processor register.
3. Use an implied register.
4. Use a special register array that maps addresses.
5. Use segmentation.

The indirection option works if the size of an indirect address is larger than an instruction address field. Then indirection can reach any virtual address, making the scheme functionally general, independent of the address sizes in either instructions or address registers. One penalty of this scheme is the memory cycles required to fetch an indirect address whenever a wide address is needed.

The second option uses base-displacement addressing whenever a wide virtual address is needed. An argument analogous to the indirection argument concludes that this option is functionally general. Base-displacement addressing is used in the IBM 370 machines and in RISC machines. It is also used, in conjunction with memory tables of addresses, to quickly load a long address into a register prior to accessing the object by using the register.

Example E-27

Suppose that register R[2] is designated to hold the address of the table of long addresses. If the second entry in that table holds the address from which we wish to load a value into R[4], we can use the following instruction sequence, in which R[3] holds the address from which the value is to be loaded:

```
LOAD    R[3],(R[2] + 2)
LOAD    R[4], R[3]
```

---

[38] But note that an individual process can manage the space it obtained from a single system allocation so that the same space holds different sets of objects at different times. Thus, smart local management reduces the number of global space allocation requests.

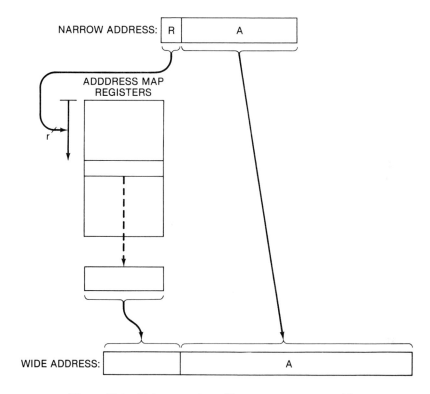

Figure E-6 Using a register file to map a narrow address into a wide address

The third option uses an extra register that holds the leftmost address bits of the wide addresses formed by the program. This option has been used to expand the addressing capabilities of older architectures, such as the DEC PDP-8 [DIGI70].

The fourth option for generating additional address bits generalizes the preceding; it includes a set of address registers in the processor. Suppose that there are 2^r such registers, so that r bits selects one of them. Now use the r most significant bits from each address to select a field register, and concatenate the contents of the selected register with the rest of the computed address. Figure E-6 illustrates this scheme, which is used in the SDS 940 to compute operand addresses [SDS66].

The fifth option relies on segmentation. A set of segment descriptors is organized in to a segment table, and then a segment number selects one descriptor, from which the origin (and length) of the segment can be extracted. The origin field can be formatted to include a wide address, and the segment lengths (and thus the offsets within the segment) can be much shorter than a complete memory address.

Notice that both the third and fourth options somewhat insulate the program's structure from the selection of the size of a complete virtual address.

E.4.3 Address Granularity

The final size issue concerns the size of each object referenced by a distinct address. The distance between two items with consecutive addresses is the machine's addressing granularity.

The designer selecting the address granularity trades the flexibility of small granularity against the additional address bits needed to specify an individual operand from a fixed amount of memory (measured in absolute units, such as bits, and not in flexible units, such as words). Most contemporary system designs address memory to the byte level. Others use words. The word width can be defined differently for different system families. Some system designs, such as the Intel iAPX 432, use bit granularity for program addressing.

It is important to note that the address granularity choice does not directly affect the size of an object accessed during one memory cycle. In Section 3.8.5, we show how the processor–memory interface can be supplemented to support different addressing granularities without changing the memory modules.

E.5 SUMMARY

In this appendix, we explored the formation and use of names in high-level languages and at the processor level. We discussed representation options for these names. We reviewed naming that can be used to access constituents parts of compound objects. We learned that a name can be interpreted either globally or within a limited context. Nested naming rules are important in this regard. Context-dependent naming and other techniques can be used to save instruction bits.

To complete our study of the design of a computer memory system, we turn to space allocation in the next appendix, and to accessing algorithms in Chapter 3.

E.6 TRENDS

Many naming issues are associated with mature resolutions. Schemes for nested naming have been in use for many years and are well-understood. The lack of static nesting in C++ and some other languages is an undesirable compromise between efficient execution and understandable program structures, but it is not likely to change.

Likewise, addressing granularity has settled down to byte-level addressing in all systems, and is not likely to change.

Parameter passing by name is difficult to implement and understand, and has largely disappeared from programming languages. It is not likely to return.

Dynamic linking schemes are easily implemented in contemporary systems by having the pointers within virtual address maps direct accesses to unallocated spaces, thereby causing an interrupt. So the underlying mechanism needed to support dynamic linking is present in all systems, and is used frequently, as in Windows operating environments. This usage is likely to continue.

Segmentation, in the two-dimensional sense, is likely to disappear as a separate addressing technique. Rather, paging schemes that allocate separate object collections on page boundaries can obtain the same effect when the address space is large enough to permit wide addresses without penalty. Capabilities are in use in some systems, but because they do not provide too much security, and might present a false sense of security, they seem likely to be used less frequently than their present infrequent use.

Registers will continue to be used to generate wide addresses via indexed address computations, as in RISC machines. This technique does not impose significant cost on the design in either logic complexity or in execution speed, because the address computation can often be overlapped with other useful activities. The only disadvantage is that wide constants need to be loaded into the registers, but a program can be generated by the code generator within a compiler to operate from register-based addresses to obtain other register-based addresses, so the cost of loading wide addresses into registers is quite small, and the practice is likely to continue.

E.7 CONCEPT LIST

1. Names, both simple and complex
2. Objects, single and compound
3. Name spaces
4. Naming contexts
5. Context-dependent names and how they are modified to move across boundaries
6. Aliasing
7. Static/dynamic and homogeneous/heterogeneous compound object structures
8. Locators (pointers)
9. Object visibility and name scope

10. Names used for linking program modules—EV and ED names
11. Nested naming environments—static and dynamic nesting rules
12. Controlled name exportation
13. Types of parameter-passing conventions—by value, reference, and name
14. Static and dynamic linking
15. Processor addressing modes
16. Two-dimensional addressing; uses with static nesting and linking
17. Tagging to identify types and to direct the memory accessing process
18. Type-based access requests
19. Capabilities
20. Use of registers and tables to construct wide addresses
21. Address compression techniques
22. Addressing granularity

E.8 PROBLEMS

E-1. A C++ procedure contains a set of declarations such that the following names are legal names for objects locally declared in the procedure. Write a set of C++ declarations that makes all of these names legal. Try to obtain the smallest set of declarations possible while meeting the legality constraint. Would your answer be changed if you were told that some of these names refer to the procedure's parameters? Explain.

a[3].b.c[4]	x[8]	a[7].g[2]
d.b.e	a[6].h	x[3]

E-2. Briefly explain why the discriminant values of an object with a dynamic structure cannot be permitted to change during the object's existence.

E-3. Explain why the allocation suggested in Figure E-1 for the variant record of Example E-9 is undesirable. Suggest a revised allocation to remove the difficulty.

E-4. In a program using static nesting (of objects and classes, called packages in Ada), a programmer would like to define an Ada package named P that will be used only in a subroutine S that is declared within a main program M. Furthermore, she does not want to use P anywhere else in the program. She has thought of two ways to organize the program; these two techniques are outlined in the following Ada program structures.

Program A

```
package P is
    ..
end P;
package body P is
    f, g : integer;
    ..
```

```
end P;
procedure M is
     a, b : integer;

       ..
     procedure S is
           m, n : integer;

              ..
       end S;
begin

      ..
end M;
```

Program B

```
procedure M is
     procedure S is
          package P is

                ..
          end P;
          package body P is
                f, g : integer;

                  ..
          end P;
          m, n : integer;
     begin

           ..
     end S;
     a, b : integer;
begin

       ..
end M;
```

The designer wishes you to compare these alternatives.
(a) Is there any logical difference between the two options?
(b) Is there any efficiency difference between the two options?

E-5.   The list structure depicted in Figure E-7 is constructed from records of the type list_bead declared in the following program fragment:

```
class list_bead {
public:
     int first;
     float second;
     list_bead *third;
}
```

For each shaded element shown in the figure, write a program fragment to read the element into a local object named value (for which you must supply a declaration). The starting point for all accessing to the list is the pointer stored in an

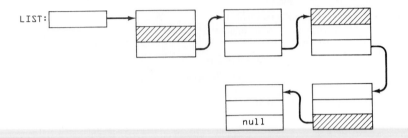

Figure E-7 A list containing some objects to be named
in Problem E-5

object declared list_bead *list. Your answer should contain three separate program
fragments.

E-6. Figure E-8 shows a simple tree structure that was created by a program that built
the tree incrementally as new data arrived. Notice the ordering among the values
at the nodes. Each bead, as shown, contains one value-holding location and two
pointers to successor nodes. Items in this tree are named by starting at the location
root, which contains a pointer to the tree's root bead. The components of each bead
are named according to the following declaration:

```
class tree_bead {
public:
        tree_bead *topson;
        tree_bead *bottomson;
        int it;
}
```

(a) What is the name of the place where the value 84 is stored?
(b) A pointer to a value in the tree contains only the address of the memory
word(s) holding the value. Given such a pointer, named here, declared int *here,
can you construct an algorithm to access the object that holds the next smaller
value in the tree without having a pointer to the root of the tree? Explain.
(c) Repeat part (b) if you also have a pointer to the root of the tree structure.
(d) Does your algorithm from part (c) work correctly if there are duplicate values
in the tree? Explain.

E-7. Consider the dynamic nesting example of Example E-12. For the given history,
construct a history of the stack in which nonvisible values are stored. Make a
separate picture showing the conditions after each context change during the
program's flow. In your diagrams, label each stack entry with the name of the
entity whose value is stored in the location. Assume that all entities have the same
size.

E-8. Consider the call-by-name parameter-passing technique. Specify the relationships
that must exist between the context where the object holding the subscript is
declared and the context of the procedure where the formal parameter is used.

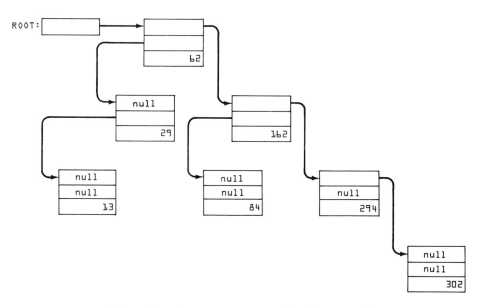

Figure E-8   A tree containing ordered integer values

E-9. The Ada specification states that a program is deemed incorrect if its correct execution relies on a particular selection of the technique used to pass parameters to subroutines. Can this correctness condition be checked by the compiler? Explain.

E-10. A system designer claims that a useful general program linking scheme could be defined as follows. Start with the usual static nesting rules and add the following linking command: "Place program Q within block y[39] of program h from file F." This command still does not clarify how the act of placing program Q in the specified block may change object naming in program h. Some interesting ways to interpret the act of nesting are as follows:

   1. The act of nesting can affect only names that were ED when h was compiled.
   2. The act of nesting can change the meaning of any name used in h.
   3. The act of nesting can change references to any procedures and subroutines but not to data-holding objects that were P when h was compiled.

   Answer the following questions for all the interpretations of the act of nesting. (It is possible that the answer to a particular question might not depend on the option chosen from the preceding list.)

   (a) Construct a set of program modules in which procedure a (defined in file FA) is statically nested within procedure b, which itself is defined within file FB, whose program has an outer block named main. Describe a (sequence of) linking command(s) that puts all of this structure together.

   (b) Under the proposed scheme, which system element (e.g., the compiler or linker) determines the final form of the linked addresses?   [*Turn for more parts.*]

---
[39]   Assume that the name y is unambiguous.

(c) Discuss the degree to which module insertion affects program modularity.

(d) Specify the information that must be contained in the symbol tables kept with filed programs. Be sure that you provide enough information in the tables so that all necessary links can be established after the insertion request has been made.

E-11. Show how indirection can be used in conjunction with the stacked implementation of dynamic nesting to handle objects that have different sizes. In your description, specify whether the program has to determine the size of each object, and, if so, how that information can be made available and accessed at the appropriate times.

E-12. Consider a processor that supports multilevel indirection. It is designed so that the programmer may specify the point in the indirection chain where indexing is performed. Only a single index value can be specified in an instruction, but the timing of the indexing operation (with respect to the indirect chain) can be specified. Consider all logically different timing options within all addressing chains that include two reads of indirect addresses.

(a) For each option, describe a data structure that is efficiently accessed by the option.

(b) Of the structures you identified in part (a), which do you think have an important effect on system speed? Discuss.

(c) Do any of these options speed accesses to parameters (stored in a stack frame)? Compare this scheme to the simple scheme in which indexing always applies only to the address used in the first read of an indirect address.

E-13. This problem is concerned with techniques that access nonlocal objects in a statically nested environment. Assume that the processor, like the B 5000, maintains pointers only to the stack frames corresponding to the most recently entered block and the outermost block. To reach an intermediate level in the static nest, the program must maintain a chain of pointers among the blocks mirroring the nesting structure, in reverse (i.e., the pointer chain reflects the search order for resolution of statically nested names). Assume that this chain has been established (i.e., while solving this problem you are not to worry about how the chain was set up). The pointer to the next ancestor block in the chain is in a fixed location (named CHAIN) within each block, declared as follows:

```
class a_record {
public:
    ..
    a_record *CHAIN;
    ..
}
```

Write an algorithm to obtain a pointer to the block at level L, given that the value of the current level is in a processor register named C. The pointer to the a_record for the current level is in a processor register named P. Leave the result in the processor register named B. Remember that the lowest level number is associated with the outermost block of the nest.

E-14. We want to design a tag-based addressing mode that supports stack data structures. On a "pop" (read) access, the processor would postincrement the last tagged indirect address object encountered along the path to the data object.[40] In a symmetric manner, on a "push" (write) access, the processor would predecrement the last tagged indirect address object along the path to the data object.

(a) Notice that to perform a "push," the processor has to read the item first before it can write to it. Explain why this is true.

(b) Write out the accessing algorithms for read and write accesses, including the updates of the indirect address object. Start with the B 5700 addressing mechanism in formulating your answer. Consider only address specifications in which the last indirection did not use a computed indirection (as designated by the presence of a tagged entry-point descriptor in the indirection chain). Design your algorithm to work correctly in the simple case in which there is no indirection in the addressing path (in this case there is no address word to be updated, and push and pop reduce to write and read, respectively).

E-15. Write out a C++ algorithm that describes accessing a data object in a system using tag-based indirection with both indirect addresses and call-by-name entry points. Notice that in order for strong typing to work, it will be necessary to use an unspecified pointer (a pointer to **void**) to a class object that includes both the value and the tag as component parts. The result of your algorithm should be the address of the data object, not the value contained therein.[41] Use three tag values to signify data, entry, and pointer. In fact, define the data class tag as an enumerated type:

enum tag { data, entry, pointer };

Under this enumeration, the words "data", "entry", and "pointer" denote the possible tag values. Design your algorithm so any arbitrary sequence (along the indirection path) of tagged access variables and tagged (call-by-name) procedure entry points will be properly interpreted.

E-16. Consider a system that supports tag-based indirection. Each indirect word can specify indexing to be applied to the indirect address within the same indirect word. Let x denote the index specification in an indirect word. The index quantities are selected by the value of x as follows:

1. If $x = 0$, there is no indexing.
2. If $x = 1$, the index value is popped from the top of an implicit stack.
3. If $x > 1$, processor register x contains the index value.

Construct an indirect path to read the value 84 in the data structure shown in Figure E-8, under the following restrictions:

(a) All index values are taken from the stack. This determines one indirection path.

(b) All index values are taken from processor registers. This determines a second indirection path.

In your answers, show all values determining the eventual address, whether located in the instruction that initiated the access, in processor registers, or in memory.

---

[40]   This statement implies that the processor must discover a data object by reading it and examining its tag before it can determine that the previously read object was in fact the last pointer in the chain leading to the data object; this is true because all objects are self-describing by virtue of their tag field contents. This comment applies to both reading and writing the data object.

[41]   Clearly, the type returned by the procedure must be *memory_object.

E-17. To support fine-grained visibility control, we could design the language to allow the declarer, the user, or both to make statements regarding either visibility or denial of visibility. Some of the possible combinations discussed in Section E.2 do not make sense. It is pointless, for example, to make a promise at the receiving end.

    (a) Make a table showing all possible combinations of the request/permission options.

    (b) Indicate which combinations have consistent semantics, and explain the meaning of each one that does make sense. Also explain why the others do not make sense.

E-18. A system with tagging marks each object with a tag containing n bits. We wish to support strong typing. This design limits the number of programmer-defined classes that can appear in one program. Explain why.

E-19. The Fairchild F8 microprocessor [FAIR75] designers reduced the bandwidth of address information flowing along the system bus by moving the contents of PC from the processor and placing it in the memory system. The processor's interface with the memory was therefore changed for instruction fetches. Two important primitive operations are provided. The first requests that the memory read the next program word. The second states that the address being sent out along the address lines is to be loaded into the PC.

    (a) This question is concerned with the need to increment the value in PC. We desire a solution such that the two operations described before are sufficient to implement arbitrary program structures. Describe which classes of machine instructions include PC incrementation. For each class of operations requiring PC incrementation, define the timing of the PC incrementation relative to the other portions of the operation's execution by the memory system.

    (b) Some instructions span more than the information fetched in one memory request. Define how such a long instruction would be fetched under this scheme.

E-20. We wish to demonstrate that using a wide indirect address to construct a wide virtual address is a general scheme, in the sense that there are no logical constraints that limit addresses under this scheme. In other words, the claim implies that any program P_w written with an arbitrarily wide address field in each instruction can be changed into an equivalent program P_n that does have a narrow address field within an instruction, using indirections through memory locations containing pointers. Discuss why this claim is true.

    Be sure that you consider all addressing modes, including indirection, that might occur in program P_w. A complete answer should specify how narrow addresses are interpreted, how wide addresses are generated as needed, and, if you use a table to hold an address map, how the table is managed (which includes finding the table, inserting entries into the table, and handling table overflow).

E-21. This problem is concerned with a scheme to change dynamically the address width in each instruction and thereby to save instruction bits. The basic idea is that programs would be shorter if the address fields were shortened so that instructions that hold addresses would become correspondingly shorter. Notice that this scheme will require bit-level addressing in the program counter, so you can assume that the PC addresses bits as you solve this problem.

The processor contains a 6-bit address field width register AFW. The value in AFW is interpreted as the number of bits in each memory address field taken from an instruction. The instruction set is augmented with a 16-bit instruction (SETAFW) whose single (6-bit) immediate operand is loaded into AFW. When the processor enters a new context, the SETAFW instruction may be executed to define the sizes of addresses that will appear in subsequent instructions.

In each addressing context, the number of distinct addresses that appear in the program for the context can be counted by the compiler. This count implies a minimum number of address bits that could be used to denote any one of these addresses. For context i, let $a(i)$ denote this minimum number of address bits required in that context. Let $n(i)$ denote the number of address specifications that appear in the representation of the program fragment executed in context i. Then $a(i)n(i)$ is the number of address bits used in the memory image of the program for context i if the dynamic width scheme discussed before is used.

Write an inequality that will be true if the AFW coding scheme reduces the overall program length compared to the base system, which has 12-bit displacement fields in each address field appearing in an instruction. Be sure to count the instruction space used to set AFW.

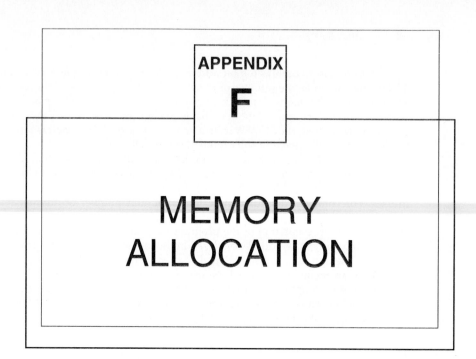

APPENDIX

F

MEMORY ALLOCATION

Have a place for everything and keep the thing somewhere else;
this is not advice, it's merely custom.

— *Mark Twain*

Yea, from the table of my memory
I'll wipe away all trivial fond records.

— *Shakespeare*, Hamlet

Allocation is a major memory system issue, naming and accessing being the other two parts of the memory puzzle. Memory naming and visibility issues can be utilized in designing processor addressing structures that are "close" to those required to implement high-level-language naming semantics (see Appendix E). Allocation policies must respect another semantic aspect of a language—the lifetimes of the named entities holding values. In this appendix, we see how the allocation semantics from high-level languages can be mapped into space allocation strategies at different system levels, ranging from the compiler's allocation of main memory to the hardware's allocation of cache memory. We see how designers can include processor and system support for allocation activities. Designs that incorporate this support are outlined in Appendix D and at other spots in the text.

After reading this appendix, you should understand important space allocation options and know how they relate (1) to the naming semantics described in Appendix E and (2) to using the system's memory resources efficiently. In contemporary systems many of these policies are implemented in software, but you should learn the connection between software allocators and features of system hardware. In addition, you should know how the inner levels of the system can be designed for automatic implementation of simple, yet adequate, allocation policies for cache memories.

In Chapter 3, we detail how actual memory accesses are completed. The accessing methods and the data supporting these methods depend on the allocation policies discussed here and the naming policies discussed in Appendix E.

F.1 THE PROBLEM

A memory object cannot be accessed until space to hold its contents has been assigned within the memory address space. The allocation act performs this essential step.

> **Definition.** *Memory allocation* is the act of assigning memory locations for specific uses.

When a translator program assigns addresses to declared objects, it allocates space. Similarly, when the linker assigns memory space to hold a module required for execution, it is performing allocation. Other allocations are performed by run-time support software and by the processor during program execution. Some of this allocation is requested directly by the program being executed; other allocation requests are implicit in the language semantics—in these cases, such as LISP or with automatic objects in C++, there are no overt allocate request in the high-level-language program.

The allocation strategy determines not only where objects will be stored but also how long the space will be allocated. The major functional requirement imposed on an allocator is as follows:

> **Lifetime Requirement**. An allocation A for the object X is *functionally correct* if the period of existence of allocation A encompasses the lifetime of X.

Most lifetime requirements are derived from high-level-language semantics.

In this appendix, we discuss allocation problems and solution techniques for single-process systems. We will see (1) how main (primary) memory space can be allocated, (2) how secondary memory allocations can be related to primary memory allocations, and (3) how these allocation decisions can be performed by a memory-management module within the operating system. The space allocation decisions concerning primary (main) and secondary memory spaces are a consequence of certain trade-offs between the speed and costs of the memory media themselves. We cannot minimize cost and maximize speed simultaneously because faster devices cost more, and larger quantities cost more. Thus, we devise techniques to combine efficiently large, slow, inexpensive memories with smaller, faster, more expensive memories. In this way, we form a *memory hierarchy*. We wish to coordinate the use of all memory resources without undue overhead or complexity. Several structured approaches to these problems have been developed, are in wide use, and may be familiar to the reader. Other, more sophisticated techniques may cost more overhead and may be used in large systems or when hardware support can be provided.

Every meaningful allocation must be respected within the system. The method for ensuring this respect depends upon the design philosophy—with the "nothing illegal" approach, the allocations will be respected, but with the "everything checked" approach, we need an *enforcement mechanism* that assures consistency with the allocations that have been made. An allocation enforcer requires sufficient information to complete its checks correctly. The information required depends upon the allocation technique.

Four aspects affecting any allocation design arise in this brief discussion:

1. The need to satisfy the lifetime requirements
2. The need for modules that handle allocate and free requests
3. The need for address validity checks
4. The need to support the illusion that each allocation gives a block of space that has contiguous addresses in some address space

The first and fourth aspects are important in support of programming illusions. It will be useful to keep all of these aspects in mind as we continue the discussion.

F.2 ALLOCATION POLICIES AND THEIR IMPLEMENTATIONS

Almost every allocation decision process can be divided into two phases. In the first phase, a space pool from which the allocation is to be taken is selected. In the second phase, some space within that pool is selected to satisfy the request. This decomposition of the allocation problem splits memory into a set of pools; a portion of a chosen pool is assigned to satisfy each individual allocate request.

F.2.1 Pool-Selection Policies

Space pools are objects and can themselves be managed as objects within larger pools. An advantage of the pool structure is that the pools themselves can be allocated and deallocated in a manner that reflects the program's structure. This structure may simplify deallocation, because frequently one can choose the pool structure so that all space allocated within a pool will be deallocated at the same time.

The following discussion is based on these three assumptions:

1. Allocated space will be divided into pools.
2. When a pool is deallocated, all of the objects contained therein are automatically deallocated.
3. Pool lifetimes and allocations mirror the program's execution structure.

These assumptions are consistent with the hierarchical allocation strategy discussed before. The third assumption implies that pool allocations do not need to change except when the program's execution point moves across a boundary separating program modules. Procedure call and return are two important actions that move execution point across a modular boundary.

The choice of the space pool that will be used to satisfy a request to allocate space for an object X is affected by the lifetime requirement, because the pools themselves have lifetimes, and no object can easily outlive the pool of which it is a part.[1]

Definition. A lifetime L_1 encompasses another lifetime L_2 if $L_1 = L_2$ or if the start of L_1 does not follow the start of L_2 and the end of L_1 does not precede the end of L_2.

Because every allocation within a pool must become invalid when the pool is deallocated, the basic pool selection policy is as follows:

Basic Pool Selection Policy. Make an object's allocation from the available pool whose lifetime is the smallest lifetime encompassing the object's lifetime.

Pool selection can become simple if each pool's existence is tied to the existence of naming or system contexts. Thus, we assume that a higher-order allocation decision has assigned an allocation pool P_i for each context C_i. Then most space allocation requests[2] ask for space to hold an object whose lifetime matches the duration of one of a set of program or system contexts $C_1 .. C_n$.

In general, the allocation pool choice is influenced by the relationship between the object's lifetime (or "extent," the C++ term) requirements and the context's (or pool's) lifetime. There are four cases (see Figure F-1):

1. The object's lifetime matches the context's lifetime.
2. The object's lifetime is nested within the context's lifetime.

---

[1]   The only possibility is to copy the object into a newly allocated space when its old allocation disappears—this is sufficiently complicated that it is not worth pursuing this option.
[2]   We note some exceptions in the following sections.

3. The context's lifetime is nested within the object's lifetime.
4. Neither lifetime is nested within the other.

Simple allocation policies suffice for the first two cases. The other two cases are handled by reduction to one of the first two, usually by finding or creating an artificial context within which the object's life is nested.

To handle the first cases, observe that if object X (in block C_j) has the same lifetime as P_j, it can be allocated within P_j on entry to C_j; then when P_j is released (on exit from C_j), the space for X will be released automatically. Under this policy, X will exist for the life of C_j.

Example F-1

Object declarations in a C++ procedure or function body define local objects with lifetimes synonymous with the lifetime of the block. Therefore, space for these objects can be allocated when the body is entered and freed when the body is exited.

In the second object–context nesting relationship, the lifetime of the object is nested within the lifetime of some context C_j. It would certainly be adequate to allocate space for X within P_j, the allocation pool corresponding to context C_j, keeping X's space allocated for the life of P_j. In this way, the lifetime of the allocation for X encompasses the required lifetime for X (see Figure F-1a). In an alternative design, the system performs a specific allocation for X when its life begins (e.g., as a consequence of encountering **new** in an executable statement) and a specific deallocation when X's life ends (e.g., as a consequence of a call to **delete** in C++) (see Figure F-1b). Even with specific allocate/deallocate requests, the space for X could be allocated within P_j, because the pool will not disappear while it is still needed to hold X.

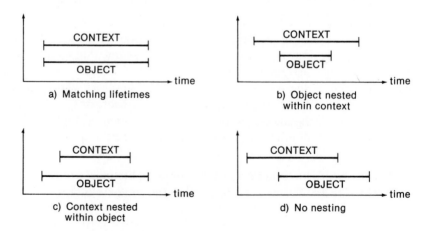

a) Matching lifetimes

b) Object nested within context

c) Context nested within object

d) No nesting

Figure F-1   Some relationships among context and object lifetimes

These simple policies can be implemented in software, but processor instructions can assist with allocations that are coupled with the lifetimes of function calls. In particular, the activation blocks for procedure calls (which are the space pool objects) can be allocated on a stack.

F.2.2 Allocation within a Pool

Any set of objects that have identical lifetimes and that are visible in the same places can be collected together for allocation purposes. Then space for the objects within the collection can be allocated just like space for an individual object.

The within-pool allocation problem has two variations:

1. Allocations for statically allocated objects
2. Allocations for dynamically allocated objects

For local automatic objects in a block-structured language with static nesting, static allocations can be made during program translation. To allocate space for object X "within" a context the translator assigns a within-context (local) address for X.

Static Allocation. A first-declared, first-allocated policy suffices for most static allocations. Under this policy, the first object (in order of declaration) is assigned to the first address, the second object to the first remaining address, and so on. For example, the objects w, x, and thing declared in the statement

    int w, x, thing;

would be assigned adjacent locations by an allocator using a first-declared, first-allocated policy.

Dynamic Allocation. Dynamic allocations are made during program execution. Dynamic allocation can improve space utilization, and may be necessary for an object whose lifetime does not match the pool's lifetime. Dynamic allocation may be necessary if the object sizes cannot be specified until the program runs; this is true for dynamically dimensioned arrays and objects having parameterized types. If the set of object lifetimes is structured so that space previously allocated for one object can be reallocated later to hold a different object, a program using dynamic allocation may require less space than a similar program using static allocation. This is the situation with stack allocations.

The selection of a dynamic allocation policy can be based on the relationships among the times of creation and deletion of the objects sharing the allocation pool. If the times of object creation and deletion are nested, the objects obey a last-in, first-out discipline (LIFO), and simple stack allocation policies can be used. If the times of object creation and deletion are slewed, the objects obey a first-in, first-out (FIFO) discipline, and a queue allocation policy can be used.

More complex heap allocation policies are required when neither of these two relationships holds among the object creation and deletion times. Four important dynamic allocation policies are as follows:

1. Allocation from a stack
2. Allocation from a queue
3. Fixed-size block allocation from a heap
4. Variable-size block allocation from a heap

We briefly survey some aspects of each allocation policy, emphasizing those aspects that influence system designs, especially instruction sets, memory management units, and caches.

Allocation from a Stack. Stack allocation can be used if the times of object creation and deletion obey a LIFO discipline. Thus, the allocate and free requests form a nested set in which every matching pair corresponds to allocation and deallocation for the same object.

Example F-2

Of these two histories,[3] one is compatible with stack allocation and the other is not. The T<letter> patterns in the histories represent object types declared in the program. The first declarations are common to both histories.

```
Ta *a;
Tb *b;
..;
Tf *f;
```

HISTORY_1	HISTORY_2
a = **new** Ta;	a = **new** Ta;
c = **new** Tc;	c = **new** Tc;
f = **new** Tf;	f = **new** Tf;
delete f;	**delete** a;
delete c;	**delete** c;
delete a;	**delete** f;

These histories are identical except for the timing of the deallocation of objects b and f. It is easy to see that HISTORY_1 obeys nesting, whereas HISTORY_2 does not.

Allocation from a Queue. At first glance, it probably seems that queue allocation would never make sense. In order for the queue structure to apply, the times of object creation and deletion must obey a FIFO discipline. Queue allocation might be forced in special situations, but you open yourself to many risks, such as deallocating space for an object just before it happens to be needed again.

---

[3]　We use a history to depict an actual sequence of (important) events that occur during the example situation. The sequence depicted in the history must be compatible with all constraints governing the situation at hand, but need not be the only such possible sequence.

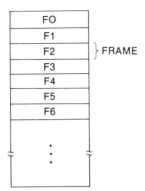

Figure F-2   A heap divided into frames

Within a memory hierarchy, forcing the FIFO order can be useful if the system can rapidly recover from allocation mishaps.

Fixed-Size Allocation from a Heap. Heap allocation is required when the allocation/deletion pattern does not obey either the LIFO or the FIFO lifetime discipline. Fixed-size allocations are appropriate if all allocation requests ask for the same amount of space. An important application of this strategy manages paged allocations in a memory hierarchy.

Because every allocation is given the same amount of space (call that amount object_size), the heap can be divided a priori into a set of *frames*, each containing space equal to object_size (see Figure F-2). The division of the pool can be made before any allocation requests are satisfied,[4] and never has to be changed. This frame structure affects hardware designs, such as page-mapping mechanisms.

The free-space pool managed by a heap allocator can become divided into disjoint blocks. With frame-based allocation, the number of entities to be managed is just the (statically known) number of frames, so free-space bookkeeping can use either a table containing a "free" bit for each frame or a linked list with each bead describing a free frame. Figure F-3 depicts these options. The details of allocation and deallocation in this environment are straightforward.

Variable-Size Allocation from a Heap. General run-time memory allocation policies must support dynamic allocations of variable-sized objects. This generality is required when (1) the allocate/free history does not obey the LIFO or FIFO disciplines and (2) individual allocate requests may ask for different amounts of space. When object sizes vary, the allocation pool cannot be divided a priori into frames with the assurance that every allocate request could be

---

[4]   The size of the divisions can be selected during system design or programming, and the divisions themselves can be made during system design, programming, or system initialization.

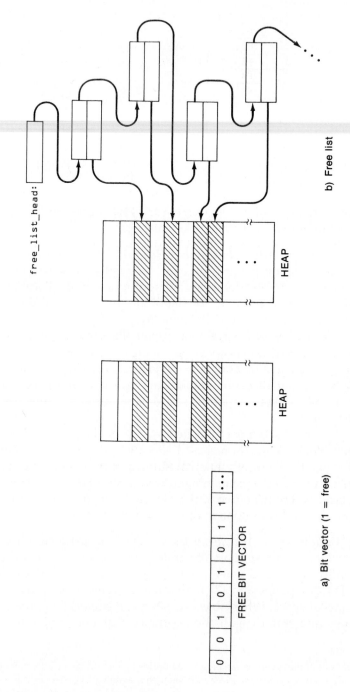

Figure F-3 Free-space bookkeeping options for fixed-size allocations. (The free space is shaded.)

a) Bit vector (1 = free)

b) Free list

satisfied by doling out a frame. The variable-size requirement implies that the allocator will have to deal with free space distributed in blocks of various sizes.

Each of the three simpler allocation policies led to an obvious implementation that intuitively seemed to be a very efficient, and perhaps the best possible, implementation. However, no simple implementation strategy stands out as the obvious best solution for all applications that require variable-size allocations from a heap. Two issues require a deeper look: (1) the strategy for selecting space to satisfy an allocate request and (2) the structure and management of the free-space database. The two issues are coupled because an allocate request could be processed more quickly if the free-space information were organized to speed the allocator's search for a block to satisfy the request. Symmetrically, the free-space data structure could be organized to simplify deallocation. Unfortunately, the structures that simplify allocation make deallocation more complex, and vice versa. A complete overhead accounting must include the overhead of both allocate and free operations [SLEA85].

We explore designs for the following necessary parts of the allocator's activities:

1. Selecting a block to use while satisfying an allocate request
2. Subdividing a large free block to create smaller free blocks
3. Combining small free blocks to create a larger free block

It may seem that the choices made in response to the first two issues affect the design of the *allocate* procedure, whereas the choices made in response to the last issue affect only the *free* procedure. However, one can defer combining free blocks until larger spaces are needed. Three important allocation policies are

1. First fit
2. Best fit
3. Buddy system

The *first-fit* allocation policy satisfies an allocate request with the first[5] free block that is larger than the requested size. Any excess space within the chosen free block may be returned to the free list if it exceeds a minimum size.

The *best-fit* allocation policy allocates the smallest free block that is larger than the space requested. The selection criterion suggests that the blocks on the free list should be ordered on the basis of their size.

The *buddy system* is like the best-fit policy in that the block with the smallest remainder after allocation is used to satisfy an allocate request. This policy is different from the best-fit policy in that the block sizes are constrained to a predetermined set of values. A block-splitting rule governs the division of a free block according to a set of fractions, specifying the fractional parts of a free block that will comprise separate blocks after block splitting. Suppose that the set of

---

[5]   Here "first" refers to the order in which the free-space list is searched.

fractions was {½, ¼, ¼}, and that the system had been initialized with a single block of free space whose size is a power of 2. Then every free block in the system will have a size that is a power of 2. The allocator will satisfy an allocate request with a block whose size is the smallest power of 2 not smaller than the requested size.

The space manager must be able to combine small free blocks to form larger free blocks in case one is requested later. To combine free blocks, the recombiner must determine whether a newly free block is adjacent to other free block(s). This check is handled easily in the buddy system, because each freed block can be combined in exactly one way with its buddies to form a larger free block that is compatible with the size ratio constraints. Therefore, it is possible to use the initial size of the free space, the origin of a free block B, and its size to compute the origins of the blocks that are candidates for constructing a larger free block using B. With the first-fit or best-fit management policies, a free list ordered by origin would be useful for finding neighboring free blocks. So one system design question concerns the choice of a data structure supporting both search strategies.

Although it may seem attractive to combine free blocks whenever possible, it is easy to see that creating an excessively large free block may, in fact, make the block too large to meet a later allocate request. Due to this possibility, it can be attractive, especially with buddy systems ([KAUF84]), to delay free-block recombination until such recombination is required to form a block large enough to meet a specific incoming allocate request.

F.2.3 Policy Summary

The memory allocation process has two parts: pool allocation and allocation of space within pools for individual objects. The problem of acquiring space for the pools is the same as the problem of acquiring space for an object within a pool.

Free-space management is central to memory allocation. Different techniques can be used, including stack and queue policies (feasible only if the lifetimes of the allocated objects have specific interrelationships), and heap management of fixed- and varying-sized objects.

Our discussion rested on two assumptions. The first assumption was that every time an object becomes free, either (1) the system or the executing program will inform the memory management module, or (2) an automatic deallocation decision can be made upon a context change. In some systems or languages, the overhead[6] required to make the notification is too great, and the memory management system must be designed differently. This situation occurs in list processing, discussed in Appendix I.

---

[6]   This overhead is incurred in the bookkeeping required to know that a space has become free.

The second assumption was that the allocator always responds to an allocate request with a contiguous block of space. This requirement makes allocation more difficult, but it simplifies the program using the space. The objects within a contiguous block of space can be accessed easily.

F.3 USER-CONTROLLED ALLOCATION IN HIGH-LEVEL LANGUAGES

The high-level-language semantics specify the lifetime requirements of all objects declared in a program. There are three different classes of object extents:

1. Static extent
2. Automatic (local) extent
3. User-controlled[7]

A *static* lifetime matches the lifetime of the executing program. Static objects in a C++ program include the program itself, all links established to bind program modules together, and all objects declared in the body of any class (not including those declared within the body of a procedure or a function). The module links are static because the search path used to resolve ED names[8] does not change during program execution. Data members inside a C++ class are static[9] because they hold the state internal to the class between invocations of program modules within the class. The seed of a random-number generator, for example, is a static value within the random-number class.

An *automatic* lifetime matches the lifetime of some invocation of a procedure, function, or block. In most languages, the lifetime of an automatic object X matches the lifetime of the procedure, function, or block that contained X's declaration. When the procedure, function, or block is invoked again, a new set of automatic objects will be allocated and reinitialized.

A *user-controlled* lifetime does not match the lifetime of any program-related module. Explicit program actions (such as an execution of the new primitive) signal the beginning and (usually) the end of the object's life. The program will invoke an allocate function when the object is to be allocated, and may invoke a free function when the object is no longer needed. Because the program's execution flow may not be discernible by the translator or may be data-dependent, the translator cannot know the lifetimes of the programmer-controlled objects appearing within the program, and static techniques will not work.

A dynamic object D must be allocated by a run-time allocator, so its location cannot be known when the program is translated. Therefore, the translator cannot replace a reference to D with a direct static address. Rather, access to D must be made through a pointer object A that contains a pointer to the actual

---

[7]   This allocation lifetime possibility is called "dynamic" in C++ terminology.
[8]   These are described in Appendix E.
[9]   These objects are shared among all invocations of the class.

space allocated for D. This indirection can slow program execution, especially with RISC architectures. However, the indirection cannot be avoided, because it is a direct consequence of the dynamic nature of the allocation.

Example F-3

In C++, the size of a programmer-allocated object is defined by its type and the pool selection is implementation-dependent (and hidden from the programmer). A dynamic allocation is made on execution of the statement

<pointer> = **new** <data_type>;

Additionally, if the data_type is a class name (possibly with parameters), the constructor function for that type will be invoked after the space has been allocated. The constructor might make additional calls to **new** to allocate related objects.

Contrast this with an allocation statement from C:

<pointer> = **malloc**(**sizeof**(<data_type>));

This C statement performs an allocation but does not initialize the object by calling the constructor for the data type. Although **malloc** may exist in some C++ libraries, its use is discouraged because it bypasses an important linguistic feature.

Example F-4

A PL/1 programmer can take control of some memory management functions by organizing memory into a set of visible pools. The programmer can control the pool selection for each allocation; a new instance of an object is created by executing a statement like

ALLOCATE RECORD TYPE **IN AREA** A **SET** POINTER;

The TYPE parameter specifies the type of the object for which space should be allocated. The area name A specifies the pool (that had been declared as a vector) from which the object is to be allocated. The pointer name POINTER in the **SET** clause states which pointer should be set to point to the new object. Notice the similarity with the **malloc** function in C (assigning the resulting pointer to a pointer object), but here the programmer chooses the allocation pool.

At the end of an object's lifetime, the programmer may request object deallocation by calling the "free" procedure with (a) parameter(s) describing the space to be deallocated. In C++, this is accomplished by calling **delete**, passing the pointer to the object as the parameter. In general, the lifetimes of the allocated space and the pointer objects are unrelated to each other, which adds complexity to a system design that attempts to support the "anything goes" approach. For example, if the deallocator were not called and the pointers to the allocated space were themselves deallocated, we would have space allocated to the program without having corresponding locators to describe the space. The space would be "lost," and a garbage collection algorithm would have to be executed to locate all useful space and retrieve the lost garbage. Conversely, it is possible to deallocate space while there still exists a pointer to that space. The remaining pointers that point to unallocated (or reallocated) space are called *dangling pointers*.

Example F-5

In C++, space is deallocated by invoking the delete function, as in

```
<type> *spaceptr = new <type>;
..
delete spaceptr;
```

This operation will leave a dangling pointer if spaceptr had been copied to another pointer object, as in

```
<type> *otherptr, *spaceptr = new <type>;
..
otherptr = spaceptr;
..
delete spaceptr;
```

This fragment leaves a copy of the pointer to the deallocated space in otherptr. Now examine this variant:

```
<type> *otherptr = new <type>, *spaceptr = new <type>;
..
otherptr = spaceptr;
..
delete spaceptr;
```

This structure leaves garbage, which is the space allocated when otherptr was initialized. After the assignment statement is performed, no pointer accessible to the program describes this space. So this space cannot be accessed or deleted, because it no longer can be described within the program.

Example F-6

Ada semantics imply that a user-controlled object created by **new** should continue to exist as long as the object or one of its components can be denoted by some name. Therefore, the object cannot exist beyond the end of the scope of the name its type. This rule implies that automatic deallocation may be performed when the type name's scope is exited. A programmer can control the deallocation by instantiating an instance of the generic Ada procedure UNCHECKED_DEALLOCATION and then calling that instance to deallocate an object. Consider this Ada program fragment:

```
type T is ..;
type aT is access T;
procedure freeT is new unchecked_deallocation( T, aT );    --See footnote10
```

---

[10]   The two parameters specified here are the actual values of the generic parameters of the procedure template unchecked_deallocation. The instantiated procedure (here called freeT) has only one parameter of the type of the second generic parameter.

```
procedure sample is
begin
     b : aT;
     ..
     b = new T;        --allocate an instance of T
     ..
     freeT( b );       --deallocate the instance
end;
```

The deallocation procedure must be instantiated for the specific object type that will be explicitly deallocated. A call to the freeT procedure that is produced by this instantiation will[11] free the object even though there might exist another locator describing the object being deallocated;[12] that is why the word "unchecked" has been placed in the label of the generic procedure to warn unwary programmers.

One difficulty with user-controlled allocations is the possibility of dangling pointers. Can the system automatically avoid them? Yes, but only with some overhead. Therefore, although language descriptions may say that a program using a dangling pointer is an illegal program, there is no inexpensive way that this type of error can be caught by an implementation.

The LISP programming language [WINS84], in which list data structures play an important role, permits list creation and reassignment of pointer values during list manipulation. As described in Appendix I, the memory in a LISP system can become filled with old lists ("garbage") that may have to be purged from the system to refresh the free-space pool. The problem arises because no linguistic structure limits object or type existence, so there is no basis for Ada-style rules governing automatic space reclamation. Furthermore, there is no language primitive that a programmer can use to request deallocation of an object.

F.4 SYSTEM-CONTROLLED ALLOCATION FOR HIGH-LEVEL LANGUAGES

The implementation of a high-level language must perform automatic run-time allocations; these provide space for several classes of objects, including the following:

1. The process
2. The program
3. Static objects
4. Automatic objects

---

[11]   Ada specifies that the implementation has the option to reclaim any space automatically deallocated, but that it is not required to do so.
[12]   If such a "dangling" locator is used to attempt an access to an object, the program is in error. (Many implementations will not detect such an error, because run-time checking of all pointer references would be required, and this would add large amounts of overhear during program execution.)

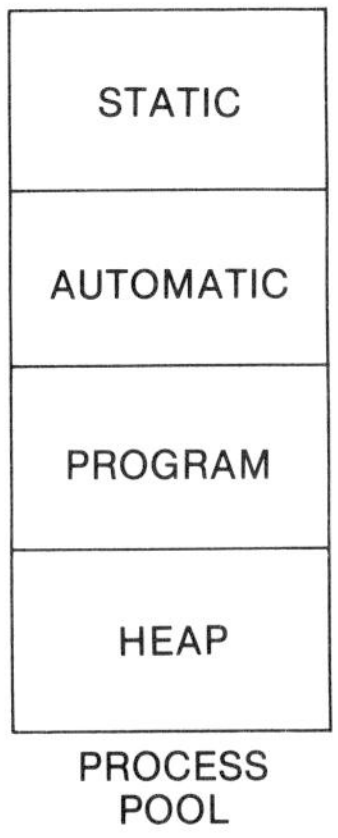

```
┌─────────────┐
│             │
│   STATIC    │
│             │
├─────────────┤
│             │
│  AUTOMATIC  │
│             │
├─────────────┤
│             │
│   PROGRAM   │
│             │
├─────────────┤
│             │
│    HEAP     │
│             │
└─────────────┘
   PROCESS
    POOL
```

Figure F-4   Static pool allocations

In this section we explore design options for these allocations. Stack allocations are useful for parameters and automatic objects, and process-private spaces are useful for static objects. Finally, we consider processor instruction sequences that may invoke or perform these important allocation functions.

F.4.1 Process-Level Allocations

Informally, a *process* is the execution of a program.[13] The system must provide memory space for the execution of each process, including space for the program itself, space for its static objects, and space for its dynamic objects, including a space pool (heap) within which programmer-controlled objects can be allocated during program execution.

If the processor supports two-dimensional addressing (see Section E.3.2), pool allocation can be simple—allocate one segment for the static object pool, one segment for the automatic object pool, one segment for the program, and a fourth segment for the heap.

If the processor supports only one-dimensional addressing, the process can be allocated a single pool that is subdivided by allocating these functionally independent pools contiguous blocks. Figure F-4 illustrates this division of allocation pools. Another approach allocates two separate static spaces for the program and the static data, plus a common space to be shared by the automatic object pool and the allocation heap, which expand in opposite directions, as shown in Figure F-5.

---

[13]   This "intuitive" explanation is actually about as precise as one can get while trying to define a process. One's intuition is certainly adequate to deal with this notion.

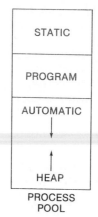

Figure F-5　The automatic
and heap pools sharing
space

F.4.2 Allocations for Automatic Objects

In a block-structured language, each automatic local object is visible and known only during the lifetime of the activation of the program block immediately enclosing its declaration. Therefore, space for all objects local to a procedure or a function block has a lifetime synonymous with the lifetime of the program block, and the corresponding space pool can be allocated when the block is entered and freed when the block is exited. This allocation pool is called the "activation block" for the invocation of the program block. Because the invocation lifetimes are nested, stack allocation can be used for the activation blocks. A stacked activation block structure is shown in Figure F-6.

How do we determine the space requirements for an activation block? If the sizes of all local objects are known at translation time, the activation record size can be computed by the translator and placed in the program as a constant. However, if the sizes cannot be determined during program translation, rather than placing the value of the block size in the program, the compiler generates

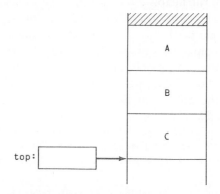

Figure F-6　An allocation block stack

instructions that compute the required space and places them in the procedure's prologue. The basic procedure calling scenario for a stack-based implementation includes the following steps:

1. Save the top of stack pointer (TOS) and the activation block pointer.
2. Copy the actual parameters to the stack.
3. CALL the procedure, updating the activation block pointer from the saved previous TOS.
4. Adjust TOS to allocate space for automatic objects.
5. Perform the procedure.
6. On completion, (a) deallocate automatic objects and restore the TOS and activation block pointers to their saved values; then (b) push the procedure's result (if any) onto the stack.

Step 4 constitutes the procedure's "prologue," which includes computing the size of the activation block. Step 6a constitutes the procedure's "epilogue."

Two problems require further study: (1) allocation for parameters and (2) allocation for the activation block itself.

Allocation for Parameters. The lifetimes of actual procedure parameters matches the lifetime of the procedure invocation, so the parameter allocation problem can be treated like the activation block allocation problem, but there is one important detail: there must exist a place to put the parameters while the calling program is executing the calling sequence. Turning this around, we ask the question, "Where do we place the parameters in relation to the local objects?" There are two options:

1. Merge the parameters with the activation block.
2. Separate the parameters from the activation block.

Figure F-7 illustrates the difference between these two options. The activation block and the parameter block in the figure are both associated with the same procedure call. The basic procedure calling scenario given before is consistent with the first allocation option and is not consistent with the second allocation option. Machine designs supporting each option—the Burroughs B 5700 design ([HAUC68] and [ORGA73]) and the HP 3000 [HEWL73]—are described in Appendix D.

Example F-7

In the Burroughs B 5700 machines, a single stack is used for saving the procedure call state, for procedure parameters, for activation blocks, and for storing temporary operand values and the results of operand manipulations. The details, showing how the parameters are joined with the activation block, are presented in Section D.1.

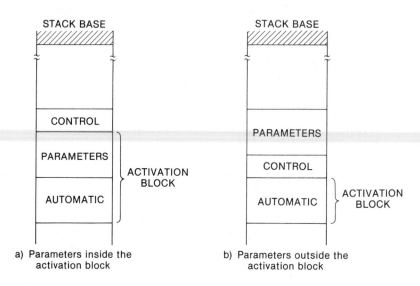

a) Parameters inside the
    activation block

b) Parameters outside the
    activation block

Figure F-7   Relationships between the parameter space
and the activation block

Example F-8

The HP 3000 activation block format separates a procedure's parameters from its automatic objects, with the parameters stacked beneath the new activation block (see Section D.2).

A similar allocation is used in the HP 9000 Series 500 system [OSEC84].

Another option is that some parameters are passed in registers, with the possibility of expanding to a stack space.

Example F-9

SPARC programs can pass up to six parameters in integer registers. Due to the use of SAVE and RESTORE[14] within subroutines, there are only eight registers available for this purpose, but two of them are preassigned for important functions: the saved program counter is in %r31 and the saved stack pointer, which serves as the frame pointer (identifying the start of the activation block for the called procedure), is in %r30. Thus, only six registers are available for parameter passing. If a procedure requires more than six parameters, the remainder must be placed on the stack before the call. If the language uses static nesting and the called block makes global references to formal parameters not declared in this (local) block, the register passing paradigm will not work.

Furthermore, the design includes space allocated so that the callee can save its register parameters on the stack. Following this block, there is a single word on the

---

[14]   See Appendix A for SPARC details.

stack for the address of the place where the callee should store its return value if that value is longer than a single word. And 16 locations are required by the system for saving the window in the event that a SAVE in the calling program happens to reach to an invalid register window. After all this space has been allocated, the frame pointer can be defined; above this, the callee's local objects can be stored.

This order of pushing, combined with the fact that stacks grow toward lower addresses, means that the address of the last parameter that was pushed on the stack before the call (call it the seventh) is %fp + 92, whereas the address of the first local object is %fp.

Comparing the B 5700 design with the HP 3000 and SPARC designs, we see that the latter designs allow the caller to push parameter values before saving any state; this removes the need for inactive state-holding words. On the other hand, the HP 3000 must support at least one more addressing mode (see Appendix D), making its implementation more complex.

Allocation for the Activation Block.   There are three ways that space for the activation block could be obtained on procedure entry. First, initial values for all local objects could be pushed onto the stack. Second, the TOS pointer could be changed to allocate space without initializing it. And third, the CALL instruction could acquire the space for the called procedure. Pushing initial values onto a stack is straightforward, so we do not discuss it here.

Changing the TOS pointer to grab stack space is simple and easily implemented; it is not very pleasing from the language point of view, because all local objects will have initial values that are residues from previous activity. To do this in the B 5700, the program adds an integer to the TOS, replacing the TOS value with the sum. The Data General Eclipse provides a catchall operation:

Example F-10

> The Eclipse operation SAVE [DATA74] has a single integer parameter, which is the amount of space to be allocated for local objects. This value is found in the program in the word following the SAVE instruction (the decision to place the value in the program makes it inconvenient to deal with dynamically allocated spaces). The operation first saves the processor registers on the stack and then increments the stack pointer by the parameter's value. The SAVE instruction thereby incorporates many of the procedure's prologue functions; it is the first instruction executed at the entry to the procedure.

The third way that the automatic space for a procedure's invocation could be allocated is to perform the allocation during the CALL operation. This is the approach used in the IBM System/38:

Example F-11

> In the IBM System/38, each procedure or function entry point has several attributes, which are stored in the descriptor of the entry point. One of these specifies the number of parameters, and another the amount of automatic storage that the

invocation will require. During the CALL instruction that invokes the procedure, the processor acquires the stated amount of stack space.

We see that a stack mechanism provides a uniform way to pass parameters and to define local storage space for each procedure. The two actions are interdependent; the design choice concerning allocation strategies affects the stack management mechanism and the call and return actions.

F.4.3 Space Allocation within the Activation Block

Space within the activation block might be needed to save the caller's processor state, and must be allocated for each automatic object declared within the program text. If the sizes of all of the local objects are known at compile time, this allocation can be performed by the compiler.

If the activation record contains an object whose size is dynamically determined, such as an array with data-dependent dimensions,[15] the block allocation problem is more complex; see Problem F-35. Similar issues arise with open-ended parameter lists, such as for the **printf** function in C and C++.

F.4.4 Comments

An executing program must acquire space for the objects that it must have present for proper execution. Static objects, automatic objects, dynamically sized objects, and user-controlled objects all require space. Some spaces can be acquired automatically by a processor with a CISC architecture by expanding the semantics of processor instructions associated with context changes (see Section F.6.1).

F.5 OPERATING SYSTEM MEMORY ALLOCATION

A computer system may serve simultaneously many processes or many threads from a single process. It should efficiently allocate its resources, including its memory, to those processes. Likewise, a computer system supporting a large virtual address space with a smaller physical memory must manage its physical memory resources. These memory management functions are performed by the operating system. In general, the operating system must be able to respond to uncertain situations. The exceptions include environments in which the particular programs to be executed are known a priori. To effectively manage memory, the system may have to relocate programs and data. We will see how the system

---

[15]   Data-dependent allocations cannot be specified in C++ or Ada through a static object declaration; the languages were designed so that all static objects within the block can be allocated during compilation.

can automatically allocate, free, and relocate user programs and data while leaving the user unaware of this underlying activity (this invisibility requires system support for run-time reinterpretation of addresses; see Chapter 3).

We present several space allocation policies for user program and data objects. First, we present a static allocation policy, with some of its inherent problems. Then we present some dynamic policies preferred in most environments.

F.5.1 Static Allocation Policies

An argument against a static allocation policy can be made similar to the one presented in Problem F-22. However compelling such arguments against static allocation may seem, they do not apply to all environments. If a system only performs a dedicated application, all program modules are known a priori and can be allocated space statically prior to execution. All interactions between scheduling and allocation can be avoided if the execution intervals of all program modules are known beforehand. Both a static execution schedule and a static memory allocation can be determined for this special situation. Most situations do not have this ideal environment that simplifies allocation problems and permits static solutions, so most systems must support dynamic allocations.

F.5.2 Dynamic Allocation Policies

In a general operating environment, the operating system must use dynamic allocation policies to manage memory space. It will benefit greatly from efficient support mechanisms, for without support mechanisms, the implementation of a dynamic allocation policy can be truly expensive! We seek a system design that permits the software designer to implement a range of different policies efficiently. We would like to select a small set of dynamic allocation policies for which we can provide low-level support in the system design.

In one simple policy, the allocator gives contiguous memory space for each individual process. There are many reasons why this policy is undesirable. A second policy option is to give each process its space as a collection of separate blocks of main memory, in which case the accessing mechanism must know how to translate virtual addresses from the program into physical addresses that relate to the set of blocks provided by the allocator. Under this policy, the total amount of space available within main memory must match the total demands from the processes. Alternatively, the system could allocate main memory space for only a portion of all objects required for the complete execution of a program module, *provided* that the system's address translation mechanism can hide this partial allocation from the programmer. Such a design would hide the system's memory allocation decisions from the programmer, who still has the illusion that the system has allocated a block for the complete program.

Detailed policy options depend on whether the system includes dynamic relocation and address mapping mechanisms that support partial allocations. In our discussion, we divide allocation and address mapping techniques in terms of the information present in or absent from main memory. Our phrases are as follows:

1. All information must be present.
2. Some information may be absent.

If all information must be present for a process to execute its program, the allocation strategies are trivial—all information must be loaded in main memory before the process can be executed. All of the information can be dumped upon process completion.

A scheme allowing absent information can be economical for two reasons:

1. Processes reference memory in patterns.
2. Inexpensive, slow memory devices can be used for secondary memory, where the system can allocate space to hold information not present in the expensive, fast main memory.

During an execution interval in which a process references only some of its objects, its execution speed will not be affected if the unreferenced information is not present in main memory. If occasionally the program does happen to attempt an access to an object that is not present in main memory, there will be a slight pause while the system makes the inaccessible information accessible by allocating space for it. If these misses are infrequent, the absence of the information will not affect execution speed significantly. This design approach is attractive because it does reduce the hardware cost because secondary memory space is cheaper than primary memory space. So we have a cheaper system that can execute programs almost as fast as an expensive system, with enough fast memory to hold all information for each process. We amplify these points before turning to specific memory allocation schemes allowing absent information.

Memory management policies allowing absent information perform well because most programs possess referencing locality, in the sense that in most program executions, the memory references tend to be limited to a small set of objects while the program executes within a small region, such as a loop body. On a larger scale, locality occurs because each program module is specialized, accessing only those (few) objects required to perform its function. This observation can be phrased in terms of the continuity of the program's behavior, as in this statement:

Principle of Locality. The memory referencing behavior of a process in the near future is likely to be similar to the memory referencing pattern it exhibited in the recent past; furthermore, this property is true at almost all times during the execution of the process.

Locality has two aspects: *temporal locality* and *spatial locality*. Temporal locality suggests that the near future will be similar to the recent past. Spatial locality suggests that in a typical short time interval, the number of objects that a large program will access will constitute a small fraction of the total set of objects accessible to the program. Spatial locality is closely related to temporal locality because time continuity suggests that the set of objects accessed recently is similar to the set of objects about to be accessed. In other words, most of the objects that are accessed are repeatedly accessed during a significant time interval, which also means that they are accessed to the exclusion of the other objects in the program's address space.

It is extremely important to realize that locality is a statistical property, not a certainty. In particular, our goal is statistically good behavior, which does not imply good behavior for each individual program that might be executed on the system. Certainly there will be exceptions—processes whose referencing patterns are problematical for the memory allocation scheme being used; such processes will exhibit poor performance. Their existence does not invalidate any statistical claims about locality or performance made for the allocation scheme. Any system design based on a statistical property of the environment may perform poorly on a specific program under a specific memory management policy, but this limited observation cannot be used to argue that the policy is bad. A valid evaluation must be based on a sufficiently large, diverse set of observations.

Referencing locality is one reason that allocation schemes allowing absent information are successful. The second reason is that memory devices can be arranged in a hierarchy based on cost and speed. The highest cost and performance memory occupies the top of the hierarchy. Each successive memory system is slower and less expensive than its predecessors. Information not needed in the fastest (primary) memory can be moved to slower (secondary) memory where it can be stored less expensively.

The designer of a dynamic relocation policy must define how the mechanism makes three important decisions:

1. *Loading*: when to load information in main memory
2. *Placement*: where to locate information being loaded
3. *Replacement*: when to replace information in main memory

Replacement is tightly coupled with placement; after all, if the system always had a place available, it would not ever have to replace any object! In some dynamic allocation schemes, loading and/or placement are trivial decisions; on the other hand, replacement decisions are difficult under most schemes. To make better replacement decisions, the system can be designed to collect usage information including the following:

1. What objects were accessed
2. What objects were modified (were *dirty*)

By knowing which objects have been accessed, the operating system can better decide which information should be allocated space closer to the top of the memory hierarchy. Further, if the system keeps track of dirty objects, and if it keeps a shadow copy of main memory within secondary memory, then an un-modified (*clean*) main memory block can be discarded without copying it out to secondary memory when its main memory space is to be reallocated. To deter-mine which objects are dirty, the supporting (hardware) mechanism sets a dirty bit when any object in the associated space is modified. Eventually, the system will copy each dirty object to secondary memory and clear the associated dirty bit. This memory cleaning could be performed speculatively; that is, in anticipa-tion of space needs. Such speculative behavior might improve system perform-ance simply because it reduces the probability that a load request will require swapping out a dirty object before the desired object can be loaded. There is, however, a cost for speculative swapping because (1) swapping consumes band-width in the primary memory–secondary memory data path and (2) swapping memory references contend with references for program execution.

The first important allocation decision concerned when to load a block into main memory. Two important loading options are (1) anticipatory loading (a block is loaded before actually being needed) and (2) demand loading (a block is loaded only when one of its members is actually accessed). In a static (dedicated) environment, the process schedule might be predetermined so that anticipatory loading could be useful. In a dynamic (general-purpose) environment, however, the process schedule and the memory needs are not known a priori, so there are three options:

1. Demand loading
2. Page set swapping managed by the operating system
3. Preloading (by the operating system) of the pages likely to be used by a process that is about to be scheduled for execution

Because memory management policies supporting demand loading use the same loading strategy, they can differ only in their placement and dumping policies.

In the following sections, we consider the placement and replacement allo-cation decisions. We emphasize the design of a general-purpose system operat-ing in an undedicated environment. Two important aspects of the memory allocation system concern the method for subdividing memory into allocatable units and the policy for managing these units of memory.

Memory Subdivision. Memory can be subdivided into variable-length segments or into fixed-length pages. A division based on segments can be related to the program's use of the objects contained therein. A division based on pages cannot be related to any properties of a user's program; the page-based division is made strictly for management convenience.

Segmentation. Segments have different sizes, despite having a fixed maximum size. Their lifetimes with respect to residence at a level of the memory hierarchy have arbitrary relationships. Thus, a segment-based allocator must use a variable-sized heap allocation policy or else something must force a queue discipline on the segment lifetimes in main memory. To force skewed lifetimes, the system dumps segments from main memory as they arrive at the end of the queue, regardless of their usage histories. In particular, when the program accesses an absent segment, that segment must be loaded, so the allocator dumps segments at the end of the queue from main memory to free enough space to hold the incoming segment. This form of queue-based allocation does not take advantage of locality.

Paging. Pages have identical sizes; under a paging system, the managed memory is divided into page frames of identical size, so any free page frame can satisfy any space request. Clearly, this space division is made for the benefit of the operating system; there is no reason to confine programs or data to fixed-size memory blocks. The assumptions permitting fixed-size heap allocation are satisfied by a paged system. Paging can be added beneath any existing memory system design because the accessing system can be designed so that all paging operations and manipulations are functionally transparent to all higher-level parts of the system.

Under paging, two management decisions have trivial answers—a page will be loaded on demand,[16] and it may be placed in any free page frame. To complete the design, we must select the page size(s), select the page dumping policy, and design hardware support for both statistics collection and address translation. Here we discuss page-size selection, dumping policies, and statistics collection mechanisms. Address translation is covered in Chapter 3.

Several costs enter into the page-size question:

1. Address translation complexity
2. Page-fault frequency
3. Waste data space
4. Descriptor table space

Address translation complexity is discussed in Chapter 3. The *page-fault frequency* measures the rate of occurrence of page faults.

Definition. A *page fault* occurs when the accessing system detects that an object that is to be accessed is, in fact, absent from main memory.

Upon detecting a page fault, the system causes an interrupt to invoke the system's memory allocation software. The total interrupt processing overhead is

---

[16]   Some systems, such as the Alpha AXP, have prefetch instruction that notifies of an upcoming need to access a cache block; when this is executed, a request to load that cache block is initiated.

proportional to the page-fault frequency. How is the page-fault frequency affected by the page size? There are two interesting aspects. First, if more pages were present in main memory, the fault probability would decrease. For a fixed main memory size, more pages can be present if each is smaller; this change might reduce the number of page faults, so one might conclude that the number of page faults would decrease as the page size decreases. However, with larger pages, more consecutive information will be moved to main memory on each page fault; having larger consecutive blocks should reduce the number of present pages, so one might conclude that the number of page faults would increase as the page size increases. Some statistical information concerning program behavior is required to determine the best page size.

Paging causes *waste data space* because the last page allocated to a block of contiguous virtual addresses will be partly empty if the entire page is not required to hold the end of the block. If the statistical distribution of object lengths is sufficiently random, the average amount of this "internal waste" will be one-half page per block of contiguous virtual addresses. The amount of this waste depends on the page size and the average size of contiguous allocation blocks (measured in units of pages).

Finally, paging consumes *descriptor table space*. These tables describe the memory allocation. They are used by the address translation and allocation modules. The table space is part of the management overhead. The amount of table space is proportional to the number of pages in the virtual address space, so the table size depends inversely on the page size. This space overhead increases with decreasing page size.

The previous factors must be balanced to determine the system's page size. How do system designers actually select the page size for a new design? A common method is to collect a set of sample programs and emulate their behavior under various page sizes. The best page size is found at the minimum cost point. The SPARC page size is 4096 bytes, whereas the Alpha AXP system [SITE92] permits four page sizes ranging from 8,192 to 65,536 bytes. For designs using memory vector streaming for high computational rates, much larger pages may appropriate. The CDC STAR-100 [CONT70], for example, has two page sizes; the large page size (for vector objects) is 65,536 words, or 524,288 bytes.

Example F-12

The Alpha AXP OSF/1 system support has page descriptors that include a "granularity hint" fieldm g. If the g is nonzero, the page may be treated as a portion of a block of naturally aligned virtually contiguous pages having identical attributes that can be managed as though it were a larger page. By loading the large page into a contiguous piece of physical space, address translation buffer entries can be saved, and faster memory accesses may be possible, especially if the processor uses streaming to process a sequence of contiguous (or nearby) memory objects. The 2-bit value in g gives the logarithm (base 8) of the number of pages in the larger page. Thus, 8, 64, or 512 pages can be considered as a larger page to be allocated contiguous physical space. Such requests do not have to be honored. The flexibility does introduce complexity into the page management module if it tries to find naturally aligned contiguous physical space to honor the hint (see Problem F-24). A net gain results because time and space can be saved if the large object is accessed frequently.

Memory Allocation Policies for Paged Systems. The memory management policy issue for a paged system concerns only page dumping, because the loading and placement policies are trivial. The page dumping policy selection affects system performance and system complexity. Consider two disparate policies: random dumping and "expert" dumping. Random dumping is easy to implement but produces poor performance; the actual program behavior, which exhibits locality, is completely ignored by a random selector. A complex "expert" dumping policy would consume processor resources (time and hardware); it would require data collection during program execution but would give better performance than random dumping. Surely, there must exist a dumping policy that gives reasonably good performance using few statistics and few processor resources. Any nonrandom policy requires that memory accessing statistics must be collected during algorithm execution. Usually, this means that some statistics are gathered during every memory access. Because different statistics are needed to support different policies, the policy selection question is more than just a software design issue. Only the execution machine can collect such statistics efficiently. Thus, the allocation policy selection affects the hardware design.

We first discuss an idealized unrealizable "optimum" page allocation policy whose performance defines the performance limit for all management policies. Then we turn to three page management policies:

1. First-in, first-out (FIFO)
2. Least recently used (LRU)
3. Working set (WS)

All but the first require some data collection during every memory access. Data collection can be simplified if there are only a few objects to manage or a few simple statistics to collect. Contemporary systems utilize use bit data collection, which simplifies the data collection hardware and yields approximate statistical information for the memory allocator.

Optimum Page Allocation. The optimum page-dumping policy [BELA66] removes that page for which the time interval to its next access is the longest. It should be obvious that this policy minimizes the number of page faults that will occur while the removed page is absent (because every other page that is present will be needed sooner than the removed page). The fundamental flaw with this fine policy is one must know the program's future behavior in order to determine which page to dump! Of course, we cannot determine future page references (without running the program itself!), so this optimum policy is unrealizable. It is useful to consider the optimal policy not because it is realistic, but because it does give an upper bound on the performance of all paged memory allocation systems.

FIFO Allocation. The FIFO allocation policy dumps the page that has been present in memory for the longest time. The entire memory can be managed as a circular buffer of pages, with the FIFO order being identical to the memory address ordering. Despite the simplicity of FIFO management, systems do not use it because it performs poorly with real programs.

LRU Management. The principle of locality states that a process's referencing behavior in the near future will be similar to its referencing behavior in the recent past. This gives us one basis for estimating the future: Measure the past. Recall that under the optimal allocation policy, the manager dumps that page for which the time to the next access is the longest. Based on the preceding interpretation of locality, the page whose next reference is furthest in the future is likely to be the page whose last reference is furthest in the past; this page is the least recently used (LRU) page in memory.

To implement LRU management, we need mechanisms for statistics collection and processing so the allocator can find the LRU page. Two options, the time stamp and stack mechanisms, show a trade-off between overhead expended on every memory access and overhead expended on page dumping.

Under the *time stamp* mechanism, during every access, the current time is copied into the accessed page descriptor. When a page must be dumped, all these time stamp values are compared to find the smallest value; the corresponding page is the LRU page that should be dumped.

Alternately, an *LRU stack* orders the page descriptors by recency of access. Whenever a page is referenced its descriptor is moved to the top of the stack and all descriptors between the top and the previous position of the promoted one are pushed one position lower in the stack. The bottom stack entry describes the least recently used page. Figure F-8 illustrates how an LRU stack changes as references are made.

Notice the trade between overhead during access and overhead during allocation: The time stamp scheme has a simple data collection scheme, but the minimum value search required to make the dumping decision is computationally complex. The stack scheme requires complex data collection because the stack must be manipulated on every access, although finding the page to be dumped is quite simple; see Section F.6.3.

One case is worthy of special note. If only a small number (n) of entries must be managed in an LRU fashion, a set of $n(n-1)/2$ recency bits can be used to collect LRU information. This mechanism is detailed in Section F.6.3.

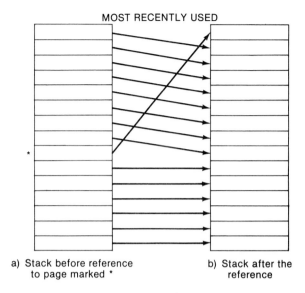

a) Stack before reference   b) Stack after the
   to page marked *   reference

Figure F-8   LRU motion of page descriptors

Use Bit Approximations. Many paging algorithm performance studies have emulated various environments. The results show that the system performance is affected more strongly by the size of the main memory than by the selection of the management policy. Of course, a "reasonable" paging policy should be used. An intuitive meaning of reasonableness is adequate: that the policy decisions should take the behavior of the executing program(s) into account.

The use bit data collection technique is a simple mechanism that provides only approximate data concerning recent referencing patterns. Usage data are collected in two stages: a simple stage requiring hardware support and a second stage possibly managed by software. In the first stage, the hardware sets a "used" bit in the page descriptor when the corresponding page is accessed. To approximate the statistics that support a particular memory management policy, the system examines the used bits and updates auxiliary data structures. The processing of the used bits is usually programmed into the page fault handler. The net result is that the auxiliary data approximates the exact behavioral data that would have been collected by a more complex data collection mechanism.

For example, to approximate the LRU algorithm, the page manager maintains a stack whose ordering approximates the recency-of-use page ordering. To update the stack, every page whose used bit is set is moved to the top of the stack, and all used bits are cleared. Thus, the set of pages referenced since the time of the last update becomes a block at the top of the stack (but the ordering within this block of pages is arbitrary). Even though the bottommost stack entry may not identify exactly the least recently used page, it certainly identifies a member of the least recently used block of pages.

A memory management policy that needs usage time information can approximate that information by sampling the used bits. More fidelity can be obtained by more frequent sampling. The used bit design presents a trade-off between implementation accuracy and implementation efficiency. As excessively accurate information is not essential for adequate page management performance, and because page dumping policies are based on the assumption that the near future will approximate the recent past—a approximation at best—a simple mechanization is often chosen. This means that the used bit data will be collected on each memory access and processed on each page fault.

F.5.3 Comments

The operating system should manage memory resources using a reasonable policy, which implies that it be based on actual behavior of the processes and programs sharing use of the system. Therefore, usage data must be collected by an underlying mechanism. These data can be used to select information to be moved down in the memory hierarchy, with the hope that the dumping decisions will produce good system performance. Usage data collection can be implemented by the hardware or by the processor microcode, but not by software, because the data collection overhead will be too great. The used bit approximation scheme employs hardware collection to obtain basic data that are processed by simple software to support memory management.

F.6 PROCESSOR SUPPORT FOR ALLOCATION POLICIES

In the preceding sections, we have explored several memory management policies and shown how certain policies can be useful at different levels of system design and implementation. We have seen how a list can be used as the free-space management database. We have seen that operating system memory management requires support from underlying mechanisms to collect usage statistics on which reasonable management policies must rely.

In this section, we present briefly several ways that processor designs might be supplemented to support memory allocation decisions and their implementation. We show how a system can be designed to make memory allocations automatically. We discuss a list searching instruction and statistical data collection mechanisms. We discuss the possible use of a coprocessor to speculatively clean memory pages that are likely swapping candidates. In addition to these specific design elements, the processor design should support efficient accessing to the allocated space; we discuss accessing in Chapter 3.

F.6.1 **Processor Support for Automatic Allocation**

The semantics of a processor's CALL instruction can be extended to include some functions from the prologue of any called procedure. In particular, the allocation of automatic space is frequently required, so it is a good candidate for inclusion within CALL.

Example F-13

> The IBM System/38 keeps the size of the automatic space as an attribute of an entry point to a procedure. When the CALL is performed, the processor fetches this space size and acquires the required amount of stack space for the new invocation, as described in Example F-11. Notice that there is no advantage to this operation if the local objects must be initialized.

Example F-14

> The MC68020 LINK instruction both sets a frame pointer for use during the execution of a procedure and adjusts the stack pointer to allocate space for the local objects of the called procedure. While executing the instruction LINK An,#d, the processor does the following:
>
> > **1.** Pushes the contents of An on the stack
> > **2.** Stores the (adjusted) stack pointer in An
> > **3.** Adds the (sign-extended) value of d to the stack pointer
>
> Because stacks grow toward low addresses in this system, a negative d is used to allocate space, and there is no meaningful reason to place a positive value in d.

Other extensions of CALL semantics to support changes of the accessing mechanisms (and thereby simplify accesses to automatic objects) are discussed in Section 4.3.1.

F.6.2 **List Searching**

Within the implementation of a heap allocation policy with variable-sized allocations, there is a linked list describing the free space. While servicing an allocate request, the allocator searches the list to find an appropriate block of free space. The best-fit policy, for example, requires finding the free block in the list whose size is the smallest value that is larger than the requested size. To implement an efficient search for a list member meeting this criterion, the list should be ordered by block size. When servicing a free request, the allocator inserts the newly freed space into the free list while maintaining its size ordering.

The allocator may merge and split free blocks to provide an appropriate block size for each allocate request. Splitting free space is not difficult; it can be built into the basic allocate and free operations. Merging free space, on the other hand, is slightly more difficult, because the allocator must find any neighboring free blocks. This task would be easy if the free list were ordered by block origins.

The general action is that the allocator searches a list to find the first entry whose value satisfies a specified search criterion. For memory allocation, the search criterion is an arithmetic comparison between the search parameter (the block size or the address) and a value in a component of the list bead. A processor operation that searches a list for the first entry whose value is not less than the value of an integer operand can support all memory allocation functions.

What result do we desire from a list search operation? We want to access the list element that met the search criterion. But it is better if the result describes the predecessor of the bead that met the search criterion; this choice supports "easy" deletion or insertion if the list is singly-linked.

To implement the list search, the locations of the value field and the next-element pointer within each list bead must be known. Standardizing these parts of the bead structure makes it easier to provide low-level support for the search operation. Two different designs are discussed in the following examples.

Example F-15

The B 5700 list search instruction ([BURR73]) requires a fixed bead format: Each bead is a single word containing both the index of the successor list entry (in bits 19 .. 0) and the integer value v associated with this bead (in bits 47 .. 20). The complete list must be stored within one segment; the successor index in a list bead specifies the successor's location relative to the segment's origin. Figure F-9 illustrates the basic list structure. The list search operation has three arguments: a descriptor of the segment containing the list, the position index of the first word of the list, and a search value S. While performing this instruction, the processor retains the position indices of recently searched list entries. It examines the next list word, comparing its value V against S. If $V < S$, the search continues to the next bead in the list. If the value in the bead is not less than S, the search is complete, and the processor returns as its result the position index of the predecessor of the list entry where the search criterion was satisfied. The design is depicted in Figure F-9.

Example F-16

The list search instruction in the HP 3000 processor has more flexibility in the list format. In particular, the locations of the value and the successor pointer do not have to have a fixed relationship to each other. The pointers contain the addresses of the pointer words in list beads, which therefore form the linked chain. There are four operands of the list search instruction; the first two, like those in the B 5700, are a pointer to the head of the list and the search value. The third operand specifies the bead format; it contains the number of words beyond the pointer where bead's value is stored. These three operands are at the top of the stack (pointed to by the processor register named S). The final operand is a count that limits the length of the search; this operand is in the index register (named X). The result of the search (left at the top of the stack) is a pointer to the bead where the completion test succeeded, and not to its predecessor, as in the B 5700. Figure F-10 illustrates the data structures, including the result of a search through the list used in Example F-15.

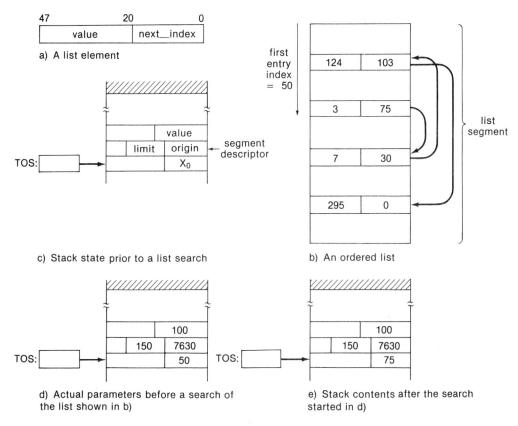

Figure F-9   B 5700 list searching

Comparing these two list search designs, we see more flexibility in the HP 3000 scheme, but two memory access are required to read the (separated) bead value and successor pointer. Having the result be a pointer to the predecessor of the bead that met the search criterion (as in the B 5700) makes bead insertion and deletion easier. These observations suggest that the B 5700 scheme is the clear winner. However, the advantage goes back to the HP 3000 design if the set of items must be ordered on more than one criterion. We examine this aspect in detail in Problem F-20.

Both the B 5700 and the HP 3000 processors can be used to search a set of beads ordered on two criteria. Therefore, these designs support memory management algorithms. List seraching is difficult to implement within a pipelined architecture due to the need for a memory accesses to determine the address for the next memory access (to the successor bead).

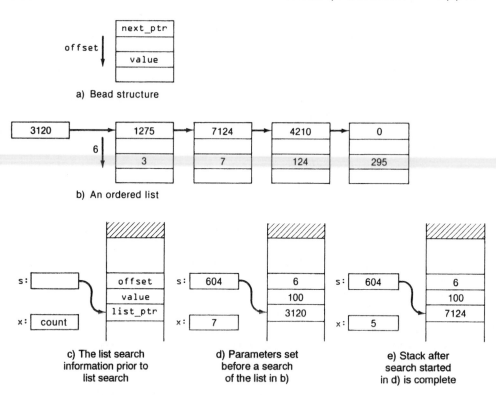

Figure F-10   HP 3000 list searching

F.6.3 Usage Statistic Collection Hardware

The hardware level is the only reasonable level at which statistics can be collected to support main memory allocation policies. The overhead inherent in implementing data collection in software is too great because data must be collected on every memory access. So we need data collection hardware.

What data should be collected? One option is to specialize the hardware for one specific management policy, such as LRU. Another option uses hardware designed to collect basic[17] usage information (such as used bits); the simple usage information could be manipulated by the memory manager to support the chosen management policy. The identical generic data collection mechanism can support many different management policies.

---

[17]   In the sense that the act of collecting information does not process (or select) information in such a way as to preclude the implementation of a specific memory management policy.

A basic statistics collection technique keeps track of the program's accessing patterns. In Section F.5.2, we saw that used bits can be set by the hardware on each access and that approximate statistics can be developed from the used bit data. The used bits are reset by the memory allocation software. In addition, the hardware can be designed to record writes (that make a page dirty) by setting a "dirty" bit in the page descriptor. This simple mechanism does not embody any management policies; thus, it is a good candidate for low-level support without biasing the choices left for the implementers.

A hardware LRU stack is a typical policy-specific hardware mechanism supporting memory allocation. Because including enough hardware to hold the entire LRU stack can be expensive, a compromise design places some topmost stack entries in a hardware module, with the less frequently referenced descriptors (lower in the stack) stored in slower memory (in a location known to the hardware mechanism). In this manner, the functionality of a complete hardware stack can be realized at a lower expense but with most of its benefits (see Problem F-27). Hardware support for LRU page stacking is provided in the CDC STAR-100 and Cyber 205 machines.

Another stack representation can be used if only a small number of blocks are to be managed—we keep a set of recency-comparison bits that record which member of each possible pair of blocks was referenced more recently. In particular, if there are n blocks in each set, the LRU information requires $n(n-1)/2$ comparison bits—bit b_{ij} ($i < j$) is set if block i has been referenced more recently than block j. While making an access, the system forces new values into $(n-1)$ of the control bits to make it appear that the block being referenced is more recent than any other block in the set. To make the set dumping decision, n AND gates, each with fan-in of $(n-1)$, are provided. The output from gate i is high if the ith item is the least recently used member of the set.

F.6.4 Coprocessor Assists for Memory Management

It is straightforward to design a coprocessor that speculatively cleans memory pages; the coprocessor examines the memory allocator's database to find candidate pages for swapping out. After a page has been swapped out, its dirty bit is cleared, and another descriptor is examined. Because the swapping activity can get in the way of useful memory traffic, it is not wise to have the processor always looking and finding pages to swap. Some statistics about the frequency of dirty pages could be used to limit these activities.

A coprocessor could be designed to maintain the approximate database using information from the used bits; a system with this type of coprocessor would incur less overhead during page fault handling.

F.7 SUMMARY

In this appendix, we covered topics related to allocating memory space for objects used by executing programs. We studied static and dynamic allocation policies and their management requirements, including free-space bookkeeping. We saw how high-level-language declarations can imply object lifetimes. We discussed ways to allocate space for static, automatic, and dynamic objects. Stacks of activation blocks are attractive for storing automatic objects and meeting the naming semantics of static nesting environments. We have seen that a process creator can allocate the spaces required to hold the programs and data for program execution. Beneath all of these mechanisms, the operating system can manage main memory space automatically using exact or approximate statistics about the actual behavior of the programs executing on the system; hardware-level data collection is required for realistic implementations of this policy option. We briefly reviewed these hardware functions, which we detail, with memory accessing techniques, in Chapter 3.

F.8 TRENDS

Memory space allocation is managed by software within the operating system, but hardware mechanisms for statistics collection will continue to be used. The used bit scheme is popular and there is no reason to supplant it with more complex mechanisms, because the predictions are not accurate anyhow. Sets of bits will continue to be used to maintain LRU information within small sets of allocation blocks, especially within cache memories and cached tables holding memory address mappings within the memory management unit. Garbage collection will remain a requirement to support languages that do not explicitly or implicitly specify execution times when deallocations should be made to avoid holding allocations for memory resources that are no longer needed.

F.9 CONCEPT LIST

    1. Allocation pools are themselves objects
    2. Object lifetime classification
    3. Allocate (**new**) and free (**delete**) requests
    4. Static versus dynamic allocations
    5. Stack, queue, and heap allocations
    6. Frame-based allocations
    7. First-fit and best-fit allocation policies

8. Buddy system allocations
9. Automatic lifetimes correlate with program flow
10. Activation block stacks
11. Parameter passing can be correlated with automatic object allocations on the stack
12. Processor instructions can reserve stack space for automatic objects
13. Users can leave dangling pointers; automatic mechanisms to find or avoid them are expensive
14. Users can abandon memory space, leaving "garbage"
15. Programs can operate even with some information absent if the system is able to support missing object faults
16. Locality and the memory hierarchy make absent information schemes interesting and feasible
17. Three basic allocation decisions concern loading, placement, and dumping
18. Paging uses frame-based allocation; dumping is the only difficult decision
19. Page fault frequency measures the efficiency of a paging system
20. Optimum page allocation is not feasible; it requires knowledge of the future
21. Approximate page allocation policies are usually adequate
22. Used and dirty bits can assist with data collection for memory managers
23. List searching processor operations can assist memory allocators
24. Least recently used information can be recorded as a set of times of access, as an LRU stack, or as the state within a set of recency bits.
25. Coprocessors might be useful for processing usage data or speculatively cleaning memory spaces by copying the modified values

F.10 PROBLEMS

F-1.   In ALGOL, it is possible to define a new naming context within a procedure body by using the keywords **declare .. end**. Such a declare context is entered when the program flow reaches the **declare** statement. On block entry (before the statements within the block are performed), the local objects declared within the declare block are allocated and initialized. In a complementary manner, the block is exited to the next statement after the **end** that terminates the block. Upon block exit, all local objects are deallocated. The previous rules define the semantics of the objects declared in an embedded **declare .. end** block. One implementation of these semantics allocates space for local objects when the block is entered and deallocates it on block exit. Figure F-11a illustrates the allocation semantics of the **declare .. end** structure.

In this problem, we introduce and study an alternate implementation of the local object semantics. In the alternate implementation, all automatic objects declared within a **declare** block are allocated at the same time as the automatic objects

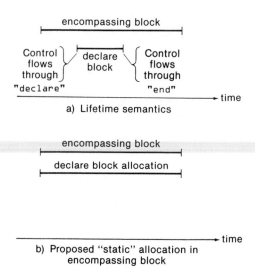

a) Lifetime semantics

b) Proposed "static" allocation in
encompassing block

Figure F-11   The **declare** .. **end** block lifetime and
allocation option

declared within the enclosing procedure or function block. Figure F-11b illustrates
this proposed allocation.

As you answer this problem, you may supplement the alternate design if necessary to match the semantics of the original design, but do preserve its basic allocation policy—that the local automatic space is allocated with the objects declared
local to the enclosing procedure or function block.

Discuss the following issues, comparing the two approaches.

(a) Object initialization.

(b) Object naming in the programming language.

(c) Object visibility in the programming language.

F-2.   This problem concerns the allocation strategy in which two stacks are allocated at
opposite ends of a single vector. The stacks are set up so that they grow toward the
middle as objects are pushed onto them.

(a) Draw a picture illustrating the two stacks in the vector's space.

(b) Write out the implementations of the push and pop operations for each stack.

(c) A designer proposes using this structure to collect the stacks for two separate
processes into a single space. The claim is that there will be a space saving
without a time penalty. Discuss this claim. In particular, is the conclusion
correct?

(d) Propose a scheme for implementing PUSH and POP processor instructions that
will work for all stacks in this system (you will have to keep the direction
somewhere—where?).

F-3.   A system uses a last-in, first-out free memory space list to allocate fixed-size blocks
from a space pool. (In other words, upon the next request for free space, the
manager will first try to use the space that was last freed.) Prove that if the

program allocates and deallocates fixed-size blocks only, this policy does maximize the amount of space that is never allocated to any object, for any given history of allocations and deallocations. Therefore, prove that the LIFO policy does minimize the amount of space that must be allocated for a given process to be able to execute. You may wish to consider an equivalent claim, namely, that there does not exist another heap-based fixed-block allocation policy which uses less space.

F-4. Write a pair of allocate and free procedures using the queue allocation policy.

F-5. In the text's discussion of queue allocation, it was claimed that if the using programs were known to be correct, one or both of the parameters of the **free** calls could be removed from the call—it was implied that the removal would not have any effect on the program's semantics. (The two parameters were the origin and length of the space to be freed.) What property must the using programs satisfy so that both parameters can be eliminated? Explain.

F-6. Write a pair of allocate and free procedures using the bit vector free-space management scheme for fixed-size allocation from a heap.

F-7. This problem compares the first-fit and best-fit allocation schemes.
  (a) Write out the allocate algorithm under each policy. For first fit, assume that a doubly linked free list is maintained in order of origins.
  (b) Discuss the differences for the first-fit algorithm between organizing the free list in order by origin and by LIFO ordering (based on the ordering of list entry times).
  (c) If you were asked to compare these schemes, what more would you like to know about the programs and their space request patterns? Explain both what you would like to know and how the information would influence your selection of an allocation policy.
  (d) How could you obtain the information that you desire [based on your answer for part (c)]?

F-8. The picture in Figure F-12 shows snapshots of four different allocation pools. The shaded regions are allocated and the clear regions are free. Fill in Table F-1 with a mark in an entry if the corresponding combination of snapshot and allocation policy are incompatible. When you are finished, the clear table entries will represent the policy-pool combinations that are compatible.

F-9. Consider a space allocator that allocates variable-sized blocks from a heap. The free requests have a parameter that is a descriptor of the space to be freed,

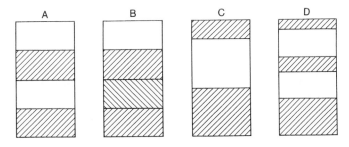

Figure F-12   Four memory allocations

TABLE F-1 COMBINATIONS OF POOL
CONFIGURATION AND ALLOCATION
POLICY (PROBLEM F-5)

	Pool Name			
Policy	A	B	C	D
Stack				
Queue				
Frames				
Segments (from heap)				

specifying both the origin and length of the space to be freed. It is possible that the information provided in such a free request is not consistent with the blocks that were previously allocated.

In the text, we did not present any algorithms that verify the consistency of free requests to an allocator. One way to include parameter checking is to perform these checks within the allocator's algorithms. Another method interposes a parameter checking package (Figure F-13) between the outside world and the allocation module. The checker changes the parameters of free requests to force them to correspond to the combination of origin and length that was doled out by the allocator in response to an earlier allocate request. You are asked to write a C++ class that serves this function. Your class will have to keep an internal (static) table that pairs each block origin with the corresponding block length. The entries to your class will be allocate_check(**int** length)[18] and free_check(space *origin, **int** length). If there is an error in the space specification of the free request received by your module, the actual allocation should be freed and an externally visible flag free_error should be set true. The system's allocation procedures that allocate and free space, without checking the parameters, are specified as

```
space *alloc( int size );     //the type space is assumed to have been declared
void free( space *loc; int size );
```

(a) Explain briefly why the checking module must be within a class.
(b) Write the class.
(c) Comment on the advantages and disadvantages of the proposed method of responding to length mismatches.

F-10. This problem concerns the design of a space allocator using variable-sized allocation from a heap such that the allocator keeps a table showing the origin-size correspondences. The free call has only a single parameter, which is the origin of the space to be freed.
(a) Show the data structures that you will use.
(b) Write the allocate and free algorithms.

---

[18] We introduce new names for the entries to avoid overloading the name of the entry point of the built-in procedure.

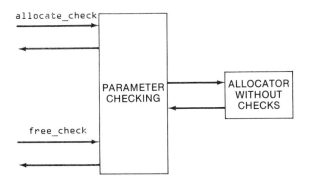

Figure F-13   A parameter-checking module interposed
between the users and the allocator

(c) Several assumptions must be made regarding the behavior of the programs using the allocated space so that the allocator will perform correctly. State two of
them.

F-11. A variation on the best-fit allocation policy places a lower limit F on the size of a
free block. It attempts to meet this constraint by choosing the free block to use in
meeting an allocate request for S words as follows:
1. If there is a free block of size S, take it.
2. Look for the best fit for size (S + F).
3. If the search in step 2 fails, look for the best fit for size S.
(a) Why is this variation attractive?
(b) Compare this allocation strategy against the ordinary best-fit policy.

F-12. A free list ordered both by size and origin requires two different link chains. The
structure shown in Figure F-14 is attractive for this purpose. This structure cannot
be described in an Ada program because one cannot perform arithmetic operations
on access objects in Ada. The structure can be described in Ada by defining the
pointers to point to the first item in each bead, with appropriate naming to specify
the location (within the bead) of the successor pointer to be used during a
particular search. For example, if org_ptr and size_ptr are the names of two access
objects in the bead's record format, a program following the address sequence
must update its current position (which we will describe as an access object named
current) by one of these two assignment statements:

```
current = current.org_ptr;
current = current.size_ptr;
```

Another design that might be used to impose two different orderings on a single
set of space descriptors uses another level of indirection. We make a separate
singly linked list to order the elements on one attribute. The "values" in the two
lists are access objects, each pointing to a space descriptor, as shown in Figure
F-15. Under this scheme, the double-list design requires two beads for each free
block. A simple processor list searching operation can be used within each list.
Describe how a newly freed block is added to the data structures. Design your

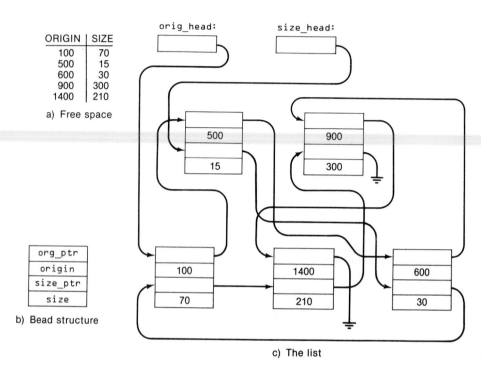

ORIGIN	SIZE
100	70
500	15
600	30
900	300
1400	210

a) Free space

b) Bead structure

```
org_ptr
origin
size_ptr
size
```

c) The list

Figure F-14 Free-space list organized using two sets
of successor pointers

algorithm to look for the possibility of combining the new free space with previously free space to form a larger free block; when this is possible, the algorithm should perform the merger.

F-13. A designer suggests the following allocation algorithm: If possible, the allocator chooses a free block close to the desired size. Failing this, it tries to split a block that is close to double the requested size. If this does not succeed, it tries for a block of four times the requested size, and so forth. If this progressive search fails, it takes the best-fit block (in relation to the original request).

    (a) Comment on any relationships between the proposed strategy and the buddy system.

    (b) Would you recommend this strategy over the best-fit strategy? If so, under what conditions? Explain your answers.

F-14. Write a space manager using the buddy system defined in the text. It can be called through the following interfaces:

```
space *alloc( int size );
void free( space *loc, int size );
```

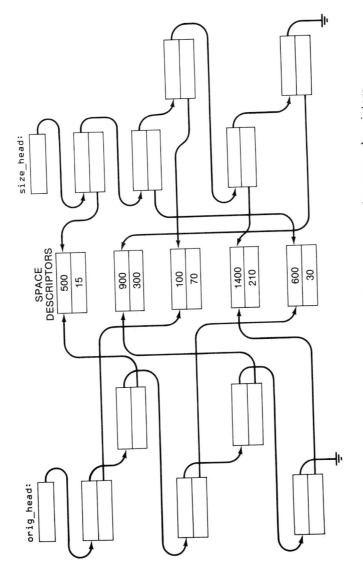

Figure F-15 Two singly linked lists pointing to free-space descriptors

Use the buddy version in which a block of size 2^n is divided into one block of size 2^{n-1} and two blocks of size 2^{n-2}. The size of the space pool is known; it is an integer located in the object named total_space.

F-15. Given a buddy system based on the fractions {½, ¼, ¼}. You are given the origin and length of a block. Specify an algorithm that computes the lengths and origins of it buddies. All addressing starts at 0, which designates the first location in the pool being allocated. Assume that you know the pool size, which is a power of 2.

F-16. In this problem we refer to the structure variants of Example E-9.
   (a) Describe a way that the implementation might distinguish the two variants. (*Hint:* You will need to have a distinguishing mechanism at both translate time and run time. Can these be identical?)
   (b) Show how the **new** statement could be implemented in a form consistent with your answer to part (a).

F-17. Pointers, descriptors, and capabilities all describe memory space. Briefly discuss their differences. For each one, describe at least one situation in which it is useful.

F-18. A designer suggests that pointer embarrassments such as dangling pointers could be removed if there were sufficient bookkeeping to keep track of pointers. One way to eliminate dangling references is to associate with each dynamically allocated object a list of all of the pointers pointing to that object. Then when the object is deleted, the system is able to go through the list and replace all the pointers by **null**. This problem concerns designs incorporating background pointer bookkeeping.
   (a) Specify such a data structure.
   (b) Show how the block epilogue could use the locator list to delete dangling references.
   (c) Write a C++ class module managing the type "safe_pointer." The package should function so that a safe_pointer object is not the same as a conventional C++ pointer object; the class implementation should guarantee that a safe_pointer object will never become a dangling reference. The trick is to chain together all objects that happen to point to the same allocated object. This structure is illustrated in Figure F-16. The chain can be used as required to find all pointers that point to an object. Design the class implementation so that all pointers that point to object X will be replaced by **null** when X is freed. Assume that all pointers point to objects created by allocate operations (in other words, a program cannot construct a pointer to an individual component of an area that was allocated by the allocator).
   (d) Discuss the reason for the pointer construction restriction stating that a program cannot construct a pointer that points to a component of a compound object. In particular, show how removing this restriction will complicate the implementation.
   (e) A designer proposes that the use of this scheme be made optional [the programmer specifies whether the locators pointing to a particular object shall be chained together by passing the value "yes" (or "no") to a third parameter of the allocate request that creates the first pointer to the object]. The proponent of this proposal claims that execution time can be saved for accesses to those objects for which dangling references will never be a problem. Comment on the designer's reasoning, and state whether anything would be lost by adopting the

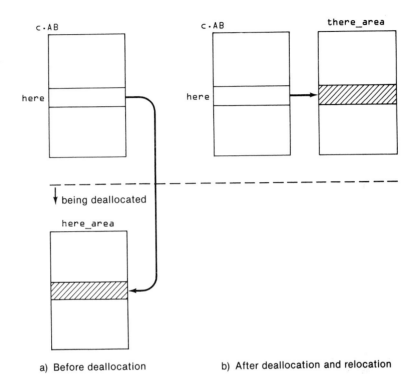

a) Before deallocation   b) After deallocation and relocation

Figure F-16   Pointer adjustments upon object relocation

proposed modification. Which design approaches (e.g. "everything checked")
apply to each design?

F-19. Suppose that a language allows a programmer to allocate objects from a global
area and place the pointers that point to them in local objects. Difficulties might
ensue if the local pointers are deallocated at block exit without freeing the allocated
spaces. To remove this problem, the system could find all pointers that are about
to disappear and deallocate the corresponding objects.

(a) Will this scheme work correctly if there exist several pointers to a single allocated object? Explain.

(b) Write a block epilogue that finds all user-allocated objects and deletes them before block exit.

(c) Specify any data structures that you create to make this function work
properly.

(d) Describe how the implementation of operations performed on pointers would
be affected by your design (it is possible that the operator implementations
would not be affected).

(e) Discuss whether the proposed scheme for automatic deallocation has any visible semantic consequences. (In other words, does the programmer ever write
different programs if he knows that the proposed scheme is used in the
implementation?)

F-20. This problem concerns a SPARC implementation of the activation block for a procedure. Draw a picture detailing the activation block allocation described in Example F-9.

F-21. Draw a picture of a reasonable allocation for an activation block in the Alpha AXP processor, which does not have register windows. Compare this structure against the structure found in your answer to Problem F-20.

F-22. Consider a trivial static allocation policy in which all programs are allocated space starting at the same physical address A. It is claimed that this policy is inefficient because it requires saving the objects for one process in order to load a different process for execution. Comment on the claim, and show an example to illustrate your arguments.

F-23. Consider reclaiming memory space in a segmented system in order to be able to load a segment into main memory. A round-robin basis is proposed. One pointer "first" describes the first allocated location, and another pointer "free" describes the first free location. A segment to be loaded is described by its descriptor, which contains

> **int** length;
> index disk_address;   //where to find it on the disk

(a) Devise and describe a data structure that chains together the descriptors of the segments loaded in main memory so that a segment descriptor can be found easily when the information it describes must be moved to secondary memory to make room for an incoming segment.

(b) Using the data structure you defined in part (a), write an algorithm that takes as a parameter the descriptor of a segment to be loaded and produces a list of descriptors of segments that have to be removed to make room for the incoming segment.

F-24. Consider a page allocator that tries to honor granularity hints as used in Alpha AXP page table entries (see Example F-12). The allocator's goal is to allocate a single large page when any small page within the large one is requested. Therefore the allocator must try to find or make a large page that is naturally aligned in physical address space.

(a) Write a function

> **space** *get_big_space(**int** hint)

that attempts to find a contiguous block of memory space whose size matches the granularity taken from the hint. Use the free-bit data structure from the original allocator (that allocates single pages and does not accept granularity hints). The hint parameter is an integer whose value is the power of 2, which is the number of pages desired (e.g., if hint = 2, a naturally aligned space containing four contiguous frames is desired). The allocator returns a pointer to the origin of the allocated space. If the allocator cannot find a naturally aligned contiguous block of space of the size requested, it returns a pointer containing zero. The allocator has access to a global object (**space** *pool_origin) containing a pointer to the (naturally aligned) origin of the space pool being managed.

(b) Using the get_big_space function, write a function

space *find_space(**int** virtual_address, hint)

that allocates the largest possible naturally aligned contiguous space (up to the size specified by the hint parameter) that includes the page containing the specified virtual address.

(c) Add statements to the previous algorithms so that they return a pointer to the page containing the virtual address, rather than a pointer to the entire contiguous block that was allocated.

F-25. One way to reduce paging overhead is to speculatively clean pages in main memory when it seems that they are likely to be overwritten to swap in a new page from secondary memory. The allocator uses a FIFO searching policy to find pages that have been modified and not cleaned out (the FIFO ordering is based on the time of page allocation). Of course, only "dirty" pages have to be swapped out. For this problem, consider the relationship between this speculative cleaning policy and the FIFO page management policy. In the first two parts of the problem, you will examine two schemes for implementing this page-cleaning strategy. The major difference between the two schemes lies in the manner in which dirty pages are found. The goal of both strategies is to keep clean at least N pages that are about to be swapped out. If a page is clean, it will not have to be written out when its frame has to be reallocated for an incoming page.

(a) In this scheme, the system maintains a pointer to the dirty page that is closest to the swap-out position in the FIFO structure (see Figure F-17). Describe how this pointer is manipulated upon page swap (information flows from primary memory to secondary memory), upon reading an object in the page (information flows from main memory to the processor), and upon writing to an object in the page (information flows from the processor to the main memory).

(b) In this scheme, the system always searches for a dirty page by scanning the dirty bits starting with the page frame about to be overwritten, and working backward toward the most recently arrived page. Describe this page swapper design, and provide descriptions of the behavior during the events mentioned in part (a).

(c) List the page manipulation operations that you believe to have the largest effect on the "performance" of these algorithms.

(d) Based on the overhead of the schemes of parts (a) and (b) involved in performing the "significant" operations you identified in part (c), what would you recommend to a system designer considering these two options?

(e) Discuss briefly how these schemes could be adapted for use in a system using an LRU memory management policy.

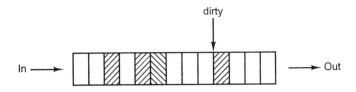

Figure F-17   Dirty pages (shaded) and the dirty-page pointer for speculative cleaning with FIFO allocation

F-26. A memory management system could process used bits either (1) periodically (based on a timer) or (2) whenever a page fault occurs. If the data reduction is performed by software, control must be passed to the data reduction program. To implement periodic data reduction, the processor will have to be interrupted regularly using a timer.

(a) Compare the total system overhead consumed by use bit data reduction under the two options.

(b) Which scheme do you recommend? Why?

F-27. The CDC STAR-100 [CONT70] uses an LRU stack to manage memory page allocation. The top part of the stack is contained in a hardware LRU stack module containing 16 page descriptors. The remainder of the stack is contained in memory starting at the address contained in a pointer named lru_stack_top.

(a) Draw a picture showing the changes in the hardware stack when it is updated to account for a memory access. Suppose that the descriptor of the accessed page was found within the hardware stack.

(b) Repeat part (a) for the case in which the matching descriptor was found in the memory portion of the stack.

(c) Describe the actions to be taken and the changes in the LRU stack for the case in which the matching descriptor is not located within either portion of the LRU stack.

F-28. The HP 3000 linked-list search instruction leaves as its result a pointer to the list bead that satisfies the matching criterion, rather than to its predecessor, as does the B 5700 linked-list lookup instruction. This difference can be significant because the processor does have to find the predecessor bead in order to insert a bead before the one found or to delete the found bead. A software designer proposes that this limitation could be alleviated by redesigning the list structure to place the search value associated with a bead B in B's predecessor in the list. Each bead's format is specified in the following record declaration:

```
class list_bead {
public:
    list_bead *next_pointer;
    int next_size;        //this field contains the search value (for the next bead)
    int present_value;
}
```

(a) Devise an algorithm to insert a bead into the list having this modified format. At the start of your algorithm, the desired place has just been found by executing the HP 3000 list lookup instruction, so you have a pointer to the first bead whose value meets the search criterion.

(b) Show an algorithm to delete a bead from the list having this modified format. As in part (a), you start with a pointer to the first bead whose value meets the search criterion.

(c) Compare the number of accesses to list entries required for the two list formats and make a recommendation for or against the proposed change in the list format.

F-29. One disadvantage of the HP 3000 linked-list search instruction was that the result pointed to the bead where the condition was met, and not to its predecessor (which is useful for insertion and/or deletion). Show how a program can obtain a pointer to the predecessor by manipulating the count in the index register (X). Illustrate the operation of your program fragment as it performs the list search depicted in Figure F-10.

F-30. The processor-supported list searching instruction requires a fixed format for the list entries. At least s, the size of the search field, is fixed by the instruction's implementation. A software designer proposes that this length limitation could be overcome by constructing a "tree" of lists. This tree is constructed as follows: Let W denote the value in the desired wide search field. Let w denote the number of bits in the wide field. Divide W into narrow search fields S_1, S_2, .. , S_p, with S_1 containing the leftmost s bits of W, S_2 the next s bits of W, and so forth. The elements of the search space are thus represented in a p-level tree of lists. In this tree, the lists at level i (level 1 is the root) are ordered by the contents of S_i.

    (a) Draw a representation of the lists in a two-level structure. Show some instances of contents with their wide field values indicated on the corresponding leaf nodes.

    (b) Specify which bead(s) you would like to obtain as a result of a list search in this tree. You want to be able to insert and/or delete an entry at the location indicated by the search. Be sure to consider the situation that arises if one of the beads at one end of a lowest-level list is the one meeting the search criterion.

    (c) Write out a search program to find the node meeting the search criterion (you can use greater than or equals, as in the B 5700 and HP 3000 machines, if you like). Your algorithm should return the result that you desired in part (b). Your algorithm can use the B 5700 search operation to find a desired entry in a list.

    (d) Write out a bead insertion program based on the algorithm you developed in part (c).

F-31. Consider a SPARC implementation of an algorithm to scan a singly linked list to find the first list bead in which the value is greater than or equal to a search value. Determine the algorithm and its translation into SPARC assembly language. Then determine the number of machine cycles required to handle a single list bead. Be sure to account for the memory references required to find both the value and the link in the bead.

ASSOCIATIVE MEMORIES

In the simple memory illusion, all objects have names that serve to identify the location of the named object within a memory space. In associative memories, objects are selected based on their contents, not on their locations. This appendix outlines techniques for implementing general associative memories, which differ from those described in Chapter 3 because the search criterion might not always be equality, as desired for the specialized (but important) name mapping problem.

Associative fetches from tables play a significant role in the implementation of memory accessing functions. The logical requirements on an associative memory are complex, and it might appear that the cost of associative fetching would be high in terms of either speed or logic gate count. Hardware and software designers have devised ways to implement the lookup features needed for memory systems without building a general associative memory; the hash table and set-associative table typify these alternatives. Despite these options, some still desire general associative memories. They may try to use an associative system to permit a large degree of parallelism in a specialized application. For example, an associative system could locate, in parallel, many situations requiring immediate attention (such as pairs of airplanes that appear too close for comfort), and the processing could then be prioritized at these critical points of the problem space.

In this appendix we explore some ways to implement a general associative memory. We start with the required operations. Then we develop a partial system design to implement the required operations. Subsequently, we outline several approaches that provide most or all of the desired associative functions.

G.1 ASSOCIATIVE MEMORY OPERATIONS

Important parts of an associative memory module include its registers, its memory array, and the operations that the module can perform. Figure G-1 depicts the memory array and the associated registers.

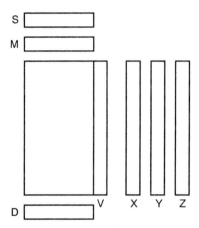

Figure G-1 Associative memory registers

Registers.   Our associative memory model contains several registers. Many registers are the same width as all memory entries; let w denote this width. Other registers have as many bits as there are entries in the memory; let h denote this height. Here are the registers with their widths (in parentheses):

1. $S(w)$, holding the selector value
2. $M(w)$, holding the mask value that selects the bits to be tested
3. $D(w)$, holding data passing to and from memory entries
4. $V(h)$, holding validity bits
5. $X(h)$, which receives search results
6. $Y(h)$, a temporary register
7. $Z(h)$, a temporary register

Memory.   For expository purposes, we use an integer index denoting the location address of memory entries (as in E[i]) even though the implementation might not provide any location-based addressing capabilities. We use vector indices as subscripts to designate the bit positions in a field within a register or location. Thus, E[i, j] denotes the jth bit of the ith entry in the memory, and D[j] denotes the jth bit of register D. The complete value in a register or location is designated by the name of the register or entry without any subscript. We will need a validity bit V(i) with each memory entry. The bit will be set ("true") if the corresponding memory entry contains meaningful information, and will be cleared ("false") otherwise. Many, but not all, associative operations are restricted to valid entries.

Operations.   We present several operations useful in a general-purpose associative memory system:

1. SEARCH
2. FIRST
3. ENTER
4. DELETE
5. READ
6. WRITE
7. Logical and copying operations

SEARCH.   This operation is expressed by

SEARCH(S, MP, M)

The parameters of a search request are a search value S, a match predicate MP, and a mask M that specifies which bit positions are to be considered when making the predicate's test. The S and M registers hold the selector value and the mask value, respectively. Only those memory entries for which X[i] is set are tested,[1] and the SEARCH will clear those X[i] bits where there is a mismatch. Thus, the result of the search operation is a set of match bits in the X register, one for each entry in the memory, specifying (for every tested entry) whether the corresponding entry meets the match condition. An additional result is a status value related to the number of entries that satisfied the match condition.

The SEARCH operation leaves status information in the associative memory condition code register (AMCC). The three bits of this register indicate the number of X bits that are set, as indicated in Table G-1. The distinctions made by the status values are important. They allow the program to test whether an upcoming associative memory operation can be meaningfully performed. For example, if AMCC(2) is set, a READ operation probably should not be performed. Because AMCC reflects the status of X, whenever X changes, AMCC has to be reevaluated.

---

[1]   This condition permits useful instruction sequences in which the first part determines the bits to be tested, and the second part determines whether they meet the condition.

TABLE G-1   ASSOCIATIVE MEMORY CONDITION CODE BITS

Bit Position	Meaning
0	No bits set in X
1	One bit set in X
2	More than one bit set in X

Any match predicate MP can be stated as a Boolean expression. The "match"[2] should succeed for all memory entries for which the match predicate MP evaluates to true. The MP governing the value of X[i] may involve the contents of the M and S registers, and the corresponding memory entry E[i]. For example, an MP requiring an exact match in all bit positions is

$$MP[i] = V[i] \text{ and } \{\forall j, (E[i, j] = S[j])\} \tag{G-1}$$

This predicate tests all entries in the memory; occasionally, it is convenient to have an equality test confined to those entries where X[i] was previously set. An MP for this test is

$$MP[i] = V[i] \text{ and } X[i] \text{ and } \{\forall j, (E[i, j] = S[j])\} \tag{G-2}$$

Another interesting match predicate requires a match only in those bit positions where the mask's bit is set. This predicate that tests all memory entries is

$$MP[i] = V[i] \text{ and } \{\forall j, (E[i, j] = S[j]) \text{ or not } M[j]\} \tag{G-3}$$

This masked equality match predicate is sufficient to implement all memory accessing algorithms presented in Chapter 3. In fact, because for memory name mapping the mask value can be fixed at design time, an explicit mask register is not required,[3] and the matching logic and algorithm can be tailored for the specific mask pattern.[4] In the following, we discuss general associative memories; this means that we will include the mask register and obtain search results in the X register.

FIRST. This important special operation finds the first bit of X that is set, setting the corresponding bit in Y, while clearing all other bits of Y. In addition, the bit of X that was selected is cleared. It is very expensive of logic, program steps, or signal delay to implement FIRST, because the value of each result bit depends on the values in all preceding bits of the operand. Therefore, we only

---

[2]   We use quotes because the English word "match" may imply that the predicate is an equality condition; in fact, equality is merely a special case of the general match predicate that is our concern here.

[3]   Because a multiple match can occur only after an error, logic to find the first match (see what follows) will not be required. (We still need logic to detect a multiple match. Why?)

[4]   This means that many gates and tests can be eliminated (compared to the design of a general associative memory) in the special-purpose design.

permit this operation to determine Y based on the values in X.[5] We choose this combination because a loop that individually processes all selected entries can be written easily. The FIRST operation would be performed after the memory finds a multiple match if one wanted to form a loop to process all entries that satisfied the search predicate. The program begins by performing the search and saving the results:

```
SEARCH (..);
if ( AMCC[0] ) {
        ..                          //handler for the no match situation
}
while ( AMCC[2] | AMCC[1] ) {        //something did match
    FIRST;
    EXCHANGE X AND Y;
    ..;                         //perform operation on one entry
    EXCHANGE X AND Y;
}
```

ENTER. This operation places the contents of D into one previously invalid entry; this operation can be emulated by a short sequence of other instructions,[6] but is so useful that we designate it as a separate operation.

DELETE. This operation clears the validity bit of every entry where X is set. In other words,

$$DELETE: V(i) = V(i) \textbf{ and not } X(i);$$

READ. This operation copies a value to the D register from the entry where X[i] is set. It is undefined if more than one bit of X is set, and it clears D if no bits of X are set.

WRITE. This operation copies the data in D to every entry E[i] where X[i] is set. The WRITE operation also sets V[i] in every entry that was written. Thus, if there is a single bit of X set at location i, the last two operations amount to

```
READ:       D = E(i);
WRITE:      E(i) = D;       V(i) = true;
```

---

[5]   We do it this way so that an implementer could use a logic circuit to perform this operation, and the logic signals propagating down the chain might stabilize during the interval after X is loaded and before Y is tested. If the operation used an intermediate register and implemented FIRST between arbitrary registers by copying, the inputs to the FIRST logic could not start propagating until the intermediate register had been loaded.

[6]   This is possible only if the contents of V can be explicitly manipulated. The design that follows does permit this kind of manipulation.

Logical And Copying Operations. These operations permit general logical and copying operations on the match information, which may be useful for application algorithms using complex entry selection criteria. Let P and Q designate any of V, X, Y, or Z. The associative memory supports the following logical and copying operations:

1. SET P;
2. NEGATE P;
3. COPY P TO Q;
4. P AND Q TO R;
5. P OR Q TO R;
6. EXCHANGE P AND Q;[7]

G.2 IMPLEMENTATION OPTIONS

We consider only the implementation of the search operation, undoubtedly the most difficult operation in an associative memory, the other operations being straightforward. The search process must examine the mask-selected bits in all memory entries with X[i] set to find all entries that satisfy the match predicate. Three searching methods can be used:

1. Fully parallel
2. Word-slice
3. Bit-slice

These names reflect the amount of memory information examined during a single access to the underlying memory.

A *fully parallel* search simultaneously compares all the mask-selected bits of all entries against the corresponding selector bits. A search of all valid entries starts by copying V to X. Then the fully parallel search is performed; it combines the outcomes of the comparisons at each bit position of word i to signal mismatch, which clears the X[i] bit; this logic is depicted in Figure G-2. Of the SEARCH implementation options, parallel search is fastest, requires the most hardware, and is the most expensive. It can be useful if fast responses are required from a small memory array.

A *word-slice* search implementation can be used to build an associative memory from a conventional location-addressed memory. The word-slice search process uses a looping sequence of accesses; each one reads a table entry and compares its mask-selected bits against the selector value. The loop terminates when a matching entry is found. With conventional memory hardware, there is

---

[7]   The set of operations embodied in this instruction set obviously greatly exceeds the logical minimum, but it makes function selection orthogonal to operand selection for these logical operations.

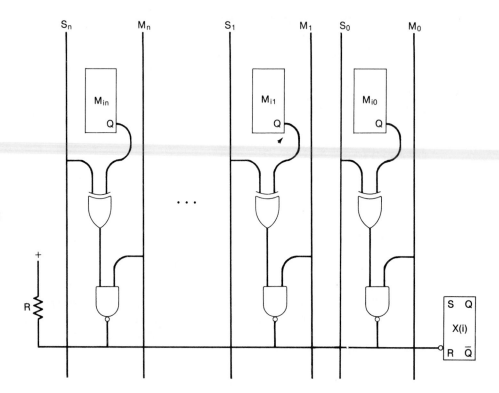

Figure G-2 Equality match logic—parallel search
(wired-OR outputs from the NAND gates)

no register analogous to the X register of the parallel design; the SEARCH result is the address of the first entry meeting the match predicate. If there is no matching entry in the memory, the search will terminate by reaching the end of the associative memory's address space. If more than one entry meets the match predicate, the search finds the first one; others can be found by restarting the search loop just after its previous (matching) position.[8]

One advantage of this implementation option is that conventional memory components can be used to implement the associative memory. Another advantage of this option is that general match predicates are easily accommodated. A disadvantage of this option is the large number of memory accesses required to complete the search.

It is interesting to compare the word-slice implementation against a hashed implementation (see Section 3.4.3) of a name table; in both schemes, individual table entries are examined to find one satisfying the desired criterion. The major differences between the hashing scheme and the word-slice search are as follows:

---

[8]   This requires defining SEARCH to have a starting word index as an operand.

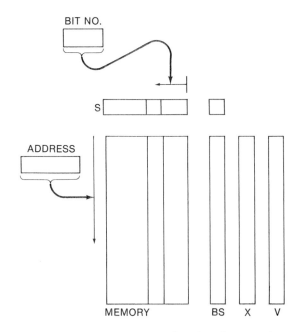

Figure G-3   Structure for a bit-slice search

1. Word-slice searching must scan all table entries if the desired entry is not in the table.
2. Word-slice searching starts at the same table entry for all search requests.

From these observations we see that, on the average, a hashed search uses fewer accesses to find the matching entry than a word-slice scan. In fact, if the hashing function is sufficiently random (i.e., if the names actually mapped hash into quite different indices), there is a good chance that the first access will succeed by finding a matching table entry. In this general context, a major disadvantage of hashing is that only one (statically chosen) search field can be accommodated in a single hash table.

A *bit-slice* search requires special hardware, but its complexity is lower than that of a fully parallel search implementation. For bit-slice searching, the memory hardware is designed so the memory can be read or written either along a slice that corresponds to a single word or along a slice that corresponds to a single bit (of every word).[9] The buffer register BS (bit slice) receives the information read from a bit slice. The structure of this bit-slice implementation is shown in Figure G-3. This memory has X and V registers (and possibly Y and Z). To search the memory, perform the following steps: (1) The X register is set to

---

[9]   Bit-slice WRITE is not necessary unless X and V are contained as columns in the memory.

define the entries that are match candidates; (2) a loop scans the bits selected by the mask. In the loop body, one mask-selected bit is read into BS and BS is compared against the corresponding bit of S; in any bit position where there is a mismatch (assuming that equality was the predicate), X is cleared. Notice that this bit-slice implementation amounts to a serial realization of the logic used in the fully parallel search.

The cost of a bit-slice memory lies between the cost of a word-slice memory and the cost of a fully associative memory. The bit-slice memory has one advantage, which is that it is easily adapted for match predicates with arithmetic comparisons, such as greater_than. An arithmetic comparison could be performed by software controlling a fully associative memory, but the program is tedious, as it must inspect bit slices and check the condition code to decide how to proceed.

G.3 SUMMARY

Associative memories are useful in memory mapping algorithms because the domain of the mapping function is large, yet only a small fraction of the domain is mapped. We have shown several alternative implementations and the basic operations of a general associative memory to support associative searches whose results can be used to enable other operations, such as arithmetic. A few have been built. The Goodyear STARAN system [BATC74] uses a variant of bit-slice searching and can be programmed as though it performs general associative operations. The details of these designs are beyond the scope of this book.

G.4 TRENDS

Although the concept of a general associative memory is quite appealing, the cost of any implementation utilizing special hardware is likely to be so high that these systems will only be implemented in software packages. In these packages, hashing and other techniques discussed in Chapter 3 can be very useful for providing efficient implementations when only equality searching is needed. If arithmetic inequality search criteria are needed, ordered lists or tables may have added appeal. The choice between ordering a table (or list) at all times or just when a search begins hinges on the relative frequencies of additions to the table and searches for entries in the table.

G.5 CONCEPT LIST

1. Location addressing versus associative addressing
2. Associative memory functions and implementation
3. Multiple matches in associative memories
4. Parallel associative search
5. Word-slice associative search
6. Bit-slice associative search
7. Complex operations implemented by associative memory programs

G.6 PROBLEMS

G-1. Write a sequence of associative memory operations (from the set listed in Section G.2) to set the bits in X according to the following predicate:

(entry.u == value_1) **or** (entry.v == value_2)

The fields u and v can be selected by using the masks u_mask and v_mask, respectively.

G-2. To answer the following questions, you will write short program fragments for associative system. Assume that the system has the structure and the functions of the systems described in Section G.2.

(a) Write a sequence of associative memory operations to set the bits in X according to the following predicate:

(entry.u == value_1) **and** (entry.v == value_2)

The fields u and v can be selected by using the masks named u_mask and v_mask, respectively.

(b) Write a search algorithm to mark all entries that meet the search criterion

entry.u < value_1

G-3. Describe the logic used to mark the first matching entry after a bit-slice associative search. Design the logic to minimize the delay while respecting a gate fan-in limit G. The logic should output a one at the position corresponding to the first entry in a vector (of length n) that is set to one, and a zero at the positions corresponding to all other entries.

G-4. An associative search has been completed and it yielded a multiple match. Suppose that each table entry contains a field dupl_position that is to be filled with an integer whose value is the ordinal position of the entry among the matching set determined by the previous search. In other words, it is desired that the ith memory entry that met the search criterion have the value i placed in its dupl_position field. Starting from the search results in the M register, specify an algorithm that places the position numbers in the dupl_position fields. Use operations from the set introduced in Section G.2.

G-5. In a general associative memory, we may wish to allow object selection based on an arithmetic comparison between the selector and the value stored in the key fields of the entry. Consider that all values are integers and describe search strategies for use in a bit-slice associative memory that use the fewest bit-slice accesses and yet implement matches wherever the key value bears the specified arithmetic relation to the selector value.

(a) key < selector.

(b) key ≤ selector.

(c) What representation do you desire for negative values? Why?

G-6. In order to speed up word-slice searching, a designer proposes a new word-slice memory with a built-in rearrangement mechanism that attempts to keep the entries most likely to be referenced at the top of the list, so that they will be found faster when a search is made. The proposed rearrangement strategy is to move an entry to the top of the memory when it is accessed, moving down one position all those entries between the top of the list and the former position of the accessed entry.

(a) Show that this policy can be implemented with only one read–modify–write access to each table entry beyond the first entry.

(b) Under what referencing patterns would you expect the redesign to pay off?

(c) Another redesign option is to consider the table as a circular list. When a search succeeds, the list pointer is left pointing to the entry that was successfully found, so that that same entry is the first to be checked during the next access attempt. What are the advantages and disadvantages of this policy compared to the list rearrangement policy?

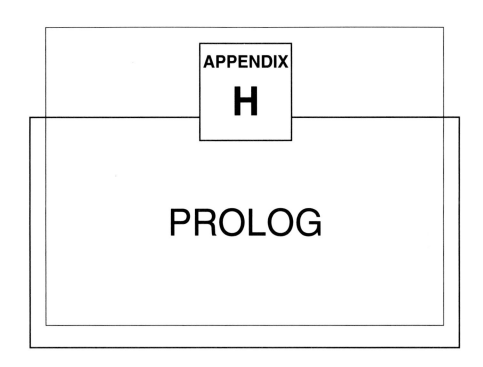

PROLOG

The conventional illusion about control structures is that there is a single "control point" progressing through a "program." Some languages, like Prolog, take a radically different view. The Prolog view is that the system consists of only a database in which searches are activated when the user asks a question. Under this view, the system tries to answer the question by database searches that seek some way to meet the "goal" specified by the question. During the search other actions might be performed, depending on the contents of the database. Prolog control structures are quite different from the conventional control structures to which most of us are accustomed. For this reason alone, we describe them apart from the conventional structures discussed in Chapter 4.

There are a number of incompatible versions of Prolog, all sharing the same control philosophy and structure; they differ with respect to their built-in functions and some representation conventions. Our presentation is based on [CLOC87], a Prolog book that has attained status for presenting a widely accepted "standard" version of the language, sometimes called "Edinburgh Prolog." Most Prolog implementations include the features we describe. A complete Prolog overview is presented in [COHE85].

Several important assumptions affect Prolog's control structure:

1. There is a single homogeneous database—a space containing both program steps and data.
2. Program execution is directed toward satisfying a specified goal.
3. A basic strategy for searching the database to satisfy a goal is built into the system.
4. Many operations work through "side effects," which are very important.

H.1 THE PROLOG DATABASE

Prolog supports reasoning about facts to draw logical conclusions, so Prolog terminology is oriented toward predicates, facts, and rules of inference. Thus, we say that the Prolog database contains *facts* and *rules*.

A *fact* states that a predicate is true. It is written like a function or a word:

```
thing.
brother(john, bob).
```

Notice that each line is terminated with a period. The first fact states that "thing" is true. Therefore, if the system is looking to find whether "thing" is true, this fact shows that it is true, and we say that that fact "satisfies" the goal. The second fact is a *structure,* which states that john and bob (in that order) satisfy the predicate brother. The ordering of the structure's parameters is important; we cannot conclude from this structure alone that bob is a brother of john. Another database entry may state that the brother predicate satisfies a commutative relationship. A rule is used to state such a general relationship.

A *rule* states a relationship between some facts or structures. Many rules contain variable names, which are distinguished from constant values by the Prolog convention that each variable name starts with a capital letter, whereas each constant starts with a lowercase letter.[1] Here is a simple rule:

```
brother(X, Y) :- brother(Y, X).
```

This rule states that the predicate brother(X, Y) is true if the predicate brother(Y, X) is true; in other words, it establishes the commutativity of the brother relationship.[2] You see that the combination ":-" can be read "if." Notice that ":-" is not read "if and only if" because there could be other rules or facts in the database that specify other ways that the brother relationship could be satisfied.

Let us look at another, more complex rule concerning the brother predicate.

```
brother(X, Y) :- father(V, X), father(V, Y), male(X), male(Y).
```

---

[1]   You may have been wondering why the proper names in the predicate were not capitalized; now you know why.

[2]   Notice that this rule is correct only if we know that both individuals are males.

This rule is read "X is the brother of Y if there is a V such that [V is the father of X] and [V is the father of Y] and [X is a male] and [Y is a male]." You see that a comma is read "and." You also see that Prolog supports existential quantification ("there exists a _____ such that _____"). As Prolog attempts to satisfy its goal, it will, in effect, choose one object whose existence was postulated, for if it cannot exhibit such an object it cannot claim that the goal can be satisfied.

An "or" relationship between two facts or rules can be stated in two different ways:

```
alphanumeric(X) :- alphabetic(X).
alphanumeric(X) :- numeric(X).
```

or

```
alphanumeric(X) :- alphabetic(X); numeric(X).
```

So the semicolon is read as "or;" it may be used to shorten the database or to express a goal that could be satisfied in several possible ways.

H.2 PROLOG GOALS

Prolog is interactive; execution is initiated when the user enters a fact, a rule, or a query. When a new fact or rule is entered, Prolog simply adds it to the end of the database and the system awaits another user input. When a query is entered, Prolog initiates its goal-satisfaction algorithm. Here is a simple query:

```
?- brother(jim, john).
```

This asks whether there is some set of facts and/or rules in the database that leads to the conclusion that the relation brother(jim, john) is true. Given a query, the Prolog system will search the database trying to find a set of facts that together imply the truth of the query. If the search is successful, the Prolog system will answer with "yes;" otherwise it will answer "no."

To complete the search the system may have to assign values to one or more variables. All such assignments have to be consistent within the scope of a single rule. If some variables were assigned particular values to satisfy the goal, the system will print out these assignments before its "yes" answer is printed. If the answer is "no," there is no way to assign values to variables to satisfy the query, so no assignment of values to variables can be printed.

One may phrase a query containing a variable name. This type of query will find a specific object (if that is necessary) that satisfies the query. For example, the query

```
-? brother(john, Brother).
```

asks for a person who is a brother of john. The identity of that person will be presented among the variable assignments listed before its "yes" answer.

Inside the system, the text of the user's query is taken as the system's goal, and the system uses its search strategy (see what follows) to determine whether the goal can be satisfied. The search terminates (1) when it finds a way[3] to satisfy the goal or (2) when the search ends in failure because there is no way to satisfy the goal. If the system indicates success, it has found one way to satisfy the goal and the user does not know whether there are other combinations that satisfy the goal. If the user responds to the "yes" answer by typing a semicolon, the system will search for a different solution. Repeated semicolon responses will produce a list of all solutions, followed by the answer "no," produced when there are no additional ways to satisfy the goal.

H.3 PROLOG'S SEARCHING STRATEGY

The execution of a Prolog program consists of a sequence of attempts to satisfy goals. There are two basic ways to satisfy a goal:

1. It matches a fact in the database.
2. It matches the left side of a rule in the database, and the right side of that rule is true.

To apply these satisfaction rules, we need a definition of "matching" between a goal and a fact or the left side of a rule. The two objects being matched are structures, which match if their corresponding components match. This recursive match condition reduces matching to a set of comparisons between pairs of "simple" elements (i.e., elements that are not themselves structures). If neither simple element contains a variable, they match only if they are identical character strings. If either or both is a variable, those variables may have to be assigned values to complete the match process. Table H-1 summarizes the possible situations. In the table, the word "free" indicates that the element in question is a variable that has not yet been assigned a specific value. An element is said to be *instantiated* if it has been assigned a specific value. The last row of the table merits special attention. When two variables need to be matched, a consistent assignment requires that both be assigned the same value. This is forced by renaming the rule's variable, (whose name is local to this rule) to match the goal's variable (whose name came from a previous goal, and may have to be matched against a another instance of the name in that rule). This renaming action does not assign a specific value to the variable; it just renames the variable. It is important to note that the name of a variable appearing in a rule is local to the rule; all rules in the database could use the same local names without conflict.

---

[3]   Some implementations find all ways to satisfy the goal, but Edinburgh Prolog and many others find just one way per query. In this text, we remain consistent with Edinburgh Prolog and terminate searching when one way to satisfy the goal has been found.

TABLE H-1 PROLOG ELEMENT MATCHING

Status		Action
Goal Free?	Rule Free?	
No	No	Match fails if they are not equal
No	Yes	Assign value of goal's entry to the rule's variable
Yes	No	Assign value of rule's entry to the goal's variable
Yes	Yes	Replace the rule's variable with the name of the goal's variable

The process for satisfying a goal can be viewed in terms of traversing a conceptual tree structure, looking for a way to *satisfy* the goal at the root of the tree. Each node is associated with a fact, rule, or a goal. We describe the tree satisfaction process recursively, as follows. A fact node is always satisfied. A rule node is satisfied if the subtree rooted at the node (call the node N_R) is satisfied. The configuration of branches from N_R is based upon the structure of the right side of the rule; the subclasses follow: First, if the right side of the rule is a single goal, that goal is the only child node of N_R. If the right side was a conjunction of some goals (that were separated by commas in the rule), the rule node becomes an "AND" node whose children are the goals within the conjunction, listed in the order of their appearance in the rule. An AND node is satisfied if all of its children are satisfied. If the right side of the rule was a disjunction of some goals (that were separated by semicolons in the rule), the rule node becomes an "OR" node whose children are the goals within the disjunction, listed in the order of their appearance in the rule. An OR node is satisfied if any one of its children is satisfied. A goal node has a child for each database entry that matches the goal. In the (conceptual) tree, the goal node is an OR node with these alternatives as its children.

The recursive goal-satisfaction algorithm makes a left-to-right depth-first search of the tree. The search progress can be controlled by recursive backtracking using a pushdown stack. Each time the system makes a choice, it records (on the pushdown stack) the search position and information about the current node. If it has to resume the search from this choice, it can pop the saved state and resume the previous scan.[4] When the user's goal succeeds, the stack's contents reflect the database entries used to satisfy the goal.

If the search to satisfy G reaches the end of the database, then G cannot be shown to be true. If G is the user's goal, the system responds "no." If G is a

---

[4]   We will see that additional information will have to be stacked for correct behavior.

subgoal, the system will back up and try again to satisfy the original goal, using new matching choices. Recursive backtracking organizes the search.

Here are a few steps that describe parts of the tree searching process:

1. If G_i is satisfied and is part of a conjunction (a list joined by commas), the next goal to check is the successor of G_i in the list. If G_i is the last entry in the list, the goal appearing on the left side of the rule has been satisfied.
2. If G_i is not satisfied, then the term in which G_i appears cannot be satisfied using the current assignment. The system must backtrack to the last point where a choice was made and retry that search.
3. A choice is made whenever one rule is chosen to be satisfied. When several terms appear in a disjunction ("or") on the right side of a rule, a choice is made when one of these terms is chosen. If it fails, the remaining terms of the disjunction must be tried before the complete rule is considered to have failed.

These steps are not a complete description of the search rules. One aspect of matching and tree searching not described before concerns managing the assignment of values to variables to be consistent with the semantic rules. Each time that a rule selection instantiates a variable or forces a rule's variable to match the goal's variable, corresponding entries in other goals may have to be changed. Making a new copy of the goal list each time that a new rule is selected is part of one solution to this consistency requirement. Another aspect concerns the use of the cut operator, discussed in the next section, that plays an important role in the language.

H.4 CONTROLLING THE SEARCH PROCESS

A Prolog programmer can control the search process in two ways:

1. By ordering the database entries
2. By using the cut operator

The order of database entries is very important because improper ordering can result in incorrect answers or infinite loops.

Example H-1

These two databases differ only in the order of their entries.

Database A:

```
brother(john, bob).
brother(X, Y) :- brother(Y, X).
```

Database B:

```
brother(X, Y) :- brother(Y, X).
brother(john, bob).
```

Given the query

```
?- brother(bob, john).
```

A Prolog system with Database A will answer "yes," having used the second entry to reverse the goal's parameters and the first entry to find its truth. In contrast, a Prolog system with Database B will loop indefinitely, repeatedly interchanging the parameters of the goal, because it always matches its subgoal when it examines the first entry in the database.

Generalizing, a Prolog programmer should order the database with more specific facts and rules placed ahead of rules expressing more general properties.

Not only must the Prolog programmer properly order the database entries, but also he needs some primitives to control the search process. Three special control terms are provided: success (expressed as "true"), failure ("fail"), and cut ("!"). Success is so simple that you might think it redundant; you are correct, but it is convenient, so it is built-in. Fail looks even more obvious, but it is absolutely necessary to be able to force a failure.[5] You will see its importance in connection with the cut operator. Cut is a very important search controller. If cut is encountered as a goal, it immediately succeeds, *and* it freezes all selections made since the parent goal (the one on the left side of the rule containing the cut) started its search through the database. This means that any options selected since the parent goal was the current goal are forced be the last possible choice once cut has been encountered as a goal. Thus, cut effectively commits the satisfaction of the parent goal to the choices that have been made in that rule up to the point of the cut. The cut states that there shall be no other ways to satisfy the parent goal, unless the search backtracks far enough to remove the parent goal from the search path. When the cut is processed, the stacked backtracking possibilities are removed from the stack back to the choice of the parent goal (of the rule containing the cut).

This database contains a simple use of the cut:

```
not(X) :- call(X), !, fail.
not(X).
wednesday.
```

---

[5]   In a strict sense, **fail** does not have to be built-in because one could simply insert a goal that does not match the left side of any rule. In fact, one could name it fail!

The primitive named "call" initiates a search with its argument (X) as the goal. We will follow the system's actions in response to two queries. The first query, not(tuesday), clearly is true. Here is how the Prolog system determines this answer:

1. Rule 1 is attempted; it matches the goal if X were assigned the string "tuesday", so the system binds tuesday to X.
2. Subgoal call(tuesday) is chosen.
3. Goal tuesday is chosen (because call always succeeds if its argument does).
4. Rule 1 is attempted; it does not match the goal.
5. Rule 2 is attempted; it does not match the goal.
6. Rule 3 is attempted; it does not match the goal.
7. There being no more rules, goal tuesday has failed.
8. Backtrack to the last choice, which was made at step 1 when rule 1 was selected. Go back to trying for the goal that was current at that point ["not(tuesday)"] and start the search just after the failure point. So the next step will try rule 2.
9. Try rule 2; this succeeds because the left side can be matched by setting the variable X to "tuesday;" this satisfies the user's goal because no unsatisfied subgoals remain on the list.
10. There being no unsatisfied goals, the question is answered in the affirmative.

   Now follow the system as it processes the false query

   ?- not(wednesday).

The process proceeds:

1. Rule 1 is attempted; it matches the goal if X were assigned the string "wednesday", so the system binds "wednesday" to X.
2. Subgoal call(wednesday) is chosen.
3. Goal wednesday is chosen (because call always succeeds if its argument does).
4. Rule 1 is attempted; it does not match the goal.
5. Rule 2 is attempted; it does not match the goal.
6. Rule 3 is attempted; it does match the goal.
7. The goal being satisfied, the system goes back to the goal list it was processing, where it finds the cut.
8. The system drops the alternatives for a retry of the parent goal "not(wednesday)" (this means that the retry of the first search starting from rule 2 is canceled).
9. Cut having succeeded, the system moves to the next goal on its list, which is "fail".
10. Clearly fail is not true, so the system tries to backtrack; there are no remaining options, so the system responds to the user's query with "no".

What would have happened if the cut were removed? In this case, the database contains

```
not(X) :- call(X), fail.
not(X).
wednesday.
```

Again we present the false query

```
?- not(wednesday).
```

Execution proceeds as in the last case through step 6. Step 7 is almost identical except that the system finds "fail" next on the list. The final search steps are as follows:

7. The goal being satisfied, the system goes back to the goal list it was processing, where it finds the fail goal.

8. Backtrack to the last choice, which was made at step 1 when rule 1 was selected. Go back to trying for the goal that was current at that point ["not(wednesday)"] and start the search just after the failure point. So the next step will try rule 2.

9. Try rule 2; this succeeds because the left side can be matched by setting the variable X to "wednesday".

10. There being no unsatisfied goals, the question is answered in the affirmative.

This result is not what we intended. Thus, we see the utility of the cut and the need for the fail goal.

It is instructive to note that the program we have just studied does not really correspond to the conventional meaning of "not," but rather the program returns "true" only if it cannot show that the argument ("X") could not be proven to be correct with the given database. This is not the same as proving that X is false.

Prolog includes other built-in predicates that allow the programmer to test conditions within variables and their values; some of these are listed in Table H-2.

The **is** operator forces the evaluation of the expression on its right side; without the **is** operator, the expression would be treated as a pattern to be matched. In a sense, the **is** operator serves as both an assignment statement and an equality test. It amounts to an assignment (to a temporary variable) when its left side is an uninstantiated variable. It amounts to an equality test if the left side is either a value or the name of an instantiated variable.

In the next subsection we look at the ways that the state of the Prolog machine can be changed and show that any general algorithm can be expressed as a Prolog program.

TABLE H-2   BASIC PROLOG PREDICATES

Predicate	True if
true	Always
fail	Never
var(X)	X has not been assigned a specific value (it is still a "free variable")
nonvar(X)	X has been assigned a specific value
integer(X)	X has a whole number as a value
atom(X)	X is not an integer and contains no spaces
atomic(X)	X is an atom or an integer
X = Y	X matches Y (also holds for integers)
X \= Y	X does not match Y (also holds for integers)
X == Y	X matches Y, but with restrictions on assignments to variables
X \ = = Y	Negation of the previous
X > Y	Both arguments are instantiated integers; the first is larger
X < Y	Use analogy with X > Y
X = < Y	Use analogy with X > Y
X > = Y	Use analogy with X > Y
A is B	B evaluated as an arithmetic expression is equal to A (see text)

H.5 OPERATIONS BY SIDE EFFECTS

The basic Prolog searching process is sufficient to answer many queries, but it does not provide general computational power or any way to modify the database permanently. In this section we show how Prolog can change its database through the side effects defined into some primitive Prolog predicates. We also will show how the execution sequence can be controlled to emulate conventional program sequencing structures. This exercise demonstrates Prolog's generality; despite this property, one should not consider Prolog for inappropriate applications, such as numerically intensive problems.

Changing the Database.   There is only one basic way that a Prolog program can permanently change the database—by scanning a built-in predicate with appropriate side effects. The value-variable assignments made during the basic Prolog matching process do not change the database; these value assignments are only temporary assignments to local variables.

TABLE H-3   SOME PROLOG OPERATORS

Action	Description
asserta(X)	Add X to the beginning of the database
assertz(X)	Add X to the end of the database
retract(X)	Find the first database entry that matches X and delete it from the database

To make permanent database changes, the scanning process must encounter one of the basic language predicates defined with side effects. Some of these basic operations[6] are listed in Table H-3. All basic operations must be considered to be goals; nonconditional operations always succeed, so the operations listed in the table always succeed.

The operators asserta, assertz, and retract modify the contents of the database; they are similar to write and read operations. Two forms of assert, which is similar to write (actually, append), are required because the order of entries within the database is crucial to the goal-matching process. The retract operator deletes a selected database entry.[7]

Conventional Sequential Execution in Prolog. We close the section on Prolog control structures with a short discussion concerning the possibility of writing conventionally expressed sequential algorithms in Prolog. To construct a simple straight-line procedure using Prolog primitive operators, place the procedure's specification (its name plus its formal parameters) on the left side of a Prolog rule and place the procedure's body, expressed as a conjunction, on the right side of the rule. Because the scanning rule will scan the members of the conjunction in the order of their appearance, the elements of the conjunction will be executed sequentially. One must be careful about the interactions between backtracking and the sequential operations, because any side effects are not retracted during backtracking.

Example H-2

The Prolog rule

$$f(X, Y, Z, A, B) :- V \text{ is } Y + Z, V \text{ is } V * (A + B), \quad X \text{ is } V * A.$$

is analogous to the following procedure

---

[6]   We have excluded input/output and file system actions to simplify the presentation.

[7]   Note that the sequence retract, assert is not analogous to a simple write that replaces the previous contents of a rule because the newly asserted entry may occupy a different position in the database than the position of the matching entry that was retracted.

```
int f( int x, y, z, a, b ) {
    int v = y + z;
    v = v * ( a + b );
    x = v * a;
}
```

Notice how the existential variable V serves as an automatic local variable.

This method for writing a Prolog analog of a conventionally expressed algorithm is adequate for a strictly sequential program, but does not work for other conventional control structures. Consider writing a Prolog program analogous to a conventional loop.

Example H-3

One way to express a loop structure uses a cut and a universal subsidiary goal. The universal subsidiary goal "repeat" defines the beginning of the loop. It really defines a pseudo choice point to which the backtracking process will return each time that the main goal (performing the loop) fails (which will occur if the termination condition has not been met). Here is the structure for an **until** loop, along with the definition of repeat:

```
loop( <var_list> ) :- repeat, <body_text>, <term_test>, !.
repeat :- true.
repeat :- repeat.
```

The meta symbols (in angle brackets) indicate where the loop body and the termination test predicate (true when the loop terminates) should be written. The cut at the end is necessary to prevent further executions of the loop if some predicate scanned after loop completion causes backtracking. This case is important for loop nesting. The reader should fill in the body and test for a simple example and trace the execution of this program.

These structures suggest a method by which one can argue that the Prolog language is general-purpose and that conventionally expressed algorithms could, if necessary, be expressed within a Prolog program. It should also be obvious, however, that thinking in terms of conventional control structures is really not appropriate for Prolog programming.

H.6 SUMMARY

The execution of a Prolog program is based on a complex internal process that attempts to certify the truth of a query on the basis of facts and rules of inference stored within its database. Conventional program execution can be specified in the language, albeit awkwardly. It may appear that the truth of falsehood of a query would be based solely on a combinatorial analysis of the facts and rules in the database. Although this is the case for simple databases, with complex rules the order of the information within the database is extremely important, for this order determines the sequence in which the facts and rules will be searched. A Prolog programmer can modify the order of scanning the database using the true, fail, and cut predicates.

The Prolog database may be modified when the scanning process encounters a predicate that has side effects. Input and output activities can be activated in a similar manner. In fact, any program can be mapped into a Prolog program, but the remapping of control constructs makes the program's structure appear to be different.

The Prolog scanning rules define a recursive left-to-right depth-first tree searching process. The implementation of this scanning process would be greatly assisted by efficient stack operations that keep account of the tree searching process. The recursive scanning process requires many stack operations. Unfortunately, it is also true that the required sequential search rules imply sequential execution; this fact makes it difficult to design a Prolog execution mechanism that effectively uses parallelism while following a strict interpretation of the defined semantics. Parallelism can be used effectively to search for all patterns that satisfy a query, or when the coupling among clauses (through variables) is weak.

It is possible to speed up the Prolog scanning process. One technique creates an internal division of the facts and rules into groups such that any one scan can be confined to a single group. Each Prolog database scan looks for a rule or fact that matches the current goal. We simply map predicate names to group identifiers; the search can be confined to the group whose identifier is the group containing the goal's predicate name (see Problem H-11).

We showed some essential parts of an argument to convince you that Prolog is indeed a general-purpose programming language. Although this generality may be reassuring, it should not be taken as an argument that every application should be programmed in Prolog.

In Appendix I, we discuss LISP, a predecessor of Prolog, with which Prolog shares many aspects. In particular, LISP is interactive, its data types include character strings, its programs can be manipulated like data, and database entries can be changed as a result of side effects within functions. Among the important differences between Prolog and LISP is the difference in emphasis on certain data types. Prolog emphasizes character strings, whereas LISP emphasizes lists.

H.7 TRENDS

Prolog structures appeal to some programmers, but the difficulty of finding efficient implementations and the demise of the touted use of Prolog within the Japanese "Fifth Generation Computer Project" will both discourage programmers from using the language except for special applications in which the fact/rule structure fits very well.

The language does remain interesting due to its nonsequential control flow rules and the predominant use of side effects to initiate important activities.

H.8 CONCEPT LIST

1. Algorithms represented within a database (e.g., in LISP, Prolog)
2. Database searches to verify a user's query
3. Facts and rules
4. Subgoals initiate further searching
5. The Prolog cut operator
6. Side effects used for system functionality
7. The importance of database ordering
8. Generality by algorithmic translation into a Prolog program

H.9 PROBLEMS

H-1. Write a Prolog program fragment that corresponds to a **while** loop. Be sure that your solution can be used inside a nest of loops.

H-2. Write a Prolog program fragment that corresponds to a C++ **switch** statement.

H-3. Write a Prolog program fragment that corresponds to an **if** <boolean> **then** <s_list> **else** <s_list> statement.

H-4. Explain why the use of the Prolog cut forces the programmer to pay attention to the order of the database entries. An example showing that the order makes a difference is sufficient.

H-5. Write a Prolog program that accepts the query

?- replace(<before>, <after>).

The intent is to change the database by replacing the fact (or rule) in the first parameter with the fact (or rule) in the second parameter. Replacement means that the search order should be the same as before, with the "after" fact (or rule) in the position in the order where the "before" fact was located. (*Hint:* It may be necessary to write a recursive routine to perform the task.)

H-6. When Prolog attempts to match two elements and finds that both are variables, it preserves the variable name that appears in the goal by changing the rule's variable name to the goal's variable name. Explain why the reverse assignment should not be used.

H-7. This problem asks you to detail the operation of a stack that tracks the progress of the search through a Prolog database as the system attempts to satisfy a goal. In general, the stack is structured with a new activation block added to the stack whenever a new subgoal is generated.

    (a) What information needs to be saved in the activation blocks? Be sure to pay attention to bound and free variables, but these might not contain all the information required for proper functionality.

    (b) What changes occur within the stack when a search for a subgoal succeeds?

    (c) Repeat part (b) for the case of subgoal failure.

    (d) Repeat part (b) for the case of the goal being a cut operator.

H-8. Write a program in a familiar conventional programming language to perform the database search inherent in Prolog's semantics. This is a large task, do not try to handle the possibility that a clause actually causes the execution of a program.

H-9. Explain the claim that Prolog is a general-purpose programming language.

    (a) Can you write a general emulator of a C++ program in Prolog? Do not try to do it!

    (b) How would you represent (i) facts and (ii) rules?

    (c) Describe how you could build a translation program to take a C++ program and produce a representation of its algorithm that conforms to the representations you defined in part (b). At the same time, try to maintain an obvious correspondence between single executable statements in the C++ program and groups of facts and rules in the Prolog database.

H-10. This problem considers the possibility of separating a Prolog program into parts that can be executed in parallel. Two major possibilities are divisions based on the logical relationships among clauses within the database. For example, if there are two "OR" alternatives for meeting a goal, two processes could simultaneously seek to satisfy the goal. A similar argument could be made for the "AND" or two subgoals on the right side of a database rule. To make the system functionally correct, certain details have to be coordinated and defined. This is the focus of the questions below.

    (a) Make a general statement about the handling of free variables that are shared in common between two AND subgoals being processed in parallel.

    (b) Make a general statement about how to handle any side effects that are encountered as the subgoals of an AND clause are processed in parallel.

    (c) Repeat part (b) for OR subgoals processed in parallel.

H-11. A designer proposes representing the Prolog database as a set of databases, separated by the hash value generated from the goal of each fact or rule.

    (a) Describe how you would hash the current goal to choose which database should be searched to satisfy the goal.

    (b) Describe briefly why this strategy might speed program execution.

    (c) Outline an argument that should convince others that your answer to part (a) does guarantee correct behavior.

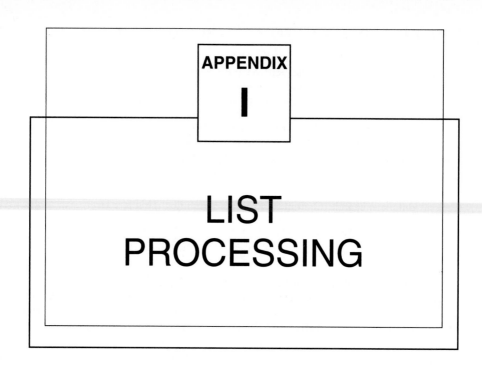

LIST PROCESSING

In Chapter 5 we saw how the creation of new object classes, operation specifications, object representations, and operation implementations could be used to support object illusions. We saw how designers could provide efficient, yet extensible, language and system implementations. To complement that presentation, we discuss the design of the LISP language ([WINS84]) and a LISP-oriented processor, with emphasis on object representations and operations on these objects. Using tagged object representations and carefully chosen representations improves the system's efficiency when performing operations that are frequently requested.

I.1 THE LISP PROGRAMMING LANGUAGE

You will not become a proficient LISP programmer from reading this summary of LISP object types, data structures, and elementary operations, but you should get the flavor of the language and see why its implementation presents an interesting challenge.

I.1.1 LISP Object Types

In addition to numbers and character strings, three important object structures in LISP are

1. Lists
2. Structures
3. Association lists

We discuss structures and association lists after we present some LISP operations in the next section.

The list is the primary LISP object class. A LISP list is structurally equivalent to a binary tree; each internal node has two successors, which themselves may be either subtrees or atomic elements. From a logical viewpoint, each list contains two elements, each one possibly being a list itself. This logical view can form the basis for constructing a (linear) parenthesized representation of any list. A two-element list is represented by the parenthesized expression (A B), where A and B are the first element and the second element of the list, respectively. The linear representation of a complete list is constructed by repeated applications of the representation rule for each internal node of the tree. This rule defines a linear representation that contains a parenthesis pair for each internal node. The linear list representations are used to express LISP objects and programs.

Example I-1

Figure I-1 contains several lists represented as trees along with the corresponding linear parenthesized representations.

Small LISP data objects that are not lists are called atoms. Data types for atoms include character_string, integer, and float.

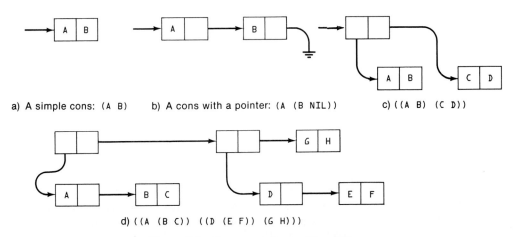

a) A simple cons: (A B)   b) A cons with a pointer: (A (B NIL))   c) ((A B) (C D))

d) ((A (B C)) ((D (E F)) (G H)))

Figure I-1   Representations of LISP lists

The pointer type is basic to a LISP list's representation. In particular, a two-element list can be represented by a two-component record containing a pointer to each of the list's components. In LISP, such records are called "cons"es. There is one cons for each internal list node. Some pointers in conses locate other cons objects, and others locate atoms.[1] One must distinguish pointers from atoms. For the moment, assume that this detail has been handled within the representation.

A common data structure represents a linear list of n elements. The LISP language provides a shortcut representation for this structure: a single list within a single pair of parentheses, such as

(A B C D E)

This list is really represented in the system as a chain of lists:

(A (B (C (D (E)))))

or

(A (B (C (D (E **NIL**)))))

The third form is a more accurate reflection of the structure, because in the representation, each atom in the list is the first element of some cons. Figure I-2 depicts the representation of this list structure. **NIL** denotes a special pointer value that indicates that the pointer object does not point to anything. A LISP list will end with a lot of right parentheses when written in this form.

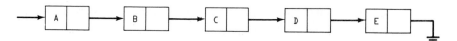

Figure I-2   The representation of the linear list (A B C D E)

I.1.2 LISP Operations

Like Prolog, LISP is an interactive language. The user can type a name, to which LISP will respond by presenting the value stored in the object whose name was given. The user can also type in an expression that will be evaluated and its value presented to the user. A LISP expression may invoke operations on LISP objects; we discuss the syntax and semantics of LISP expressions in this section.

Because LISP uses prefix notation to specify operations and their operands, the first element of a LISP object that is treated as an expression is interpreted as a function (or operation) name. The remaining list elements are interpreted as the function's actual parameters, passed by value.[2] The manner of handling

---

[1]   One may save space by substituting a short atom for the pointer that otherwise would locate it; this refinement is not important in this discussion, which focuses on LISP's logical properties.

[2]   But lists are passed by copying only the pointer to the root of the list, and not by copying the entire list.

function parameters is affected by the function name. If the function is user-defined, all of its parameters will be evaluated before the function is called.[3] If the function is a LISP primitive, the language specifies whether one or more of its arguments should not be evaluated before calling the function.

The single quote mark is a very important element in LISP programs; it defers the evaluation of the expression that follows the quote. The scope of the single quote extends to the next (unmatched) right parenthesis or space. In effect, the characters within the string preceded by the quote are treated as a character string, and not as an expression to be evaluated. If the object starting with the quote mark were to be evaluated, the result would be the enclosed character string.

Now we are ready to describe simple LISP operations to create and manipulate list objects. Each LISP operation returns a value. An operation without side effects simply computes one value that it returns. The basic LISP list operations include assembling a list, disassembling a list, and testing whether an object is an atom. Table I-1 lists some of these operations. In the table, we use L and M to denote object names.

TABLE I-1   SOME BASIC LISP OPERATIONS WITHOUT SIDE EFFECTS

Operation	Value is
(**CAR** L)	The first element of L
(**CDR** L)	A list containing the second element of L as a list
(**CONS** L M)	A list whose first element is L and the second is M
(**ATOM** L)	**T** (true) if L is an atom; **NIL** (false) otherwise

A sequence of **CAR** and **CDR** operations can be used to "walk around" a list, selecting an element by its position within the list. The **CDR** operator always returns a pointer to a list, which will be empty if the list that is the operand contains only one entry.[4] The **CONS** operation obtains a new instance of a cons node (from the global heap) and fills it with pointers to the two arguments (which may have been lists themselves). Because the **CONS** operator does not recopy the list components, any subsequent operation that changes one of these components will also change the composite list created by **CONS**. Every operation that returns a list value actually returns a pointer to the list, except that when the result is presented on the terminal, the user sees a copy of the contents of the list, expressed in the linear parenthesized form.

---

[3]   Numbers, of course, do not need to be evaluated. If you insist that there should be no distinction between numbers and other objects, you can adopt the attitude that each number is a name for a location that always contains the value of the number.

[4]   The empty list is the same as the **NIL** pointer; this object is considered to be both an atom and a list; it is the only object value having this peculiar property.

The **SETQ** operation performs an assignment as a side effect and returns the value of the expression that was assigned to the named location. For example, (**SETQ** L M) assigns the value of M to L (i.e., like the C++ assignment statement L = M) and returns the value of M. There is a rule stating that the first parameter of **SETQ** is not evaluated before **SETQ** is called. This convention saves writing a quote mark in front of the destination name. **SETQ** can also be called with any number of argument pairs (expressed as a single list); each odd parameter is not evaluated and is taken as the name to which the value of the next parameter will be assigned. These evaluations and assignments are performed sequentially.[5]

The **EVAL** operator evaluates its single argument. It is the left inverse of the quote operator because the following two expressions are equivalent.

> (**EVAL** 'S)
> S

A sequence of operations can be written as a list containing those operations in the order of their execution. The value of the sequence is the value of the last operation executed.

Example I-2

The "expression"

> ((**SETQ** C 'B M 'D)
> (**CONS** C M))

sets C to point to a list having one element whose value is the string "B", sets M to pcint to another one-element list containing "D", and then constructs a new list from those two. The value of the expression is the list (B D).

Notice the use of returns and spaces to depict the logical structure of the expression.

The **COND** (conditional) operator tests whether a predicate is true and, if so, it evaluates a corresponding expression. This is similar to a C++ **if** statement; the value returned by **COND** is the value of the evaluated expression, or **NIL**, if the predicate is false. A list generalization of **COND** has several parameters, each being a list containing two expressions. The first expression is a condition; if its value is non-**NIL**, the condition is true. The list **COND** is evaluated by sequentially evaluating the conditions until one of them is found to be true. Then the corresponding expression is evaluated. The value of the **COND** expression is the value of the expression chosen to be evaluated. If all of the conditions are false, the value of the **COND** expression is **NIL**.

---

[5]   The built-in operator **PSETQ** performs similar assignments in parallel; all expressions are evaluated before any assignments are performed.

Example I-3

Consider the following program fragment:

```
( ( SETQ L ’( A ( B ( ( C D ) ( E ( F G ) ) ) ) ) )
  ( SETQ M L )
  ( SETQ N ( CONS M M ) )
  ( COND ( ( ATOM M ) ( SETQ N L ) )
    ( ( ATOM ( CAR L ) ) ( SETQ M ( CONS N L ) ) )
    ( T NIL ) ) )
```

The first three lines of this program establish the environment in which the **COND** expression will be evaluated. The **COND** states that if M is an atom, then set N to point to L; if M is not an atom and the first element of L is an atom, then set M to point to a new list constructed from a copy of N concatenated with L; and otherwise (the predicate T always being true) return **NIL** as the result. Without looking at the values in L, M, and N, we can state (weakly) that the overall result returned by this program fragment is the value returned by the last function executed (which is the value of L, the value of M, or **NIL**, depending on the predicate evaluations).

Given the values established in the first three lines, what is the program's actual behavior? Because M is not an atom, the first element of L is examined. Because it is an atom, M is set to point to **CONS**(N L), and that is the value of the program, because this assignment was the last action executed within the program.

Table I-2 lists a few basic LISP predicates. Three have obvious meanings. The difference between **EQL** and **EQUAL** is analogous to the difference between a default equality test that checks bit patterns and a programmer-defined equality test that reflects the semantics of the objects. In particular, the (**EQL** A B) predicate test can be evaluated by comparing the pointers within A and B, but to evaluate the (**EQUAL** A B) predicate test, the system must examine the complete data structures that start from the A and B pointers to determine whether they represent identical structures with identical values at their leaves.

TABLE I-2   SOME LISP PREDICATES

Predicate	True if
(**ATOM** A)	A is an atom
(**EQL** A B)	A and B are structures represented by the same memory object
(**EQUAL** A B)	A and B are "matching" lists[a]
(**LISTP** A)	A is a list
(**NUMBER** A)	A is a number

[a] In particular, A and B represent lists with identical logical structures, but they do not have to be represented by the same memory cells.

LISP formats effectively place operand names and operator names on an equal footing. Thus, a LISP program can make an assignment (during program execution) to an operator name. The next example illustrates this option.

Example I-4

A LISP expression is a prefix list whose first element, considered as a symbol string, is the symbolic name of the function that performs the operation. Thus, the three-element list (+ 3 6) represents the addition of three and six.

The contents of a variable could be interpreted as a program fragment and executed; the **APPLY** primitive function initiates this activity. **APPLY** interprets its (single) argument (which is a list) as a program fragment and performs the indicated operations. Table I-3 shows a few LISP program fragments and the corresponding values and/or effects. The (**RPLACA** X Y) operation replaces the first element of the list named in the first argument (X) with the value of the second argument (Y). The LISP expression (**APPLY** X) requests the interpretation of the contents of X as a LISP expression, which is to be evaluated to find the value of the **APPLY** expression.

Notice that in order to permit run-time interpretation of the string in a variable as a program fragment, LISP's run-time support must include a compiler or an interpreter for the language.

TABLE I-3   SOME LISP PROGRAM FRAGMENTS AND THEIR EFFECTS

LISP Fragment	Effect
(**APPLY** '(+ 3 4))	7
(**SETQ** A '(+ 3 4)) (**APPLY** A)	(Assigns prefix list to A) 7
(**SETQ** A '(+ 3 4)) (**RPLACA** A '-) (**APPLY** A)	(Assigns prefix list to A) (Replaces "+" with "–" in A) –1

Example I-5

This expression is similar to the one shown in Example I-2.

```
(( SETQ  R
    (( SETQ C ( CONS B F)  M 'D )
     ( CONS C M )))
    ( RPLACA C 'AB ))
```

What is the final value within R? Notice that the representation of R contains a pointer to the C and M objects, and the **RPLACA** operation changes the first element of the C object to which R points. Thus, the answer to the question is

((AB F)D)

Because there was only one assignment operation that appears to affect the value in R, it is difficult to quickly scan the program and ascertain the result.

I.1.3 More Lisp Data Structures

With our understanding of some basic Lisp operations, we are ready to discuss structures and association lists, two important Lisp data types.

The Lisp *structure* construct is analogous to a Pascal or Ada record or a C++ structure. However, a Lisp structure is created not by a declaration, but by executing the definition function **DEFSTRUCT**. The fact that a Lisp structure is defined (or declared) during program execution is only one of several important differences between the Lisp and C++ versions of structures; some others are as follows:

1. The Lisp **DEFSTRUCT** operator is an executable function.
2. While executing **DEFSTRUCT**, Lisp creates an instance creation routine that can be called to create an instance of the structure.
3. While executing **DEFSTRUCT**, Lisp creates a set of accessing functions that can be used to access the components of an instance of the structure.

The following example will clarify these features.

Example I-6

```
(( DEFSTRUCT ( THIS )
   ( NAME NIL )
   ( VALUE 3 )
   ( COMMENT 'Here it is ) )          //here is the end of the first statement
 ( SETQ HERE ( MAKE-THIS ) )
 ( SETQ M ( THIS-VALUE HERE ) )
 ( SETF ( THIS-NAME HERE ) 'thing )
 ( SETQ TWO ( MAKE-THIS :NAME 'SIX :COMMENT '6 ) )
```

The first statement defines the class THIS; each instance of an object of class THIS will have three components named NAME, VALUE, and COMMENT, with default initial values **NIL**, 3, and "Here it is", respectively. The second statement creates an object of class THIS and assigns to the object named HERE a pointer to the new instance. Notice how the name of the creation operator was constructed from the class name. The third statement illustrates how a value is read from a named record's field; the statement reads the field named VALUE of the object HERE and assigns it to M. The fourth statement assigns a new value to the NAME field of HERE. The fifth statement shows how a "function," which obtains a pointer to the field, can be used as a destination specification for an assignment in a **SETF** operator. (It cannot be used as a destination in a **SETQ** operation.) Finally, the last statement illustrates how the default initial values can be overridden when an object is created; the value of (THIS-NAME TWO) is "SIX" after this statement has been evaluated.

The *association list*, which is a list of lists, is another important LISP data type. This type is supported by an associative lookup operation **ASSOC**, which searches in an association list (which is the value of the second argument of **ASSOC**) for a list whose first element matches the value of **ASSOC**'s first argument (its key); the result is the entire list of which the specified key is the first element. Observe the behavior:

Example I-7

((**SETQ** A '((FIRST this) (SECOND thing) (THIRD is)))
  (**SETQ** M (**ASSOC** 'SECOND A)))

The first expression assigns an association list to the object named A. The second expression looks in the value of A for a component list whose first entry is "SECOND" and returns that entire sublist. So the value assigned to M is the list

(SECOND thing)

I.1.4 LISP Functions

LISP functions differ from C++ functions in several ways. LISP functions are defined during program execution. When called, a function receives all of its parameters by value. If a parameter is a list, it is passed by passing the value of a pointer to the list, and not by copying the list itself; this rule saves memory space, but it also determines the semantics of functions that modify a list that was a parameter without copying it to a local object.

A LISP program defines a new function by executing the **DEFUN** function. **DEFUN** has three parameters, which are not evaluated before **DEFUN** is called. The parameters are the name of the function, a list of its formal parameter names, and a list that is the body of the function. The following example should be obvious:

(**DEFUN** SQUARE (X) (* X X))

LISP utilizes dynamic nesting for name resolution. The set of declarations local[6] to a function f includes both f's formal parameters and those names assigned values by the **LET** primitive during f's execution. In Appendix E, we showed how an implementation of dynamic nesting can use a stack onto which the old values of all newly declared objects are pushed during procedure call and from which they are popped during procedure return. In a similar manner, a LISP system pushes the old values of the objects whose names match the formal parameters of the new procedure during call. The old values of objects that become local by virtue of the execution of the **LET** operation are pushed when **LET** is executed. In many respects, **LET** is similar to **SETQ**, but it does have four important differences beyond the value-saving attribute:

---

[6]   The objects that we call "local" are called "bound" objects in LISP terminology.

1. **LET**'s list parameter is not evaluated before **LET** is called.
2. **LET** takes one argument, which is a list of name-value pairs enclosed in parentheses.
3. **LET** performs parallel assignments if given a list of assignments.
4. **LET** allows a name without a value in place of an argument pair—a **NIL** value will be stored in the designated location.

As in all implementations of dynamic nesting, the previous (i.e., external) values of all local objects are popped off the stack when the function returns.

During program execution, a function will be called if the name of the function is the first entry in the expression being evaluated. Also, a function can be called by executing the primitive **FUNCALL**. This primitive accepts any number of parameters. It evaluates them all and then uses the value of the first one as the name of the function to be called. The values of the remaining list entries become the actual parameters passed to that call.

Example I-8

We can combine **FUNCALL** with association list retrieval operations to implement object-oriented programming in the manner of the "message to the first parameter" school. Under this version, the general function name and the type of the first operand are converted into the name of the specific procedure that handles the operation when the first operand has the specified type. The value of the first operand, along with the values and types of the other operands, is passed to the selected function.

Suppose that we wish to implement this by representing each operand by a pair of operands, of which the first contains the value and the second the type of the operand. In the following implementation, all versions of the first portion of the calling sequences of the specific functions are placed in an association list named FLIST. An entry in FLIST would look like (integer fint), where integer is the name of an operand type. We name the overloaded function OFCN. When a function call is to be made, the OFCN function searches the association list to find a match against the type of the first actual parameters passed to the overloaded version of the function. After finding a match, the generic procedure then executes **FUNCALL** to call the function whose first part of the calling sequence is found in the association list. This program fragment shows this style of dispatching within the overloaded function definition

```
( DEFUN OFCN ( x xtype y ytype )
  ( ( FUNCALL ( CDR ( ASSOC FLIST xtype ) ) x y ytype ) ) )
```

Notice the use of **CDR** to remove the parameter class list that served as the search key, leaving only the last atom of the pair in the association list, which contained the function name. Thus, making the call

```
( OFCN 6 'integer 8 'integer )
```

results in a call (fint 6 8 integer).

I.1.5 Comments

The Lisp programming language emphasizes lists as both data and program objects. All operations are expressed in prefix notation. Basic Lisp functions include those that construct lists, select from them, call functions, and test predicates.
    Several aspects of this language make its implementation difficult:

1. Objects are created dynamically from free storage, which has to be managed as a heap.
2. Object types and functions can be defined during program execution.
3. The data structures contain many pointers.
4. The implementation must distinguish pointers from other objects.
5. Object sizes vary.
6. Dynamic nesting is used for name resolution.
7. The set of objects local to a procedure may grow during procedure execution (while executing **LET**).
8. There is no way to program object deletion, so the system will accumulate *garbage*, which is data that cannot be accessed any longer.

    These aspects introduce requirements that make it difficult to realize an efficient implementation of the language. Now we see how one design team designed an efficient host for the Lisp language.

I.2 A Lisp PROCESSOR ARCHITECTURE

The Symbolics 3600 family of machines ([SYMB86] and [MOON87]) was designed to support Lisp. We discuss the following aspects of the machine's design:

1. Object representation
2. Operator selection
3. Operator implementation
4. Internal processor state
5. Garbage collection

I.2.1 Object Representation

Each Symbolics 3600 word contains 36 bits, of which some may be used for tag information. Every object is either directly tagged or belongs to a structure whose header defines the types of the components. Directly tagged words have a 2-bit tag called the "cdr code," which occupies bits 35 and 34. We illustrate the important cases, starting from the bottom with representations of atoms.

TABLE I-4   TYPE TAG INTERPRETATIONS IN THE SYMBOLICS 3600

Short Name	Meaning
r	Word contains a 32-bit float value
i	Word contains a 32-bit integer value
hp	The minor tag (bits 31 .. 28) plus 1 bit from the major tag determine the meaning of the word as a pointer or a header

Atoms. The interpretation of an atom does not depend on the cdr code. Thus, all atoms have to be represented within 34 bits, including their type tags. A 34-bit indirect pointer is used to access an atom if its representation will not fit within 34 bits.

Figure I-3 illustrates three important object types and their representations. Our short tag names for these object types are listed in Table I-4. Single-precision floats and integers have 32-bit encodings, with floats conforming to the IEEE standard format. Because these data types are used so frequently, the designers sacrificed pointer space so that integers and floats could be accessed quickly. A pointer contains a 6-bit type tag and a 28-bit virtual address. The pointer's type tag specifies the type of object located at the indicated address. Table I-5 lists some interpretations of the pointer's type tag.

One important special case is the indirect[7] pointer used to signify that the object that was expected here actually exists elsewhere (namely, at the address

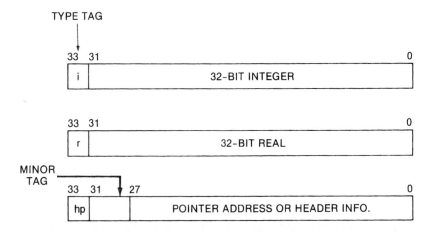

Figure I-3   Simple object representations in the Symbolics 3600 (after [MOON87], Figure 1; © IEEE 1987)

---

[7]   These are called "forwarding pointers" in Symbolics literature.

TABLE I-5   SELECTED CASES OF MINOR TAG VALUES IN THE SYMBOLICS
3600 LISP PROCESSOR

Name of Tag Value	Type of Thing in the Remaining 28 Bits of the Word
Symbol	Pointer to a "value"
List	Pointer to the next entry in a list
Nil	Pointer to nothing
Prog header	Word contains the length of the program object
String	Pointer to the string's representation in an array
Array	Pointer to an array header
Type instance	Pointer to an array defining a type (a "flavor")
Indirection	Pointer to the value that logically belongs here

contained within the pointer). Indirect pointers are introduced to implement operations that change the structure of an existing list without recopying the entire list. Any indirect pointers are automatically traversed by the processor when needed to access the proper object. Special operators are provided to manipulate indirect pointers.

Lists. Because LISP is a list processing language, the list is a very important object class. Thus, it is important to choose an efficient representation for list objects. The obvious choice is a machine representation that mirrors a literal interpretation of the list as a set of two-element beads linked together by pointers. Such a representation is logically correct, but a machine using this list representation scheme would spend many cycles fetching pointers from memory and using their contents as addresses to direct further fetches. Clearly, we need to seek a better way to represent the most common list structures.

The linear list is an important common case. In a linear list, the cdr of each cons points directly to the next cons in the list (see Figure I-4a). The general list representation seems particularly inefficient in this case, because a linear list can be compressed to a vector. Introducing a special format for this simple case alone might not be effective, because any node in the list could be changed, which would destroy the simple linear structure. The Symbolics system uses the cdr tag to define the relationship between the word associated with the cdr tag and the remainder of the list of which it is a part. In essence, the cdr tag specifies whether a simple case applies, and, if so, which case does apply. The cdr tag codes are listed in Table I-6. The representation of a linear list uses two of the cdr tag codes. The "next" tag indicates that the next word contains the list element that is the cdr of this word. The "end" tag indicates that the cdr of this word would

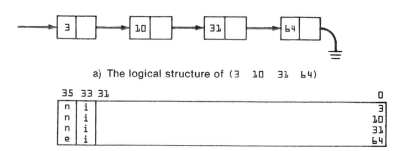

a) The logical structure of (3 10 31 64)

b) A compressed representation of (3 10 31 64)

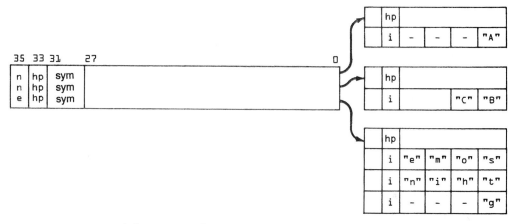

c) A compressed representation of (A BC something).
("Sym" denotes the tag for a pointer to a symbol).

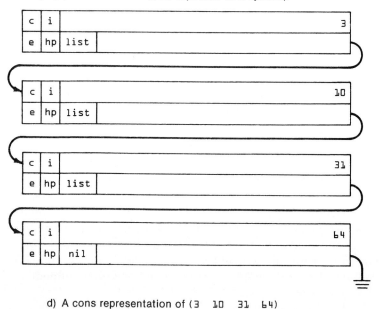

d) A cons representation of (3 10 31 64)

Figure I-4 Compressed list interpretations in the Symbolics 3600 (after [MOON87]; © IEEE 1987)

TABLE I-6   INTERPRETATIONS OF THE CDR TAG (BITS 35 AND 34) IN THE SYMBOLICS 3600

Short Name	Abbreviation in Figures	Meaning of Appended Tag
next	n	The next word contains the CDR of this entry
cons	c	The next word contains the *value* of the CDR of this entry
end	e	The next word is not part of this structure
other	—	This word's contents are not necessarily part of a list entry

be null, which means that this element is the last word of this construct. Figure I-4b illustrates the use of the next and end tags to compress the linear list. In this simple example, each integer list entry does fit into the single tagged word provided for each list element in the compressed structure. If a list entry were a character string, the tagged word in the compressed structure would contain a pointer to a structure containing the character string (see Figure I-4c).[8]

To represent a general list node, we need two words, the first tagged with the cons cdr code, and the second with the end cdr code. The Symbolics 3600 representation of our simple list using cons nodes is shown in Figure I-4d. The generalization to other list structures should be obvious.

Now suppose that the entry holding 10 in our list were changed so that its successor becomes an existing list containing (2 -7 13). Figure I-5a illustrates the logical structures after that change. Logically, the system should replace the entry holding 10 with a general cons structure. Unfortunately, the needed cons structure takes more space than the compressed node representation that it logically replaces. We cannot just overwrite the next entry (containing 31), because that entry might be accessible through one or more pointers elsewhere in the system. This reasoning shows that the (single word) entry that previously held 10 has to (logically) hold its larger replacement. In the Symbolics 3600, this difficulty is handled by replacing the old entry (10) with an indirect pointer that specifies the location where the new, larger entry is located. Figure I-5b illustrates the modified list.

Structures.   Recall that a structure is a collection of diverse kinds of objects. Structures have a very straightforward representation in the Symbolics 3600 machines. The first word of the structure is typed as an array header; it contains information about the size and type of the structure. Because the header word cannot be a member of a list, its cdr code bits will not be used to decide how to interpret the word as a list member, so the cdr code bits are used to extend its type code field. The consecutive words immediately following the

---

[8]   This indirection is used even if the character string is short and could be stored in the single word.

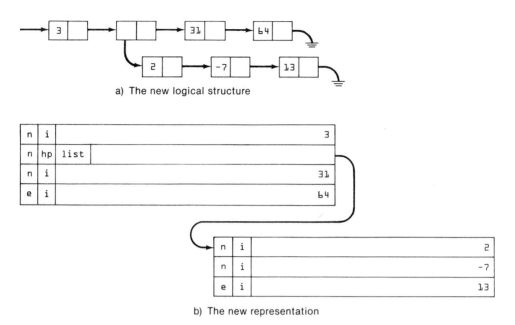

a) The new logical structure

b) The new representation

Figure I-5   Replacing an entry in a compressed list may change its structure

header hold the structure's contents; each is self-describing, thanks to its own tag. None of the components of a structure can serve as an element in the middle of a list. Thus, there is no need for the cdr codes associated with the structure's entries. The Symbolics 3600 representation of a three-element structure is illustrated in Figure I-6.

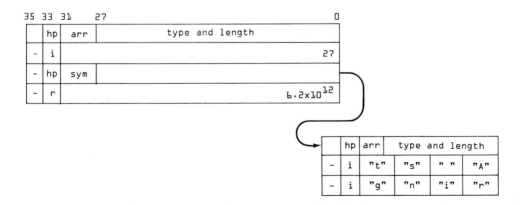

Figure I-6   The Symbolics 3600 representation of a three-element structure containing (27 "A String" 6.2 x 10^{12})

Special structure types are used to hold character strings and programs. A character string is stored in an array packed four characters to each word, each one tagged as an integer. The leftmost character code is stored in the rightmost byte. Because the processor makes many accesses to character strings and programs, having representations that are easily accessed enhances processor speed.

Program Representation.   Each function occupies a separate array (see Figure I-7). Thus, most programs occupy several arrays. The header and first word of a program array together specify the type of the array, its overall size, the size of the constants region within the program (see what follows), the number of arguments expected by the function, and the location of the first instruction within the array. Space following this header is reserved for use during debugging; any information in the debugging space is not interpreted during function execution. The debugging information is followed by the constant values used by the function. Instruction words occupy the remainder of the array.

Two 17-bit instructions are encoded within the 34 bits of instruction word plus its two cdr tag bits; its minor tag indicates that the array element is an integer (see Figure I-8). There are two instruction formats; one has a 9-bit function code and an 8-bit operand field, whereas the other has only a 7-bit function code and a 10-bit specification of the location of a bit field (i.e., its first bit position and width). The latter format is used for a few bit field instructions.

The function code determines the interpretation of the operand field contents. Table I-7 lists some of the possible uses of the operand field information. Because the function code determines the use of the operand field information, the operation code and addressing selections are not orthogonal.

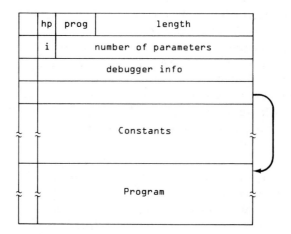

Figure I-7   The Symbolics 3600 representation of a function body

I.2.2 Operator Selection

The Symbolics instruction set was selected so that its operators would be close to
LISP primitives. It contains the usual arithmetic operators, list manipulation operators, several operators to support fast function calling, and many operators
that manipulate pointers. The instructions were carefully chosen so that

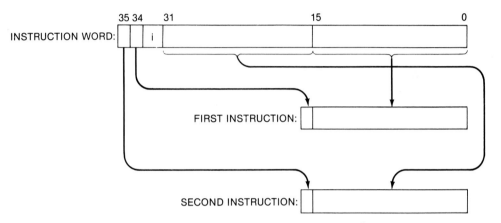

Figure I-8   A Symbolics 3600 instruction word contains two 17-bit instructions

TABLE I-7   ALTERNATE INTERPRETATIONS OF THE OPERAND FIELD IN SYMBOLICS
3600 INSTRUCTIONS

Case	Operand Field Usage
PC-offset address	Offset (range –128 .. +127)
Local operand	Unsigned offset within local stack frame
Temporary result	Unsigned offset back from top of stack
Flavor instance component	Unsigned offset within flavor instance
Indirect flavor instance component	Indirect through an unsigned flavor instance offset
Link operand	Unsigned offset within program's constants
Indirect link operand	Indirect through a program constant offset
Structure component	Offset from structure origin
Global reference	Unsigned offset from link pointer
Immediate unsigned	Value (range 0 .. +255)
Immediate signed	Value (range –127 .. +128)
Function	Extension of the function code

Source: After [MOON87], Table 1; © 1987 IEEE.

operations occurring most frequently would complete quickly. Tagging reduces the number of different operators, because a function code can be overloaded such that its effect depends on the types of its operands.

I.2.3 Operator Implementation

The Symbolics 3600 implementation of frequently executed operators attempts to use parallelism as much as possible. In this spirit, the add instruction feeds its operands directly to the integer adder (and the optional float adder, if present) and checks their types while the two additions are performed. The type check determines which result is valid, if either suffices. If no result obtained from the hardware can be used for the sum, the controller will issue an additional (stream of) microinstructions to perform the desired operation.

Other techniques used to speed instruction execution are closely related to the representation of each process's internal state.

I.2.4 Process State

The Symbolics 3600 machines do not have any programmer-visible registers; all operations are stack-oriented, so operands are popped from the stack and results are pushed on the top of the stack. This "control" stack is cached in a local memory that contains four 256-word pages. The (control) stack cache memory is designed so that words near the top of the stack can be accessed quickly. An implementation restriction demands that functions be compiled such that the activation record remains small enough so that the entire block can be held in the 4 pages of the control stack cache.

Each Symbolics 3600 process has three stacks. One stack holds binding information (values pushed to retain the external state of the LET and parameter objects), one holds program-allocated information, and the third (the control stack) holds the usual combination of control information, parameter values, and saved stack pointers plus small local objects. The control stack configuration is similar to the B 5700 stack configuration, except that a complete copy of the parameter values is present in both the old and new stack frames (see Figure I-9). The procedure calling instructions are analogous to the B 5700 set; there is a "start-function-call" instruction, a push instruction (to store parameters at the top of the stack), and a "complete-function-call" instruction that actually transfers control to the new procedure. These instructions are similar to the analogous B 5700 instructions, except that the Symbolics 3600 versions have a parameter whose value states how many parameters are being passed. During the execution of the call instruction, the processor checks the number of actual parameters against the number of formal parameters (obtained from the procedure's header), and inserts default values for any missing parameters.

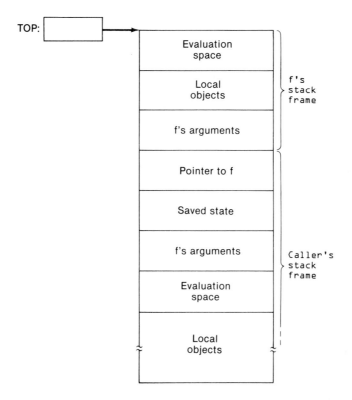

Figure I-9   The Symbolics 3600 stack format for
calling procedure f

During function call and return the stack buffer may be changed so that
the new block will fit in the stack buffer. During call, the bottommost stack page
in the processor's cache memory may be copied to main memory to free a buffer
page for the new top of the stack. During return, an old page may be read from
main memory to the buffer so that the entire block will be present in the buffer.

I.2.5 Garbage Collection

All LISP implementations use heap allocations to acquire the spaces that hold
conses and other dynamically created objects. Whenever a new cons is created,
space is obtained from the heap. No LISP operations explicitly deallocate any
storage. In fact, space becomes free only after all pointers to that space have been
deallocated or overwritten, but no implementation of LISP tracks pointers to discover this condition. Thus, garbage collection is essential in LISP systems; it en-
tails traversing all "live" pointers to ascertain which space is indeed free.

LISP garbage collection algorithms typically follow these phases:

1. Scan: Recursively follow all "live" pointers to find and mark all values currently in use.
2. Compress: Compress space by relocating all live objects to a contiguous space at low addresses, changing all pointers accordingly.
3. Free: Initialize the free-space descriptors to make the free space at high addresses available to the space allocator.

The Symbolics 3600 architecture includes several low-level mechanisms that assist garbage collection. First, each physical page has an associated tag that is set when a pointer to reclaimable space is written into the page. A scan of these tags during garbage collection uncovers those pages that must be scanned in detail to find pointers. Second, a similar table is kept by the software for all disk-resident pages; this table determines which disk pages must be copied from the disk during the garbage collector's scan phase. Third, it is possible to run programs during the compression phase because objects that have been relocated can still be accessed from their old locations through indirect pointers that replace the original entries. Setting this up requires additional work to install the indirect pointers; it may be easier and faster to just permit garbage collection to complete with all user programs suspended. The programmer may control whether garbage collection shall complete without interruption. The negative aspect of uninterruptible garbage collection is that the complete garbage collection process could take many minutes.

I.3 SUMMARY

The LISP language presents some unique architectural challenges due to dynamic typing, dynamic nesting, garbage generation, and a large number of function calls. The Symbolics 3600 designers chose an efficient representation for the common linear list structure, designed self-describing data objects, designed a LISP-oriented instruction set, designed operation implementations that perform frequently executed instructions quickly, and designed tables to track pointers to assist with garbage collection. By these means, they produced a machine architecture tuned to LISP program execution.

I.4 TRENDS

List processing will continue to be an important alternative for structuring some computer applications. Efficient implementations of list processing languages will probably utilize fast programs executed on RISC processors. It seems difficult to automatically find opportunities for parallelism within LISP programs;

this should be an important future challenge. Any realistic implementation will probably use an efficient list representation such as the one used within the Symbolics processors.

The complexity of implementing a fast contemporary processor, which requires a VLSI implementation with over a million devices on the same die, precludes implementing processors targeted for specialized languages. This means that the development cost for a new processor design is so high that a very large number of copies must be sold to recover that cost and then make a profit. Thus, the Symbolics style, designing a processor for a language, is likely to die out.

I.5 CONCEPT LIST

1. List structures
2. Lists are both programs and data, creating a von Neumann architecture
3. Run-time structure definition
4. Run-time function definition
5. Run-time local object declaration through **LET**
6. Structures modified by side effects (as with **RPLACA)**
7. Efficient representations of linear lists
8. Indirect pointers in structures
9. Tag-based operation selection
10. Efficient software coding for pointer management
11. Need for garbage collection
12. Use parallel implementations, choose the appropriate result later
13. Stack blocks cached in a known manner within the processor

I.6 PROBLEMS

I-1. Draw a diagram illustrating the logical data structures that exist at the completion of the program in Example I-5.

I-2. Figure I-10 shows the LISP data structures in the machine at the start of the execution of some LISP program fragments. Draw a picture of the LISP data structures in the machine after each of the following LISP program fragments completes execution. The conditions of Figure I-10 pertain at the start of each program fragment.

(a)   ((**SETQ** B (B F)))
(b)   ((**SETQ** G (CAR C)))
(c)   ((**RPLACD** F (**CDR** (**CDR** G))))
   See Problem I-6 for an explanation of **RPLACD**.
(d)   ((**SETQ** G (**CAR** C))
         (**RPLACD** F (**CDR** (**CDR** G))))

NAMED OBJECTS

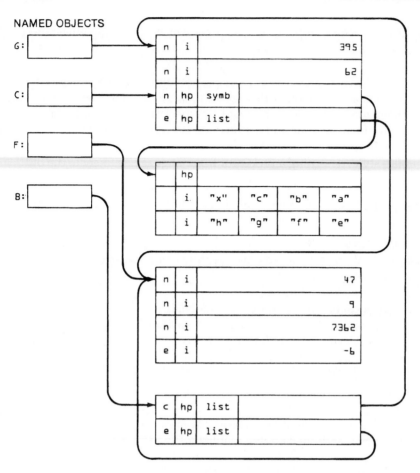

Figure I-10   A snapshot of the Symbolics 3600 memory

I-3.   Write a LISP function that compares two lists to see whether they have the same structure, but without comparing the values at the leaves of the structure. The function should return T if the structures are the same, and F otherwise.

I-4.   Draw diagrams illustrating the representation of each of the following LISP lists in the Symbolics 3600.

   (a) $(((A3($64))F)(X(Y((NX)G))))$
   (b) $(((12)(34))((56)(78)))$
   (c) $(((AB)(CD))((EF)(GH)))$

I-5.   Modify the Symbolics 3600 list element representation rules so that a short character-string list element can be stored in a single word. The goals are to save space and memory accesses by avoiding the overhead of an array structure for each short character string. Your solution must conform with the other Symbolics 3600 object representation conventions; this means that you will have to use a new minor tag field value to denote your special case. How long is the longest character string that will fit into your representation?

I-6. The two LISP primitives **RPLACA** and **RPLACD** replace the contents of the first (A) or second (D) part of a list cons without changing anything else in the list.
   (a) Draw a picture illustrating the transformation that the Symbolics 3600 must make on its internal representation of the target list to perform **RPLACA**.
   (b) Repeat part (a) for the case that the machine is performing **RPLACD** and the affected node is a cons memory cell.
   (c) Repeat part (a) for the case that the machine is performing **RPLACD** and the target list is represented as a compressed list.
   (d) Write a series of steps that the Symbolics 3600 could use to perform **RPLACD**.

I-7. Discuss the following claim: The Symbolics 3600 processor could handle a reference to a component within a LISP structure as an indexed reference to the array holding the structure.
   Point out the similarities and differences between (1) accessing a LISP structure component and (2) accessing a component of a C++ structure.

I-8. This problem is concerned with devising effective support for user-defined object classes within LISP. In particular, we desire processor support for these classes. We start by devising some internal formats for objects having user-defined types. We build up from the Symbolics 3600 representations for untyped lists and their elements. We want each user-defined class to be defined by a list of functions that manipulate objects of the corresponding type, in the style of a C++ class interface. We propose to list the actual procedure names in a data object of type structure. Then the class is described by this structure.
   (a) Draw figures representing the data structures and object representations implementing this class definition scheme. Represent each object as a two-component LISP list of the form (type value).
   (b) Draw figures representing the data structures and object representations implementing this class definition scheme. Represent each object as a two-component word containing codes for the type and value. Use the compressed format shown in Figure I-11.
   (c) Design an efficient representation and the corresponding interpretation rules to cover the situation when the value of an object may be small enough to fit in the compressed word format developed in part (b), but sometimes might require a full word to hold the value alone.
   (d) A designer claims that the representation developed in part (c) is both comprehensive (it covers all situations) and efficient in both space and time. Comment on these claims.

I-9. It has been claimed (with some justification) that memory references are less local when executing a LISP program than when running an algorithm expressed in a "conventional" language like C++. Thus, a LISP machine designer devises the following schemes in an attempt to localize the reference string; this would be

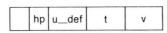

Figure I-11   An encoding proposed for short objects having user-defined types (u_def is a new minor tag)

useful if the system used paging for memory management. Discuss each scheme, particularly covering its space and time efficiencies and inefficiencies, if any.

(a) Each process is confined to a contiguous partition of (virtual) memory space.

(b) During execution of function f, all space is allocated from a heap for f; each of these heaps is managed using a stack discipline.

(c) Keep a separate heap within each memory page. When space is needed, the new space is allocated (if possible) within the page where a pointer to the space will be stored. What criteria would you use to decide when to allocate a new object in a different page?

I-10. Explain why one could claim that the Symbolics machine has $(512 - 3b)$ possible function codes within its instruction set (b denoting the number of bit field instructions).

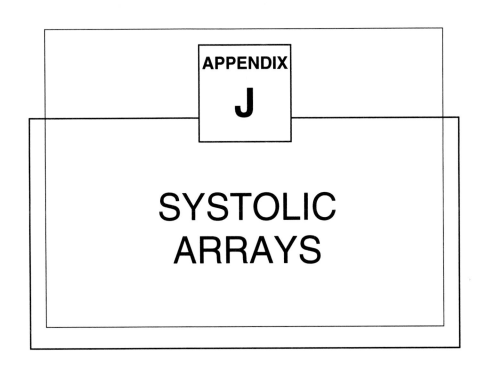

APPENDIX J

SYSTOLIC ARRAYS

The basic idea behind the systolic array architecture is that data flow through a computational array. Contrast this with the basic idea behind conventional architectures, that a program moves across data stored in memory. In this respect, the systolic array is like a data flow system (see Appendix K). The two are not the same, because (1) all modules in a systolic array are active all the time; (2) events in the systolic array occur in synchronism with an external clock; (3) in the systolic system, there is a separate memory outside the array that serves as the source and destination of all values; and (4) in the systolic system, the internal state can be stored within the modules between clock pulses. Furthermore, many systolic designs contain only one or two types of modules. The systolic structure is useful for executing specialized algorithms on homogeneous data structures.

A simple systolic array [KUNG82] is a regular array of identical modules connected through data paths according to a regular structure. Each module performs a computation, using its arriving input data and its internal state, to generate results that may affect both the retained state and the data sent on outgoing data links. Some systolic arrays include a variety of module types with different interconnection structures in different sections of the array.

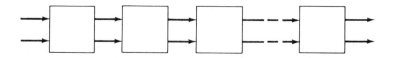

Figure J-1   A linear systolic array

All operations within the systolic array are synchronized by an external clock, which becomes the reference for controlling and describing the systolic array's operation. In each module on each clock pulse, data are read from the module inputs and computations are performed to determine the values to be passed out during the next clock pulse.[1] The internal module states are also updated on each clock pulse so that the modules are prepared to process the data arriving on the next clock pulse. The flow of values through the system can be depicted in a space–time diagram that emphasizes the positions of the first and last components of each traveling component or partial result.

In this appendix, we describe a straightforward method to obtain a mathematical description of the computation performed by a systolic array and some structural options for systolic arrays.

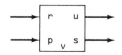

Figure J-2   A systolic array
module

J.1 FUNCTIONAL DESCRIPTIONS

Figure J-1 illustrates a simple systolic array containing identical modules interconnected using a linear pattern. Figure J-2 illustrates our notation for a single module's state and data values. We see two inputs (with internal names p and r), two outputs (with internal names s and u), and an internal state (v). We use subscript k to denote the clock time. Each module's operation satisfies a set of relations such as[2]

$$s_k = p_{k-2} \tag{J-1}$$

$$u_k = r_{k-1} \tag{J-2}$$

---

[1]   This makes the behavior analogous to the Moore model of sequential machine behavior.
[2]   Note that a module meeting this particular specification includes a register holding v and also a register holding the previous value of p.

$$v_k = v_{k-1} + r_{k-1}p_{k-1} \tag{J-3}$$

To identify individual modules, we add a subscript denoting the module's position within the array. Thus, $r_{i,k}$ denotes the r input to the ith module at time k. The constraints due to the interconnection structure can be formalized in a set of relations such as[3]

$$u_{i,k} = r_{i+1,k} \tag{J-4}$$

$$s_{i,k} = p_{i+1,k} \tag{J-5}$$

These five relations specify a set of partial difference equations whose solution gives the states within the modules in the systolic array, plus the array's outputs.

Before we can solve these partial differential equations, we need spatial boundary conditions concerning the external array inputs and temporal initial conditions concerning the internal module states. These states include not only the initial values of v_i, but also the values of the signals being propagated through the array on the p, r, s, and u signal paths. In our example, suppose that the internal states are all zero at time zero. Let w_i and x_i denote the external inputs applied at the r and p inputs, respectively, of the module at spatial index zero. This set of boundary conditions is expressed in the relations

$$r_{1,k} = w_{k-1} \tag{J-6}$$

$$p_{1,k} = x_{k-2} \tag{J-7}$$

$$v_{i,0} = 0 \tag{J-8}$$

For this set of boundary conditions, the solution of the set of partial difference equations [(J-1) .. (J-5)] is this set of relations:

$$r_{i,k} = w_{k-i} \tag{J-9}$$

$$p_{i,k} = x_{k-2i} \tag{J-10}$$

$$v_{i,k} = \sum_{m=2i+1}^{k-1} w_{m-i} x_{m-2i} \tag{J-11}$$

This exercise demonstrated a general technique: One can express all values within any systolic system by solving the combination of three elements: (1) the

---

[3]   If we were being mathematically precise, we would describe the interconnection signals with external names and then we would describe the wiring by relating the internal names to the external signal names. The net effect, after substitution to remove the external names from the equations, is the pair of relations shown here.

partial difference equations expressing the relationships among the inputs and outputs of the modules, (2) the equations defining the interconnection structure, and (3) the boundary conditions describing the external inputs and the initial conditions.

J.2 ARRAY STRUCTURE OPTIONS

Many computations that fit into the systolic mold can be made to correspond to many optional structures within the systolic paradigm. There are several basic ways in which the options differ; one systolic array design issue concerns the relative motion of operands and results across processing modules. In one option, operand streams move, with result streams spatially distributed across the module set. Another option assigns one operand's components in a fixed pattern to processing modules and the other operands and results move. Another option relies on spacing apart the operand components; the system speed may be reduced because no computations can be performed in the modules receiving null inputs. However, in some of these spaced-out systolic array designs, one may interleave data from another problem instance in the gaps, thereby replacing the "lost" cycles with useful computations for other problem instance(s).

J.2.1 Linear Array Structures

We illustrate some structural options for linear arrays that compute the convolution of two signals w(t) and $x(t)$, represented by digitized samples w_m and x_j, with $w_m \neq 0$ only for $1 \leq m \leq h$ and $x_j \neq 0$ only for $1 \leq j \leq n$. The convolution y_i is nonzero for delays in the range $1 - h \leq i \leq n + 1$. For simplicity, we compute

$$y_i = \sum_j w_j x_{i+j} \tag{J-12}$$

There are many ways to subdivide this computation and map it onto a systolic array.

Example J-1

Our first design is based on the observation that the value of y_i is the dot product of two vectors (one delayed) w_j and x_{j+i}. So we could use a dot product module that multiplies together its two inputs and adds their product to an accumulating (internal) sum. One of these modules directly produces a single y_i, if the inputs are streamed appropriately. The computation of y_{i+1} is similar, but requires a further (unit) relative delay between the inputs. This can be provided by placing a second dot product module next to the first and inserting an extra unit delay on one input being passed through the module. To make the timing work properly, the input values must be separated by two time units. Zeroes can be interspersed. This thinking leads to the structure shown in Figure J-3. In the figure, the "hat" atop a symbol

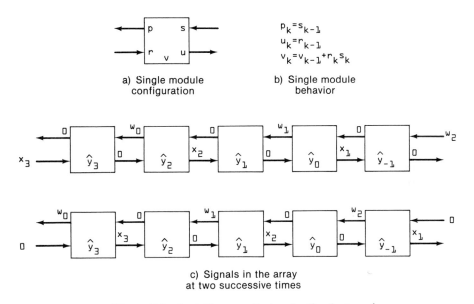

a) Single module
configuration

b) Single module
behavior

c) Signals in the array
at two successive times

Figure J-3   Systolic array timing for the design of
Example J-1 (after [KUNG82]; © 1982 IEEE)

denotes a value that is an intermediate result; its final value is denoted by the symbol beneath the hat.

Another way to visualize the activities in a linear systolic system is to construct a space–time diagram like the one in Figure J-4. The lines show the position of the components of the input vectors as time progresses. From the picture, you can determine the number of modules required to perform a computation and the amount of time from start to finish of the computation.

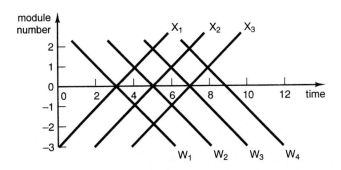

Figure J-4   A space–time diagram illustrating signal
motion in the systolic array of Figure J-3 for $h = 4$, $n = 3$

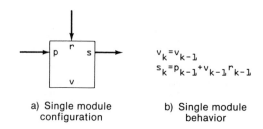

a) Single module configuration	b) Single module behavior

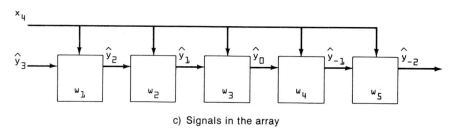

c) Signals in the array

Figure J-5   Systolic array timing for the design of Example J-2 (after [KUNG82]; © 1982 IEEE)

Example J-2

In our second convolution design (Figure J-5), one operand stream is presented in parallel to all processing modules. The other operand stream is stored in the processing modules. The results are shifted across the array.

Other alternative designs are based on moving the streams through the array at different rates. If two streams move in the same direction at the same speed, the same combinations of components will be presented to all modules, which is not appropriate for the convolution problem. Therefore, either one stream must move in the opposite direction, or both must move at different rates in the same direction.

Example J-3

A third design (Figure J-6) uses motion at half the clock speed to effect the necessary relative shift between two data streams. This design was discussed in our introductory example.

Example J-4

The preceding design moved the two operand streams through the array in the same direction; a design moving one operand stream and the result stream in the same direction is also possible. The module structure is shown in Figure J-7.

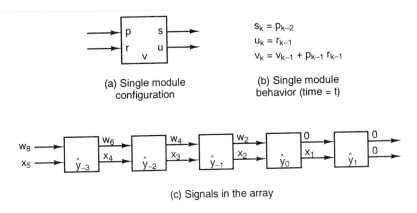

$$s_k = p_{k-2}$$
$$u_k = r_{k-1}$$
$$v_k = v_{k-1} + p_{k-1} \, r_{k-1}$$

(a) Single module
configuration

(b) Single module
behavior (time = t)

(c) Signals in the array

Figure J-6 Systolic array timing for the design of
Example J-3 (after [KUNG82]; © 1982 IEEE)

J.2.2 Hexagonal Arrays

A hexagonal interconnection of processing modules can be configured to perform matrix multiplication (Figure J-8). The elements of the two operand matrices pass diagonally downward through the array, and the components of the product matrix pass upward. The operand values are passed through each module with unit delay in each module, but without modification. Each module forms the product of the two operands arriving from above and adds the product to the value entering from below. The result and the components to be forwarded are held in the module until they are moved onward on the next clock pulse. Figure J-8 illustrates this timing; it shows the positions of various

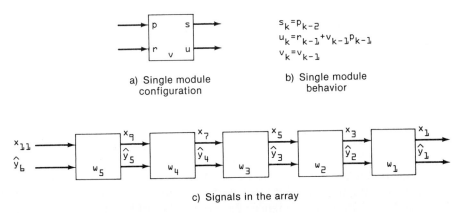

$$s_k = p_{k-2}$$
$$u_k = r_{k-1} + v_{k-1} p_{k-1}$$
$$v_k = v_{k-1}$$

a) Single module
configuration

b) Single module
behavior

c) Signals in the array

Figure J-7 Systolic array timing for the design of
Example J-4 (after [KUNG82]; © 1982 IEEE)

components at two successive times. This pattern follows a cycle of length three. While processing a single problem, each value path holds data in only one-third of its positions. This observation suggests that three independent matrix multiplication problems can be processed simultaneously by this array (see Problem J-6). This style for handling multiple problem instances is easily achieved in this array because no state is saved in the modules between clock pulses.

J.3 SUMMARY

The systolic array strategy could be viewed as a combination of the pipeline and array strategies. A systolic system is similar to a pipeline, in that operand values and intermediate results flow through a set of computational modules. Each module performs a single computation in one time unit, and the systolic array operates synchronously under control of a central clock whose role is similar to the role of the pipeline's central clock. In a pipeline, the information flows in one direction along one dimension of a linear module interconnection structure. In a systolic array, however, information may flow in any direction along any dimension, and the flow rates along different paths can be different. This flexibility allows one to design a systolic array so that different combinations of vector components interact in different modules at different times. Flow rates are determined by the delays in the modules.

Pipeline stages perform different functions, but systolic array modules are more homogeneous. A simple systolic array, like the ones in our introductory examples, contains replications of a single module type in a regular interconnection structure. Most systolic array proposals have used rectangular, linear, or hexagonal interconnection patterns. For some applications, all modules are identical, while for others, a small number of module varieties is required.

Systolic arrays usually operate on vectors or arrays of data objects; individual components of each single object may be passed sequentially through the array, and the components of others may reside in array modules. The flows may move at the basic array speed or at submultiples of the basic speed. They may be in the same direction or in related, but different directions. The operand and result components may have individual flow patterns.

It is instructive to note some other differences between a systolic array and a pipeline. In the systolic array, most processing elements are identical, or the complete array is divided into regions such that all processing modules within a single region are identical. In the systolic array, the value of one operand component entering the array interacts with more than one component of the other operand, and as a consequence, its value may affect the values of many result components. In the systolic array, each module performs a complete operation

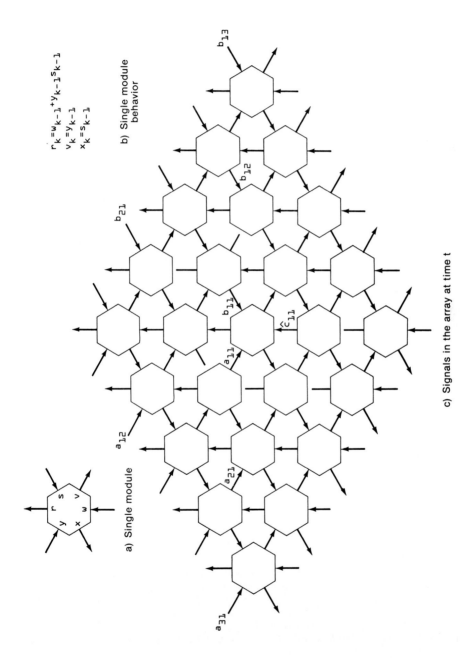

a) Single module

$$r_k = w_{k-1} + y_{k-1} s_{k-1}$$
$$v_k = y_{k-1}$$
$$x_k = s_{k-1}$$

b) Single module behavior

c) Signals in the array at time t

Figure J-8   A hexagonal systolic array for matrix multiplication C = AB (after [HAYN82]; © 1982 IEEE.)

on its inputs.[4] This feature is a necessary consequence of the fact that the operand component streams may pass through the array in different directions or at different speeds.[5]

Systolic array machines can provide speedy execution of computations expressed in recurrence relations. Each array's structure is "tuned" to a particular recurrence structure, and is not appropriate for other computations. Therefore a systolic machine can be very efficient for one specialized problem class, and inefficient for unrelated problems. A systolic array might be installed as a coprocessor attached to a general-purpose processor.

J.4 TRENDS

Systolic arrays are useful for a small number of specialized algorithms, and might be considered for the structure of a high-performance attached processor. Otherwise, it seems that the systolic scheme will not be used in the future. It is interesting to observe that most published examples of systolic arrays utilize modules that perform multiply–accumulate operations. In this connection, note that the multiply–add operation has been incorporated into vector pipelines. Thus, such a pipeline might help perform the same algorithms quickly without the need for specialized interconnections of specialized modules.

Despite the fact that the systolic array concept has probably become a passing phase in general computer system design, it should remain interesting to designers implementing special-purpose modules, such as those used in signal processing systems.

J.5 CONCEPT LIST

1. Systolic array processing
2. Data flow through an array of processing modules
3. Optional flow patterns—do operands move or results move?
4. Linear interconnection structures
5. Flows at different rates
6. Hexagonal interconnection structures

---

[4]   The passing components could be fed into a pipeline at each module, and one would have a pipelined systolic array. The clock speed for such a pipelined array could be faster than the clock for the systolic array in which each module performs a complete operation.

[5]   The argument is that any pair of interacting components will be present in the same module only during one clock interval, and therefore must be completely processed before another component combination arrives. We noted in the previous footnote that pipelining may be possible, in which case, this requirement for a complete operation during a clock cycle is replaced by a requirement concerning the timing of the initiation of the pipeline's operations.

7. Difference equations describe the activity and the result
8. Space–time diagrams
9. Interleaving multiple problem instances

J.6 PROBLEMS

J-1.   Figure J-9 shows a systolic arrangement of nonidentical modules. Each module performs the transformations specified in the figure. The inputs are the vector components x_i and y_j, with the subscripts lying in the ranges $1 \leq i \leq m$ and $1 \leq j \leq n$. Whenever required, the x components corresponding to subscripts outside the specified range are input as 1, and the y components corresponding to subscripts outside the specified range are input as 0. The results are the values v_k stored in the modules when the computation terminates.

   (a) How wide should the array be made so that every nontrivial component of v is computed within the array?

   (b) Find a formula expressing the nontrivial values of v_k in terms of the components of x and y.

J-2.   Expand the timing information of Figures J-5 and J-6 by drawing snapshots showing the locations of all data on the next four successive clock pulses for the computation of the convolution of two vectors.

J-3.   Construct a table showing the array sizes and execution times for the computation of the convolution of two vectors using each of the systolic systems discussed in

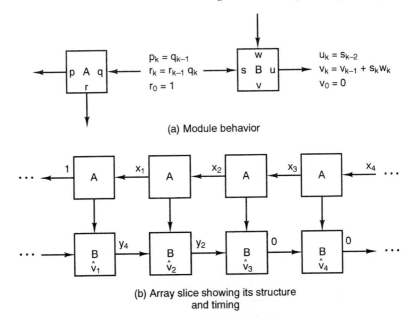

(a) Module behavior

(b) Array slice showing its structure
and timing

Figure J-9   A systolic array

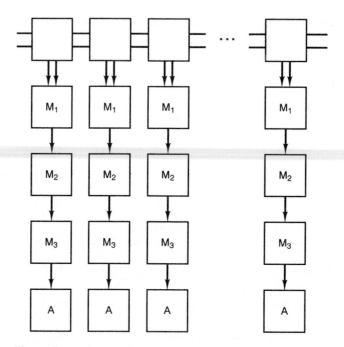

Figure J-10   A convolution array with multiplication
pipelines in the array (*Key:* A = accumulate; M_i = pipe stage)

Section J.2.1. Express your answers as functions of the lengths (k and n) of the two
input vectors. (*Hint:* For each design, look at the space-time diagram depicting the
data flowing within the array.

(a) Find the number of processing modules.

(b) Find the number of minor cycles required to compute all nonzero components
of the convolution. The first clock cycle to count is the one in which the first
vector component enters the array; the last cycle to count is the cycle in which
the last result component leaves the array.

J-4.   A designer proposes building a systolic array to compute the convolution of two
vectors with 3-stage multiplication pipelines, as depicted in Figure J-10. Describe
the pattern(s) of operand/result flows for which this structure would be
appropriate.

J-5.   Draw timing diagrams that show three successive minor cycles of the matrix
multiply systolic array of Figure J-8 when three independent matrix multiplications are interleaved. Suppose that all three problems involve 3 × 3 matrices,
and that the array was designed for a maximum size of 3 × 3 arrays.

J-6.   The matrix multiply systolic array structure depicted in Figure J-8 is configured
(keeping the same interconnect structure) to multiply two matrices of sizes $n \times p$
and $p \times m$ to produce an $n \times m$ result. Express the answers to the following
questions in terms of m, n, and p.

(a) How many processing modules are used in the whole array?

(b) How many clock cycles are required to compute the answer? The first cycle to count is the one in which the first matrix element enters the array; the last cycle to count is the one in which the last result element leaves the array.

J-7. Repeat Problem J-6 if the $p \times m$ matrix B has all of its nonzero entries restricted to a band defined by the relation

$$B_{ij} = 0 \quad \text{if} \quad j - i > 2 \quad \text{or} \quad i - j > 3$$

J-8. A designer proposes connecting two hexagonally connected systolic matrix multiplication arrays to compute the product of three matrices A, B, and C. His idea is to use one array to compute the product AB and then feed its output directly into an input of the second array, which computes the final result by multiplying the product matrix AB by matrix C. He proposes that the output paths from the AB array be connected to the input paths of the ABC array, possibly through delay elements. Each component passing through a given data path will experience the same delay, which could be different from the delay along any other path in the system. Will the proposed scheme work? Explain your answer.

J-9. In this problem, you will justify the correctness of the hexagonal systolic array shown in Figure J-8 for performing matrix multiplication.
   (a) Write difference equations expressing the interconnections of the array and the operation of the modules themselves.
   (b) Specify the boundary conditions on the array equations.
   (c) Show that the set of equations has a solution corresponding to the claimed operation of the array (namely, that the array produces the product of the input matrices).

J-10. The text described a simple strategy by which one could utilize the idle cycles of an array to compute the result for the set of input data values for another problem instance. This strategy worked because there no state was retained in any processing module between clock pulses. This problem explores a generalization of that strategy to permit any modules to retain instance-specific state between clock pulses. You should describe the implementation strategy, paying particular attention to the management of the state within each module. Your approach should assure correct functional behavior for each independent problem instance passing through the array. Comment on the relationship of this strategy to barrel processing.

DATA FLOW SYSTEMS

The basic idea behind the data flow paradigm is that data flow through an arrangement of computational modules whose structure parallels the flow of dependencies within the algorithm being performed. This is "dual" to the idea behind a conventional programming paradigm in which the control point flows through a series of algorithm steps that move across the data in memory. Unlike the systolic array paradigm, the data flow paradigm is completely general in that all algorithms can be expressed within the data flow paradigm. Unlike the systolic array paradigm, most modules within a data flow system are not replicated. After you read this appendix, you will understand the data flow paradigm, its limitations, and one approach toward its implementation. You will also see how the data flow paradigm might remind one of the optimizations performed within many compilers.

K.1 DATA FLOW SYSTEM STRUCTURE

The virtual structure of a data flow system can be described by a *data flow graph*. A data flow system[1] is constructed from modules, each performing a piece of a computation, connected by message-passing links, each communicating packets

---

[1] Basic references to this paradigm can be found in [ARVI86], [DAVI82], [DENN74], [GURD85], [TREL82], [TREL84], and [WATS82].

(called *tokens*) containing result objects. Each path originates at an output from a module and terminates at some module input. Each token carries a single object.

> **Definition.** A *module* performs a computation on its input data to produce output data. A data flow module does not retain internal information between its computations (unless it is an explicit memory module).

In data flow diagrams, the shape of a module indicates the type of computation performed by the module. For example, a processing module is represented by a rectangular box, and a decision module by a diamond-shaped box. Other shapes will be presented later.

> **Definition.** A *path* is a directed connection from an output of one (source) module to an input of another (destination) module.

The basic interaction between two modules occurs along a path between them and consists of passing a data token from the path's source module to its destination module. If there is no path between modules A and B, there is no direct way that actions within A can affect B, or vice versa.

The interpretation of a data flow graph is quite different from the interpretation of a conventional flow chart; edges in the latter depict control flow (rather than data flow) and conventional flow charts do not depict parallelism. Furthermore, there is no memory within the modules of a data flow system.

Example K-1

Figure K-1 illustrates a regular array of computational modules that performs a bubble sort of the input data values. Each module accepts two data objects and produces a copy of the larger input value at its upper output port and a copy of its smaller input value at its lower output port. Even though the internal realization of this module requires a data-dependent decision, its external behavior does not depend on the data values.

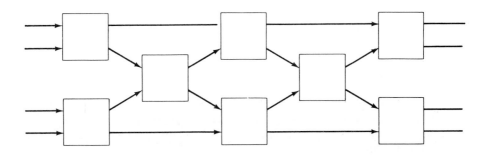

Figure K-1   A data flow system for bubble sorting

K.1.1 Basic Activities in Data Flow Systems

The basic actions in a data flow system are (1) module computation and (2) token transfer along a path between modules. First, consider module computations.

Module Computation. Four aspects require attention: (1) module activation, (2) rules governing usage of input tokens, (3) rules governing the production of output tokens, and (4) timing of the output production process.

A module computation interval begins with *module activation* and ends with *module completion*. When a module is activated, we sometimes say that it has "fired." Module activation may occur at any time when the inputs that are present satisfy the module's *activation condition*. The simplest activation condition states that an input token must be present at every module input; other possibilities will be discussed later. When a module fires, it consumes some input tokens.

An *input usage rule* specifies the pattern of token consumption. The simplest input usage rule states that the module uses an input token from each of its inputs when it fires. The third module computation rule describes the production of output data objects. There could be two aspects to this rule: the timing of the result production and the extent of output production. The timing rule states only that a module completes its computation at some time after it has fired. The actual delay is not specified in the model, and could depend on the operand values. When the module has completed its computation, it produces output tokens according to its *output production rule*. The simplest output production rule states that a module produces an output token at every one of its output ports. The values contained in the output tokens may be identical or different—the actual values are defined by the specification of the module's computation.

Token Flows. When a token is delivered to an output port, it is "launched" along the path connected to that output and arrives at some later time at the input port(s) at the other end(s) of the path. Each simple path connects one output port to one input port. Because it is trivial to build a "fan-out" module that replicates its single input at all of its output ports, without loss of generality, we can draw paths with one input and many outputs. This simplification eliminates the replication modules that might be required within an implementation. When a source module places a token on a multidestination path, a copy of the token is delivered to each destination of the path.

Several tokens may be waiting at a single input port. A rule governs any ordering constraints among the tokens waiting on the path. In simple data flow systems, the ordering rule states that tokens on a path are queued and released in FIFO order.

Overall System Specifications. Any data flow computation can be specified by its module connections, the module semantics, the activity rules, the path behavior, and the initial token configuration. Inputs and outputs to and from the system are represented by paths that extend outside the graph, each of these paths having only one termination within the graph.

K.1.2 Decision-Free Data Flow Systems

In a decision-free data flow system, no module ever makes a data-dependent decision visible outside the module. All modules in a decision-free data flow system obey simple behavioral rules: (1) Each module requires an input token at each input port to satisfy its activation condition, (2) each module takes an input token from each of its input ports when it is activated, and (3) each module produces an output token at each of its output ports when it has finished its computation. Notice that the module firing and result production rules are independent of the values in the input objects. Because the previous rules governing module enabling, token usage, and result production did not involve data dependencies, every module in a decision-free data flow system is a computational module. Computational modules are represented by rectangular boxes.

Example K-2

> Figure K-2 illustrates a simple tree structure that utilizes three-input computational modules to perform a commutative operation on n input values.

Behavior. To describe the actual behavior of a data flow system, we record the sequence of events from outside the system. We ignore relativistic effects; they manifest themselves as uncertainties concerning observations from within the system of the relative timing of events that occur at two different places in the system.

The module activity rules limit the possible order of events in a data flow system. The event sequence must meet the following constraints:

1. A module cannot start execution unless its activation condition is satisfied.
2. When a module is activated, it consumes input tokens in accordance with its input usage rule and the input ordering rules applicable to the input paths.
3. A module finishes execution some (arbitrary, unknown) time after it starts execution.
4. When a module finishes execution, it produces result tokens at its outputs in accordance with its result production rule.
5. Each path transmits each result token to each input connected to that path.
6. Each token sent along a path arrives after some (arbitrary, unknown) delay.

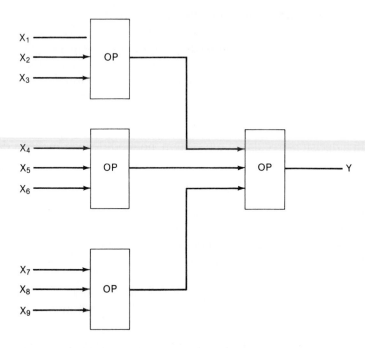

Figure K-2   A simple data flow system for a commutative operation

These rules define a simple procedure determining the set of enabled modules; an emulation program can be written easily. The starting configuration may show tokens conveying input values at the input places; other initial tokens may appear on branches as stated in the system's specification. The emulation determines successive system configurations as the computation progresses. The emulator picks an enabled event and emulates its effect to find each new token configuration.

The data flow constraints are equivalent to a set of permissive scheduling constraints; together these define a set of *feasible schedules*. The actual schedule for a particular computation is a feasible schedule chosen by a scheduling mechanism. For example, the emulator's choice of the enabled activity to be emulated next is a scheduling decision.

From an external viewpoint, the significant events in an actual schedule are module activation (start) and termination (finish). We can depict the order of these events in the actual schedule by constructing a string of symbols s_k and $f_{k'}$ denoting, respectively, the start and finish[2] of the execution by module k.

---

[2]   These symbols will be adequate because a module can be activated no times, one time, or an uncountable number of times in any feasible schedule of a decision-free system.

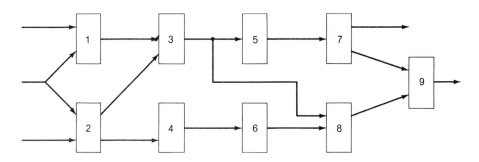

Figure K-3   A decision-free data flow graph

Example K-3

The following are two feasible schedules for the data flow graph of Figure K-3:

$$E_1 = s_1 f_1 s_2 f_2 s_3 f_3 s_4 f_4 s_5 f_5 s_6 f_6 s_7 f_7 s_8 f_8 s_9 f_9 \tag{K-1}$$

$$E_2 = s_1 s_2 f_2 s_4 f_1 s_3 f_4 s_6 f_3 s_5 f_5 s_7 f_6 s_8 f_8 f_7 s_9 f_9 \tag{K-2}$$

Programs Corresponding to Data Flow Systems.   One simplification that results from the absence of data-dependent decisions in a data flow system is that either a computation never terminates or else only a single value arrives at each particular path during a single computation. This observation can be used to formulate an algorithm that constructs a program corresponding to a given decision-free data flow system. First, associate an object name N_i with each path A_i in the system. Second, note that performing an assignment statement places a value in a named location. So performing an assignment to N_i corresponds to computing the value on path A_i. Therefore, if path A_i receives only one value during the complete computation, then during the execution of the entire program, only one assignment statement with the name N_i on the left side will be executed, and that one exactly once. A program meeting this constraint is called a single-assignment program.

> **Definition.**   A *single-assignment program* may contain, for each data object, only one statement that assigns a value to that object.

The statements in the single-assignment program must be ordered to correspond to a feasible schedule of the data flow system. In particular, the statement order must place the statement that makes an assignment to a variable before all statements that use that variable to evaluate another expression.

It is easy to see that any single-assignment program is equivalent to a non-looping data flow graph. It should be clear that one can construct a data flow system from any single-assignment program by defining a computational module corresponding to each assignment statement and connecting these modules according to the appearance of object names on the right sides of the assignment statements. By using arguments similar to those presented in Section L.2, one can prove the independence of the results computed by a decision-free data flow system from the actual (feasible) schedule. One uses an induction argument based on the distance of each assignment statement from the input values.

K.1.3 Data Flow Systems with Decisions

Visible data-dependent decisions are required to model most interesting algorithms. Realistic algorithms require loops and therefore we must incorporate data-dependent decisions. In the data flow model, these are handled by data routing modules and data-dependent decisions. Sequencing decisions manifest themselves as the values of Boolean variables within control tokens appearing at module inputs. Control tokens may exist in the initial configuration, they may be computed from other control tokens (by performing logical operations), or they may be computed by relational test modules. A relational test module producing a Boolean result is represented in a data flow graph by a diamond symbol, as in a conventional flowchart. The inputs to the test module may be data or control tokens; the result is a control token. Figure K-4 depicts a relational test module.

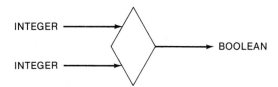

Figure K-4   A relational test module

Data Routing Modules. Data-dependent decisions may change token flow patterns. Special data routing modules model data-dependent sequencing.[3] The data routing modules, shown in Figure K-5, include two varieties of gate modules and a merge module; each has a single control input. A gate module blocks data flow (absorbing a token) when conditions are incorrect, and passes data (by copying the input token to the output) when conditions are correct.

---

[3]   Although it might seem sufficient to add a control terminal to each module to control its activation directly and thereby achieve data-dependent computations, under such a model, residual values do not leave the system at the termination of a computation. For reentrancy, we need a mechanism that conditionally routes data through the network, and thus indirectly controls module activation.

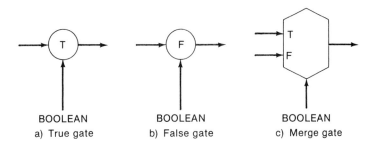

Figure K-5   Data routing modules

Conditions are "correct" when the symbol within the circle matches the truth value arriving at the control input. The merge module allows data from two different sources to be selectively presented on one data line.

The firing and result production rules for data routing modules are described in Figure K-6. The activation and result production rules for data routing modules depend on the value of the (Boolean) control input. Because a gate module may block token flow, its result production process is regulated by the control value. The activation condition for a merge module must test the value in its control token because the input that is to be forwarded needs to be present to activate the module, but the other input port can be empty. Both the value token that will be forwarded and the control token are consumed by the merge module when it fires; any token at the opposite (value) input remains there after the module has fired; this is shown in the figure.

Feasible Schedules.   The schedule feasibility rules for looping data flow graphs are similar to those for decision-free data flow graphs. We do need minor modifications to handle multiple activations of modules within loops. Let i denote an instance index used to identify the loop iteration and let $f_{k,i}$ and $s_{k,i}$ denote the ith occurrences of f_k and s_k, respectively. Assume that loop instance indices are integers counting upward from one. The loop instance index must be incremented for each iteration of a loop. Thus, we need to designate one path within the loop to be the point where the instance index changes. The sequencing rules for modules in the loop are analogous to those of decision-free graphs, adding a condition requiring matching instance indices on both members of a precedence relationship. For example, if there is a path from module p to module q, we constrain $f_{p,i}$ to precede $s_{q,i}$. This rule does not work across the path where the instance index changes. Let module e denote the module at the destination of the path P where the index changes, and let m denote the index of the module that is the source of path P. The loop's scheduling precedence rule for path P is that $f_{m,i}$ must precede $s_{e,i+1}$.

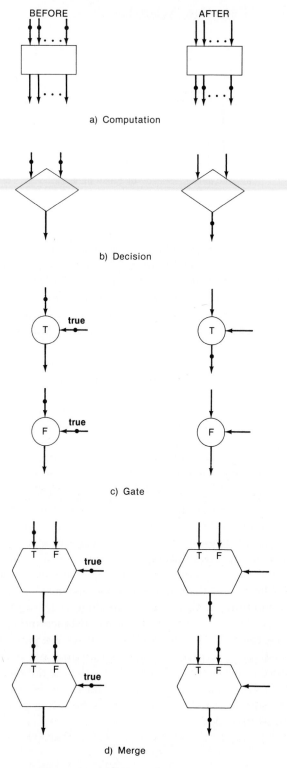

Figure K-6 Effects of firing modules

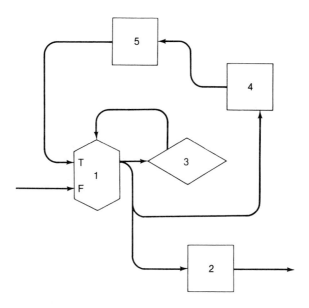

Figure K-7   An uninitialized data flow loop

Example K-4

Consider the data flow system depicted in Figure K-7. Modules 1, 3, 4, and 5 belong to a loop structure. There must exist an initial token within this structure, because otherwise there would not be any way to start the computation (module 1 would never be able to fire). We choose the path from module 5 to module 1 as the place where the index instance changes. Then module 5 must fire for the first time before module 1 can fire for the second time. From this reasoning, we obtain the sequencing constraint that $f_{5,k}$ must precede $s_{1,k+1}$ in every feasible schedule.

Loop Structures.   The following examples illustrate some basic computational structures in the data flow model.

Example K-5

We want to produce an unending stream of tokens holding an identical (i.e., constant) value V. The structure of Figure K-8 does this task; the initial external token carries the value that is replicated in all the output tokens.

A stream of identical tokens can be used for constant initial values in a loop.

Example K-6

We wish to modify the data flow system of Figure K-8 so that it will produce another copy of the value that arrived to initialize the loop only as long as a true

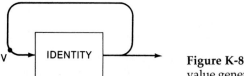

Figure K-8   A constant value generator

control token arrives and will stop when a false control token arrives. Upon termination, the system should be prepared to accept another (external) value token and restart its replication activity with the new value. The requisite structure is shown in Figure K-9.

The structure of the token replication system contains the elements of a general loop structure—we need an initial value, a sequence of subsequent values, and a controlled way to clean out the structure, thereby making the graph reentrant. An initial control token at the control input of the merge module passes the first value into the loop. After the loop has terminated, a copy of the final control token remains at the merge module input, waiting for the arrival of a subsequent input value; that next token arrival initiates a new instance of the computation.

Example K-7

```
float f( int arg, float threshold ) {
    int index = 1;
    float result = 0, change = 100;      //Assume 100 forces the first interaction
    while ( change > threshold ) {
        change = g(arg, result, index);  //g assumed to be declared elsewhere
        result = result + change;
        index++;
    }
    return result;
}
```

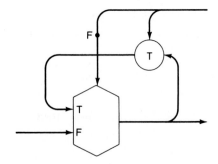

Figure K-9   A data flow system providing controlled replication of an input value

Figure K-10 illustrates a data flow graph of this computation. Notice how the looping structure of the program is reflected in the graph structure.

The data flow graph corresponding to a counting loop structure has three major sections: an input replication section, a loop control section, and a computation section. The *input section* creates copies of the token holding the loop limit value; this loop has one gate module and one merge module. The loop continuation Boolean variable controls the replication process; its initial value (false) allows the input value to enter the loop. Although the continuation Boolean is true, the old value is replicated. When the loop is complete, the Boolean value will be false, and the next external input value will be allowed to enter the loop.

The *loop control section* computes the loop index and compares it with the count limit. The resulting Boolean values control data flows within the remainder of the loop's modules. The loop within the loop control section is similar to the input replication loop with an incrementer inserted to increment the count in the loop index tokens.

The *computation section* also has a loop. Gate and merge modules insert the initial value, route the final result out of the net, and destroy all old partial results so that they will not influence the next computation.

Minimal interactions connect the three sections. In fact, some sections can "get ahead" of other sections. One feasible schedule mirrors the execution of the program fragment following the conventional pattern of sequential execution from a single control point. Many other schedules are possible—in one, all loop control tokens are generated before any loop body computations are performed; this is possible within a counting loop (but not within a general loop structure utilizing other termination conditions).

Example K-8

```
int x = 0;
for ( int i = 1, i <= n,  i++ )
    x = x + i;
```

This program has a single input n and a single output x. Its data flow graph representation is shown in Figure K-11.

Try tracing the computation for several representative small values of n. Be sure to keep your mind open for all feasible scheduling options.

K.1.4 Comments

The data flow model is a useful tool for describing the functional interrelationships among a set of processes or modules that together comprise a functional system. In Section K.2, we discuss some options for implementing data flow systems. In Section L.2, we show how one could reason about the functionality of data flow systems. Although this paradigm is conceptually appealing, the

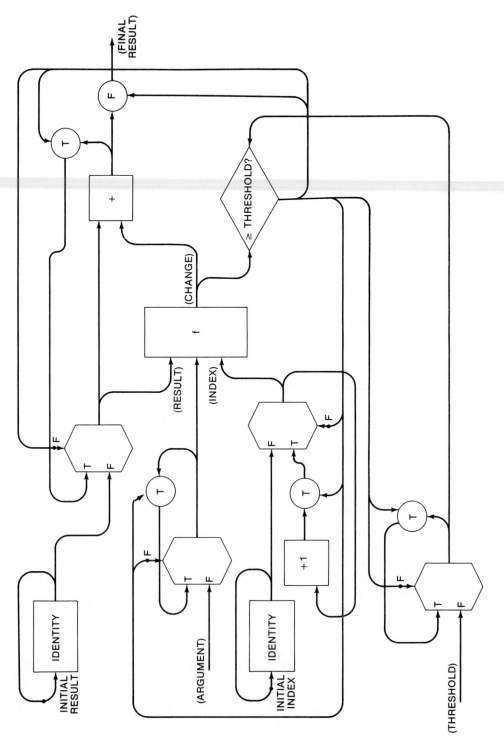

Figure K-10 A data flow graph for an iterative functional computation

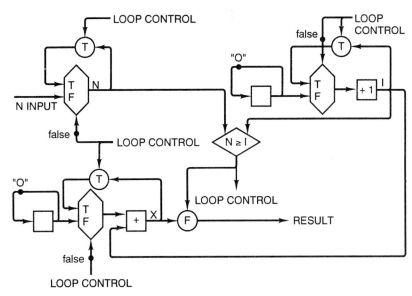

Figure K-11   Data flow graph for Example K-8

implementation overhead for coordinating message-passing and -checking module activation conditions can exceed the effort required to perform the computations within modules unless the modules themselves perform high-level functions.

K.2 IMPLEMENTATIONS OF DATA FLOW SYSTEMS

In this section, we show how the communicating process model discussed in Chapter 7 could be used to construct a host that emulates general data flow systems.[4] We will construct a data flow host that can emulate any data flow machine. To simplify the implementation, we impose certain conditions restricting the graph's structure. First, we show a procedure by which any data flow system can be transformed into an equivalent one meeting the conditions; the existence of the transformation shows that the restrictions do not lose the generality of the implementation that we present. Then we present the design.

It is tempting to implement a specific data flow machine (the *target system*) by using a *host system* consisting of a physical interconnection of hardware modules that parallels the virtual (logical) structure of the data flow graph. This approach is clearly inefficient, because each module in the host system will be idle until its activation condition is satisfied, which means that the module is likely to be idle most of the time. To overcome this limitation and build an efficient host

---

[4]   See [VEEN86] for a survey of data flow implementations.

system, we design the host system to pass messages among a set of general-purpose modules that are programmed to mirror the target system. In this manner, we design a general data flow host system on which any data flow target system can be programmed.

The first step in the process is to transform the target data flow system so that it fits the constraints on target systems that can be programmed on our host.

K.2.1 Transformations of Data Flow Systems

In this section we describe some transformations of data flow systems that reduce the number of different classes of modules required in the host system.[5] These changes simplify the design of the host system. In fact, making these transformations may simplify things enough that it will speed the execution of all steps within the host system. Usually, the transformed target system will have more modules than the original target, so there will be more modules to emulate, but we hope that the speedup of all operations will more than compensate for the increased module count.[6] In any case, we emphasize logical capabilities and not speed.

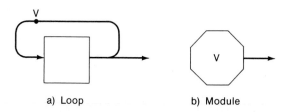

a) Loop   b) Module

Figure K-12   Removing constant replication loops

We make three basic transformations of the target system:

1. Removing recirculating constant tokens
2. Restricting module fan-out to two inputs
3. Limiting each module to two inputs

The first transformation introduces a single module generating a constant value to replace a set of modules using recirculating tokens to replicate the constant value. The new module type will be designated by an octagon with the constant value written inside the octagon. The modification replaces each constant replication loop in the target graph with an octagon module. The basic transformation is illustrated in Figure K-12.

---

5   These transformations are based on [GURD85].
6   Notice the similarity of this argument with the argument supporting the RISC approach.

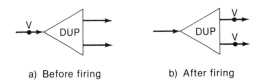

a) Before firing   b) After firing

Figure K-13   A DUP module duplicates its input token

The second transformation limits module fan-out, restricting the flow of results from one module output to not more than two module inputs. This change uses a DUP (duplicate) module type whose function is to duplicate its input value at its two outputs (see Figure K-13). To model a fan-out greater than 3, we build a tree of DUP modules to produce the additional copies. This change is illustrated in Figure K-14; it introduces additional modules and tokens.

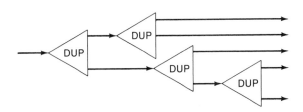

Figure K-14   A tree of DUP modules to increase fan-out

The third, and most difficult, transformation changes module definitions so that every module has only one or two inputs. We all use a similar transformation when we perform when we reduce complex arithmetic expressions in a program for a conventional processor to a series of primitive operations that take only one or two operands. This analogy suggests that replacing computational modules with sets of unary and binary modules is a straightforward modification. The difficult part of this transformation is to modify or remove merge modules from the graph; they need three logically independent inputs that have significantly different roles in the activation condition, and this requirement exceeds the input port limit. To replace a merge module, we change the token flow rules to allow tokens from more than one source to arrive at the same module input. In pictures, we draw converging paths to the input where the tokens converge. One network equivalent to a merge module is shown in Figure K-15; the reader should convince herself that the equivalence holds.[7]

---

[7]   An alert reader will notice that making this transformation violates the no fan-in requirement that is crucial for our arguments in Appendix L about data flow system functionality. All is not lost, however, because fan-in is used only to replace the merge module function; clearly, this replacement does not violate functionality. Thus, although proof details would require modification, the transformed

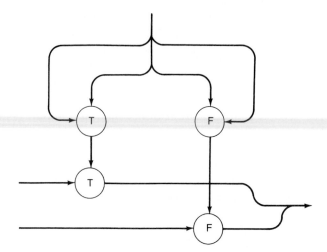

Figure K-15 A gate network equivalent to a merge module

Example K-9

Consider transforming the system illustrated in Figure K-16 (the system of Figure K-10). The original system has two zero-carrying constant tokens; the transformed system contains two octagon modules that produce these constants. In the original system, only the loop control token is destined to more than two inputs; a tree of DUP modules added at the output of the loop termination test module provides the necessary fan-out. To complete the transformation of the graph into the desired form, the original merge modules are replaced by equivalent gate networks. The graph shown in Figure K-17 was constructed using the strict equivalence rules explained before.

Actually there is a more efficient implementation of the general loop structure, illustrated in Figure K-18.

K.2.2 Tagging in Data Flow Systems

Practical applications perform algorithms expressed by modular programs using simple subroutines, nested subroutines, and (possibly) recursive subroutines. A subroutine presents difficulties in a data flow system because the subroutine's graph must replace each call within the computation graph. A reusable graph must be implemented in a reentrant manner or replicated in the system description. Obviously, replication is unattractive.

---

system could still be proved to be functional.

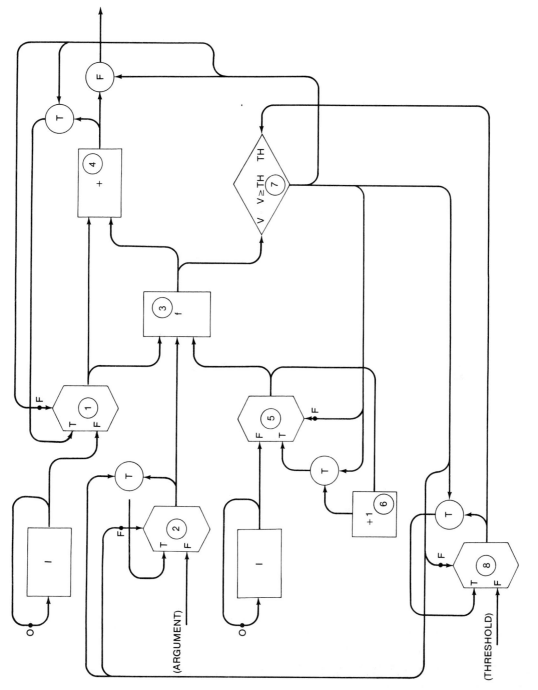

Figure K-16 The data flow system of Figure K-11 with module numbers

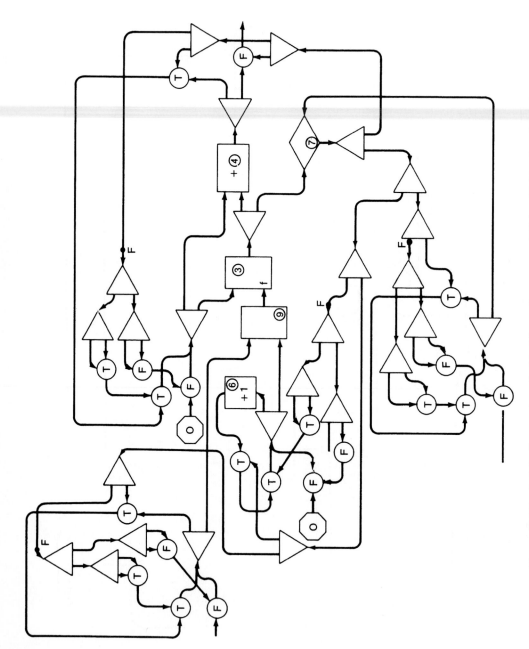

Figure K-17   A data flow system derived from the system of Figure K-16 using the strict module equivalences

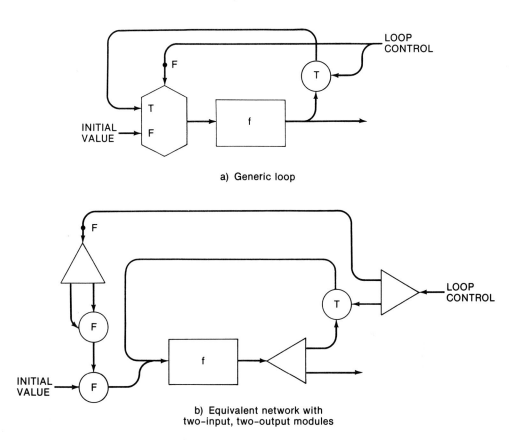

a) Generic loop

b) Equivalent network with
two–input, two–output modules

Figure K-18   A simpler loop equivalence

We can introduce tagging to convert a program block to a reentrant form. After [GAJS82], we use the term "graph block" to denote the portion of the graph that is to be made reentrant. Each graph block satisfies the serial reentrancy property: It correctly performs a single activation of its function provided that it is never invoked unless every previous invocation has completed execution. In other words, for correct behavior at most one invocation of the block can be active at any one time. An inductive argument shows that each subblock used to build the graph block must itself satisfy the serial reentrancy property.

Two design questions are as follows:

1. How can we design the system so that it forces a delay in the invocation of a graph block until all previous invocations of that block have been completed?

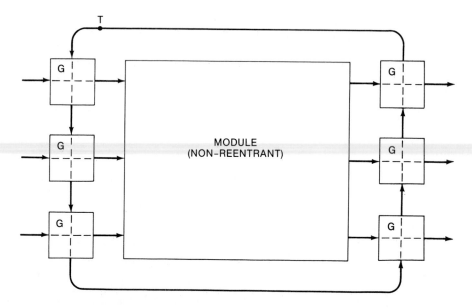

Figure K-19 A guard token ring controls reentrancy for a data flow block

2. How can we design the system to permit reuse of the same copy of the graph block in more than one place in the complete graph?

Five approaches to these problems are outlined in [GAJS82]:

1. Prohibit reentrant graphs.
2. Add control structures to serialize block invocations.
3. Require that all output paths from a module M be empty before enabling M's operation.
4. Queue tokens in FIFO order on each branch.
5. Add "tags" to tokens.

The first "approach" is not really an approach at all—it defines the problem into nonexistence! Because our objective is to solve the problem, we immediately dismiss this "option."

A design based on the second approach introduces a "guard" token that circulates in a loop around the block; this gating structure is illustrated in Figure K-19. The gate (G) module has two inputs; when the module is enabled, it simply copies the two input values to the two outputs, as suggested by the dashed lines through the module's symbol. Assume that initially the graph block has not been activated and the guard token is waiting at the input to the gate module that admits the first input token to the block (see Figure K-19). Then the reader can easily convince herself that this graph configuration both prevents there being more

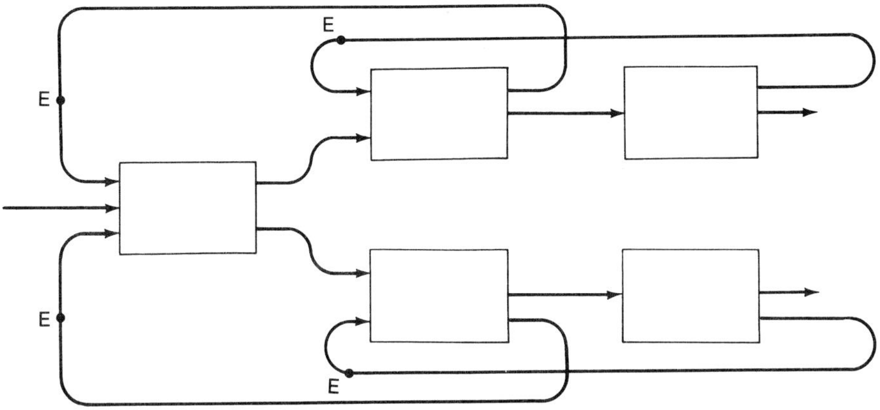

Figure K-20   Preventing token queues in a set of data flow modules. (The E tokens are present when the outputs are empty.)

than one invocation of the block in progress at any moment and also limits the amount of parallelism within the execution of the complete graph.

The third approach requires the insertion of acknowledgment paths and additional module inputs. Each module has an additional input corresponding to each of its outputs, and an extra output corresponding to each input. The extra paths are connected as exemplified in Figure K-20. In this approach, the preceding and succeeding modules affect the enabling conditions for module M to ensure that the empty output path requirement is met every time module M fires. A similar strategy can be used at the block level to force serialization of its activity—we prohibit the activation of the first modules of the block until the last modules have produced their outputs from the previous activation of the block.

As we noted earlier, the fourth approach requires that each branch be handled in the host as a FIFO queue, which requires a lot of hardware. Another method introduces position values within the tokens; these are similar to the tags that we will introduce in the sequel.

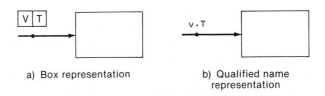

a) Box representation

b) Qualified name representation

Figure K-21   A tagged value token

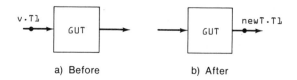

a) Before   b) After

Figure K-22   Obtaining a new unique tag

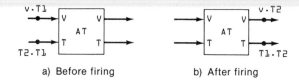

a) Before firing   b) After firing

Figure K-23   The apply tag (AT) module

In the remainder of this section, we develop the use of tags to distinguish block invocations. A token holding value V associated with a tag value T will be denoted V.T and may be drawn as a rectangle with two fields (see Figure K-21).

The module enabling rule for modules in a tagged system includes the condition that the tag values must match across the entire set of input tokens used to activate the module. The set of tokens (with matching tags) that activated the module is consumed by the module when it fires. Actually, this rule makes it difficult to build a system without the constant replication loops that we removed in the first transformation step before. To circumvent this problem, we introduce a distinguished tag value V_D and modify the matching rules slightly: First, the tag value V_D matches any other tag value. Second, any input token with a tag V_D should not be consumed when the matching succeeds and the module is activated.

New tag values are obtained from a module called GUT (get unique tag),[8] depicted in Figure K-22. The GUT module's input token enables its operation and the tag from the input is the tag value to be associated with the GUT module's output; the value portion of the input token is ignored by the GUT module. If the GUT's input token is in.old_tag, the output of the GUT module is new_tag.old_tag.

A new tag value can be attached to a problem value by an apply tag (AT) module, illustrated in Figure K-23. The tag input (T) to the AT module carries the value new_tag.old_tag. The value input (V) to an AT module carries the token

---

[8]   We are taking a pedagogical approach to this problem by assuming that there is a unique tag generator that, whenever it is invoked, produces a new tag value different from any other tag value ever created. This tag generator can be invoked from any GUT module in the system. Implementing this design may be far from trivial if the functions are implemented in a host system with parallelism.

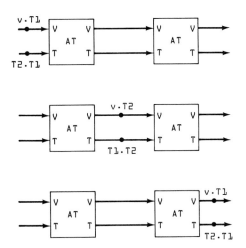

Figure K-24   The AT operation is its own inverse

value.old_tag. There are two results: value.new_tag and old_tag.new_tag. Figure K-24 shows that the AT operation is its own inverse; thus, another AT module can be used to remove a new_tag, replacing it with the old_tag value.

What situations will require tag changing?

1. Procedure entry and exit
2. Loop entry, exit, and iteration

With procedure entry and exit, we also have to handle control flow convergence (upon entry) and divergence (upon exit). We consider these problems in the following order:

1. Tagging value tokens within a reentrant section
2. Flow convergence at procedure entry
3. Flow divergence at procedure exit
4. Loop iteration
5. Loop exit

The next example illustrates the essence of this tagging approach to provide graph block reentrancy.

Example K-10

We want to reuse a graph block for a simple subroutine call. This requires a new tag value for each new invocation; the internal tag value must be removed from the results returned from the invocation. To establish the new tag value on the invocation, all parameters must be assigned the same tag value; the structure of Figure K-25 makes this assignment. On return, all results must be retagged with the

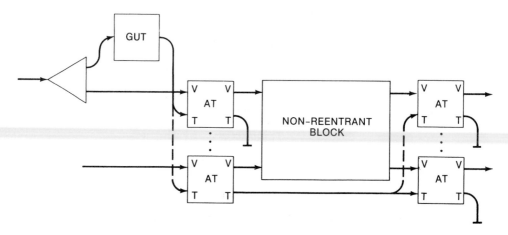

Figure K-25   Applying unique tags to a single invocation of a module

tag value of the calling block; this can be accomplished by AT modules at the block's outputs, as shown in the figure.

This example illustrates how to obtain and assign new tag values for an individual invocation of a subroutine; the same technique can be used to force serial reentrancy upon any reentrant graph block.

The second and third problems concern token flow on subroutine call and return. We must direct the result tokens to the branches corresponding to the return point associated with the point from which the routine was called. A solution to this problem must uniquely label each calling point and it must direct the return to the calling point. For unique labeling, we simply design the system to obtain a unique tag value before making each call. To direct the return token flow, we build paths from the routine exit to all return points and then gate the tokens according to their unique tag values. In addition, a result token that might arrive at an unintended return point must be destroyed. The structure shown in Figure K-26 illustrates one approach to the subroutine problem. A dead end branch indicates a module output whose token should be destroyed. The structure in the middle of the network produces true and false tokens and routes them to the output gates (1) to destroy the results that would go to the incorrect return points and (2) to gate out the result at the return point that does correspond to the point from which the call was made. The generalization of this approach to handle reentrant modules with multiple inputs and outputs should be obvious.

The last two reentrancy issues concern looping behavior. First, one needs a unique tag value to discriminate among the values associated with different loop iterations. We need to choose a place in the loop where we declare that a new

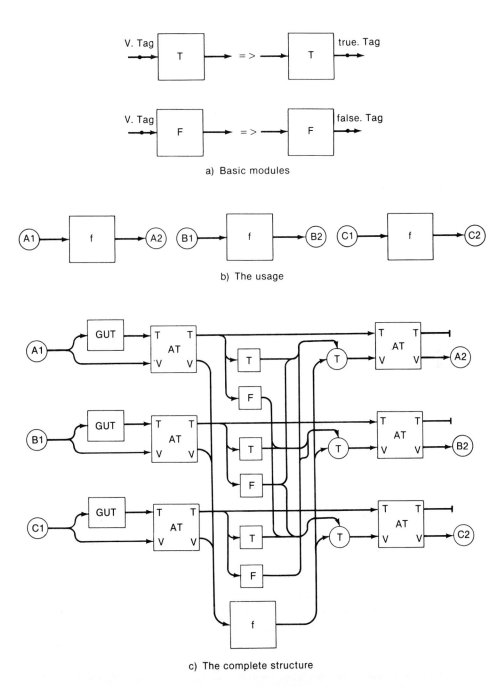

a) Basic modules

b) The usage

c) The complete structure

Figure K-26   Emulating a subroutine call structure with a one-input/one-output functional block

iteration begins and the previous one ends. The choice is arbitrary; we select the recirculating input of the merge module that initiates the loop. This choice is analogous to the choice of the path at which the loop iteration identifier is changed. Consider the simple loop shown in Figure K-27a. Figure K-27b shows how a "next iteration" module (NIM) is placed inside the loop. Notice that the standard loop merge module is not needed because the unique tag values guarantee correct flow control.

The second loop problem concerns restoration of the tag value after loop completion. We need the tag that corresponds to the environment enclosing the loop. This value must be propagated around the loop so that it will have the proper tag to match the result on loop exit. The connection shown in Figure K-27c shows how each new loop tag can be assigned to the environment tag value in such a manner that the proper tag assignment can be made on loop completion. The following example illustrates another approach to these tagging issues.

Example K-11

The unique tag generator for a program that contains only one loop and no function calls can be reduced to a simple counter embedded in the program. Let the count portion of the tag be called the *iteration level*. Two operators can be defined to set the iteration level and add to the iteration level (i.e., increment it). On loop completion, the iteration level parts of the value tags must be reset to their values for the loop's environment. By performing a static program analysis, we can assign a constant tag value to the external environment and this assignment can be made from a constant value.[9]

To handle procedure calls, another tag component, the environment, can be added. It is necessary that the environment tag values be uniquely distinguishable within the context(s) in which that tag value may appear. If this condition is true, a tagged token cannot be mistaken for a tagged token from a different environment. One could perform a static analysis of the structure of a given program graph to find the scope of appearance of each tag value and then statically assign tag values to guarantee the uniqueness condition.[10]

Comments.   Tagging can be added to a data flow model to permit reentrancy and to provide the possibility of reentrant blocks within the data flow system. Several basic strategies can be used, but their overhead is high enough that one might restrict their use to large reused blocks within the system. One cost of tagging is the added comparisons required to check module activation conditions. Another drawback concerns the possibility of queue overflow in the implementation if one portion of the system advances too far ahead of the remainder

---

[9]   This approach is used in the Manchester Prototype Data Flow Computer [GURD85].
[10]   This approach cannot handle recursive subroutines, because a static analysis cannot unfold all nested calls of the routine.

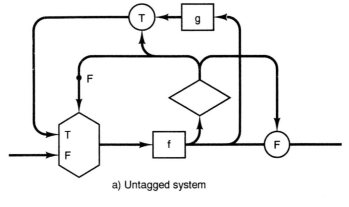

a) Untagged system

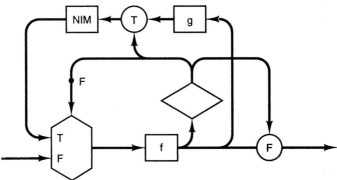

b) Positioning the next iteration module (NIM)

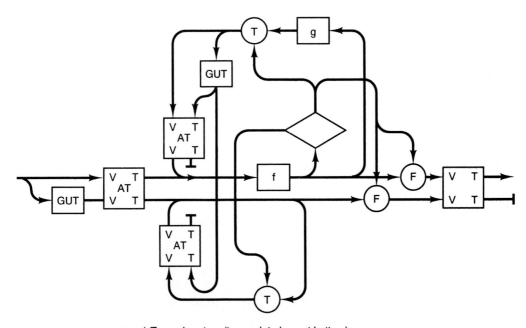

c) Tagged system (tag update loop at bottom)

Figure K-27 Adding tagging to support simultaneous execution of several iterations of a loop body

of the system. A blocking mechanism must be introduced to handle this possibility.

K.2.3 Data Flow Host Architecture

By transforming a data flow graph and introducing tagging, one can reduce any data flow system to one handling tagged tokens that contains modules with two (or one) input port(s). Here we illustrate some implementation options for such a data flow system. We start with the basic execution sequence within the host and then turn to implementation details. Our implementation uses two kinds of tokens: "value" tokens and "function" tokens. Value tokens appeared in the original data flow graph. Each value token contains a value and a tag. A function token describes an enabled module that is ready for execution. The function token includes a function identifier, a set of parameter values, and the corresponding tag value.

The host machine repeats a cyclic pattern. If we choose to think that the execution cycle begins when a value token T arrives, the cyclically executed steps are as follows:

1. Check the new token T against other unmatched value tokens to see whether a module enabling condition was met by the new arrival. If there was a match or if T is headed to the input of a one-input module, form a function token and queue it; otherwise, store T in the token memory.
2. If the function token queue is not empty, select a function token from the queue and proceed to step 3. If the function token queue is empty and there is no activity in the remainder of the host, halt this stream. If there is other (parallel) activity, wait for a new function token to arrive.
3. Perform the computation specified in the selected function token, producing value tokens representing the results. If the function does not produce any output tokens, proceed to step 2.
4. Distribute the output tokens, performing step 1 for each one.

To start an emulation, the program memory is loaded with a description of the target system. The value and function memories are loaded to reflect the target's initial configuration. Value tokens representing the computation's parameters are inserted as though they had been produced as results from step 5; performing step 1 on these parameter tokens will generate some function tokens, and the host system can then commence computation. The host repeats its cycle until activity ceases and the function token queue becomes empty.

One could simply implement all of the steps of the cycle in a single-processor computer, but the management overhead required to handle all of the interprocess messages would swamp the system and degrade its performance. To reduce the token-handling overhead, we introduce hardware parallelism.

The first parallelism opportunity concerns the memory; the host can have three logically separate memories. One holds value tokens that are waiting at module inputs. The second holds function tokens that correspond to enabled modules. The third memory holds the "program," a description of the target system comprised of two parts: (1) the function performed by each module and (2) the module interconnections.

Now design a cyclic hardware structure mirroring the steps of the algorithm. The host could be implemented in the style of a data flow system; there would be a cyclic connection of four modules (see Figure K-28). These modules cyclically pass messages among themselves. These messages contain the host's value and function tokens.

The token-matching subsystem contains a memory holding the unmatched value tokens waiting at module inputs. This subsystem operates cyclically; in each cycle, the subsystem accepts an incoming value token, which contains a destination (module number, pin number), a tag value, and the value. The subsystem examines the incoming token to determine first whether the destination module has only a single input. This test succeeds when the pin number matches a reserved value. In this case, the matching module constructs a function token containing the value token[11] as the first operand, an empty second operand, and

TABLE K-1   TOKEN FIELDS FOR THE MACHINE OF FIGURE K-28

Location	Fields
Q1	value1, value2, tag, module#
Q2	value1, value2, tag, program, dest1, dest2
Q3	result1, result2, tag, dest1, dest2
Q4	result, tag, dest

the module number. If the incoming token is destined for a module with two inputs, the match subsystem searches in its memory for a value token having the same module number, the same tag value, and the opposite input number. The search can be implemented using any of the associative lookup techniques discussed in Appendix G. If the search succeeds, a function token is constructed according to the Q1 format shown in Table K-1. If the search fails to find a match, the incoming token is stored in the value token memory. The token-matching subsystem then waits for another incoming token to process on the next cycle.

The instruction fetch subsystem contains the system's program memory. When this subsystem is ready, it obtains another function token from the function queue. The module number from the new token is used to access the

---

[11]   The value token is copied to preserve its tag value.

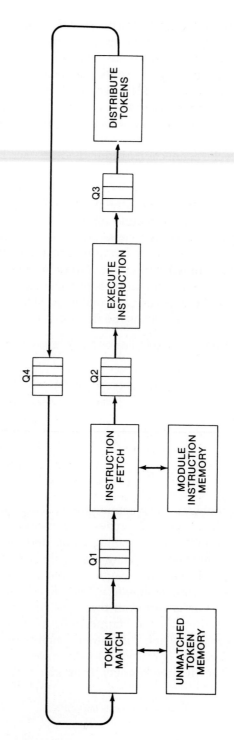

Figure K-28   Basic data flow host architecture

program memory. The fetch module replaces the module number with the corresponding program and result destinations. The instruction-bearing token is queued in Q2 for execution.

The instruction execution subsystem performs the instruction stored in the incoming token, replacing the operand values and instruction with the result. The result's tag is identical to the operand tags, unless the module performs the AT operation. The result's format corresponds to the Q3 entry in Table K-1.

The value token creation subsystem separates the result token obtained from instruction execution into one or two tokens, depending on the destination module numbers. These tokens are then recirculated to the token-matching subsystem. These tokens are represented in format Q4.

This completes the basic design of the data flow processor. To improve the emulator's efficiency, one could ask two design questions: (1) Is it worthwhile to duplicate any host subsystems, and (2) if so, how do we assign target modules to the replicated modules of the host system? Notice that expanding the host system is easy: Just insert parallel modules. This simple strategy works because every processing stage is (or could be) preceded by a memory holding independent tokens ready for processing in the next stage. By duplicating subsystems that are bottlenecks, the designer can improve the performance of the host system.

If the designer decides to duplicate some subsystem, she must also decide whether to impose a static mapping from target module numbers to the host subsystem copies. One advantage of making a static assignment is that the instruction fetch modules can access separate small memories. If there is to be such an assignment, what should that assignment be? This question is best studied by simulation. If target modules are assigned to host modules, the designer must answer two questions: What part of the host system is assigned a particular set of target modules? Where is the distribution of tokens among the copies made? An attractive option is to replicate the entire host for each set of target modules. Then the second question is easily answered because only the value tokens (format Q4) move among target modules. Therefore, they may have to cross from one host copy to another only when passing between the value token-creating and value token-matching stages.

K.2.4 Comments

One drawback of the data flow paradigm is that, although the scheme is general and completely functional, it is grossly inefficient in handling data structures. This problem is basic to the data flow notion, in which values flow among modules, and no module has any saved state. A module that serves as a memory holding any data object (particularly a data structure) does not fit into this mold. One way out of this dilemma is to design data flow systems that can handle data structures as objects held within special modules that have memory. One difficulty with this approach is that it is contrary to the simple token-passing model.

Considerable controversy exists concerning the efficiency of data flow designs. Proponents claim that the parallelism in the host system can speed algorithm execution. Opponents claim that the hardware used for token management could better be used to implement a more "conventional" execution engine. The balance between execution and control hardware obviously depends on the complexity of the operations performed by single target system modules. As these modules become more complex, the fractional overhead goes down, but the implementation of the execution unit necessarily becomes more complex, because it must include a program counter and program memories.

If the host system provides only low-level functions in its execution modules, the message-passing module could easily become the system performance bottleneck. To alleviate bottlenecks, the message-signaling paths within the emulator might be replicated, which would cut the message communication time and improve the system's performance.[12] One would expect that the execution times of the low-level instructions might not greatly exceed the time for transmitting operand values, which themselves were only a portion of the instruction message. Therefore, levels of higher granularity should be explored. But notice that with high granularity, the data flow model becomes similar to passing messages among processes; within this model token-passing is analogous to process scheduling.

K.3 SUMMARY

In this appendix, we explored data flow systems, starting with the data flow model of computation. We showed several ways that a data flow system could be implemented.

K.4 TRENDS

The data flow model appeals to people because they can visualize the tokens flowing through the computation and because parallelism shows up among the modules in the virtual network performing the computation. If the modules perform simple computations, the overhead involved in managing token flows and module activations seems to overcome any performance benefits that might accrue from parallelism among the modules. On the other hand, if the module computations are large, they seem to be like threads in a program, and can be

---

[12] However, the time required to distribute result tokens and check module enabling rules may become the performance bottleneck.

managed by conventional task-scheduling mechanisms. Thus, despite the ease of reasoning about system functionality in data flow models, it seems likely that the data flow paradigm will fade from the mainstream view. Because the logic of data flow analysis is similar to the dependency analysis performed within optimizing compilers, one might take the view that a compiler's optimizer will find a good schedule for implementing a data flow structure on a conventional processor.

K.5 CONCEPT LIST

1. System components: paths and modules
2. Module activation conditions
3. Module timing not specified
4. Rules for token production from modules
5. Single-assignment languages correspond to simple data flow systems
6. System transformations reduce the number of different cases in the system
7. Tagging can label tokens with unique values distinguishing the activations of loop and subroutine structures
8. Barrel implementation of an emulator for data flow systems
9. Similarities between data flow structures and compiler optimization strategies.

K.6 PROBLEMS

K-1. For this problem, you may assume without proof that a reentrant data flow graph whose modules obey the "standard" input and output rules given in the text (all inputs are used and all outputs are produced) always behaves functionally. For this problem, consider a data flow system containing generalized modules with modified enabling conditions and modified output production rules. The new module enabling condition consists of a list of input subsets. If all members of one of the listed subsets of input leads contain a waiting token, the module is enabled. When the module is enabled, it consumes all tokens that were used to meet the enabling condition. In a similar manner, one could generalize the output production rules to a list of subsets of the set of output ports. When the module finishes its computation, it chooses one of the listed subsets and places an output token on each path in the chosen subset. All subset choices are independently made for each activation of a module.

In an interesting special case of these general rules, the module enabling list includes all input subsets with n_1 members. In other words, the module will be enabled if there exists input data at n_1 of its input leads. By using a similar rule applied to the outputs, output will be produced at a set of n_2 output leads.

(a) Let us simplify the output token production rule so that the same subset of output leads receives tokens at the completion of any computation in the module. Will the system containing these modules with generalized enabling conditions be functional?

(b) Now consider the case in which the following is true for all modules in the network: The choice of the members of the set of output ports where results appear is uniquely determined by choice of the members of the set of inputs from which inputs were taken for this invocation of the module. Is this type of system functional?   [*Turn the page for part* (c).]

(c) Now consider the case in which the set of outputs produced is determined in part by the values contained within the selected input tokens. Is this type of system functional?

K-2. Specify at least four significantly different ways in which the data flow and systolic array parallelism models are not the same.

K-3. Develop an argument to show the similarities between (1) the data flow network transformations that modify the paths and modules to have a limited number of inputs and outputs, and (2) the division of a long message into packets for transmission along a path.

K-4. Find at least four different feasible schedules for the data flow system described in Figure K-3.

K-5. Consider changing the data flow module enabling rules to permit one to use a variable e_i (that is true when there are no tokens in input place p_i) in the module enabling rule. Does this change affect system functionality? (*Hint:* Consider the enabling rules for the output module of the system shown in Figure K-3.)

K-6. Write out a definition of a feasible schedule for a decision-free data flow system.

K-7. In this problem, you will devise a scheme for numbering the iterations within a nested loop structure.

(a) Suppose that you know an upper limit on the number of activations of each loop in the nest. Devise a scheme that gives a unique number by concatenating the iteration numbers of the active loops.

(b) Devise a general scheme for uniquely numbering the iterations within the nest. One possibility is that the numbers are computed by a generalization of the formula $2^i 3^j 5^k$, where i, j, and k are the iteration numbers for three nested loops. Explain why you believe that the iteration numbers determined by your scheme are unique.

(c) Give an example to explain why the iteration numbers need to be unique.

K-8. It is claimed that blocking **receive** operations are adequate for this exercise. You are trying to implement processes that emulate data flow modules. For example, the program fragment for receiving the inputs for a three-input computational data flow module would be

```
a = receive( A );        receive(a, A);
b = receive( B );
c = receive( C );
```

Write program fragments for value reception for the gate and merge data flow modules. Do not worry about token queueing or about performing the module's computations.

K-9. Write a program for a set of processes that emulates the data flow structure of Figure K-11. Emulate each computational module within a separate task. With module numbers used in task name identifiers, it should be easy to construct a main program that uses the **one_of** construct to select an enabled module for execution. In addition, the main program can handle result distribution and check for machine enabling to update the list of enabled tokens. Parts (a), (b), and (c) ask for three different programs designed under the stated guidelines regarding the merge and gate module functions.

(a) Also use a separate task for each merge or gate module.

(b) Incorporate the merge and gate functions into the computational tasks at their outputs.

(c) Incorporate the merge and gate functions into the computational tasks at their inputs.

(d) Comment on the differences between the control philosophies in designs (b) and (c).

K-10. This problem concerns the relationships between data flow parallelism specifications and the Ada rendezvous construct (see Section 7.2.1). The claim is that the two constructs are equivalent. This claim could be shown to be correct by presenting two algorithms—each converts a system specification from one format to the other, but they make the conversions in opposite directions. Here we consider only the mapping of a data flow specification into a set of tasks using the Ada rendezvous construct for synchronization. The construction will create a separate Ada task that emulates each module in the data flow system.

(a) Briefly describe how a functional module with more than two inputs would be modeled in the Ada program.

(b) Describe how a merge module's control structure would be emulated in the Ada program.

(c) Discuss the validity of the proposition that the rendezvous construct is consistent with functional programming because its blocking rule prevents confusion between messages. Also comment on the claim that an Ada implementation using the rendezvous construct will have fewer feasible schedules than a data flow implementation of the same system.

K-11. Define a relationship between the behavior in a data flow system and the states of processes being scheduled by a conventional scheduler (one designed for general process multiplexing based on process state transitions, rather than one specially designed for the data flow scheduling problem). Associate a separate process with each module in the data flow system.

(a) Define a set of rules that relates changes of scheduling state to activities in the data flow system.

(b) Select a feasible schedule for the data flow system of Figure K-3 and show the corresponding combinations of scheduling states of the processes that emulate the behavior of the modules in the data flow system.

K-12. Transform the data flow system of Figure K-10 into an equivalent one satisfying the conditions for emulation on the host described in Section K.2.

K-13. This problem concerns the tagging scheme introduced in Section K.2 for data flow emulation.

    (a) Modify the data flow system of Figure K-10 to add tagging to the tokens. Show the modules that manipulate tag values.

    (b) Pick a schedule for the activity in the system if the loop is traversed four times before it is completed. Trace the tag values used in the system. Assume that GUT gives out consecutive integers starting with 1.

    (c) Repeat parts (a) and (b) if the computation of the function requires a function call.

K-14. Show that the tag values that go with a calling program in a data flow system can be statically fixed if the implementation prohibits more than one invocation of the calling procedure to be active at one time. Discuss the implementation of this rule while transforming a data flow graph into a canonical form.

K-15. Write a specific rule that defines how a data flow implementation should encode, detect, and handle outputs that are directed to a dead end.

K-16. Does the choice of the queueing discipline for the function queue in the data flow emulator affect any of the following? Explain each answer.

    (a) The values in the result tokens.

    (b) The speed of emulating the target system. Ignore the overhead imposed by any actions necessary to implement the selected queueing discipline.

K-17. Consider the design of the token-matching module associated with the data flow host system described in Section K.2. The proposed implementation uses a memory table in which one location is associated with each module input in the target data flow system. The value stored at the designated location is the bead at the head of a list of tokens waiting at that input port. The other tokens on the list, if any, are stored in other memory locations outside the table allocated for the list heads.

    (a) Describe the module's response to the arrival of a new result token containing a value, a tag, and a destination module number and pin number.

    (b) Why must there be a list for each module input?

K-18. It is proposed that a data flow machine be implemented using a pipelined barrel processor. Each individual process sharing the barrel corresponds to one module among those modules that are shown in the data flow system (i.e., in the diagram of the application, not of any emulator of general data flow systems). All data flow modules are implemented in the same barrel.

    (a) Discuss the performance of this design in comparison with one in which the same logical processing elements are implemented in physically separate modules.

    (b) Are there any disadvantages to the pipelined barrel implementation for this system structure? Explain.

APPENDIX

L

REASONING
AND PROOFS

In this appendix we discuss several ways one could structure one's thinking about the behavior of computer systems, especially multiprocess systems. Our specific objective is to be able to reason about system properties. Often, but not always, the objective is to prove that the system is functional—that indeed it satisfies certain functional specifications. The structuring techniques depend upon the model for interprocess interactions. We set the stage by looking at uniprocess and data flow systems before we look at message-passing and shared-resource systems in detail. The latter two models suggest a common technique—a matrix holding the "history" of all objects that participate in interprocess interactions.

A system should exhibit functional behavior, which we define to be *correct*. A detailed correctness definition depends upon the programming model. With some simple system structures or special applications having simple properties, it will be obvious that all feasible execution sequences give correct behavior. Defining correctness in terms of sequentially consistent behavior is commonplace because it is easily understood and its consequences easily determined. With realistic complex systems, there may be no obvious way to know what constitutes correct behavior. Clearly, we need programmer specifications concerning functionality and correctness (these may be implicit in how the program is written).

One important aspect of any descriptive technique is its utility for reasoning about the properties of the system it describes. Suppose that we wish to prove that property P holds in a particular system. To prove P, we probably have to reason about the system's actual schedule. We could try to structure the proof by enumerating all feasible schedules $\{S_i\}$ and proving P for each S_i. Clearly, this is a poor approach. It would be better to construct a proof from general properties that relate the system's behavior to its configuration.

L.1   SINGLE CONTROL POINT PROGRAMS

As mentioned in Chapter 4, one can reason about program behavior by creating semantic descriptions concerning the behavior of each type of program statement; these descriptions start from assumptions about conditions prior to the execution of the statement and construct a true statement concerning the machine's state after the statement has been completed.

One desires maximum generality in the semantic description of each instruction, which means that one desires the minimum *preconditions* on the prior machine state such that one can determine the maximum amount of information concerning the posterior machine state.

To reason about a multistep sequencing structure, such as a loop structure, the prover states a property that is invariant during the loop's execution; then the prover shows that this property is preserved through every execution of the loop body. Again, the sequencing among the loop's instructions is critical to this demonstration.

There do exist automatic programs that take a program's code as input and generate pre- and postconditions and use statement properties to attempt to prove those properties; their details are beyond the scope of this book. The basic reference for this material is [HOAR69].

L.2   DATA FLOW SYSTEMS

Without a single control point, many different schedules may be feasible. Thus, general proofs are based on the fact that the system's execution schedule must be feasible, meaning that it satisfies certain constraints. In a data flow system, schedule feasibility implies certain relationships between set of the modules that are enabled and the system's token configuration. In this case, (1) the module enabling rules must be satisfied for a module to be enabled and (2) when a module fires it must consume the input tokens according to a specified usage rule. The rules governing the production of output tokens complete the specification.

We can prove that a decision-free data flow graph does produce the same results for all feasible schedules. The proof uses an induction based on the "distance" of a particular internal node or path from the nodes where initial (external) values were presented. Let the distance of path A from an initial place be equal to the number of paths that must be traversed on the longest nonlooping

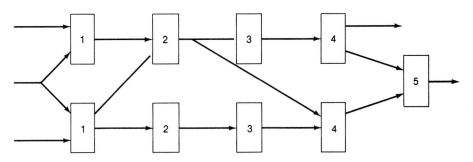

Figure L-1 A decision-free data flow system with
module distances

path from an input place to A. We assign a distance to each module that is equal
to the distance of its output paths. Figure L-1 shows some module distances.

We first argue that each path receives a data object only once in any computation. Then we show that the value associated with that object is identical for
every feasible schedule. A proof of these properties using an induction on the
path distances follows.

Basis: All external inputs are at distance zero; they receive input values
only once, and these values, being the initial ones, are the same in any schedule.
Thus, all paths at level zero satisfy the assertion.

Induction Step: Assume that the assertion is satisfied by every path at all
distances up to and including n. Path A at distance $n + 1$ receives the output of a
computation C whose inputs come from paths at distances n or less. Because
each input to C receives only one value during any computation (by the induction hypothesis), there is only one activation of C in any feasible schedule. By the
induction hypothesis, its input values are the same in all feasible schedules.
Therefore, the object in the packet on path A is the same in all feasible schedules.
The same argument applies at all paths at distance $n + 1$, so the assertion is true
for distance $n + 1$, and, hence, for all paths in the graph.

The data flow system's results are objects arriving at output nodes, and the
unique value property holds there, so the system's results are independent of the
actual schedule, provided that it is a feasible schedule. Q.E.D.

A similar argument can be applied to a data flow system that includes decisions. The major problem introduced by decision modules is that loops and
conditional execution can be present; many tokens can pass along the same path
(in FIFO order, according to the assumptions), and they have to be distinguished
from each other. One approach for dealing with this complexity introduces a history matrix, identifying the individual messages passing on the path. The detailed reasoning becomes similar to that used with message-passing systems.

L.3 MESSAGE-PASSING SYSTEMS

After we present basic notions underlying arguments about the behavior of message-passing systems, and some important assumptions about the behavior of each component of the system of communicating processes, we present the basic structure of a functionality proof for a message-passing system. Data flow systems are message-passing systems that obey simple sequencing constraints between message transactions and computations in modules. In a general message-passing system, each module's program may specify an individualized pattern of computations interleaved with message interactions.

L.3.1 Basic Notions

Because the system passes messages, the sequence of messages passed on each message path is important. Arguments about the message sequences will form the basis for our correctness proof. We assign globally unique numbers to identify all processes and communication paths.

   We attribute a few simple static properties to each process in the system. Each process P_i has some private memory; the collective contents of P_i's memory constitutes the *state of process P_i*, designated S_i. We introduce an auxiliary term:

> **Definition.** Process P_j *interferes* with process P_i if its state S_i is directly affected by some computation performed in P_j.

   We wish to avoid interprocess interference, limiting interprocess interactions to overt ones such as those occurring through messages passed between two processes. There are many possible scenarios, but certainly interference will occur if process P_j directly writes to a portion of S_i.

   We assume that a message-passing system possesses this property and then prove that it is functional. In the proof, we examine process histories. The history of each process can be divided into intervals during which no interprocess messages are passed, punctuated by message-passing events. Figure L-2 depicts this pattern; message passing events are indicated by x's along the time lines, and directed arrows show message flows. Between two consecutive x's, the process is not interacting with other processes; we say that it is performing *introverted actions*. At an x, the process is performing an *extroverted action*. Now we give a formal definition of the noninterference property:

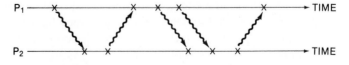

Figure L-2   A pair of processes passing messages

The Noninterference Property. A system possesses the noninterference property if, for every process pair (P_i, P_j), no introverted action by process P_i affects the state of process P_j.

L.3.2 Assumptions

Now we describe the class of systems under study. The assumed properties are divided into four categories:

    A. Properties of the static interprocess interconnections

    B. Dynamic properties of the processes

    C. Dynamic properties of the paths

    D. Dynamic properties within the processes

The static interconnection properties are as follows:

A1. For every process pair (P_i, P_j), P_i does not interfere with P_j.

A2. The association between ports and message paths is static.

A3. Each path is unidirectional.

The properties concerning dynamic process behavior are as follows:

B1. Each process performs in a functional manner during each introverted interval.

B2. Each time that a message is received by process P_i, its contents affect S_i in a functional manner.

B3. The sequence of execution of each process is a function of the state of that process.

These assumptions reflect the determinism of process behavior when the process is not interacting with the message-passing system.

The dynamic properties of the message paths are as follows:

C1. Each path contains an unbounded message queue.

C2. Each path delivers messages in the same order that they were presented to the path.

C3. Each path never loses a message.

C4. Each message is delivered exactly as it was presented.

The properties concerning the process-port dynamics are as follows:

D1. For each message that is sent by process P_j, the contents of the message and the identity of the port through which it is conveyed are functions of S_i at the time the message is sent.

D2. A process receiving a message blocks[1] until the message has been sent.

D3. The selection of the message path from which a particular message will be received depends only on the state of the receiving process.

Together these assumptions assure determinism in all interactions between the message-passing system and the processes that comprise the system. Many proof techniques will not work without determinism in the system.

Conditions B imply that each process executes a fixed order[2] of introverted segments in any feasible schedule. We use this ordering to number the introverted segments within each process. We denote the execution point of a process by the index of the last completed introverted segment.

L.3.3 History Matrix

Now we prove that a system satisfying the previous constraints will be functional. The proof utilizes a port history matrix (PHM) and a process state matrix (PSM). Each row in PHM corresponds to a message port; the entry $PHM(i, j)$ contains the jth message sent out of output port i. This will also be the jth message received at input port i. Each row in PSM corresponds to a process; the entry $PSM(i, j)$ contains the state of process P_i after it completes the execution of its jth introverted sequence. To prove functionality, we will show that the PHM and PSM entries do not depend on the schedule S, provided that the schedule is feasible. This fact will prove the independence of the system's results from its (feasible) schedule.

L.3.4 The Functionality Proof

Our proof assumes a uniprocessor implementation. In such an implementation there is virtual parallelism, but no real parallelism, because there is only one activity at any time, and this slightly simplifies the reasoning. We choose an actual (feasible) schedule and follow the progress of the computation, arguing that each step is functional. By induction, the complete schedule and the system must be functional.

In addition to schedule feasibility, we add a restriction that no process will be interrupted in the midst of an introverted sequence of operations. This condition implies that process switching occurs only when processes interact through

[1] Without blocking, the proof we will outline does not work and cannot be generalized. In fact, without blocking, one can construct a nonfunctional system.
[2] The order is fixed for the values in the given computation, but it is not known a priori.

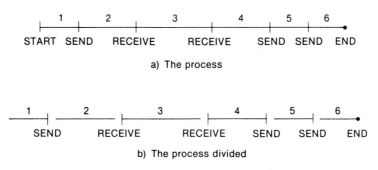

a) The process

b) The process divided

Figure L-3   Dividing a process into introverted sequences

passed messages; imposing the condition simplifies our reasoning but does not affect the generality of the proof. Two introverted sequences are separated with either a **send** or a **receive**. In the former case, we associate the **send** with the preceding introverted sequence, and in the latter case, we associate the **receive** with the following introverted sequence. Figure L-3 illustrates the decomposition of the execution sequence of a communicating process into introverted segments. Figure L-4 shows the four possible combinations of message passing events with

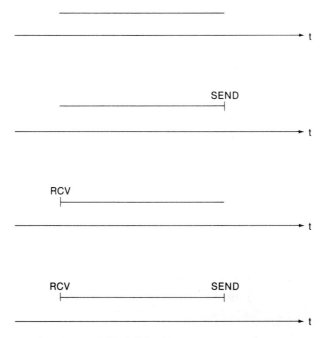

Figure L-4   Relationships among introverted segments and message-passing activities

a single introverted sequence. These four combinations will be the basis for an enumeration within the proof.

The induction will be based on the number n of introverted sequences that have been completed. The inductive assertion contains three parts: (1) message PHM(i, j), if it has been sent or received during the history, is identical for all n-sequence histories based on feasible schedules that include the passing of message PHM(i, j); (2) the state PSM(i, j), if it has been reached during the history, is identical for all n-sequence histories based on feasible schedules that include the execution of introverted sequence j by process i; and (3) the choice of the port used by process i at the end of its jth introverted segment is identical for all histories that include the execution of introverted segment j by process i. To complete the induction argument, one must show that all of these properties hold at each stage of the proof.

The basis for the induction is that the set of initial states of the processes is identical in all histories. Thus, the conclusion is correct for a history containing no executions of an introverted sequence.

In the induction step, we add an introverted sequence to the history. Let p and s denote the process number and sequence number of the introverted sequence added to the n-segment history. Because the schedule is a feasible one, process p must have executed ($s - 1$) introverted segments previously, and, by the induction hypothesis, the state of P_p on starting the new introverted segment is PSM(p, $s - 1$), which is independent of the (feasible) schedule chosen. Furthermore, the choice of the port used by the process at the end of segment ($s - 1$) is independent of the schedule. To show that the same actions are completed during the added segment S, we consider all possible combinations of message interactions during S.

Case 1: There is no message interaction during S. In this case, P_p starts from PSM(p, $s - 1$) and progresses, updating its own state, to the end of S. Because P_p does not interact with any other process, its state at the end of S is a function $f_{p, s}$ of its state at the beginning of S. Therefore, the final state is

$$\text{PSM}(p, s) = f_{p, s}(\text{PSM}(p, s - 1))$$

This function is identical for all schedules in which the ($n + 1$)st segment is the execution of process p in segment s. It is also identical to the state PSM(p, s) in any schedule whose length is not greater than n. Furthermore, the port number used for the **receive** that terminates the segment is a function only of the state of process s at the beginning of the segment, and therefore is identical for all schedules whose lengths are less than $n + 1$. The induction has been extended for the first type of segment, because the entry added to PSM meets the condition and no entry was added to PHM.

Case 2: Segment $(n + 1)$ starts with a **receive** by P_p and ends with no interaction with the message system. In this case, let m denote the message path used for this **receive**. First, we know that the port number used for this **receive** is identical in the schedules that are shorter than n, by the induction hypothesis. Because every port number used for **receive** in the first s segments of process p is independent of the schedule, the sequence numbers on the uses are also identical, and therefore the sequence number of the use of the port at the beginning of the segment is independent of the schedule. So we let j be an integer denoting the number of times that P_p executed a **receive** on path m in its earlier segments. Then the contents of the received message are PHM(m, j). These contents must have been in the PHM before adding the segment to the history, because otherwise the process could not have been scheduled (process P_p would still be waiting for the message to arrive). So the information that P_p works on during the segment is fixed by the contents of the PHM, which satisfies the induction hypothesis, and the PSM at the end of the segment is fixed, by the same argument that we used in case 1. Also, the port number used for the **receive** at the end of the new segment is independent of the schedule. Again, no entry was added to PHM, and the induction is complete for case 2.

Case 3: Segment $(n + 1)$ starts with no message interaction and ends with a **send**. In this case, the initial state of the process must be correct, and, therefore, the final state must be identical independent of the schedule; this argument parallels the one used in case 1. Then the selection of the path for the message and the contents of the message depend only on the initial state information. It is a simple step to argue that the message destination and contents are independent of the schedule. So we have added entries to both PHM and PSM and shown that they are functional, which completes the induction for this case.

Case 4: Segment $(n + 1)$ starts with a **receive** and ends with a **send**. The arguments in this case are similar to the previous case, with the addition of an argument that the starting information is the same, as we argued under case 2.

Having shown that the process states are all independent of the (feasible) schedule after the completion of each execution segment, we have completed the proof that this system is completely functional. Q.E.D.

L.3.5 Comments

By limiting interprocess communication to blocking communication operations and demanding that there are no other interprocess interactions within the system, we proved that the system will exhibit functional behavior. When the system contains shared resources, such as shared memory, reasoning about the system becomes more complex.

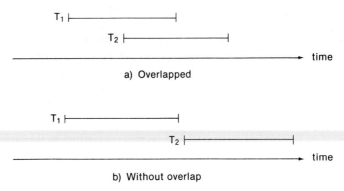

$T_1 \vdash\!\!\!\longrightarrow\!\!\!\dashv$

$T_2 \vdash\!\!\!\longrightarrow\!\!\!\dashv$

→ time

a) Overlapped

$T_1 \vdash\!\!\!\longrightarrow\!\!\!\dashv$

$T_2 \vdash\!\!\!\longrightarrow\!\!\!\dashv$

→ time

b) Without overlap

Figure L-5   Two arrangements of two transactions

L.4 TRANSACTION-BASED SYSTEMS

Transaction-based systems are a simple version of a shared-resource system, because the programmer has structured the system's interactions with the shared objects, and we may be able to reason about the transactions as atomic actions. One important technique for reasoning about system functionality is *transaction serialization*; the serialization process modifies the actual schedule to place the transactions into a functionally equivalent canonical schedule in which no transactions overlap. If the steps in the serialization procedure do not change the computation's results, given that the original schedule was feasible, then every feasible schedule can be serialized, and the system will be functional.

The following basic argument concerns the semantics of a transaction serialization procedure. First, consider the values computed by process P as it executes transaction T_i. The values computed during T_i are functions of the values read from the transaction's read set R_i, and values in S_P, the (private) state of P when the transaction began. Transaction T_i may write new values to shared objects in T_i's write set W_i, and perhaps into objects private to P. These values depend only on the contents of R_i and S_P.

Second, consider two transactions T_1 and T_2 with overlapping execution intervals. What would be the effect of adjusting the actual schedule S by delaying the second transaction until the first has been completed, as shown in Figure L-5? In particular, would the computation's results change? If T_1 and T_2 satisfy the empty intersection property, this schedule adjustment would not change any values stored in a shared resource.

Third, consider the effects of an exchange of two nonoverlapping transactions performed by different processes. If the transactions are commutative, this change will not affect the results of the computation.

Fourth, we can use swapping and overlap removal to transform the actual feasible schedule into a schedule in which each process executes to completion

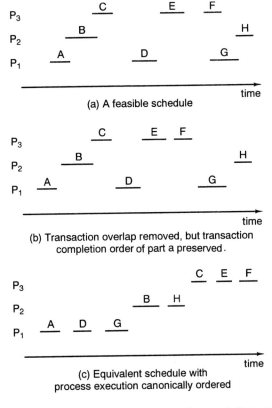

(a) A feasible schedule

(b) Transaction overlap removed, but transaction
completion order of part a preserved.

(c) Equivalent schedule with
process execution canonically ordered

Figure L-6 Illustrating the equivalence of all feasible
schedules when transactions commute

without interruption. Furthermore, we can arrange things so that all transactions of the ith process precede the transactions of the $(i + 1)$st process. This canonical schedule can be produced from any feasible schedule that satisfies the empty intersection property. Figure L-6 illustrates the schedule transformations leading to a canonically ordered schedule.

This argument shows that if the system obeys the empty intersection property and each pair of transactions executed by different processes commutes, the system will be functional.

L.5 SHARED-RESOURCE SYSTEMS

A key part of every proof devises a method for describing system configurations in such a way that one can prove desired properties of these configurations. In a message-passing scheme, the important state information describes messages within the visible message paths. In a system with shared resources that hold state, it is difficult to identify the important places, because there is no a priori reason to single out any locations. We need to handle the composite state that includes the set of the states of each of the shared resources. We can use a history matrix construct that is similar to the path history matrix used in the previous section. We might use the history matrix as the basis for a data flow model of the interactions; this may help with certain proofs.

First, we introduce the history matrix for a shared resource system and then we show how this structure can be related to take-grant and more general interprocess coordination schemes.

L.5.1 The History Matrix

The *history matrix* represents all interactions between sharing processes and shared objects. It holds the history of all values assigned to each data object. There is a row in the history matrix for each object, and each entry in that row corresponds to a write access to that object; the history matrix entry holds the value that was written. Every write is represented in the matrix. We might consider that the history matrix "explodes" the memory to produce a separate object that receives each value that is stored. In effect, we have created an artificial single-assignment system that has a simple relationship to the original system.

To distinguish among the various write accesses to each shared object, we introduce *version numbers*; there is a version number for each entry in the history matrix. Version numbers within each row must be unique, but they can have duplicates in other rows of the matrix. A simple version numbering scheme counts across each row of the history matrix. Under this scheme, the ith write to an object produces version i of the object. More generally, let $v_{i,x}$ denote the version number associated with the ith write[3] to object x. A minimum constraint on version numbering is that $v_{k,x} > v_{j,x}$ if the kth write occurs after the jth write. In other words, version numbers should be monotonically increasing across each row of the history matrix. A similar version numbering scheme can be used to synchronize distributed sets of objects that cooperate to give the illusion of a single object (see Section 8.7.3), and to form internal identifiers that assist in understanding the data flows within superscalar processors as they reorder activity, rename registers, and buffer action requests (see Section 6.6).

The history matrix will be useful in some functionality proofs and will be helpful for understanding some synchronization schemes.

---

[3]   The index in the subscript is defined by the version numbering system using a counter in each row.

L.5.2 Take-Grant Capability Schemes

When reasoning about a take-grant scheme, one must track the possession of each capability. It is difficult to track the system state if capabilities can be copied, thereby creating multiple places from which the same object can be accessed. Despite the complexity, it may be possible to use the empty intersection property to decide which types of simultaneous accesses could be allowed without harming functionality. In this manner, one might be able to find scheduling constraints that assure functional behavior. Then one could argue that the way that the capabilities are passed around does make the system satisfy the desired property. One approach reasons about system events (particularly those involving the shared objects) enabled by possession of capability C_i. In this approach, we find the schedule feasibility constraints forced by the take-grant interactions that pass the capabilities among the processes. A second approach utilizes artificial transactions that correspond to the intervals during which a particular process holds capability C_i.

A third approach to reasoning about the take-grant design views the acts of taking and granting a capability as message communication acts. The system's properties might be proved by constraining the schedule based on the history of messages passed among the set of interacting processes. This will be easier if capabilities cannot be copied, because then there is a unique capability for each resource and passing that capability to a process is analogous to passing the contents of the resource that the capability describes. Because this scenario is equivalent to passing the contents of the object as a message, one might be able to apply the reasoning strategies that work well with message-based designs to this other design.

L.5.3 General Sharing Schemes

The absence of structure limiting access to shared objects in general sharing systems makes reasoning about their properties more difficult because there is no basis for ordering accesses to a shared object within the sharing control mechanism.

Some functionality proofs are based on the following simple observation: the system will be functional if a particular module M_i that reads a shared variable x will in fact read the same value from x independent of the schedule being followed, provided that the system is obeying a feasible schedule. In particular, consider two feasible schedules S_1 and S_2, and let $x_{i,j,k}$ denote the value of x read during the kth read of x by module M_i in schedule j. We want to show that $x_{i,j,k}$ is independent of j. Whether the system obeys this property may depend on many other interactions within the schedule. Now skip ahead and suppose that we could prove that this property were true for all inputs to all modules. Then we would know that each module obtains identical inputs under any (feasible) schedule. Therefore, the module would perform the identical computation (assuming that the modules themselves are functional entities)[4] in all feasible schedules, and it would produce the same results in all feasible schedules. These results become the system's output or the inputs for other modules. This logic provides the structure for an induction proof of the system's functionality.

A general system will be functional if its specification constrains the ordering of all read and write accesses to each shared object, at least to the extent that a particular read operation accessing a shared variable V reads the same version of V, and a particular write operation writes the same version of V. For a particular specification technique, if we could argue that this condition will be satisfied for every shared object if a feasible schedule were followed, we would have the basis for a functionality proof.

Consider a "single-assignment" system. In Section K.1, we discussed the fact that in such a system, each object receives a value only once during a computation. A schedule for a single-assignment system is feasible if the following trivial ordering constraint is met: An object must not be read until after it has been written. This rule is similar to the data flow module enabling rule. As with decision-free data flow systems, we can inductively prove that the value in every object will be independent of the (feasible) schedule in a single-assignment system if the ordering constraint is met. This argument shows that the system is completely functional.

In general, one would like to prove that a given programming scheme is so constrained that every program specified using that scheme must be functional. Because most sharing specification schemes do not satisfy the convenient single-assignment property, one would like to know how to show functionality despite multiple assignments to a single variable.

If the history matrix is identical for all feasible schedules, the system always produces the same outputs, and the system is functional.

How could we prove that fact? Consider the information flows among the history matrix entries. We start with a system of programs P and a feasible schedule S. Given P and S, one can emulate the system's behavior and determine which version of an object is actually used as the input for each computation that is performed.[5] In addition, one can determine which version of an object contains the result of each computation performed by the system. Now we construct a data flow system DF(P, S) whose semantics will correspond to the behavior of P under S. To construct DF(P, S), associate a module output with each history matrix entry and a computational module with each computation in the system. Each matrix entry will have a single input branch from the computational

---

⁴   If this were not the case, then clearly the system is nonfunctional.

⁵   We are dividing the programs into a set of "computations," where each computation produces a value that is stored in memory. The inputs to the computation consist of all values read from memory that affect the result.

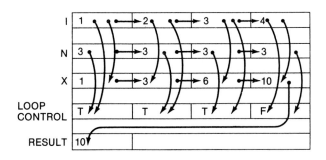

Figure L-7   A history matrix with data flow paths added

module corresponding to the computation that wrote that value in the indicated memory location. The fact that DF(P, S) exists is not adequate to prove anything about the correctness of the computation. One must consider the set of histories across the set of data flow systems {DF(P, S) | S is a feasible schedule for P}. This set of data flow systems corresponds to the set of system behaviors consistent with the scheduling constraints imposed by the semantics of the programs P. If the results are independent of S, the system is functional. It might be true that the structure of DF(P, S) is independent of S; in this situation, the existence of a *unique* DF(P) suffices to show the functionality of P. To complete a functionality proof, one has to consider the scheduling constraints imposed by the synchronization constructs to show the uniqueness of the data flow system derived from the history matrix.

Example L-1

Figure L-7 shows a history matrix for the computation of the program fragment of Example K-8, along with the flows for one feasible schedule of the data flow structure shown in Figure K-11. We do not show the details of the feasible schedule for this example. The structure happens to be completely functional, so that the history matrix and the flows are identical for all feasible schedules.

A necessary condition for functionality is that at any step in the computation, in any feasible schedule, only a single activity that can write in a particular element of the history matrix will be enabled.[6] The reader can easily construct examples to show the necessity of this condition (see Problem L-2). Unfortunately, the condition is not sufficient for functionality.

---

[6]   If a processor can issue multiple instructions, this rule implies that two instructions that write to the same location cannot be issued together.

L.6 SUMMARY

To reason about system properties, one needs logical statements about the effects of each important interaction. When a single control point determines the order of execution, things are simple. We use preconditions to develop postconditions regarding the system's state after completing the execution of a statement.

A system containing interacting processes presents challenges to people trying to reason about the system's properties. If the interactions are structured by visible steps, the reasoning can be structured around these identified steps. For example, capability-passing systems (without capability copying) define the program regions within which particular shared objects might be accessed. Transaction specifications can help impose structure in a similar manner. Auxiliary notions, such as history matrices, can be used to structure thinking about the system's progress, and therefore about the results available at the completion of the computation. But there remain several difficulties, including (1) identifying process steps that cause interprocess interactions, (2) dividing processes into intervals that can be treated as atomic actions for proof purposes, and (3) determining event ordering among the interactions. We showed several programming paradigms that impose constraints that limit the scheduling and interaction flexibility.

These reasoning steps become simpler if all interprocess interactions occur through visible mechanisms, such as communication paths. The identification of all interactions is easier if the process steps that can cause interactions are distinguished from "normal" processing steps (such is the case with message-passing statements). In a system using shared resources for interprocess communication, any read or write action can be an interprocess interaction, so it is more difficult to identify processing phases that can be treated as atomic actions.

L.7 TRENDS

It is difficult to find or predict trends in the evolution of proof techniques. Clever people may devise new ways to visualize interprocess interactions at any time, thereby changing this landscape. With increasing processing power, opportunities for automating assertion generation and proofs will expand. However, people have to decide that making a proof is worthwhile. Right now there is excessive reliance on testing without adequate reasoning about system properties. We end up with systems that fail due to event combinations and timings that were not foreseen (and therefore not tested), which is unfortunate.

L.8 CONCEPT LIST

1. Preconditions and postconditions
2. Path properties for functionality
3. History matrices: for paths and for shared object states
4. Version numbering
5. Divide processing into phases based on the points of interaction
6. Conditions for noninterference among processes
7. Capability passing (without copying) delimits interaction intervals
8. Similarities with message-passing may simplify proofs
9. Transaction serialization makes proofs simple

L.9 PROBLEMS

L-1. Consider the functionality proof for packet-based message-passing systems.
    (a) Discuss how the proof could be modified to show the functionality of a stream-based system. *Do not attempt to complete such a proof.*
    (b) In your proof, what would you choose for the granularity of the elements in the history matrix?

L-2. Construct an example to prove the necessity of the functionality condition that states that a system will be functional if it is never true that there is more than one operation enabled at the same time that wishes to write to the same shared object.

L-3. Describe the similarities and differences between proofs or reasoning based on the following system properties:
    (i) A path history matrix
    (ii) A transaction-based system
    (iii)A take-grant capability system

L-4. Show how the functionality proof for decision-free data flow systems can be generalized to cover data flow systems with decisions. The statement to be proved is: The output values from the data flow system are identical for every feasible schedule, depending only on the values in the input tokens.

    You may assume that each module (except merge and gate modules) requires that there be a token at each input before it fires, that when it fires, it consumes an input token from each input path, and that it produces an output token at each output port when its computation is completed. The merge and gate modules obey the rules given in the text. (*Hint:* Use induction on the "distance" from the external inputs in a dynamic interpretation of the system graph.)

REFERENCES

[AMDA67] Amdahl, G. M., "Validity of the Single Processor Approach to Achieve Large Scale Computing Capabilities," *AFIPS Conference Proceedings 30*, 483–485, 1967.

[ANDE67] Anderson, D. W., F. J. Sparacio, and R. M. Tomasulo, "The IBM System/360 Model 91: Machine Philosophy and Instruction Handling," *IBM Systems Journal 11*(1), 8–24, January 1967.

[ARVI86] Arvind, and D. E. Culler, *Dataflow Architectures*, MIT Technical Report MIT/CS/TM-294, Massachustees Institute of Technology, Cambridge, MA, February 1986.

[BARN68] Barnes, G. H., R. M. Brown, M. Kato, D. J. Kuck, D. L. Slotnick, and R. A. Stokes, "The Illiac IV Computer," *IEEE Transactions on Computers C-17*(8), 746–757, August 1968.

[BATC74] Batcher, K. E., "STARAN Parallel Processor System Hardware," *Proceedings of the National Computer Conference*, 405–410, 1974.

[BELA66] Belady, L. A., "A Study of Replacement Algorithms for a Virtual-Storage Computer," *IBM Systems Journal 5*(2), 78–101, 1966.

[BELL75] Bell, D. E., and L. J. LaPadula, *Secure Computer Systems: Unified Exposition and Multics Interpretations*, Technical Report MTR-2997, MITRE Corp., Bedford, MA, July 1975.

[BELL76] Bell, C. G., and W. D. Strecker, "Computer Structures: What Have We Learned from the PDP-11?" *Proceedings of the Third Annual Symposium on Computer Architecture*, 1–14, January 1976.

[BERS79] Berson, T. A., and G. L. Barksdale, Jr., "KSOS–A Development Methodology for a Secure Operating System," *Proceedings of the National Computer Conference 48*, AFIPS Press, Montvale, NJ, June 1979.

[BIBA77] Biba, K., *Integrity Considerations for Secure Computer Systems*, Mitre Technical Report TR-3153, Mitre Corp., Bedford, MA, April 1977.

[BOEB84] Boebert, W. E., "On the Inability of an Unmodified Capability Machine to Enforce the *-Property," *Proceedings of the Seventh DoD/NBS Computer Security Conference*, 291–293, September 1984.

[BOEB85] Boebert, W. E., R. Y. Kain, W. D. Young, and S. A. Hansohn, "Secure Ada Target: Issues, System Design, and Verification," *Proceedings of the 1985 IEEE Symposium on Security and Privacy*, 176–183, April 1985.

[BOUK72] Bouknight, W. J., S. A. Denenberg, D. E. McIntyre, J. M. Randall, A. H. Sameh, and D. L. Slotnick, "The Illiac IV System," *Proceedings of the IEEE 60*(4), 369–388, April 1972.

[BURR61] *The Operational Characteristics of the Processors for the Burroughs B5000*, Document 5000-21005-D, Burroughs Corp., Detroit, November 1961.

[BURR69] *Burroughs B5500 Information Processing Systems Reference Manual*, Document 1021326, Burroughs Corp., Detroit, 1969.

[BURR72] Burroughs Corp., *Burroughs B1700 Systems Reference Manual*, Publication 1057155, Detroit, 1972.

[BURR73] Burroughs Corp., *Burroughs B7700 Information Processing Systems Reference Manual*, Order No. 1060233, Burroughs Corp., Detroit, 1973.

[CLAR87] Clark, D., and D. Wilson, "A Comparison of Commercial and Military Computer Security Policies," *Proceedings of the 1987 IEEE Symposium on Security and Privacy*, 184–194, May 1987.

[CLOC87] Clocksim, W. F., and C. S. Mellish, *Programming in Prolog*, 3rd ed., Springer-Verlag, Berlin, 1987.

[COHE85] Cohen, J., "Describing Prolog by Its Interpretation and Computation," *Communications of the ACM 28*(12), 1311–1324, December 1985.

[COLW87] Colwell, R. P., R. P. Nix, J. J. O'Donnell, D. B. Papworth, and B. K. Rodman, "A VLIW Architecture for a Trace Scheduling Compiler," *Proceedings of the Second Conference on Architectural Support for Programming Languages and Operating Systems*, IEEE Computer Society, Palo Alto, CA, March 1987.

[CONT66] Control Data Corp., *Control Data 6400/6600 Computer Systems Reference Manual*, Publication No. 60100000, Control Data Corp., St. Paul, MN, 1966.

[CONT70] Control Data Corp., *Control Data STAR-Computer System, Hardware Reference Manual*, CDC Publication No. 60256000, Control Data Corp., Arden Hills, MN, 1970.

[COX83] Cox, G. W., W. M. Corwin, K. K. Lai, and F. J. Pollack, "Interprocess Communication and Processor Dispatching in the Intel 432," *ACM Transactions on Computer Systems 1*(1), 45–66, February 1983.

[CRAG92] Cragon, Harry C., *Branch Strategy Taxonomy and Performance Models*, IEEE Computer Society Press, Los Alamitos, CA, 1992.

[CRAY85] *CRAY-2 Computer System Functional Description*, Publication No. HR-2000, Cray Research, Inc., Mendota Heights, MN, 1985.

[DAHL95] Dahl, P. J., *Compiler and Architecture Issues with CRegs*, Ph.D. Thesis, University of Minnesota, Minneapolis, MN, February 1995.

[DATA74] Data General Corp., *Programmer's Reference Manual: ECLIPSE Computer*, Order No. 015-000024-00, Data General Corp., September 1974.

[DAVI82] Davis, A. L., and R. M. Keller, "Data Flow Program Graphs," *Computer* 15(2), 26–41, February 1982.

[DENN74] Dennis, J. B., J. B. Fosseen, and J. P. Linderman, *Data Flow Schemas*, Lecture Notes in Computer Science, Vol. 19, Springer-Verlag, New York, 1974.

[DENN88], Denning, D., T. Lunt, R. Schell, W. Shockley, and M. Heckman, "The SeaView Security Model," *Proceedings of the 1988 IEEE Symposium on Security and Privacy*, 218–233, May 1988.

[DIGI70] Digital Equipment Corp., *PDP8/e Small Computer Handbook 1971*, Digital Equipment Corp., Maynard, MA, 1970.

[DIGI75] Digital Equipment Corp., *PDP-11/70 Processor Handbook*, Digital Equipment Corp., Maynard, MA, 1975.

[DIGI77] Digital Equipment Corp., *VAX11-780 Architecture Handbook*, Vol. 1, Digital Equipment Corp., Maynard, MA, 1977.

[DIJK68a] Dijkstra, E. W., "Go To Statement Considered Harmful," *Communications of the ACM* 11(3), 147–148, March 1968.

[DIJK68b] Dijkstra, E. W., "Cooperating Sequential Processes," in F. Genuys, ed., *Programming Languages*, pg. 43, Academic Press, London, 1968.

[DOD85] Department of Defense, *Trusted Computer System Evaluation Criteria*, Document DoD 5200.28-STD, U.S. Department of Defense, Washington, DC, 1985.

[DORA80] Doran, R. W., and L. K. Thomas, "Variants of the Software Solution to Mutual Exclusion," *Information Processing Letters* 10(4), 206–208, July 1980.

[EDLE85] Edler, J., A. Gottlieb, C. P. Kruskal, K. P. McAuliffe, L. Rudolph, M. Snir, P. J. Teller, and J. Wilson, "Issues Related to MIMD Shared-Memory Computers: The NYU Ultracomputer Approach," *Proceedings of the 12th Annual Symposium on Computer Architecture*, 126–135, June 1985.

[ELLI90] Ellis, M. A., and B. Stroustrup, *The Annotated C++ Reference Manual*, Addison-Wesley, Reading, MA, 1990.

[ENGL72] England, D. M., "Architectural Features of System 250," in *Infotech State of the Art Report on Operating Systems*, London, 1972.

[ENGL74] England, D. M., "Capability Concept Mechanisms and Structure in System 250," *Proceedings of the International Workshop on Protection in Operating Systems*, 63–82, IRIA, Paris, August 1974.

[FABR74] Fabry, R. S., "Capability-Based Addressing," *Communications of the ACM* 17(7), 403–412, July 1974.

[FAIR75] Fairchild Semiconductor, *F8 Preliminary Microprocessor User's Manual*, Fairchild Semiconductor, Palo Alto CA, 1975.

[GAJS82] Gajski, D. D., D. A. Padua, D. J. Kuck, and R. H. Kuhn, "A Second Opinion on Data Flow Machines and Languages," *Computer* 15(2), 58–69, February 1982.

[GARE79] Garey, M. R., and D. S. Johnson, *Computers and Intractability: A Guide to the Theory of NP-Completeness*, W. H. Freeman, San Francisco, CA, 1979.

[GEHR86] Gehringer, E. F., and R. P. Colwell, "Fast Object-Oriented Procedure Calls: Lessons from the Intel i432," *Proceedings of the 13th Annual Symposium on Computer Architecture*, 92–101, June 1986.

[GLIG79] Gligor, V. D., "Review and Revocation of Access Privileges Distributed through Capabilities," *IEEE Transactions on Software Engineering SE-5*(6), 575–586, November 1979.

[GOLD79] Gold, B. D., et al, "A Security Retrofit of VM/370," *AFIPS Conference Proceedings 48*, 335–342, 1979 National Computer Conference, 1979.

[GOLD83] Goldberg, A., and D. Robson, *Smalltalk-80: The Language and its Implementation*, Addison-Wesley, Reading, MA, 1983.

[GOTT83] Golltieb, A., R. Grishman, C. P. Kruskal, K. P. McAuliffe, L. Rudolph, and M. Snir, "The NYU Ultracomputer—Designing an MIMD Shared Memory Parallel Computer," *IEEE Transactions on Computers C-32*(2), 175–189, February 1983.

[GURD85] Gurd, J. R., C. C. Kirkham, and I. Watson, "The Manchester Prototype Dataflow Computer," *Communications of the ACM 28*(1), 34–52, January 1985.

[HAUC68] Hauck, E. A., and B. A. Dent, "Burroughs B6500/B7500 Stack Mechanism," *Proceedings of the 1968 Spring Joint Computer Conference 32*, 245–251, 1968.

[HAYN82] Haynes, L. S., R. L. Lau, D. P. Siewiorek, and D. W. Mizell, "A Survey of Highly Parallel Computing," *Computer 15*(1), 9–24, January 1982.

[HEWL73] Hewlett-Packard Co., *HP 3000 Computer System Reference Manual*, Part No. 03000-90019, Hewlett-Packard Co., Palo Alto, CA, September 1973.

[HOAR69] Hoare, C. A. R., "An Axiomatic Basis for Computer Programming," *Communications of the ACM 12*(10), 576–580, October 1969.

[HOAR74] Hoare, C. A. R., "Monitors: An Operating System Structuring Concept," *Communications of the ACM 17*(10), 549–557, October 1974.

[HOLL59] Holland, J. H., "A Universal Computer Capable of Executing an Arbitrary Number of Sub-Programs Simultaneously," *Proceedings of the Eastern Joint Computer Conference 1959*, 108–113, 1959.

[HOLT72] Holt, R. C., "Some Deadlock Properties of Computer Systems," *Computing Surveys 4*(3), 179–195, December 1972.

[HONE60] Honeywell, Inc., *Honeywell 800 Programmer's Reference Manual*, Honeywell, Inc., Wellesley Hills, MA, 1960.

[HONE80] Honeywell, Inc., *Honeywell Level 6 Minicomputer Systems Handbook*, Order No. CC71a, Honeywell, Inc., Billerica MA, June 1980.

[HUFF52] Huffman, D. A., "A Method for the Construction of Minimum-Redundancy Codes," *Proceedings of the IRE 40*(9), 1098–1101, September 1952.

[IBM55] IBM, *704 Electronic Data-Processing Machine Manual of Operation*, Form No. 24-6661-2, IBM Corp., New York, 1955.

[IBM80] IBM Corp., *IBM System/38 Functional Concepts Manual*, Document GA21-9330-0, IBM Corp., New York, June 1980.

[IBM81a] IBM Corp., *IBM System/38 Functional Reference Manual*, Document no. GA21-9331-1, File No. S38-01, IBM Corp., New York, February 1981.

[IBM81b] IBM Corp., *IBM System/370 Principles of Operation*, Document No. GA22-7000-7, IBM Corp., New York, March 1981.

[IEEE85] Institute of Electrical and Electronic Engineers, *Binary Floating-Point Arithmetic*, IEEE Standard 754-1985, IEEE, New York, 1985.

[INTE89] Intel Corp., *386 SX Microprocessor Programmer's Reference Manual*, Intel, Osborne/McGraw-Hill, New York, 1989.

[JAME90] James, D. V., A. T. Laundrie, S. Gjessing, and G. S. Sohi, "Scalable Coherent Interface," *IEEE Computer* 23(6), 74–77, June 1990.

[JOHN91] Johnson, M., *Superscalar Microprocessor Design*, Prentice Hall, Englewood Cliffs, NJ, 1991.

[KAIN86] Kain, R. Y., and C. E. Landwehr, "On Access Checking in Capability-Based Systems," *Proceedings of the 1986 IEEE Symposium on Security and Privacy*, 95–100, April 1986. Also published (with minor changes) in *IEEE Transactions on Software Engineering SE-13*(2), 202–207, February 1987.

[KAIN89] Kain, R. Y., *Computer Architecture: Software and Hardware* (2 vols.), Prentice Hall, Englewood Cliffs, NJ, 1989.

[KANE92] Kane, G., and J. Heinrich, *MIPS RISC Architecture*, Prentice Hall, Englewood Cliffs, NJ, 1992.

[KAUF84] Kaufman, A., "Tailored-List and Recombination-Delaying Buddy Systems," *ACM Transactions on Programming Languages and Systems* 6(1), 118–125, January 1984.

[KLAP86] Klapp, O. E., *Overload and Boredom: Essays on the Quality of Life in the Information Society*, Greenwood Press, Westport, CT, 1986.

[KOEN94] Koeninger, R. K., M. Furtney, and M. Walker, "A Shared Memory MPP from Cray Research," *Digital Technical Journal* 6(2), 8–21, Spring 1994.

[KOHL81] Kohler, W. H., "A Survey of Techniques for Synchronization and Recovery in Decentralized Computer Systems," *ACM Computing Surveys* 13(2), 149–184, June 1981.

[KSR92] Kendall Square Research, *KSR1 Technology Background*, Kendall Square Research, Cambridge, MA, 1992.

[KUCK82] Kuck, D. J., and R. A. Stokes, "The Burroughs Scientific Processor (BSP)," *IEEE Transactions on Computers C-31*(5), 363–376, May 1982.

[KUNG81] Kung, H. T., and J. T. Robinson, "On Optimistic Methods for Concurrency Control," *ACM Transactions on Database Systems* 6(2), 213–226, June 1981.

[KUNG82] Kung, H. T., "Why Systolic Architectures?" *Computer* 15(1), 37–46, January 1982.

[LAMP71] Lampson, B. W., "Protection," in *Proceedings of the Fifth Princeton Symposium on Information Sciences and Systems*, 437–443, Princeton University, March 1971, reprinted in *ACM Operating Systems Review* 8(1), 18–24, January 1974.

[LAMP86] Lamport, L. A., "The Mutual Exclusion Problem: Part II - Statement and Solutions," *Journal of the ACM* 33(2), 327–348, April 1986.

[LAND83] Landwehr, C. E., "The Best Available Technologies for Computer Security," *Computer 16*(7), 86–100, July 1983.

[LAWR75] Lawrie, D. H., "Access and Alignment of Data in an Array Processor," *IEEE Transactions on Computers, C-24*(12), 1145–1155, December 1975.

[LAWR82] Lawrie, D. H., and C. R. Vora, "The Prime Memory System for Array Access," *IEEE Transactions on Computers C-31*(5), 435–442, October 1982.

[LEVY84] Levy, H. M., *Capability-Based Computer Systems*, Digital Press, Bedford, MA, 1984.

[LILJ94] Lilja, D. J., and P. L. Bird, *The Interaction of Compilation Technology and Computer Architecture*, Kluwer, Boston, 1994.

[LIND76] Linden, T. A., "Operating System Structures to Support Security and Reliable Software," *ACM Computing Surveys 8*(4), 409–445, December 1976.

[MAY83] May, D., "Occam," *ACM SIGPLAN Notices 18*, 4, 69–79, April 1983.

[MOON87] Moon, D. A., "Symbolics Architecture," *Computer 20*(1), 43–52, January 1987.

[MOTO84] Motorola, Inc., *M68020 32-bit Microprocessor User's Manual*, Prentice Hall, Inc., Englewood Cliffs, NJ, 1984.

[MOTO93] Motorola, Inc., *PowerPC 601: RISC Microprocessor User's Manual*, Motorola, Inc., Phoenix, AZ, 1993.

[NEED77] Needham, R., M., and R. D. H. Walker, "The Cambridge CAP Computer and Its Protection System," *Proceedings of the 5th ACM Symposium on Operating System Principles*, 1–10, 1977.

[NEUM80] Neumann, P. G., R. S. Boyer, R. J. Feiertag, K. N. Levitt, and L. Robinson, *A Provably Secure Operating System: The System, Its Applications, and Proofs*, Report CSL-116, 2nd ed., SRI International, Menlo Park, CA, May 1980.

[ORGA72] Organick, E. I., *The MULTICS System*, MIT Press, Cambridge, MA, 1972.

[ORGA73] Organick, E. I., *Computer System Organization: The B5700/6700 Series*, Academic Press, New York, 1973.

[ORGA83] Organick, E. I., *A Programmer's View of the Intel 432 System*, McGraw-Hill, New York, 1983.

[OSEC84] Osecky, B. D., D. D. Georg, and R. J. Bucy, "The Design of a General-Purpose Multiple-Processor System," *HP Journal 35*(3), 34–38, March 1984.

[PATT82] Patterson, David A., and Carlo H. Sequin, "A VLSI RISC," *Computer 15*(9), 8–21, September 1982. t

[PATT93] Patterson, D. A., and J. L. Hennessy, *Computer Organization and Design: The Hardware/Software Interface*, Morgan Kaufmann, San Mateo, CA, 1993.

[POTT85] Potter, J. L., ed., *The Massively Parallel Processor*, MIT Press, Cambridge, MA, 1985.

[RAND64] Randell, B., and L. Russell, *Algol60 Implementation*, Academic Press, London, 1964.

[RAND75] Randell, B., "System Structure for Software Fault Tolerance," *IEEE Transactions on Software Engineering SE-1*, 220–232, June 1975.

[SAYD87] Saydjari, O. S., J. M. Beckman, and J. R. Leaman, "Locking Computers Securely," *Proceedings of the 10th NBS/NCSC Computer Security Conference*, 129–141, September 1987.

[SCHR72] Schroeder, M. D., and J. A. Saltzer, "A Hardware Architecture for Implementing Protection Rings," *Communications of the ACM 15*(3), 157–170, March 1972.

[SDS66] Scientific Data Systems, *SDS 940 Computer Reference Manual*, Publication 900640A, Scientific Data Systems, Santa Monica, CA, August 1966.

[SHER84] Sherburne, R. W., Jr., M. G. H. Katevenis, D. A. Patterson, and C. H. Sequin, "A 32-Bit NMOS Processor with a Large Register File," *IEEE Journal of Solid-State Circuits SC-19*(5), 682–689, October 1984.

[SITE92] Sites, R. L., *Alpha Architecture Reference Manual*, Digital Press, Maynard, MA, 1992.

[SITE93] Sites, R. L., A. Chernoff, M. B. Kirk, M. P. Marks, and S. G. Robinson, "Binary Translation," *Communications of the ACM 36*(2), 69–81, February 1993.

[SLEA85] Sleator, D. D., and R. E. Tarjan, "Amortized Efficiency of List Update and Paging Rules," *Communications of the ACM 28*(2), 202–208, February 1985.

[SMIT83] Smith, J. E., and J. R. Goodman, "A Study of Instruction Cache Organizations and Replacement Policies," *Proceedings of the 10th Annual Symposium on Computer Architecture*, June 1983.

[SPAR92] SPARC International, *The SPARC Architecture Manual, Version 8*, Prentice Hall, Englewood Cliffs, NJ, 1992.

[SUPN84] Supnik, R. M., "MicroVAX 32, a 32 Bit Microprocessor," *IEEE Journal of Solid-State Circuits SC-19*(5), 675–681, October 1984.

[SYMB86] Symbolics, Inc., *Internals, Processes and Storage Management*, Document No. 999008, Symbolics, Inc., Cambridge, MA, July 1986.

[TANN84] Tannenbaum, A. S., *Structured Computer Organization*, 2nd ed., Prentice Hall, Englewood Cliffs, NJ, 1984.

[THIN91] Thinking Machines Corp., *The Connection Machine CM-5 Technical Summary*, Thinking Machines Corp., Cambridge, MA, 1991.

[THOM79] Thomas, R. H., "A Majority Consensus Approach to Concurrency Control for Multiple Copy Databases," *ACM Transactions on Database Systems 4*(2), 180–209, June 1979.

[THOR70] Thornton, J. E., *Design of a Computer: The Control Data 6600*, Scott, Foresman, Glenview, IL, 1970.

[TOMA67] Tomasulo, R. M., "An Efficient Algorithm for Expoiting Multiple Arithmetic Units," *IBM Journal 11*(1), 25–33, January 1967.

[TREL82] Treleaven, P. C., D. R. Brownbridge, and R. P. Hopkins, "Data-Driven and Demand-Driven Computer Architecture," *Computing Surveys 14*(1), 93–144, March 1982.

[TREL84] Treleaven, P. C., and I. Gouveia Lima, "Future Computers: Logic, Data Flow, ... Control Flow," *Computer 17*(3), 47–58, March 1984.

[TYNE81] Tyner, P., *iAPX 432 General Data Processor Architecture Reference Manual*, Order No. 171860-001, Intel Corp., Aloha, OR, January 1981.

[UNGE58] Unger, S. H., "A Computer Oriented Towards Spatial Problems," *Proceedings of the IRE 46*(10), 1744–1750, October 1958.

[VEEN86] Veen, A. H., "Dataflow Machine Architectures," *ACM Computing Surveys 18*(4), 365–396, December 1986.

[VONE92] Von Eicken, T., D. E. Culler, S. C. Goldstein, and K. E. Schauser, "Active Messages: A Mechanism for Integrated Communication and Computation," *Proceedings of the 19th Annual Symposium on Computer Architecture*, 256–266, May 1992.

[WATS82] Watson, I., and J. Gurd, "A Practical Data Flow Computer," *Computer 15*(2), 51–57, February 1982.

[WEAV94] Weaver, D. L., and T. Germond, eds., *The SPARC Architecture Manual, Version 9*, Prentice Hall, Englewood Cliffs, NJ, 1994.

[WHIT85] Whitby-Strevens, C., "The Transputer," *Proceedings of the 12th Annual Symposium on Computer Architecture*, 292–300, June, 1985.

[WILK53] Wilkes, M. V., and J. B. Stringer, "Microprogramming and the Design of the Control Circuits in an Electronic Digital Computer," *Proceedings of the Cambridge Philosophical Society 49*, 230–238, 1953.

[WILK56] Wilkes, M. V., "The Best Way to Design an Automatic Calculating Machine," *Report of Manchester University Computer Inaugural Conference*, 16–18, Ferranti, Ltd., London, 1956.

[WILN72] Wilner, W. T., "Design of the Burroughs B1700," *Proceedings of the AFIPS Fall Joint Computer Conference 41*, 489–497, 1972.

[WINS84] Winston, P. H., and B. K. P. Horn, *LISP*, 2nd ed., Addison-Wesley, Reading, MA, 1983.

[WISE86] Wiseman, S., "A Secure Capability Computer System," *Proceedings of the 1986 IEEE Symposium on Security and Privacy*, 86–94, April 1986.

[WONG85] Wong, R. M., T. A. Berson, and R. J. Feiertag, "Polonius: An Identity Authentication System," *Proceedings of the 1985 Symposium on Security and Privacy*, 101–107, April 1985.

[YOUN86] Young, W. D., P. A. Telega, W. E. Boebert, and R. Y. Kain, "A Verified Labeller for the Secure Ada Target," *Proceedings of the 9th DoD/NBS Computer Security Conference*, September 1986.

INDEX

NOTE: A page number in boldface type indicates where a significant idea is presented or a term is defined.